Indexing and Abstracting
in
Theory and Practice

Indexing and Abstracting
in
Theory and Practice

F. W. Lancaster

Third Edition
2003

University of Illinois
Graduate School of Library and Information Science
501 East Daniel Street
Champaign Illinois 61820-6211

Distributed exclusively by the University of Illinois
Graduate School of Library and Information Science Publications Office
501 East Daniel Street
Champaign Illinois 61820-6211 USA

http://www.lis.uiuc.edu/puboff/

ISBN 0-87845-122-6

Designed and typeset by Robert Chapdu, IntelliText Corporation,
Champaign Illinois 61826 USA

Printed and bound by Thomson-Shore Inc.,
Dexter Michigan 48130 USA

CONTENTS

For Shane, Aaron,
Rachael, Maddie, Alex,
Joshua, Evan, and Emma,
as well as
Lakshmi and Rajeshwari

PREFACE

The first edition of this work, which received the Best Information Science Book award from the American Society for Information Science, was published in 1991; the second appeared in 1998. The earlier editions were well received by reviewers and the book has been widely used as a text in North America, the United Kingdom, and elsewhere.

Between 1991 and 1998 this field changed considerably, necessitating completely new chapters, especially chapters on the Internet and on indexing and abstracting for image and sound databases. The changes since 1998 have been less dramatic. Nevertheless, developments have occurred, necessitating a third edition

The entire text has been updated although the earlier chapters, which deal more with basic principles, remain quite similar to those of the second edition. On the other hand, some of the later chapters have been substantially or completely rewritten. These are Chapters 13-17 dealing respectively with image and sound databases, text searching, automatic indexing and related activities, indexing and the Internet, and the future of indexing and abstracting.

I have not changed many of the figures because I feel that those used in the second edition are still fully applicable to illustrate the points I want to make. This is even true of Chapter 10, dealing with printed indexing and abstracting services. While I could have updated the sample pages, I felt it quite unnecessary to do so.

While indexing and abstracting were once seen as procedures of interest only to libraries and certain publishers, their relevance and value are now much more widely recognized, for they clearly have applicability to all types of information resources in digital form. Thus, this edition, while still intended primarily as a text for use in schools of library and information science (and related programs), should have some interest to a much wider audience: database producers of all kinds, and those involved in such areas as intranet design, portal design, management information systems, and knowledge management in general.

I feel that I should also say something about the sources cited. One reviewer of the first edition criticized me for continuing to cite "old" sources. While I have tried to completely update the sources cited (through early 2003), I make no apologies for continuing to cite older, and even much older, material. It is inconceivable to me that a book on this topic would fail to cite (for example) Cutter (1876) and Ranganathan (1930s). Furthermore, many people writing on these topics today seem to have no interest in, or knowledge of, the earlier contributions to this field. I feel that it is important, especially for students, to understand how the field has developed and to recognize that many of the ideas presented as new today can actually be found in the literature, in a somewhat similar form, thirty or more years ago.

As with earlier editions, this one does not attempt to deal with back-of-the-book indexes. This subject is well covered in other works written by people with much more experience in that particular area than I have.

This edition should still be considered as primarily an introductory text. While I believe that Chapters 1-12 are rather comprehensive, complete books have been written on the topics dealt with in Chapters 13-15, so these, in particular, should be viewed as introductions to these subjects.

F. W. Lancaster
Urbana, Illinois
March 2003

ACKNOWLEDGMENTS

Permission to reprint various figures from other sources is acknowledged in the figure captions. In addition, I would like to thank: Elsevier Science for permission to reproduce some extensive quotations from *Information Processing and Management*; OCLC Inc. for permission to reproduce extensive quotations from an article by O'Neill et al. (2001); John Wiley and Sons for permission to reproduce several lengthy quotations from *Journal of the American Society for Information Science and Technology* (and its predecessors); Information Today Inc. (<www.infotoday.com>) for permission to reproduce extensive quotations from Hock (2001), from *EContent* and from *Online*; IBM for permission to reproduce an extensive quotation from the *IBM Systems Journal*; Thomas Craven for permission to reproduce quotations from several of his articles; Getty Research Institute for extensive quotations from Layne (2002); IOS Press for permission to reproduce an extensive quotation from Nielsen (1997); and ACM Publications for permission to quote from Wactlar et al. (2002).

The terms and definitions taken from ISO 5963:1985 are reproduced with the permission of the International Organization for Standardization, ISO. This standard can be obtained from any ISO member and from the Web site of the ISO Central Secretariat at the following address: <www.iso.org.> Copyright remains with ISO.

Finally, I would like to thank various people for help on this edition— Bella Weinberg for drawing my attention to some sources I might otherwise have overlooked, Bryan Heidorn for reading an early draft of Chapter 13, Susanne Humphrey and Lou Knecht for updating my information on the National Library of Medicine, June Silvester of the Center for AeroSpace Information, Chandra Prabha for input from OCLC, the staff of the Library and Information Science Library at the University of Illinois (and especially Sandy Wolf), for their patient help in finding me materials, and Kathy Painter for doing her usual excellent job in getting the revision into electronic form.

F. W. Lancaster
Urbana, Illinois
April, 2003

A NOTE ON TERMINOLOGY
(and the Rediscovery of Wheels)

I have worked in or around libraries for very many years. Much of this time I have been involved, in one way or another, with subject analysis. In 1957 I began work writing abstracts, covering a wide range of science and technology, for an industrial abstracts bulletin, a job that also involved a detailed level of subject indexing of the abstracted items. In 1958, I became editor of the bulletin. I had earlier had experience in the classification of books for a public library, as well as the writing of locally-relevant annotations to appear on catalog cards (cooperative or centralized cataloging was not the norm in the 1950s). I got myself involved in the field of "information retrieval" around 1961, and published my first paper in this area in 1963 and my first book in 1968.

In other words, I have had a very long involvement with the areas of subject analysis/information retrieval, have seen very many changes, and have known many of the principal actors on this particular stage.

Until the late 1940s and early 1950s, the field that we now think of as "information retrieval" was almost exclusively the domain of the library profession. The occurrence of two important international conferences, plus the recognition that computers might make a significant contribution to the information retrieval problem, made the field more glamorous, and brought researchers into the field from very many other areas.

Over a period of more than 50 years, contributions to the literature of information retrieval have come from virtually every academic field, including mathematics, computer science, psychology, statistics, law, and medicine (medical informatics).

While new faces and new approaches are always welcome, it is unfortunate that many now working in the field have absolutely no previous background and, thus, no firm foundation upon which to build. The greatest problem is caused by the fact that many now working in information retrieval seem completely unaware that procedures other than fully automatic ones have been applied, with some success, to information retrieval for more than 100 years, and that there does exist an information retrieval literature beyond that of the computer science community. A glaring example of this can be found in Agosti et al. (1995), who define the "steps of indexing" as "term extraction, stop-term removal, conflation, and weighting."

Many ideas appearing today have obvious antecedents in the literature of 30 or 40 years ago, yet these pioneering works are completely unknown to current investigators. A case in point is the research on visual maps or "browsers" to facilitate navigation in hypermedia systems (e.g., Fowler et al., 1996; Zizi, 1996) which is basically a rediscovery of the "semantic road maps" of Doyle (1961).

The image retrieval field seems to be worse than most in rediscovering the wheel. For example, a paper by Schreiber et al. (2001) describes a scheme for indexing photographs (they call it "ontology-based photo annotation") that is essentially based on a rather simple set of facets. They seem to believe that facet analysis originated with them or, at least, with others working in the same area. Ironically, their paper appears in a journal devoted to "intelligent systems."

Computer scientists writing on information retrieval seem to recognize and cite only other computer scientists writing on information retrieval. An obvious example is the almost invariable recognition and citation of Salton as the authority for recall and precision measures in the evaluation of information retrieval activities. Gerard Salton, important though he has been in the information retrieval field, most certainly did not introduce these measures which, in fact, can be traced back to the 1950s.

This rediscovery phenomenon has been highlighted by Holmes (2001), himself a computer scientist, who reminds us of George Santana's warning that those who cannot remember the past are condemned to repeat it. Holmes goes on from this to state:

> . . . what we think to be innovations will often be mere repetitions . . . our profession can develop faster and better through cumulative innovation, building on its past instead of ignoring it. (Page 144)

He claims that, in particular, the works of Vannevar Bush and Hans Peter Luhn, dating from forty to sixty years ago, contain ideas that have since been reinvented.

My worst experience with this particular problem occurred several years ago when I came across an article by a European scholar, essentially a mathematician, dealing with a topic that I had published on earlier. When I wrote to point out that he failed to cite my earlier work, and several by other researchers, he blithely wrote back to say that he never searched the literature unless he was writing a review article! What kind of egotistical non-scholarship is that?

Another result of the multiplicity of professions now contributing to the subject analysis/information retrieval literature is the fact that well-accepted and appropriate terminology from the library profession has been needlessly replaced. One obvious example is "metadata." The Oxford English Dictionary (online) traces this term back to 1968. Then it was used to refer to data describing sets of data (numerical or statistical). Since then it has become virtually a replacement for "bibliographic description," a perfectly good term that has been with us for very many years and is recognized in international standards. One could argue, of course, that "bibliographic" applies properly only to books. However, its extension to other documentary forms (as in "bibliographic database" and "bibliographic reference") has been with us for a long time.

Some writers, to be sure, have highlighted the same problem. Milstead and Feldman (1999), for example, make the point cogently:

> Whether you call it cataloging, indexing, or metadata, the concept is a familiar one for information professionals. Now the electronic world has finally discovered it. Until a few years ago, only a few philosophers had ever heard of the word "metadata." Today, it is hard to find a publication about electronic resources that ignores it. . . . Like the man who had been writing prose all his life without knowing it, librarians and indexers have been producing and standardizing metadata for centuries. Ignoring this legacy, an immense variety of other players have recently entered the field, and many of them have no idea that someone else has already "been there, done that." Different systems are being developed for different—and sometimes the same—kinds of information, resulting in a chaotic atmosphere of clashing standards. (Page 25)

Nevertheless, they seem disposed to accept the new terminology.

People from our own field, who surely should know better (and be more responsible), contribute to this situation. For example, Greenberg (2003) tells us that human metadata generation takes place when a person such as a professional metadata creator or content provider produces metadata. By "professional metadata creator" she means "cataloger" or "indexer," as she admits later in her article (although she also includes "web master" in this category). I was profoundly shocked (and not really pleased) to learn that I had spent several years of my life as a professional metadata creator, albeit unknowingly.

Many people writing in the image retrieval literature use the term "annotation" for the assignment of text labels, such as keywords, to describe what the image represents, which is clearly "indexing." This is doubly unfortunate because "annotation," for very many years, has been used to refer to what is essentially a very brief abstract (appearing at one time on catalog cards). Liu and Li (2002) refer to index terms assigned to video clips as "annotation tags." These seem to constitute a "semantic description" and are arrived at through "semantics extraction," which presumably means identification of subject dealt with.

Some of the confusion in terminology is caused by sloppy editorial work. I recently came across an article in which the word "indexation," appearing even in the title, is used as a synonym for "indexing." "Indexation" does exist in the English language but only in an economic context (e.g., having to do with such variables as wages or interest rising or falling at the same rate as the cost of living index); it most certainly is not a synonym for indexing. The authors, in this case, have an excuse because they are French ("indexation" is the French equivalent of "indexing") but there is no excuse for the editors of an English language journal to allow this misuse. I am now waiting for the word "indexation" to replace "indexing" in the computer science literature.

Santini (2002), another computer scientist, has urged his profession to use language more responsibly. He goes so far as to warn that:

Computing's rampant misuse of language threatens to isolate our profession from society and make our achievements incomprehensible. (Page 128)

Santini agrees with the point I am trying to make:

Other words make more sense but are being inexplicably abandoned in favor of less fitting terms. (Page 126)

The terms he singles out for contempt include "data warehouse" and "data mart" in place of "database."

A word I have some difficulty in accepting is "mining" (as in data mining, text mining, speech mining, or Web mining), which is often used as a synonym for "knowledge discovery" or, at least, the central operation of knowledge discovery. My father spent many years as a hewer in a coal mine in the north of England. He worked long hours, for much of the year seeing daylight only once a week. Often he hewed coal in a "wet seam," lying on his back or side in water in a passage with a very low ceiling. I'm not sure that this type of laborious extraction in semi-darkness is the analogy that "data miners" really want to use.

My biggest complaint, however, is the fact that the noun "classification" has virtually been replaced by (shudder!) "taxonomy," (double shudder!!) "ontology," or even (triple shudder!!!) "taxonomized set of terms." The way these terms are defined in recent articles clearly shows that they are used synonymously with "classification scheme." Typical is an article by Hovy (2003) who defines:

. . . an ontology simply as a taxonomized set of terms, ranging from very general terms at the top . . . down to very specialized ones at the bottom. (Page 48)

Hovy's "ontology" becomes a "concept hierarchy" in Meng et al. (2002). They define it as "a large number of concepts organized into multiple levels such that concepts at higher levels have broader meanings than those at lower levels." When I went to library school, umpteen years ago, these would have been accurate, although very simplistic, definitions of hierarchical classification.

Soergel (1999) has also decried the replacement of "classification" with "ontology," and has done it very well:

But a classification by any other name is still a classification. The use of a different term is symptomatic of the lack of communication between scientific communities. The vast body of knowledge on classification structure and on ways to display classifications developed around library classification and in information science more generally, and the huge intellectual capital embodied in many classification schemes and thesauri is largely ignored. Large and useful systems are being built with more effort than necessary. Examples are the CYC ontology (<www.cyc.com/cyc-2-1/intro-public.html>), whose presentation could be vastly improved, or WordNet (<www.cogsci.princeton.edu/~wn> or <www.notredame.ac.jp/cgi-bin/wn.cgi>), a wonderful system whose construction would have profited from applying experience in thesaurus construction and whose synset (concept) hierarchy should be made more easily accessible using standard methods for classification display. Another example is the ANSI Ad Hoc Group on Ontology Standards (<www-ksl.stanford.edu/onto-std/index.html>), which does not seem to have any information scientist concerned with classification among its numbers. (Page 1120)

"Classification" as an action is also being replaced in the information science literature, by "categorization" (as in "text categorization") but this, while annoying, does not seem quite so outrageous.

Some of the newer terminology is superficially attractive. I was reasonably receptive to the word "summarization" (because it could be used to embrace "abstracting," "extracting," and even "annotating") until I found that a major book dealing with the subject (Endres-Niggemeyer, 1998) includes subject indexing as a form of summarization. Although a set of index terms can, in fact, act as a kind of summary of content, summarization is certainly not the major purpose of indexing.

In this book I have clung to the older terminology whenever possible. For clarity, I have used a few newer terms, such as metadata, but I use them reluctantly.

LIST OF FIGURES

Part I

Theory, Principles, and Applications

CHAPTER 1

Introduction

THE MAIN PURPOSE of indexing and abstracting is to construct *representations* of published items in a form suitable for inclusion in some type of *database*. This database of representations could be in printed form (as in an indexing/abstracting publication such as *Chemical Abstracts* or the *Engineering Index*), in electronic form (in which case the database will often be roughly equivalent to a printed service), or in card form (as in a conventional library catalog).

The role of the indexing/abstracting operations within the larger framework of information retrieval activities in general is illustrated in Figure 1. First, the producer of the database selects from the population of newly published documents those that meet certain criteria for inclusion. The most obvious criterion is the subject dealt with, but others, such as type of document, language, or source, may also be important. For those databases that deal primarily with articles from journals, the selection criteria will usually focus on the journal rather than the article; that is, certain journals will be covered and others not (although some journals may be indexed in their entirety and others selectively). To a large extent, the coverage of many databases is governed by considerations of cost-effectiveness. Particularly in the case of databases dealing with a highly specialized field, only those journals that publish most on the subjects of interest will be included.

The items selected for inclusion in the database must be "described" in various ways. Descriptive cataloging procedures (not explicit in Figure 1) identify authors, titles, sources, and other bibliographic elements; indexing procedures identify the subject matter dealt with; and abstracting may be used to summarize the contents of the item. The terms used in indexing will frequently be drawn from some form of controlled vocabulary, such as a thesaurus (the "system vocabulary" of Figure 1), but may instead be "free" terms (e.g., drawn from the document itself).* These description activities create document representations in a form suitable for inclusion in the database. The documents themselves will usually go to a different type of database (document store) such as the shelves of a library.

---

*The terms applied may be referred to generically as "index terms,"although the word "descriptors" is frequently used also, especially when thesaurus terms are referred to. The two terms are used interchangeably in this book.

Members of the community to be served use the database primarily to satisfy various information needs. To do this they must convert an information need into some form of "search strategy," which may be as simple as selecting a single term to consult in a printed index or card catalog, or may involve the combining of many terms into a more elaborate and sophisticated strategy used to interrogate a database held locally or online to some network.

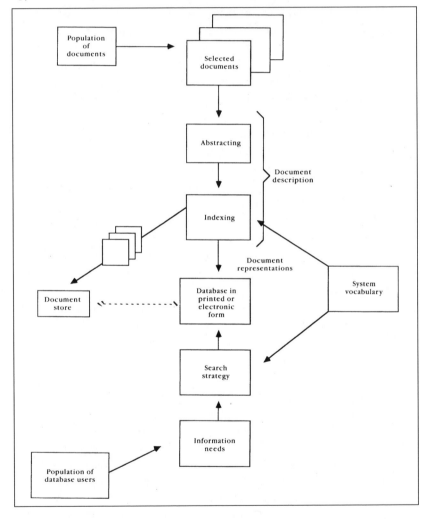

FIGURE 1

The role of indexing and abstracting in the larger information retrieval picture.

In searching a database, of course, one wants to find items that are useful in satisfying some information need, and to avoid retrieving items that are not useful. Terms such as "relevant" and "pertinent" are frequently used to refer to "useful" items, and these terms have been defined in several different ways. There is a lot of disagreement as to what "relevance" and "pertinence" really mean (Lancaster and Warner, 1993). In this book I will consider as synonymous the expressions "useful," "pertinent," and "relevant to an information need." That is, a pertinent (useful) item is one that contributes to the satisfaction of some information need.

The information retrieval problem is depicted graphically in Figure 2. The entire rectangle represents a database and the items it contains. The plus (+) items are those that a hypothetical requester would find useful in satisfying some current information need and the minus (−) items are those that he would judge not useful. For any particular information need there will be many more − items than + ones. Indeed, if the diagram were drawn "to scale" one would expect that the eleven useful items might be accompanied by a whole wall of useless ones. The problem is to retrieve as many as possible of the useful items and as few as possible of the useless ones.

The smaller of the two interior rectangles of Figure 2 represents the results of a search performed in the database. It retrieved 57 items, of which 6 were useful and 51 not useful. The ratio of useful items to total items retrieved (6/57, or about 10%, in this case) is usually referred to as a *precision ratio*. The ratio commonly used to express the extent to which all the useful items are found is the *recall ratio*. In this case the recall ratio is 6/11, or about 54%.

To improve recall in this situation one would probably need to search more broadly. This search is depicted by the larger of the two interior rectangles. Through searching more broadly, recall has been raised to 8/11 (73%) but precision has declined further to 8/112, or about 7%. It is an unfortunate characteristic of the information retrieval situation that an improvement in recall will usually cause a deterioration in precision, and vice versa.

Figure 2 suggests another phenomenon. It might be possible to search sufficiently broadly to find all the useful items (i.e., achieve 100% recall) but precision would probably be intolerable. Furthermore, the larger the database the less tolerable will be a low precision. A user who might be willing to look at abstracts of, say, 57 items to find 6 useful ones, may be much less willing to examine 570 abstracts for 60 useful ones. With very large databases, then, it becomes increasingly difficult to achieve an acceptable level of recall at a tolerable level of precision, a situation that has reached a critical state in searching for information on the Internet.

In this book I use the term *recall* to refer to the ability to retrieve useful items and *precision* to refer to the ability to avoid useless ones. There are other measures of the performance of searches in a database (see, for example, Robertson, 1969), some more mathematically exact, but *recall* and *precision* give the general picture and still seem to be the obvious measures to use to express the results of any search that simply divides a database into two parts (retrieved and not retrieved).* It is clear from Figure 1 that many factors determine whether a search in a database is successful or not. These include the coverage of the database, indexing policy, indexing practice, abstracting policy and practice, the quality of the vocabulary used to index, the quality of the search strategies, and so on. This book makes no attempt to deal with all of these factors (although they are all interrelated) but focuses on the important activities of document description or, at least, those concerned with the content of documents.

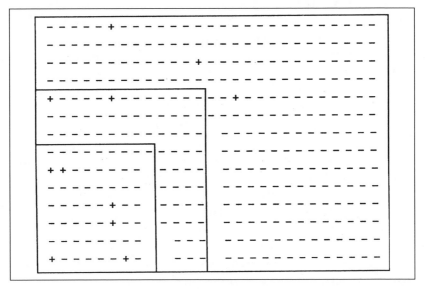

FIGURE 2
The problem of retrieving pertinent items from a database.

In principle, the database depicted in Figure 1 could be the entire content of the World Wide Web (hereafter simply the Web). However, the diagram does not represent the Web situation as well as it represents databases such as the catalog of an academic library or a database of bibliographic records for journal articles such as the MEDLINE database of the National Library of Medicine. Since any organization or individual can establish a Web site, there is no real selection process involved. Moreover, although Web

---

*A search that ranks output in order of "probable relevance" requires a somewhat different measure that in effect compares the ranking achieved with some ideal ranking.

sites may include some type of descriptive data about their contents (usually referred to as "metadata"; see the note immediately preceding this chapter), many do not, and the descriptive data are integral with the Web pages themselves, not in a separate database. Furthermore, human indexing and abstracting of Web content is the exception rather than the rule, so most Web searching is performed on the full text of the sites accessed by a particular search engine. Where indexing and/or abstracting operations are performed, they are likely to be performed "automatically" through various computer processing steps. Such automatic procedures, along with the searching of complete text and the special case of the Web, are dealt with in the concluding chapters of this book. While Figure 1 does not exactly correspond to the Web situation, Figure 2 does. That is, the search problem shown is equally relevant to Web searching except multiplied by orders of magnitude.

CHAPTER 2

Indexing Principles

WHILE THE TITLE OF THIS BOOK refers to "indexing," the scope is actually restricted to subject indexing and to abstracting. Subject indexing and abstracting are closely related activities in that both involve preparing a *representation* of the subject matter of documents. The abstractor writes a narrative description or summary of the document, while the indexer describes its contents by using one or several index terms, often selected from some form of controlled vocabulary.

The main purpose of the abstract is to indicate what the document is about or to summarize its contents. A group of index terms can serve the same purpose. For example, the following set of terms gives a fairly good idea of what is dealt with in some hypothetical report:

> Information Centers
> Resource Sharing
> Union Catalogs
> Cooperative Cataloging
> Online Networks
> Interlibrary Loans

In a sense, such a list of terms can be considered to act as a kind of mini-abstract. It would serve such a purpose if all the terms were listed together in a published index or were printed out or displayed to represent an item retrieved from some database as a result of an online search.

More obviously, the terms assigned by an indexer serve as access points through which an item can be located and retrieved in a subject search in a published index or electronic database.* Thus, in a printed index, one should be able to find the hypothetical item mentioned earlier under any one of the six terms. In a computer-based retrieval system, of course, one would expect to be able to find it under any one of these terms or, indeed, any combination of them.

---

*Other writers may use different terminology to refer to indexing and to index terms without significantly changing the meaning as presented in this book. For example, Anderson (1985) regards terms as "indicators" of content; indexing is "the process of indicating the content and related features of a document." O'Connor (1996) prefers the term "pointing": index terms are pointers; indexing is the task of providing useful pointers to sources of information.

The distinction between indexing and abstracting is becoming increasingly blurred. On the one hand, a list of index terms can be printed or displayed to form a mini-abstract. On the other, the text of abstracts can be stored in a computer-based system in such a way that searches can be performed on combinations of words occurring in the text. Such abstracts can be used instead of index terms, to allow access to the items, or can supplement the access points provided by the index terms. To some extent this changes the role of the abstractor, who must now be concerned not only with writing a good clear description of the contents of a document but also with creating a record that will be an effective representation for retrieval purposes.

If indexing and abstracting were looked upon as fully complementary activities, the character of the indexing operation might change somewhat. For example, the indexer could concentrate on assigning terms that supplement the access points provided in the abstract. However, such complementarity must be fully recognized and understood by the user of the database. Otherwise a set of index terms alone would give a very misleading picture of the content of an item.

Length of Record

One of the most important properties of a representation of subject matter is its length. The effect of record length is illustrated in the example of Figure 3. At the left are various representations of the content of a journal article in the form of narrative text; at the right are two representations in the form of lists of index terms.

The title is a general indication of what the article is about. The brief abstract gives more detail, indicating that survey results are presented in the article and identifying the major questions addressed. The extended abstract carries this further, identifying all of the survey questions and giving the size of the sample used in the study.

The more information given, the more clearly the representation indicates the scope of the article and the more likely it is to indicate to a reader whether or not it satisfies some information need. For example, one might be looking for articles mentioning U.S. attitudes toward various Arab leaders. The title gives no indication that this specific topic is discussed and the brief abstract, by focusing on other topics, suggests that it may not be. It is only the extended abstract that shows that the article includes information on this subject.

The longer the representation, too, the more access points it provides. If title words were the only access points, this item would probably be missed in many searches for which it might be considered a valuable response. As the length of the representation is increased, so is the retrievability of the item. Only with the extended abstract, presumably, would one be likely to retrieve this item in a search for information on U.S. attitudes toward Arab leaders.

Title	**Indexing** (selective)
Nation-wide public opinion survey of U.S. attitudes on the Middle East	PUBLIC OPINION TELEPHONE SURVEYS UNITED STATES
Abstract (brief)	ATTITUDES
A telephone survey held in 1985 presents views on such matters as: U.S. aid to Israel and to Egypt; whether the U.S. should side with Israel, the Arab nations, or neither; whether the PLO should participate in a peace conference; and whether an independent Palestinian State is a prerequisite for peace.	MIDDLE EAST **Indexing** (exhaustive) PUBLIC OPINION TELEPHONE SURVEYS UNITED STATES ATTITUDES MIDDLE EAST ISRAEL
Abstract (expanded)	EGYPT ARAB NATIONS
Telephone interviews were conducted in 1985 with 655 Americans sampled probabilistically. Answers were obtained to the following questions: is the establishment of a Palestinian State essential for peace; should U.S. aid to Israel and Egypt be reduced; should the U.S. participate in a peace conference that includes the PLO; should the U.S. favor neither Israel nor the Arab nations but maintain friendly relations with both? Opinions were also expressed on major Middle East leaders (Hussein, Arafat, Peres, Mubarak, Fahd, Assad), especially their peace efforts, and whether or not respondents felt they had enough information on the various national groups in the region.	PALESTINE LIBERATION ORGANIZATION PEACE CONFERENCES PEACE PALESTINIAN STATE FOREIGN AID POLITICAL LEADERS

FIGURE 3

Effect of record length on retrievability.

The same situation applies to indexing. The selective indexing, involving only five terms, gives a very general indication of what the article is about (roughly equivalent, in this case, to the title) and a very limited level of access.

The more exhaustive indexing provides a much better indication of the specific subject matter dealt with, as well as allowing many more access points.

Steps in Subject Indexing

Subject indexing involves two principal steps:

1. Conceptual analysis, and

2. Translation.

These are intellectually quite separate, although they are not always clearly distinguished and may actually occur simultaneously.

Conceptual analysis, first and foremost, involves deciding what a document is about—that is, what it covers. The terms listed on the right of Figure 3 represent this author's conceptual analysis of a particular article—what he considered it to be about.

This statement on conceptual analysis is oversimplified. Subject indexing is usually performed to meet the needs of a particular audience—the users of a particular information service or of a particular publication. Effective subject indexing involves deciding not only what a document is about but also why it is likely to be of interest to a particular group of users. In other words, there is no one "correct" set of index terms for any item. The same publication could be indexed rather differently in different information centers and should be indexed differently if the groups of users are interested in the item for different reasons.*

The indexer, then, must ask several questions about an item:

1. What is it about?

2. Why has it been added to our collection?

3. What aspects will our users be interested in?

The point is well illustrated in Figure 4. This hypothetical example refers to a report issued by the National Aeronautics and Space Administration (NASA) and dealing with a manned space flight. When NASA adds this report to its own database, it will presumably be interested in all facets and may index it exhaustively, trying to cover all of the aspects, perhaps at a fairly general level. One section of the report may deal with the clothing used by the astronauts, mentioning some new synthetic rubber compounds used in part of the clothing. This makes the report of interest to a rubber company. When added to this company's collection, however, the report will be indexed quite differently. Highly specific terms will be used to index the

---

*Dabney (1986a) recognized this in the distinction he makes between document-oriented and request-oriented indexing. It is also implicit in the "gedanken" approach advocated by Cooper (1978).

new compounds and the general term *space suits* may be used to indicate the particular application of the compounds. A metals company may be interested in this report for another reason: it mentions a new welding technique developed to join some alloys in the construction of the space vehicle. Here it is indexed under the welding terms, the appropriate metals terms and perhaps the general application term *space vehicles*. The rubber company indexes the report quite differently from the metals company and neither set of terms resembles the more exhaustive list used by NASA itself.

NASA Technical Report Describing a New Manned Space Mission		
NASA	**Rubber Company**	**Metals Company**
_____ Exhaustive	_____ New	_____ New welding
_____ indexing	_____ synthetic	_____ techniques
_____ covering	_____ rubber	_____ and metals
_____ all aspects	_____ compounds	_____ involved
_____ at a	_____	_____
_____ somewhat		
_____ general level	SPACE SUITS	SPACE VEHICLES
_____		
_____		
_____		
_____		
_____		
_____		

FIGURE 4
Example of an item indexed from various points of view.

This is as it should be. The more specialized the clientele of an information center, the more likely it is that the indexing can and should be tailored to the precise interests of the group. It is only in more general institutions— e.g., general academic libraries—that one might expect to find one organization indexing an item in exactly the same way as another. Fidel (1994) uses the term "user-centered indexing" to refer to the principle of indexing on the basis of requests expected from a particular audience.

Hjørland (2001) agrees that indexing must be tailored to the needs of a particular clientele:

> Because any document can, in principle, provide answers to an infinity of questions, subject analyses should establish priorities based on the specific user groups served (or specific services provided in the information ecology). The subject of a document is thus relative to the aim of the specific information service. I define subject . . . as the epistemological or informative *potentials* of documents. The best subject analysis is the one that makes the best prognosis of the future use of the document. (Page 776)

This point has also been addressed by Bates (1998):

> . . . the challenge for the indexer is to try to anticipate what terms people with information gaps of various descriptions might search for in those cases where the record in hand would, in fact, go part way in satisfying the user's information need. This can be seen to be a very peculiar challenge, when one thinks about it. What kinds of information needs would people have that might lead them to want some information that this record would, in fact, provide? (Page 1187)

Mai (2001), who uses semiotics in his analysis of the subject indexing process, gives a clear description of the difficulties involved in trying to recognize why a document might be of interest to future users:

> It would be nearly impossible, of course, for any single person or, in this case, any single indexer, to determine *all* of the ideas and meanings which might be associated with any particular document, since there might always be potential ideas and meanings which different people at different times and places might find in the document. Furthermore, it would be well nigh impossible to predict precisely which of the many possible ideas and meanings that could be associated with the document would be specifically valuable to the users or would have some sort of lasting value for the document. To recognise and accept this fundamental openness is of utmost importance. The indexer must realise from the start that he or she will never discover all the ideas and meanings that could be associated with the document and that, therefore, it is not possible to describe all these ideas and meanings. (Page 606)

Referring specifically to the indexing of art images, Layne (2002) also recognizes the need for different indexing, with different terminology, for different audiences:

> The second aspect of vocabulary choice for art images is that any given image may be of interest to different disciplines with different vocabularies. For example, *The Birth of Esau and Jacob* might be of interest to historians of medicine who might wish to use a medical vocabulary, rather than a more general vocabulary, when searching for images. Clearly, it is not practical to use all possible vocabularies when providing subject access to art images, but if it is known or intended that a particular collection of art images will be used by a particular discipline, it may be worth considering the use of a specialized vocabulary in addition to a general vocabulary. For example, an image of tulips might be indexed as "tulips" or even "flowers" for general users, but scientific species names such as *Tulipa turkestanica* might be used as indexing terms if botanists are among the intended users. (Page 15)

For certain types of materials, user-oriented indexing may be even more important than it is for journal articles, books, or technical reports. For example, writers such as Shatford (1986) and Enser (1995) point out that collections of images can be viewed quite differently by different groups of users. Thus, each group has different indexing needs. This led Brown et al. (1996) to suggest the need for a "democratic" approach to indexing, with users of the images adding their own terms to a record where necessary and appropriate.

Hidderley and Rafferty (1997) present one approach to democratic indexing. A sample of users is given an object (book, article, image) along with a "public view" indexing of it (e.g., a set of terms drawn by experienced indexers from a thesaurus). They modify the public view to reflect their own "private view." On the basis of multiple private views of a set of objects, a new public view emerges. A reconciliation process is used to arrive at the final public view. This process takes into account how many users have associated a particular term with a particular object. In particular, they advocate a "democratic" approach to the indexing of fiction because, as they point out, "fictional text may be read in a number of different ways."

Collaborative or "democratic" approaches are most often advocated in the case of the indexing of images (see Chapter 13).

Collaborative approaches to indexing are obviously more feasible in a digital library environment. That is, users of a particular library could provide new index terms for the items they consult, and user-supplied terms could then be stored in a new field in the record. Villarroel et al. (2002) propose an approach in which users highlight sections of digital text that they judge of importance and this highlighting can lead to the revision of "weights" (see Chapter 11) associated with the index terms or text words.

There is an important lesson to be learned from the principles of user-oriented indexing. Indexers need to know much more than the principles of indexing. In particular, they must be thoroughly familiar with the interests of the community served and the information needs of members of that community. Indeed, it will usually be desirable that the indexers should not remain "behind the scenes" but should also work in other capacities, such as that of a reference librarian, in which they participate in searching the records they have created.

One can carry the user-oriented indexing principle even further by claiming that, in relation to a particular collection of documents and group of users, any optimum set of index terms would be optimum *only at a particular point in time*. A few years later, the same group of users may need access to the same collection (or one closely similar) from different perspectives. An obvious example might be a collection of technical reports within a research organization: changing priorities of the organization, and of its research interests, may change the way in which the collection is useful to the community. This might be particularly true in the case of interdisciplinary research. In fact, one could argue that, in an ideal world, a collection of documents would be organized (i.e., indexed) around the interests of a particular research initiative. When the initiative changes, the collection would be reorganized around the new requirements. Of course, the cost of re-indexing, and reorganization in general, makes this an economically unattractive proposition. Weinberg (1992) is one author who has pointed to the impermanence of subject access and the fact that it is "relative." However, she bases this on the fact that vocabularies (e.g., subject headings, classifications) change rather than the fact that user needs and interests do.

Mai (2000) also warns that user-oriented indexing can only be directed toward a particular set of users at a particular point in time:

> If one focuses solely on the representation aspect and ignores future users, one might risk representing documents in a way that would be of no use for the users. An indexer who does not pay much attention to the users might choose to represent subjects of documents that are of no interest to the users, or might use a different vocabulary from the users, or might represent the subject on a level that is too broad or too narrow for the users. However, if the indexer pays too much attention to the users of the system, the indexer might represent documents in such a way that the subject representation of the documents only serves the current users and those current information needs. (Page 294)

Aboutness

In the previous discussion no attempt was made to define "about": the expression "is about" was merely a synonym for "covers." That is, "what a document is about" was used to mean the same as "what a document covers." These expressions may not be very precise and the terms "about" and "covers" are not easily defined. Nevertheless, they are expressions that seem acceptable to most people and to be understood by them. It is not my intention to enter into a philosophical discussion on the meaning of "about" or "aboutness." A number of authors have already done so. In so doing, they have failed to clarify the situation, at least as far as the task of subject indexing is concerned. Beghtol (1986) and Hutchins (1978) both draw upon text linguistics in discussing the subject, Maron (1977) adopts a probabilistic approach, and Swift et al. (1978) are careful to point out that aboutness in indexing may not coincide with the aboutness that searchers for information are concerned with. Wilson (1968) goes so far as to imply that subject indexing faces "intractable" problems because it is so difficult to decide what a document is about.

Moens et al. (1999) take the position that a text does have an intrinsic "aboutness" but that it also has different "meanings" in accordance with "the particular use that a person can make of the aboutness at a given time."

Layne (2002) makes a distinction between "of-ness" and "aboutness" in the case of art images:

> Less obvious than the *of-ness* of a work of art, but often more intriguing, is what the work of art is *about* . . . Sometimes the *about-ness* of a work of art is relatively clear, as in Georg Pencz's *Allegory of Justice* . . . This image is *of* a naked woman holding a sword and scales, but the title tells us that the image is an allegorical figure representing justice or, in other words, that the image is *about* the abstract concept "justice." In Goya's drawing *Contemptuous of the Insults* . . . the *about-*

ness is slightly less obvious, but it is still clear that this work of art has some meaning beyond simply what it is *of*. Indeed, a description of what it is *of*—a man, perhaps Goya himself, gesturing toward two dwarfs wearing uniforms—is not really sufficient to make sense of this image; it symbolizes something else, it is *about* something else: the relationship between Spain and France at the beginning of the nineteenth century or, more specifically, Goya's personal attitude toward the French occupation of Spain. (Page 4)

She believes this distinction is a valuable one and that, in retrieval, it should be possible to separate the two:

> . . . it makes it possible to retrieve, for example, just those images that are *of* "death" and to exclude those images that are *about* "death." It also permits the subdivision of large sets of retrieved images based on these distinctions. For example, a search on "death" as a subject could result in a retrieval of images subdivided into groups based on whether the image explicitly depicts "death" or is *about* the theme of "death." (Page 13)

Bruza et al. (2000) deal with aboutness from a logical perspective. They "attempt to formalize logical relevance by formalizing commonsense properties describing the aboutness relation." They also deal with "nonaboutness" and the interaction between aboutness and nonaboutness. In the information retrieval context, nonaboutness is actually a simpler situation because the great majority of items in any database clearly bear no possible relationship to any particular query or information need (i.e., they are clearly "nonabout" items).

The subject of aboutness is very much related to that of "relevance" — i.e., the relationship between a document and an information need or between a document and a statement of information need (a query). The subject of relevance/pertinence has generated a great deal of debate and literature. A very complete overview can be found in Mizzaro (1998). Hjørland (2000) points out that relevance is dependent on the theoretical assumptions that guide the behavior of the person seeking information.

As Harter (1992) has pointed out, however, a document can be relevant to some information need without being "about" that information need. For example, if I am writing on the subject of barriers to communication, a history of Latin may have some relevance, especially if it deals with the present use of Latin in the Catholic Church and with those organizations that are now trying to promote its wider use. Nevertheless, although I might be able to draw upon this source in my article, few people would claim that it is "about" international communication and it is unlikely to be indexed in this way unless the author explicitly makes reference to the international communication aspect.

Wong et al. (2001) treat "aboutness" as more or less synonymous with "relevance":

> . . . if a given document D is *about* the request Q, then there is a high likelihood that D will be relevant with respect to the associated information need. Thus the information retrieval problem is reduced to deciding the aboutness relation between documents and requests. (Page 338)

They relate aboutness directly to recall and precision measures.

Articles on aboutness continue to appear in the literature. Hjørland (2001) and Bruza et al. (2000) are examples. While these may have some academic interest (Hjørland goes to great length to try to distinguish such terms as "subject," "topic," "theme," "domain," "field," and "content"), they have no practical value to the indexer, who would do well to ignore such semantic differences and simply give an item the labels that will make it usefully retrievable by members of a target community.

Put differently, do we really need to understand "aboutness" in order to index effectively? Is it not enough to be able to recognize that a document is of interest to a particular community because it contributes to our understanding of topics X, Y, and Z? The recognition that it does contribute in this way exemplifies the process we have called "conceptual analysis," while the process of "translation" involves a decision on which of the available labels best represent X, Y, and Z. "Concept" is another word that some writers like to philosophize around (see, for example, Dahlberg (1979)). In this book I use it to refer to a topic discussed by an author or represented in some other way (e.g., in a photograph or other image). "Conceptual analysis," then, means nothing more than identifying the topics discussed or otherwise represented in a document. Preschel (1972) has a very practical approach. She takes "concept" to mean "indexable matter" and defines "conceptual analysis" as "indexer perception of indexable matter." Also practical is Tinker (1966):

> By assigning a descriptor [i.e., an index term] to a document, the indexer asserts that the descriptor has a high degree of relevance to the content of the document; that is, he asserts that the meaning of the descriptor is strongly associated with a concept embodied in the document, and that it is appropriate for the subject area of the document. (Page 97)

Wooster (1964) is even more pragmatic. He refers to indexing as assigning terms "presumably related in some fashion to the intellectual content of the original document, to help you find it when you want to."

I find nothing wrong with these pragmatic definitions or descriptions of subject indexing. Purists will no doubt quibble with them on the grounds that such expressions as "indexable matter," "relevance," "meaning," "associated with," "concept," "appropriate for," "related to," and "intellectual content" are not precisely defined to everyone's satisfaction. However, if one must reach agreement on the precise definition of terms before pursuing any task, one is unlikely to accomplish much—in indexing or any other activity.

Weinberg (1988) hypothesizes that indexing fails the researcher because it deals only in a general way with what a document is "about" and does not focus on what it provides that is "new" concerning the topic. She maintains that this distinction is reflected in the difference between "about-ness" and "aspect," between "topic" and "comment," or between "theme" and "rheme." She fails to convince that these distinctions are really useful in the context of indexing or that it might be possible for indexers to main-tain such distinctions.

Swift et al. (1978) discuss the limitations of an aboutness approach to index-ing in the social sciences. They recommend indexing documents accord-ing to the "problems" to which they seem to relate. It is difficult to see how the distinction they make differs from the distinction, made earlier in this chapter, between what an item deals with and why a particular user or group of users might be interested in it. Crowe (1986) maintains that the indexer should address the "subjective viewpoint" of the author. One of her exam-ples deals with the topic of depression which can be discussed in books or articles from several different viewpoints (e.g., treatment through psy-chotherapy, through drug therapy, and so on). Again, it is difficult to see how this differs from normal indexing practice as exemplified by the National Library of Medicine's use of subheadings.

Breton (1981) claims that engineers make little use of databases because indexers label items with the *names* of materials or devices while engineers are more likely to want to search for their *attributes* or the *functions* they perform. In other words, they would like to locate a material or device that satisfies some current requirement (for strength, conductivity, corrosion resis-tance, or whatever) without being able to name it. This is not a condem-nation of subject indexing per se but of the indexing policies adopted by the majority of database producers. If a new material or alloy described in a report is said to have a certain tensile strength, the property may be indexed (e.g., by assigning the term *tensile strength*), but the particular *value* of the property (i.e., the strength attainable) would not be indexed by most data-base producers, although it may well be mentioned in the abstract. Of course, there is no reason why values could not be indexed (e.g., the term *tensile strength* might be subdivided into twenty more specific terms, each one representing a range of tensile strength values) and they would be in cer-tain databases, such as a company's indexes to its own contract files, indexes to data compilations, or certain patent databases. Some of Breton's objections, then, could be countered by indexing at a much higher level of specificity. Functions can also be indexed as long as the possible functions of a device are identified by an author, and appropriate terms exist in the vocabulary of the database, but it is altogether unreasonable to expect the indexer to be able to recognize applications not specifically claimed by the author.

Later, Breton (1991) reported research on an indexing system that embodied his ideas and was intended to aid "invention." The experimental system was derived from the indexing of several thousand industrial products according to the functions they perform and their "distinctive attributes." The attributes include such things as "lighter," "cheaper," "safer," and "stronger."

Some writers suggest that retrieval may be improved in certain contexts by indexing only particular characteristics in a text. For example, Oh (1998) suggests that, in psychology, the indexing only of "empirical facts" (variable names, correlation values, and significance level information) would improve the retrieval situation. While highly specialized indexing of this type may be justified in a few unusual situations, it is unlikely to be a majority requirement and will probably be much more expensive than a more conventional approach.

It has become fashionable in recent years to view the information retrieval problem as primarily one of matching the "anomalous state of knowledge" of a requester with the more "coherent" state of knowledge of authors (see, for example, Belkin et al., 1982), the implication being that the problems lie more with system output (searching) than with input. This is somewhat misleading. If one accepts that indexing is most effective when oriented toward the needs of a particular group of users, the indexer's role is to predict the types of requests for which a particular document is likely to be a useful response. This is probably more difficult than predicting what types of documents are likely to be useful responses to a particular request, which is in a sense what the searcher's function is. One could argue, then, that the "anomalous" state of knowledge applies more to the input side of the retrieval system than it does to the output. Olafsen and Vokac (1983) make the point clearly:

> The indexer has to make guesses at what questions the future user of the system will put. Regardless of how cleverly the guesswork is construed, they are still guesses, while the user approaches the system with his own concrete question, and his associations may be different from those of the indexer. (Page 294)

They too oversimplify in referring to user questions as "concrete" when, in fact, many will be far from it. Nevertheless, they are probably correct in implying that the problems of effective input to a retrieval system exceed the output problems. As Fairthorne (1958) pointed out many years ago: "Indexing is the basic problem as well as the costliest bottleneck of information retrieval."

In some indexing applications it may be possible to be rather more precise on what should be considered "indexable." In discussing the indexing of an encyclopedia, for example, Preschel (1981) offers the following guidelines:

> All text information of a substantive nature should be indexed. "Substantive" is here defined as information that covers 8-10 text lines *or* that is *unique* or *outstanding* and will almost certainly not occur elsewhere in the encyclopedia. (Page 2)*

In other situations it is not always possible to be so precise.

In fact, the question of what an item is about gets much more difficult when one considers the indexing of imaginative works, such as fiction or feature films, or images in general. Aboutness in these contexts is treated in later chapters.

Of course, the whole "aboutness" question has become much more complex in the current hypertext/hypermedia environment. When one item can be linked to several others, it is no longer clear where one ends and another begins. Is a document only about what it deals with directly, or is it also about the topics dealt with in the associated items? Little has been written on hypertext indexing per se, although it is touched upon to some extent in the hypertext/hypermedia literature. Savoy (1995) and Salton et al. (1997) discuss possible methods for establishing hypertext links automatically, which can be considered a form of automatic indexing. This subject is dealt with in later chapters.

Translation

Translation, the second step in subject indexing, involves the conversion of the conceptual analysis of a document into a particular set of index terms. In this connection, a distinction can be made between indexing by *extraction* (derivative indexing) and indexing by *assignment*. In indexing by extraction, words or phrases actually occurring in a document are selected to represent its subject matter. For example, the item in Figure 3 might be indexed with the following terms:

PUBLIC OPINION	ISRAEL
TELEPHONE SURVEYS	EGYPT
UNITED STATES	AID
ATTITUDES	PEACE
MIDDLE EAST	

all of which appear in the title or abstract. An early form of derivative indexing, known as *Uniterm*, used only single words to represent subject matter. If strictly observed, the Uniterm system brought some strange results, such as the splitting of Middle East into *Middle* and *East*.

Assignment indexing involves assigning terms to a document from a source other than the document itself. The terms could be drawn from the

---

*This quotation, from an unpublished work, is reproduced by permission of Funk & Wagnalls.

indexer's head; e.g., an indexer might decide that the terms *foreign aid* and *foreign relations*, which do not appear explicitly in either abstract, might be good terms to use with the item in Figure 3.

More commonly, assignment indexing involves trying to represent the substance of the conceptual analysis by the use of terms drawn from some form of controlled vocabulary.

Controlled Vocabularies

A controlled vocabulary is basically an authority list. In general, indexers can only assign to a document terms that appear on the list adopted by the agency for whom they work. Usually, however, the controlled vocabulary is more than a mere list. It will generally incorporate some form of semantic structure. In particular, this structure is designed to:

1. Control synonyms by choosing one form as the standard and referring from all others.
2. Distinguish among homographs. For example, *Turkey (country)* is a term quite distinct from *Turkey (bird)*.
3. Bring or link together those terms whose meanings are most closely related. Two types of relationships may be explicitly identified: the hierarchical and the nonhierarchical (or associative) relationship. For example, the term *working women* is related hierarchically to *women* (as a species of this term) and to *housewives* (also a species of the term *women*), as well as being *associated* with such terms as *employment* or *single parent families*, which appear in quite different hierarchies.

Three major types of controlled vocabularies can be identified: bibliographic classification schemes (such as the *Dewey Decimal Classification*), lists of subject headings, and thesauri. All attempt to present terms both alphabetically and "systematically." In the bibliographic classifications, the alphabetical arrangement is secondary, in the form of an index to the major arrangement, which is hierarchical. In the thesaurus, the overt arrangement of terms is alphabetical but a covert hierarchical structure is built into the alphabetical list through the use of cross-references. The traditional list of subject headings is similar to the thesaurus in that it is alphabetically based. It differs from the thesaurus because it incorporates an imperfect hierarchical structure and fails to distinguish clearly between the hierarchical and the associative relationship. All three types of vocabulary control synonyms, distinguish among homographs and group related terms together, but they use somewhat different methods to achieve these ends.

A more complete discussion of these matters can be found in Lancaster (1986).

Indexing as Classification

In the literature of library and information science, a distinction is some-times made among the three terms *subject indexing, subject cataloging,* and *classification.* *Subject cataloging* usually refers to the assignment of subject headings to represent the overall contents of complete biblio-graphic items (books, reports, periodicals, and so on) within the catalog of a library. *Subject indexing* is a term used more loosely; it may refer to the representation of the subject matter of *parts* of complete bibliographic items as in the case of an index at the back of a book. Thus, a library may "cata-log" a book under the subject heading *dogs* to indicate its overall subject matter; the detailed contents of the book are only revealed by the back-of-the-book *subject index.* This distinction between the terms *subject cata-loging* and *subject indexing,* one referring to complete bibliographic items and the other to parts of items, is artificial, misleading, and inconsistent. The process by which the subject matter of bibliographic items is repre-sented in published databases—printed or electronic form—is almost invari-ably referred to as *subject indexing,* whether overall items or their parts are being discussed. Thus, the *subject index* to, say, *Chemical Abstracts* might refer to complete books or complete technical reports as well as referring to parts of bibliographic items (chapters in books, papers within confer-ence proceedings, articles in periodicals). On the other hand, libraries may choose to represent parts of books (e.g., chapters or papers) within the cat-alog; this is usually referred to as *analytical cataloging.* When applied to subject matter, this activity would be analytical subject cataloging.

The situation is even more confusing when the term *classification* is con-sidered. Librarians tend to use the word to refer to the assignment of class numbers [drawn from some classification scheme—e.g., Dewey Decimal (DDC), Universal Decimal (UDC), Library of Congress (LC)] to bibliographic items, especially for the purpose of arranging these items on the shelves of libraries, in filing cabinets, and so on. But the subject catalog of a library can be either alphabetically based (an *alphabetical subject catalog* or a *dic-tionary catalog*) or arranged according to the sequence of some classification scheme (a *classified catalog*). Suppose a librarian picks up a book and decides that it is about "birds." He or she might assign the subject heading *birds* to this item. Alternatively, the class number 598 may be assigned to it. Many people would refer to the first operation as *subject cataloging* and to the second as *classification,* a completely nonsensical distinction. More con-fusion occurs when one realizes that *subject indexing* may involve the use of a classification scheme or that a printed subject index might follow the sequence of some classification scheme.

These terminological distinctions are quite meaningless and only serve to cause confusion (see Acton, 1986, for a typical example). The fact is that *classification*, in the broadest sense, permeates all of the activities associated with information storage and retrieval. Part of the terminological confusion is caused by failure to distinguish between the *conceptual analysis* and the *translation* stages in indexing.

Suppose that an information specialist picks up some item and decides that it deals with the subject of "robots." The intellectual activity involved in the decision is the same whatever the item dealt with—book, part of book, periodical, article in a periodical, conference proceedings, conference paper, photograph, or whatever. The information specialist has *classified* the item, i.e., put it into the conceptual class of "items discussing robots."

As previously discussed, the process of *translation* involves the representation of the conceptual analysis by means of a term or terms drawn from some vocabulary. A term assigned to an item is merely a *label* identifying a particular class of items. This label could be the English term *artificial intelligence* drawn from a thesaurus, a list of subject headings or from the document itself, an equivalent word in another language, or a label such as 006.3 drawn from some classification scheme.

The process of deciding what some item is about and of giving it a label to represent this decision is conceptually the same whether the label assigned is drawn from a classification scheme, a thesaurus, or a list of subject headings, whether the item is a complete bibliographic entity or a portion of it, whether the label is subsequently filed alphabetically or in some other sequence (or, in fact, not filed at all), and whether the object of the exercise is to organize items on shelves or records in catalogs, printed indexes, or electronic databases.

In the field of information storage and retrieval, document *classification* refers to the formation of classes of items on the basis of their subject matter. Thesauri, subject headings, and bibliographic classification schemes are primarily lists of the *labels* by which these classes are identified and, perhaps, arranged. The process of searching for information involves deciding which classes to consult in a printed index, card catalog, or electronic database. A search can involve the examination of a single class (e.g., everything appearing under the heading *robots*) or it can involve combinations of classes (e.g., items appearing under *robots* and also under *artificial intelligence*). How much combination is possible, or how easily various classes can be combined, is very much dependent on the format of the tool used for searching, especially on whether it is in printed or electronic form.

In short, *subject indexing* is conceptually identical to *subject cataloging*. The activity involved is that of *subject classification*, i.e., forming classes of objects on the basis of their subject matter. In this text, the term *subject indexing* or even *indexing* is used as a matter of convenience to refer to all activities of subject classification.

Specificity of the Vocabulary

Figure 5 shows a conceptual analysis prepared for a journal article and the translation of this conceptual analysis into three different types of vocabulary. The article deals with the use of robots in industry, specifically their use in manufacturing and materials handling applications. It also discusses the use of artificial intelligence techniques in the design and operation of robots, as well as the special problems involved in getting robots to move properly (i.e., problems of locomotion).

Conceptual Analysis	Dewey Decimal Classification	Library of Congress Subject Headings	INSPEC Thesaurus
Industrial robots		ROBOTS, INDUSTRIAL	INDUSTRIAL ROBOTS
Artificial intelligence	670.427263 Artificial intelligence applied to robots in factory operations	ARTIFICIAL INTELLIGENCE	ARTIFICIAL INTELLIGENCE
Manufacturing operations		MANUFACTURING PROCESSES— AUTOMATION	MANUFACTURING PROCESSES
Materials handling	621.86 Materials handling equipment	MATERIALS HANDLING	MATERIALS HANDLING
Locomotion	531.112 Kinematics	ROBOTS—MOTION	KINEMATICS

FIGURE 5
Conceptual analysis translated into three controlled vocabularies.

In all respects, the conceptual analysis can be translated effectively into any one of the vocabularies. It should be noted that the ideas conveyed by the conceptual analysis in Figure 5 are covered *collectively* by the groups of terms listed under the three vocabularies. For example, the three DDC class numbers, taken together, cover the subject matter of this article clearly and completely, although there is no one-to-one relationship between the individual elements of the conceptual analysis and the DDC terms. While earlier editions of the DDC did not permit very much synthesis of notations (i.e., number building), the later editions permit more and more of this. Thus, 670.4272, robots in factory operations, can be subdivided by 004-006. Since 006.3 represents artificial intelligence, the numbers can be combined to form the highly specific 670.427263.

The conceptual analysis in Figure 5 is covered equally completely and specifically in each vocabulary when entire groups of terms are considered. At the single term level, of course, differences do exist. If only one term could be assigned to this article, DDC would do better than the other vocabularies since a single class number can be built to express the major topic of the article.

This example illustrates two important points. First, the type of controlled vocabulary (classification scheme, subject headings, thesaurus) is not the most important factor affecting the translation stage of indexing. Much more important are the scope (coverage) and specificity of the vocabulary. In this indexing exercise, all three vocabularies can cover the subject quite well, although in somewhat different ways. The second point illustrated is that, while specificity is a very important property of a controlled vocabulary, it can be achieved in different ways in different vocabularies. In particular, it is important to consider the properties of *combinations* of index terms rather than the properties of single terms.

Consider, as an example, an article discussing mental health services. Vocabulary *A* contains the specific descriptor *mental health services*, while Vocabulary *B* has the term *health services* but not the more specific term. Nevertheless, *B* also includes the term *mental health*, so the idea of "mental health services" can be specifically covered by indexing under *health services* and *mental health*. With regard to this topic, then, vocabulary *B* is as specific as *A*. Vocabularies *C* and *D* are less specific: *C* contains the term *mental health* but has no health services term while *D* contains *health services* but lacks a mental health term, so neither one has the ability to express specifically the idea "mental health services." When it comes to searching the systems represented by the various vocabularies, it should be possible to achieve effective results in *A* and *B*, but it will be impossible to restrict the search in *C* and *D*—either everything on mental health or everything on health services will be retrieved.

This chapter has dealt with indexing principles in the abstract since no single information service has been used as a model. Large information services are likely to produce their own indexing guidelines and these are worth examination to see how rules apply in a particular context. A good example for study is the indexing/abstracting manual for the International Nuclear Information System (Bürk et al., 1996).

CHAPTER 3

Indexing Practice

INDEXERS RARELY HAVE THE LUXURY of being able to read a document carefully from cover to cover. The requirement that they index a certain number of items per day will usually dictate that they must accept less than a complete reading. A combination of reading and "skimming" is usually advocated. The parts to be carefully read will be those likely to tell the most about the contents in the shortest period of time: the title, abstract, summary, and conclusions. Section headings and captions to illustrations or tables are also worth more attention. The rest of the text should be skimmed to ensure that the more condensed parts give an accurate picture of what the item is about. Nevertheless, the indexer should usually take into account the entire document (parts read, parts skimmed) and the terms assigned should reflect the whole. The exception would be the case in which only part of the document (e.g., a lengthy multitopical item) is of interest to the user group to be served.

Jones (1976), quoting Anderson (1971), points out that some parts of a document are especially rewarding to an indexer: "Opening paragraphs (in chapters or sections) and opening and closing sentences of paragraphs seem to be particularly rich in indexable words." This agrees with the findings of Baxendale (1958) in her work on the development of procedures for the automatic indexing of documents.

An international standard on subject indexing (*Methods for Examining Documents*, 1985) offers further guidance on the examination of the document:

> A complete reading is often impracticable, nor is it always necessary, but the indexer should ensure that no useful information has been overlooked. Important parts of the text need to be considered carefully, and particular attention should be paid to the following:
>
> a. the title;
> b. the abstract, if provided;
> c. the list of contents;
> d. the introduction, the opening phrases of chapters and paragraphs, and the conclusion;
> e. illustrations, diagrams, tables, and their captions;
> f. words or groups of words which are underlined or printed in an unusual typeface.

All these elements should be scanned and assessed by the indexer during his study of the document. Indexing from the title alone is not recommended, and an abstract, if available, should not be regarded as a satisfactory substitute for an examination of the text. Titles may be misleading; both titles and abstracts may be inadequate; in many cases neither is a reliable source of the kind of information needed by an indexer. (Page 2)

In their comprehensive study of how indexers actually operate, Oliver et al. (1966) discovered that the majority do follow a read/scan approach:

> The largest group of indexers (about 85 percent of the total) stated that they routinely examine the entire document. However, these indexers stressed that certain sections of the document were examined more carefully than others. These sections included the abstract, introduction, summary, conclusion, methodology, findings, and charts and graphs. If one or more of these "condensed" sections were considered adequate by the indexer, he might lightly scan, or simply "page through" other parts of the document. The major reasons given for looking at the body of the document were to see if anything was overlooked, to facilitate greater depth in indexing, and to clarify any doubts or questions. (Page 4-14)

More recently, Chu and O'Brien (1993) found that novice indexers made heavy use of an abstract, when available, in determining the subject of articles; however, while they used more than a hundred indexers, they used only three articles.

One assumption underlying all of this is that the item to be indexed can be read. As ISO 5963 (*Methods for Examining Documents*, 1985) points out, different procedures will apply to other types of item:

> Non-print documents, such as audio-visual, visual, and sound media, including realia, call for different procedures. It is not always possible in practice to examine a record in its entirety (for example by running a film). Indexing is then usually carried out from a title and/or synopsis, though the indexer should be allowed to view or hear a performance of the medium if the written description is inadequate or appears to be inaccurate. (Page 2)

A book by Šauperl (2002) describes how catalogers in libraries go about determining the subject of a book and choosing which subject headings and class numbers to apply to it. It is based on in-depth observation of the work of twelve individuals.

Indexing of sources in electronic form presents special problems. Browne (2001), for example, has pointed out the problems of indexing sites on the Web:

> The first step in indexing a Web site is to get a feel for the amount and type of material to be indexed. You can hold the page proofs of a book in one hand and flick through them. You can't do this with the Web, so you have to systematically examine the site, taking note of the sort of information, the amount of detail, and the quality of the navigation links. Check the size of files in megabytes. Ask the Webmaster to provide as much information as possible about the files, including the number of authors who have contributed Web pages. The more authors, the more variation you can expect, and the more sampling you should do. (Page 32)

The reason for examining the document, of course, is to decide what to include in the indexing (in the terms of Preschel (1972), this is the identification of the "indexable matter").*

As suggested in Chapter 2, to do this effectively the indexer must know a great deal about the interests of the community served. Within a particular organization, indexers may be instructed to look for certain predefined elements in a document; if these occur they *must* be covered in the indexing. Depending on the type of organization, such essential elements might include: materials of construction, temperatures involved, age group involved, educational level, and so on. In some cases the more essential elements may be preprinted onto an indexing form (or, more likely today, displayed online) to remind the indexer that the appropriate terms must be used if they apply to a particular document. For example, the National Library of Medicine uses "checktags" of this kind to account for age groups, gender, types of animals used in experiments, and so on.

This "conceptual analysis" stage of indexing should not be influenced by the characteristics of the vocabulary to be used in the translation stage. That is, indexers must first decide what topics need to be represented; only later (momentarily perhaps) should they consider whether or not the vocabulary can represent these topics adequately. Put somewhat differently, indexers should not ignore a topic because they know or suspect that it cannot be expressed adequately. It is possible that a careful examination of the vocabulary may prove them wrong in this. Moreover, an important function of the indexer is to improve the controlled vocabulary by bringing its inadequacies to the attention of those responsible for its maintenance. This is unlikely to occur if the indexer is encouraged to "think" in the controlled terms. In this respect I am in complete disagreement with ISO 5963, which states that "Both analysis and transcription should be performed with the aid of indexing tools such as thesauri and classification schemes." The transcription, to be sure, cannot be performed without such tools but the analysis should be completely independent of them.

A related factor to bear in mind is that the terminology used by an author may not correspond exactly to the terms of the controlled vocabulary. Even though author terms and controlled terms coincide, the way they are used may differ. For example, an author may use the term "epidemiology" in a rather loose way but the vocabulary may define the term much more precisely and the assignment of the term, although used by the

---

*See Milstead (1984) for another discussion on how to examine a text to determine its "indexable matter."

author, may be erroneous. It is the ideas dealt with by an author, rather than the words used, that must be indexed.

Hjørland (2001) addresses the translation stage of indexing as follows:

> A second decision is which descriptors from the controlled vocabulary should be assigned to the document. This decision could (and should) be seen from the reverse perspective: under which descriptors would it appear relevant for a user to find this document? (Page 777)

While I completely agree that indexing must be related to the needs of a particular user group, I feel that Hjørland may be confusing the conceptual analysis and translation stages here. It is in the former that user needs are identified. That is, the indexer decides which aspects of the document are likely to be of interest to users. Then, the indexer selects the controlled terms that best represent these aspects.

Exhaustivity of Indexing

Factors affecting the performance of an information retrieval system that are directly attributable to indexing can be categorized as follows:

1. Indexing policy.
2. Indexing accuracy

      Conceptual analysis
      Translation

Policy decisions are established by the managers of the information service and are thus outside the control of the individual indexer; the accuracy factors are under the individual indexer's control.

The major policy decision is that relating to the *exhaustivity* of the indexing, which roughly corresponds to the number of terms assigned on the average. The effect of exhaustivity was illustrated earlier in Figure 3. Exhaustive indexing implies the use of enough terms to cover the subject matter of a document rather completely. Selective indexing, on the other hand, implies the use of a much smaller number of terms to cover only the central subject matter of a document. The more terms used to index a document, the more accessible it becomes and, presumably, the more it will be retrieved. An information center will want to index exhaustively if its users frequently ask for comprehensive searches to be performed. A requester wanting to find all items dealing in any way with the PLO will expect to retrieve the item depicted in Figure 3, but this will be possible only if the indexing has been fairly exhaustive.

Policy decisions on exhaustivity should not take the form of absolute limits on the number of terms to be assigned. Rather, the policy might suggest a range of terms—e.g., "most items will be indexed with 8 to 15 terms." In a large information center, dealing with many different kinds of material, the policy may vary with type of document. For example, the information center of a large company might establish a policy as follows:

Company's own technical reports	15-25 terms
Other technical reports	10-15 terms
Patents	15-20 terms
Journal articles	5-10 terms

and so on. Alternatively, the policy could be based on subject matter, the subjects of most interest to the company being indexed with most terms.

Although a database indexed exhaustively will tend to allow for comprehensive searches (high *recall*),* exhaustive indexing is likely to be more expensive than selective indexing. Moreover, exhaustive indexing will cause lower *precision* in searching. That is, more items will be retrieved that a requester judges not pertinent to his information need. This may occur for two reasons:

1. "False associations" will increase with the number of terms assigned. For example, the item in Figure 3 might be retrieved in a search on telephone surveys in Egypt but it has nothing whatever to do with this topic.
2. The more terms used to index an item, the more it will be retrieved in response to search topics dealt with in only a very minor way. The item in Figure 3 is likely to be retrieved in a search for articles discussing political leaders of Arab states but the person requesting such a search may decide that it contributes so little to this topic that it can hardly be considered useful.

The idea of "exhaustivity" can also apply to a retrieval system operating on the basis of searchable text (see Chapter 14). The title of the item in Figure 3 is not a very exhaustive representation of its subject matter. The exhaustivity increases with the number of words in the representation.

The term "depth" is frequently used to refer to the number of terms assigned to a document. That is, "depth" is used in place of "exhaustivity". Both terms are imprecise and can be misleading. To better understand the effect of increasing the number of terms used to index a document, one may consider it as having two dimensions, as illustrated in Figure 6. Let us say that an indexer is able to identify ten related topics discussed in the item. One can regard this as the breadth of coverage of the document. If the indexer attempts to cover all of these topics, the indexing can be considered *exhaustive* (i.e., it is an exhaustive representation of the subject matter). The

---

*This has been demonstrated on numerous occasions; e.g., by Boyce and McLain (1989).

more topics covered, the more exhaustive is the indexing. On the other hand, the fewer topics covered, the more *selective* the indexing. Clearly, exhaustive indexing will require the use of more terms.

The second dimension of the document, from the indexing point of view, is referred to as *specificity* in Figure 6. That is, some of the topics identified could be indexed at more than one level of specificity. Suppose that the first topic is "architecture of cathedrals." This might be indexed under the term *ecclesiastical architecture* which is not completely specific. To increase specificity the indexer might add a second term, *cathedrals*. The joint use of the two terms precisely represents the topic of discussion. On the other hand, addition of *domestic architecture* would increase exhaustivity rather than specificity because it is introducing a new concept into the indexing.

In other words, the addition of further index terms might increase the exhaustivity of a representation or might increase its specificity. Therefore, while it is true to say that "exhaustivity" roughly corresponds to the number of terms assigned, no exact, one-to-one relationship exists between exhaustivity and number of terms. In this book "exhaustivity" refers to the breadth of coverage in indexing as illustrated in Figure 6. "Depth" is a less satisfactory term because it denotes the opposite of breadth and is more appropriately applied to the specificity dimension illustrated in Figure 6.

The number of terms assigned to a document is really a cost-effectiveness consideration. Generally speaking, the more exhaustive the indexing the greater the cost,* and there is little sense in indexing more exhaustively than warranted by the needs of the users of the service. A high level of exhaustivity will be needed if many requests are made for really comprehensive searches. If comprehensive searches are the exception, rather than the rule, a much lower level of exhaustivity will suffice.

It is clear that the more terms used per document (i.e., the greater the exhaustivity), the greater the probability that it will be retrieved and the more characteristics it has to distinguish it from other documents. However, the distribution of documents over terms will also affect the discrimination: terms that apply to many documents will not discriminate much; those applied to few documents will be good discriminators.

---

*In actual fact, of course, this is an oversimplification. In dealing with a lengthy document, an indexer may need more time to cover the subject matter exhaustively. In other cases, it may be faster to use many terms rather than try to select fewer from a group in which the terms may be closely related or even overlap in meaning. In general, however, the more terms used, the more expensive it will be to enter them into the database and process them subsequently. Moreover, increasing the number of terms will add substantially to the costs of indexes in card or printed form.

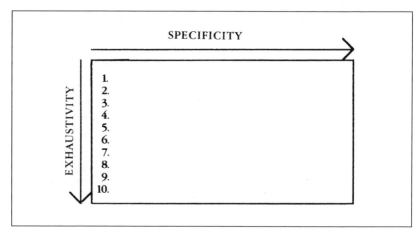

FIGURE 6
The two indexing dimensions of a document.

Wolfram and Zhang (2002) have used computer simulation to study the effects of varying both exhaustivity levels and term distributions (the average number of items to which a term applies). They conclude that:

> Low exhaustivity and shallow term distributions produce fewer distinctions among documents because fewer terms are assigned per document and more common terms are shared among documents, resulting in more terms with a low term weight. Higher exhaustivity provides additional opportunities for extra, distinctive terms to be added to a document. Similarly, a steeper term distribution, where a lower average rate of specific term assignment to the document set is found, adds to the document's distinctiveness. With high exhaustivity to more completely describe a document and steeper term distributions, defining more unique sets of terms, the lowest document densities are encountered, making it easier to distinguish documents from one another. The results for each model demonstrate that similar document space densities may be achieved with different combinations of indexing exhaustivity and term distributions. For example, a high exhaustivity/shallow term distribution combination and a low exhaustivity/steep term distribution combination resulted in similar document space density levels. (Pages 950-951)

Methods for automatic indexing and abstracting (see Chapter 15) are based largely on statistical criteria (the counting of word occurrences in text) so "density" measures can be applied (i.e., the number of index terms or the length of an abstract related to the length of the text). Connolly and Landeen (2001) propose and apply a similar measure (number of index entries related to the total number of lines of text) to back-of-the-book indexes.

It is obvious that, as databases increase in size, the number of items appearing under any particular term will also tend to increase. Therefore, it becomes necessary to index using more terms (and also to make them increasingly specific) so that the indexing is more discriminating to allow searches in which an adequate level of recall can be achieved at a tolerable level of precision. Unfortunately, this has not been taken into account in subject cataloging practice in the United States library community. The subject matter of books is represented at a very general and superficial level (an average of fewer than two subject heading/subheading combinations per item as reported by O'Neill and Aluri, 1981). While this may have been tolerable fifty or so years ago, when collections were much smaller, and still may be for very small collections, it is virtually useless in catalogs covering several million items. The conversion of card catalogs to online catalogs gave users a great potential advantage—the ability to search on terms in logical combinations. But the potential value of this is greatly reduced by the low level of exhaustivity of the representations in the catalog. Consequently, online searches in the catalogs of large academic libraries frequently result in hundreds of items retrieved, most of which may be completely unwanted by the searcher (Lancaster et al., 1991). This "large retrieval phenomenon" has stimulated considerable experimentation on means of searching large catalogs in a more discriminating way (see, for example, Prabha, 1991), such as restricting by date, language, and other criteria. The fact that most online catalogs allow searches on title words (and perhaps classification numbers), as well as subject headings, seems to have had surprisingly little effect on the exhaustivity of the representation since title words, subject headings and classification numbers frequently duplicate each other (Xu and Lancaster, 1998).

A number of studies have looked at the extent to which subject headings in OPACs duplicate keywords in book titles. Voorbij (1998), for example, looked at this question in a Dutch context. In effect, he was looking for evidence that assigning subject descriptors to books, a costly process, was worthwhile. That is, how much do they contribute that title keywords do not? The subject descriptors were able to retrieve almost twice as many relevant items as the keywords. Not only are many titles inadequate indicators of what a book is about but, Voorbij points out, the same topic can be represented in many different ways in titles. The vocabulary control imposed by subject headings is important. The study was done in the humanities and social sciences which may, on the average, have less descriptive or complete titles than is true of the hard sciences.

Figure 7 demonstrates the law of diminishing returns as applied to indexing. For the hypothetical information service illustrated, the assignment of X terms, on the average, will satisfy about 80% of user needs. To raise this to 90-95% would require much greater exhaustivity in the indexing. Where point X on such a curve lies, and what X represents in number of terms, will depend very much on considerations that are system-specific. The managers of an information service prepare guidelines on exhaustivity of indexing that derive from their knowledge of the needs of users. These tend to be based on intuition, although controlled experiments could be conducted in which samples of information needs are matched against a collection of documents indexed with varying numbers of terms.

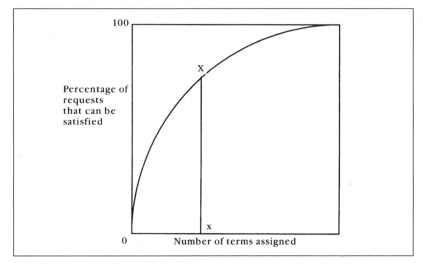

FIGURE 7
Diminishing returns in indexing.

Of course, the idea of an optimum level of exhaustivity applying to all items in a database is somewhat misleading since widely different optima would apply to different items depending on the requests actually made by system users (Maron, 1979). Optimum exhaustivity is entirely request-dependent.

For some types of indexable items it will be unusually difficult to agree what they are "about." For these, it will not be at all easy to achieve any agreement and consistency in indexing and, thus, they may need to be indexed at an exhaustive level to provide for differing viewpoints. This might be true, for example, in the indexing of images, which can be looked at by indexers at different levels from the highly concrete to the highly abstract (Enser, 1995).

Intner (1984) has pointed out that, in deciding what to include and how many terms to use, an indexer could actually exercise a form of censorship, perhaps by failing to cover some aspect of the work the indexer does not approve of. The reverse situation, of course, is the use of an unwarranted number of terms to get an item retrieved as often as possible, a temptation that might occur when some financial or other gain is associated with its retrieval. This phenomenon has been noted within the Internet environment (see Chapter 16), where it has been referred to as "spoofing" or "spamming." Price (1983) may have been first to recognize this as a potential problem.

Bell (1991a) discusses a similar situation with regard to back-of-the-book indexes: indexers, or possibly publishers, can show bias, by omitting certain topics from the index, by reinforcing (or otherwise) the ideas of the author, or by introducing the indexer's own attitudes. Several examples are given.

The number of terms assigned to a document is a critical factor in determining whether or not a particular item will be retrieved. But other related factors also come into play. Most obviously, one expects that the number of items retrieved will decline as more terms are combined in an *and* relationship in a search strategy. Clearly, the extent to which terms can be combined successfully in a search is heavily dependent on the number of terms used in indexing. To take a trivial example, the combining of three terms (A·B·C) may retrieve a large number of items when an average of 20 terms per item is used in indexing but is unlikely to retrieve many from a database in which only three terms are assigned to each item on the average. (For reasons mentioned earlier, it would not retrieve much, if anything, in a search of an online library catalog.) The more selective the indexing, the more it will be necessary to combine terms in an *or* relationship in order to improve recall. The interactions between exhaustivity of indexing and the characteristics of search strategies have been discussed by Sparck Jones (1973). Studies of the effect of exhaustivity in more automatic approaches to retrieval (see Chapter 15) can be found in Shaw (1986, 1990a,b) and Burgin (1991, 1995).

In a number of information services, indexing may be performed for two somewhat different purposes: (a) to allow access to an item in a printed index, and (b) to allow access to that same item in an electronic database. In this situation, the indexer may be required to index at some pre-established level of exhaustivity for the latter and to select a subset (perhaps 2-4) of the index terms thus assigned to provide access points in the printed index. The terms in the subset will be those the indexer considers to best represent the most important aspects of the item. This can be considered as a crude form of "weighted" indexing: a term can carry one of two weights—"major" (central subject matter for printed index) or "minor" (all other terms). Weighted indexing is discussed more fully in Chapter 11.

Principle of Specificity

The single most important principle of subject indexing, traceable back to Cutter (1876), is that a topic should be indexed under the most specific term that entirely covers it. Thus, an article discussing the cultivation of oranges should be indexed under *oranges* rather than under *citrus fruits* or *fruit*.

Usually, it would be better to use several specific terms rather than a term that is more general. If an article describes the cultivation of lemons, limes, and grapefruit, it is better indexed under the three specific terms rather than the more general *citrus fruits*. This term should be used only for articles discussing citrus fruit in general and for those in which virtually all citrus fruit are discussed. This guideline could be extended to the situation in which several citrus fruit are discussed but not in enough detail (in the indexer's judgement) to warrant use of the specific terms. In some cases, too, the audience served may be interested only in certain fruit. In this situation it would be legitimate to index these only and not to include terms for the others.

Some students of indexing make the mistake of indexing redundantly. Having indexed an article on oranges under the term *oranges*, they want also to assign *citrus fruits* and even *fruit*. This is quite unnecessary. Indeed, it is poor indexing practice. If the generic terms are assigned every time a specific term is used, it becomes difficult to distinguish general articles from specific ones. For example, the user who searches an index under the term *fruit* should expect to find items on fruit in general rather than items on individual fruit.

In the manual retrieval systems that were the predecessors of computer-based systems, it was in fact necessary to "post up" from specific to generic terms; e.g., the use of the term *oranges* in indexing an item caused *citrus fruits, fruit,* and even, perhaps, *crops*, to be assigned also. This was done to allow for generic searches. Were it not done, it would be virtually impossible to perform a complete search on, say, all fruit. If a computer-based system is properly designed, however, posting-up in this way should not be necessary, at least when a controlled vocabulary is in use. For example, it should be possible to ask the computer to search on the term *fruit* and *everything below it in the hierarchical structure* (all of the narrower terms, NTs, in the case of a thesaurus).

In general, then, one would not expect the terms *citrus fruits* and *oranges* to be applied to the same item. The only situation in which this combination is justified would involve an article dealing with citrus fruit in general, but including a lengthy discussion on oranges, or one on citrus fruit that uses oranges as an example (e.g., the irrigation of citrus fruit with examples drawn from the irrigation of oranges).

The indexer must remember that specificity may be achieved through the use of combinations of terms. If no single term exists, an appropriate combination should be sought in the controlled vocabulary. Some hypothetical examples:

> Medieval French Literature
>> indexed under MEDIEVAL LITERATURE and FRENCH LITERATURE

Medical Libraries
indexed under SCIENCE LIBRARIES and MEDICAL SCIENCES

Canadian Literature
indexed under LITERATURE and CANADA

Groundnut Oils
indexed under VEGETABLE OILS and GROUNDNUTS

Note that the indexer must look for the most appropriate combination in each case. In theory, Medieval French Literature could be expressed by *medieval literature* and *France*, but the combination of *medieval literature* and *French literature* expresses the idea more accurately. Likewise, *medical sciences* is combined with *science libraries*, rather than *libraries*, to express the idea of medical libraries, since medical libraries are clearly scientific, and *groundnuts* is combined with *vegetable oils* rather than *oils*, since groundnut oil is a vegetable oil.

Sometimes the controlled vocabulary will not include a term at the level of specificity demanded by a particular document. In such a case indexers must use the most specific term available (e.g., *citrus fruits* rather than *fruit* for an article on oranges). They may also want to suggest, to the group maintaining the vocabulary, the need for more specific terms in this category.

Other Guidelines

The process of subject indexing seems not to be susceptible to precise rules. Beyond the principle of specificity, no real rules for the assignment of terms have been developed, although many exist for what to do with index terms once they are assigned (e.g., establishing the sequence in which they are listed to form headings in a printed index). A number of "theories" of indexing have been put forward, and several have been reviewed by Borko (1977), but these tend not to be true theories and they offer little practical help for the indexer.

Fugmann (1979,1985) has presented several axioms of "indexing and information supply" but not all of these are directly related to indexing per se. The only real indexing principle put forward, referred to as "mandatory indexing," states that an indexer is to use the most appropriate terms available to describe the subject matter discussed in a document. Since this will usually mean the most specific terms, this is essentially a restatement of the principle of specificity. Most of Fugmann's axioms are really factors affecting the performance of information retrieval systems rather than elements of indexing theory, although several have implications for indexing. For example, the axiom of definability relates to the ability to define an information need clearly and unambiguously. This can obviously be extended to the ability to define the subject matter of documents clearly and unambiguously. Fugmann's axiom of predictability states that the success of a search in a retrieval system depends largely on the predictability with which subject matter is described, which points to the importance of consistency in indexing. The axiom of fidelity states that another factor affecting performance is the ability to precisely and accurately describe subject matter (of information needs and, by extension, documents), which relates more to the vocabulary used to index than it does to indexing itself.

In fact, I have not been able to find any real theories applicable to the process of indexing although there are some theories (see, for example, Jonker (1964)) that relate to the characteristics of index terms. Furthermore, I believe that it is possible to identify only two fundamental rules of indexing, one related to the conceptual analysis stage and the other to the translation stage, as follows:

1. Include all the topics known to be of interest to the users of the information service that are treated substantively in the document.
2. Index each of these as specifically as the vocabulary of the system allows and the needs or interests of the users warrants.

Of course, these rules are subject to interpretation. For example, what does "substantively" really mean? One possible guideline would be that topic X should be indexed if it is felt that the majority of users seeking information on X would find this item of interest. It is clear that "substantively" is not a property that can be expressed or measured in any precise way. Whether or not a particular topic is worth indexing will depend largely on three factors: (a) the amount of information given on the topic, (b) the degree of interest in the topic, and (c) how much information already exists on the topic: a single, brief mention of a compound may be worth indexing if the compound is known to be quite new; years later much more information would be needed to warrant inclusion.

The statement "needs or interests of the users" in the second rule implies that the principle of specificity can and should be modified when it is known that users of a particular system or tool would be better served by indexing a particular topic at a more general level under certain circumstances. For example, in a medical database, articles on veterinary medicine applied to dogs might be indexed under the names of the breeds of dogs involved. On the other hand, articles discussing the use of dogs in laboratory experiments might simply be indexed under *dogs*, even though the specific breed might be identified.

A corollary to the first rule mentioned above is that topics not discussed in the document should not be covered by the indexer. While this may seem self-evident and trite, it is not necessarily so. Some indexers, particularly those who consider themselves to be subject "experts," may be tempted to see things in a document that the author never intended (e.g., applications of a device beyond those claimed in the document). While it may be an important function of certain information specialists (e.g., those in industry) to bring potential applications to the attention of users of an information service, this is not really the function of the indexer per se. It is much better that indexers stick to the text and the author's claims. The *ERIC Processing Manual* of 1980 gave good advice on this:

> Index the document in hand, not the document the writer *would like* to have written or *intends* to write the next time. Do not confuse speculation, or referrals to implications and possibilities, with real content. (Page VII-13)

"Results not claimed by the author," of course, should not be confused with negative results. It will usually be desirable to index the latter. For example, if a study shows that a particular material is not suitable for use in a certain application, the application mentioned should certainly be included in the indexing if other criteria (e.g., how much information is given) are met.

In certain more specialized applications, indexers may be encouraged to look for implications. For example, Schroeder (1998), referring to experience at the General Motors Media Archives, stresses the importance of an "implication layer" in the indexing of images. For example, a photograph of a particular vehicle may show it crossing a very rocky landscape, and it is necessary not only to identify the vehicle but also to use terms indicating its ability to perform in a rocky environment.

Klement (2002) makes a distinction between "open-system" and "closed-system" indexing. The latter (most obvious are back-of-the-book indexes) refers to indexes to a single item; such indexes are noncontinuous. Open-system indexing, in contrast, applies to many items and is continuous, as in the indexing of periodical articles in databases such as MEDLINE. When indexing applies to many items, and is continuous, the terms used in index entries must be standardized. Standardization is not really an issue in closed-system indexing although it is obviously necessary to use consistent terminology throughout the single index. Closed system indexing may use terms that are noncontinuous: "Leonardo da Vinci, dies" may be perfectly appropriate in such an index but is unlikely to appear in an open-system index (although "Leonardo da Vinci" would).

Postcoordinate Indexes

The subject matter discussed in a document, and represented by index terms assigned to it, is multidimensional in character. Consider, for example, an article discussing labor migration from Mozambique to the mines of South Africa, indexed under the following terms:

MOZAMBIQUE
SOUTH AFRICA
MIGRANT WORKERS
MINERS
ECONOMIC RELATIONS

Although the terms are given here in the form of a list, they actually represent a network of relationships:

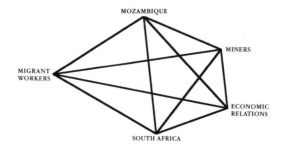

One should be able to retrieve this document in a search involving any single term or any combination of them: any two terms, any three, any four, or all five. An information retrieval system that allows a searcher to combine terms in any way is frequently referred to as *postcoordinate* (*postcombination* or *manipulative* are other terms that have been used).

Postcoordinate systems emerged in the 1940's, when they were implemented by use of various types of cards. A modern computer-based system, operated online, can be considered a direct descendant of these manual systems. It can be thought of conceptually as a matrix as shown in Figure 8.

The files of an online system comprise two major elements:

1. A complete set of document representations: bibliographic reference, usually accompanied by index terms or abstract or both.

2. A list of terms showing which documents have been indexed under them (sometimes referred to as an *inverted file* or a *postings file*). The documents are identified by numbers as shown in Figure 8.

What happens in an online search can be demonstrated through reference to the matrix of Figure 8. Suppose the searcher enters the term *Mozambique* at a terminal and that this is represented by P in the diagram. The system responds by indicating that seven items have been indexed under the term. The searcher enters *migrant workers* (L in the diagram) and is told that four items appear under this term. If the searcher now asks that L be combined with P, the system compares the document numbers on these two lists and indicates that three items satisfy the requirement. When told to do so by the searcher, the computer finds these records by their identifying numbers (4, 8, 10) and displays them or prints them out.

TERMS (CLASSES)	1	2	3	4	5	6	7	8	9	10	11	12	13	14	15
A	X									X					
B		X			X		X		X						X
C					X	X					X				
D					X					X					
E	X		X				X	X	X					X	X
F	X														
G			X	X			X					X			
H	X										X			X	
I													X		
J	X		X				X		X					X	X
K	X	X	X				X			X	X	X			
L				X				X		X			X		
M		X				X				X					X
N	X			X	X			X	X			X	X		
O		X	X			X	X	.							X
P	X			X	X			X	X	X				X	

FIGURE 8

Information retrieval system represented as a matrix.

This procedure remains the same however many terms are involved and whatever the logical relationships specified by the searcher. If F *or* G is asked for, the system will indicate that five items satisfy the requirement. The searcher may then ask that this list of five items be combined with the list under N—i.e., (F *or* G) *and* N—resulting in the retrieval of three items.

Of postcoordinate systems, it is possible to say that:

1. Terms can be combined in any way when a search is performed.
2. The multidimensionality of the relationships among terms is retained.

3. Every term assigned to a document has equal weight—one is no more important than another (although weighted indexing, as discussed in a later chapter, may be used).

These characteristics do not apply to precoordinate indexes, which are dealt with in the next chapter.

Indexing Aids

The indexer must have some way of recording the results of the indexing operation. Four possibilities exist:

1. Recording on the document itself
2. Completing some kind of form printed on paper
3. Recording on an audiotape
4. Completing a form displayed online.

While indexing directly online, using some type of structured display, is now the norm, other possibilities were once common and are still used in places.

In some organizations, the indexer merely marks up the document at hand and a typist transcribes the indexer's markings. This mode would usually be appropriate only to situations in which a relatively simple approach to indexing is employed—e.g., the augmentation of titles coupled with the addition of a relatively small number of index terms or codes.

Until online systems became commonplace, it was usual for an indexer to enter terms into a printed form. Figure 9, for example, shows a version of a form used at the National Library of Medicine. Note the use of "checktags." These are terms potentially applicable to many documents in the database. It is efficient and economical to preprint these on the form so that the indexer need only check off those that are applicable. Not only does this save the indexers time, but it reminds them that these terms must be assigned when they apply to a particular document. Because of this reminder, checktags are assigned more consistently than other terms (Lancaster, 1968a; Funk et al., 1983).

In some highly specialized indexing environments, it might be possible to preprint the entire controlled vocabulary onto an indexing form, allowing all terms to become essentially checktags. The pioneer of this approach was probably Mooers. Figure 10 (from Brenner and Mooers, 1958) shows a typical Mooers indexing form. Note how the descriptors are grouped together systematically. In analyzing a document, the indexer essentially considers every descriptor in the schedule as potentially applicable. In effect, the indexer asks the questions posed by the indexing form itself. If, for example, the answer to "are there specific aerodynamic loads?" is "yes" (i.e., the document at hand discusses specific loads), the indexer must account for this by assigning the most appropriate aerodynamic load descriptor or descrip-

① C | ⑧ PAGINATION | ⑨ LANGUAGE ENG. ___ ___ ___ | ANONYMOUS A □ | ⑰ REFS | ⑮ SUBJECT NAME

⑩ AUTHOR DATA

⑬ TITLE *(Eng or Transl)*

⑭ TITLE *(Vernac or Translit)*

⑲	⑳				⑫ AUTHOR
A □ HIST ART	A □ PREGN	J □ CATS	V □ HUMAN	f □ 15th CENT	□ AFFIL
B □ HIST BIOG	B □ INF NEW (to 1 mo)	K □ CATTLE	W □ MALE	g □ 16th CENT	
C □ BIOG OBIT	C □ INF (1–23 mo)	L □ CHICK EMBRYO	X □ FEMALE	h □ 17th CENT	⑫ AUTHOR
G □ MONOGR	D □ CHILD PRE (2–5)	M □ DOGS	Y □ IN VITRO	i □ 18th CENT	□ ABST
H □ ENG ABST	E □ CHILD (6–12)	O □ GUINEA PIGS	Z □ CASE REPT	j □ 19th CENT	
	F □ ADOLESC (13–18)	P □ HAMSTERS	b □ COMP STUDY	k □ 20th CENT	㉔ NIH/PHS GRANT NO
	G □ ADULT (19–44)	Q □ MICE	c □ ANCIENT	l □ NIH/PHS SUP	
	H □ MID AGE (45–64)	S □ RABBITS	d □ MEDIEVAL	m □ OTHER US GOVT SUP	
	I □ AGED (65 +)	T □ RATS	e □ MODERN	n □ NON-US GOVT SUP	
		U □ ANIMAL			

㉑
1
2
3
4
5
6
7
8
9
10
11
12
13
14
15
16
17
18
19
20
21
22
23
24
25
26
27
28
29
30
31

NIH–1416 Rev. 6–80 | INDEXED CITATION FORM | GPO : 1985 O – 476-504

FIGURE 9

Index form once used by the National Library of Medicine.

tors. The descriptor list, presented in this way, simplifies the indexing process because it takes some of the intellectual burden from the indexer. The potential uses of a document of interest to the organization are represented by the list of "leading" questions, which has been carefully compiled by senior scientific personnel. The indexer merely follows the leads given in this list.

What material was studied?	Is the process dynamic (rather than static)?	Are there specific aerodynamic loads?	Is structural strength and elasticity involved?
Metals			
Gases	Vibrations	Lift	
Plastics	Transient response	Drag	Stress and strain
Aluminum	Impact	Moment	Plasticity
Magnesium	Stability	Gust	Failure
Titanium	Velocity	Pressure	Ultimate properties
Air		Center of application e.g., aerodynamic center, center of pressure, etc.	Material properties
			Aeroelasticity
			Flutter
What is the type of fluid flow?	**Is it a stability and control problem?**	**Or is there another aerodynamics problem?**	**Is a thermal process involved?**
Fluid flow			Thermodynamics
Internal flow	Stability		Thermodynamic constants
Subsonic	Control	Boundary layer	Combustion
Transonic	Static	Aeroelasticity	Heat transfer
Supersonic	Dynamic=trans. resp.	Flutter	Cooling
Hypersonic	Longitudinal	Downwash	Convection
Laminar	Lateral	Stall and buffet	Thermal
Turbulence	Derivatives	Interference	Radiation
Slip flow	Damping	Hydraulics	Aerodynamic heating
Compressibility	Weight and balance e.g., center of gravity, moments of inertia, etc.	Trajectory	
Viscosity		Droplets	
Vortices		Modifying technique	
Shock waves		Performance	
Finite span			

FIGURE 10

Typical Mooers indexing form.

Reprinted from Brenner & Mooers (1958) by permission of Van Nostrand Reinhold.

In the past, the U.S. Patent and Trademark Office developed small retrieval systems restricted to a single class, or limited number of classes, in the patent art. Specialized vocabularies were devised for these areas and they were small enough to be printed on a few sheets. Figure 11 illustrates part of such a vocabulary for the patent subclass dealing with general purpose digital computers. As with the Mooers descriptor schedules, the entire vocabulary can be easily scanned, preventing the indexer from overlooking an important term and eliminating the need for entering terms on an indexing sheet. In this case, multiple copies of the term list are available, and a patent is indexed merely by circling the appropriate terms or their codes on a copy of the list. All subsequent processing is clerical. The "microthesaurus" of the Air Pollution Technical Information Center, as described by Tancredi and Nichols (1968), was also designed for use by circling of terms. A portion of the microthesaurus is illustrated in Figure 12.

```
            SYSTEM ARCHITECTURE
228         .Plural processors with different
             internal structures (28/0)
228.1       .Shared memory (28/1)
228.2       .Virtual processor/machine (28/2)
228.3       .Plural (redundant) central processors
             (28/3)
228.4       .Central processor combined with
             terminal processor (28/4)
228.5       .Central processor combined with
             interface processor (28/5)
228.6       .Central processor combined with
             coprocessor (28/6) *
228.7       .Multiple instruction multiple data
             (MIMD) (28/7) *
228.8       ..Loosely coupled MIMD (28/8) *
228.9       ..Tightly coupled MIMD (28/9) *
229         .Multiprocessor interconnection (29/0)
229.1       ..Direct (29/1)
229.2       ..Parallel (common bus) (29/2)
229.3       ..Loop (29/3)
229.4       ..Reconfigurable (29/4)
229.41      ..Tree structure (29/A) *
229.5       ..Other specific multiprocessor
             interconnection (29/5)
230         .Multiprocessor/Processor control (30/0)
230.1       ..Priority assignment (30/1)
230.2       ..Interrupt handling (30/2)
230.3       ..Task assignment (30/3)
230.4       ..Supervisory (master/slave) (30/4)
230.5       ..Other specific multiprocessor control
             (30/5)
230.6       .Other specific multiprocessor system
             (30/6)
231         .Mini/Micro/Personal computer (31/0)
231.1       ..Portable (31/1)
231.2       ...Hand-held/Carried on person (31/2)
231.3       ...Other portable computer (31/3)
231.31      ..Other specific mini/micro/personal
             computer (31/A) *
231.4       .Timeshared (31/4)
231.5       ..Peripheral devices (31/5)
231.6       ..Plural programs (Multiprogrammed)
             (31/6)
231.7       ..Other specific timeshare (31/7)
231.8       .Pipelined (31/8)
231.9       .Parallel array/Single Instruction
             Multiple Data (SIMD) (31/9)
232         .Orthogonal (32/0)
232.1       .Virtual (32/1)
232.2       .Adaptive (32/2)
232.21      .Vector processor (32/A) *
232.22      .Data flow (32/B) *
```

FIGURE 11

Portion of a specialized vocabulary on digital computers as used by
the U.S. Patent and Trademark Office.

Reproduced by permission of the U.S. Patent and Trademark Office.

Success has also been achieved in some organizations by having the
indexer dictate terms into a tape recorder for future transcription by typists.
This approach does have some problems associated with it. Many typing

errors may occur when a large technical vocabulary, unfamiliar to the typist, is used, necessitating very careful editing. Some indexers do not work well in this mode because they have trouble remembering which terms they have already assigned to an item.

BK-65   BIOMEDICAL TECHNIQUES & MEASUREMENT

```
BK-66   ABSENTEEISM
BK-67   ATTACK RATES
BK-68   BIOCLIMATOLOGY
BK-69   EPIDEMIOLOGY
BK-70   GENETICS
BK-71   HEALTH STATISTICS
BK-72   HEMATOLOGY
BK-73     BLOOD CHEMISTRY
BK-74     BLOOD GAS ANALYSIS
BK-75     CARBOXYHEMOGLOBIN
BK-76     HEMOGLOBIN INTERACTIONS
BK-77   IMMUNOLOGY
BK-78     ANTIBODIES
BK-79     ANTIGENS
BK-80   LIFE SPAN
BK-81   MORBIDITY
BK-82   MORTALITY
BK-83   OCCUPATIONAL HEALTH
BK-84   OUTPATIENT VISITS
BK-85   PATHOLOGICAL TECHNIQUES
BK-86   RADIOLOGICAL HEALTH
BL-48   TISSUE CULTURES
BK-87   TREATMENT & AIDS
BK-88     ARTIFICIAL RESPIRATION
BK-89     BREATHING EXERCISES
BK-90     DIAGNOSIS
BK-91       AUTOPSY
BK-92       BIO-ASSAY
BK-93       BIOPSY
BK-94       SKIN TESTS
BK-95     DRUGS
BK-96       ANTIDOTES
BK-97       BRONCHODILATORS
BK-99     INHALATION THERAPY
BL-00     MEDICAL FACILITIES
BL-02     PHYSICAL THERAPY
BL-03     RADIOGRAPHY
BL-04     SURGERY
BL-05     VETERINARY MEDICINE
BK-22   URINALYSIS
```

BL-06   BODY CONSTITUENTS & PARTS

```
BL-07   BODY FLUIDS
BL-08   BONES
BL-13   CELLS
BL-14     BLOOD CELLS
GR-41       LEUKOCYTES
BL-17       LYMPHOCYTES
BL-15     CHROMOSOMES
BL-16     CILIA
BL-18     SPERMATOZOA
BL-09   CIRCULATORY SYSTEM
BL-10     BLOOD VESSELS
BL-11     HEART
BL-19   DIGESTIVE SYSTEM
BL-20     ESOPHAGUS
BL-21     INTESTINES
BL-22     LIVER
BL-23     MOUTH
BL-24     STOMACH
BL-25   ENZYMES
BL-46     EPITHELIUM
BL-26   EXCRETIONS
BL-27   EYES
BL-28   GLANDS
BL-29   HISTAMINES
BL-30   HORMONES
BL-31   KIDNEYS
BL-32   LIPIDS
BL-33   MEMBRANES
BL-34   NERVOUS SYSTEM
GY-29   NUCLEIC ACIDS
BL-35   PROTEINS
BL-36     AMINO ACIDS
BL-37   RESPIRATORY SYSTEM
BL-38     BRONCHI
BL-39     LARYNX
BL-40     LUNGS
BL-41       ALVEOLI
BL-42     NOSTRILS
BL-43     SINUSES
BL-44     TRACHEA
BL-45   SKIN
BL-46     EPITHELIUM
BL-47     TISSUES
```

BL-49   BODY PROCESSES & FUNCTIONS

```
BL-50   ADAPTATION
BL-52   BLOOD PRESSURE
BL-53   CELL GROWTH
BL-54   CELL METABOLISM
BL-55   DIGESTION
BL-56   INGESTION
BL-57   INHIBITION
BL-58   METABOLISM
BL-59   PULSE RATE
BL-60   REPRODUCTION
BL-61   RESPIRATORY FUNCTIONS
BL-62     BREATHING
BL-63     COMPLIANCE
GY-51     DEPOSITION
GY-98     LUNG CLEARANCE
BL-64     OXYGEN CONSUMPTION
BL-65     PULMONARY FUNCTION
BL-66       OXYGEN DIFFUSION
BL-67       PULMONARY RESISTANCE
BL-68       VENTILATION (PULMONARY)
BL-69     RETENTION
BL-71   SYNERGISM
BL-72   THRESHOLDS
BL-73   TOXIC TOLERANCES
```

BL-74   DISEASES & DISORDERS

```
BL-75   ALLERGIES
BL-76   ANEMIA
BL-77   ANOXIA
BL-79   ASPHYXIATION
Y-71    BERYLLIOSIS
BL-80   BLINDNESS
BL-81   CANCER
BL-82     BRONCHIAL
BL-83     LEUKEMIA
BL-84     LUNG
BL-85     SKIN
BL-86     TRACHEAL
Y-78    CARCINOGENS
BL-87   CARDIOVASCULAR DISEASES
BL-88   ERYTHEMA
BL-89   EYE IRRITATION
BL-90   FLUOROSIS
BL-91   HEADACHE
BL-92   HEALTH IMPAIRMENT
BL-93   HYPERSENSITIVITY
BL-94   HYPERVENTILATION
BL-95   HYPOXIA
BL-96   INFECTIOUS DISEASES
BL-97   LACHRYMATION
BL-98   METAL POISONING
BL-99   MUTATIONS
GR-00   NAUSEA
GR-01   ORGANIC DISEASES
GR-02   RESPIRATORY DISEASES
GR-03     ADENOVIRUS INFECTIONS
GR-04     ASTHMA
GR-05     BRONCHITIS
GR-06     BRONCHOCONSTRICTION
GR-07     BRONCHOPNEUMONIA
GR-08     COMMON COLD
GR-09     COUGH
GR-10     EMPHYSEMA
GR-11     HAYFEVER
GR-12     INFLUENZA
GR-13     LARYNGITIS
GR-14     PLEURISY
GR-15     PNEUMOCONIOSIS
P-84        ANTHRACOSIS
BL-78       ASBESTOSIS
S-72        BYSSINOSIS
S-84        FARMER'S LUNG
GR-18       SILICOSIS
GR-16     PNEUMONIA
GR-17     PULMONARY EDEMA
GR-19     TUBERCULOSIS
GR-20   STERILIZATION
GR-21   TUMORS
```

FIGURE 12

Section of microthesaurus of the Air Pollution Technical Information Center.

From *American Documentation* (Tancredi & Nichols [1968]).
Copyright 1968 John Wiley & Sons, Inc. Reprinted by permission of John Wiley & Sons, Inc.

Today, however, the majority of database producers use online indexing procedures. In this, various formatted displays are presented on the screen and the indexer enters data into the fields thus displayed. This mode of operation offers significant advantages over its predecessors: the indexer can be prompted in various ways, some indexer mistakes can be recognized by error detection programs and the indexer informed immediately, and the intermediate clerical step of converting the work of the indexer into electronic form is avoided. Moreover, it should also be possible for the indexer to switch from an input mode to a retrieval mode. Thus, precedence can be used to guide certain indexing decisions. That is, the indexer can switch into the database to find out how a particular term has been used in the past or how an earlier document, related to one at hand, was indexed.

A typical online indexing system, known as DCMS (Data Creation and Maintenance System), is in use at the National Library of Medicine for input to the MEDLINE database. The indexer works by completing various displayed "panels". See, for example, Figure 13, a panel in which the current version of the checktags is presented. Note that the indexer has ticked (✓) the tags that apply to this article from the journal *American Journal of Human Genetics*, namely *adult, middle age, aged, human, male,* and *female.* Figure 14 shows the next panel in which the checktags selected by the indexer are displayed. Several descriptors (subject headings alone or with subheadings) have also been selected by the indexer. The system has a capability to give prompts to the indexer. For example, if the checktag *pregnancy* is used, DCMS will automatically tell the indexer to add *female* and will prompt the indexer to use either *animal* or *human.* DCMS will also prompt for the use of certain checktags on the basis of a limited number of words occurring in titles or abstracts. For example, if the word "feline" occurs in text, the indexer is prompted to consider use of the *cats* checktag.

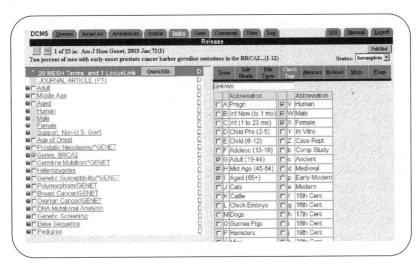

FIGURE 13
Checktag display on DCMS.

DCMS has other features that facilitate the indexing process. The vocabulary (*Medical Subject Headings*) can be displayed and an indexer can select terms from it without rekeying. For any term selected, the system can be asked to display an explanatory annotation or, alternatively, a list of the subheadings that can be used with it. The system will also convert ("map") from a nonapproved term to an approved one by means of the cross references appearing in *Medical Subject Headings*.

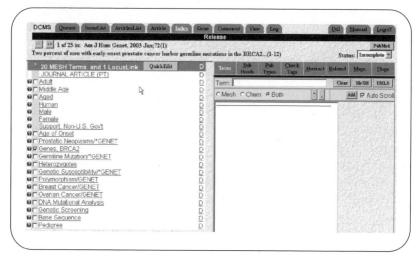

FIGURE 14
Finished indexing record on DCMS.

Obviously, the controlled vocabulary used by an information service will be a tool of paramount importance to the indexer. It should be organized and displayed in such a way that it gives the indexer positive assistance in the selection of the terms most appropriate to use in a particular situation. While closely related to the subject of indexing, the construction and properties of controlled vocabularies are topics outside the scope of this book. They have been dealt with in detail elsewhere (Lancaster, 1986; Soergel, 1974).

A published thesaurus will usually incorporate a limited *entry vocabulary* in the form of *see*, *use*, or *see under* references. A large information center may also develop a separate entry vocabulary for in-house use by indexers, searchers, and lexicographers. Such a vocabulary may be available in printed and/or online form.

For example, the National Library of Medicine (NLM) makes use of several tools that are rich in entry vocabulary components and indexing guidelines. Most obvious is the electronic MeSH (*Medical Subject Headings*) Browser. This Web-based tool, which is intended for use by indexers, sub-

Depressive Disorder

F3.600.300+

do not confuse with DEPRESSION: see note there; depression lasting over 2 years = DYSTHYMIC DISORDER

81; DEPRESSION, NEUROTIC was DEPRESSIVE NEUROSES see DEPRESSION, REACTIVE 1979-80, see under DEPRESSION, REACTIVE 1969-78

X   Depression, Endogenous
X   Depression, Neurotic
X   Depression, Unipolar
X   Depressive Syndrome
X   Melancholia
X   Neurosis, Depressive
X   Unipolar Depression

Depressive Disorder, Major see Depression, Involutional

Depressive Symptoms see Depression

Depressive Syndrome see Depressive Disorder

Depth Intoxication see Inert Gas Narcosis

Depth Perception

F2.463.593.200+   F2.463.593.932.869.255+
G11.697.911.860.317+

disord of depth perception: coord IM with PERCEPTUAL DISORDERS (IM)

X   Stereopsis
X   Stereoscopic Vision

Dequalinium

D3.438.810.824.200

1991(1976); see QUINOLINIUM COMPOUNDS 1976-1990; for DECHALINIUM & DEQUALONUM see DEQUALINIUM 1976-1993

Dercum's Disease see Adiposis Dolorosa

Derealization see Depersonalization

Dermabrasion

E4.680.250

mechanical planing of the skin; do not use /util except by MeSH definition

Dermacentor

B1.131.166.132.832.400.200

infestation: coord IM with TICK INFESTATIONS (IM)

91(73); was see under TICKS 1973-90

FIGURE 15

Sample entries from *Medical Subject Headings—Annotated Alphabetic List* (2003).

cyst, teratoid - TERATOMA

cyst, teratomatous - TERATOMA

cyst, thyroglossal
        - THYROGLOSSAL CYST (not neo-
        plastic)

cyst, umbilical
        - URACHAL CYST (not neoplastic)

cyst, urachal - URACHAL CYST (not neoplastic)

cystadenocarcinoma (unspecified)
        - CYSTADENOCARCINOMA

cystadenocarcinoma, bile duct
        - CYSTADENOCARCINOMA +
        CHOLANGIOCARCINOMA

cystadenocarcinoma, endometrioid
        - CARCINOMA, ENDOMETRIOID

cystadenocarcinoma, mucinous
        - CYSTADENOCARCINOMA, MUCINOUS

cystadenocarcinoma, mucinous papillary
        - CYSTADENOCARCINOMA, MUCINOUS

cystadenocarcinoma, papillary (unspecified)
        - CYSTADENOCARCINOMA,
        PAPILLARY

FIGURE 16
Sample entries from the *Tumor Key*, a specialized entry vocabulary formerly used
at the National Library of Medicine.

ject catalogers, and searchers, is much more elaborate than *Medical Subject Headings*, which is intended as a guide to the use of the printed *Index Medicus*. Another tool, in printed form, is *Medical Subject Headings— Annotated Alphabetic List*. Figure 15 shows some sample entries from this annotated version. This rather complex tool has entry vocabulary components (e.g., *depth intoxication* is referred to *inert gas narcosis*) as well as other indexing guidelines or instructions: related terms (see, for example, the fact that *depressive disorder* is to be distinguished from *depression*), terms that were used in the past (e.g., in the period 1973-1990 the term *dermacentor* existed for online searching only; for printing in *Index Medicus* this organism had to be indexed also under the more general *ticks*), and even some definitions (see, for example, *dermabrasion*).

More specific entry vocabularies that were developed by NLM include the *Tumor Key*, which gave guidance on the indexing of neoplastic diseases. Sample entries are shown in Figure 16. Note how this can be considered a true entry vocabulary with both one-to-one and one-to-many references. For example, a teratoid cyst is to be indexed under *teratoma* but bile duct cystadenocarcinoma is to be indexed under *cystadenocarcinoma* and also under *cholangiocarcinoma*. Such specialized vocabularies are no longer maintained by NLM.

Most published thesauri include entry vocabulary components but they are unlikely to have the richness (or the complexity) of the Figure 15 example.

Published reference works can be of great value to the indexer, most obviously in defining the meaning of unfamiliar terms. Specialized and general dictionaries and encyclopedias, and glossaries of all kinds, will be of particular importance. Bakewell (1987) produced a list of reference tools of potential use to the indexer but this is now very much out of date. In some organizations the work of the indexer may be aided by online access to terminological data banks.

CHAPTER 4

Precoordinate Indexes

THE FLEXIBILITY associated with postcoordinate systems is lost when index terms must be printed out on paper or on conventional catalog cards. Printed indexes and card catalogs are *precoordinate*; they have the following characteristics:

1. The multidimensionality of the term relationships is difficult to depict.
2. Terms can only be listed in a particular sequence (A, B, C, D, E), which implies that the first term is more important than the others.
3. It is not easy (if not completely impossible) to combine terms at the time a search is performed.

The crudest form of information retrieval system is probably the traditional card catalog as used for centuries in libraries. Consider the item mentioned earlier: a book on labor migration from Mozambique to the mines of South Africa. Suppose this were given three subject headings: *Mozambique, South Africa* and *migrant workers*. The bibliographic description of the book would appear under all three headings in an alphabetical subject catalog in card form. This makes the book accessible under any one of these headings. However, it will be extremely difficult to perform a search on any *combination* of these terms. For example, a library user looking for books on political or economic relations between Mozambique and South Africa would need to look under all the entries under the heading *Mozambique* or all those under the heading *South Africa*. Even if this were done the user would not necessarily be able to recognize the pertinent items. If looking under *Mozambique*, the searcher would only be likely to recognize a book as pertinent if it had the term "South Africa" in its title (and vice versa if looking under *South Africa*), or if the bottom of the catalog card showed the other headings assigned to the book (only very sophisticated catalog users would be likely to look at these anyway). Another possibility would be to look under all the *Mozambique* entries and all the *South Africa* entries to try to find titles appearing under both—a very tedious process if many entries are involved.

It is possible to improve this situation in card catalogs by using one heading as subheading (i.e., terms are *precoordinated* in an entry). Thus, one might find an entry as follows:

> Mozambique—Economic Relations

or even

> Mozambique—Economic Relations—South Africa

However, subheadings tend to be used rather sparingly in library catalogs and it would be an unusual catalog that put together a whole string* of terms as in the precoordinate entry:

> Mozambique, Economic Relations, South Africa, Migrant Workers, Miners

Detailed entries of this type are more likely to appear in printed indexes than they are in library catalogs. In this respect, printed indexes can be considered more effective retrieval tools than conventional library catalogs. In certain printed indexes, a user could scan the entries under Mozambique to see if any also mention South Africa. Examples of various forms of printed index appear in Chapter 10.

But an entry such as that illustrated has one obvious problem associated with it: it provides access to the document only for someone searching under the term *Mozambique* and would not allow access in a search relating to South Africa, miners, or migrant workers. To provide additional access points requires that more entries be provided in the index.

There is no way that a printed index can economically provide the level of access to a document provided by a postcoordinate retrieval system. As shown earlier, a postcoordinate system allows access through any *combination* of terms assigned to a document. The number of combinations is 2^n-1, where n represents the number of terms. Thus, for an item indexed under five terms, there are 2^5-1 combinations—a total of 31. In theory, then, a printed index could provide for all combinations of five terms if it printed 31 entries. It would be economically impractical to create a printed index having so many entries for each item, and the number of entries will increase dramatically with the number of terms—there are 255 combinations of eight terms!

Moreover, because terms must be printed out one after the other in an entry (i.e., in a linear sequence), printed indexes are governed by *permutation* rather than *combination*. For example, the sequence *Mozambique, South Africa* is not the same as *South Africa, Mozambique*. The number of permutations is *n factorial*, where *n* is the number of terms. For example, the number of permutations of eight terms is 40,320 (8x7x6x5x4x3x2x1).

The situation is not quite as dismal for printed indexes as this discussion implies. Various computer programs have been developed for taking a string

---

*Consequently, indexing of this type is sometimes referred to as *string indexing* (Craven, 1986).

of terms and generating a set of index entries automatically. One such procedure is known as SLIC (Selective Listing in Combination). The program, devised by Sharp (1966), first arranges the string of terms in alphabetical order. This string (see Figure 17) becomes the first index entry. The program then generates all further entries deemed necessary, following two simple rules:

1. Terms are always listed in alphabetical order.
2. Redundant sequences are eliminated (e.g., the entry, Migrant Workers, Miners, is not needed if Migrant Workers, Miners, South Africa, is already there).

When this rule is followed, the number of entries is reduced from 2^n-1 to 2^{n-1}.

Economic relations, Migrant workers, Miners, Mozambique, South Africa
Economic relations, Migrant workers, Miners, South Africa
Economic relations, Migrant workers, Mozambique, South Africa
Economic relations, Migrant workers, South Africa
Economic relations, Miners, Mozambique, South Africa
Economic relations, Miners, South Africa
Economic relations, Mozambique, South Africa
Economic relations, South Africa
Migrant workers, Miners, Mozambique, South Africa
Migrant workers, Miners, South Africa
Migrant workers, Mozambique, South Africa
Migrant workers, South Africa
Miners, Mozambique, South Africa
Miners, South Africa
South Africa

FIGURE 17
Entries for a SLIC index.

The SLIC method is ingenious in that it allows for all useful juxtapositions of terms, at least as long as the terms are kept in alphabetical order. It also has disadvantages: it still generates a rather large number of entries; to use the index effectively a searcher must mentally re-arrange the search terms in alphabetical order (e.g., one can find Migrant workers, Mozambique, but not Mozambique, Migrant workers); it loses context for terms appearing near the end of the alphabet (e.g., someone looking at all entries under South Africa would have no idea what this item is about).

Other indexes are based on a set of entries arrived at systematically by cycling, rotation, or shunting. In *cycling* each term in a string is moved to the leftmost position to become an entry point, the remaining terms being listed after it:

> ABCDE
> BCDEA
> CDEAB
> DEABC
> EABCD

Note that the entry term is followed first by those terms that followed it in the original string and then by the terms that originally preceded it. In a cycled index the sequence of terms in a string need not be in any obvious order, although they are frequently arranged alphabetically and could be arranged "systematically" (as discussed later).

Rotation is essentially the same as cycling except that the entry term is highlighted in some way (e.g., italicized or underlined) rather than being moved to the leftmost position:

> *A*BCDE
> A*B*CDE
> AB*C*DE
> ABC*D*E
> ABCD*E*

Cycling and rotation both provide some "context" for a term but the relationships among some of the terms may still be obscure or ambiguous. An index based on *shunting* uses a two-line display in an attempt to reduce ambiguity (i.e., be more precise in depicting how one term relates to another), as in the examples:

> A   B.A
>   B.C.D   C.D

The prime example of this, PRECIS, is referred to later.*

A simple method of producing a printed index, based on alphabetical order and the systematic "cycling" of terms to the entry position, as used in *Excerpta Medica* publications, is illustrated in Figure 18. Again, the first entry is derived by putting all terms in alphabetical order. The additional entries are derived by moving each term, in turn, to the entry position and listing the other terms after it (always in alphabetical order) as a string of modifiers. While this does not provide for every possible juxtaposition of terms, it does offer some obvious advantages over SLIC: it is more economical (no more entries than the number of terms assigned) and every entry has full "context." With this type of printed index, it is possible to recognize two types of terms: those that generate index entries and those that do not. Terms that are not to generate entries are marked in some way by the indexer (or could be recognized automatically). Such terms are used as modifiers only.

---

*The terminology relating to precoordinate indexes is not really standardized. For example, Craven (1986) seems to make no distinction between cycling and rotation.

They appear at the end of the string of terms and can be recognized by being out of alphabetical sequence and perhaps being printed in a different type face (see the "bibliography" example in Figure 18).

The indexes illustrated in Figures 17 and 18 assume the use of index terms rather than free text, although in principle they could be produced by computer after programs have been used to extract "significant" phrases from narrative text. Some even simpler approaches to the production of printed indexes have been devised to operate on text and especially on words appearing in the titles of publications. The approaches most commonly used are KWIC (keyword in context), KWOC (keyword out of context), and variations on these.

Economic relations, Migrant workers, Miners, Mozambique, South Africa, *Bibliography*

Migrant workers, Economic relations, Miners, Mozambique, South Africa, *Bibliography*

Miners, Economic relations, Migrant workers, Mozambique, South Africa, *Bibliography*

Mozambique, Economic relations, Migrant workers, Miners, South Africa, *Bibliography*

South Africa, Economic relations, Migrant workers, Miners, Mozambique, *Bibliography*

FIGURE 18
Entries for an index based on systematic cycling (*Excerpta Medica* model).

The KWIC index (Luhn, 1959) is a rotated index most commonly derived from the titles of publications. Each *keyword* appearing in a title becomes an entry point and is highlighted in some way, usually by being set off at the center of a page as in the example of Figure 19. The remaining words in the title are "wrapped around" the keyword. The KWIC index is the simplest approach to the production of printed indexes by computer, yet it has some power since each keyword can be viewed in its "context." For example (Figure 19), one can scan down the "crystals" entries to find any that seem to deal with elastic or plastic properties. KWIC indexes normally refer only to some form of document number; it is necessary to look up the number to get full bibliographic details on the item represented.

Note that the computer program that produces the index identifies keywords through a "reverse" procedure: it recognizes the words that are not keywords (those appearing on a "stop list") and avoids using these as entry points. The stop list contains words that serve a syntactic function (articles, prepositions, conjunctions, and so on) but do not in themselves indicate subject matter. The KWIC index is an inexpensive approach to providing some level of subject access to the contents of a collection. It is useful to the extent that titles are good indicators of content (so it is likely to work better for some subjects or types of materials than for others), although in principle there is no reason why KWIC indexes should not be derived from other text—e.g., sentences from abstracts or even strings of subject headings. Many studies of the value of titles in retrieval have been performed (see Hodges, 1983, and Hjørland and Nielsen, 2001). Titles can also be made more informative through *augmentation* or *enhancement*. That is, further words can be added to the title, usually parenthetically, to explicate it or make it a more complete description.

```
LE TECHNIQUE FOR THE STUDY OF THE ELASTICITY OF CRYSTALS.                                    A SIMP
            STRUCTURAL IMPERFECTIONS IN QUARTZ CRYSTALS.
      LINEAR CUMPRESSIBILITY OF FOURTEEN NATURAL CRYSTALS.
THE LINEAR CUMPRESSIBILITY OF THIRTEEN NATURAL CRYSTALS.
                  TRANSLATION GLIDING IN CRYSTALS.
                            TWINNED CRYSTALS.
              BENDING CREEP OF ICE SINGLE CRYSTALS.
DIRECT MEASUREMENTS OF THE SURFACE ENERGY OF CRYSTALS.
          THE GROWTH AND DEFORMATION OF ICE CRYSTALS.
RELIMINARY EXPERIMENTS ON THE PLASTICITY OF ICE CRYSTALS.                               RESULTS OF P
            PROPAGATION OF CLEAVAGE CRACKS IN CRYSTALS.
S. IN DISLOCATIONS AND MECHANICAL PROPERTIES OF CRYSTALS.        THE DIRECT CBSERVATION OF DISLOCATION PAT
AL GRAINS, PETROFABRIC AND INTERFACE STRUCTURE. CRYSTALS.        THE ELASTIC CONSTANTS OF ROCKS IN TERMS O
    DISLOCATIONS AND MECHANICAL PROPERTIES OF CRYSTALS.  TEXTBCOK.
                        DISLOCATIONS IN CRYSTALS. TEXTBCOK.
                  STRENGTH OF CRYSTALS.TEXTBOOK.IN GERMAN.
            PHYSICAL PROPERTIES OF CRYSTALS.TEXTBOOK.
                  PLASTICITY OF CRYSTALS.TEXTBOOK.
      IMPERFECTIONS IN NEARLY PERFECT CRYSTALS.TEXTBOOK.
    DISLOCATION AND PLASTIC FLOW IN CRYSTALS.TEXTBOOK.


        ANNEALING RECRYSTALLIZATION IN CALCITE CRYSTALS AND AGGREGATES.
BRICS.SEMINAR.          FLOW OF ROCK FORMING CRYSTALS AND AGGREGATES. KINK BANDS.  MINERALS.PETROFA
THE EFFECT OF ORIENTATION ON STRESSES IN SINGLE CRYSTALS AND OF RANDOM ORIENTATION ON STRENGTH OF POLY
                THE FAILURE OF CAVITIES IN CRYSTALS AND ROCKS UNDER PRESSURE.
    EXPERIMENTAL DEFORMATION OF QUARTZ SINGLE CRYSTALS AT 27-30 KB. CONFINING PRESSURE AT 24 DEG.C.
AN.                          DEFORMATION OF CRYSTALS AT HIGH PRESSURE AND HIGH TEMPERATURE.IN GERM
.IN RUSSIAN.    OBSERVATION OF DISLOCATIONS IN CRYSTALS BY THE METHOD OF SELECTIVE ETCHING.CONFERENCE
RAY ANALYSIS OF PREFERRED ORIENTATION OF QUARTZ CRYSTALS IN 3 LINEATED QUARTZITE.              X-
ICE CRYSTALS IN GLACIERS COMPARED WITH QUARTZ CRYSTALS IN DYNAMICALLY METAMORPHOSED SANDSTONES.
CYNAMICALLY METAMORPHOSED SANDSTONES.        ICF CRYSTALS IN GLACIERS COMPARED WITH QUARTZ CRYSTALS IN
ND GEOTHERMOMETRIC CONSIDERATIONS ON THE QUARTZ CRYSTALS IN RHYOLITE OF THE ROSIA MONTANA. IN RUMANIAN
METHOD IN STUDY OF STATISTICS IN ORIENTATION OF CRYSTALS IN ROCKS AND ORES.            DIFFRACTION
MA.              PREFERRED ORIENTATION OF OLIVINE CRYSTALS IN TROCTOLITE OF THE WICHITA MOUNTAINS,OKLAHO
S.      COMPRESSIONAL WAVE VELOCITIES IN SINGLE CRYSTALS OF ALKALI 'FELDSPAR AT PRESSURES TO 10 KILOBAR
          ELASTIC PROPERITES OF SINGLE CRYSTALS OF ANHYDRITE.
ON THE INHOMOGENEITY OF PLASTIC DEFORMATION IN CRYSTALS OF AN AGGREGATE.
              THE DEFORMATION OF SINGLE CRYSTALS OF ICE.CONFERENCE.
          MECHANICAL PROPERTIES OF SINGLF CRYSTALS OF ICE
                  CREEP OF SINGLE CRYSTALS OF ICE.
SURE ON VELOCITY OF SHEAR DEFORMATION OF SINGLE CRYSTALS OF ICE.      EFFECT OF HYDROSTATIC PRES
        PLASTIC DEFORMATION OF SINGLE CRYSTALS OF QUARTZ.
```

FIGURE 19

Sample entries from a KWIC index.

Reprinted from the *KWIC Index of Rock Mechanics Literature* by permission of the American Institute of Mining, Metallurgical, and Petroleum Engineers, Inc.

The KWOC index is similar to KWIC with the exception that the keywords that become access points are repeated out of context, usually by setting them off in the left hand margin of the page (Figure 20) or using them as though they were subject headings (Figure 21). Sometimes a distinction is made between KWOC indexes and KWAC (keyword and context) indexes. Those who make this distinction would call the indexes illustrated in Figures 20 and 21 KWAC indexes. A KWOC index would then be one in which the keyword used as an entry point is not repeated in the title but is replaced by an asterisk (*) or some other symbol. One can find very little justification for this strange practice (using some symbol to replace the keyword) so the distinction between KWOC and KWAC is not a very useful one. Several variations on KWIC/KWOC exist, including Double-KWIC (Petrarca and Lay, 1969). Related to the KWIC/KWOC family are "permuted term" indexes, best exemplified by the Permuterm index associated with the citation indexes produced by the Institute for Scientific Information. In Permuterm each keyword in a title is associated, one at a time, with each other keyword occurring in that title, as in the following example:

CRYSTALS
ALUMINUM	20071
ANALYSIS	18024
BALANCE	17853
COBALT	00409
DISLOCATIONS	04778
FERRITE	04778
GROWTH	20071
HEXAGONAL	30714

With such an index it is easily possible to correlate keywords in a search—for example, to look down the "crystals" column to see if any title seems to deal with cobalt crystals. Note that all keywords in a title are exhibited in pairwise associations (for instance, the common document number, 04778, indicates that "crystals," "dislocations," and "ferrite" all occur in the same title) and that each keyword becomes an entry point in the index: "aluminum" will be an entry point, as will "analysis," "balance," and so on.

Somewhat related to the KWIC/KWOC/permuted group of indexes is the "articulated subject index" exemplified by the subject index to *Chemical Abstracts*. In this type of index, a brief narrative description of a document is used to generate entries. This could be a statement written by an indexer or, instead, a title or sentence extracted from the text. Certain words or phrases appearing in this statement are selected as entry points in the index, the remainder of the statement being retained as a modifier to provide the necessary context.

Armstrong and Keen (1982) describe the process of constructing entries for an articulated index as follows:

> Input terms are re-arranged such that each is linked to its original neighbour by a function word or by special punctuation so that the sentence-like structure remains although often re-ordered. (Page 6)

The following examples, from Armstrong and Keen, illustrate the principle:

Indexing of Chemical Periodicals by Researchers
Chemical Periodicals, Indexing of, by Researchers
Periodicals, Chemical, Indexing of, by Researchers

Note that the syntax of the original text is retained so that the meaning of the original statement is not obscured. Index statements such as these can be prepared by an indexer following a prescribed set of rules, or computer programs can be written to generate entries of this type (Armitage and Lynch, 1968; Lynch and Petrie, 1973).

```
NONEQUILIBRIUM  SCALE EFFECTS FOR NONEQUILIBRIUM CONVECTIVE HE
                AT TRANSFER WITH SIMULTANEOUS GAS PHASE AND SU
                RFACE CHEMICAL REACTIONS. APPLICATION TO HYPER
                SONIC FLIGHT AT HIGH ALTITUDES
                            AD-291 032(K)   $1.60 0025
NONLINEAR       APPLICATION OF VARIATIONAL EQUATION OF MOTION
                TO THE NONLINEAR VIBRATION ANALYSIS OF HOMOGEN
                EOUS AND LAYERED PLATES AND SHELLS
                            AD-289 868(K)   $2.60 0667
NONLINEAR       EXTENSIONS IN THE SYNTHESIS OF TIME OPTIMAL OR
                BANG-BANG NONLINEAR CONTROL SYSTEMS. PART I.
                THE SYNTHESIS OF QUASI-STATIONARY OPTIMUM NONL
                INEAR CONTROL SYSTEMS
                            PB 162 547(K)   $4.60 0235
NONLINEAR       EXTENSIONS IN THE SYNTHESIS OF TIME OPTIMAL OR
                BANG-BANG NONLINEAR CONTROL SYSTEMS. PART I.
                THE SYNTHESIS OF QUASI-STATIONARY OPTIMUM NONL
                INEAR CONTROL SYSTEMS
                            PB 162 547(K)   $4.60 0235
NONLINEAR       NONLINEAR FLEXURAL VIBRATIONS OF SANDWICH PLAT
                ES          AD-289 871(K)   $2.60 0669
NONLINEAR       OPTIMUM NONLINEAR CONTROL FOR ARBITRARY DISTUR
                BANCES      NASA N62-15890(K)  $2.60 0682
NONRECURRENT    A TECHNIQUE FOR NARROW-BAND TELEMETRY OF NONRE
                CURRENT PULSES  AD-290 697(K)  $2.60 0577
NONUNIFORM      ELECTROMAGNETIC SCATTERING FROM A SPHERICAL NO
                NUNIFORM MEDIUM. PART II. THE RADAR CROSS SECT
                ION OF A FLARE  AD-289 615(K)  $2.60 0747
NONUNIFORM      ELECTROMAGNETIC SCATTERING FROM ASPHERICAL NON
                UNIFORM MEDIUM. PART I. GENERAL THEORY
                            AD-289 614(K)   $2.60 0748
NORMAL          PROBABILITY INTEGRALS OF MULTIVARIATE NORMAL A
                ND MULTIVARIATE-T  AD-290 746(K)  $8.60 0760
NORMAL          RESONANCE ABSORPTION OF GAMMA-RAYS IN NORMAL A
                ND SUPERCONDUCTING TIN
                            AD-289 844(K)   $3.60 0826
NORMS           NORMS FOR ARTIFICIAL LIGHTING
                            AD-290 555(K)   $1.10 0734
NORTH           FACTORS INFLUENCING VASCULAR PLANT ZONATION IN
                NORTH CAROLINA SALTMARSHES
                            AD-290 938(K)   $7.60 0603
NORTH           SONAR STUDIES OF THE DEEP SCATTERING LAYER IN
                THE NORTH PACIFIC  PB 162 427(K)  $2.60 0587
NORTH           THE DEVELOPMENT OF RESCUE AND SURVIVAL TECHNIQ
                UES IN THE NORTH AMERICAN ARCTIC
                            PB 162 410(K) $12.00 0085
NOSE            THE FLORA OF HEALTHY DOGS. I. BACTERIA AND FUN
                GI OF THE NOSE, THROAT, AND LOWER INTESTINE
                            LF-2(K)   $2.60 0458
NOZZLE          FABRICATION OF PYROLYTIC GRAPHITE ROCKET NOZZL
                E COMPONENTS  PB 162 371(K)  $1.10 0351
NOZZLE          FABRICATION OF PYROLYTIC GRAPHITE ROCKET NOZZL
                E COMPONENTS  PB 162 370(K)  $1.10 0353
NOZZLE          FABRICATION OF PYROLYTIC GRAPHITE ROCKET NOZZL
                E COMPONENTS  PB 162 372(K)  $2.60 0352
NOZZLE          THIRD SYMPOSIUM ON ADVANCED PROPULSION CONCEPT
                S SPONSORED BY UNITED STATES AIR FORCE OFFICE
                OF SCIENTIFIC RESEARCH AND THE GENERAL ELECTRI
                C COMPANY FLIGHT PROPULSION DIVISION CINCINNAT
                I, OHIO OCTOBER 2-4, 1962. PLASMA FLOW IN A MA
                GNETIC ARC NOZZLE  AD-290 082(K)  $2.60 0147
NOZZLES         HEAT TRANSFER AND PARTICLE TRAJECTORIES IN SOL
                ID-ROCKET NOZZLES  AD-289 681(K)  $5.60 0030
```

FIGURE 20

Sample entries from a KWOC index.

Reprinted from *U.S. Government Technical Reports*, Volume 1, 1963, by permission of the National Technical Information Service.

```
GLYCIDE

    MATERNAL GLYCIDE NORMAL ASSIMILATION. TOMATO BABY, PRECEDENTS
    OF MACROSOMIA AND FETAL MORTALITY. • B SALVADORI,
    G CAGNAZZO, A DELEONARDIS • MINERVA PEDIAT V12 P117,
    11 FEB 60 IT

GLYCINE

    AN INSULIN ASSAY BASED ON THE INCORPORATION OF LABELLED
    GLYCINE INTO PROTEIN OF ISOLATED RAT DIAPHRAGM. •
    K L MANCHESTER, P J RANDLE, F G YOUNG • J ENDOCR V19 P259-62,
    DEC 59

    MAINTENANCE OF CARBOHYDRATE STORES DURING STRESS OF COLD AND
    FATIGUE IN RATS PREFED DIETS CONTAINING ADDED GLYCINE. •
    W R TODD, M ALLEN • USAF ARCTIC AEROMED LAB TECHN REP V57-34
    P1-16, JUNE 60

GLYCINE C14

    RATE OF ASSOCIATION OF S35 AND C14 IN PLASMA PROTEIN FRACTIONS
    AFTER ADMINISTRATION OF NA2S3504, GLYCINE-C14, OR GLUCOSE C14.
    • J E RICHMOND • J BIOL CHEM V234 P2713-6, OCT 59

GLYCOGEN

    GLYCOGEN OF THE ADRENAL CORTEX AND MEDULLA. INFLUENCE OF AGE
    AND SEX. • H PLANEL, A GUILHEM • C R SOC BIOL PAR V153 P844-8,
    1959 FR

    EFFECT OF DIET ON THE BLOOD SUGAR AND LIVER GLYCOGEN LEVEL OF
    NORMAL AND ADRENALECTOMIZED MICE. • B P BLOCK, G S COX •
    NATURE LOND V184 SUPPL 10 P721-2, 29 AUG 59

    LIVER GLYCOGEN AND BLOOD SUGAR LEVELS IN ADRENAL-DEMEDULLATED
    AND ADRENALECTOMIZED RATS AFTER A SINGLE DOSE OF GROWTH
    HORMONE. • C A DE GROOT • ACTA PHYSIOL PHARMACOL NEERL V9
    P107-20, MAY 60

    A MICROMETHOD FOR SIMULTANEOUS DETERMINATION OF GLUCOSE AND
    KETONE BODIES IN BLOOD AND GLYCOGEN AND KETONE BODIES IN
    LIVER. • O HANSEN • SCAND J CLIN LAB INVEST V12 P18-24, 1960

    AN INVERSE RELATION BETWEEN THE LIVER GLYCOGEN AND THE BLOOD
    GLUCOSE IN THE RAT ADAPTED TO A FAT DIET. • P A MAYES • NATURE
    LOND V187 P325-6, 23 JULY 60

    LIVER GLUCOSYL OLIGOSACCHARIDES AND GLYCOGEN CARBON-14
    DIOXIDE EXPERIMENTS WITH HYDROCORTISONE. • H G SIE,
    J ASHMORE, R MAHLER, W H FISHMAN • NATURE LOND V184 P1380-1,
    31 OCT 59

    STUDIES ON GLYCOGEN BIOSYNTHESIS IN GUINEA PIG CORNEA BY
    MEANS OF GLUCOSE LABELED WITH C14. • R PHAUS,
    J OBEMBERGER, J VOTOCKOVA • CESK FYSIOL V9 P45-6, JAN 60 CZ

    GLYCOGEN CONTENT AND CARBOHYDRATE METABOLISM OF THE LEUKOCYTES
    IN DIABETES MELLITUS. • G MAEHR • WIEN Z INN MED V40 P330-4,
    SEPT 59 GER

    GLYCOGEN LIVER.  AN IATROGENIC ACUTE ABDOMINAL DISORDER IN
    DIABETES MELLITUS. • A SCHOTTE, H K LANKAMP, M FRENKEL •
    NED T GENEESK V103 P2258-62, 7 NOV 59 DUT

    ACUTE GLYCOGEN INFILTRATION OF THE LIVER IN DIABETES MELLITUS.
    2.  THE EFFECTS OF GLUCAGON THERAPY. • A SCHOTTE, H K LANKAMP,
    M FRENKEL • NED T GENEESK V104 P1288-91, 2 JULY 60 DUT
```

FIGURE 21

Alternative format for a KWOC index as used in the *Diabetes-Related Literature Index*, a supplement to *Diabetes*, Volume 12, 1960.

One example of the articulated subject index, and in fact the one described in detail by Armstrong and Keen (1982), is NEPHIS (Nested Phrase Indexing System), a system devised by Craven (1977). In the simplest form of NEPHIS, the indexer uses angular brackets to indicate a phrase "nested within" a larger phrase and thus to be used to generate index entries. For example the phrase

Research Productivity of <**Sleep Researchers**>

will generate the two entries:

Research Productivity of Sleep Researchers
Sleep Researchers, Research Productivity of

Craven builds upon this simple principle by the addition of further symbols and conventions to be used by the indexer to create index entries that are consistent and unambiguous as well as useful. The report by Armstrong and Keen (1982) gives one an appreciation of the capabilities of this relatively simple approach to indexing. Quite similar to NEPHIS is the PASI (Pragmatic Approach to Subject Indexing) system described by Dutta and Sinha (1984).

One other indexing system is worth brief mention. SPINDEX (Selective Permutation Index), which was designed for the indexing of collections of archives, was originally no more than a KWAC or KWOC index (Burke, 1967). In later versions, it was modified to produce two-level index entries consisting of main and qualifying keywords as in the examples ARIZONA, Indian affairs and INDIAN AFFAIRS, Arizona (Cook, 1980). Unfortunately, the SPINDEX acronym, standing for Subject Profile Index, was also used for a different format by producers of several printed indexes including the American Bibliographical Center (publisher of *Historical Abstracts* and *America: History and Life*). This approach, later referred to as ABC-SPINDEX (American Bibliographical Center's Subject Profile Index) to distinguish it from the quite unrelated SPINDEX, seems virtually identical with the cycled indexes used by *Excerpta Medica* (Falk and Baser, 1980).

Classification in Subject Indexes

All of the indexes discussed so far use approaches that are "alphabetical" rather than "systematic." Other types of indexes require that entries be constructed according to "logical" principles. Such approaches can be traced back to Cutter (1876) who presented rules on such matters as direct versus inverted entry (Ancient History or History, Ancient?). A more sophisticated approach was introduced by Kaiser (1911), who recognized three categories of terms: concretes, processes, and locality terms. "Concretes" are terms that relate to "things," real or imaginary, while "processes" covers activities. Kaiser required that indexing "statements" should arrange terms in a systematic sequence, rather than alphabetically. Only three sequences were permitted:

1. Concrete—Process (as in Tubes—Welding or Steel Tubes—Welding)

2. Locality—Process (as in Argentina—Trade)

3. Concrete—Locality—Process (as in Coffee—Brazil—Export)

In order to follow Kaiser's rules, the indexer might have to supply an implicit concrete term. For example, the term *desalination* would become Water—Desalination.

The next major development is attributable to Ranganathan. Although Ranganathan's name is primarily associated with theories of classification and with his own bibliographic classification scheme, the *Colon Classification*, he has also made a significant contribution to modern practice in alphabetical subject indexing. His *chain indexing* is an attempt to arrive at a procedure for systematically developing an alphabetical subject index for a classified catalog (in card or book form). The principles of his classification scheme, and his theories of classification, are beyond the scope of this book. Suffice it to say that a major characteristic of classification schemes constructed on Ranganathan's principles is that of "synthesis" or "number building." That is, the class number that represents some complex subject is arrived at by joining the notational elements that represent more elemental subjects. For example, the topic "manufacture of woollen clothing in Germany in the nineteenth century" might be represented by the notation $AbCfHYqZb$, where Ab represents "clothing," Cf "woollen," H "manufacture," Yq "Germany," and Zb "nineteenth century," all of these notational elements being drawn from different parts of the classification scheme and combined in a sequence ("preferred order" or "citation order") specified by the maker of the scheme.

It should be obvious that the alphabetical index to a classified catalog constructed on these principles must be arrived at systematically, otherwise it might appear chaotic and impossible to use. Ranganathan's solution to this problem, chain indexing, involves indexing each step of the hierarchical chain from the most specific to the most general. Thus, an item represented by the class number $AbCfHYqZb$ would generate the following index entries:

> Nineteenth century, Germany, Manufacture, Woollen goods,
> Clothing $AbCfHYqZb$
> Germany, Manufacture, Woollen goods, Clothing $AbCfHYq$
> Manufacture, Woollen goods, Clothing $AbCfH$
> Woollen goods, Clothing $AbCf$
> Clothing Ab

Clearly, the user of an index of this type must also search according to a predefined sequence of terms. For example, if seeking information on clothing in Germany in the nineteenth century, the searcher would get little help from the index if the term *clothing* were consulted.

In determining the sequence in which class numbers should be combined in an "analytico-synthetic" classification scheme (frequently referred to, somewhat misleadingly, as "faceted"), Ranganathan arrived at five "fundamental categories" and a formula for putting them together. The categories, Personality, Matter, Energy, Space, and Time, are combined in this sequence and the formula is sometimes referred to simply as "PMEST."

Personality is best thought of as "the thing itself." Matter is the material of which the thing is composed. Energy is the action performed on or by the thing, Space is where the action takes place, and Time is when it takes place. The sequence $AbCfHYqZb$ observes the PMEST order. It follows, then, that the chain index entry for an item thus categorized will be in the reverse of this order.

Ranganathan's "logical" sequencing of facets in number building can be carried also into alphabetical subject catalogs and indexes. Thus, one could build a logical index entry, following the PMEST formula, as follows:

Clothing: Woollen goods: Manufacture: Germany:
Nineteenth Century

Unfortunately, the PMEST formula is a little simplistic. In indexing highly complex subject matter, a particular category may occur more than once (e.g., the stressing of a structure could lead to the cracking of that structure which implies two different occurrences of the "energy" category); some of the categories need to be further subdivided (e.g., to indicate different types of activities); moreover, the PMEST formula does not clearly handle certain attributes that are important in indexing, such as the *properties* of materials.

Nevertheless, Ranganathan's theories have had a profound effect on modern practice in subject indexing. One can see this clearly in the work of Coates (1960) who advocates a catalog or index free from the rigidity of pre-established subject headings. An index entry should be made fully co-extensive with the subject matter discussed, as in the example

Power transmission lines, Overhead, Conductors, Icing, Prevention, Heating

Coates uses a "significance formula" to establish the sequence in which component terms are put together. The basic sequence he adopts is Thing, Part, Material, Action, Property, but this may be modified under certain circumstances. The heading used above, for example, adopts the sequence Thing, Kind, Part, Action, Agent. The procedures developed by Coates were adopted by the *British Technology Index* (later the *Current Technology Index*), of which Coates was the first editor. Some sample entries from this index are shown in Figure 22. Note that an item appears only once in the index. Additional approaches are provided through the use of cross references.

Ranganathan's theories can also be considered to have influenced PRE-CIS (Preserved Context Index System) as developed by Austin (Austin, 1984). In PRECIS, computer programs generate a complete set of index entries and cross references for an item from a string of terms and instruction codes provided by an indexer. The subject matter of a document is described by a series of terms that are put in a "context-dependent" sequence. Austin and Digger (1977) use the following example:

India, Cotton industries, Personnel, Training

The logic claimed for this is that each term is essentially dependent on the term immediately before it. Thus, "training" applies only to the context of "personnel," "personnel" applies only to the context of "cotton industries" and this applies only in the context of India.

In PRECIS the relationships among component terms in an index entry are presented as a two-line display:

Personnel. Cotton industries. India
Training

This is justified on the grounds that it provides a practical way of showing, simultaneously, the relationship between the term used as an entry point in the index and the terms that are (a) of wider context and (b) of narrower context. In the example above, "Personnel" is modified by "Cotton indus-tries" and "India" to show the broader context, while "Training" is displayed as a dependent of "Personnel."

As illustrated in this example, a PRECIS entry has three components:

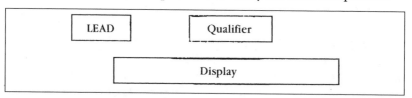

The "lead" term is the entry point in the index and it is printed in bold face. the "qualifier" provides the broader context and the "display" shows the terms of narrower context. While the lead position will obviously always be occu-pied, the other positions need not always be.

Entries of the general type illustrated above can be generated by com-puter from a string of terms presented in a context-dependent sequence. Thus, the string India, Cotton industries, Personnel, Training would generate the following entries:

India
     Cotton industries. Personnel. Training.
Cotton industries. India
     Personnel. Training

Unfortunately, the procedure is not as simple as suggested in this one example. There are many instances in which the sequence in a string of terms does not in itself illustrate the dependencies unambiguously. In point of fact, a PRECIS indexer must use "operators" (codes tacked onto component terms) in order to represent term relationships unambiguously. For the example used earlier, the input string would be

(0)	India
(1)	cotton industries
(P)	personnel
(2)	training

where (2) represents "transition action," (P) "object of action, part of key system," (O) "location," and (1) "key system" (object of transitive action). These operators show the "role" that a term plays in relation to other terms (providing a kind of syntax) and thus can be regarded as "role indicators" or "role operators."

Austin and Digger list 26 operators of this type. Clearly, use of such a scheme greatly complicates the indexing operation and adds to its cost and, in fact, a very substantial manual of indexing instructions is needed to implement PRECIS.

Somewhat related to PRECIS is POPSI, the Postulate-based Permuted Subject Indexing system (Bhattacharyya, 1981), which derives from Ranganathan's theories of classification.

The indexing scheme of Farradane (1967, 1980), which predated PRECIS, is similar in that it also uses a scheme of role indicators. Whereas PRECIS uses its roles solely as a means of generating consistent indexing statements by computer, the roles are retained in Farradane's system to show precise relationships among the terms. The relationships are drawn from work on the experimental psychology of thinking by Piaget, Vinacke, Isaacs, and others, and reinforced by the work of Guilford on the "structure of intellect."

Nine explicit relations exist in Farradane's scheme, each represented by an "operator." The complete set of these operators is given in Figure 23. The scheme represents stages in the development of thinking drawn from child psychology; i.e., the stages through which a child develops in associating objects and in discriminating among them. There are two sets of gradation: in associative mechanisms and in discriminating mechanisms. The first associative stage is simple awareness without reference to time; the second is temporary association between ideas; and the third is the fixed (permanent) association of ideas. The stages of discrimination are: simple concurrence (concepts hard to distinguish), not-distinct (concepts having

FABRICS
  Related Headings:
    WEAVING
FABRICS, Cellulosic ,, Crease resistant : Cross linking :
Dimethylol-1,3-propylene urea
  Deferred curing [BP 1,107,796 : Sun Chemical Corp., USA] Dyer,
    Textile Printer, Bleacher & Finisher, 141 (2 May 69) p.614+
FABRICS, Cellulosic ,, Crease resistant : Finishing
  Crease-resist and wash-and-wear finishing. B.C.M. Dorset. Textile
    Manufacturer, 95 (Apr 69) p.156-63
FABRICS, Cellulosic ,, Knitted ,, Crease resistant : Finishing
  Permanent press processes for knitted fabrics. D. Haigh. Hosiery Trade
    J., 76 (May 69) p.127+. il.
FABRICS ; Cellulosic—Nylon : Dyeing, High temperature : Dyes, Reactive
  "Hot-dyeing" reactive dyes on blends [Drimarene X and Drimafon X :
    Sandoz Products Ltd, Horsforth, Leeds] [summary] P.F. Bell. Dyer,
    Textile Printer, Bleacher & Finisher, 141 (2 May 69) p.622+
FABRICS ; Cellulosic—Polyester fibres : Dyeing, High temperature :
Dyes, Reactive
  "Hot-dyeing" reactive dyes on blends [Drimarene X and Drimafon X :
    Sandoz Products Ltd, Horsforth, Leeds] [summary] P.F. Bell. Dyer,
    Textile Printer, Bleacher & Finisher, 141 (2 May 69) p.622+
FABRICS, Coated : Clothing. See CLOTHING : Fabrics, Coated
FABRICS : Finishing : Weft straighteners : Control system, Photoelectric
  Fabric straightening [BP 1,107,822] H. Elcken. Dyer, Textile
    Printer, Bleacher & Finisher, 141 (2 May 69) p.612+
FABRICS, Foamback : Laminating
  Versatility the key: different cloths call for different techniques. P.
    Lennox-Kerr. Hosiery Times, 42 (Apr 69) p.107-9. il.
FABRICS ; Man made fibres ,, Pile : Knitting
  Manufacture and use-development of pile fabrics in Du Pont fibres.
    J. Rest & M.R.B. Addison. Hosiery Times, 42 (Apr 69) p.88+. il.
FABRICS ; Mohair : Suitings. See SUITINGS : Fabrics ; Mohair
FABRICS : Tape. See TAPE : Fabrics
FABRICS, Warp knit : Dyeing, High temperature : Heating : Heat
transfer oil
  HT process heating in the modern dyehouse [Kestner-Stone-Vapor at
    Nyla-Raywarp, Long Eaton] Dyer, Textile Printer, Bleacher &
    Finisher, 141 (18 Apr 69) p.542+
FABRICS, Warp knit : Knitwear. See KNITWEAR : Fabrics, Warp knit
FABRICS ; Wool ,, Knitted ,, Shrink resistant : Finishing : Solvents :
Perchloroethylene : Machines
  'Bentley Rapide' solvent finishing machine for knitwear and piece-goods.
    A.G. Brooks. Hosiery Times, 42 (Apr 69) p.45+. il.
  Milling machine for knitwear [Bentley Rapide] Hosiery Trade J., 76
    (May 69) p.130+. il.

FIGURE 22
Specimen entries from the *British Technology Index.*
Reprinted by kind permission of CSA.

much in common), and distinct conceptualization (concepts that can be completely distinguished).

Indexing statements are constructed by joining terms ("isolates") together by means of these operators. An indexing statement, consisting of terms related by means of operators, is called an "analet." Some simple examples are:

Birds /* Migration
Iron Ore /—Smelting

and a more complex one:

Glass/(Oxygen/)Fluorine/—Substituting

which represents the substitution of fluorine for oxygen in glass. Two-dimensional display is used where necessary, as:

Beets/—Storing   The storage of washed
/;   beets
Washing
          {Sucrose   }   Rats fed on sucrose
Rat /*   {Coconut Oil} /—Feeding   with coconut oil

Farradane (1977) has compared his relational indexing system with PRECIS, NEPHIS, and POPSI, all of which he refers to loosely as producing "permuted" indexes; he claims that his two-dimensional diagrams can be converted by computer into permuted alphabetical index entries.

		Associative mechanisms		
		Awareness	Temporary association	Fixed association
Discriminatory mechanisms	Concurrent conceptualization	1 /θ Concurrence	4 /* Self-activity	7 /; Association
	Not-distinct conceptualization	2 /= Equivalence	5 /+ Dimensional	8 /(Appurtenance
	Distinct conceptualization	3 /) Distinctness	6 /— Action	9 /: Functional dependence (causation)

FIGURE 23
Farradane's system of relations.
Reproduced from Farradane (1980) by kind permission of CSA.

Gardiner et al. (1995) acknowledge the influence of Farradane in their approach to the searching of text databases. That is, their search procedures look for text in which sought terms appear to relate to each other in the precise way required by the search statement.

The Symbolic Shorthand System (Selye, 1966; Selye and Ember, 1964) is another indexing system that expresses relationships among terms by means of role indicators. The indexer draws terms from a classification scheme comprising 20 main classes organized principally on the basis of body system. Throughout the scheme, mnemonic symbols are used to represent subjects. For example, *Adr* represents the adrenal gland, *Hypt* hypothalamus, *BMR* basal metabolic rate, and so on. Selye's basic role indicator is an arrow

($\leftarrow$) showing direction of action, as in:

Cer $\leftarrow$ ACTH	Effect of adrenocorticotrophic hormone on the brain

or the more complex:

Adr $\leftarrow$ Hyp $\leftarrow$ ACTH+TX	Effect on the adrenal of hypophysectomy in conjunction with adrenocorticotrophic hormone and thyroxin

Other role indicators show other relationships. For instance, the symbol < is used to indicate content or component (Glu < B represents blood sugar) and the colon (:) is used for the comparison role. Quite complex subject matter can be represented concisely and unambiguously in this system, as the following examples show:

R $\leftarrow$ ('B/Rb $\leftarrow$ R/Duck')/Rat

(Injection of renal substance of duck into a rabbit's blood and injection of serum thus formed into rats, thus producing renal changes)

Glu < B (:Ur) $\leftarrow$ CON

(Effect of cortisone on sugar content of blood compared with sugar content of urine)

Level of Coordination

A distinction has been made between precoordinate and postcoordinate systems. In point of fact, however, a modern information retrieval system is likely to incorporate precoordinate features as well as postcoordinate capabilities. Some precoordination is likely to exist in the vocabulary used for indexing. For example, the descriptor *population growth*, drawn from a thesaurus, represents the precoordination of the terms *population* and *growth*. In some systems, an indexer may be allowed to use certain terms as subheadings of others. Thus, he might create:

population growth/statistics

Finally, the searcher can freely combine terms in logical relationships, e.g., "retrieve items indexed under *population growth/statistics* and also under *South America*."

Some coordination (of concepts or terms representing them) occurs, then, in the characteristics of the vocabulary, and some further coordination may occur at the time of indexing. These can be considered as forms of *precoordination* in that the coordination is built into the records that are input into a database. The final level of coordination is that achievable through the manipulation of terms in the conduct of a search (i.e., *postcoordination*).

While this chapter has presented examples of various types of precoordinate indexes, it certainly has not exhausted the possibilities. A more complete analysis of the characteristics of precoordinate indexes can be found in Keen (1977a) and in Craven (1986). Keen (1977b) also discusses the subject of search strategy as applied to such indexes.

Back-of-the-Book Indexes

Although many of the principles discussed in this book are valid for indexes of all types, the major focus of attention is the indexing of databases of bibliographic items—postcoordinate indexing for databases in electronic form and precoordinate indexing for those in printed form. No attempt is made to present detailed instructions on the indexing of individual books. This topic is well covered elsewhere (e.g., Mulvany, 1994; *Guidelines for Indexes*, 1997). Diodato (1994) presents results of a study of user preferences for book indexes; the opinions of librarians and teaching faculty are compared.

The most complete studies of book indexes appear to be those reported by Bishop et al. (1991) and Liddy et al. (1991). In this pair of related studies, the former analyzes the characteristics of a sample of indexes (format, arrangement, and suchlike) while the latter surveys the policies of publishers (e.g., who prepares the index, style requirements); this paper also includes some information on index characteristics and includes conclusions from the whole project. Liddy and Jörgensen (1993a) used student volunteers to study how they actually used a book index.

Precoordinate Versus Postcoordinate Indexes

Printed indexes of the type discussed in this chapter can be very effective in locating one or "a few" items on a topic rather quickly. However, some writers seem to go overboard in extolling the virtues of precoordinate indexes. They criticize postcoordinate retrieval on the grounds that it can give poor results (see Weinberg, 1995, for example), such as too much irrelevancy, although this can be true of all approaches, and that many users have trouble understanding search logic. The latter claim is certainly true but it is equally true that many people have great difficulty in understanding and using even the simplest of printed indexes (see, for example, Liddy and Jörgensen, 1993a,b). Given the choice, library users seem overwhelmingly to prefer postcoordinate searching in electronic databases over use of printed indexes (see, for example, Massey-Burzio, 1990) although, in fact, they may get very poor results from their searches (see pp. 121-127 of Lancaster and Sandore, 1997).

CHAPTER 5

Consistency of Indexing

IT IS QUITE CLEAR that indexing is a subjective rather than an objective process. Two (or more) individuals may disagree on what some publication is about, what aspects of it deserve indexing, or what terms best describe the topics selected. Moreover, a single individual may make different indexing decisions at different times. *Consistency* in indexing refers to the extent to which agreement exists on the terms to be used to index some document. *Inter-indexer consistency* refers to agreement between or among indexers while *intra-indexer consistency* refers to the extent to which one indexer is consistent with himself.

Several different measures of consistency have been used or proposed; these have been well reviewed by Leonard (1975). Perhaps the most common measure is the simple ratio *AB/(A+B)*, where *A* represents the terms assigned by indexer *a*, *B* represents the terms assigned by indexer *b*, and *AB* represents the terms on which *a* and *b* agree. Consider the situation depicted in Figure 24. Five individuals have indexed the same item, with the number of terms assigned varying from four (indexer *b*) to eight (indexer *e*). The terms assigned by any pair of indexers can be compared. Hooper (1965) refers to pair consistency values as *consistency pairs* (CPs). For indexers *a* and *b*, the CP is 3/6, or .5 (there are six unique terms assigned and three of these are assigned by both). Each pair in the group can be treated in the same way. From the data supplied, one can derive the following CPs: *ab*, (.5); *ac*, 4/7 (.57); *ad*, 4/6 (.75); *ae* 4/9 (.44); *bc*, 3/7 (.43); *bd*, 2/7 (.29); *be*, 4/8 (.5); *cd*, 3/8 (.37); *ce*, 5/9 (.56); *de*, 3/10 (.30).

A measure of inter-group consistency can be obtained by averaging the results for each pair of indexers. For the group *a-e* the overall consistency is about .47.

If the sequence of terms in Figure 24 reflects priority of assignment, one can see that reasonable agreement exists as to the most important terms. All five indexers assign term *A* and four of the five assign both *A and B*. Much less agreement exists on the secondary aspects of the document or what terms to assign to these aspects. Note also how the number of terms assigned affects the consistency score: the more terms assigned (at least up to a point), the lower will tend to be the consistency. Zunde and Dexter (1969b) and Rolling (1981) suggest that consistency measures should take

68

into account the importance of various terms to the subject matter of a document. Inconsistency in assignment of minor terms will be much less important than inconsistency in assignment of major terms and this should be reflected in any scoring method.

a	b	c	d	e
A	A	A	A	A
B	B	C	B	B
C	E	D	C	D
D	F	E	D	E
E		E	D	F
		F	H	G
		G		I
				J

FIGURE 24

Terms (*A-J*) assigned to the same document by five different indexers (*a-e*).

The data of Figure 24 could also represent intra-indexer consistency: the situation where one individual indexes the same document on five different occasions.

Cooper (1969) looks at inter-indexer consistency in a different way—at the term level. That is, he measures the degree to which a group of indexers agree on the assignment of a particular term to a document. With respect to this term, inter-indexer consistency is defined as the proportion of indexers who assign the term minus the proportion who do not. In the Figure 24 example, there is 100% agreement on term *A*, 60% agreement on *B* (80%-20%), 20% agreement on *C* (60%-40%), and so on.

Many studies of inter-indexer consistency have been performed, although they are not as common now as they once were; they tend to reveal that a high level of consistency is very difficult to achieve. Hooper (1965) summarized fourteen different studies and found values ranging from 10% to 80%. For the six studies in which he was able to recompute the values from the data supplied (to ensure that consistency was calculated in the same way for each), the results ranged from 24% to 80%.

Virtually all of the studies of inter-indexer consistency that have taken place so far treat each term as equal although, as suggested earlier, it might be more sensible to give greater "weight" to consistency in assigning the more important terms. Another complication is the fact that, with certain types of controlled vocabularies and indexing procedures, a partial match could occur. For example, two indexers might agree on the same main heading but not on a subheading. Consider the following example in which upper case letters represent headings, the lower case letters represent subheadings, and the asterisk is used to mark the headings the indexer considers most important:

Indexer 1	Indexer 2	Indexer 3
*A/b	*A/c	*A/b
*B/b/c	*B/c	B/c
C/f	C/f	*D/f
D/f	D/r	F
E	F	*H/q
	G	I

This is actually a realistic situation. For example, it closely resembles indexing practice at the National Library of Medicine where more than one subheading may be assigned to a term and major descriptors are distinguished from minor ones.

It is clear that this type of indexing presents significant problems in the performance of consistency studies. The simple consistency pair approach is meaningless here. In indexing of this type, greater "credit" should be given for a perfect agreement between two indexers. For example, indexers 1 and 3 should be given great credit for the fact that both agree on the main heading/subheading combination A/b and that this should be a major descriptor. While a numerical scoring method could be devised to express consistency (5 points for a perfect main heading/subheading match, 10 points for a main heading/subheading match if both indexers use as a major descriptor, and so on), it is difficult to get agreement on what the score should be and even more difficult to interpret what the scores really mean. Scoring of this type is more likely to be usable in studies of indexing *quality*, as discussed in the next chapter.

Factors Affecting Consistency

This variability in consistency scores leads one to ask "what are the factors that have most effect in determining consistency in indexing?" An attempt is made to identify possible factors in Figure 25.

The number of terms assigned was already mentioned. If indexers are asked to assign terms in order of perceived "importance" to the subject matter of the document, one would presumably get a fair degree of agreement on the terms at the top of the list. As one goes down the list, this agreement can be expected to decline. Put somewhat differently, one would expect more agreement on what are the main topics of the document than on which of the minor topics are worth inclusion.

But this may be a little simplistic. Figure 26 suggests a possible relationship between consistency and number of terms assigned. Assuming that terms are assigned in order of priority, it is hypothesized that agreement may peak at the level of two terms and then begin a gradual decline up to a point when so many terms have been assigned that agreement will again increase. This can be illustrated by the example of Figure 27.

1.	Number of terms assigned
2.	Controlled vocabulary versus free text indexing
3.	Size and specificity of vocabulary
4.	Characteristics of subject matter and its terminology
5.	Indexer factors
6.	Tools available to indexer
7.	Length of item to be indexed

FIGURE 25
Possible factors affecting consistency of indexing.

This figure shows ranked lists of terms assigned by indexers a and b. That is, a believes that A is the most important term, B is next most important, and so on. Another way of looking at this is to say that, if indexer a could only assign one term to the document that term would be A. Each indexer eventually assigns sixteen terms. Note that, while the indexers agree on the top two terms, they do not agree on the number one term. This is not surprising. Many documents involve a relationship between two major concepts. It may be possible to agree on what these concepts are but not to agree on which should take precedence. For example, in an article on welding of titanium does the metal or the process take precedence? (Of course, such decisions are very much related to the characteristics of the database. In one devoted exclusively to titanium, the term *titanium* has little or no value.) This is a little like betting on greyhounds (or racehorses): it is frequently easier to guess which two dogs will finish in the first two positions than to guess which one will be first.

After all sixteen terms have been assigned, perfect agreement has been reached. This is due to a type of "saturation" effect. There are only so many terms that could plausibly apply to any item, at least if these terms are drawn from a controlled vocabulary. If enough terms are assigned, a high consistency will eventually be reached. Note, however, that consistency declines between the two term level and the sixteen term level. For example, after five terms, the CP is 5/6 (.83), after ten terms it is 6/14 (.43), and so on.

The relationship shown in Figure 26, then, seems plausible, although it has not been confirmed experimentally. At least, the shape of the curve is plausible if the results for many indexers are taken into account. If few indexers were considered, of course, the decline in consistency would probably be less smooth (e.g., greater consistency may exist for four terms than for three).

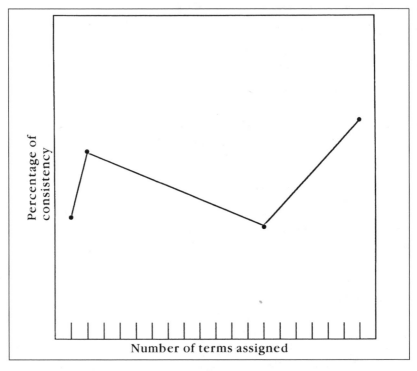

FIGURE 26
The relationship between consistency and number of terms assigned.

Harris et al. (1966) report results that differ somewhat from those hypothesized in Figure 26. Consistency was greater after ten terms than after five but declined at the 20 term and 30 term level, increasing again when 40 terms had been assigned. They claimed to have found little evidence of any saturation effect, but their indexers were using uncontrolled keywords and not selecting from a limited set of controlled terms. Fried and Prevel (1966) discovered a decline in consistency with the number of terms assigned, but Leonard (1975) found inconclusive evidence on this point—true for one database but not another.

In a study of consistency within agricultural databases, Reich and Biever (1991) found evidence of the effect of exhaustivity on consistency: in a sample of articles indexed with an average of 8-9 thesaurus terms, consistency was 24%; it was 45% for a sample having an average of 5-6 thesaurus terms.

a	b
A	B
B	A
C	D
D	E
E	K
F	C
G	G
H	L
I	M
J	N
K	O
L	P
M	F
N	H
O	I
P	J

FIGURE 27

Effect of number of terms assigned on indexer consistency (two indexers).

The second factor affecting consistency (Figure 25) is the type of vocabulary used in indexing. One of the major advantages claimed for a controlled vocabulary is that it will improve consistency in the representation of subject matter. However, the relationship between vocabulary control and indexer consistency is not as straightforward as it might seem at first sight. Suppose I take a few medical articles and ask a group of high school students to index them. First, I require them to index by extracting words and phrases from the items themselves. I would expect a reasonable level of consistency here. Presumably, the students will behave in more or less the same way that a computer would in this task: they will look for words or phrases that occur frequently and/or appear in the title or other prominent places.

As a second step in this exercise, I now ask the students to translate their free text indexing into terms selected from the National Library of Medicine's *Medical Subject Headings (MeSH)*. Almost certainly, consistency will deteriorate. In this situation, the controlled vocabulary will have an adverse effect. This is because the textual expressions selected will not always be identical with the controlled terms. The students will have trouble in selecting the appropriate controlled terms because they lack sufficient knowledge of medicine and its terminology and because some of the controlled terms will have been given a special "meaning" (scope) by the compilers of the vocabulary. A controlled vocabulary should improve consistency of indexing in the long run but it can only be applied consistently by experienced indexers knowledgeable in the subject matter and fully familiar with the terms.

Another thing to note is that a controlled vocabulary should improve consistency of indexing over a group of documents but may well reduce it at the single document level. That is, the terminology adopted in a particular article should be internally consistent—an author will tend not to use a variety of terms to describe the same topic, at least in articles of a technical or scholarly nature. It is quite possible, however, that two indexers might differ on what controlled term to use to represent this topic. On the other hand, different authors may use different terminology so the controlled vocabulary, by reducing the amount of choice, has a beneficial effect on consistency of indexing over a large group of documents.

If interindexer consistency is low when two people index items using the same vocabulary, one obviously expects even lower consistency when the same items are indexed into different databases because variations in the vocabularies used adds another dimension to the problem. Qin (2000), for example, took a group of articles on the subject of antibiotic resistance and, for these, compared MEDLINE indexing with citation-based indexing in the *Science Citation Index* (*Key Words Plus*). Not surprisingly, similarity was low, even when "partial similarity" was the criterion used, although the three keyword terms that occurred most frequently were conceptually equivalent to the two most frequently occurring MEDLINE subject headings.

It should be noted in passing that a comparison of free text indexing with controlled term indexing is not as simple as it may seem at first sight. A controlled term either is assigned or it is not. With free text indexing, however, one faces the problem of deciding whether or not two expressions are identical. For example, is "electric power" to be considered identical to "electrical power," or how do you score a situation in which one indexer selects the term "medieval French literature" and a second uses both "medieval literature" and "French literature"? This, of course, brings us back to the distinction between conceptual analysis and translation. The effect of these stages on consistency will be mentioned later.

Fugmann (1985) raises a very interesting issue related to consistency. He points out that, while consistency studies focus on selection of terms for a particular document, the seeker of information (searcher) is more concerned about consistency *among* documents. This implies that a different type of consistency analysis might be useful—one that measures the extent to which the same topic is indexed consistently throughout a database.

The third factor identified in Figure 25 is the size and specificity of the vocabulary. The larger the vocabulary, the more specific it is likely to be;

and, the greater its specificity the more difficult it will be to use consistently (Tinker, 1966, 1968). For example, two indexers may be more likely to agree that a document is about corrosion than they are to agree on what type of corrosion is discussed. The finer the shades of meaning that a vocabulary can express, the more difficult it will be to achieve consistency. In my evaluation of MEDLARS (Lancaster, 1968a), I included a small consistency study. I discovered that consistency in the assignment of subject headings (*MeSH*) was 46.1% when the results for three indexers were averaged over 16 articles. When subheadings were also used, however, consistency dropped to 34.4%. In an earlier study it was found that role indicators had an even more drastic effect in reducing consistency of indexing (Lancaster, 1964), a finding that was confirmed by Sinnett (1964) and by Mullison et al. (1969).

In their study of indexing consistency within agricultural databases, Reich and Biever (1991) conclude that "Consistency . . . appears to be more difficult to attain with increasing vocabulary specificity."

Slamecka and Jacoby (1963) make a distinction between "prescriptive" and "suggestive" vocabularies. The latter give the indexer some latitude in the choice of terms while the former give the indexer virtually no choice. On the basis of some experiments with vocabularies of different types (subject headings, thesaurus, classification scheme), they concluded that:

> Inter-indexer consistency improves significantly with the use of prescriptive indexing aids containing a minimum of variable semantic relationships among terms. The use of indexing aids which enlarge the indexer's semantic freedom of term choice is detrimental to indexing reliability. Quality of indexing is best improved by vocabularies which formalize relationships so as to uniformly and invariably prescribe the choice of indexing terms. (Page 30).

Note that they appear to consider consistency and quality as more or less equivalent. This point will be discussed in the next chapter.

It is hardly surprising that prescriptive vocabularies produce greater consistency. Indeed, it seems probable that the greatest consistency would be achieved in the assignment of those terms that might be preprinted on an indexing form or displayed online (as in the case of the "checktags" of the National Library of Medicine) to remind an indexer that they *must* be used whenever applicable. Leonard (1975) has produced some evidence in support of this, as have Funk et al. (1983).

Leininger (2000), based on 60 items that were accidentally indexed twice into the PsycINFO database, found 66% consistency in the assignment of checktags, whereas overall consistency (all terms considered) was only 55%. The most surprising result was that only 44% consistency was achieved in the assignment of broad classification codes. With only 22 classes and 135 subclasses, and with an average of only 1.09 assignments per record (most records are put into only a single class, a few into a maximum of two), much greater consistency might have been expected. The most likely explanation is that many psychology articles may seem equally relevant to two or more categories: while different indexers might agree on which two or three categories to assign, there might be much less agreement on the single "best" category. Racehorses and greyhounds again.

The fourth factor identified in Figure 25 is the nature of the subject matter dealt with and, more particularly, its terminology. One must assume that greater consistency will occur in the indexing of more concrete topics (e.g., physical objects, named individuals) and that consistency will decline as one deals increasingly with abstractions. Tibbo (1994) points out that authors in the humanities tend to be imprecise in their terminology and that they may prefer to make their writing "dense" rather than readable. Zunde and Dexter (1969a), however, did not find that consistency increased with "document reading ease". Certain types of materials may cause special problems vis-a-vis indexing consistency. For imaginative works, such as fiction, feature films and some types of pictures, there is likely to be an unusually high level of disagreement on what the work is about and how it should be indexed. Different groups of people may have quite different interests in materials of these types. For example, art scholars and scholars of the film may want indexing that is quite different from the indexing wanted by the general public. Markey (1984) and Enser (1995) present some evidence to suggest that the indexing of images may produce unusually low levels of consistency.

The fifth factor has to do with the indexers as individuals. One would expect that two indexers with very similar backgrounds (education, experience, interests) will be more likely to agree on what should be indexed than two with widely differing backgrounds. Related to this is the type and extent of training given to the indexers. If all indexers take part in the same rigorous training program, this may serve to reduce the significance of earlier background as a factor influencing consistency. Knowledge of the subject matter dealt with is also important. If two indexers have about the same level of subject expertise, they may be more consistent with each other than would be the case if one is very knowledgeable and the other has only slight acquaintance with the subject matter. More important than subject knowledge per se, however, might be a detailed knowledge of the needs and interests of the users to be served.

Jacoby and Slamecka (1962) found higher consistency among experienced indexers than among beginning indexers in dealing with patents; the experienced indexers also used fewer terms. Leonard (1975) found that consistency increased with the experience of the indexers but found no positive correlation between consistency and educational background of the indexers. That is, improved familiarity with the subject matter (presumed from the educational background) did not increase consistency. Korotkin and Oliver (1964), in an experiment with abstracts in psychology, could detect no significant differences in consistency among two groups of indexers, one familiar with the subject matter and one not. In this case, however, the study was conducted with several artificial constraints that would affect the outcome: no controlled vocabulary was used, abstracts rather than full articles were involved, and indexers were told to assign exactly three terms (no more, no less) to each item.

A more recent study, by Bertrand and Cellier (1995), also looked at the effect of indexer experience. However, their study included so many variables that it is difficult to interpret their results.

Data in Stubbs et al. (1999) illustrate the effect that an "extreme" (i.e., atypical) indexer can have on consistency scores.

Another factor identified in Figure 25 relates to the tools used by the indexer. If a group of indexers shares a common set of indexing tools (dictionaries, glossaries, handbooks), these may tend to improve consistency among the group. Most important would be some form of *entry vocabulary*, constructed by the information center, that serves to map terms occurring in documents to the appropriate controlled terms.

Finally, the length of the item indexed should affect consistency: the shorter the item, the fewer the terms that might plausibly apply. Not surprisingly, Harris et al. (1966) found that consistency was greater in indexing questions (short textual statements) than it was in indexing journal articles. Rodgers (1961), Fried and Prevel (1966), Leonard (1975), and Horký (1983) also found some evidence of declining consistency with length of item, while Tell (1969) discovered that consistency when indexing from the full text of articles was lower than when indexing from titles or abstracts.

Consistency in Conceptual Analysis
Versus Consistency in Translation

The type of consistency study discussed in this chapter blurs the distinction between the conceptual analysis and the translation stages of indexing. However, Preschel (1972) attempted to separate these two stages to determine whether indexers were more likely to agree in their conceptual analysis than they were in the translation into index terms. The results of her investigation indicated that indexers were much more likely to agree on what should be indexed (conceptual analysis) than on how concepts should be described (translation). It is important to recognize, however, that the indexers in this study did not use a controlled vocabulary but made up their own "verbal labels" for topics. Quite different results might have been achieved had the normalizing influence of a controlled vocabulary been present in this study.

Figures 28-31 show examples of sets of index terms assigned to articles by two different indexers. In all cases the vocabulary used was the *Thesaurus of ERIC Descriptors*. These are all real examples of alternative approaches to indexing. The indexing was done, as part of a homework assignment, by students in the Graduate School of Library and Information Science at the University of Illinois. The examples were selected from a larger set collected by the author over a period of years. Students were free to choose any articles they wished to index and it was pure chance that more than one student should pick the same article. They are reproduced here because they do illustrate some of the problems involved in achieving agreement among indexers.

Indexer A	Indexer B
Major terms	*Major terms*
Crime victims	Assistance (social behavior)
Assistance (social behavior)	Impression formation
Apathy	Participation
Help seeking behavior	Witnesses
Minor terms	*Minor terms*
Crime	Crime prevention
Citizenship	Involvement
Avoidance	Laws
	Social behavior
	Social perception

FIGURE 28

Two approaches to indexing an article entitled *When Bystanders Just Stand By.*

Figure 28 is an extreme example: only one term in common among sixteen assigned. The article deals with the phenomenon of people who refuse to intervene when they witness a crime. Notice how the two indexers view the article from different perspectives—*B* more from the social and legal viewpoint and *A* more from the psychological.

The example of Figure 29 is not much better. Among the major terms, the indexers agree on only one. The article deals with a program, offered by a public library, to teach parents of preschool children about literature suitable for that age group. Indexer *B* regards this as preschool education, although it is the parents and not the children who are being educated, while *A* (probably more correctly) interprets it as adult parent education. Indexer *B*, although a student of library science, fails to indicate that the program takes place in a library. Indexer *A*, on the other hand, fails to indicate that the article is related to very young children. Note how closely related terms are selected by the two indexers: *reading interests* versus *reading attitudes*, *literature appreciation* versus *literary criticism*, *reading materials* versus *reading material selection*.

Indexer A	Indexer B
Major terms	*Major terms*
Children's literature	Children's literature
Library extension	Preschool education
Adult education	Parent aspirations
Parent education	Literary criticism
Reading material selection	
Minor terms	*Minor terms*
Parent student relationship	Early experience
Recreational reading	Early childhood education
Literature appreciation	Reading materials
Reading interests	Young children
Fiction	Reading attitudes
Fantasy	Literature
Public libraries	Parent responsibility

FIGURE 29

Two approaches to indexing an article entitled *A Children's Literature Course for Parents.*

This illustrates the problems involved in applying a controlled vocabulary that contains many closely related or partially overlapping terms, especially when the indexers are not fully familiar with the intended scope of these terms.

Figure 30 shows more consistency in that two of the major terms coincide. Nevertheless, some translation differences are evident here. Indexer *A* expresses "graduate schools of education" by use of the terms *schools of education* and *higher education*, while *B* selects *schools of education* and *graduate study*. Similarly, where *B* uses *teacher attitudes*, *A* uses *opinions*, and where *B* uses *student-teacher relationship*, *A* uses *interprofessional relationship* and *faculty advisors*.

It is difficult to believe the indexing results of Figure 31. There is no term in common among twelve assigned. Again, the problems associated with the use of related and/or overlapping terms are shown clearly here: five "reading" terms are used but they all differ. In this case, however, *A*'s indexing must be regarded as rather poor: the educational level is not indicated and the item is indexed too generally under *audiovisual education* when, specifically, it deals with television. At the time this item was indexed the term *closed captioned television* did not exist in the thesaurus.

The eight anonymous students whose work is compared in Figures 28-31 were not highly experienced indexers, although they were intelligent, interested, and motivated. It is quite likely that indexers of greater experience, especially with greater experience in use of this thesaurus, would have achieved more consistent results. Nevertheless, these examples do serve to illustrate some of the barriers to consistent indexing.

Indexer A	Indexer B
Major terms	*Major terms*
Mentors	Mentors
Higher education	Schools of education
Opinions	Graduate study
Schools of education	Teacher attitudes
Minor terms	*Minor terms*
Professional development	Student-teacher relationship
Faculty advisors	Graduate school faculty
Career guidance	Graduate students
Interprofessional relationship	

FIGURE 30

Two approaches to indexing an article entitled *Mentoring in Graduate Schools of Education.*

Indexer A	Indexer B
Major terms	*Major terms*
Audiovisual education	Captions
Reading research	Television teachers
	Elementary education
Minor terms	*Minor terms*
Nontraditional education	Remedial programs
Reading strategies	Television curriculum
Student motivation	Reading skills
	Reading instruction

FIGURE 31

Two approaches to indexing an article entitled *Closed Captioned Television: A New Tool for Reading Instruction.*

Figure 32 is a different kettle of fish. Here two students have recorded words and phrases representing their conceptual analysis of an article before attempting to translate into controlled terms. The comparison is very instructive. Apart from the fact that both sets of terms relate to Harlequin romances, they seem to have little in common. *A*'s interpretation is a "soft" and romantic one while *B*'s is, to say the least, harsh. *A* includes only three negative terms (conflict, dominance, resentment) while *B* includes many extreme terms. The fact that such radically different interpretations of the meaning of an article are possible argues, perhaps, for the use of indexing as a tool in psychoanalysis.

Indexer A	Indexer B
Romance fiction—Harlequin romances	Women as readers of contemporary fiction
Women's romantic fiction	Harlequin novels
Conflict between men and women	Heroines
Male/female love relationships	Female fantasy
Feminine self-perception	Masochism—rape
Male dominance over women	Gothic novels
Romantic novels as outlet for women's resentment	Sex roles—stereotyping
	Psychoanalysis
	Female self-image
	Narrative
	Schizophrenia
	Hysteria
	Social roles

FIGURE 32

Differences in conceptual analysis for an article entitled *The Disappearing Act: A Study of Harlequin Romances.*

While two or more individuals may not agree closely on which terms to assign to a document, this phenomenon is not peculiar to indexing. Saracevic et al. (1988) found that the terms used by different searchers for the same request showed remarkably little overlap.* Moreover, items retrieved by different searchers showed low overlap and each searcher tended to find some relevant items not found by the others.** Saracevic suggests the need

---

*Fidel (1985) also found that experienced searchers showed little agreement in the selection of terms for use in complex searches. Earlier, Lilley (1954) and Bates (1977) had shown that users of card catalogs also tend not to agree much on what terms to use in searching.

**Katzer et al. (1982) found that different document representations caused different sets to be retrieved and that these showed little overlap even when the representations were very similar.

for multiple searches, by different individuals, for the same request, with the results pooled and ranked—the items retrieved by most searchers at the top of the ranking, those retrieved by only one searcher at the bottom. By the same token, an ideal approach to indexing might involve team effort, with a consensus reached for each document as a result of discussions among a group of indexers. While this approach has been possible in a few highly specialized environments (such as the specialized systems existing within the U.S. Patent and Trademark Office), it is too costly for most applications. A "democratic" approach to the indexing of images, with terms contributed by users of the image database, has been proposed by Brown et al. (1996), among others.

Bates (1986) suggests that indexing is "indeterminate and probabilistic" and that this is more or less inevitable, being "rooted in the nature of the human mind." Rather than bewailing the fact that a high level of consistency in indexing is never likely to be attained, at least when human indexers are involved, we should concentrate on compensating for this at the search end of the process. Searching should not be based on the exact matching of terms but on methods that rank documents by the degree to which they match some form of search statement. Various aids should be available to allow a searcher to select from a variety of methods for generating semantic associations among terms.

While many consistency studies have been performed over the years, there has been rather little research on *why* different indexers select different terms, admittedly a more difficult type of investigation. Two related papers by David et al. (1995) and Bertrand-Gastaldy et al. (1995) address this problem but arrive at rather nebulous conclusions.

Consistent indexing is not necessarily the same as indexing of high quality. The quality of indexing is discussed in the next chapter, which also compares quality and consistency.

CHAPTER 6

Quality of Indexing

INDEXING IS NOT AN END IN ITSELF. "Good" indexing can be defined in a very pragmatic way as indexing that allows items to be retrieved from a database in searches in which they are useful responses and prevents them from being retrieved when they are not. Cooper (1978) carries this somewhat further:

> The assignment of a term to a document is justified if the average utility associated with that assignment is positive and unjustified if it is negative. (Page 110)

He uses the word "utility" here as more or less synonymous with "benefit."

As implied by the relationships depicted in Figure 1, several subsystems interact to control the performance of an information retrieval system. Another way of considering this is in terms of a sequence of events governing the performance of a search. This is illustrated in Figure 33.

In a typical information center situation, an information need arises in the mind of some customer of the center who discusses this need with an information specialist. The result of this dialog can be referred to as a *request* (i.e., the specialist's understanding of what the user really wants). On the basis of this request, the information specialist prepares a search strategy using index terms, text words, or some combination of these. The search strategy is then matched against the database (of course, in many cases, the search strategy and the match with the database will be intertwined, since the strategy will be developed interactively online). As a result of the search, certain items are retrieved. These may be screened by the searcher to eliminate any that seem obviously irrelevant, and a final set of documents or references is delivered to the user.

The diagram, of course, represents "delegated" searches—those in which customers ask an information specialist to find certain information for them. While this was the norm twenty or so years ago, it is becoming less so as more and more individuals perform their own searches in databases accessible online, and especially sources accessible through the Web.

Apart from the first and last steps, however, the diagram still represents the important factors affecting the performance of a subject search in a database. In the case of the nondelegated search, the information need is converted directly into a search strategy at a terminal without the intermediate "request" stage.

It is clear from this diagram that many factors affect the quality of the search as measured, for example, by recall and precision. First and foremost, the searcher needs to understand what the user really wants. If the request is an imperfect representation of the information need, it hardly matters that all other elements—vocabulary, search strategy, indexing, and so on—are satisfactory.

Given that the request is a reasonable approximation of the information need, the next factor affecting performance is the quality of the search strategy. Major influences here are the experience, intelligence, and ingenuity of the searcher. However, the vocabulary of the database also comes into play. If a controlled vocabulary is in use, one cannot search more specifically than the vocabulary allows, although additional specificity may be achieved through use of text words. Unfortunately, it is difficult to think of all the terms necessary to achieve a complete search. The problem in all searching is to try to balance recall and precision. The need is usually to achieve maximum recall but still to operate at an acceptable level of precision.

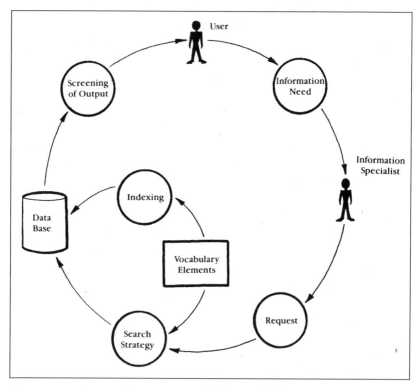

FIGURE 33
Factors affecting the results of a search in a database.

When the search strategy is matched against the database, clearly, the quality of the database itself is a major factor affecting performance. It is here, of course, that the quality of the indexing comes into play. The vocabulary elements also affect indexing since an indexer cannot use terms that do not exist.

The effectiveness of a "screening" of output, if such an operation is performed, will depend primarily on two factors:

1. How well the searcher understands what the user really wants.
2. How well the document representations stored in the database indicate what the documents are about.

It is not appropriate here to present a detailed analysis of all the factors affecting the performance of a retrieval system, as depicted in Figure 33, but only to consider those factors attributable to indexing. An indexing "failure" could occur in the conceptual analysis phase of indexing or in translation.

Conceptual analysis failures could be of two types:

1. Failure to recognize a topic that is of potential interest to the user group served.
2. Misinterpretation of what some aspect of the document really deals with, leading to the assignment of a term (or terms) that are inappropriate.

Translation failures are also of two types:

1. Failure to use the most specific term available to represent some subject.
2. Use of a term that is inappropriate to the subject matter because of lack of subject knowledge or due to carelessness.

In practice, of course, the evaluator of an information service could not draw some of these distinctions. For example, if term X is assigned to an item when it should not be, there is no way of knowing if the indexer misinterpreted what the document is about, did not really understand the meaning or scope of X, or simply assigned this term out of carelessness.

If an indexer fails to assign X when it should be assigned, it is obvious that recall failures will occur. If, on the other hand, Y is assigned when X should be, both recall and precision failures can occur. That is, the item will not be retrieved in searches for X, although it should be, and will be retrieved in searches for Y, when it should not be.

The careless omission of a term that should be assigned to a document can have a profound effect on the results of a particular search, even when the term omitted may not seem too important at first sight. Figure 34 presents a simple illustration of this, based on one of many examples uncovered in the evaluation of MEDLARS (Lancaster, 1968a). The article deals with the effect on growth of the cerebral cortex of being born into darkness and never experiencing light. The indexer covers all the major aspects except that of growth. This simple omission could be very important. In this case, the article is considered highly relevant to a request for information on factors affecting growth of the central nervous system. A searcher can only use the "growth" term to approach this topic, since it is unrealistic to expect someone to be able to predict what the factors might be, so this important article remains unretrieved.

In the MEDLARS study, few examples of indexers using incorrect terms were found; rather more cases of omissions of important terms by indexers occurred. This is likely to be typical of the situation in other information services.

Article	**Search**
Topic	*Request*
Effect of visual deprivation on growth of the visual cortex in mice	Factors affecting growth, regeneration and degeneration in the central nervous system
Indexing	*Strategy*
SENSORY DEPRIVATION	CENTRAL NERVOUS SYSTEM (complete
DARKNESS	hierarchy)
CEREBRAL CORTEX	*and* (GROWTH *or* REGENERATION *or*
VISION	DEGENERATION)
MICE	

FIGURE 34
Example of important item missed by simple indexer omission.

Recognizing "Good" Indexing

The discussion so far in this chapter implies that quality of indexing can only be judged *ex post facto*—i.e., as a result of experience in the operation of a retrieval system and, more particularly, its evaluation. To a very large extent this is true. A set of index terms assigned to a document cannot be judged "correct" or "incorrect" in any absolute sense. That is, there is no one "best" set of terms. To claim that such a set exists implies a foreknowledge of all the requests that will be put to the database in which the document is represented.

Nevertheless, errors do occur in indexing and it should be possible for a senior indexer (or "revisor") to spot some, at least, of these errors before a record is added to a database and thus to impose some quality control over the process. The senior indexer might identify errors of the following types:

1. The indexer contravenes policy, especially policy relating to the exhaustivity of indexing.

2. The indexer fails to use the vocabulary elements in the way in which they should be used (e.g., an incorrect main heading/subheading combination).
3. The indexer fails to use a term at the correct level of specificity. In most cases this will mean that the term selected is not the most specific available.
4. The indexer uses an obviously incorrect term, perhaps through lack of subject knowledge (e.g., *liquid rocket fuels* when it is gaseous fuels that are discussed).
5. The indexer omits an important term.

Usually the revisor will not spend as much time checking the indexing of an item as the indexer spent in the first place. It may be relatively easy to recognize an incorrect term, which is likely to "jump out" at the experienced indexer, but it might be quite difficult to recognize the fact that an important term has been omitted unless it is very obvious (e.g., the term appears in the title).

It is possible to test the work of indexers in a more rigorous way than merely looking over the terms assigned, which is the most that one can expect from a routine checking operation. The most obvious approach is to conduct a simulation of a true evaluation. This can be achieved as follows:

1. Select a group of documents from the normal input stream before these reach the indexers.
2. For each document compose, say, three questions for which the item can be considered an important response. One question could be based on the central theme of the document while the others would be based on secondary, but still important, themes.
3. Have experienced search analysts construct search strategies for each question. Of course, these would not be the same individuals whose indexing is being studied.
4. Have the items indexed in the normal way.
5. Compare the indexing to the search strategies to determine whether or not the relevant items are retrievable on the terms assigned.

As a method of evaluating the performance of a group of indexers this procedure should work rather well if the sample of documents is large enough and the best possible search strategies are used. The whole test could take place over a series of weeks. It would be desirable, of course, if the same set of documents was indexed several times, once by each indexer, so that the performance of the indexers could be compared on the same basis, but this may not always be possible because of subject specialization within the group.

In large information services built on the work of many indexers, especially when the indexing is decentralized, it will probably be essential to impose some form of quality control. If the volume of documents indexed is very great, it may well be economically infeasible to check all records before entry into the database so some form of sampling would be necessary. Completely random sampling of the records would be possible but not very efficient, especially if the error rate is likely to be low. What is needed is some automatic procedure for "flagging" records for expert inspection based on the fact that these records appear "suspicious."

Todeschini has developed an ingenious method for identifying such suspicious records (Todeschini and Farrel, 1989; Todeschini and Tolstenkov, 1990). The procedure has been in use at the International Atomic Energy Agency, Vienna, for quality control of input to the INIS database (Todeschini, 1997). The method is made possible by the fact that items added to the database are indexed by means of descriptors from the INIS thesaurus (an average of around eleven per item in 1990) as well as being assigned to one of 237 broad subject categories. In essence, the system is capable of identifying records in which the descriptors assigned are atypical of the descriptors strongly associated with the assigned category in the past. If the descriptors assigned to a particular document, which has been assigned to category X, are atypical of the previous descriptor "profile" for X, the record is a good candidate for quality review since either categorization or indexing may be in error.

Factors Affecting the Quality of Indexing

Regrettably, not much research has been performed on the factors that are most likely to affect the quality of indexing. An attempt has been made to identify such factors in Figure 35 but this is based more on common sense or intuition than on hard evidence.

Indexers should have some familiarity with the subject matter dealt with, and understand its terminology, although they need not necessarily be subject experts. Indeed, some organizations have had problems with indexers who are too "expert"—they tend to interpret too much and perhaps to go beyond the claims of the author (e.g., to index a possible application not specifically identified in the article) or even to exhibit prejudices by not indexing claims that they are unwilling to accept (see Intner, 1984, and Bell, 1991a, for discussions of bias and censorship in indexing). However, lack of subject knowledge may lead to overindexing. Unable to distinguish between two terms, perhaps, the indexer assigns both when only one is needed or only one is correct. Loukopoulos (1966) referred to this as indexer *indecision*.

Indexer factors	*Document factors*
Subject knowledge	Subject matter
Experience	Complexity
Concentration	Language
Reading ability and comprehension	Length
	Presentation and summarization
Vocabulary factors	*"Process" factors*
Specificity/syntax	Type of indexing
Ambiguity or imprecision	Rules and instructions
Quality of entry vocabulary	Required productivity
Quality of structure	Exhaustivity of indexing
Availability of related aids	
	Environmental factors
	Heating/cooling
	Lighting
	Noise

FIGURE 35

Factors that may affect the quality of indexing.

For the idea behind this figure the author is indebted to Oliver et al. (1966).

Mai (2000) identifies five stages in the development of an indexer: novice, advanced beginner, competent, proficient, and expert. He maintains that only the expert has the ability "to index the same document using different approaches." This would imply, for example, that only an expert would have the ability to index document A for audience X and differently for audience Y. While this sounds plausible on the surface, it must also be recognized that a computer could be programmed to index a text differently (i.e., for different audiences) by linking word/phrase occurrences to different sets of index terms.

Of course, a special type of expert is the author of a document. Some studies of the author as indexer have taken place. For example, Diodato (1981) studied consistency in term selection among three groups: authors, indexers, and readers of mathematics papers. Ebinuma et al. (1983) translated author-assigned keywords into thesaurus terms and compared these with terms already assigned by experienced indexers. The author-derived indexing seemed to produce better precision but lower recall. Mulvany (1994) discusses the pros and cons of authors indexing their own books.

Rasheed (1989) performed a study to compare terms assigned by authors of medical articles with terms assigned by MEDLARS indexers. He found that the indexers assigned many more terms and the terms they used were more specific than those used by authors. Other studies have dealt with the indexing of individual books. Diodato and Gandt (1991) found that professional indexers provided indexes that were more thorough than those produced by authors, although the differences (e.g., in number of entries per page of text) were not as great as one might expect.Authors have also been found to be deficient in writing abstracts for their articles, a point dealt with in a later chapter.

Knowledge of the interests of the users of the database is especially important because "good" indexing should be tailored to the needs of a particular community wherever possible. Years of experience as an indexer should also be a factor affecting quality, as should such characteristics as the individual's ability to concentrate, to read rapidly, and to comprehend quickly. Finally, and perhaps most important of all, a good indexer should enjoy the work. One is unlikely to get good indexing from people who hate what they are doing.

Document factors also come into play. Some subjects are more difficult to comprehend than others. Usually the theory is much more difficult than the practice, as in the differences between applied mechanics and engineering. Related to this, of course, is the degree of "match" between the subject matter of a document and the knowledge or interests of the indexer.

"Language" can be interpreted in more than one way. Clearly, the indexer who knows no Russian can hardly index Russian articles effectively unless they have unusually clear and complete abstracts in the indexer's own tongue. Another aspect is the clarity of the author's language. Some authors present their thoughts or findings more clearly than others, making the indexer's job less difficult. Finally, there are some presentation factors that will influence how easy it is for the indexer to find out what the document is about: is the title accurate or misleading, is there an abstract or some other summarization and does this fully reflect the contents of the item?

Vocabulary factors can also be expected to influence the quality of indexing. The more specific the vocabulary, the finer the shades of meaning it can express; and, the finer the shades of meaning, the more difficult it becomes to make distinctions among closely related terms and to use these terms consistently. Added syntactical elements such as subheadings or role indicators increase specificity and may complicate the indexing task.

Terms that are ambiguous or imprecise (lacking adequate context or scope notes) are difficult to interpret and use correctly and the vocabulary must have a sufficiently complete structure (e.g., the BT/NT/RT structure of the conventional thesaurus) that it guides the indexer to the term most appropriate to represent a particular topic. The size and quality of the entry vocabulary will also be important, as will the availability of various related aids, such as technical dictionaries or glossaries.*

---

*An entry vocabulary is a list of nonpreferred terms, occurring in the literature, that are mapped to the appropriate preferred terms through *see* or *use* references. The importance of this is discussed elsewhere (e.g., in Lancaster, 1986).

Other factors that may affect quality have to do with the indexing process itself. Some types of indexing, such as the extraction of words or phrases from text, do not require much concentration, intellectual effort, or experience, while other types, particularly those requiring the establishment of precise conceptual relationships (through role or relational indicators), are at the opposite end of the spectrum of difficulty. In general one would expect indexers to perform more effectively when they are given precise rules and instructions rather than operating under laissez-faire conditions. Required productivity should be another significant factor. If required to deal with a specified number of items a day, the indexer may feel under pressure and this may lead to careless errors, especially if the organization expects too much in the way of daily output. Exhaustive indexing may require more time than selective indexing.

Finally, indexing requires concentration and adverse environmental conditions seem likely to have a negative impact on the accuracy of this intellectual task.

Another way of considering factors that affect the quality of indexing is in terms of the difficulties encountered by indexers. Oliver et al (1966), in an interview survey involving 61 indexers, found that "making decisions about how to best describe the content of documents" was (not surprisingly) the problem most frequently mentioned. Unfortunately, this problem is general, pervasive, and not susceptible to easy solutions. Other significant problems mentioned were "understanding new or unfamiliar material" and lack of appropriate terms in the controlled vocabularies. Chu and O'Brien (1993) studied the conceptual analysis stage of indexing, using more than a hundred novice indexers (students), but they made use of only three short articles in their research so it is difficult to reach any firm conclusions from their data.

Is Quality Related to Consistency?

Quality and consistency are not the same: one can be consistently bad as well as consistently good! Nevertheless, one intuitively feels that consistency and quality should be related. For example, if three indexers tend to agree with each other, but a fourth indexes in a quite different way, one is inclined to believe in the consensus.

In a provocative article, Cooper (1969) questions the value of consistency as an indicator of quality. The point he makes can be illustrated by reference to Figure 36. An information center employs four indexers, *A-D*. *B* and *C* are quite consistent with each other but *A* and *D* are both idiosyncratic. However, for one reason or another, *D*'s view of the world is closest to that of the users of the center and the terms he assigns better reflect their interests. One assumes that his indexing is the best, at least for this particular audience. In this case, then, the indexers most consistent with each other do not produce the best work, although they are not as bad as *A* whose indexing is furthest away from the interests of the users.

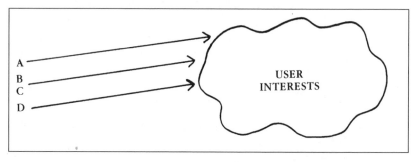

FIGURE 36
Indexer consistency related to user interests.

While this situation is plausible, it may not be highly so. It is difficult to understand why *B* and *C* would be more consistent with each other unless this reflected the fact that they are the more experienced indexers. If they are, logic suggests that it is these two who would know most about the users. Studies that relate in any way to Cooper's contentions are few and far between. However, Diodato (1981) did find that consistency between authors of mathematics papers and professional indexers was greater than the consistency between authors and readers of the papers.

Leonard (1975) has made the only serious attempt to study the relationship between quality and consistency in indexing. "Quality" was defined in terms of retrieval effectiveness—the ability to retrieve what is wanted and to avoid what is not wanted. Leonard worked with two separate collections of data, subsets from previous evaluation studies. These collections consisted of documents, requests, search strategies, and relevance assessments. For each request it was known which items had been judged relevant and which not. The sets of terms assigned to documents by indexers participating in the study could thus be compared with search strategies previously constructed, allowing the investigator to determine whether or not a particular document would be retrieved by a particular strategy.

The comparison between consistency and retrieval effectiveness proved more difficult than anticipated. A major problem is caused by the fact that the "effectiveness" of indexing is normally associated with the work of a single indexer while consistency, by definition, is a measure that relates to the work of two or more indexers (Leonard measured group consistency as well as indexer pair consistency). Leonard combined the "effectiveness" scores for two (or more) indexers and then compared this score with the consistency measure for these indexers. The effectiveness score takes into account the number of relevant documents retrieved and the number of irrelevant documents retrieved, and these scores can be combined by averaging the results for the two indexers or by aggregating them. If the aggregation method is used, only unique items are counted, which in effect treats the two indexers as though they were a single individual.

Leonard observed a "moderate to strong" positive relationship between consistency and retrieval effectiveness, with a "clearly defined positive relationship" between consistency and the recall ratio.

The Value of Consistency Studies

The research performed by Leonard (1975) does suggest that a positive relationship exists between consistency and quality of indexing, where "quality" refers to retrieval effectiveness. Even if no such relationship had been discovered, consistency studies still have some value. Hooper (1966) has suggested several applications, including:

1. In the selection or training of indexers. The indexing of trainees is compared with some pre-established standard.
2. In the ongoing quality control of indexing activities.*
3. To detect problems in the use of a controlled vocabulary; for example, identification of terms or types of terms that are frequently used inconsistently because of ambiguities or overlapping.
4. To detect any problems that might exist with regard to indexing rules.
5. To determine whether or not consistency may be lower in handling certain subject fields or document types.

In this chapter, quality of indexing has been assumed to mean the same as "retrieval effectiveness" of indexing. Not everyone defines it in this way. Rolling (1981), for example, claims that "Indexing quality can be defined as the degree of agreement between the terms assigned by the indexer and an 'ideal' or 'optimum' group of terms." He goes on to point out that the ideal is best achieved through some form of expert consensus. The work of one indexer can be compared with the consensus and he would be "penalized" for not using terms that the experts had agreed on as well as for using terms that had not been agreed on. Rolling, who appears unaware of Leonard's work, claims that effectiveness measures are "not practicable," while consistency studies are "not reliable." He advocates studies of quality, based

---

*Stubbs et al. (1999) discuss how interindexer consistently studies can be used in ongoing monitoring of indexing in an organization. They combine consistency calculations with the use of "control charts" as employed in industrial engineering.

on the consensus approach, with consistency studies used only to investigate "influences and trends." An example of the scoring of indexing, based on Rolling's suggestions, is given later in the chapter.

Various other investigators have attempted to evaluate indexing outside the context of the retrieval system in which it occurs. For example, White and Griffith (1987) describe an approach in which methods external to the indexing system being studied are used to establish a set of documents judged to be "similar in content." Using sets of this kind (they call them *criterial document clusters*) as the basis for evaluation, they look at three characteristics of the index terms assigned to items in the set within a particular database:

1. The extent to which terms link related items. The obvious measure of this is the number of terms that have been applied to all or a majority of items in the set. The items can be considered closely linked if several subject terms have been applied to all of them.

2. The extent to which terms discriminate among these sets within the database. The most obvious measure of this is the frequency with which terms that apply to most documents in the set occur in the database as a whole.* Very common terms are not good discriminators. For example, in MEDLINE the term *human* may apply to every item in a set but is of little value in separating this set from others since it applies to so many items in the database. On the other hand, terms that occur very rarely in the database as a whole will be useful in highly specific searches but of little use in the identification of somewhat larger sets.

3. The extent to which terms discriminate finely among individual documents. Rarity is an applicable measure here also. So is the exhaustivity of the indexing: a term may apply to all items in a set but cannot discriminate among its members; the more additional terms that are assigned to each member, the more individual differences can be identified.

To look at quality in this way one must first establish the test sets, retrieve records for the members of each set from some database, and study the characteristics of the terms assigned. White and Griffith used the technique to compare the indexing of their test sets in different databases. A comparison of databases in this way is a check on the assumption that test set items are in fact similar in content. White and Griffith used co-citation

---

*Ajiferuke and Chu (1988) are critical of the discriminating index used by White and Griffith because it fails to take account of the size of the database; they propose an alternative measure that does. In a related paper (Chu and Ajiferuke, 1989), they apply the White/Griffith evaluation criteria, with their own modified discriminating index, to the evaluation of indexing in library science databases.

as the basis for establishing their test sets, although other methods, including bibliographic coupling, could also be used.

The value of this work is limited by the fact that only very small clusters (range of three to eight items) were used. Moreover, the validity of the method as a test of human indexing depends entirely on one's willingness to accept a co-citation cluster as being a legitimate standard. One could make a persuasive argument that it would make more sense to use expert indexers as a standard for judging the legitimacy of the co-citation cluster.

White and Griffith claim that the method is useful to a database producer as a check on the quality of indexing, and present examples of terms that should perhaps have been used by MEDLINE indexers or added to the controlled vocabulary. However, such "quality" checks can be done more simply: sets of items defined by a particular term or terms (e.g., "superconductors" or "superconductivity" occurring as index terms or text words) can be retrieved from several databases and their indexing compared without the use of co-citation as a standard. In fact, this type of study has also been done by the same group of investigators (McCain et al., 1987). For eleven requests, posed by specialists in the medical behavioral sciences, comparative searches were performed in MEDLINE, Excerpta Medica, PsycINFO, SCISEARCH, and SOCIAL SCISEARCH. In the first three databases, the searches were performed on (a) controlled terms and (b) natural language. In the citation databases, searches were performed (a) using the natural language of titles and (b) using citations to known relevant items as entry points. While the purpose of the investigation was to study the quality of MEDLINE indexing, little was discovered that could be turned into recommendations to the National Library of Medicine on indexing practice, although some recommendations on indexing coverage could be made.

The most important findings of the study were (1) that the incorporation of natural language approaches into search strategies resulted in significant improvements in recall compared with use of controlled terms only, (2) that citation retrieval should be considered an important adjunct to term-based retrieval because additional relevant items can be found using the citation approach, and (3) that no single database is likely to provide complete coverage of a complex multidisciplinary literature.

Quality Measured by Use of a Standard

In a study performed for the National Library of Medicine (Lancaster et al., 1996), I developed a method of evaluating the quality of indexing for MEDLINE, along the lines proposed by Rolling (1981), by comparing the work of indexers against a "standard," this being a set of terms agreed upon by highly experienced indexers. Figure 37 shows an example of the standard for an article and Figure 38 shows terms selected by two different indexers for this same article.

Score	Headings/subheadings
9 (6+3)	Autoantibodies/analysis
9 (6+3)	Blood Platelets/immunology
6	Case Report
6	Chronic Disease
9 (6+3)	Hodgkin's Disease/surgery
6	Human
6	Male
6	Middle Age
6	Recurrence
26 (15+5+3+3)	Spleen/*abnormalities/radiography/radionuclide
6	Splenectomy
20 (15+5)	Technetium/*diagnostic use
23 (15+5+3)	Thrombocytopenia/*immunology/surgery
15	*Tomography, X-Ray Computed
Total 153	

FIGURE 37

Indexing "standard" for a medical article, showing scores associated with the assignment of various types of terms.

The standard represents the consensus of a group of senior indexers on what the "ideal" indexing should be for this item. They arrived at fourteen terms. Some are subject headings and some are checktags, and some of the subject headings are given one or more subheadings. In addition, a subject heading or a subject heading/subheading combination can be selected as "major." That is, these are the terms that the indexers consider most important for the article and they are the terms that this article will appear under in the printed *Index Medicus*. These terms are identified by use of the asterisk. For example, *tomography, x-ray computed* is selected as a major term and so is the combination *spleen/abnormalities*. Note that an asterisk applied to a subheading is automatically carried to the heading to which it is attached.

The scoring reflects the importance of the various terms and term combinations as judged by the expert indexers, as follows:

6 points for a correctly assigned subject heading without an asterisk

6 points for a checktag (to which asterisks do not apply)

3 points for a subheading without an asterisk

15 points for a subject heading with an asterisk

5 points for a subheading with an asterisk

INDEXER A

Score	Headings/subheadings
6	Case Report
-13 (-7,-1,-4,-1)	Choristoma/complications/*radiography/radionuclide
-4 (-3,-1)	Erythrocytes/radionuclide
8 (6,-1,+3)	Hodgkins Disease/complication/surgery
6	Human
6	Male
6	Middle Age
6	Recurrence
-3	Retroperitoneal Space
15	*Spleen
6	Splenectomy
7 (8,-1)	Technetium/diagnostic use
10 (15,-4,-1)	Thrombocytopenia/*etiology/therapy
8	Tomography, X-Ray Computed

Total 64

INDEXER B

Score	Headings/subheadings
6	Case Report
-15 (-7,-4,-4)	Choristoma/*radiography/*radionuclide
6	Chronic Disease
5 (6,-1)	Hodgkin's Disease/therapy
6	Human
-4 (-3,-1)	Immunoglobulins/therapeutic use
-13 (-7,-1,-4,-1)	Immunologic Diseases/radiography/*radionuclide/therapy
-3	Laparotomy
6	Male
6	Middle Age
-4 (-3,-1)	Prednisolone/therapeutic use
-3	Remission Induction
-4 (-3,-1)	Retroperitoneal Space/radionuclide
15	*Spleen
4	*Splenectomy
6 (15,-4,-4,-1)	Thrombocytopenia/*radiography/*radionuclide/therapy
15	*Tomography, X-Ray Computed

Total 29

FIGURE 38

Scoring of two indexers against the standard of Figure 37.

The total possible score for the item is 153. That is, in the very unlikely event that an indexer would exactly duplicate the standard, he or she would receive the full score. Any deviations from the standard—failure to assign a wanted term, failure to use the asterisk appropriately, or use of a term outside the standard—results in loss of points. Note how the really important terms and combinations contribute heavily to the score. The term *spleen* carries three subheadings, one of them asterisked. *Spleen* itself scores 15 points because it receives an asterisk from the asterisked subheading *abnormalities*, so the total score for this combination is 15 for the asterisked main heading, 5 for the asterisked subheading, and three each for the other two subheadings, a total of 26.

This item has been indexed twice, once by indexer A and once by indexer B (Figure 38). Scoring the work of indexers is a little more complicated because they are given positive scores for correctly assigning terms in the standard and negative scores for assigning terms not in the standard. When an indexer exactly matches the standard for a term, the score for that term is transferred to the indexer's score. Any deviation results in a reduced score or, at worst, a negative score.

The full scoring is as follows:

> Exact match with standard: carry over score from standard
> −7 for asterisked heading not in standard
> −4 for asterisked subheading not in standard
> −3 for nonasterisked heading not in standard
> −1 for nonasterisked subheading not in standard
> 4 for a heading asterisked by indexer but not asterisked in standard (as opposed to 6 if asterisk were not assigned by indexer)
> 8 for a heading asterisked in standard but not by the indexer (as opposed to 15 if correctly asterisked)
> −1 for subheading asterisked in standard but not by indexer.

While this sounds rather complex, it is not really so because, once the scoring method has been established, rather simple programs can be (and have been) written both to score the standard and to score the work of indexers against the standard.

Scoring for the indexing of the National Library of Medicine is more complicated than scoring would be for many other situations, because of the use of subheadings and the distinction between major and minor descriptors, so it is also more difficult to get agreements on what the scores should be. While the actual numerical scores used in these (real) examples can be considered somewhat arbitrary, they do reflect the perceived enormity of various types of indexer error.

Once the scores have been agreed to, this method of assessing indexing is quite discriminating. That is, it clearly reflects deviations from the standard. While, in this particular example, neither indexer A nor indexer B did very well, A is clearly closer to the standard than B is, and the scores reflect this. B suffers for missing completely a term judged "major" by the standard and also for introducing several terms not included there.

As emphasized earlier in the chapter, the quality of indexing is best assessed within the context of a complete evaluation of the retrieval system in which real user requests are used, as in the MEDLARS study (Lancaster, 1968a). Nevertheless, use of the "gold standard" approach can be effective, especially in assessing the progress of trainee indexers and in comparing the work of one group of indexers against another.

This single example also illustrates how agreement on the use of check-tags is much easier to achieve than agreement on other terms and that, the more refined the indexing (through use of multiple subheadings and asterisks), the more difficult it becomes to achieve complete agreement.

Susanne Humphrey (1995), of the National Library of Medicine, has proposed a scoring method that uses quality scores in measuring consistency of indexing. In this approach, once indexers have been scored against the standard, each indexer's scored work for an article becomes the standard against which each other indexer is measured, in turn, for consistency purposes. Use of this method can be illustrated by means of a simple example, as follows:

Indexer A		Indexer B	
A/a	6+3	A/a	6+3
B/c/d	6+3+3	C/*c	15+5
C/*c	15+5	D/d	6+3
		E	6
Total	41	Total	44

Using A as a standard, indexer B scores 29 (the scores for the terms in which B agrees with A) so the consistency is expressed as 29/41, or 70.7. Using B as a standard, A scores 29/44, or 65.9. When the two comparisons (A with B, B with A) are combined, the average achieved is 68.3. While this is ingenious, it is not completely clear what the score really means. Basically, while "quality" scores have been retained, quality is not being measured directly (since neither indexer score is compared with the standard). It is merely an alternative measure of consistency which, as suggested in the preceding chapter, at least has the merit of taking into account the relative importance of terms. That is, if one indexer fails to use a high scoring combination used by another indexer, this will reduce the consistency score between them much more than would the failure to agree on a low scoring term.

CHAPTER 7

Abstracts: Types and Functions

AN ABSTRACT is a brief but accurate representation of the contents of a document. Endres-Niggemeyer (1998) uses a similar definition: "a short coherent text which has to inform a user about the essential knowledge conveyed by a document."

A distinction should be made between the words *abstract* and *extract*. An extract is an abbreviated version of a document created by drawing sentences from the document itself. For example, two or three sentences from the introduction, followed by two or three from the conclusions or summary, might provide a good indication of what a certain journal article is about. A true abstract, while it may include words occurring in the document, is a piece of text created by the abstractor rather than a direct quotation from the author. The term "summarization" is now widely used to refer to any process that produces a condensed representation of a text and so can be applied to both abstracting and extracting.

Abstracts can be characterized in a number of different ways, including length. In Figure 3 (Chapter 2), for example, two different abstracts are presented, one longer than the other. There is absolutely no reason why all abstracts should be approximately the same length. Factors affecting the length of an abstract might include the following:

1. *The length of the item being abstracted* (Craven, 1990, however, found no correlation between article length and abstract length, but he worked in a very limited subject area);
2. *The complexity of the subject matter;*
3. *The diversity of the subject matter.* For example, an abstract prepared for the proceedings of a conference may need to be rather long if the papers presented cover a wide range of topics;
4. *The importance of the item to the organization preparing the abstract.* As with the exhaustivity of indexing, an industrial information center may want to prepare longer abstracts for the company's own reports than it does for other items.
5. *The "accessibility" of the subject matter.* In a published abstracting service, in particular, it might be sensible to prepare more complete abstracts for items that are less accessible physically (e.g., limited dis-

tribution reports or papers presented at conferences) or intellectually (e.g., those written in obscure languages).

6. *Cost.* Longer abstracts are not necessarily more expensive to prepare than short ones. Indeed, it may take much longer to prepare a good condensation of 200 words than one of 500. Nevertheless, it is obvious that the cost of a printed abstracting service would increase significantly if the average length of an abstract were increased by, say, 50%. Typesetting, paper and mailing costs would all be affected.

7. *Purpose.* An abstract primarily used to access a document for retrieval purposes might need to be longer to provide sufficient access points.

A very brief abstract (e.g., one that attempts to describe a document by means of a single sentence) is sometimes referred to as an *annotation*, but this is a rather imprecise term.*

A distinction is frequently made between *indicative abstracts* (sometimes called descriptive abstracts) and *informative abstracts*. The distinction is illustrated in Figures 39 and 40 which show two different types of abstract prepared for the item first depicted in Figure 3. The indicative abstract simply describes (indicates) what the document is about, whereas the informative abstract attempts to summarize the substance of the document, including the results.

Telephone interviews were conducted in 1985 with 655 Americans sampled probabilistically. Opinions are expressed on whether: (1) the establishment of a Palestinian state is essential for peace in the region; (2) U.S. aid to Israel and to Egypt should be reduced; (3) the U.S. should (a) participate in a peace conference that includes the PLO, (b) favor neither Israel nor the Arab nations, (c) maintain friendly relations with both. Respondents indicated whether or not they had sufficient information concerning various national groups in the region.

FIGURE 39
Indicative abstract.

That is, an indicative abstract might mention what types of results are achieved in a study but the informative abstract would summarize the results themselves. Cremmins (1996) explains that indicative abstracts may contain information on purpose, scope, or methodology but will not present results, conclusions, or recommendations. On the other hand, the informative abstract may include information on purpose, scope, and methods but must also contain results, conclusions, or recommendations. For some

---

*Moreover, the field of video indexing and retrieval tends to use "annotation" in place of "indexing," which is inexcusably misleading.

purposes, a good informative abstract might act as a reasonable substitute for reading a document.* An indicative abstract is unlikely to serve as a substitute in this way. Its main purpose would be to indicate to readers of the abstract whether or not they would be likely to want to read the original. For obvious reasons, informative abstracts tend to be longer than indicative. They are also more difficult to write. Indeed, while it will usually be possible to write an informative abstract for an experimental study, it may be almost impossible to do so for a theoretical study or an opinion piece. For this reason, informative abstracts occur more frequently in science and technology than they do in the social sciences or humanities.

Telephone interviews conducted in 1985 with 655 Americans, sampled probabilistically, brought these results: most (54-56%) think U.S. aid to Israel and Egypt should be reduced; most (65%) favor U.S. participation in a peace conference that includes the PLO; more than 80% consider it important that the U.S. should maintain friendly relations with both Israel and the Arab
Countries; 70% believe that the U.S. should favor neither side; most (55%) think that the establishment of a Palestinian state is essential to peace in the region. The Israelis are the best known of the national groups and the Syrians the least known. The Arab-Israeli situation is second only to the conflict in Central America among the most serious international problems faced by the U.S.

FIGURE 40
Informative abstract.

A single abstract may incorporate indicative and informative elements (Cremmins refers to these as indicative-informative), depending on the interests of the intended readers. For example, consider a report on air pollution abstracted in a publication designed for chemists. Much of the abstract, covering the environmental aspects, is merely indicative, but a part of it may be truly informative (e.g., presenting results from analyses performed on atmospheric samples). Indicative and informative abstracts may both be included in a single published abstracting service. In general, however, indicative abstracts are more common. Fedosyuk (1978) describes detailed procedures for distinguishing between indicative and informative abstracts, using linguistic criteria, and even presents an algorithm for this task. While this is ingenious, it is not clear why one would want formal procedures for making such distinctions.

---

*This is not without its dangers. For example, Haynes et al. (1990) present some evidence to suggest that physicians sometimes make patient care decisions on the basis of reading less than the full text of medical articles. This danger is compounded by the fact that more recent studies have shown that abstracts in medical journals, even major ones, tend to be quite deficient (see Chapter 9).

The term *subject slanting* is sometimes used in connection with abstracts. The implication of the term is that the abstract should be "slanted" to the interests of the intended users. That is, in abstracting, as in indexing, a guiding question should be, "Why are our users likely to be interested in this item?" Abstracts prepared by an organization for its own internal use should always be slanted to local needs and interests. The situation is a little more complicated in the case of published abstracting services.

A distinction can be made between services that are *discipline-oriented* and those that are *mission-oriented*. The former attempt to serve the needs of a particular discipline (e.g., chemistry, biology, the social sciences) while the latter try to meet the needs of a particular industry or group of individuals (e.g., abstracts for the rubber industry or abstracts for nurses). Subject slanting is more relevant and feasible in the case of mission-oriented services than it is for discipline-oriented, because the interests of users of the former tend to be more homogeneous and specialized than the interests of users of the latter. At least one study has indicated that rather little slanting occurs in published services (Herner, 1959).

Another type of abstract is the *critical abstract*. Such an abstract is really a "condensed critical review." Applied to reports, journal articles, and other relatively brief items, a critical abstract serves much the same purpose as a critical book review. A critical abstract is evaluative. The abstractor expresses views on the quality of the work of the author and perhaps contrasts it with the work of others. For example, a critical abstract of the item illustrated in Figure 3 might mention weaknesses of the methodology used—the way the population was sampled, the size of the sample, the wording of the questions—or compare the results with those of earlier surveys. Because the writers must be true experts, critical abstracts are rather uncommon.

Two publications that claim to include critical abstracts are *Mathematical Reviews* and *Applied Mechanics Reviews* (AMR). Figure 41 shows a true critical abstract from the latter. Note that the abstract is signed and that it combines descriptive and critical elements. An examination of AMR reveals, however, that true critical abstracts have always been very much the exception rather than the rule, and no critical abstracts are included today. AMR is now available only in online form.

Nowadays abstracts frequently appear in scholarly journals, along with the articles to which they relate; they are usually written by the authors of the articles. In many cases these abstracts are picked up and reproduced by the indexing and abstracting services. Some journals include abstracts in more than one language. For example, several Russian and Japanese journals include English abstracts.

Purpose of Abstracts

Many different purposes could be mentioned. First and foremost, perhaps, abstracts facilitate selection. That is, they help the reader decide whether a particular item is likely to be of interest or not. In this way, they save the time of the reader—e.g., by preventing him from acquiring articles that would not be of any interest. In some cases, too, a good informative abstract may actually substitute for the reading of an item that is of interest to the user. Abstracts are particularly useful in illuminating the content of items written in languages unfamiliar to a particular reader. Janes (1991) discovered, not surprisingly, that abstracts were more effective than other parts of a record, such as titles and index terms, in judging the relevance of an item.

The printing and distribution of abstracts is effective in keeping people informed of newly published literature in their fields of interest (i.e., providing for *current awareness*). As mentioned earlier, abstracts appearing within the articles or reports to which they relate are useful to indexers in helping them identify the central subject matter of the item as rapidly as possible. Borko and Bernier (1975) imply that abstracts can substitute for the full text in indexing activities but this may not always be a desirable practice.

Finally, abstracts now play an important role in computer-based retrieval systems, by facilitating the identification of pertinent items and by providing access to stored items (in systems in which the text of abstracts is stored in searchable form). Taking both recall and precision into account, automatic retrieval procedures based on abstracts have been shown to be more effective than those based on complete document texts (Lam-Adesina and Jones, 2001), although more evidence is needed on this point.

Hartley and Benjamin (1998) claim that abstracts have grown in importance over the years as the research literature has grown:

> Indeed, the nature of abstracts has changed over the years as more and more research articles have come to compete for their readers' attention. Today readers have to skim and search for more than they had to do in the past, and the abstract is continually evolving as a gateway into the research literature. (Pages 451-452)

In science, they point out, abstracts have been getting larger and more results-oriented.

For certain purposes, a *structured abstract* may be preferred to one in the form of narrative text. A hypothetical example of a "frame" for a structured abstract is shown in Figure 42. The subject matter dealt with is that of irrigation. In this case, the abstractor is told to look specifically for the items listed. Abstracting involves putting the appropriate "values" into the frame. That is, for each article, the type of irrigation, soil type, crops involved, climatic conditions, and location are indicated, and codes are used

1989. Pao, Y. C., Dept. of Eng. Mech., Univ. of Nebr., Lincoln.
Shy, D. S., et al., **On relationship between bulk modulus and relative volume of lung during inflation-deflation maneuvers,** p 136-
142, *Journal of Biomechanical Engineering, Transactions of the
ASME* v 104, n 2 (May 1982).
The paper presents an equation relating the bulk modulus of the
lung to the relative volume during inflation and deflation. The average bulk modulus of the lung was obtained by injecting air via a
6-mm-i.d. cannula in the main lobar bronchus. "Regional lobe"
volume changes were measured by roentgen-videographically determined placement of 25 metal markers implanted in the excised
lower lobes of three dogs. Whole lobe volumes at various transpul-
monary pressures were measured by water displacement. Pressure
and volume measurements were used to calculate bulk modulus
($K = \Delta V P/\Delta V$). The "most satisfactory least squares curve-fit" of
bulk modulus (K) vs. relative volume (V/V_{max}) was obtained with
the equation $K = C/(1 - V/V_{max})^n$. Substituting for bulk modulus.
with the equation $K = V dP/dV$, and integrating enabled computer-
generated pressure-volume plots. This equation provided a better
pressure-volume curve-fit than previously obtained, especially at
low values of pressure and volume. Also, as expected, the bulk
modulus was smaller at low volume, but the rate of change of
modulus was greater during deflation than during inflation.

The authors assumed, without giving sufficient justification, that
the "regional lobe" (the area bounded by the 25 markers) included
a higher density of airways than the rest of the lobe. Using this
assumption, the authors claimed that the modulus and rate of change
of modulus were different for parenchyma tissue and the airways
during both inflation and deflation. No mention, however, was made
of paired t-tests or any other statistical tests. In fact, if they had
done a paired t-test, they would have discovered that none of these
differences were significant, even at the 90 percent confidence level.

Other sources of error which were not addressed include: the difference in the properties of excised lung and intact lung due to
blood in the vessels, surrounding tissue, negative pressure, etc.; the
effect of the markers on the pressure-volume relationship; the effect
of strain rate on the modulus of lung tissue, which is a viscoelastic
material; the time elapsed between regional volume measurement
and whole volume measurements (this is important for viscoelastic
material); the difference between the true regional ΔV and the
measured ΔV; and the differences between the mechanical properties of dog and human lung tissue.

Despite its limitations, the paper presents a step forward in the
understanding of mechanical properties of the lung, and, thus, lung
diseases. Therefore, it should be of benefit to researchers interested
in respiratory mechanics and physiology.

D. S. Feldman, USA

FIGURE 41

Example of a critical abstract.

Reprinted from *Applied Mechanics Reviews*, 37, 1984, by permission of the publisher.

to represent the type of results achieved. This type of abstract has value in
the compilation of handbooks summarizing a large number of studies performed in a particular field. However, it would only work for a subject area

in which the essential elements would remain more or less the same from one study to another. Zholkova (1975) describes how facet analysis might be used to create a structured abstract but is somewhat unconvincing on the value of this approach.

Hartley et al. (1996) compared structured abstracts with unstructured ones in an information seeking task. They found that the subjects in their experiment could use the structured abstracts more effectively (i.e., more rapidly and/or with less error) in locating answers to questions or in identifying abstracts relevant to a particular topic. However, their use of the term "structured" is very different from mine. To them, a structured abstract is merely one with subheads (background, aim, methods, results, conclusions) to facilitate scanning (and as used today in many medical journals), whereas I have used the term to refer to an abstract in non-narrative form. The type of structured abstract represented in Figure 42 could conceivably be produced by use of a computer program designed to identify and extract the appropriate values from text (see discussion of the template-filling approach to text extraction and summarization as discussed in Chapters 14 and 15). In some places, the type of abstract discussed by Hartley et al. has simply been referred to as a "more informative abstract" (Haynes et al., 1990; Haynes, 1993) and I believe this to be a better term. This type of structured abstract is dealt with in more detail in the next chapter.

TYPE OF IRRIGATION	SOIL TYPE	CROPS	CLIMATIC CONDITIONS	PLACE	RESULTS

FIGURE 42
Framework for a structured abstract.

A completely different type of structured abstract, in diagrammatic form, was proposed by Broer (1971). As the completely fictitious example (Figure 43) shows, the abstract resembles a block diagram, or flowchart, in which interconnected word blocks with standard titles are used to convey the substance of the article. Broer claims easier scanning and comprehension for an abstract in this form and presents a conventional abstract for comparison purposes (Figure 43). The approach is intriguing but it has never been

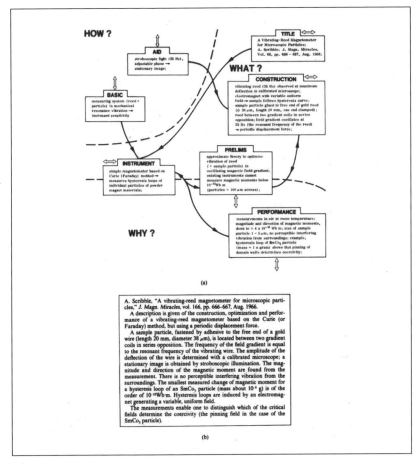

FIGURE 43

"Block diagram" abstract for a hypothetical article with "conventional" abstract
for comparison.

Reprinted with permission from J. W. Broer, "Abstracts in Block Diagram Form," *IEEE Transactions
on Engineering Writing and Speech* (© 1971, Institute of Electrical and Electronics Engineers).

popular. One disadvantage, the space occupied on the printed page, would
not be a disadvantage for online display so perhaps the Internet may revive
interest in such a format.

Bernier and Yerkey (1979) have described and illustrated the use of
highly abbreviated statements each of which encapsulates the major "point"
of some publication. They refer to these generically as "terse literatures"
and to the most condensed of them as "ultraterse literatures." One variety
is the ultraterse conclusion, a very brief statement on the major conclusion
reached in some piece of research. For example:

Theoretical linguistics has had no significant impact on information science

This type of summarization is not an abstract in the conventional sense; nevertheless, terse literatures are certainly related to abstracts. They have a number of potential applications. For example, it would be possible to produce a handbook summarizing what is known about some phenomenon (e.g., disease) as a series of ultraterse statements, each statement linked to a bibliographic reference identifying the source from which it is derived.

Modular Abstracts

In 1964 Herner and Company undertook a study for the National Science Foundation on the feasibility of "modular content analyses" (Lancaster et al., 1965). These had two components: modular abstracts and modular index entries. A specimen is included as Figures 44-45.

Citation

Rosensweig, R. E., and Beecher, N. Theory for the ablation of fiberglas-reinforced phenolic resin. American Institute of Aeronautics and Astronautics Journal, vol. 1, No. 8, August 1963, pp. 1802-1809.

Annotation

A theoretical model is developed, for a charring and melting composite material, combining glassy ablation and the char layer-molten glass chemical reaction effects.

Indicative

The variables associated with the ablation of a typical resin-glass system are examined. These include glass ablation and plastic pyrolysis, flow in both the reacting and non-reacting parts of the melt, mass loss and heat absorption due to chemical reaction, mass injection effects, and coupling between the external pressure and the assumed chemical reaction. The mathematical development is traced and the approximations utilized are discussed. Parametric examinations are made.

Informative

Pyrolysis, melting, and chemical reaction are taken into account in this theory of the ablation of phenolic-fiberglas. It postulates a very thin, isothermal, surface reaction zone, where the char layer (carbon) formed during the pyrolysis of the organic binder reacts chemically with the molten silica. Other assumptions are conventional.
Calculations for typical IRBM re-entry conditions showed little temperature drop in the reaction zone, 6% maximum and usually less than 1%. Depth of the zone was three orders of magnitude less than the thermal thickness. The unreacting run-off in the melt zone ranged from 40-80% as a function of the possible reaction enthalpy level. However, more than 99% of the material reaching the reaction zone was affected. At the expected temperatures of 1400-2000° C., the theory assumed the reaction
$$SiO_2 + 3C \rightarrow SiC + 2CO$$
Earlier experiments had yielded the reaction kinetics. Significant effects, up to 25% increase, on the ablation rate appeared only at the lower reaction rates. Changing the reaction enthalpy by a factor of three changed the ablation rate by less than 10%. When compared with a peak re-entry ablation rate, the value given by this theory was reported to be 38% in defect.

Critical

This theory extends the classic work of Bethe and Adams (Avco-Everett Research Lab., Res. Rept. 38, Nov. 1958) on ablation of pure glasses. Thus it treats the problem as concerning carbon-contaminated glass rather than, as is more usual, a char-layer. In the only comparison given between the theory and experimental data, revealing 38% underprediction by the theory, a thorough error analysis was not included. Spalding (Aero. Quart., Aug. 1961, pp. 237-274) and Scala (General Electric Co. (MSVD), Rept. R59SD401, July, 1959; ARS Jnl., June, 1962, pp. 917-924) have treated similar problems.

FIGURE 44
Modular abstracts.

Modular abstracts were intended as full content descriptions of current documents. Each abstract consists of five parts: a citation, an annotation, an indicative abstract, an informative abstract, and a critical abstract. The set was so designed that an abstracting service could process it to conform to its own unique requirements with a minimum of effort: any one of the abstracts could be used intact, or the modules edited to form, for example, a partially indicative, partially informative abstract, or a partially informative, partially critical abstract.

Physical and Mathematical Systems

Axisymmetric and Blunt Body Systems
Re-entry Bodies

Thermodynamics

Coupled Reactions
Carbon-Silica Reactions

Environment

Atmospheric Entry
Re-entry Conditions
Space Flight

Materials

Phenolics, Fiberglas Reinforced
Glass Fibers
Rocket and Missile Materials
Ablation Materials
Reinforced Plastics
Thermal (Re-entry) Shields
Phenolic Resin

Mass Transfer

Ablation, Analytical
Ablation, Charring
Ablation, Melting
Ablation of Glasses
Chemical Reaction Effects
Thermal Thickness
Reaction Zone
Reaction Thickness
Gasification Ratio

Means and Methods

Parametric Analysis

Authors

Rosensweig, R. E.
Beecher, N.

Affiliations

Massachusetts Institute of Technology
National Research Corporation

FIGURE 45
Modular index entries.

The prime purpose of modular abstracts was to eliminate the duplication and waste of intellectual effort involved in the independent abstracting of the same documents by several services, without any attempt to force "standardized" abstracts on services whose requirements may vary considerably as to form and subject slant. Both abstracts and index entries were prepared by subject specialists, and it was intended that they would reconcile the requirements for speed of publication with the thoroughness of abstracts prepared by experts. Their standardized format and treatment would also reduce repetitive handling and speed the flow of work within recipient abstracting services.

The modular index entries would suggest descriptive terms, drawn from representative index vocabularies, that could be used intact, with refinement or with augmentation to index the abstract derived from the modular package. The representative index vocabularies used as sources for the modular index entries were to be derived from the current indexes or authority lists of the recipient abstracting and indexing services, and would thus be reflective of the indexing styles and policies of these services.

SUMMARY

1. A method is described for the determination of strontium and barium in human bone by radioactivation analysis.

2. Results of analyses of 35 bone samples, from normal persons of both sexes and different ages, are given. The concentrations of barium and strontium were found to be of the order of 7 and 100 µg./g. of ashed tissue respectively.

3. No relationship between sex or disease of individuals with strontium and barium concentration was noted. The concentration of strontium in the age group 0-13 years was significantly lower than that in the group 19-74 years.

4. No significant difference was found in the concentrations of strontium and barium in the various bones of those individuals examined.

5. Results obtained in this survey are discussed and compared with those of other workers.

/00193/
/METHOD/DETERM/STRONTIUM/BONE/HUMANS/RADIOACTIVATION ANALYSIS/
/00193/
/NO RELAT BETW/STRONTIUM/HUMANS/AND/SEX/OR/DISEASE/
/00193/
/NO RELAT BETW/BARIUM/HUMANS/AND/SEX/OR/DISEASE/
/00193/
/METHOD/DETERM/BARIUM/BONE/HUMANS/RADIOACTIVATION ANALYSIS/
/00193/
/DETERM/STRONTIUM/BONE/HUMANS/RADIOACTIVATION ANALYSIS/ 7 UG PER G ASHED TISSUE/
/00193/
/DETERM/BARIUM/BONE/HUMANS/RADIOACTIVATION ANALYSIS/100 UG PER G ASHED TISSUE/
/00193/
/INCR/STRONTIUM/HUMANS/ADULTS/AGE 19-74/COMP W/CHILD-REN/0-13/

FIGURE 46, PART 1

Comparison of mini-abstract, author's summary and abstracts from *Chemical Abstracts* and *Biologial Abstracts* (see part 2 of Figure).

Reproduced from Lunin (1967) by permission of Drexel University. The abstract from *Biochemical Journal* is reprinted by permission of the Biochemical Society, Portland Scientific Press; the abstract from *Biological Abstracts* by permission of BIOSIS; and the abstract from *Chemical Abstracts* by permission of Chemical Abstracts Service. Note that one abstract follows the author's summary very closely and the other is merely a further abbreviation of it.

A test of the concept was performed in the field of heat transfer, this being a highly interdisciplinary subject of potential interest to a large number of abstracting services. Sets of abstracts/index entries were prepared and submitted to several services for routine processing. The services completed questionnaires to evaluate the concept. It was concluded that it was possible to produce a content analysis, in modular form, that could be used as input to a variety of abstracting services but that the majority of services were reluctant to relinquish their autonomy in order to participate in the type of clearinghouse implied by the modular approach.

Craven (1987) discusses a rather different modular approach. In this case, an analyst marks and codes a text to form an "intermediate representation" which can then be used, semi-automatically, to produce abstracts customized to the needs of different audiences.

BA 32: 18857, 1958
18857. SOWDEN, ELEANOR M., and B. R. STITCH. (Med. Res. Council Radiobiol. Res. Unit, Atomic Energy Res. Establishment, Harwell, Didcot, Berks, Eng.) Trace elements in human tissue. 2. Estimation of the concentrations of stable strontium and barium in human bone. Biochem. Jour. 67(1): 104-109. 1957.--A method is described for the determination of strontium and barium in human bone by radioactivation analysis. Results of analyses of 35 bone samples, from normal persons of both sexes and different ages, are given. The concentrations of Ba and Sr were of the order of 7 and 100 µg/g of ashed tissue respectively. No relationship between sex or disease of individuals with Sr and Ba concentration was noted. The concentration of Sr in the age group 1-13 years was significantly lower than that in the group 19-74 years. No significant difference was found in the concentrations of Sr and Ba in the various bones of those individuals examined. Results obtained in this survey are discussed and compared with those of other workers.--Auth. summ.

CA 51: 18184, 1957
II. Estimation of the concentrations of stable strontium and barium in human bone. Eleanor M. Sowden and S. R. Stitch. *Ibid.* 104-9.—A method based on the technique of Harrison and Raymond (*C.A.* 49, 12571g) has been used for the detn. of Sr and Ba in human bone by radioactivation analysis. Results of analyses of 35 bone samples, from normal persons of both sexes and different ages, are given. The concns. of Ba and Sr were found to be of the order of 7 and 100·/g. of ashed tissue, resp. No relation between sex or disease of individuals age group 0-13 yrs. was significantly lower than in the group 19-74 yrs. No significant difference was found in the concns. of Sr and Ba in the various bones of those individuals examined. The results obtained in this survey are discussed and compared with those of other workers.

Roland F. Beers, Jr.

FIGURE 46, PART 2

Mini-Abstracts

The term "mini-abstract" is rather imprecise. It could mean merely a short abstract. As used by Lunin (1967), however, the term refers to a highly structured abstract designed primarily for searching by computer. It is, in fact, a kind of cross between an abstract and an index entry, and Lunin defines it as a "machine-readable index-abstract." The terms used in the abstract are drawn from a controlled vocabulary and are put together in a specified sequence. For example, the statement "There is a decreased amount of zinc in the blood of humans with cirrhosis of the liver" would be written:

/DECR/ZINC/BLOOD/HUMANS/CIRRHOSIS/LIVER

Note that the abstractor tries to keep to a sequence of terms as close as possible to the normal sentence structure. The contents of a document may be described in some detail through the use of a series of such stylized statements. While intended primarily to facilitate searching by computer, Lunin's mini-abstracts can also make sense to the intelligent reader. Figure 46, taken from Lunin, compares the results of the mini-abstract technique with abstracts from *Biological Abstracts* and *Chemical Abstracts* and with the author's summary.

Telegraphic Abstracts

The term "telegraphic abstracts" is also imprecise. It implies a document representation that is presented very parsimoniously: not in complete sentences and resembling a telegram. Indeed it might just be a string of terms without syntax. Lunin's mini-abstracts are telegraphic in style. The term "telegraphic abstract" was used to refer to an essential component in the early computerized retrieval system developed at Western Reserve University (see Chapter 11).

CHAPTER 8

Writing the Abstract

AS WITH INDEXING, one learns to be a good abstractor only through practice. The most that can be done in a book of this type is to give some general guidelines.

Again similar to indexing, the good abstractor will learn to read/skim an item to identify the salient points quickly. Cremmins (1996) discusses in detail how to read an article to pick out the most important points as efficiently as possible, and presents some rules for this purpose. Much of this is self-evident and, in any case, different individuals prefer different techniques for getting to the heart of a text.

The characteristics of a good abstract can be summarized as brevity, accuracy, and clarity. The abstractor should avoid redundancy. In particular, the abstract should build upon the information in the title of the item, not duplicate it. For example, the title of the article used as an illustration in Figures 3, 39, and 40 is *Nationwide Public Opinion Survey of U.S. Attitudes on the Middle East*. The first line of a published abstract is:

> The results of a survey conducted in February, 1985, of U.S. public attitudes on the Middle East.

Clearly, this adds little to the title, except for giving the date. Note how the abstracts in Figures 3, 39, and 40 build on the title rather than duplicating it.

The abstractor should also omit other information that readers would be likely to know or that may not be of direct interest to them. This might include background or historical information—e.g., why a study was undertaken or details of the previous experience of the company conducting the study. Borko and Bernier (1975) stress that the abstractor should indicate what the author did rather than what he tried to do, but failed to accomplish, or intends to do next.

The shorter the abstract the better, as long as the meaning remains clear and there is no sacrifice of accuracy. Unnecessary words such as "the author" or "the article" can be left out. For example, "This article examines . . ." can be reduced to "Examines . . ." Standard abbreviations and acronyms can be used whenever these are likely to be well known to readers (e.g., PLO). In other cases, an abbreviation can be used once its meaning has been defined. For example:

> . . . within the framework of European Political Cooperation (EPC). The achieve-
> ments . . . by EPC . . .

Abstracts in some fields of science may use many abbreviations. While this saves space it can reduce intelligibility and actually increase the amount of time required of the reader. Despite the need for brevity, abstracts should be self-contained; a major purpose of the abstract is defeated if a reader needs to consult the original to understand the abstract!

Jargon is best avoided. Jargon words may mean different things to different groups of readers and may not be understood at all by some people.

Some abstractors feel that they must change the words of an author. While paraphrase is frequently necessary to achieve brevity, nothing is gained by chang-ing the author's words in striving for originality. Indeed it is easy to distort the meaning of the original by deliberately seeking, for stylistic reasons, to find substitute expressions. This point is made forcefully by Collison (1971):

> It is important that the abstractor should use the vocabulary of the author as far
> as possible; paraphrase is dangerous and can lead the reader to channels of
> thought not intended by the author. (Page 11)

Nevertheless, Craven (1990) found that abstracts make little use of "longer verbatim word sequences from full texts," although he was dealing in a very limited subject area. An abstract is utilitarian and need not be a work of art, although Cremmins (1996) believes that abstracts should have "grace" as well as clarity and precision.

The U.S. national standard on abstracts (*Guidelines for Abstracts*, 1997) specifies that verbs should be used in the active voice (e.g., "Role indica-tors reduce recall" rather than "Recall is reduced by role indicators") when-ever possible but that the passive voice may be used for "indicative statements and even for informative statements in which the receiver of the action should be emphasized." This qualification is very imprecise and is best forgotten: in most cases the preferred tense will be obvious for stylistic reasons. Borko and Chatman (1963) suggest use of the past tense in describing experimental procedures and conditions but the present tense for conclu-sions derived from the experiments. This is logical: the activities reported by an author are things of the past while the results and conclusions are still with us. Borko and Bernier (1975) are more explicit, recommending active voice and past tense for informative abstracts and passive voice and present tense for indicative.

Many sets of abstracting rules have been produced in the past. Perhaps the most concise set of abstracting principles is the one issued by the Defense Documentation Center (1968), which is reproduced in Figure 47. In a few brief statements this encapsulates the center's rules for what to include, what not to include, how long the abstract is to be, and what type of terminology is to be used. A more complete statement, but still in concise form, is given in a report by Payne et al. (1962). This is reproduced in Appendix 1.

OUTLINE

In brief:
  1. Always an informative abstract if possible
  2. 200-250 words
  3. Same technical terminology as in report
  4. Contents
      a. Objectives or purpose of investigation
      b. Methods of investigation
      c. Results of investigation
      d. Validity of results
      e. Conclusions
      f. Applications
  5. Numerals for numbers when possible
  6. Phrases for clauses, words for phrases when possible
  7. No unconventional or rare symbols or characters
  8. No uncommon abbreviations
  9. No equations, footnotes, preliminaries
  10. No descriptive cataloging data
  11. Security Classification
  12. Dissemination controls, if any
  13. Review it.

FIGURE 47
Abstracting principles published by the Defense Documentation Center (1968).
Reproduced by permission of the Defense Technical Information Center.

Content and Format

What should be included in an abstract, of course, depends very much on the type of publication involved. A long indicative abstract of some type of research report might mention the objectives of the research, experimental or other procedures used, the types of results achieved (an informative abstract would present the results themselves, at least in condensed form), and the author's conclusions on the significance of the results. The treatment of a historical article, on the other hand, would be quite different. The abstract might, for example, emphasize the author's thesis or conclusions, being sure to mention the periods, geographic locations, and individuals involved.*

---

*Tibbo (1992) has shown that published standards relating to the writing of abstracts are much more relevant to the sciences than to the humanities.

In specialized subject areas, an abstractor may be given precise instructions on certain things to look for in an article and to bring out clearly in the abstract. These might include such varied items as drug dosage, climatic conditions, age of individuals, soil types, equations used, or alloying element involved. Abstracts tend to be easier to write when the subject matter deals with concrete objects and become more difficult to write the more abstract or nebulous the subject.

The majority of abstracts are presented in the conventional format of bibliographic reference followed by the text of the abstract. In some publications, however, the abstract precedes the bibliographic reference and the first line of the abstract is highlighted in some way, as in the following example:

LABOUR MIGRATION FROM MOZAMBIQUE TO THE MINES OF SOUTH AFRICA remains a significant element in the economic relationship between these countries. . . .

Brockman, G. Migrant labour and foreign policy: the case of Mozambique. *Journal of Peace Research*, 22, 1985, 335-344.

This is a more dramatic form of presentation, rather like a newspaper headline, and may attract a reader's attention more readily. Weil et al. (1963) refer to this as a "reader-oriented" abstract, a "topical-sentence first" abstract, or a "findings-oriented" abstract (although the headline need not necessarily relate to findings). If it is suitable, the title of the article could become the headline, to be followed by an amplifying topic sentence.

A complete abstract may be considered to have three parts: the bibliographic *reference*, identifying the item abstracted; the *body* of the abstract (the text); and the *signature*. This last element is the attribution of the source of the abstract—e.g., the abstractor's initials, or an indication that the abstract was prepared by the author of the item, is a modified author abstract, or is derived from some other source such as another abstracting service.

Many abstracts seem to fall in the 100-250 word range but, as discussed earlier, it makes sense that the length should vary with such factors as the length of the item itself, its range of subject matter, its perceived importance, its physical availability, and its intellectual accessibility (e.g., items difficult to locate, such as conference papers, or items in obscure languages, might be abstracted in more detail than other items). Borko and Bernier (1975) suggest that abstracts of science literature should usually be between one tenth and one twentieth the length of the original, although Resnikoff and Dolby (1972) indicate that one thirtieth may be more common.

Sound advice on the sequencing of content is given by Borko and Bernier (1975):

The body of the abstract can be arranged to save the reader's time. Conclusions placed first may satisfy the reader and save further reading. (S)he may accept or reject the conclusions without needing to know the findings upon which the conclusions were based. Amplifying information should be placed last. Labeling each part of an abstract as, for example, *conclusions*, *results*, or *procedures*, has been found to be unnecessary; readers understand what part they are reading. The arrangement of parts of the body of an abstract is done for the same purpose that parts of an item in a newspaper are organized—to communicate more information more rapidly.

Paragraphing is not desirable. The abstract is short; it should express a homogeneity of thought, and should be written as a single paragraph. (Page 69)

In point of fact, the recent tendency has been to break abstracts up into smaller chunks through paragraphing and even the use of subheadings. This has occurred particularly in medical journals. An example, from the information science literature itself, and discussing this very situation, is shown in Figure 48. This type of abstract has become known as a "structured abstract" although this use of the term differs markedly from mine.

Curiously, from 1988 to the present, the medical literature probably includes more articles on "abstracts" than does the information science literature. "Structured" abstracts of medical articles were first introduced in *Annals of Internal Medicine*, where authors were requested to prepare abstracts in a prescribed format, and rather elaborate rules for creating them have been established (see, for example, Haynes et al., 1990). Figure 49 gives a summary of the type of information sought, but the actual instructions to authors are much more detailed.

Structured abstracts in medical journals have not been introduced without controversy. Haynes et al. (1990) suggest that the rather rigid formatting may encourage some authors to claim more than they should. For example, having a *method* or *design* heading to catch the reader's attention may force some to claim a more rigorous approach than really justified.

Froom and Froom (1993a,b) showed that structured abstracts in *Annals of Internal Medicine* do not always contain all of the information requested in the guidelines for authors, even when the information needed was present in the article itself. Haynes (1993) is critical of their study but unconvincing in his criticism. Taddio et al. (1994), based on a larger study of 300 abstracts from three journals, found that the structured abstracts were more likely to contain more complete information of research importance than unstructured abstracts were. Evaluation aspects are dealt with in the next chapter.

While structured abstracts of this type may have merit, the claims for them are often inflated. For example, Haynes et al. (1990) claim that they "can facilitate peer review before publication, assist clinical readers to find articles that are both scientifically sound and applicable to their practices, and allow more precise computerized literature searches," although not all of these claims are substantiated.

ABSTRACT.

BACKGROUND: Structured abstracts—which, like the present one, contain several subheadings—have replaced traditional abstracts in most medical journals. Evaluation studies have shown that such abstracts usually provide more information, are of a higher quality, facilitate peer review and are generally welcomed. AIM: The aim of the studies reported here was to investigate an additional possible advantage for structured abstracts—namely, whether or not they are easier to search.

METHOD: Two studies are reported. In Study 1, using an electronic database, 52 readers were asked to find the answers to two questions for each of eight abstracts in one format (say, traditional) followed by two questions for each of eight abstracts set in the other format. Time and error data were recorded automatically. In Study 2, using a printed database, 56 readers were asked to find five abstracts that reported a particular kind of study (e.g., studies with school-children and reading tests) and then to find five more that reported another kind of study. Again, the order and presentation of the format of the abstracts was counterbalanced. Time and error data were recorded manually.

RESULTS: In Study 1, the participants performed significantly faster and made significantly fewer errors using the structured abstracts. There were, however, some unexplainable practice effects. In Study 2, the participants again performed significantly faster and made significantly fewer errors with the structured abstracts. In Study 2, however, there were asymmetrical transfer effects: participants who responded first to the structured abstracts responded more quickly to the following traditional ones than did those participants who responded first to the traditional abstracts.

CONCLUSIONS: The overall findings, notwithstanding certain caveats, support the hypothesis that it is easier for readers to search structured abstracts than it is to search traditional ones.

FIGURE 48
Example of highly formatted abstract.
Reprinted from Hartley et al. (1996) by permission of the *Journal of Information Science*.

Interestingly enough, at about the time the medical literature was discovering this type of abstract, Trawinski (1989) discussed methods for producing similar abstracts in the information science field. Moreover, he compared the detail of abstracts produced in this way with abstracts drawn from the INSPEC database.

The literature related to structured abstracts continues to grow. Hartley (1998) presents a case for the use of structured abstracts more widely in scholarly journals. He (Hartley, 2000b) also makes the point that some form of structured abstract is needed to accompany systematic literature reviews in medicine. He claims that such abstracts need to be easier to read than those for medical research articles because systematic reviews are targeted at a wider audience.

Original Articles
1. Objective: the exact question(s) addressed by the article
2. Design: the basic design of the study
3. Setting: the location and level of clinical care
4. Patients or participants: the manner of selection and number of patients or participants who entered and completed the study
5. Interventions: the exact treatment or intervention, if any
6. Main outcome measures: the primary study outcome measure as planned before data collection began
7. Results: the key findings
8. Conclusions: key conclusions including direct clinical applications.

Review Articles
1. Purpose: the primary objective of the review article
2. Data sources: a succinct summary of data sources
3. Study selection: the number of studies selected for review and how they were selected
4. Data extraction: rules for abstracting data and how they were applied
5. Results of data synthesis: the methods of data synthesis and key results
6. Conclusions: key conclusions, including potential applications and research needs

FIGURE 49

Key information needed by clinicians in assessing the relevance and quality of articles and therefore important for inclusion in structured abstracts. From Haynes et al. (1990) by permission of *Annals of Internal Medicine*.

One objection to structured abstracts, expressed by some journal editors, is that they take up more space. This issue has been investigated by Hartley (2002). He concluded that structured abstracts do take up more space (they are typically 21% or more larger than traditional ones) but that this would only affect those (relatively rare) journals in which articles run on after each other and not journals in which each article begins on a new page.

The broad types of error that can occur in subject indexing can also occur in abstracting: points that should be included are not and others may be included that are better omitted. Transcription errors can also occur, especially when formulae or numerical values are involved. The work of inexperienced abstractors should always be checked and edited by a more senior person. Borko and Bernier (1975) affirm the value of a good editor:

> Editors of abstracts seem to develop a sixth sense as to when some content of importance is missing. They look for, and expect to see, certain categories of information, such as methods and equipment used, data collected, and conclusions. (Page 12)

A particular abstracting service will probably adopt some guidelines on such things as spelling, punctuation, and capitalization. Much of this is a matter of individual preference so it seems pointless to give examples here.

To aid the work of the abstractor, particularly in a training program, it may be desirable to prepare some type of worksheet to prompt the abstractor on what to look for in a publication. A worksheet* of this kind might include such headings as:

Types and Purpose [Type of investigation, such as experimental, theoretical, review, basic or applied research, development. Purpose: a statement of the problem, a definition of what exactly is investigated.]

Experimental Set-up or Theoretical Model [Salient features, new approaches, hypothesis to be proven, results anticipated when work was begun. What differentiates this work, either experimentally or analytically, from that of other investigators?]

Conditions Examined [Parameters varied, ranges involved, controls imposed.]

Procedures [New techniques utilized, transformations used or developed, how results were obtained.]

Assumptions [What are the direct and indirect assumptions and are they standard?]

Main Conclusions [Author's principal conclusions, other conclusions supported by the data, significant negative results.]

Secondary Conclusions [Minor points, or those in peripheral areas of the investigation, may be reported if they are deemed sufficiently useful. Interpretations and reasonable inferences and extrapolations may be reported. Loose theoretical linkages and speculative questions are not desired.]

Importance or Utility [Importance and competence of the work performed. Potential applications.]

Limitations and Shortcomings [Are the assumptions unduly restrictive or confining? Is the theoretical model too far removed from possible practical application? Are there flaws in the technique? Were limitations imposed on the results by the approach to the problem? What degree of sophistication was employed? Has there been sufficient analysis of the data, particularly with respect to possible errors?]

Critical Comments [Possible fundamental error, and magnitude of the errors. Possible previous publication of this information. Are there any similar investigations and what is the position of the present work in the literature? Which features are particularly praiseworthy? Is the interpretation of results reasonable?]

Clearly, not all of these categories will apply to every item to be abstracted and the last three would apply only to critical abstracts. The use of this type of questionnaire approach to abstracting is discussed by Solov'ev (1971).

Today, of course, some form of online, interactive aid to the abstracting process is likely to be more attractive than the use of this type of structured approach, even if it were displayed online. Craven (1996) has developed a prototype system to assist abstractors, and has tested it in at least a preliminary way. The abstracting aid includes a thesaurus component (Craven, 1993).

---

*The headings and descriptions for the worksheet illustrated here are based on those used in the Herner and Company modular abstracts project (Lancaster et al., 1965).

Some writers have attempted to produce guidelines for abstracting particular types of documents. For example, Solov'ev (1981) suggests that abstracts of doctoral dissertations should address the following points: current significance of the subject, the problem dealt with and the goal of the research, scientific novelty, methodology, results achieved, and conclusions (including implementation of the results).

Although it is somewhat unclear and thus difficult to interpret in places, the UNHCR Refugee Documentation Centre has compressed the essentials of abstracting into a single diagram (Figure 50). Particularly useful are the evaluation criteria listed on the left of the diagram. Note that the abstract is to be evaluated on the basis of its language and content, its conformity to "house style" (length, structure, spelling, and punctuation conventions), and, most importantly, the degree to which it satisfies user needs.

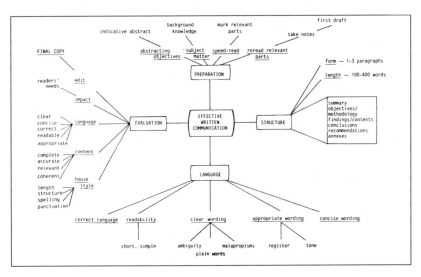

FIGURE 50

Essentials of abstracting.

From UNHCR Refugee Documentation Centre (1985). Reproduced by permission of the UNHCR Centre for Documentation on Research.

More formal "models" of the abstracting process have been prepared (e.g., by Karasev, 1978). While these may aid our understanding of the steps that an abstractor goes through intuitively, they seem of little practical value to abstractors.

Although one can recognize some general principles involved in the task of abstracting, it is clear that individual abstractors will each have their own ways of implementing the principles. Indeed, Endres-Niggemeyer (1994,

1998) claimed to identify 453 different strategies based on tape recording the thinking-aloud protocols of only six abstractors.

The theoretical aspects of abstracts and abstracting are dealt with more frequently by European authors, particularly Endres-Niggemeyer (1998) and Pinto. The latter presents a complete study of abstracting in its broader linguistic context in a book in Spanish (Pinto, 2001). Partial versions appear in Pinto (1995) and in Pinto and Lancaster (1999). She has also discussed the roles of semiotics, logic, and cognitive psychology in the content analysis of text (Pinto, 1994). Pinto and Gálvez (1999) analyze abstracting in terms of communicational, physical, cognitive, and systemic paradigms.

Abstractors

Abstracts can be prepared by authors, other subject specialists or professional abstractors. Many scholarly journals require authors to prepare abstracts to accompany their papers. Increasingly, these abstracts are adopted by published abstracting services in place of preparing a new abstract.

As in the case of indexing, abstractors must have some understanding of the subject matter dealt with although they need not be subject experts. Writing and editing skills are important requirements, and the ability of an abstractor to read and understand quickly is a definite asset.

Borko and Bernier (1975) caution that authors do not necessarily write the best abstracts for their papers. Authors usually lack training and experience in abstracting as well as a knowledge of abstracting rules. The more prestigious abstracting publications are usually able to recruit subject specialists as abstractors. These experts may agree to write abstracts in their field of specialization without pay or for a modest honorarium. Borko and Bernier claim that "Those who are trained in abstracting and are also expert in a field write the best abstracts," a claim that is difficult to quarrel with. Because these subject specialists are usually volunteers, it may be difficult to get them to abstract promptly. The professional abstractor is expensive but prompt and can do excellent work when dealing with subject areas that are not totally unfamiliar.

At the present time, authors and publishers have little incentive for "embroidering" abstracts to make the underlying work seem more attractive than it really is. Price (1983) has argued that this could become a danger in a completely electronic environment (see Chapter 16). Publishers would want to promote use because they would probably be paid on this basis. Authors would want to promote use if this factor became, as it might, a criterion used in promotion and tenure decisions. The term "spoofing" or "spamming" has been used to refer to the embroidering of Web pages to increase their retrievability (Chapter 16).

Abstracting and indexing are closely related activities and a strong argument can be made for combining them. It is a small step from the conceptual analysis stage of indexing to the preparation of an acceptable abstract. Moreover, the additional discipline involved in writing the abstract can help in deciding what should be covered in the indexing and what can be omitted. The fact that some combination of reading and skimming is involved in both activities is another reason why it is efficient to combine them in a single individual wherever it is practical to do so.

Quality and Consistency in Abstracting

No two abstracts for a document will be identical when written by different individuals or by the same individual at different times: what is described may be the same but how it is described will differ. Quality and consistency are a bit more vague when applied to abstracts than when applied to indexing. There seem to be two major facets of quality:

1. Are the major "points" of the document brought out in the abstract?
2. Are these points described accurately, succinctly, and unambiguously?

To some extent, then, the quality of abstracting may be judged according to criteria that are very similar to those used in the evaluation of indexing. The first step in abstracting, as in indexing, is really conceptual analysis-—what points should be brought out?—and the second step is the translation of this conceptual analysis into sentences (usually).

The quality of the conceptual analysis, presumably, can be judged against the content-related instructions of the organization for which the abstract is prepared; for example:

1. Is the purpose and scope of the work covered?
2. Are the results indicated or summarized?
3. Are the author's conclusions summarized?
   and so on.

The consistency between two abstracts can then be judged, at this conceptual level, on the degree to which the abstractors have agreed on what points to include.

Judging the quality of the "translation" phase of abstracting is a bit more tricky, because accuracy, ambiguity, and brevity are somewhat subjective criteria. Nevertheless, it is possible for a senior abstractor to use them in judging the work of more junior people. Consistency applied to the translation phase of abstracting should not be a major concern: it should be possible to make the same point in several different ways, each accurate and unambiguous and, perhaps, equally brief.

	Full Text	Abstracts
Number of items judged relevant	12	15
Number of items judged nonrelevant	38	35
Total	50	50

FIGURE 51
Hypothetical results from a test of relevance predictability.

The ultimate test of a good abstract is simply "does it allow a reader to accurately predict whether or not the item abstracted is relevant to his or her present interests or not?" For a particular reader, and a particular information need, it is possible to test this on the basis of, say, 50 abstracts printed out as the result of an online search. The results of the study might be those presented in Figure 51: the abstracts suggested that 15 items might be relevant but only 12 turned out to be. Moreover, if it is discovered that not all of the 12 judged relevant from text were also judged relevant from the abstracts, the abstracts have failed in both ways: they suggested some items to be relevant when they were not and others not to be relevant when they were.

Of course, this kind of study is somewhat difficult to do. Moreover, the results apply only to a particular user and information need; change the user or information need and the results change. Most users of abstracting services, or of online databases, will have experienced the situation, perhaps fairly frequently, in which an abstract whets the appetite for a document that subsequently turns out to be quite different from what was expected. In these cases, then, the abstracts have failed these users, although they might have served other users quite adequately.

The value of abstracts in predicting the relevance of documents to a particular user is discussed in more detail in the next chapter. While several relevance predictability studies have been performed, investigations of the activities of abstractors are few and far between. In fact, more work may have been done on the evaluation of extracting than on the evaluation of abstracting. For example, both Rath et al. (1961b) and Edmundson et al. (1961) discovered that humans were not very consistent (with each other or with themselves) in selecting from a text the sentences that were judged to be the best indicators of its content.

Edmundson et al. (1961) suggest several possible approaches to the evaluation of abstracts:

1. Intuitive, subjective judgment;
2. Comparison with an "ideal" abstract;
3. Determining to what extent test questions about a document can be answered from the abstract;
4. Retrievability of the document by the abstract.

Clearly, abstracts are evaluated by editors and others working within information centers or publishing houses, presumably by the intuitive method. It would seem likely that, as more and more use is made of text searching in place of human indexing, the "retrievability" approach to evaluation becomes increasingly important. The criteria for judging an abstract on "retrievability" are not necessarily the same as those used to judge it on the basis of relevance predictability (see "Compatibility issues" discussion).

Vinsonhaler (1966) proposes behavioral methods for judging the quality of abstracts on the basis of "content validity" or "predictive validity." In a content validity study, the subjects judge the degree to which the document and the abstract are "similar," using perhaps a 7-point similarity scale. Alternatively, a test may be used to determine to what extent an abstract discriminates among documents, especially when the subject matter of the documents may be quite similar. To measure discriminability Vinsonhaler proposes a test in which subjects examine a particular document and then try to identify the appropriate abstract from a booklet of abstracts. One test of predictive validity determines to what extent decisions made on the similarity of abstracts agree with similarity decisions made on the basis of the documents themselves: if the abstracts are "good," groupings of abstracts on the basis of similarity should coincide with groupings of the documents on the basis of similarity. The second test of predictive validity is more conventional: the extent to which abstracts correctly predict the relevance of documents is determined. Vinsonhaler suggests a crossover test in which one group of subjects judges the relevance of a set of documents to a search request statement and then, after a suitable time interval, does the same thing with the abstracts of the documents. The second group of subjects works in reverse sequence, judging abstracts first and documents second.

Mathis (1972) has proposed that abstracts be evaluated on the basis of a "data coefficient" (*DC*). The *DC* is expressed by the formula C/L, where C is a "data retention factor" and L a "length retention factor." C is a measure of the extent to which all of the "concepts" (Mathis refers to them as "data elements") of the document are retained in the abstract. L is simply the number of words in the abstract divided by the number in the document. The *DC* is a numerical value, the higher the value the better. It favors concentration and compression: ability to retain all of the essential elements of the text in the fewest words. The value can be improved by either increasing the number of data elements present or reducing the number of words in the abstract. Mathis suggests that a *DC* value below one would indicate an abstract of unacceptable quality. The approach is ingenious although it is entirely dependent on the ability to identify "data elements." Mathis proposes that they can be identified through syntactic criteria.

As with any other type of text, abstracts can be evaluated on the basis of "readability," using standard readability formulae. Dronberger and Kowitz (1975) used the Flesch Reading Ease formula to compare abstracts from *Research in Education* with the reports from which they were derived. The abstracts were found to have significantly lower readability levels, presumably due to their lack of redundancy. Similarly, King (1976), using a "cloze" criterion, found abstracts from *Child Development Abstracts* to be less readable than the items on which they were based.

Hartley (1994) used both Flesch readability scores* and cloze (comprehension) tests in comparing four different versions of the same abstracts. He concluded that abstracts could be improved (i.e., made more clear) by changing type size, by structuring (into paragraphs with headings), and by rewriting. Later, Hartley and Sydes (1996) studied reader preferences for the layout of structured abstracts.

Hartley (2000c) identifies three factors affecting the clarity of abstracts: language (readability), way in which information is presented (sequence or structure), and the typography. He also describes different typographical approaches to the presentation of structured abstracts.

Salager-Meyer (1991) analyzed a sample of medical abstracts from a linguistic perspective, finding almost half to be "poorly structured" (i.e., having discoursal deficiency). Since "discoursal deficiency" can include such things as conceptual scatter (e.g., results reported in different places in the abstract), as well as omission of an important element (e.g., purpose of research) from the abstract, the author implies that abstracts flawed in this way will be less effective in conveying information.

Borko and Bernier (1975) have provided what is perhaps the most comprehensive list of possible criteria for the evaluation of abstracts, as follows:

1. A global rating of quality (by human judges).

---

*The Flesch Reading Ease (R.E.) score takes into account the length of the sentences and the length of the words in the text. The original formula is R.E. = 206.835 - 0.846w - 1.015s (where w is the average number of syllables in 100 words and s is the average number of words per sentence. The scores usually fall in the range 0-100 with the lowest scores reflecting greater difficulty (Hartley, 2000c).

2. The extent to which the NISO (ANSI) or some other standard is observed (also a major component in the approach to evaluation recommended by Mathis (1972).*
3. The inclusion of significant information and the exclusion of unimportant information.
4. Lack of errors.
5. Consistency of style and readability.
6. Relevance predictability.
7. Ability to serve as a surrogate for the original (informative abstracts).
8. Adequacy as a source of index terms.

Obviously, the list represents various levels of criteria. For example, criteria 3-5 would presumably all have to be taken into account in any "global" rating. One approach to the evaluation of the extent to which an abstract can serve in place of the original (criterion 7) is to compare the ability of groups of individuals to answer questions based on (a) abstracts and (b) full text. Studies of this type have been reported by Payne et al. (1962).

In fact, the Payne studies involved three different approaches to evaluation:

1. *Consistency*. Subject specialists were used to compare abstracts on the basis of similarity in the amount of information given.
2. *The amount of text reduction achieved.*
3. *Utility*. Students answered technical questions based on papers in their area of specialization. Some students read the papers, others only the abstracts. Answers of the two groups were compared. This method was also used by Hartley et al. (1996) to compare different types of abstracts: it was found that structured abstracts (formatted in separate paragraphs, each with its own heading) could be used more effectively.

Within the TIPSTER program (see Chapter 14), two methods of evaluation of abstracts are used: (1) using the abstract to judge the relevance of documents, and (2) using the abstract as the basis for the categorization of documents (i.e., categorization based on abstract compared with categorization from full texts).

Evaluations of the quality of abstracts published in the last few years have mostly concentrated on structured abstracts. Hartley and Benjamin (1998) compared traditional and structured abstracts written by authors of papers submitted to four British psychology journals. Psychology students participated in the evaluation. The structured abstracts were judged significantly more readable, significantly longer, and significantly more informative.

---

*But see also the discussion on standards in Chapter 9.

Little work has been done to evaluate published abstracts by comparing them to the texts they refer to. However, one useful study of this type has been reported by Pitkin et al. (1999). They evaluated 88 abstracts published in six major medical journals in this way. Abstracts were considered "deficient" if they included data that differed from the data in the article itself or if they failed to appear in the article at all. By these criteria, significant numbers of abstracts were judged deficient, about 18% in the best case journal and 68% in the worst case.

As a result of this study, *JAMA (Journal of the American Medical Association)* introduced a quality improvement program (Winkler, 1999). The following quality criteria were adopted:

1. Abstract headings are consistent with structured abstract format.
2. Data in abstract are consistent with text, tables, and figures.
3. Data or information in the abstract are presented in the text, tables, or figures.
4. Years of study and length of follow-up are provided.
5. Results for Main Outcome Measures are presented in Results section (avoid selective reporting).
6. Results are quantified with numerators, denominators, odds ratios, and confidence intervals where appropriate.
7. Absolute differences rather than relative differences are presented wherever possible (e.g., "Mortality declined from 6% to 3%" rather than "Mortality declined 50%").
8. For randomized trials, analysis is identified as intent-to-treat or evaluable patient analysis.
9. For surveys, response rate is provided in Results or Design.
10. For multivariate analysis, factors controlled for in model are briefly summarized.
11. Conclusions follow from information contained within the abstract.

These criteria are now used to review and edit the abstracts. Winkler reported a dramatic improvement in the quality after this program was implemented, and Pitkin et al. (2000), in an independent investigation, also found considerable improvement, although not at the dramatic level reported by Winkler. Earlier, Pitkin and Branagan (1998) had reported, as a result of a randomized controlled trial, that specific instructions presented to authors who were revising their manuscripts were not effective in reducing abstract deficiencies. It appears that distributing instructions on abstract quality to authors is not in itself a guarantee of improvement, although such instructions may be effective when used by journal editors in the evaluation of abstracts.

Hartley (2000a) compared the accuracy of structured abstracts with that of "traditional" abstracts for the same articles submitted for publication in journals of the British Psychological Society. This was possible because the authors included traditional abstracts with their submissions but were required to submit structured versions after their papers were accepted for publication. Hartley reports few inaccuracies in either type of abstract and that the structured abstracts were neither better nor worse than the others. The latter finding may not be too surprising given that most of the authors simply converted their original abstract to structured form. The fact that these abstracts in psychology appear more accurate than the medical abstracts in the Pitkin studies is more difficult to explain.

The predictability value of abstracts (i.e., their ability to indicate the relevance of the parent item to the interests of some user) is discussed in the next chapter.

Compatibility Issues

Fifty years ago the sole reason for writing abstracts was to create a representation of a document to be read by humans. However, abstracts are now used for a second purpose—to provide a representation that can be searched by computer. Unfortunately, these two purposes are not fully compatible. For retrieval purposes redundancy is desirable. That is, a topic is best represented in more than one way. For example, including the synonyms "triangular wings" and "delta wings" in some abstract increases the probability that the item will be retrieved—one searcher may use "triangular" while another may think of "delta." For the human reader, on the other hand, consistency rather than redundancy is desirable. Indeed, a user may be very confused if ideas are described in a number of different ways within an abstract.

For retrieval purposes, the longer the abstract the better. At least, the longer the abstract the more access points it provides, and the more access points the greater the potential for high recall in retrieval. At the same time, it must be recognized that precision is likely to deteriorate: the longer the abstract, the more "minor" aspects of the document that will be brought in and the greater the potential for false associations (see Chapters 6, 11, and 14). For the human reader, of course, brevity is desirable. It is also desirable for the subscribers to printed tools since longer abstracts lead to more expensive publications.

For the human reader, negative references are valuable: "but excludes cost considerations" tells the reader what not to expect in the document. Inclusion of the word "cost" in the abstract, of course, will cause it to be retrieved in searches in which cost is an important facet—exactly the situation in which it should not be retrieved.

For retrieval purposes, too, certain words are best avoided. The common word "aids" will create problems in many databases for it will cause retrieval of items on the disease AIDS, while "to lead" will cause retrieval of items in a search on the metal *lead*. For more effective retrieval, then, abstractors should avoid terms known to create problems of this type.

Even the conventions of punctuation and syntax that make sense to the human reader may create problems for the computer. Consider, for example, a sentence ending with the word "acid" and followed immediately by one beginning with "Rain." In many systems this item will be retrieved in a search on "acid rain," although it may have nothing at all to do with this subject.

The mini-abstracts of Lunin (1967) (see preceding chapter), unlike the conventional abstract, are designed primarily to facilitate searching by computer. While they can be interpreted by intelligent users, they are definitely more difficult to read and understand, and it is not known how a stylized statement of this kind would be accepted by the users of a retrieval system.

All of this points to the fact that an abstract "optimum" for the human reader may not be optimum for searching by computer. Within the foreseeable future, however, abstracts will continue to serve both purposes. Even if the importance of printed services declines, abstracts will still be needed as an intermediate output in computer-based searches. One implication of this is that the publishers of secondary services need to revise their instructions so that abstractors are led to create abstracts that, as far as possible, are effective surrogates for searching as well as for reading.

Fidel (1986) has done a great service by analyzing the abstracting instructions prepared by 36 producers of databases. Her summary of instructions that appear relevant to the retrievability characteristics of abstracts is reproduced as Figure 52. More than anything else, her summary reveals some polarities of opinion: use author language, do not use author language, use language identical with the language of assigned index terms, use language that complements the assigned terms, and so on. The most sensible rule is probably the one that specifies that the abstract should include relevant terms that are missing from the descriptors and from the title. Frequently these will be terms more specific than the controlled vocabulary terms.

Booth and O'Rourke (1997) investigated structured medical abstracts in an information retrieval context. By downloading records from MEDLINE, they were able to establish two searchable databases, one of full abstracts, and one of abstracts partitioned into various components (objectives, design, conclusions, and so on) of the structure. Searches in the partitioned database, not surprisingly, give greater precision but lower recall. Searchers also had difficulty in deciding which partitions to search.

Nomoto and Matsumoto (2001) advocate the evaluation of the quality of automatically produced abstracts (actually extracts) in terms of how well they can substitute for the full text in information retrieval tasks. They seem to believe that this idea originates with them, when in fact it is quite an old one.

The Content of Abstracts

General statements
Use 'important' concepts and terms (e.g., those which will enhance free-text retrieval, those for which a document gives enough information, or key words).
Index terms
Co-ordinate concepts used in abstracts with assigned descriptors.
   (a) Assign concepts in abstracts that are identical to descriptors.
   (b) Assign concepts in abstracts that complement descriptors (e.g., relevant terms that are missed in descriptor indexing and in titles, terms that are more specific than descriptors, or a particular type of term that is important to the subject area, such as geographic names).
   (c) Assign concepts in abstracts that both complement and are identical to descriptors.
Enhance indexing independent of any index language used.

Check lists
Follow a list of retrieval-related elements that should be included in abstracts.
Forms of check lists:
   (a) Categories that should be included in abstracts (e.g. materials, properties and processes) and the conditions under which they should be included (e.g. only when they are discussed elaborately, or whenever mentioned).
   (b) Specific and particular guidelines (e.g. 'whenever dealing with a new product, mention the company name').

The Language of Abstracts

Use of author language
Use author language.
Do not use author language.
   (a) Use standardised and concrete terms specific to a subject area.
Use both author language and synonyms.

Relationship to index language used
Co-ordinate terms in abstracts with descriptors.
Complement descriptors with terms in abstracts (e.g. use synonyms or more specific terms).
Use specific and well-accepted terms for particular categories (such as materials, processes and products).

Practices to avoid
Do not use the negative (e.g. use *sick* instead of *not healthy*).
Do not list terms which have a common last word as a series (such as 'upper, middle, and working class').

Word forms
Follow local language practices (e.g. change American spelling for British database).
Always spell out terms in certain categories (such as processes, materials, products).
When a term and a descriptor are the same, record the term in the form used by the descriptor.
Express terms both in their abbreviated form and in their complete form.

FIGURE 52

Rules for abstractors that relate to retrievability characteristics of abstracts.

Reproduced from Fidel (1986) by permission of Emerald.

The Inhouse Bulletin

The fact that bibliographic databases are available in virtually all fields of endeavor, and that for some fields several competing databases exist, does not necessarily eliminate the need for an inhouse abstracting bulletin. The information center of a company, or other organization having a strong research program, may want to produce its own bulletin because:

1. Published abstracting journals may not be sufficiently current in covering the core material of greatest interest to the organization.
2. No single database, in printed or electronic form, is likely to embrace all the material of interest to the organization. Indeed, many databases may be relevant to organizational interests when diversity of subject matter and of documentary forms are taken into account.
3. No external database will cover certain materials of importance, most obviously the organization's own internal reports, manufacturers' literature, advertising material of competitors, and so on.

In order to optimize the procedures used to produce the inhouse bulletin, it will be necessary to identify those materials that should be abstracted directly. These would presumably include the company's own internal reports and external material judged of particular importance. For example, one member of the center's staff might review all new patents and prepare abstracts for those of possible interest to the company—an art in itself. Using the methods discussed in the next chapter, a "core" of journals that are expected to be unusually productive in terms of the interests of the organization can be identified. These too will be abstracted directly.

It is possible that the sources regularly scanned in this way will yield, say, 80 to 90% of the literature that should be included in the internal bulletin. To push this coverage well above the 90% level will require the use of more general published sources. The team members who scan the core journals for articles of interest should also scan appropriate indexing/abstracting services in printed form. This should reveal other relevant items—e.g., from sources not subscribed to directly. A comprehensive science source such as *Chemical Abstracts* is particularly useful in the location of more obscure items of potential interest.

The question may be raised as to why, in 2003, one would scan secondary services in printed form rather than performing regular online searches in the appropriate databases. This would be the preferred mode of operation for an organization whose interests are clearly circumscribed and can be expressed rather comprehensively in a search strategy. But some organizations may have such a diversity of heterogeneous concerns that it becomes very difficult to locate items of potential interest except by the browsing of broad sections of published sources. Moreover, serendipity can play an important role here: a good information specialist can identify items of relevance to a company that may fall outside its interest profile—e.g., a potential new application for a company product.

Anyway, the inhouse bulletin should be compiled by the scanning of both primary and secondary sources, the latter complementing the coverage of the former. In a large information center the team responsible for scanning the literature might include some individuals whose main task is to scan foreign materials, prepare English abstracts, and undertake complete translations when items are judged of sufficient importance.

As to abstracting itself, the individuals responsible can save a lot of time by marking up the text of the item so that input can be made directly from the publication. In some cases it will be possible to use author abstracts directly, or the author abstract may require some alteration—editing or augmentation. In other cases, a perfectly good "abstract" can be prepared by extracting portions of the text—perhaps from the summary or conclusions section. Of course, there will always be some items for which original abstracts must be prepared—because no good abstract exists, extraction is inadequate, or some aspect of great interest to the company, but of minor interest to the author, needs to be given emphasis.

Abstracts prepared for internal use can be disseminated in several ways. Most obviously, a duplicated bulletin can be issued on a regular basis. Since this can be considered an intelligence tool of major importance to the company, it should be issued weekly if at all possible. The abstracts should be organized into sections that remain more or less the same from week to week to facilitate scanning. An analytical contents page, showing section and subsection breakdown, should be included. A bulletin of this type might contain in the range of 80 to 150 abstracts. Each abstract should be given a unique number for identification and ordering purposes. Included in the bulletin should be a form to allow recipients to place orders for items abstracted.

The abstracts bulletin will go out on a distribution list. For certain key individuals in the organization the information center may go one step further, attaching a memorandum to the front of the bulletin to draw attention to items that may be particularly relevant to each recipient's interests. The standard form can be worded somewhat as follows: "If you have time to look at only a few items, the following will probably be of particular interest."

One alternative to the bulletin per se, of course, is to disseminate the abstracts as discrete items. This implies that the disseminators have a clear and comprehensive picture of individual interests—so that each individual receives only items likely to be pertinent—or that some computer program is used to match characteristics of the abstracts with individual interest profiles.

The distribution of separate abstracts is not really recommended. It requires a lot more work on the part of the information center and eliminates the possibility of browsing. A well-organized bulletin is a more effective dissemination tool. The highlighting of selected items in the bulletin to save the time of key individuals is an effective substitute for the dissemination of separate abstracts.

In creating an inhouse bulletin, of course, the information center is building a database. Moreover, it is a database that should be of great potential value to the organization. It should be accessible online within the company in a form amenable to effective searching. Each abstract can be indexed (by the same individuals who prepare the abstracts), the text of the abstracts can be searchable, or the retrieval system can operate on a combination of index terms and text expressions.

Of course, the enterprise's own intranet can be used to disseminate abstracts electronically to individuals and/or to make the complete bulletin accessible for online browsing. Nevertheless, there is still much to be said for the browsing value of a bulletin distributed in some paper form.

Subject Slanting

Subject slanting was referred to in the previous chapter. Where an abstracting publication is designed for use by a group of individuals with clearly defined and specialized interests (as would be true for an inhouse bulletin), it is clearly desirable that each abstract be tailored to the precise interests of the group. This was recognized in the modular content analyses project (Lancaster et al., 1965), as described in Chapter 7. To make these analyses of maximum use to a diverse group of secondary services, it was proposed that they should incorporate "subject modules." A content analysis would include a "basic" abstract plus supplementary paragraphs, each of these tailored to the interests of a particular group. The index entries supplied would also reflect this diversity of interests. Appendix 2 illustrates the approach: the basic abstract on flame impingement is supplemented by paragraphs relating the work to interests in physiology and medicine, the plastics industry, the rubber industry, and the protective clothing and aircraft industries.

CHAPTER 9

Evaluation Aspects

THE SUBJECT OF EVALUATION is treated in several chapters of this book. For example, Chapter 1 touches upon criteria for evaluating the results of searches performed in a database, while Chapter 6 deals with the quality of indexing and the criteria by which quality may be judged.

Indexing and abstracting are not activities that should be looked upon as ends in themselves. It is the results of these activities that should be evaluated and this can only be done within the context of a particular database, whether in printed or electronic form. In this context, the indexing can be judged successful if it allows searchers to locate items they want without having to look at many they do not want. Abstracts are successful if they correctly predict which documents will be useful to a searcher and which will not, or if they are useful as document substitutes in text searching.

A bibliographic database cannot be evaluated in isolation but only in terms of its value in responding to various information needs. In relation to a particular information need, a database can be evaluated according to four principal criteria:

1. *Coverage*. How much of the literature on a topic, published within a particular time period, is included in the database?
2. *Retrievability*. How much of the literature on the topic, included in the database, can be found using "reasonable" search strategies?
3. *Predictability*. Using information in the database, how well can a user judge which items will be useful and which not?
4. *Timeliness*. Are recently published items retrievable or do indexing/abstracting delays lead to a situation in which items retrieved represent "old" rather than "new" research results?

Coverage

Evaluating the *coverage* of a database is very similar to evaluating the completeness of the collection of a library on some topic. Indeed, the collection of books in a library is itself a database, as is the catalog of the library—one a database of artifacts and the other of representations of these artifacts.

One way to evaluate the coverage of a library's collection on some subject is to find reliable bibliographies on the subject and to check these against the collection. This technique can also be used to evaluate the coverage of indexing/abstracting services. Martyn (1967) and Martyn and Slater (1964) have illustrated the use of this method. Suppose, for example, that you want to evaluate the coverage of *Index Medicus* on the subject of feline leukemia. If you are lucky, you might find a bibliography that looks or claims to be comprehensive on this subject for some period. In this case, the task is easy: entries in the bibliography are checked against the author index to *Index Medicus* to determine which items are included and which not. As a result of this one might conclude that *Index Medicus* covers, say, 84% or so of the literature on this subject. Of course, one needs to know something about the policies of the database being evaluated—e.g., that *Index Medicus* is devoted almost exclusively to periodical articles and includes no monographs.

This technique is not without its problems. In the first place, comprehensive bibliographies are not that easy to find. Moreover, one may know nothing about how a bibliography was compiled. If the feline leukemia bibliography were compiled primarily from the use of *Index Medicus* (or its electronic equivalent) it would be of very little use in evaluating this tool.

The fact is, of course, that we do not really need a comprehensive bibliography in order to estimate the coverage of a database on some subject; all we need is a representative sample of items. One way of obtaining such a sample is to use one database as a source of items through which to evaluate the coverage of another. For example, suppose one wanted to know how complete is the coverage of the *Engineering Index* on the subject of superconductors. One might go to *Physics Abstracts* to identify, say, 200 items that this service has indexed under "superconductors" or "superconductivity" and use this set to estimate the coverage of the *Engineering Index*. After checking these against the author indexes of *Engineering Index* one might find that 142/200 are included there, giving us a coverage estimate of 71%. The fact that the 200 items are not *all* the items published on superconductors is not important; it is, in some sense, a "representative" set of superconductor items and may be a perfectly legitimate sample to use in the estimation of coverage.

Clearly, it would be possible to go in the reverse direction, using items drawn from the *Engineering Index* to assess the coverage of *Physics Abstracts*. In this way one can also determine overlap and uniqueness in two (or more) services, as represented in the diagram at the end of this paragraph. These results might be achieved by drawing a random sample of superconductor items from *A* and checking them against *B* and drawing a random sample of superconductor items from B and checking them against A. Such samples would allow us to estimate A's coverage (181/200, or about 90% in the hypothesized example), B's coverage (168/200, or about 84%), the overlap between the services (149/200, or about 75%), and the uniqueness (about 16% of the items included by A, that is 32/200, appear in that service only while the comparable figure for B is a little below 10% (19/200)). The same kind of results could be achieved, and in some ways more easily, if we could draw a sample from a third source, C, to estimate the coverage, overlap, and uniqueness of A and B.

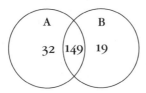

In the above discussion the evaluation of a database in printed form was assumed. The procedures would not differ significantly were they applied to one in electronic form. It is tedious, of course, to enter perhaps hundreds of author names in order to determine the coverage of some online source. The solution to this problem is to first perform a broad subject search (needed anyway if one wants to determine retrievability—see later) and then do supplementary searches by author. Using the same example, one could draw a sample of items indexed under *superconductors* or *superconductivity* from the INSPEC database in order to evaluate the coverage of this topic in COMPENDEX. The first step would be to search COMPENDEX on the superconductor terms to see how many of the sample items were retrieved. The next step would be to perform author searches to determine whether or not the other sample items appear in COMPENDEX and, if they do, discover how they were indexed.

There is a possible problem associated with drawing a sample of items from one database to evaluate the coverage of another. In some cases a database in printed form will index items only under the terms considered "most important." This is true for *Index Medicus*, for example, so items indexed under the term *feline leukemia virus* there will only be those dealing centrally with the subject and not those dealing with it peripherally. In using a sample drawn from *Index Medicus* to evaluate some other service, then, we must recognize that the estimate of coverage for this service relates only to coverage of journal articles dealing "centrally" with the topic. If we draw our sample from the MEDLINE database (essentially the electronic equivalent of *Index Medicus*), on the other hand, this problem will not arise since an index term such as *feline leukemia virus* may be used there to refer to this subject when treated peripherally as well as when treated centrally. In certain printed indexes, too, no distinction is made between "major" and "minor" terms. For example, a subject sample could be drawn from one of the *Excerpta Medica* indexes with a reasonable expectation that the items chosen would include some in which the subject is dealt with less than centrally.

Obviously, in drawing samples from one indexing/abstracting service to evaluate another, one must take into account publication dates. For instance, one might draw a sample of items included in *Excerpta Medica* in the year 1997. If using this to evaluate the coverage of *Index Medicus* one would presumably check the author indexes for 1997 first. Any items not found there should be checked against 1998 (and even perhaps later) or 1996 (and even, in some cases, earlier) to account for the fact that the National Library of Medicine will not necessarily have indexed things in the same time frame used by the Excerpta Medica Foundation. In doing this, of course, one might get some idea of the relative timeliness of the two tools. The topic of timeliness is discussed later in the chapter.

There is another source that can be used to assess the coverage of a database: the bibliographic references that appear in journal articles. To return to the example already used, suppose that we can identify a number of recently published articles, appearing in scholarly journals, that deal with feline leukemia. The bibliographic references included in these papers can be used to form a bibliography that could be applied to assess the coverage of *Index Medicus* or one of the *Excerpta Medica* indexes.

There is one obvious difference between using items from bibliographies on feline leukemia (or items indexed under this term in some bibliographic tool) and using bibliographic references from journal articles: the former, presumably, are items dealing with feline leukemia per se while the latter are the sources needed by researchers working in the area of feline leukemia. The latter sources can be expected to extend well beyond the specific subject and, indeed, may encompass a broad area of the biological sciences and perhaps even other fields. The evaluator may choose to exclude any items that seem peripheral to the topic of the evaluation or may include them on the grounds that a bibliographic tool useful to investigators on this subject should provide access to all related materials needed to support their research.

In the evaluation of a database that restricts itself almost completely to journal articles (as is the case with *Index Medicus*) one could take an obvious shortcut to arriving at an estimate of coverage. Having drawn a sample from some other source, or sources, one could identify the journal articles and then simply check to see if these journals are routinely covered in *Index Medicus*. In all probability this would give an acceptable estimate of coverage. If one wanted to be more precise, however, the sample items (or at least a subset picked at random) should be checked by author to account for the fact that some journals may be indexed only selectively and that some articles (and perhaps even complete issues of some journals) that should have been indexed were not indexed for some reason.* The journal title shortcut is of less use in evaluating the coverage of a database that includes published items of all types and of no use at all in the case of a highly specialized database that attempts to include everything on some topic, from whatever source, and does not restrict itself to a particular set of journals.

There are several possible reasons why an evaluation of coverage might be performed. For example, some information center may want to know if a particular database, say that of *Chemical Abstracts*, covers the center's area of specialization comprehensively or if it would need to draw upon several databases for more complete coverage. The producer of a database, too, may be interested in knowing how well it covers a particular subject area. In this case, it would be important to determine which types of publications are covered well and which less well. To do this one would need to categorize the items covered, and those not covered, by such characteristics as document type, language, place of publication, and journal title.

From these data one could determine how the coverage might be improved in the most cost-effective manner. In considering the coverage of databases it is important to be aware of the phenomenon of *scatter*. This phenomenon works against the highly specialized database, and the highly specialized library or information center, and favors the more general database, library, or center. Consider, for example, a specialized information center on AIDS (acquired immunodeficiency syndrome) that wants to collect the literature on this subject completely and thus to create a comprehensive database. The dimensions of this problem are illustrated in Figures 53-59, based on searches performed in the MEDLINE database in 1988. Figure 53 shows that only 24 journal articles had been published on AIDS up to the end of 1982; by 1987 this literature had grown to 8510 items. In 1982 all the AIDS literature was embraced by three languages but by 1987 there were 25 languages involved and 54 countries contributing to the literature (Figures 54 and 55). Most telling is Figure 56, which shows that the entire

---

*For example, Thorpe (1974), studying the rheumatology literature, got a somewhat different coverage estimate for *Index Medicus* on the basis of journal titles than he did on the basis of journal articles. Brittain and Roberts (1980) also present evidence on the need to study coverage and overlap at the article level.

AIDS literature could be found in only 14 journals in 1982 but by 1987 almost 1200 journals had contributed!

All of these Figures demonstrate the phenomenon of *scatter*. As the literature on some subject grows it becomes increasingly scattered (more countries involved, more languages involved, more journals involved, more document types involved) and thus more difficult to identify, collect, and organize.

Year	Number of items published	Cumulative number of publications
1982	24	24
1983	641	665
1984	1,158	1,823
1985	1,707	3,530
1986	2,117	5,647
1987	2,863	8,510

FIGURE 53
Growth of the scholarly literature on AIDS, 1982-1987.
Source: MEDLINE.

	1982	1983	1984	1985	1986	1987
Number of languages	3	14	21	21	20	23
Cumulative number of languages	3	14	22	25	25	25

FIGURE 54
AIDS literature: coverage by language, 1982-1987.
Source: MEDLINE.

	1982	1983	1984	1985	1986	1987
Number of contributing countries	5	30	38	43	39	42
Cumulation of contributing countries	5	30	39	48	52	54

FIGURE 55
AIDS literature: coverage by country, 1982-1987.
Source: MEDLINE.

The most dramatic aspect of scatter relates to the dispersion of journal articles over journal titles. It was Bradford who first observed this phenomenon in 1934 and the phenomenon is now referred to as Bradford's Law

Year	Number of journals	Cumulative number of journals
1982	14	14
1983	228	234
1984	257	464
1985	492	719
1986	582	952
1987	676	1,170

FIGURE 56

Number of journals that published articles on AIDS, 1982-1987.

(Source: MEDLINE)

No. of journals	No. of articles	Cumulative no. of journals	Cumulative no. of articles	No. of journals	No. of articles	Cumulative no. of journals	Cumulative no. of articles
1	550	1	550	2	29	42	3,954
1	351	2	901	3	28	45	4,038
1	307	3	1,208	5	27	50	4,173
1	303	4	1,511	2	26	52	4,225
1	289	5	1,800	7	25	59	4,400
1	217	6	2,017	3	24	62	4,472
1	200	7	2,217	3	23	65	4,541
1	104	8	2,321	3	22	68	4,607
1	98	9	2,419	2	21	70	4,649
1	97	10	2,516	5	20	75	4,749
1	83	11	2,599	4	19	79	4,825
1	78	12	2,677	7	18	86	4,951
1	70	13	2,747	7	17	93	5,070
2	67	15	2,881	4	16	97	5,134
1	60	16	2,941	7	15	104	5,239
1	59	17	3,000	8	14	112	5,351
1	54	18	3,054	14	13	126	5,533
1	52	19	3,106	12	12	138	5,677
1	49	20	3,155	13	11	151	5,820
1	48	21	3,203	11	10	162	5,930
2	47	23	3,297	15	9	177	6,065
2	46	25	3,389	14	8	194	6,101
2	40	27	3,469	40	7	234	6,481
1	39	28	3,508	42	6	276	6,733
1	36	29	3,544	50	5	326	6,983
2	34	31	3,612	87	4	413	7,331
4	33	35	3,744	117	3	530	7,682
1	32	36	3,776	188	2	718	8,058
4	30	40	3,896	452	1	1,170	8,510

FIGURE 57

Scatter of the journal literature on AIDS in 1987.

Source: MEDLINE.

of Scattering. It is demonstrated clearly in Figure 57, which shows the scatter of periodical articles on AIDS for the period 1982-1987. The top journal on the list contributed 550 papers in a six-year period, the second contributed 351 papers, and the third 307 papers. Note that two journals each contributed 67 papers, two contributed 47 each, and so on down to the bottom of the list where we have 452 journals each of which contributed only a single paper to the AIDS literature in six years. Rather more than a third of the literature is concentrated in as few as 15 journals. To get the next third, however, one needs to add a further 123 journals, while the final third is scattered over more than a thousand additional journals. This distribution provides a dramatic demonstration of the law of diminishing returns. This is revealed even more clearly in Figure 58, which plots the percentage of articles against the percentage of journals contributing. Note that, as one moves up the curve, the scatter of articles over titles increases at an approximately geometric rate: the first third of the articles from 15 journals, the second from 123 journals (15 x 8.2), and the final third from 1008 journals (very roughly 15 x 8.2^2). Such a distribution is typically Bradfordian.

It is clear that an information center establishing a database on the subject of AIDS could not form such a resource on the basis of direct subscriptions to all contributing journals. However, the ranked list of journals contributing (Figure 57) can be used to identify some core of journals that should be worth purchasing and scanning on a regular basis. Figure 59 shows what the top of this list would have looked like based on data from 1982-1987. How far down the ranked list the information center can afford to go will partly depend upon its financial resources. However, even with unlimited resources the center could not acquire all the journals that publish on AIDS. As one goes down the ranked list, the predictability of the journal titles diminishes. Thus, the top ten titles for 1982-1987 may be the top ten for the next five years. Even this is not certain. In the case of AIDS, for example, new journals devoted exclusively to this subject now exist and would presumably appear in the top ten for the period 1987 onwards, perhaps even in the first position. Nevertheless, it is quite likely that all of the journals in Figure 59 will continue to be among the most productive journals on AIDS for some time to come. The journals in the middle of the distribution (i.e., around the middle of the table in Figure 57) are much less predictable—they may continue to publish AIDS-related articles or they may not. Those titles at the bottom of the table are quite unpredictable: a journal that has contributed only one paper on AIDS in five or six years may never contribute another on the subject.

In trying to build a specialized database on AIDS, then, the information center must cover some of this literature by direct subscription—perhaps one hundred or so journals—and identify the other AIDS-related items by regular searches in other databases of wider scope: MEDLINE, BIOSIS, and so on.

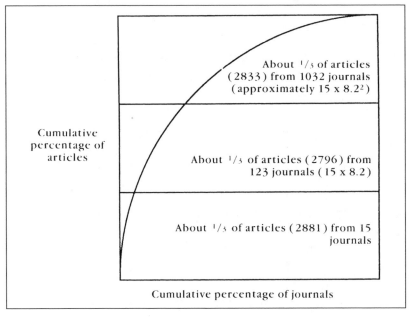

FIGURE 58
Plot of the scatter of the AIDS literature.

Rank	Title	Yield
1	*Lancet*	550
2	*Journal of the American Medical Association*	351
3	*New England Journal of Medicine*	307
4	*Annals of Internal Medicine*	303
5	*Nature*	289
6	*Science*	217
7	*British Medical Journal*	200
8	*MMWR*	104
9	*American Journal of Medicine*	98
10	*Journal of Infectious Diseases*	97

FIGURE 59
Scholarly journals that published the most papers on AIDS, 1982-1987.
Source: MEDLINE.

Martyn (1967) and Martyn and Slater (1964) have performed the "classic" studies of the coverage of indexing/abstracting services, but many other studies of coverage or overlap exist in the literature. For example, Goode et al. (1970) compared the coverage of *Epilepsy Abstracts*, a product of the Excerpta Medica Foundation, with that of *Index Medicus*, while Wilkinson and Hollander (1973) compared the coverage of *Index Medicus* and the *Drug Literature Index*.

Two studies have compared the coverage of *Biological Abstracts, Chemical Abstracts* and *Engineering Index* and their electronic equivalents: Wood et al. (1972) compared the coverage of the three tools in terms of journal titles while Wood et al. (1973) compared them in terms of journal articles selected for coverage.

Probably the largest of overlap studies was one reported by Bearman and Kunberger (1977); it looked at fourteen different services and almost 26,000 journals indexed by them and considered overlap and uniqueness of coverage.

While *Index Medicus* may have been looked at more often than any other tool, the *Bibliography of Agriculture* has been the subject of the most intensive coverage study. In two related reports, Bourne (1969a,b) compared the coverage of this tool with that of fifteen other services and estimated its coverage on specific topics using bibliographies accompanying chapters in annual reviews.

Montgomery (1973) studied the coverage of the literature of toxicology in *Chemical Abstracts, Biological Abstracts, Index Medicus, Excerpta Medica, Chemical Biological Activities* and the *Science Citation Index*. Her study was unusual in that it assembled a set of 1873 references to the toxicology literature (1960-1969) from 221 members of the Society of Toxicology and used these as the basis of her comparison of the various tools.

O'Connor and Meadows (1968) studied the coverage of astronomy in *Physics Abstracts*, Gilchrist (1966) the coverage of the literature of documentation (specifically items on the evaluation of information systems) in six services, and Fridman and Popova (1972) the coverage of experimental primatology in the *Referativnyi Zhurnal*. Brittain and Roberts (1980) focus on overlap in the field of criminology and Robinson and Hu (1981) compare the coverage of databases in the field of energy. Edwards (1976) included coverage as one aspect of his study of indexes in library and information science. La Borie et al. (1985) study the overlap of four secondary services in library/information science, based on journal titles, and compare the titles covered by these services with those covered by six services in the sciences and the social sciences. Other investigators have looked at the coverage of particular types of publications (e.g., Hanson and Janes (1961) investigated the coverage of conference papers in several services and Oppenheim (1974) looked at the *Chemical Abstracts* coverage of patents), or at the coverage of a highly specific topic (e.g., Smalley's (1980) comparison of two databases in their coverage of the literature on operant conditioning).

Coverage studies are less frequent today but a few continue to appear in the literature. Brown et al. (1999), for example, compare coverage of the *Current Index to Journals in Education* with the *Education Index*.

Studies of coverage or overlap are not necessarily mere intellectual exercises. Some are performed with definite goals in mind, most obviously how to improve the coverage of some service. Another purpose might be to identify a "core" of journals in some field, identified by the fact that they are all judged to be worth indexing by several different services. One example of a study of this type is reported by Sekerak (1986), who was able to identify a core list of 45 journals in the field of psychology from a study of overlap among five services in the psychology/health care area.

Retrievability

For someone seeking information on a particular subject, the coverage of a database on that subject will be important, especially if a comprehensive search is required. Also important, of course, is retrievability; given that a database includes n items on a subject (which can be established through a study of coverage) how many of these is it possible to retrieve when searching the database?

This can be tested by a study that is supplementary to an investigation of coverage. Suppose we want to study coverage and retrievability in a variety of subject areas falling within the scope of the AGRICOLA database. For each of ten topics we have a set of bibliographic items (established by one of the methods described earlier) and, for each set, know which items are included in AGRICOLA and which not. For each topic we could have a search performed by an information specialist familiar with AGRICOLA and can judge retrievability on the basis of the proportion of the known items that the searcher is able to retrieve. For example, in the first search, on insects hazardous to soybeans, we know of 80 items on this topic that are included in AGRICOLA. The searcher, however, was able to find only 60 of these, a *recall* (see Chapter 1) of only 75%.

Of course, this type of study is testing more than the database and its indexing; it is also testing the ability of a particular searcher. The effect of this variable can be reduced by having the same search performed independently by several information specialists to determine what results can be expected in a search on this subject *on the average*. The results could also be considered as probabilities: e.g., 50/80 were found by all three searchers (probability of retrieval 1.00), 6/80 by two of the three searchers (probability of retrieval .66), 4/80 by only one of the searchers (probability of retrieval .33), and 20/80 by none of them (probability of retrieval zero).

Note that retrievability (recall) is judged only on the basis of the items known in advance to be relevant to the search topic and to be included in the database. The search on insect pests affecting soybeans may retrieve a total of 200 items, of which, say, 150 seem relevant. If only 60 of the 80 "known relevant" items are retrieved, the recall estimate is .75, implying that the 150 items retrieved represent roughly 75% of the total relevant items in the database.

Of course, the recall ratio relates to only one dimension of the search. To establish a *precision ratio* (see Chapter 1) one would need to have all retrieved items judged for relevance in some way (e.g., by a group of subject specialists). An alternative would be to measure cost-effectiveness by determining the cost per relevant item retrieved. For example, the total cost of an online search (including time of the searcher) might be $75. If 150 relevant items are retrieved, the cost per relevant item is $0.50.

There is an alternative way of studying the retrievability of items from a database; it involves a type of simulation. Suppose we are aware of 80 items relevant to topic X that are included in a database and that we can retrieve and print out records to show how these items were indexed. We can then, as it were, simulate a search by recording the number of items retrievable under various terms or term combinations. A hypothetical example of this is shown in Figure 60. In this case, 38/80 items known to be relevant to the subject of superconductors appear under the term *superconductors*, while a further twelve can be found under *superconductivity*. Additional items cannot be found under these two terms but only under terms *A-J*. One might conclude from an analysis of this type that 50/80 items are easily retrievable and that 62/80 should be found by an intelligent searcher because terms A and B are either closely related to "superconductors" or are explicitly linked to the term *superconductors* by cross references in the database. One might further conclude that 18/80 would probably not be retrieved because they appear only under terms not directly related to "superconductors" (e.g., they may represent applications of the principle of superconductivity).

Albright (1979) undertook a detailed study of this type using *Index Medicus*. Simulated searches, performed for ten different topics, revealed that, on the average, 44 different terms would have to be consulted to retrieve all items known to be relevant to a particular topic. While some of these were linked, through the hierarchical or cross-reference structure of the system vocabulary, many were not so linked and it would be unlikely that even a persistent and ingenious searcher would consult them. Figure 61 shows one exam-

Term	Number of items retrievable
Superconductors	38
Superconductivity	12
A	7
B	5
C	3
D	3
E	3
F	2
G	2
H	2
I	2
J	1
TOTAL	80

FIGURE 60

Hypothetical example of distribution of "superconductor" items
under terms in a printed index.

Term	Number of items retrievable	Cumulative number of items retrievable
LYMPHOCYTES	23	23
B-LYMPHOCYTES	7	30
THYMUS GLAND	6	36
CELL MEMBRANE	2	38
SWINE	2	40
ANTIGENS	1	41
ANTIBODY FORMATION	1	42
HISTOCOMPATIBILITY	1	43
GENES	1	44
ANTILYMPHOCYTE SERUM	1	45

FIGURE 61

Distribution of items on cellular immunology in the pig
under terms in *Index Medicus*.

From Albright (1979) by permission of the author.

ple from Albright's work. It would indeed be a very knowledgeable and persistent searcher who would achieve high recall in a search on this topic in
Index Medicus.

Just as journal articles are scattered over journal titles, items on a topic
included in a database may be scattered over many different terms. This is
represented diagrammatically in Figure 62. It may be that, for any particular topic, a relatively high percentage of the relevant items can be found under

a small number of "obvious" terms (e.g., *superconductors* or *superconductivity* for a search on superconductors). By adding other closely related terms, perhaps linked to these terms in the structure of the vocabulary of the database, recall might be pushed up to, say, 70 to 80 percent. There remains, in this hypothetical case, an elusive 20 to 30 percent of the covered items that the searcher would be unlikely to find.

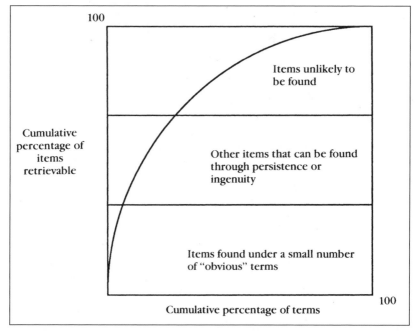

100

Cumulative
percentage of
items
retrievable

Items unlikely to
be found

Other items that can be found
through persistence or
ingenuity

Items found under a small number
of "obvious" terms

100

Cumulative percentage of terms

FIGURE 62
Scatter of items under index terms.

This discussion on simulations has been deliberately simplified in that it has mostly assumed that a search will have only a single facet or, at least, it will be a search performed in a printed index where only one term at a time can be consulted. The simulation of a search in an online database, which will usually involve more than one facet, will be a little more complicated. For example, in a search on insect pests affecting soybeans one would have to assume that an item would be retrieved only if it had been indexed under an "insect" term as well as a term indicating "soybeans."

Albright (1979) has performed the most complete study of retrievability, but using only a single tool, *Index Medicus*, Martyn (1967) and Martyn and Slater (1964) looked at the scatter of relevant material under index terms for several printed services, and Bourne (1969a,b) also looked at scatter in his studies of the *Bibliography of Agriculture*. Carroll (1969) looked at the scatter of the literature of virology in *Biological Abstracts* and found papers on this subject dispersed over 20 sections of this tool beyond those dealing directly with virology. O'Connor and Meadows (1968) found similar scatter of the astronomy literature in *Physics Abstracts*.

Davison and Matthews (1969) looked at retrievability of items on computers in mass spectrometry in eleven services, as well as coverage of these services on this subject. Thorpe (1974) estimated recall and precision for searches on rheumatology in *Index Medicus* and Virgo (1970) used the subject of ophthalmology to compare retrieval from the MEDLARS database with that from its printed product, *Index Medicus*. Jahoda and Stursa (1969) compared the retrieval capabilities of a "single entry" subject index with an index based on keywords in titles, Yerkey (1973) compared the retrieval capabilities of a KWIC index with the *Engineering Index* and the *Business Periodicals Index*, and Farradane and Yates-Mercer (1973) evaluated the *Metals Abstracts Index* by means of simulated searches.

One approach to the evaluation of printed indexes is to use human subjects in the performance of finding tasks. Different indexes can then be compared in terms of success and efficiency (e.g., searching time) in task performance. A study of this kind, comparing different formats for the presentation of printed indexes of the back-of-the-book type, is reported by van der Meij (2002).

Olason (2000) also deals with the usability of printed indexes, restricting her study to book indexes. Her study involved the cooperation of volunteer participants who were given information-seeking tasks requiring use of particular indexes. Times taken to complete the tasks were recorded, as were the access paths used by the participants; their comments were also solicited. Olason focuses primarily on the effects of index format on efficiency of use.

The most thorough studies of retrieval performance in printed indexes have been reported by Keen (1976), using the subject of library and information science. Searches were performed by students and the results were evaluated in terms of recall, precision, and search time. Keen (1977b) has also presented an analysis of search strategy as applied to printed indexes.

Conaway (1974) has developed a single figure of merit for a printed index, the Coefficient of Index Usability (CIU), which reflects how long it takes for a searcher to locate the full bibliographic details for a particular item. A subject search was judged successful if a searcher was able to find an item known in advance to be "relevant" to a given topic. If the item was located, the time taken to find the full bibliographic data was recorded. Using Conaway's methods, numerical scores can be given to different indexes by averaging the results achieved on a number of topics by several searchers. The CIU is essentially a measure of cost-effectiveness. However, it is a very weak one since effectiveness is determined solely on the basis of whether or not a single known item is retrieved. A much better cost-effectiveness measure is the unit cost (in $ or in user time) *per relevant item retrieved*.

Predictability

The discussion on evaluation of retrievability made a major assumption: that it is possible to recognize a "relevant" item from the information on that item contained in a database. This information may comprise:

1. The title of the item
2. Title plus a list of index terms
3. Title plus an abstract
4. Title plus terms plus abstract

In general, the longer the representation the more clues it provides as to whether an item will be of interest to a user or not. The least information provided by a database would be the title of the item. How well the title reflects the subject matter is very largely dependent on the type of publication involved. In general, articles from scholarly journals tend to have quite descriptive titles while, at the other extreme, newspaper articles may have titles that are cute or eye-catching but not very descriptive of their contents. Technical or trade publications also tend toward the cute title: the *Journal of Metals* may have very descriptive titles while *Iron Age* is less likely to.

Titles are not provided in isolation, of course. In a printed index, for example, the title may be considered within the context of the index term under which the title appears. The title "A rare complication of tuberculosis" tells us little about the contents of an article, even if it appears under the heading *tuberculosis, pulmonary*. If this title appears under the subject heading *amyloidosis*, however, one has a much better idea of what it deals with. In some cases, too, a clue to the subject matter may be provided by the title of the journal (or book) in which an article appears. Thus, an article entitled "Effects on the presentation of information" has little meaning on its own. Within a book entitled "Electronic Publishing," on the other hand, the title is much more predictive of its content.

It is somewhat rare for a printed index to include a complete list of the index terms associated with an item (although the *Excerpta Medica* indexes do so) but it is usually possible to generate such a list in a printout from an online database in which human indexing has been employed. The combination of title and index terms may be quite powerful in indicating what a publication is about.

Abstracts, of course, should be the best indicators of content. How well they perform as predictors is the major criterion by which their quality can be judged.

To test the value of various forms of document surrogate as indicators of content requires that one present to users of a retrieval system (or to individuals substituting for such users under experimental conditions) various document representations of increasing length. For example, suppose a search in a database has retrieved 30 records. Representations of these items could be submitted to the requester of the search in a sequence of increasing length of record, with the results shown at the end of this paragraph. In this hypothetical situation the requester, on viewing the full text of the journal articles, judges 14 to be relevant and 16 not. His predictions of relevance got better as the length of the document representation increased, although the addition of index terms to abstract did not differ from use of the abstract alone. Even the best surrogate (title plus abstract) was not perfect; it underrepresented the relevant items and overrepresented the irrelevant ones.

Record presented	Items presented	Items judged clearly irrelevant	Items judged relevant or possibly relevant
Title of article	30	12	18
Title of article plus title of journal	30	13	17
Title of article (and journal) plus list of index terms	30	15	15
Title of article (and journal) plus abstract	30	18	12
Title of article (and journal) plus abstract and index terms	30	18	12
Full text of articles	30	16	14

Investigations of effect of document surrogates on relevance predictability have been performed by several investigators, including Rath et al. (1961a), Resnick (1961), Kent et al. (1967), Dym (1967), Shirey and Kurfeerst (1967), Saracevic (1969), Marcus et al. (1971), and Keen (1976). Marcus et al. showed clearly that the "indicativity" of a document surrogate is directly related to its length in number of words. On the other hand, there may well be an optimum length beyond which it is uneconomical to go, at least for purposes of predictability. Hagerty (1967), for example, found that, while the length of an abstract improved relevance predictions, the effect of increasing the length was surprisingly slight.

Investigations of the value of abstracts in predicting the relevance of documents generally assume that the abstract is separate from the document, appearing in a printed abstracting service or in the output of a retrieval operation. Thompson (1973), however, looked at the use and value of abstracts accompanying documents (at the head of journal articles or at the beginning of technical reports). He gathered data on disposition decisions made by engineers and scientists, at three military laboratories, for documents crossing their desks in the normal course of events over a four week period. He was not able to confirm that disposition decisions for documents having abstracts were made more rapidly than decisions made for those without abstracts. Moreover, when the subjects of the experiment were given copies of the document again, at a later time, for "deliberate re-examination," their earlier relevance decisions for documents having abstracts were no more likely to agree with the later, more deliberate decisions than was true for the documents without abstracts. These results do not cast doubt on the value of abstracts per se, or even on the value of abstracts accompanying articles or reports (since these are frequently adopted or modified by secondary services), but they do suggest that abstracts may have limited use in initial screening decisions. Many recipients of publications may prefer to judge their relevance to current interests by glancing through the text, looking at tables or figures, or even checking the bibliographic references (e.g., to see if they themselves have been cited!).

The quality of abstracts per se is discussed in Chapter 8, while the subject of automatic abstracting is dealt with in Chapter 15.

In a more recent study, Salton et al. (1997) compare summaries of complex documents prepared automatically on the basis of paragraph extraction with a similar paragraph extraction procedure applied by humans. They justify the automatic approach on the grounds that an automatically prepared summary is as likely to agree with a humanly prepared one as a summary prepared by one human is to agree with a summary prepared by another.

Similar procedures have been used for the evaluation of translations prepared automatically or by humans. Brew and Thompson (1994), for example, argue that "good translations will tend to be more similar to each other than will bad ones."

Timeliness

Timeliness or "currency" is a measure of the speed with which new publications are listed in an indexing/abstracting service. It is a criterion that is immediately visible to users, because the date of publication of a printed index is known and the date (or at least the year) of first publication of each item included is part of the bibliographic reference for that item. Timeliness is less apparent to users of online systems but is still perceptible.

This visibility is unfortunate, because it usually leads to invalid conclusions. One human tendency is to note exceptional cases, and another tendency is to give expectations undue weight in making a judgment. A user of a printed volume of abstracts may scan a number of references. On observing that some of them refer to material published perhaps two or three years earlier, the user may unjustifiably conclude that the service is generally very slow in identifying and processing new items.

There are many reasons why inclusion of an item in a database may be delayed. The interval between publication of a journal and its receipt by the secondary service may be long for geographical or economic reasons; for example, a U.S. service may receive U.S. journals through the mails a day or so after publication, but foreign journals may take six or seven weeks to arrive. Some classes of material, such as conference proceedings, are difficult to locate and, once located, may be difficult to acquire. Documents in some languages may require longer-than-average processing times because of a shortage of qualified translators. "Fringe" material, which usually means material published in journals or other publications not routinely scanned by the service, takes longer to locate than core material, because it is often identified by scanning other secondary services and therefore suffers a double set of processing delays. Some services have faster processing systems than others, and some delays are attributable to system inefficiency. When an indexing/abstracting service is used for current awareness, the judgment of users may be influenced by the number of items in the latest issue of which they are already aware. The presence of some known items tends to promote confidence in the reliability of the service but too many erode confidence in its timeliness.

From the evaluator's point of view, timeliness has great charm as a criterion of effectiveness. Timeliness is relatively easy to measure and is incontrovertible when measured, because it does not depend on subjective judgments. The only influence the evaluator exerts on the measure is in the choice of which dates to use. For printed databases, date of appearance of the reference is normally taken as the date of publication of the service. For an online service, the date should be that on which the reference is entered into the database, but this date cannot always be ascertained retrospectively. A possible solution is to determine from the publisher the interval between release of the update for the electronic database and its equivalent printed version, and to adjust the measurements accordingly. For date of appearance of the primary publication to which the secondary service refers, the evaluator can choose between the date of actual publication and the date of availability.

Actual publication date presents some problems, because it is seldom given exactly in secondary services. One may have to refer to a copy of the publication, and, in most cases, the date is given only to the nearest month. The actual day of publication may be found only by asking the publisher. Unfortunately, the date on a journal cover is not always reliable, some journals being published in the month preceding the nominal month of issue, most appearing later than the nominal date of issue.

The availability date is, in some countries, a trouble-free alternative. Although the availability date does not truly measure timeliness of a service, it provides a measure of the effective timeliness from the viewpoint of users in the country in which availability dates are taken. Journal availability dates in the U.S.A. could be taken as the dates of receipt at the Library of Congress or one of the other national libraries. These dates may be stamped on the journal covers or would likely be available in some check-in record maintained by the library. The lag between availability of a journal in the United States and notification of its existence by some secondary service can thus be measured. Strictly, the availability date of the secondary service should be taken rather than its publication date, but there is seldom a large difference. The update of the electronic database will usually occur before the printed index to which it relates.

Data collection entails drawing a random sample of items from the latest issue of some secondary service, noting the date of publication (or update) of the service, and adding to this, usually from a different source, the original publication or availability data. If, as is often desirable, breakdowns by language, country of origin, and form of publication (e.g., journal article, thesis, or monograph) are required, sample sizes will have to be larger than would be true if only an overall estimate of timeliness is desired.

Timeliness is probably the most easily measured characteristic of a secondary service. It is also probably the least important. Publishers may be concerned with timeliness as a measure of the effectiveness of their activities, but users, although often expressing a desire for speed in service, may be less affected. When the interval between the performance of a piece of research and its first publication is taken into consideration, the additional delay of using a secondary service to locate the research is relatively insignificant.

Standards

In theory, an obvious approach to the evaluation of indexes and abstracts is to compare them with published standards. The relevant standards for the English-speaking world are:

> ANSI/NISO Z39.14-1997 *Guidelines for abstracts* (reissued 2002)
> ANSI/Z39.4-1984 *Basic criteria for indexes*
> ISO 999 : 1996 *Guidelines for the content, organization, and presentation of indexes*
> ISO 5963-1985 (E) *Methods for examining documents, determining their subjects, and selecting indexing terms*

BS 3700 : 1988 *Preparing indexes to books, periodicals, and other
documents*
BS 6529 : 1984 *Examining documents, determining their subjects,
and selecting indexing terms*

Note that these standards tend to focus on the product rather than the process: indexes and abstracts rather than indexing and abstracting. Only the ISO 5963 and BS 6529 address the process. Because they look at the most difficult aspect of indexing, deciding what the "indexable matter" of a document really is, they are in many ways the most useful of all the standards dealing with content analysis of documents.

In point of fact, of course, while these various publications are issued by standards organizations, one can hardly consider them as true standards. A true standard should be exact (e.g., one for the composition of an alloy) and enforceable (e.g., one that specifies that a particular steel must have a tensile strength of x). Clearly, indexing and abstracting are activities that are neither exact nor enforceable (except under very limited conditions such as requirements that might be imposed by the editors of a particular journal). The inexactness and obvious subjectivity of indexing is well demonstrated by the fact that the NISO Standards Development Committee, charged with revising ANSI Z39.4, could not reach agreement on a standard and thus could only issue a report "to serve as a current resource on indexing" (*Guidelines for Indexes*, 1997). Consequently, this report simply receives a report number and not an official Z39 standards designation. It is difficult to understand such hairsplitting since, as mentioned earlier, true standards cannot (and probably should not) be imposed on intellectual activities, and most of the "standards" call themselves something else anyway ("guidelines" or "criteria"). Call them what you will, these standards are not precise enough to use in the evaluation of indexes or abstracts, or indexing and abstracting, except at the most superficial level. Moreover, the indexing standards focus primarily on printed indexes in general and back-of-the-book indexes in particular.

Other Evaluation Aspects

Various other approaches have been employed to look at the performance and use of printed indexes. For example, Torr et al. (1966) describe four methods that can be used to "observe" index users: (1) have users keep a written record of their thought processes and strategy in performing a search, (2) have the searcher use a tape recorder for the same purpose,* (3) have an observer accompany the searcher, and (4) use a combination of human

---

*Keen (1977b) has also used this technique.

observation and a camera to study index use. These investigators found it difficult to get "real users" to cooperate in such studies, which was also the experience of Hall (1972).

Other investigators have used interviews or questionnaires to solicit the opinions of users concerning various indexing/abstracting services, including Hall (1972a,b), Keen (1976), Drage (1969) and Cluley (1968).

In considering retrievability, this chapter has focused more on printed indexing and abstracting services than on retrieval from electronic databases. This partly reflects the focus of the present book: indexing and abstracting rather than other aspects of information retrieval. Clearly, methods used to study coverage, predictability, and timeliness are relevant to all types of databases, printed or electronic. Coverage studies and timeliness studies are completely objective, predictability studies somewhat less so. Studies of retrievability are inherently subjective in that they are dependent on human decisions regarding which items are relevant (or pertinent)* and which not. In studying retrieval effectiveness, one needs to use a measure reflecting the proportion of the relevant items that are retrieved in a search (recall ratio) as well as some measure of the *cost* of retrieving this much of the relevant literature. The precision ratio is commonly used as an indirect measure of the cost since it reflects the number of items that a user must somehow look at in order to identify n useful ones. Another indirect measure of cost is the expected search length, as described by Cooper (1968). Of course, cost can be measured in a more direct way by taking all costs of a search, including the time of the searcher and costs of database access, into account (see, for example, Elchesen, 1978). The cost of the search can then be related to the number of relevant (or pertinent or useful or "new") items retrieved; the "cost per relevant reference retrieved" is a good measure of the cost-effectiveness of a search.

Effectiveness measures such as recall and precision (or others as described, for example, by Robertson, 1969) are applicable to studies of retrieval from any type of database, whether in printed or electronic form. However, when we study retrieval effectiveness it is quite difficult to isolate the effects of indexing/abstracting from other factors such as the vocabulary of the database, the search strategies used, and the user/system interaction. This was touched upon in Chapter 6. A detailed account of evaluation methodology (measurement of precision, estimation of recall, diagnostic analysis to determine the precise causes of recall and precision failures) is

---

*The relevance/pertinence issue has been discussed by many writers. See, for example, Wilson (1973), Swanson (1986), Lancaster and Warner (1993), and Mizzaro (1998).

outside the scope of this book. The subject is fully treated in Lancaster and Warner (1993).

Evaluations of printed indexing/abstracting services, or their electronic equivalents, are less common today than they once were, partly because more attention is now devoted to Web-related studies (e.g., evaluations of search engines or Web sites). Nevertheless, a few evaluations do still appear. Examples include Brown et al. (1999), who compare the coverage of the *Current Index to Journals in Education* with the *Education Index*. Brettle (2001) compared different databases on their coverage of information on the rehabilitation of people with severe mental illness and Green (2001) included coverage (along with timeliness) in an evaluation of music periodical databases. Both concluded that multiple databases were needed for an adequate coverage of these subjects.

Azgaldov (1969) has identified a number of criteria that can be used for assessing the quality of printed indexes. These are: *adequacy* (which covers a whole host of properties, including coverage, characteristics of the vocabulary used in indexing, and such indexing factors as exhaustivity and consistency), *generality* (which relates primarily to the diversity of searches that can be performed), *ergonomicity* (ease of use), *currency* (how up-to-date the tool is), and *cost*. He points out, quite correctly, that:

> The most efficient printed index will be a failure with the users if its convenience parameter [ergonomicity and currency] is low, and vice versa, an index that is simple and easy to use will gain wide popularity even if its retrieval performance is not very high. (Page 281)

This quotation provides a good lead-in to Chapter 10, which looks at the characteristics of various printed indexing and abstracting services.

Approaches Used in Printed Indexing and Abstracting Services

THE PURPOSE OF THIS CHAPTER is to illustrate various approaches to the implementation of indexing and abstracting services in printed form. In particular, it looks at printed databases in terms of their properties as tools for information retrieval.*

Basically, two major approaches to the organization of such tools can be identified. In one, entries appear under relatively specific subject headings or descriptors arranged in alphabetical order. Entries may be duplicated under more than one heading and/or cross references can be used to link related headings. In this approach no subject index is needed but other types, most obviously author indexes, will be required.

In the other major approach, some form of classification is used: entries can be arranged under highly specific class numbers or grouped under relatively broad subject categories (possibly with subcategories). In either case, subject indexes are needed to allow alternative approaches or more specific access to the subject matter.

Alphabetico-Specific Indexes

One of the best examples of this approach is the monthly *Index Medicus* and its cumulation, *Cumulated Index Medicus* (Figure 63). Various characteristics of this index are worth attention:

1. Note how subheadings are used to give greater specificity.
2. No abstracts are provided so that it is feasible to duplicate the bibliographic reference under more than one heading. For example, the first entry under the subheading *administration & dosage* (Figure 63) would presumably be duplicated under *osteoarthritis*.
3. The combination of heading, subheading and article title usually gives a fairly clear picture of what an item deals with.
4. Two types of cross-reference appear in the printed index: *see* is used to link terms considered synonymous or almost synonymous and *see related*

---

*In point of fact, these printed tools are much less used today than they were when the earlier editions of this book were published. Many libraries have cancelled subscriptions to printed versions in favor of online access and, in some cases, the printed versions, or parts of them, have been discontinued by publishers.

to link closely related terms. To get a complete picture of the network of associations among the terms used, however, it is necessary to consult two other tools: *Medical Subject Headings* (MeSH) and the *MeSH Tree Structures.* Figure 64 shows a sample page from *MeSH*. Note how *MeSH* displays the *see* reference (and its reciprocal *X*) as well as *see related* references (reciprocal *XR*) used to link two semantically related terms, usually from different hierarchies. More importantly, perhaps, each heading in *MeSH* is given one or more class numbers to indicate where it appears in the hierarchical tree structures (Figure 65). Thus, while the vocabulary used by the National Library of Medicine is quite rich in associations, *Index Medicus* is not self-contained in that the associations are not displayed there. Consequently, it is a useful tool in relatively specific searches but difficult to use in broader searches that would require the consultation of many different headings.

Figure 66 shows sample entries from an author index to *Cumulated Index Medicus*. Note that this is completely self-contained in that it is not an index to the subject section. Indeed, for any particular item found in the author index it is frequently quite difficult to determine what subject headings it appears under. Note also that the author index, unlike the subject section, lists all authors of each article and gives the title of the article in its original language (at least for those in the Roman alphabet), not in translation. The *Cumulated Index Medicus* is no longer published but the monthly *Index Medicus* is.

The many printed indexes produced by the H. W. Wilson Co. (of which the *Reader's Guide to Periodical Literature* and *Library Literature* are good examples) are similar in many ways to *Index Medicus* in that they use specific headings with subheadings and incorporate *see* references. (They differ from *Index Medicus* by using rather more *see also* references to link semantically related terms, making it somewhat easier to perform broad searches that might involve several different headings. For example (see Figure 67) a user consulting the term *magnetohydrodynamics* (in the *Applied Science and Technology Index*) is told to look also under *plasma, plasma waves* and *synchrotron radiation.*

The *Engineering Index* also used to arrange entries under specific headings and subheadings and include some *see* and *see also* references. Now, however, it is arranged under descriptors without subheadings (see Figure 68). The major difference between this index and the ones previously illustrated, of course, is that it includes abstracts. Each abstract is given a unique identifying number. The author index, then, is a true index to the subject arrangement, leading from the name of an author to the numbers of the abstracts with which the name is associated. In addition, since many entries will accumulate under the headings in the annual volume, a more specific subject index is also provided. Figure 69 shows sample entries from the sub-

---

CYCLONAMINE see ETHAMSYLATE

CYCLOOXYGENASE see
PROSTAGLANDIN-ENDOPEROXIDE SYNTHASE

CYCLOOXYGENASE INHIBITORS
see related
ANTI-INFLAMMATORY AGENTS,
NON-STEROIDAL

ADMINISTRATION & DOSAGE
Meloxicam in osteoarthritis: a 6-month, double-blind comparison with diclofenac sodium. Hosie J, et al.
Br J Rheumatol 1996 Apr;35 Suppl 1:39-43
Peri-operative administration of rectal diclofenac sodium. The effect on renal function in patients undergoing minor orthopaedic surgery. Irwin MG, et al.
Eur J Anaesthesiol 1995 Jul;12(4):403-6
Transdermal modification of platelet function: an aspirin patch system results in marked suppression of platelet cyclooxygenase. McAdam B, et al.
J Pharmacol Exp Ther 1996 May;277(2):559-64
[What dose of aspirin should be prescribed in patients with coronary disease?] Montalescot G, et al.
Ann Cardiol Angeiol (Paris) 1995 Oct;44(8):469-72 (Eng. Abstr.)   (Fre)

ADVERSE EFFECTS
Tolerability of imidazole salicylate in aspirin-sensitive patients. Senna GE, et al. Allergy Proc 1995 Sep-Oct; 16(5):251-4
Doppler echocardiographic findings of indomethacin-induced occlusion of the fetal ductus arteriosus. Takahashi Y, et al. Am J Perinatol 1996 Jan; 13(1):15-8
Impact of preexisting health conditions on the outcome of an adverse drug reaction alerting program: gastrointestinal disorders before piroxicam and sulindac therapy. Rawson NS. Ann Pharmacother 1995 Jul-Aug;29(7-8):676-80
Abnormally high platelet activity after discontinuation of acetylsalicylic acid treatment. Beving H, et al.
Blood Coagul Fibrinolysis 1996 Jan;7(1):80-4
Effects of free radical scavengers on indomethacin-induced aggravation of gastric ulcer in rats. Naito Y, et al.
Dig Dis Sci 1995 Sep;40(9):2019-21
Effect of ketorolac tromethamine on bleeding and on requirements for analgesia after total knee arthroplasty [letter; comment] Dodenhoff RM.
J Bone Joint Surg Am 1996 Jun;78(6):968. Comment on: J Bone Joint Surg Am 1995 Jul;77(7):998-1002.
Effect of ketorolac tromethamine on bleeding and on requirements for analgesia after total knee arthroplasty [letter; comment] Linville D. J Bone Joint Surg Am 1996 Jun;78(6):967-8. Comment on: J Bone Joint Surg Am 1995 Jul;77(7):998-1002.
NSAIDs, Cox-2 inhibitors, and the gut [letter; comment] [see comments] Bennett A, et al. Lancet 1995 Oct 21; 346(8982):1105. Comment on: Lancet 1995 Aug 26;346(8974):521-2. Comment in: Lancet 1995 Dec 16;346(8990):1629.
NSAIDs, Cox-2 inhibitors, and the gut [letter; comment] Vane JR. Lancet 1995 Oct 21;346(8982):1105-6. Comment on: Lancet 1995 Aug 26;346(8974):521-2.
[Sensitivity to acetylsalicylic acid] Elverland HH.
Tidsskr Nor Laegeforen 1996 Feb 28;116(6):754-6 (22 ref.) (Eng. Abstr.)   (Nor)

CHEMICAL SYNTHESIS
Diarylspiro[2.4]heptenes as orally active, highly selective cyclooxygenase-2 inhibitors: synthesis and structure-activity relationships. Huang HC, et al.
J Med Chem 1996 Jan 5;39(1):253-66
Design, synthesis, and biochemical evaluation of N-substituted maleimides as inhibitors of prostaglandin endoperoxide synthases. Kalgutkar AS, et al.
J Med Chem 1996 Apr 12;39(8):1692-703

CHEMISTRY
Hydroxylamine analogs of 2,6-di-t-butylphenols: dual inhibitors of cyclooxygenase and 5-lipoxygenase or selective 5-lipoxygenase inhibitors. Kramer JB, et al.
Bioorg Med Chem 1995 Apr;3(4):403-10
Involvement of arginine 120, glutamate 524, and tyrosine 355 in the binding of arachidonate and 2-phenylpropionic acid inhibitors to the cyclooxygenase active site of ovine prostaglandin endoperoxide H synthase-1. Bhattacharyya DK, et al. J Biol Chem 1996 Jan 26;271(4):2179-84
A single amino acid difference between cyclooxygenase-1 (COX-1) and -2 (COX-2) reverses the selectivity of COX-2 specific inhibitors. Gierse JK, et al.
J Biol Chem 1996 Jun 28;271(26):15810-4
The structural basis of aspirin activity inferred from the crystal structure of inactivated prostaglandin H2 synthase [see comments] Loll PJ, et al. Nat Struct Biol 1995 Aug; 2(8):637-43. Comment in: Nat Struct Biol 1995 Aug;2(8):605-6.

IMMUNOLOGY
Oral aspirin and ibuprofen increase cytokine-induced synthesis of IL-1 beta and of tumour necrosis factor-alpha ex vivo. Endres S, et al. Immunology 1996 Feb;87(2):264-70

METABOLISM
Indomethacin, esculetin and nordihydroguaiaretic acid modify arachidonate biosynthesis in rat adrenocortical cells. de Gómez Dumm NT, et al.
Acta Physiol Pharmacol Ther Latinoam 1995;45(3):155-64
Tyrosine kinase inhibitors prevent cytokine-induced expression of iNOS and COX-2 by human islets. Corbett JA, et al. Am J Physiol 1996 Jun;270(6 Pt 1):C1581-7
Synthesis and use of iodinated nonsteroidal antiinflammatory drug analogs as crystallographic probes of the prostaglandin H2 synthase cyclooxygenase active site. Loll PJ, et al. Biochemistry 1996 Jun 11;35(23):7330-40
In vivo inhibition profile of cytochrome P450TB (CYP2C9) by (+/-)-fluvastatin. Transon C, et al.
Clin Pharmacol Ther 1995 Oct;58(4):412-7
Reactions of prostaglandin endoperoxide synthase and its compound I with hydroperoxides. Bakovic M, et al.
J Biol Chem 1996 Jan 26;271(4):2048-56
Effects of indomethacin and arachidonic acid on sister chromatid exchange induction by styrene and styrene-7,8-oxide. Lee SH, et al. Mutat Res 1995 Oct; 348(2):93-9

PHARMACOKINETICS
The pharmacokinetic and pharmacodynamic interactions between the 5-lipoxygenase inhibitor zileuton and the cyclo-oxygenase inhibitor naproxen in human volunteers. Awni WM, et al. Clin Pharmacokinet 1995;29 Suppl 2:112-24
Pharmacokinetics and pharmacodynamics of tepoxalin after single oral dose administration to healthy volunteers. Waldman SA, et al. J Clin Pharmacol 1996 May;36(5):462-8

PHARMACOLOGY
Inhaled lysine acetylsalicylate (L-ASA) attenuates histamine-induced bronchoconstriction in asthma. Crimi N, et al. Allergy 1996 Mar;51(3):157-63
Influence of indomethacin on bone turnover related to orthodontic tooth movement in miniature pigs. Giunta D, et al. Am J Orthod Dentofacial Orthop 1995 Oct; 108(4):361-6
High-dose tumor necrosis factor alpha produces an impairment of hamster diaphragm contractility. Attenuation with a prostaglandin inhibitor. Wilcox P, et al. Am J Respir Crit Care Med 1996 May;153(5):1611-5
Effect of flunixin meglumine on endogenous prostaglandin F2 alpha secretion during cloprostenol-induced abortion in mares. Daels PF, et al. Am J Vet Res 1995 Dec; 56(12):1603-10

FIGURE 63
Sample of entries from *Cumulated Index Medicus* (1996).

Receptors, Cyclic AMP
D12.776.543.750.720.700.150   D12.776.543.750.810.150

77

see related
    Cyclic AMP-Dependent Protein Kinases
    Cyclic AMP Receptor Protein
X   cAMP Receptors
X   Cyclic AMP Receptors
XR Cyclic AMP

Receptors, Cytoadhesin
D12.776.543.750.705.408.460+   D24.611.834.408.460+

90

X   Receptors, Extracellular Matrix Glycoprotein
XR Extracellular Matrix Proteins

Receptors, Cytokine
D12.776.543.750.705.852+   D24.611.834.852+

94

X   Cytokine Receptors

Receptors, Cytoplasmic and Nuclear
D12.776.826+

94

see related
    Transcription Factors
X   Cytoplasmic and Nuclear Receptors
X   Cytosolic and Nuclear Receptors
X   Nuclear and Cytoplasmic Receptors

Receptors, delta see Receptors, Opioid, delta

Receptors, delta Opioid see Receptors, Opioid, delta

Receptors, Diazepam see Receptors, GABA–A

Receptors, Diiodotyrosine see Receptors, Thyroid Hormone

Receptors, Dioxin see Receptors, Aryl Hydrocarbon

Receptors, Dopamine
D12.776.543.750.600.300.400+   D12.776.543.750.720.300.300.400+

77

X   Dopamine Receptors
XR Dopamine
Receptors, Dopamine/agonists see Dopamine Agonists
Receptors, Dopamine/antagonists & inhibitors see Dopamine Antagonists

Receptors, Dopamine D1
D12.776.543.750.600.300.400.400   D12.776.543.750.720.300.300.400.400

93; DOPAMINE–D1 RECEPTOR was indexed under RECEPTORS,
DOPAMINE 1982–92
X   Dopamine D1 Receptors

Receptors, Dopamine D2
D12.776.543.750.600.300.400.500   D12.776.543.750.720.300.300.400.500

93; DOPAMINE–D2 RECEPTOR was indexed under RECEPTORS,
DOPAMINE 1982–92
X   Dopamine D2 Receptors

FIGURE 64

Sample of entries from *Medical Subject Headings* (1996).

Leukemia			
Leukemia by Immunologic Marker (Non MeSH)			
Leukemia, B–Cell			
Leukemia, B–Cell, Chronic			
Leukemia, B–Cell, Chronic	C4.557.337.150.125.250	C4.557.337.	
Leukemia, Pre–B–Cell	C4.557.337.150.125.650		
Leukemia, Mixed–Cell	C4.557.337.150.500	C4.557.337.	
Leukemia, Null–Cell	C4.557.337.150.550	C4.557.337.	
Leukemia, T–Cell	C4.557.337.150.800		
Leukemia, T–Cell, Acute	C4.557.337.150.800.100	C4.557.337.	
Leukemia–Lymphoma, T–Cell, Acute,			
HTLV–I–Associated	C4.557.337.150.800.100.300	C2.782.815.	C4.557.337.
		C20.673.483.	
Leukemia, T–Cell, Acute	C4.557.337.150.800.250	C4.557.337.	
Leukemia, T–Cell, HTLV–II–Associated	C4.557.337.150.800.350	C2.782.815.	C4.557.337.
		C20.673.483.	
Leukemia, Experimental	C4.557.337.372	C4.619.531	
Avian Leukosis	C4.557.337.372.216	C2.782.815.	C2.928.120
		C4.619.531.	C4.619.935.
		C4.925.120	C22.131.94
Leukemia L1210	C4.557.337.372.594	C4.619.531.	
Leukemia L5178	C4.557.337.372.602	C4.619.531.	
Leukemia P388	C4.557.337.372.782	C4.619.531.	
Leukemia, Feline	C4.557.337.385	C2.782.815.	C22.180.500
Leukemia, Hairy Cell	C4.557.337.415	C15.604.515.	C20.683.515.
Leukemia, T–Cell, HTLV–II–Associated	C4.557.337.415.700	C2.782.815.	C4.557.337.
		C20.673.483.	
Leukemia, Lymphocytic	C4.557.337.428	C15.604.515.	C20.683.515.
Leukemia, Lymphocytic, Acute	C4.557.337.428.511		
Leukemia, B–Cell, Acute	C4.557.337.428.511.100	C4.557.337.	
Leukemia, CALLA–Positive	C4.557.337.428.511.225		
Leukemia, Lymphocytic, Acute, L1	C4.557.337.428.511.400		
Leukemia, Lymphocytic, Acute, L2	C4.557.337.428.511.410		
Leukemia, Mixed–Cell	C4.557.337.428.511.500	C4.557.337.	
Leukemia, Null–Cell	C4.557.337.428.511.550	C4.557.337.	
Leukemia, T–Cell, Acute	C4.557.337.428.511.800	C4.557.337.	
Leukemia–Lymphoma, T–Cell, Acute,			
HTLV–I–Associated	C4.557.337.428.511.800.300	C2.782.815.	C4.557.337.
		C20.673.483.	
Leukemia, Lymphocytic, Chronic	C4.557.337.428.550		
Leukemia, B–Cell, Chronic	C4.557.337.428.550.250	C4.557.337.	
Leukemia, Prolymphocytic	C4.557.337.428.550.675		
Leukemia, T–Cell, Chronic	C4.557.337.428.550.800	C4.557.337.	
Leukemia, Mast–Cell	C4.557.337.440	C4.557.337.	
Leukemia, Myeloid	C4.557.337.539	C15.378.190.	C15.604.515.
		C20.683.515.	

FIGURE 65

Sample entries from *Medical Subject Headings* Tree Structures (1996).

ject index for 1993. It uses both controlled descriptors (in bold face) and free text terms (in light face). The index refers to the entries in both the annual volume (numbers beginning with A) and the monthly issues (numbers beginning with M). Note how one of the entries of Figure 69 relates to entry 073654 in Figure 68, providing access to this item under the alternative access point *beam plasma interactions.*

Many (but by no means all) of the printed indexes are based on some form of controlled vocabulary—a thesaurus or list of subject headings. The vocabulary used in the *Engineering Index* is the *Engineering Index Thesaurus.* Such controlled vocabularies can be of great value to someone searching the printed index, especially in cases where the index itself includes little cross-reference structure, as is true of *Index Medicus.*

Classified Indexes

There are basically two types of classified index. In one, entries appear under highly specific class numbers derived from a general or special-pur-

Colquhoun J. Dental caries among children in New Zealand [letter; comment] Community Dent Oral Epidemiol 1995 Dec;23(6):381. Comment on: Community Dent Oral Epidemiol 1994 Aug;22(4):226–30.

Colquhoun JP. Heartsink revisited. Aust Fam Physician 1995 Oct;24(10):1964–5

Colquhoun JP. That was the week that was. Aust Fam Physician 1996 Aug;25(8):1333–4

Colquhoun JP. The index theory and the magic of medicine. Aust Fam Physician 1996 Jun;25(6):978–9

Colquhoun K see Mahmood R

Colquhoun KO, Timms S, Fricker CR. Detection of Escherichia coli in potable water using direct impedance technology. J Appl Bacteriol 1995 Dec;79(6):635–9

Colquhoun MC, Waine C, Monaghan MJ, Struthers AD, Mills PG. Investigation in general practice of patients with suspected heart failure. How should the essential echocardiographic service be delivered? [editorial] [see comments] Br Heart J 1995 Oct;74(4):335–6. Comment in: Heart 1996 Jun;75(6):642; discussion 643. Comment in: Heart 1996 Jun;75(6):642–3. Comment in: Heart 1996 Jun;75(6):643. Comment in: Heart 1996 Jun;75(6):643–4.

Colquhoun MC, Waine C, Monaghan MJ, Struthers AD, Mills PG. Investigation in general practice of patients with suspected heart failure: how should the essential echocardiographic service be delivered? [editorial] Br J Gen Pract 1995 Oct;45(399):517–9

Colquhoun S see Swanson C

Colquhoun SD. Hepatitis C. A clinical update. Arch Surg 1996 Jan;131(1):18–23 (49 ref.)

Colquhoun SD see Imagawa DK

Colquhoun–Flannery W, Carruth JA. Diet-modified sex hormone metabolism: is this the way forward in recurrent respiratory papillomatosis and squamous carcinoma prophylaxis? J Laryngol Otol 1995 Sep;109(9):873–5

Colquitt WL, Zeh MC, Killian CD, Cultice JM. Effect of debt on U.S. medical school graduates' preferences for family medicine, general internal medicine, and general pediatrics. Acad Med 1996 Apr;71(4):399–411

Cols Jiménez M see Tuneu Valls L

Colson AM see Brasseur G

Colson AM see Meunier B

Colson C see Hublet C

Colson KL see Zein N

Colson P, Bailly C, Houssier C. Electric linear dichroism as a new tool to study sequence preference in drug binding to DNA. Biophys Chem 1996 Jan 16;58(1–2):125–40

Colson P, Damoiseaux P, Brisbois J, Duvivier E, Levecque P, Roger JM, Bouilliez DJ, McKenna P, Clement J. Epidémie d'hantavirose dans l'Entre-Sambre-et-Meuse: année 1992–1993 Données cliniques et biologiques. Acta Clin Belg 1995;50(4):197–206 (Eng. Abstr.)   **(Fre)**

FIGURE 66

Sample entries from author index to *Cumulated Index Medicus*.

pose classification scheme. This was the method used in *Library and Information Science Abstracts* (LISA) until 1993. In LISA, entries were arranged according to a faceted classification scheme devoted to the special field of library and information science. Figure 70 shows some sample entries relating to CD-ROM. Note how the notation relating to databases in CD-ROM form (*Zjjc*) is subdivided by notations from elsewhere in the classification scheme (*Rn, Vtic*) to give greater specificity, and how an alphabetical label is used to explain each specific notation. Figure 71 shows specimen entries from the alphabetical subject index, including some entries relating to the items shown in Figure 70. Note how the terms used as alphabetical labels in Figure 70 become entry points in the subject index. The principle followed is that of chain indexing (see Chapter 4); each step in the hierarchical chain is indexed from the most specific up to the most general:

Cost-benefit analysis, Information services, Data bases, CD-ROMs, Computerized information storage and retrieval

Information services, Data bases, CD-ROMs, Computerized information storage and retrieval

Data bases, CD-ROMs, Computerized information storage and retrieval

---

Magnetohydrodynamics
See also
Plasma (Physics)
Plasma waves
Synchrotron radiation
Alpha-torque forces. P. Graneau. bibl il diags *Electron Wirel World* 95:556-9 Je '89; Discussion. 95:875-6 S '89
Drop-on-demand operation of continuous jets using EHD techniques. D. W. Hrdina and J. M. Crowley. bibl flow chart diags *IEEE Trans Ind Appl* 25:705-10 Jl/Ag '89
Hydrodynamics of double-charged ions in a plane low-pressure discharge. D. A. Shapiro. bibl *J Phys D* 22:1107-13 Ag 14 '89
Iodine laser creates plasma X-rays. B. Dance. *Laser Focus World* 25:26+ Je '89
The magnetohydrodynamical instability of a current sheet created by plasma flow. A. I. Podgorny. bibl diags *Plasma Phys Control Fusion* 31:1271-9 Jl '89
A personal-computer-based package for interactive assessment of magnetohydrodynamic equilibrium and poloidal field coil design in axisymmetric toroidal geometry. W. P. Kelleher and D. Steiner. bibl diag *Fusion Technol* 15:1507-19 Jl '89
Why Extrap? B. Lehnert. bibl(p38-43) il diags *Fusion Technol* 16:7-43 Ag '89
Mathematical models
Induction electrohydrodynamic pump in a vertical configuration. J. Seyed-Yagoobi and others. bibl diags *J Heat Transf* 111:664-74 Ag '89
Mass transport and the bootstrap current from Ohm's law in steady-state tokamaks. J.-S. Kim and J. M. Greene. bibl *Plasma Phys Control Fusion* 31 no7:1069-94 Je '89
Reduction of thermal expansion in Z-pinches by electron beam assisted magnetic field generation. J. A. Heikkinen and S. J. Karttunen. bibl *Plasma Phys Control Fusion* 31 no7:1035-48 Je '89
Magnetometers
Scanner can detect brain damage. il *Engineer* 269:49 Ag 31-S 7 '89
Design
Electronic balancing of multichannel SQUID magnetometers. H. J. M. ter Brake and others. bibl diags *J Phys E* 22:560-4 Ag '89

FIGURE 67

Sample entries from the *Applied Science and Technology Index*, 1986.

graphite basal planes. A considerable fraction of the He gases desorbs at room temperature, implying that they are relatively mobile inside the lattice. (Author abstract) 32 Refs. English.

Choi, W. (Pohang Inst of Science and Technology, Pohang, SOUTH KOREA); Kim, C.; Kang, H. *Surf Sci* v 281 n 3 Feb 1 1993 p 323-335.

073651   Light scattering as a probe of thermodynamic quantities in a binary mixture. The authors have shown recently how Rayleigh-Brillouin light scattering can be used to extract certain thermodynamic quantities of a binary mixture in an approximate way. An approach which yields exact results is described here, although it requires knowledge of additional thermodynamic data. This information can be obtained either from other experiments or from a thermodynamic model prediction. Since we are dealing with a model system that can be described by a van der Waals equation of state, that model is preferred here. The results for the osmotic compressibility for a He + Xe mixture obtained in this way from the Landau-Placzek ratio are in good agreement with calculations. (Edited author abstract) 27 Refs. English.

Bot, Arjen (FOM, Amsterdam, Neth); Wegdam, Gerard H. *Fluid Phase Equilib* v 77 Sep 15 1992 p 285-295.

073652   Role of the buffer gas in the ArF laser chemical vapour deposition of silicon oxide. Inert gases are commonly used in thin film deposition methods as a diluent of the gas mixture or as a purging gas. However, several workers have determined the influence of the buffer gases on the film growth mechanism which has consequences for the film properties. In this paper, a study of the influence of argon, used as the reactor window purging gas, on the silicon oxide film growth and properties is presented. Films are deposited from silane and nitrous oxide by ArF-laser-induced chemical vapour deposition. By purging the beam entrance window with Ar, not only is window film formation or powder deposition avoided, but also reductions in the H and OH contents and thus better optical properties are achieved. (Author abstract) 28 Refs. English.

Gonzalez, P. (Univ of Vigo, Vigo, Spain); Pou, J.; Fernandez, D.; Garcia, E.; Serra, J.; Leon, B.; Perez-Amor, M. *Thin Solid Films* v 230 n 1 Jul 15 1993 p 35-38.

INERTIAL CONFINEMENT FUSION

073653   Analysis of radiation symmetrization in hohlraum targets. Symmetrization of illumination non-uniformity by thermal radiation in spherical hohlraum targets has been studied systematically for indirectly driven inertial confinement fusion. Numerical calculations have shown that the effect of X-ray re-emission on the illumination uniformity is quasi-linear. On the basis of a linear theory it is found that the non-uniformity of each mode of the X-ray source considerably smoothed out by three different effects. The first is the geometrical effect, which accounts for the configuration and the number of X-ray converters. The second is the effect of single emission, which depends only on the hohlraum structure (area ratio). The third is the effect of multiple re-emission, which is equal to the reciprocal of the average circulation number of radiation in a hohlraum target. The paper gives practical solutions regarding the required number of converters, N_C, in particular for heavy ion fusion systems. It is shown that $N_C = 6$ (hexahedron) is a necessary and sufficient condition to ensure tolerable symmetrical illumination (≤ 1-2% rms). (Author abstract) 19 Refs. English.

Murakami, M. (Inst for Laser Technology, Osaka, Jpn). *Nucl Fusion* v 32 n 10 Oct 1992 p 1715-1724.

073654   Experimental testing of thin-shell stable acceleration for ICF schemes with direct and indirect drive. The present review is of the experimental investigations on laser-plasma interaction being carried out in past years at IAE. Experiments were conducted on the 'Mishen' facility. The laser system of 'Mishen' consists of two channels with output beam

parameters as follows: the main beam-output energy 100-200 J ($\lambda = 1.054$ µm) in 3-ns pulse, divergence approx. 2×10^{-4} rad, contrast ratio approx. 10^6, power density at the target surface approx. 10^{13}-10^{14} W/cm²; the diagnostic beam - output energy 10-20 J ($\lambda = 1.054$ µm) and 5-10 J ($\lambda = 0.53$ µm) in 0.3-ns pulse, divergence approx. 10^{13}-10^{14} W/cm². Our aim in this experiment is to study the different aspects of the ICF processes in flat geometry. The main issues of our studies are hydrodynamic aspects, including acceleration efficiency, high-velocity impact in cascade targets, hydrostability, and X-ray physics-conversion efficiency, heat transfer, and X-ray-driven targets. Refs. English.

Bolotin, V.A. (Branch of Kurchatov Atomic Energy Inst, Moscow, Russia); Burdonsky, I.N.; Velikovich, A.L.; Gavrilov, V.V.; Golberg, S.M.; Goltsov, A.Yu.; Zhuzhukalo, E.V.; Zavjalets, S.V.; Kondrashov, V.N.; Kovalsky, N.G.; Pergament, M.I.; Koshevoi, M.O.; Rupasov, A.A.; Shikanov, A.S. *Laser Part Beams* v 11 n 1 1993 Japan-US Symposium on Physics of High Power Laser Matter Interaction, Kyoto, Jpn, p 127-135.

073655   Heavy-ion-driven targets for small-scale inertial confinement fusion experiments. Two regimes of hydrodynamic evolution are found in the analysis of the performance of small-scale heavy-ion-driven targets. One leads to high density and high compression with moderate temperatures (approximately I keV) for driving energies of 100 kJ for 0.1-mg deuterium-tritium targets. Ignition can then be triggered by a second ion pulse (approximately 50 kJ). Breakeven could be obtained if a burnup fraction as small as 1% is obtained. The second regime leads to very high temperatures in the central part of the fuel, while the rest of the fuel remains at moderate temperatures (<1 KeV), and the density is very low everywhere. Propagated ignition cannot occur in this case because of the small optical thickness of the compressed fuel (<0.1 g/cm²). (Author abstract) 36 Refs. English.

Martinez-Val, Jose M. (Madrid Polytechnic Univ, Madrid, Spain); Piera, Mireia. *Fusion Technol* v 23 n 2 Mar 1993 p 218-226.

073656   High gain DT targets for heavy ion beam fusion. In a parametric study of reactor size DT targets driven by beams of heavy ions it was found that spark ignition and high energy gains can be achieved in four-layer single-shell targets irradiated by a non-shaped box pulse of 10 GeV ^{209}Bi ions. With an input energy of E_{in}=6 MJ delivered in t_m≤10 ns, one-dimensional energy gains of G≥400 are possible in the optimum cases. It is shown that, to obtain spark ignition and high energy gain, two conditions must be necessarily met: (1) a high enough implosion velocity, $U_v \geq 6.2 \times 10^7$ $\Omega^{-1/2}$ cm/s, must be reached, and (2) the fuel compression must be accomplished with a low enough pusher/fuel mass ratio, M_p/M_{DT}≤5-7 (Ω is a dimensionless parameter determined by the density distribution in the compressed target core). It was found also that when the ($\rho\Delta r$) of the cold part of the compressed fuel is ≈2-5 g/cm², the main portion of the fuel is ignited owing to the heating by 14 MeV neutrons emitted from the central hot region. (Author abstract) 36 Refs. English.

Basko, M.M. (Max-Planck-Inst fur Quantenoptik, Munich, Ger). *Nucl Fusion* v 32 n 9 Sep 1992 p 1515-1529.

073657   Low activation structural materials for ICF reactors: differences with MCF environments. Activation calculations considering the neutron flux and spectrum of a first structural wall (FSW) in an inertial confinement fusion reactor (ICF) are performed for all stable elements, using a recently upgraded data base. Surface γ dose rate and waste disposal ratings (WDR) are employed as indices to compare the merit of elements and compute the concentration limits corresponding to hands-on processing, remote recycling and shallow land burial (SLB). The performance of steels, vanadium alloys and silicon carbide as candidate structural materials has also been explored. The materials with less waste/recycling concerns are identified, and the influence that impurities

FIGURE 68

Sample entries from annual volume of *Engineering Index* (1993).

BEAM INTENSITY
Gamma-rays and half-life of ^{157}Pm. A126649 M135315
Improvement in the output characteristics of a large-bore copper vapor laser by hydrogen. A081088 M062316

BEAM IONS
Collisional slowing down of beam ions in non-Maxwellian plasmas. A114673 M009756

BEAM IRRADIANCE
Probability density and autocorrelation of short-term global and beam irradiance. A144826 M024330

BEAM LEAD DEVICES
Fabrication of YBaCuO-Josephson-junctions on MgO-substrates damaged by a focused ion beam prior to film deposition. A010031 M124258
Wideband balanced frequency doublers - a proposed novel planar MIC structure. A058505 M031433

BEAM LIGHTING SYSTEMS
Assessment of beam lighting systems for interior core illumination in multi-story commercial buildings. A036142 M126596

BEAM LOAD PARAMETERS
Equilibrium configurations of cantilever beams subjected to inclined end loads. A010091 M027319

BEAM LOADING
Extended theory of beam loading in electron linac. A082418 M145995

BEAM LOSS MONITOR (BLM)
Beam loss monitor for superconducting accelerators. A110073 M105803

BEAM LOSS RATES
Beam loss rates with an internal gas target in an electron-cooled storage ring. Implications for luminosity optimization. A150352 M121627

BEAM LUMINOSITY
Further results on cerium flouride crystals. A110243 M164229

BEAM MEASURING SYSTEM
Beam measuring system for quality assurance in electron beam welding. A046800 M003927

BEAM MILLS
Designing for maintenance. The Lackenby beam mill. A131819 M149717

BEAM MODE BUCKLING
Beam mode buckling of buried pipelines in a layered medium. A114085 M148540

BEAM MODE STABILITY
Study on beam mode stability of high power CO_2 laser. A015671 M056712

BEAM MODEL
Approximate methods for dynamic response of multi-module floating structures. A103193 M092466

BEAM OPTICS
Beam optics studies transport from USP pelletron exit to linac entrance. A082409 M076422
Selection of charge for the ECR Alice without forming a waist. A077380 M103545

BEAM OPTIMIZATION DISPLACEMENT APPROXIMATIONS
Displacement approximations for optimization of beams defined in nonprincipal coordinate systems. A010076 M000761

BEAM PARAMETERS
Dependence of photorefractive beam fanning on beam parameters. A080600 M130920

BEAM PLASMA
Simulation of water vapour beam plasma. A114793 M164677

BEAM PLASMA DISCHARGES
Kinetics of molecular oxygen $(a^1\Delta_g)$-state formation in beam-plasma discharge. A095477 M063491

BEAM PLASMA INTERACTIONS
Ablation characteristics of material by excimer laser under different gas pressure and species. A000007 M123369
Bandwidth effects on laser-plasma interaction with a 1/4-μm laser. A010032 M111486
Charge distribution and structure of an inhomogeneous plasma, located between two surfaces of opposite charges. A114672 M164682
Collisional redistribution in Hg-Kr. Polarization spectrum of the redistributed light. A010033 M111485
Cooling of atoms in colored vacua. A080492 M116493
Depth profiles of trapped deuterium in nickel bombarded with helium-3. A036978 M086631
Divertor neutral pressure enhancement with a baffle in DIII-D. A159586 M138718
Effect of hydrogen in the CuBr- and CuCl-vapor lasers. A059902 M046432
Electron and ion collisions with water vapour. A010034 M056241
Enhancement of heat transfer from a rarefied plasma flow to thermoemitting particle. A065838 M032120
Excitation of quintet states VII by an electron shock. A010035 M084242
Experimental testing of thin-shell stable acceleration for ICF schemes with direct and indirect drive. A073654 M115971
In-beam tests of proximity mesh dynode tubes for the STAR TOF subsystem. A110256 M118475
Japan-US Seminar on Physics of High Power Laser Matter Interaction. A010036 M111484
Kinetics of molecular oxygen $(a^1\Delta_g)$-state formation in beam-plasma discharge. A095477 M063491
Laser-plasma research at MPQ. A010037 M111487
Neutral beam source design and beam kinetic energy activated SiO_2 etching. A050108 M158013
New model for the floating potential of fine particle in plasma. A114584 M164659
Novel materials synthesis using an intense pulsed ion beam. A077135 M160498
One-dimensional beam stability analysis based on the waterbag model. A110153 M148205
Optical emission spectroscopy of plasma etching of GaAs and InP. A050115 M127880
A plasma diagnostics system in magnetic traps with spatial axis. A114444 M093541
Plasma etching of polysilicon/nitride/polysilicon sandwich structure for sensor applications. A050122 M127881
Spectroscopic system for measurements of turbulent electric fields originating from intense relativistic electron beam-plasma interactions. A010038 M098598
Study of combined NBI and ICRF enhancement of the D-^{3}He fusion yield with a Fokker-Planck code.

FIGURE 69

Sample entries from the subject index to *Engineering Index* (1993).

ZjjcRaNak—CD-ROMs. Data bases. Information services.
Economic aspects   88/5339
   The CD-ROM marketplace: a producer's perspective. Christopher
Pooley. *Wilson Library Bulletin*, 62 (4) Dec 87, 24-26.
   Contribution to a special issue devoted in part to CD-ROM. When
laser disc technology was first introduced to libraries, librarians recognised
the great possibilities of the medium, especially its vast storage capacity.
Examines the major differences between print, on-line and CD-ROM versions
of the same data base which fall in 3 key areas: content, currency or update
frequency, and pricing. Discusses competition in the marketplace and emphas-
ises that the future for CD-ROM in libraries is excellent with more products,
more new products offering combinations of data bases, better software and
networking systems available to stimulate the growing use of CD-ROM products. (A.G.)

ZjjcRaNko—CD-ROMs. Data bases. Information services.
Cost-benefit analysis. PsycLIT   88/5340
   Justifying CD-ROM. Ralph Alberico. *Small Computers in Libraries*, 7
(2) Feb 87, 18-20.
   Considers data bases on CD-ROM in terms of costs and benefits, by
examining PsycLIT, an abbreviated CD-ROM version of the PsycINFO data
base. PsycLIT was one of the first CD-ROM data bases and is one of the
best and one of the most expensive. Compares the CD-ROM version to print
and on-line products and stresses that as the number of users grow prices will
decrease. (P.B.)

ZjjcVtic—CD-ROMs. User-System interface   88/5341
   Entering unchartered territory: putting CD-ROM in place. Nancy
Crane, Tamara Durfee. *Wilson Library Bulletin*, 62 (4) Dec 87, 28-30. illus.
   Contribution to a special issue devoted in part to CD-ROM. Discusses
considerations that need to be raised before implementing end-user CD-ROM

and offers some proposals as to how solutions may be found. These include:
assessing the environment; choice of a CD-ROM system; components needed
in setting up a workstation; vendor services; placement; user constraints; training for searching; statistics and ongoing assessment; effects on staff; and
desired features of CD-ROM services. The rationale for end-user CD-ROM is
presented. (A.G.)

FIGURE 70

Sample entries from *Library and Information Science Abstracts* (before 1993).

Reproduced by permission of the editor.

Computerized information storage and retrieval (this most general entry does not
appear in Figure 71).

PsycLIT (the name of a database) in Figure 70 was not a bona fide index
term in LISA and thus did not generate an entry in the subject index,
although it did generate one in the separate name index.

While LISA employed a special-purpose classification scheme, other
printed indexes have been based on general schemes, the one most commonly used being the *Universal Decimal Classification* (UDC).

In the other classified approach to the organization of a printed database,
entries are grouped under relatively broad subject categories and more specific subject access is provided by means of indexes. The present LISA format is one example. Figure 72 shows the broad subject categories under
which abstracts were organized as of 1997 and Figure 73 shows some sample entries. The subject index is still based on chain indexing procedures
(see Figure 74) although they are no longer tied to a classification scheme.

Chemical Abstracts resembles LISA in that entries are organized under subject categories and subcategories. However, the subject index is quite different, based on the principle of articulation (see Chapter 4): strings of terms assigned by human indexers are manipulated in a standard way to provide a group of consistent access points for each item (Figure 75). While this articulated subject index appears only in the cumulations of *Chemical Abstracts*, a keyword index appears in each weekly issue (see Figure 76). *Chemical Abstracts* also includes an index by chemical formula (see Figure 77).

CD-ROMs
Computerised cataloguing 387
Computerised information storage and retrieval
    422—441, 978—983, 1540—1542,
    2088—2091, 2093, 2612—2617, 3155—3165,
    3669—3674, 4222—4226, 4699—4710,
    5319—5341, 6241—6260
Computerised information storage and retrieval:
    Comparison with On-line information
    retrieval 1570, 4702, 4704, 5321—5322,
    6244—6245
Computerised information storage and retrieval:
    Comparison with On-line information retrieval
    and Printed information services 5323
Computerised union catalogues 5292
Computers 491—494, 1052, 1591, 2653,
    3206—3207, 3765, 4292, 4831—4833, 6434
Computers: Library equipment 205, 1837,
    2391—2392, 3451—3452, 4499, 5067, 5799
Document delivery: On-line information
    retrieval 4825

Cost benefit analysis
Computerised acquisitions 1968
Computerised information work 3025
Information services: Data bases: CD-ROMs:
    Computerised information storage and
    retrieval 5340
Of Business information: Information services:
    Data bases: On-line information retrieval 471
Reference work 2471

Data bases
See also Computerised bibliographic records
CD-ROMs: Computerised information storage
    and retrieval 428—440, 979—983, 1542,
    2089—2091, 2613—2616, 3157—3165,
    3672—3673, 4222—4226, 4703—4710,
    5327—5340, 5344—5345, 6248—6259
CD-ROMs: Computerised information storage
    and retrieval: *Comparison with* On-line
    information retrieval 1570, 4702, 4704,
    5321—5322, 6244—6245
CD-ROMs *and* Videodiscs: Computerised
    information storage and retrieval 2093
Command languages: User-system interface:
    On-line information retrieval 1585
Computerised information storage and retrieval
    419, 2606
Concepts: Computerised subject indexing 5313
Free text searching: On-line information
    retrieval 2136

Full text searching: On-line information
    retrieval 480, 1038, 2640, 3748, 3750—3751
Gateway facilities: On-line information
    retrieval 3704—3705
Hypertext: On-line information retrieval 6417
In-house systems: On-line information retrieval
    6262
Laser optical discs: Computerised information
    storage and retrieval 977, 5318
Laser optical discs: *Use for* Periodicals: Subject
    indexing 2061
Multiple data base searches: On-line
    information retrieval 2643
On-line information retrieval 460—479,
    1019—1036, 1558—1580, 2108—2128, 2623,
    2626—2638, 3182—3195, 3727—3746,
    4256—4279, 4766—4809, 5344, 5357—5370,
    6321—6382

Information services
Data bases: CD-ROMs: *Comparison with*
    On-line information retrieval 4704
Data bases: CD-ROMs: Computerised
    information storage and retrieval 428—440,
    980—983, 1542, 2089—2091, 2613—2616,
    3157—3165, 3672—3673, 4223—4226,
    4703—4710, 5327—5340, 5344—5345,
    6248—6258
Data bases: CD-ROMs *and* Videodiscs:
    Computerised information storage and
    retrieval 2093
Data bases: Command languages: Man-machine
    interface: On-line information retrieval 1585
Data bases: Computerised information storage
    and retrieval 419, 2606
Data bases: Computerised subject indexing
    5313
Data bases: Free text searching: On-line
    information retrieval 2136
Data bases: Full text searching: On-line
    information retrieval 480, 1038, 2640, 3748,
    3750—3751
Data bases: Gateway facilities: On-line
    information retrieval 3704—3705
Data bases: Laser optical discs: Computerised
    information storage and retrieval 977, 5318
Data bases: Laser optical discs: *Use for*
    Periodicals: Subject indexing 2061
Data bases: Multiple data base searches:
    On-line information retrieval 2643
Data bases: On-line information retrieval
    460—479, 1019—1036, 1558—1580,
    2108—2128, 2626—2638, 3182—3195,
    3727—3746, 4256—4279, 4766—4809, 5344,
    5357—5370, 6321—6382

FIGURE 71

Sample entries from the subject index to *Library and Information Science Abstracts* (before 1993).

Reproduced by permission of the editor.

1.0 LIBRARIANSHIP AND INFORMATION SCIENCE
1.1 PUBLICATIONS AND DATABASES
1.11 BOOK REVIEWS
1.12 CONFERENCES
1.13 RESEARCH
1.14 WORLD LIBRARIANSHIP
2.0 PROFESSION
2.1 ORGANIZATIONS
2.11 BIOGRAPHIES
2.12 EDUCATION AND TRAINING
2.13 LIBRARY AND INFORMATION STAFF
2.14 TYPES OF STAFF
3.0 LIBRARIES AND RESOURCE CENTRES
3.1 WORLD LIBRARIES
3.11 NATIONAL LIBRARIES AND STATE LIBRARIES
3.12 PUBLIC LIBRARIES
3.13 ACADEMIC LIBRARIES (NOT SCHOOL LIBRARIES)
3.14 GOVERNMENT LIBRARIES
3.15 LIBRARIES OF OTHER ORGANIZATIONS AND PRIVATE LIBRARIES
3.16 SPECIAL SUBJECT LIBRARIES, RESEARCH LIBRARIES
3.17 SOCIAL SCIENCES, BUSINESS LIBRARIES
3.18 HUMANITIES LIBRARIES
3.19 SCIENCE, TECHNOLOGY, MEDICINE LIBRARIES
3.2 ARCHIVES
3.21 NATIONAL AND GOVERNMENT ARCHIVES
3.22 BUSINESS ARCHIVES
3.23 CHURCH ARCHIVES
3.24 ARCHIVES OF OTHER ORGANIZATIONS AND PRIVATE ARCHIVES
3.25 SOUND AND FILM ARCHIVES
3.26 SPECIAL SUBJECT ARCHIVES
3.27 MUSEUMS
4.0 LIBRARY USE AND USERS
4.1 LIBRARIES AND SERVICES BY TYPES OF USER
4.11 USERS - CHILDREN AND YOUNG PEOPLE
4.12 SCHOOL LIBRARIES
4.13 USERS - SOCIAL GROUPS
4.14 USERS - OCCUPATIONAL GROUPS
4.15 USER SERVICES
4.16 USER TRAINING
4.17 PROMOTION
4.18 ACTIVITIES
4.19 EXHIBITIONS
4.2 DOCUMENT DELIVERY
4.21 INTERLOANS AND PHOTOCOPYING SERVICES
4.22 LOANS
5.0 MATERIALS
5.1 OLD AND RARE MATERIALS
5.11 MATERIALS BY PUBLISHER
5.12 MATERIALS BY LANGUAGE AND GEOGRAPHICAL AREA
5.13 PERIODICALS AND NEWSPAPERS
5.14 GREY LITERATURE
5.15 OTHER PRINTED DOCUMENTS
5.16 NON PRINT MATERIALS
5.17 AUDIOVISUAL MATERIALS
5.18 ELECTRONIC MEDIA
5.19 MICROFORMS
5.2 SUBJECTS
5.21 SOCIAL SCIENCES, BUSINESS MATERIALS
5.22 HUMANITIES MATERIALS
5.23 SCIENCE, TECHNOLOGY, MEDICINE MATERIALS
5.24 BIBLIOMETRICS, SCIENTOMETRICS, INFORMETRICS
6.0 ORGANIZATION
6.1 COOPERATION
6.11 MANAGEMENT (OTHER THAN PERSONNEL MANAGEMENT)
6.12 FINANCE
6.13 PUBLIC RELATIONS
6.14 OTHER MANAGEMENT PROCEDURES AND OPERATIONS
7.0 LIBRARY BUILDINGS
7.1 REMOVALS
7.11 PLANNING AND DESIGN OF LIBRARY BUILDINGS
7.12 NEW AND RENOVATED LIBRARY BUILDINGS
7.13 FURNITURE
7.14 VEHICLES
8.0 LIBRARY TECHNOLOGY
8.1 TELECOMMUNICATIONS
8.11 NETWORKS
8.12 COMPUTERS
8.13 SOFTWARE
8.14 OTHER MACHINES
9.0 TECHNICAL SERVICES
9.1 CIRCULATION CONTROL
9.11 ACQUISITIONS
9.12 COLLECTION DEVELOPMENT
9.13 WITHDRAWALS
9.14 STOCKTAKING
9.15 PRESERVATION

9.16 SECURITY
9.17 SHELF ARRANGEMENT
9.18 OTHER TECHNICAL SERVICES
10.0 INFORMATION COMMUNICATION
10.1 INFORMATION WORK
10.11 SOCIAL SCIENCES, BUSINESS INFORMATION WORK
10.12 HUMANITIES INFORMATION WORK
10.13 SCIENCE, TECHNOLOGY, MEDICINE INFORMATION WORK
10.14 INFORMATION SERVICES
10.15 REFERENCE WORK
11.0 BIBLIOGRAPHIC CONTROL
11.1 BIBLIOGRAPHY
11.11 BIBLIOGRAPHIES
12.0 BIBLIOGRAPHIC RECORDS
12.1 PERIODICALS CONTROL
12.11 CATALOGUING AND INDEXING
12.12 COOPERATIVE CATALOGUING, BIBLIOGRAPHIC UTILITIES
12.13 CATALOGUING RULES
12.14 BIBLIOGRAPHIC DESCRIPTION
12.15 MANUAL CATALOGUES
12.16 COMPUTERIZED CATALOGUES
12.17 ONLINE CATALOGUES
12.18 CD-ROM CATALOGUES
12.19 INDEXING
12.2 BOOK INDEXING
12.21 SUBJECT INDEXING
12.22 SEARCHING
12.23 INDEX LANGUAGE AND SYSTEMS
12.24 SUBJECT HEADING SCHEMES
12.25 THESAURI
12.26 CLASSIFICATION
12.27 CLASSIFICATION SCHEMES
12.28 COMPUTER ASSISTED INDEXING
13.0 COMPUTERIZED INFORMATION STORAGE AND RETRIEVAL
13.1 ECONOMIC AND COMMERCIAL ASPECTS
13.11 NETWORKS
13.12 SOFTWARE
13.13 AUTOMATIC TEXT ANALYSIS, AUTOMATIC INDEXING, MACHINE TRANSLATION
13.14 SEARCHING
13.15 DOWNLOADING
13.16 DATABASES IN GENERAL
13.17 NON BIBLIOGRAPHIC DATABASES, DATABANKS
13.18 BIBLIOGRAPHIC DATABASES
13.19 IMAGE DATABASES
13.2 FULL TEXT DATABASES
13.21 MULTIMEDIA
13.22 ONLINE SYSTEMS
13.23 ONLINE DATABASES
13.24 DISC STORED SYSTEMS
13.25 CD-ROMS
13.26 CD-ROM DATABASES
13.27 OTHER DISC STORED SYSTEMS
13.28 OTHER STORAGE SYSTEMS
13.29 VIDEOTEX
14.0 COMMUNICATIONS AND INFORMATION TECHNOLOGY
14.1 COMPUTER INDUSTRY
14.11 NETWORKS
14.12 COMPUTER SCIENCE
14.13 COMPUTERS
14.14 SOFTWARE
14.15 IMAGING TECHNOLOGY
14.16 ONLINE SYSTEMS
14.17 DISC STORED SYSTEMS
14.18 TELECOMMUNICATION AND BROADCASTING TECHNOLOGY
14.19 COMPUTER APPLICATIONS
15.0 READING
15.1 LITERACY
16.0 MEDIA
16.1 COPYRIGHT
16.11 PRINTING, PUBLISHING AND BOOKSELLING
16.12 PRINTING
16.13 PRINTING HISTORY AND ANALYTICAL BIBLIOGRAPHY
16.14 PUBLISHING HISTORY AND BOOKSELLING
16.15 AUTHORSHIP
16.16 PUBLISHING
16.17 PUBLICATIONS
16.18 ELECTRONIC PUBLISHING
16.19 BOOKSELLING
16.20 AUDIOVISUAL MATERIALS
16.21 BROADCASTING
17.0 KNOWLEDGE AND LEARNING
17.1 RESEARCH
17.11 EDUCATION
18.0 RECORDS MANAGEMENT
19.0 OTHER FRINGE SUBJECTS

FIGURE 72

Subject categories used by *Library and Information Science Abstracts* (1997).
Reproduced by permission of the editor.

Other Indexes

Most of the other services in printed form are variations on the types already illustrated. *Sociology of Education Abstracts*, unlike *Library and Information Science Abstracts* and *Chemical Abstracts*, simply lists abstracts in numerical order without grouping under broad subject categories. The subject

---

14.18 TELECOMMUNICATIONS AND BROADCASTING TECHNOLOGY

7363
The impact of EC competition law on satellite broadcasting. D.
Rhodes. *Tolley's Communications Law*, 2 (2) 1997, p.66-73. refs.
Broadcasting technologies offer an unprecedented extension of consumer
choice. However, although the market structure of the broadcasting sector
has been gradually liberalised, private initiative is still lacking mainly
because companies have faced significant barriers to entry. Discusses EU
policies relating to competition, broadcasting, advertising, and
telecommunications; and the application of EU competition rules to treaty
provisions, guidelines and the control of essential facilities. Presents 7 major
cases decided by the Commission and the European Court which have had a
great impact on broadcasting. GLC

7364
**To foster residential area broadband Internet technology: IP
datagrams keep going, and going, and going...** M. Laubach.
Computer Communications, 19 (11) Sep 96, p.867-875. il.refs.
Contribution to a special issue devoted to recent advances in networking
technology. Overviews the notion of sending small, fixed sized packets over
the cable television (CATV) networks plant. These small packages are 53
octet asynchronous transfer mode (ATM) cells. Summarizes 2 of the
standardisation efforts: the ATM over HRC definition work taking place in
the ATM Forum's Residential Broadband Working Group; and the standards
progress in the IEEE P802.14 Cable TV Media Access Control and Physical
Protocol Working Group. Overviews and summarizes delivery of a viable
Internet service to a Cable TV based subscriber community. Original
abstract-amended.

7365
**A novel MAC protocol for broadband communication over
CATV-based MANs.** D-C. Twu and K-C. Chen. *Computer
Communications*, 19 (11) Sep 96, p.888-900. il.refs.
Contribution to a special issue devoted to recent advances in networking
technology. To overcome difficulties in serving reverse link integrating
service traffic in tree and branch cable television (CATV) networks, proposes
a novel protocol known as the Spatial-Group Randomly Addressed Polling
with Reservation (SR-GRAP) protocol. The potential large service area and
the large number of end users, demonstrates its significant efficiency for
reverse link multiple access communication in CATV networks, so that a
good variety of constant/variable bit rate applications with different Quality
of Service and multimedia local area networks/metropolitan area network
communications can be fully supported. Original abstract-amended.

7366
Digital TV: the all-new Internet? P. Dwer. *net*, (32) May 97,
p.97-9. il.
Discusses the potential of digital television for providing a range of
interactive information services direct to the home. (The author may be
contacted by electronic mail at phil@dwer demon co uk) LT

7367
**The regulation of conditional access for digital television
services.** J. Landau. *Tolley's Communications Law*, 2 (2) 1997,
p.74-6. refs.

FIGURE 73

Sample entries from *Library and Information Science Abstracts*.

Reproduced by permission of the editor.

index, described as a "modified keyword index," indexes the abstracts under
key words or phrases appearing in the title or the abstract itself. Proper
names are also indexed. Figure 78 shows two sample abstracts and Figure 79
shows sample index entries, including some (e.g., black dropouts, class cutting, compulsory education) relating to the abstracts of Figure 78.

The many abstracts bulletins produced in the Excerpta Medica Series (Elsevier Science Publishers) also group items under broad subject categories.
The subject indexes are highly specific. All of the terms assigned (from a
thesaurus) by indexers appear in an index entry. Most of the terms become
entry points in the index, the other terms being carried as modifiers. The
modifiers are arranged in alphabetical order in two sequences: terms that

will themselves become entry points precede the terms that are modifiers only and will not be entry points. Figure 80 provides an example. Note how the string of terms acts as a kind of mini-abstract, providing a clear indication (in most cases) of what each item is about. The Excerpta Medica subject indexes are discussed more completely in Chapter 4.

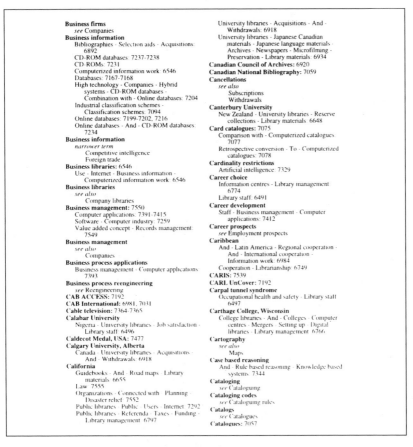

Business firms
  see Companies
Business information
  Bibliographies - Selection aids - Acquisitions: 6892
  CD-ROM databases: 7237-7238
  CD-ROMs: 7231
  Computerized information work: 6546
  Databases: 7167-7168
  High technology - Companies - Hybrid systems - CD-ROM databases - Combination with - Online databases: 7204
  Industrial classification schemes - Classification schemes: 7094
  Online databases: 7199-7202, 7216
  Online databases - And - CD-ROM databases: 7234
Business information
  narrower term
  Competitive intelligence
  Foreign trade
Business libraries: 6546
  Use - Internet - Business information - Computerized information work: 6546
Business libraries
  see also
  Company libraries
Business management: 7550
  Computer applications: 7391-7415
  Software - Computer industry: 7259
  Value added concept - Records management: 7549
Business management
  see also
  Companies
Business process applications
  Business management - Computer applications: 7393
Business process reengineering
  see Reengineering
CAB ACCESS: 7192
CAB International: 6981, 7031
Cable television: 7364-7365
Calabar University
  Nigeria - University libraries - Job satisfaction - Library staff: 6496
Caldecot Medal, USA: 7477
Calgary University, Alberta
  Canada - University libraries - Acquisitions - And - Withdrawals: 6918
California
  Guidebooks - And - Road maps - Library materials: 6655
  Law: 7555
  Organizations - Connected with - Planning - Disaster relief: 7552
  Public libraries - Public - Users - Internet: 7292
  Public libraries - Referenda - Taxes - Funding - Library management: 6797

University libraries - Acquisitions - And - Withdrawals: 6918
University libraries - Japanese Canadian materials - Japanese language materials - Archives - Newspapers - Microfilming - Preservation - Library materials: 6934
Canadian Council of Archives: 6920
Canadian National Bibliography: 7059
Cancellations
  see also
  Subscriptions
  Withdrawals
Canterbury University
  New Zealand - University libraries - Reserve collections - Library materials: 6648
Card catalogues: 7075
  Comparison with - Computerized catalogues: 7077
  Retrospective conversion - To - Computerized catalogues: 7078
Cardinality restrictions
  Artificial intelligence: 7329
Career choice
  Information centres - Library management: 6774
  Library staff: 6491
Career development
  Staff - Business management - Computer applications: 7412
Career prospects
  see Employment prospects
Caribbean
  And - Latin America - Regional cooperation - And - International cooperation - Information work: 6984
  Cooperation - Librarianship: 6749
CARIS: 7539
CARL UnCover: 7192
Carpal tunnel syndrome
  Occupational health and safety - Library staff: 6497
Carthage College, Wisconsin
  College libraries - And - Colleges - Computer centres - Mergers - Setting up - Digital libraries - Library management: 6766
Cartography
  see also
  Maps
Case based reasoning
  And - Rule based reasoning - Knowledge based systems: 7344
Cataloging
  see Cataloguing
Cataloging codes
  see Cataloguing rules
Catalogs
  see Catalogues
Catalogues: 7057

FIGURE 74

Sample entries from the subject index to *Library and Information Science Abstracts*.

Reproduced by permission of the editor.

Most alphabetico-specific indexes arrange bibliographic references under subject headings, perhaps with subheadings, and duplicate entries under two or more such headings (as in *Index Medicus*), or they organize abstracts under subject headings and use some form of index to provide alternative subject access approaches to individual items (as in the *Engineering Index*).

Some variations on this alphabetico-specific approach exist. For example, the former *British Technology Index* (BTI), as described in Chapter 4, used index entries consisting of a string of controlled terms in a "systematic order." Figure 22 (Chapter 4) provides an example. A bibliographic reference appeared in only one place in the index, this being determined by the

Mandarin orange
amino acids of, of Australia, 153016z
ascorbic acid and dehydroascorbic acid detn. in, by
  dichlorophenolindophenol titrn. and
  fluorometry, 22364p
canned, nickel of, of Germany, 56322p
carotenoids and vitamin A activity of, of Finland,
  211229j
Clementine, compn. of, Wenzhou Honey orange oil
  in relation to, 230387a
desulfurizing agents contg., for hydrogen sulfide
  removal from gases, P 138523u
eastern dodder control on, with glyphosate, 187753c
fertilizer expt. with, with zinc, 230615y
fruit thining in, 90511j
juice, limonin detn. in, by HPLC, 211054y
nitrification in krasnozem soil under, nitrogen
  fertilizer form effect on, 191706g
Satsuma
  antioxidative activity and tocopherols in flavedo
    of, rind spot effect on, 72661d
  ascorbic acid and sugars in peel of, in growth and
    development, 21199b
satsuma, disease, rind spot, antioxidative activity
  and tocopherols of flavedo in relation to,
  72661d
Satsuma
  ethylene formation by, during fruit development,
    cyanide metab. in relation to, 21201w
  fertilizer expt. with, with potassium rates,
    38196w
  flavonoid glycosides and adenosine of peels of,
    hypotensive effect and structure of, 69120w
  flavonoid glycosides of peel of, isolation and
    structure and hypotensive effect of, 189403n
  glycosides from leaves of, citrosides A and B as,
    189387k
  juice, ascorbic acid and sugars in peel and, in
    growth and development, 21199b
  juice, potassium fertilizer effect on yield and
    compn. of, 38196w
  naringinase of waste of, treated with brewers'
    yeast, 6335z
  Penicillium digitatum inhibition on,
    thiabendazole effect enhancement by
    carbohydrate fatty acid esters in, 6616s
  pollen fertility induction in, by nitrosoethylurea,
    189619n
  terpenoids and terpenoid glycosides from, 54482s
  vitamin B$_{12}$ detn. in, by *Alteromonas*
    thalassomethanolica bioassay, 171865e
tangerine
  aroma, energy food contg. leucine and isoleucine
    and valine and, P 211346v
  canned, tin detn. in, by oscillog. polarog. titrn.,
    56109z
  juice, carotenoids detn. in concs. of, by HPLC,
    orange juice adulteration in relation to,
    56052a
  juice, glucose and sucrose of, 211250j
  pectins of, extn. of, with use of microwave, P
    175439s
  preservation of, ethylene-decompg. compns. in, P
    56330q
  puree conc., provitamin A carotenoids detn. in by
    HPLC, 73937k
  tissue culture of, essential oil manuf. with, P
    55999c
  volatile acids detn. in, by distn. and titrn.,
    133781s
wastewater from processing of, treatment of,
  Penicillium janthinellum and activated sludge
  process in, 44290p

FIGURE 75

Sample entries from the subject index to *Chemical Abstracts*.

Reprinted by permission of Chemical Abstracts Service.

Thermolytic
    dissocn water hydrogen oxygen
        P 136408h
Thermolyzed
    chalk polymn filling 134413g
Thermomagnetic
    material iron rhodium manuf 137011k
Thermomech
    analysis coating characterization
        135519h
    chem pulp tissue 135751c
    property polyamide fiber 135343w
    pulp mech property 135752d
    pulp storage latency 135761f
    pulp thiol bleaching 135763h
    strengthening copper alloy 138017d
    treatment aluminum alloy aging
        138016c
    treatment austenite transformation review
        137609m
    treatment austenitized maraging steel
        137685h
    treatment steel silicon structure
        137688m
Thermometer
    automated helium 3 melting 140908p
    electronic silicon transistor sensor
        136035j
    NMR samarium acetate hydrate
        144753g
    noise ceramic resistor 144278f
Thermometric
    titrn anionic surfactant 135953v
Thermometry
    noise thermocouple high temp 140909q
Thermonuclear
    neutron scattering plasma 141608c
Thermooptical
    liq crystal display P 143716k
    time resolved spectrochem analysis
        145099k
Thermoperlite
    bending strength metal oxide P 138826s
Thermophoresis
    sol gel coating 138577m
Thermophys
    property data bank 140925s
    property data center London 140926t
    property fabric 135346z
    property process simulation 140762m
    property study China review 140860s
Thermopiezic
    analysis absorption desorption 140310n
Thermoplastic
    elec conductive blend P 134864e
    electromagnetic interference shielding
        P 144516g
    polyester blend adhesive sheet
        P 135111u
    polyester elastomer blend molding
        P 135276b
    resin film manuf P 135110t
    resin magnetic fluid recording
        P 143692z
    resin polyolefin electrophotog toner
        P 143539e
    surface treatment flame 135013p

FIGURE 76

Sample entries from the keyword index to *Chemical Abstracts.*

Reprinted by permission of Chemical Abstracts Service.

sequence in which terms are combined. Other approaches were provided by systematic cross-referencing based on chain indexing principles. For example, *see* references were used to provide alternative access points for the "fabrics" items illustrated in Figure 22 (from such terms as "finishing," "dyeing," "laminating," and so on). Note also how this index links terms judged

to be semantically related ("related headings"). While the principles underlying the indexing remained the same, a later version of this publication,
known as the *Current Technology Index* (CTI), used a somewhat different
approach to the presentation of the references. This change was made to
save space and to avoid the rather densely packed page that was characteristic
of the BTI. The differences between the BTI and CTI layouts are illustrated
in Figure 81.

$C_{52}H_{44}N_3O_2P_2Tc$
Technetium, [1,3-bis(4-methylphenyl)-1-=
triazenato-N^1,N^3]dicarbonylbis=
(triphenylphosphine)-
(*OC*-6-14)- *[99354-95-7]*, 14057b
$C_{52}H_{44}N_4O_6P_2$
Phosphonic acid, (3,3',4,4',6,6'-hexaphenyl[6,6'-=
bi-6*H*-pyrrolo[1,2-*b*]pyrazole]-2,2'-diyl)bis-
tetramethyl ester, (*R**,*S**)- *[100418-78-8]*,
88671u
tetramethyl ester, (*R**,*S**)-, compd. with
trichloromethane (1:1), monohydrate
[100418-79-9], 88671u
$C_{52}H_{44}N_6OZn$
Zinc, [4-(diethylamino)-*N*-[2-(10,15,20-=
triphenyl-21*H*,23*H*-porphin-5-yl)phenyl]=
butanamidato(2-)-$N^{21},N^{22},N^{23},N^{24}$]-
(*SP*-4-2)- *[102497-59-6]*, 224763e
$C_{52}H_{44}N_6O_4$
2-Naphthalenecarboxamide, 4,4'-[(3,3',5,5'-=
tetramethyl[1,1'-biphenyl]-4,4'-diyl)bis=
(azo)]bis[3-hydroxy-*N*-(4-methylphenyl)-
[81287-27-6], P 196932p
$C_{52}H_{44}N_6O_6$
2-Naphthalenecarboxamide, 4,4'-[(3,3',5,5'-=
tetramethyl[1,1'-biphenyl]-4,4'-diyl)bis=
(azo)]bis[3-hydroxy-*N*-(2-methoxyphenyl)-
[81287-28-7], P 196932p
$C_{52}H_{44}N_8O_4$
2-Naphthalenecarboxamide, 4,4'-[1,4-piperazine=
diylbis(4,1-phenyleneazo)]bis[3-hydroxy-=
N-(4-methylphenyl)- *[101701-09-1]*, P
196932p
$C_{52}H_{44}N_8O_6$
2-Naphthalenecarboxamide, 4,4'-[1,4-piperazine=
diylbis(4,1-phenyleneazo)]bis[3-hydroxy-=
N-(3-methoxyphenyl)- *[101701-10-4]*, P
196932p
$C_{52}H_{44}O_5Sb_2$
Antimony, bis(benzeneacetato-*O*)-μ-=
oxohexaphenyldi-
stereoisomer *[99825-05-5]*, 50926t
$C_{52}H_{44}P_2Rh$
Rhodium(1+), [[1,1'-binaphthalene]-2,2'-=
diylbis[diphenylphosphine]-*P*,*P*][(1,2,5,6-=
η)-1,5-cyclooctadeiene]-
chloride, stereoisomer *[101627-26-3]*, 168628a
——, [[1,1'-binaphthalene]-2,2'-diylbis=
[diphenylphosphine]-*P*,*P*][(1,2,5,6-η)-1,5-=
cyclooctadiene]-
stereoisomer, perchlorate *[82822-45-5]*, 168628a
$C_{52}H_{45}CoN_4O_3S$
Cobalt, (1-butanol)(ethyl mercaptoacetato-*S*)[5,=
10,15,20-tetraphenyl-21*H*,23*H*-porphinato=
(2-)-$N^{21},N^{22},N^{23},N^{24}$]-
(*OC*-6-23)- *[100203-75-6]*, 64759c

FIGURE 77

Sample entries from the formula index to *Chemical Abstracts*.

Reprinted by permission of Chemical Abstracts Service.

This index is now in its third format, and abstracts are now included, the current title being *Abstracts in New Technologies and Engineering*. The inclusion of abstracts has necessitated a major format change, and this publication now closely resembles the present format of *Library and Information Science Abstracts*.

A number of printed indexes have made use of PRECIS (the Preserved Context Index System). One example was the *British Education Index*. Some

---

88S/037   **Compulsory education and home schooling: truancy or prophecy?** M. A. PITMAN, *Education and Urban Society*, 19(3), 1987, pp 280—289.

Starting from the premise that American schooling is experiencing a crisis of meaning, the author looks at the increased incidence of in-school truancy or class cutting, and the increase in home schooling. Approximately 25 percent of the school population are educated at home, though at least another 9 percent are persistent truants, and up to 20 percent in-school truants. A variety of research is cited throughout the article. Home schoolers are defined as falling into three main categories: religious; progressive; and academic. Religious concerns centre upon the poor quality of public schooling, the moral education of the children and a desire for closer parent-child relationships. The author has carried out a survey of a New Age or Progressive community in the northeastern United States, where the emphasis is on Green politics and alternative lifestyles and approaches. For these people, home schooling makes sense as it allows for unorthodox views and treatment to be provided. The academic home-schoolers are concerned about the academic quality (or lack of it) in public schools. Surveys do show that home-schooled children do perform on average better than public school educated children, though the parents themselves tend to be more highly educated than the population at large. Legally, the laws concerning schooling do not compel education; rather they compel attendance, so home-schoolers tend to receive a disproportionate amount of school superintendent time and activity. In the history of society, the emphasis on compulsory attendance is very recent, and is occurring at the precise time when parents are questioning the quality and nature of public education provided.   —*NM*

88S/038   **A comparative study of black dropouts and black high school graduates in an urban public school system.** S. B. WILLIAMS, *Education and Urban Society*, 19(3), 1987, pp 311—319.

A sample of 50 black male and female dropouts from an urban southeast Texan school district in 1985–86 is compared with 50 black male and female graduates from the same school in the same year to ascertain significant differences between them. Data was collected from records, tests and home visits. All the students lived in the attendance zone for the school, which provided an homogeneous socioeconomic background. The researcher was a participant observer, having been a resident in the community for 30 years. Church attendance was found to be a significant factor, with 72 percent of the graduates and 14 percent of the dropouts attending. Graduate status, however, did not help the students in gaining social security assistance. There was a higher incidence of detentions and grade retentions (being kept down a year) for the dropouts than for the graduates, and a lower attendance at vocational educational programmes. Though there was no significant difference in the occupational levels of parents, the parents of the graduates were more highly educated. Similar sibling attainment, and the friendship of other graduates were also significant factors in the background of the graduates. The graduates also had more positive views towards the school than the dropouts, who felt alienated and on the periphery of school and community life. The dropout experiences pervasive feelings of isolation, disconnectedness and rejection, and these must be addressed if the dropout is to be rehabilitated to schooling.   —*NM*

FIGURE 78

Sample abstracts from *Sociology of Education Abstracts*.

Reproduced by permission of Taylor & Francis

<http://www.tandf.co.uk>.

sample entries are shown in Figure 82. A bibliographic reference would appear under all of the "significant" terms appearing in a subject statement, each one being "shunted" to the entry position as described in Chapter 4. For example, the second "aggression" entry in Figure 82 will be duplicated under "Pupils" and under "Primary schools." Since 1986, PRECIS is no longer used as the basis of indexing in the *British Education Index*.

ability grouping, 109, 112, 127
ability grouping research, 111
Aboriginal schooling, 024
academic achievement, 035, 081, 101
academic marketplace, 113
academic performance, 120
academic women, 148
achievement, 046, 084, 108, 121
adolescence, 060, 079
adolescents, 047
adult claimants, 139
adult education, 002, 003, 140
Afro-Caribbean students, 138
Alabama, 042
Alaska, 080
amalgamation, 019
America, 080
American school policy, 144
American society, 118
anti-social behaviour, 030
appraisal, 145
apprenticeships, 023
Arab-Israeli students, 125
art, 044
Asian students, 138
assistant professors, 133
Atlanta, 007
Australia, 015, 019, 105
Austria, 045

best-evidence synthesis, 109, 111
biology, 072
black adults, 085
black children, 007, 081, 083, 084
black dropouts, 038
black males, 030
black school politics, 007
black students, 051, 120
black youths, 086
Botswana, 035
Brazil, 062
Brazilian education, 062
British universities, 075
building design, 145
business schools, 029

Canada, 025, 026, 027, 028
Canadian census figures, 028
career opportunities, 118
careers advice, 141
careers guidance, 018
Caribbean, 033
Caribbean homes, 043
Catania, 090
chemistry, 072
childbirth, 133
church, 086
civic education, 067
class cutting, 037
classroom advice, 142
classroom instruction, 111

classroom interactions, 072
classroom research, 014
classroom teaching, 105
classrooms, 046, 055
college opportunities, 117
college quality, 077
Commonwealth Caribbean, 069
community education, 089
community educators, 089
competency testing, 005
comprehensive schools, 060
compulsory education, 037
computing, 018
continuing education, 140
corporal punishment, 115
counselling, 017
creativity, 101
Cuba, 064
cultural diversity, 044
cultural influences, 065
culture, 011
curriculum, 057, 057, 070, 075, 096, 105, 145
curriculum changes, 116
curriculum development, 015

decision making, 042, 094
design education, 044
developing countries, 068

FIGURE 79
Sample of index entries from *Sociology of Education Abstracts*.
Reproduced by permission of Taylor & Francis
<http://www.tandf.co.uk>.

Citation Indexes

The Institute for Scientific Information (ISI) now publishes three citation indexes: the *Science Citation Index*, the *Social Sciences Citation Index* and the *Arts and Humanities Citation Index*. Since these are quite different from the other printed indexes described in this chapter, they deserve some attention in their own right.

---

haloperidol, aminophylline, amphetamine, anticonvulsive agent, arecoline, bicuculline, cocaine, convulsant agent, kindling, n methyl dextro aspartic acid, neurotransmitter, tetracaine, mouse, 989
- behavior disorder, carbamazepine, fluphenazine decanoate, phenytoin, schizophrenia, adult, blood level, drug therapy, 1110
- central nervous system, electroencephalogram, evoked visual response, lithium, myoclonus, neuroleptic agent, neurotoxicity, side effect, 969

head injury, central nervous system, computer assisted tomography, epidural hematoma, epilepsy, incidence, skull fracture, subdural hematoma, complication, 1001
- electrocardiography, emergency medicine, glucose blood level, hematocrit, migraine, orthostatic hypotension, seizure, syncope, childhood, epidemiology, etiology, morbidity, 1086

heart arrhythmia, asystole, electrocardiogram, electroencephalogram, epilepsy, seizure, adult, etiology, pacemaker, 1108

heart graft, convulsion, cyclosporin a, risk assessment, adult, drug therapy, etiology, 994

heart infarction, acidosis, bleeding tendency, brain disease, coma, convulsion, diarrhea, hemorrhagic shock, hypovolemic shock, syndrome, diagnosis, infant, kidney function, liver function, pathogenesis, 1087

heart rate, amygdaloid nucleus, convulsion, epileptogenesis, hippocampus, respiration control, single unit activity, adult, diagnosis, etiology, 1040
- blood pressure, convulsion, timolol, aged, animal model, cat, drug therapy, 939

heat shock protein, brain region, epileptic state, kainic acid, seizure, histochemistry, rat, 904

hematocrit, electrocardiography, emergency medicine, glucose blood level, head injury, migraine, orthostatic hypotension, seizure, syncope, childhood, epidemiology, etiology, morbidity, 1086

hemiparesis, anosognosia, epilepsy, seizure, transient ischemic attack, adult, aged, diagnosis, etiology, 1010
- behavior disorder, brain abscess, mental deficiency, neurologic disease, seizure, age, child, complication, electroencephalograpphy, follow up, infant, sex difference, surgery, 1084

FIGURE 80

Sample entries from the subject index in *Epilepsy Abstracts.*
Reprinted by permission of Elsevier Science Publishers.
This index is typical of the subject indexes produced in the *Excerpta Medica* series.

The primary use of a citation index is to find, for a particular bibliographic item known to the searcher, later items that have cited it. Figure 83 shows some sample entries from the *Social Sciences Citation Index* (the other citation indexes observe the same principles). Suppose we know that an article by W. E. Lambert, beginning on page 44 of the *Journal of Abnormal and Social Psychology*, volume 60, 1960, is highly relevant to a current research interest. By entering the SSCI under the name of the author (Figure 83) we can locate this article and find later ones that have cited it. In this example the article is cited by two other items published in 1989 (by Hogg and by Spears).

Figure 83 is taken from the Citation Index section of the *Social Sciences Citation Index.* Note that, under the name of each author, entries appear

BTI Heading STEEL : Production : Furnaces, Arc : Ladles
References   LADLES : Arc furnaces : Steel production.
            See STEEL : Production : Furnaces,
            Arc : Ladles
         ARC FURNACES : Steel production. See
            STEEL : Production : Furnaces, Arc
         FURNACES, Arc : Steel production. See
            STEEL : Production : Furnaces, Arc

CTI Heading STEEL : Production : Furnaces, Arc : Ladles
References   LADLES
            See
            Steel : Production : Furnaces, Arc : Ladles
         ARC FURNACES
            See
            Furnaces, Arc
         FURNACES, Arc
            See
            Steel : Production : Furnaces, Arc

FIGURE 81

Differences in presentation of references between *British Technology Index* (BTI)
and *Current Technology Index* (CTI) for an item on ladles for arc furnaces
producing steel.

The author is grateful to Tom Edwards, former editor of the *Current Technology Index*,
for this example. Both examples are reproduced by kind permission of CSA.

AGGRESSION
    See also
       Violence
AGGRESSION. Children
    Coping by adults
       Coping with physical violence : some suggestions / John Jamieson.
       — *Mal. Ther. Educ.*, Vol.2, no.2 : Autumn 84. — p39-45
       Bibliography: p45

AGGRESSION. Pupils. Primary schools
    Identification
       Identification of aggressive behaviour tendencies in junior age
       children : first stage in a study of aggression / C. Gilmore ... [et
       al.]. — *Educ. Rev.*, Vol.37, no.1 : Feb 85. — p53-63
       Bibliography: p63

AGRICULTURAL COLLEGES
    Curriculum. Innovation — Australasia — Case studies
       Learning to be a capable systems agriculturist / Richard Bawden
       and Ian Valentine. — *Program. Learn. Educ. Technol.*, Vol.21,
       no.4 : Nov 84. — p273-287
       Education for Capability. — Bibliography: p286-287

AGRICULTURAL COLLEGES
    Management (curriculum subject). Courses. Development — Nigeria
       Development of management courses for the agriculture sector in
       Nigeria / A.E. Shears. — *Program. Learn. Educ. Technol.*,
       Vol.21, no.2 : May 84. — p88-94
       Dissemination and Diffusion. — Bibliography: p94

AGRICULTURAL COLLEGES
    Teaching aids: Microcomputer systems — Case studies
       Computers in agricultural education / by Andrew Todd. —
       Comput. Educ., No.48 : Nov 84. — p24

AGRICULTURAL LECTURERS
    Lecture notes. Inclusion of new material — Case studies
       Sources of new materials included in lectures by lecturers in
       agriculture / J.T. Smith, B.W. Rockett
       Bibliography: p299
       Pt 2: An analysis of published sources used. — *High. Educ.*,
       Vol.13, no.3 : Jun 84. — p289-299

FIGURE 82

Sample PRECIS entries as formerly used in the *British Education Index.*

Reproduced by permission of the British Library.

LAMBERT RA			VOL	PG	YR
KWALL RR	TEX LAW REV		67	685	89
LAMBERT RD					
71 SEX ROLE IMAGERY CHI					
BURKE PJ	SOC PSYCH Q		52	159	89
79 CANADIAN REV SOCIOLO 16 47					
GUIMOND S	CAN R SOC A		26	193	89
86 TRANSFORMATION INDIA					
DRIVER ED	CONT SOCIOL	B	18	366	89
86 1984 CANADIAN NATION					
CURTIS JE	CAN J SOC		14	143	89
87 CANADIAN REV SOCIOLO 24 529					
BRUCE PG	IND RELAT		28	115	89
LAMBERT RS					
87 S CAROLINA LOYALISTS					
POTTER J	AM HIST REV	B	94	513	89
LAMBERT RW					
82 SOC NEUR ABSTR 8 318					
GABRIEL M	EXP BRAIN R		76	441	89
88 PATIENT EVALUATION C					
HALEY SM	T EAR CHILD		9	106	89
LAMBERT S					
86 CD ROM NEW PAPYRUS					
COOPER LKD	INF PR MAN		25	161	89
87 ASPECTS PRINTING 160					
LAMBERT S	PAST PRESEN			36	89
87 CDI INTERACTIVE VIDE					
HUGHES H	FOREIGN LAN		22	283	89
LAMBERT VA					
85 J NURSING SCHOLARSHI 17 50					
REVENSON TA	J CONS CLIN		57	344	89
LAMBERT W					
68 READINGS SOCIOLOGY L					
HORNBERG NH	APPL LING		10	214	89
LAMBERT WE					
59 AM J PSYCHOL 72 77					
LEMMON CR	APPL PSYCH		10	133	89
60 J PERS 28 350					
KOHN PM	J RES PERS		23	214	89
60 J ABNORMAL SOCIAL PS 60 44					
HOGG MA	GENET SOC G		115	153	89
SPEARS R	EUR J SOC P		19	101	89
67 CHILDRENS VIEWS FORE					
SILVERST B	AM PSYCHOL	R	44	903	89
69 SUBSTANCE STRUCTURE					
NELDE PH	J MULTILING		10	73	89
72 BILINGUAL ED CHILDRE					
LEAVER BL	FOREIGN LAN		22	269	89
WAGNER DA	APPL PSYCH		10	31	89
72 BILINGUAL EDUCATION					
SNOW MA	TESOL QUART		23	201	89
72 LANGUAGE PSYCHOL CUL					
WATTS RJ	J PRAGMATIC		13	203	89
74 CULTURAL FACTORS LEA					
HOGG MA	GENET SOC G		115	153	89
75 ED IMMIGRANT STUDENT					
CUMMINS J	J MULTILING		10	17	89
75 INT J SOCIOL LANG 4 127					
HOGG MA	GENET SOC G		115	153	89
76 TU VOUS USTED					
BROWN R	LANG SOC		18	159	89
77 BILINGUALISM PSYCHOL 15					
MIONI AM	J PRAGMATIC	B	13	467	89
79 CHILD REARING VALUES					
EDWARDS CP	YOUNG CHILD		44	15	89
ROSENTHA DA	INT J BEHAV		12	207	89
79 LANGUAGE SOCIAL PSYC 186					
HOGG MA	GENET SOC G		115	153	89
80 PATTERNS BILINGUALIS 3					
OKSAAR E	J MULTILING		10	33	89
86 CAN J BEHAV SCI 18 35					
87 ETHNICITY LANGUAGE 58					
MOGHADDA FM	CAN J BEH S		21	160	89

FIGURE 83

Sample entries from the *Social Sciences Citation Index*.

Reprinted with permission from the *Social Sciences Citation Index*. Copyright © 1989 by the Institute for Scientific Information®, Philadelphia, PA, USA.

JARADAT D

RELIABILITY VALIDITY AND GRADING
EDUC PSYC M 48(3) 627 635 88 9R Q3592
YARMOUK UNIV IRBID JORDAN

JARADIAZ SR

MULTIOUTPUT ANALYSIS OF TRUCKING OPERATIONS USING SPATIALLY DISSAGGREGATED FLOWS
TRANSP R B 22(3) 159-171 88 16R P0196
UNIV CHILE DEPT CIVIL ENGN CASILLA 228 3 SANTIAGO CHILE

FARAH M—VALUATION OF USERS BENEFITS IN TRANSPORT-SYSTEMS
TRANSP REV 8(3) 197 218 88 32R P3529
UNIV CHILE DEPT INGN CIVIL CASILLA 228 3 SANTIAGO CHILE

FIGURE 84

Sample entry from the source index to the *Social Sciences Citation Index*.

Reprinted with permission from the *Social Sciences Citation Index*. Copyright © 1989 by the Institute for Scientific Information®, Philadelphia, PA, USA.

in order of publication date. Only brief bibliographic details are given for the citing items. To get more complete bibliographic data we must go to another section of the SSCI, the *Source Index*. For example, the citing item by Spears appears in the *European Journal of Social Psychology*, volume 19, 1989, and begins on page 101. To get more complete bibliographic details (title and full page numbers) we must look under Spears in the *Source Index*.

FIGURE 85

Sample entry from the Permuterm Subject Index to the
Social Sciences Citation Index.

Reprinted with permission from the *Social Sciences Citation Index.* Copyright © 1988 by the Institute for Scientific Information®, Philadelphia, PA, USA.

The source indexes to the *Social Sciences Citation Index* and to the *Arts and Humanities Citation Index* (but not to the *Science Citation Index*) provide, for each item included, a list of the bibliographic references appearing at the end of the article (see Figure 84 for an example).

In the citation indexes, a novel form of keyword index provides a subject approach to the citing (source) items. Known as the Permuterm Subject Index, it is based on keywords occurring in the titles of citing items. Figure 85 shows a sample entry under terms beginning with the root "debt" as they appear in the titles of several citing items. Note that a few compounds (e.g., debt-financed) are used, as well as single words. Each entry shows, in alphabetical order, other keywords that have co-occurred with it in the titles of citing items. Thus, one item under *debts* (by Giguere) deals with Third World debts, one (by Garfield) with intellectual debts, and so on. Note that entries will be repeated under each significant keyword in a title (e.g., one entry under the keyword "Third World" will be modified by the term "debts"). Of course, the effectiveness of this type of subject index is entirely dependent on the descriptive quality of the titles used to generate it and on the ingenuity of the searcher since no form of vocabulary control is used.

The various sections make such citation indexes quite powerful searching tools. Several different search approaches are possible. A search can begin with the bibliographic reference to an item known to be of interest or it can begin with a keyword. Keywords can lead to other possible keywords and the titles of citing items can also suggest further keywords that might be useful in the search. To take a hypothetical example, a keyword search of the SSCI for 1996 might yield a highly relevant item that can be followed up to find later items that have cited it. These might then suggest further keywords that could lead to other papers that can also be followed for later citations, and so on in a series of iterations. For those citation indexes in which the source index includes the bibliographic references (see Figure 84) other forms of iteration are possible. For example, a search on an item known to be highly relevant can lead to a highly relevant citing item. Some of the references in the citing item can then be followed up to locate other items that cite them, and so on.

The printed citation indexes have equivalent databases in electronic form. These, and many of the other indexes mentioned in this chapter, are now accessible through the Web. The citation principle—one bibliographic item citing (referring to) an earlier one—can also be used to link publications in other ways—by bibliographic coupling or co-citation (see Chapter 15).

Another well known product of the Institute for Scientific Information is *Current Contents*, a weekly published in various subject-related sections, that reproduces the contents pages of a wide range of journals. Figure 86 shows a sample page. Each issue of *Current Contents* includes a very simple keyword index, as illustrated in Figure 87; one of the terms in this Figure ("glucose") relates to one of the items in Figure 86. Note that the index includes some phrases and names as well as single keywords. Each entry leads to a page in *Current Contents* and to a page number in the journal represented there. For example, one of the entries under "glucose" refers to the item beginning on page 3214 of the December 1989 issue of *Applied and Environmental Microbiology* (Figure 86). This simple index can be used in one of two ways. Obviously, one can simply follow up all references to a particular keyword. However, a more sophisticated searcher, looking for

CC666 **Applied and Environmental Microbiology** Amer. Soc Microbiol
Articles and Abstracts in English

VOL. 55 NO. 12 DECEMBER 1989 (L,A)

GENETICS AND MOLECULAR BIOLOGY

Characterization of a Plasmid from the Ruminal Bacterium *Selenomonas ruminantium*. Scott A. Martin and Roger G. Dean 3035–3038

Organization of Genes Required for the Oxidation of Methanol to Formaldehyde in Three Type II Methylotrophs. C. Bastien, S. Machlin, Y. Zhang, K. Donaldson, and R. S. Hanson 3124–3130

Cloning and Expression of a *Schwanniomyces occidentalis* α-Amylase Gene in *Saccharomyces cerevisiae*. Tsung Tsan Wang, Long Liu Lin, and Wen Hwei Hsu 3167–3172

Cloning and Characterization of Two Genes from *Bacillus polymyxa* Expressing β-Glucosidase Activity in *Escherichia coli*. L. González-Candelas, M. C. Aristoy, J. Polaina, and A. Flors 3173–3177

Two *Bacillus* β-Mannanases Having Different COOH Termini Are Produced in *Escherichia coli* Carrying pMAH5. Toshiro Akino, Chiaki Kato, and Koki Horikoshi 3178–3183

Expression of the Insecticidal Protein Gene from *Bacillus thuringiensis* subsp. *aizawai* in *Bacillus subtilis* and in the Thermophile *Bacillus stearothermophilus* by Using the α-Amylase Promoter of the Thermophile. Keiko Nakamura and Tadayuki Imanaka 3208–3213

Development of Enterobacterium-Specific Oligonucleotide Probes Based on the Surface-Exposed Regions of Outer Membrane Proteins. Gonnie Spierings, Harm Hofstra, Jos Huis in't Veld, Wiel Hoekstra, and Jan Tommassen 3250–3252

ENZYMOLOGY AND PROTEIN ENGINEERING

Induction and Purification of Endo-β-*N*-Acetylglucosaminidase from *Arthrobacter protophormiae* Grown in Ovalbumin. Kaoru Takegawa, Masanao Nakoshi, Shojiro Iwahara, Kenji Yamamoto, and Tatsurokuro Tochikura 3107–3112

PHYSIOLOGY AND BIOTECHNOLOGY

Factors Affecting Adhesion of *Fibrobacter succinogenes* subsp. *succinogenes* S85 and Adherence-Defective Mutants to Cellulose. Jianhua Gong and Cecil W. Forsberg 3039–3044

Degradation of Barley Straw, Ryegrass, and Alfalfa Cell Walls by *Clostridium longisporum* and *Ruminococcus albus*. V. H. Varel, A. J. Richardson, and C. S. Stewart 3080–3084

Fermentation of Cellulosic Substrates in Batch and Continuous Culture by *Clostridium thermocellum*. Lee Rybeck Lynd, Hans E. Grethlein, and Richard H. Wolkin 3131–3139

Beneficial Effects of Nickel on *Pseudomonas saccharophila* under Nitrogen-Limited Chemolithotrophic Conditions. Wilfredo L. Barraquio and Roger Knowles 3197–3201

Competition for Glucose between the Yeasts *Saccharomyces cerevisiae* and *Candida utilis*. Erik Postma, Arthur Kuiper, W. François Tomasouw, W. Alexander Scheffers, and Johannes P. Van Dijken 3214–3220

FOOD MICROBIOLOGY

Mechanism of Proteinase Release from *Lactococcus lactis* subsp. *cremoris* Wg2. Harry Laan and Wil N. Konings 3101–3106

MYCOLOGY

Physiological and Environmental Studies of Sclerotium Formation and Maturation in Isolates of *Morchella crassipes*. Thomas J. Volk and Thomas J. Leonard 3095–3100

CONTINUED

86 ©1990 by ISI® CURRENT CONTENTS ®

FIGURE 86

Sample page from *Current Contents.*

Reprinted with permission from the *Current Contents*®, Copyright © 1990 by the Institute for Scientific Information®, Philadelphia, PA, USA.

more specific information, might choose to combine keywords. For example, if one were looking for articles on glucose in the context of yeasts, one could compare the numbers appearing under the term "glucose" with those appearing under "yeast" and "yeasts" to see if any numbers appear under both terms. If they do, they presumably refer to items that deal precisely with the topic of the search, including one of the articles appearing in Figure 86. This is essentially a variant of the Uniterm system (or at least the physical implementation of that system), as referred to in Chapter 2. The Uniterm system was a very early form of postcoordinate retrieval system.

CC Pg	J Pg	CC Pg	J Pg	CC Pg	J Pg	CC Pg	J Pg
GLUCOSE		**GLUCOSE-UTILIZING**		**GLUTAMATE-IMMUNOREAC-TIVITY**		**GLUTEAL**	
41	1421	79	6808	262	118	211	875
..	1507	**GLUCOSE-1,6-BISPHOSPHATE**		**GLUTAMATE-PYRUVATE**		..	884
45	9447	68	1229	55	1420	**GLUTEN-SENSITIVE**	
48	20910	**GLUCOSE-6-PHOSPHATASE**		**GLUTAMATERGIC**		23	1093
55	1240	189	692	288	516	**GLYBURIDE**	
59	263	**GLUCOSE-6-PHOSPHATE DEHYDROGENASE**		**GLUTAMINE-RICH**		39	1741
..	331	75	429	77	827	**GLYCATED**	
86	3214	**GLUCOSIDE-PHOSPHATI-DYLCHOLINE**		**GLUTAMINE-SYNTHETASE**		45	9464
..	3234	51	225	29	2623	**GLYCATION**	
89	467	**GLUCOSIDES**		270	223	48	20947
105	3661	297	3361	**GLUTARALDEHYDE**		**GLYCEMIC**	
172	1370	41	1507	136	205	55	1415
181	683	**GLUCOSINOLATE**		**GLUTATHIONE**		..	1474
186	465	**GLUCOSYLCERA-MIDE**		32	1371	223	665
215	J 24	89	573	43	437	..	694
223	725	**GLUCURONIDES**		..	613	**GLYCERALDE-HYDE-3-PHOSPHATE**	
235	998	57	1673	52	203	79	6696
252	638	**GLUTAMATE**		65	353	**GLYCERALDE-3P-DEHYDROGE-NASE**	
271	361	51	150	67	449	134	2065
284	881	79	6776	..	455	**GLYCEROL**	
GLUCOSE-H-2		113	1213	105	3653	193	371
224	253	262	5	..	3697	..	393
..	254	263	293	..	3807	290	987
GLUCOSE-HOMEOSTASIS		277	363	108	4291	**GLYCERYL**	
223	709	290	1039	..	4307	113	1296
GLUCOSE-INDUCED		291	1143	112	1025	**GLYCINE**	
48	20910	294	397	121	209	51	257
GLUCOSE-TRANSPORT				159	6917	86	3119
43	389			..	7020	97	39
GLUCOSE-UPTAKE				**GLUTATHIONE-S-TRANSFERASES**			
79	6808			64	113		
266	1302						
GLUCOSE-UTILIZATION							
110	69						

FIGURE 87

Sample entries from the title word index to *Current Contents*

Reprinted with permission from the *Current Contents*®, Copyright © 1990
by the Institute for Scientific Information®, Philadelphia, PA, USA.

Conclusion

Several different approaches to the implementation of an indexing/abstracting service in printed form have been illustrated in this chapter. While some individuals will prefer one approach, and others another, no one approach is ipso facto better than the rest. It very much depends on how the tool is to be used.

For current awareness purposes, those tools that use some form of classified approach will usually be superior to the alphabetico-specific indexes, at least to the extent that the classification scheme corresponds to the interests of a particular user. For example, someone interested in keeping current with new developments in parasitology in general would probably find

Biological Abstracts, which devotes a section to this topic, more useful than *Index Medicus* where references to the subject are likely to be scattered over a wide variety of subject headings. Nevertheless, for someone whose current awareness interests are highly specific, the alphabetico-specific approach might actually be more convenient. For example, *Index Medicus* would probably be a very useful tool for keeping up with the literature of, say, retinitis pigmentosa.

In considering these various tools as search and retrieval devices, of course, all of the performance factors discussed elsewhere in this book will come into play. That is, the effectiveness of a printed index as a search tool will depend on the number of access points provided, the specificity of the vocabulary used to index, the quality and consistency of the indexing, and the extent to which the tool offers positive help to the searcher (e.g., by linking of semantically related terms). Because the *Excerpta Medica* indexes provide more subject access points per item than *Index Medicus*, they are likely to give better recall. On the other hand, *Index Medicus*, since it indexes each item under only the "most important" terms, may well give greater precision.

Printed tools that include abstracts are superior to those that do not in that they provide more information to help the user decide whether or not a particular item is really likely to be useful. This is especially valuable in the case of hard to find items or those in languages unfamiliar to the searcher. Nevertheless, abstracts are not always essential. For example, the combination of the title of an item, together with the subject heading and subheading under which it appears, as in the *Index Medicus* example, is often enough to indicate its potential relevance.

Finally, it is obvious that indexes based only on title words offer a rather limited approach to retrieval. However, even these have their advantages. For example, a highly specific search involving, say, a name, might actually be more successful in a title word index than in one based on a broader controlled vocabulary. Moreover, when items are retrieved on keyword-in-title searches, providing the keyword is highly specific, there is a very good chance that they will be "relevant."

Because most librarians and other information professionals find printed indexes easy to use, they often assume that this is universally true. In fact, a number of studies have shown that the general public may have trouble using or understanding even the "simplest" of indexes, such as those appearing at the backs of books (see, for example, Liddy and Jörgensen, 1993a,b).

Over the last decade or so, an attempt has been made to make indexing and abstracting services more "simple," as in the abandonment of a faceted classification approach in *Library and Information Science Abstracts* and of PRECIS in the *British Education Index*. However, making these tools more user friendly may not save them. The fact that many libraries are canceling print subscriptions, in favor of access to electronic versions, suggests that sources of this kind in printed form may now have a very short life expectancy.

CHAPTER 11

Enhancing the Indexing

THROUGHOUT THIS BOOK, it has generally been assumed that the end result of indexing a particular document is a simple list of terms, perhaps selected from some controlled vocabulary, that collectively describe the subject matter discussed. Frequently, all terms in the list are considered equal (i.e., the indexer does not specify that some are more important than others) and, usually, no explicit relationships among the terms are specified.

But indexing can be a bit more sophisticated than this: terms can be weighted to reflect the indexer's perception of their importance and/or an attempt can be made to add some "syntax" to the terms so that their inter-relationships become more clear.

Weighted Indexing

Much subject indexing entails a simple binary decision: a term is either assigned to a document or it is not. While this simplifies the process of index-ing, it does create some problems for the user of a database, who cannot devise a search strategy that will distinguish items in which a topic receives substantial treatment from those in which it is dealt with in a very minor way.

In weighted indexing, indexers can assign to a term a numerical value that reflects their opinion on how important that term is in indicating what a particular document is about. Usually, the more central the subject matter, or the more detail that is given on this subject, the higher will be the weight. Consider, as an example, a numerical scale having five points with five being the highest score. Applied to the item illustrated in Figure 3 (Chapter 2), the terms *public opinion, telephone surveys, attitudes,* and *Middle East* might be given a weight of 5, *United States* a weight of 4, *Israel* and *Egypt* a weight of 3, and so on. Clearly, this is subjective and different indexers will arrive at different weights. Nevertheless, most could be expected to give *Middle East* a high weight but *political leaders* or *foreign aid* a low one.

Weighted indexing of this type can be used in two ways in retrieval from a database. One way is simply to allow a searcher to specify that only items indexed under a term carrying a particular weight should be retrieved. Thus, someone interested in articles directly on the subject of Middle Eastern leaders might require that both terms, *middle east* and *political leaders*, should carry at least a weight of 4. This should prevent retrieval of the item illustrated in Figure 3, which deals with political leaders in only a very minor way, and presumably many others like it.

The alternative application is to use the weights to rank the items retrieved in a search. Thus, in a search requiring the co-occurrence of *middle east* and *political leaders*, items in which both terms carry a weight of five (total weight of ten) would be printed out or displayed first, with items scoring nine appearing second, and so on down to items scoring only two.

The assignment of numerical weights to terms has long been advocated by Maron (Maron and Kuhns, 1960; Maron et al., 1959; Maron, 1988), who refers to this type of indexing as "probabilistic." Despite this advocacy, I know of no conventional retrieval systems (i.e., based on human indexing) that employ numerical weights in quite this way, although the weighting of terms is implicit in certain automatic or semi-automatic retrieval systems such as SMART (see Chapter 15).

Nevertheless, some databases do incorporate a simple weighting technique by distinguishing between "major" and "minor" descriptors, which is tantamount to adopting a numerical scale having two values. This practice may be tied to the production of a printed index, the major descriptors being those under which an item appears in the printed index and the minor descriptors those that are associated only with the database in electronic form. This has been the practice, for example, at the National Library of Medicine (*Index Medicus* and the MEDLINE database), the National Technical Information Service (NTIS), and the Educational Resources Information Center (ERIC). Even this simple weighting method allows some of the flexibility in searching alluded to earlier. A searcher can specify that items should be retrieved only when a term (or terms) appears as a major descriptor. Alternatively, a crude ranking of output can be achieved, as in the example:

$$M * M$$
$$M * m$$
$$m * m$$

That is, items in which two terms, used by a searcher in an *and* relationship, and both major (M) descriptors, appear first, followed by those in which only one of the two is a major descriptor, and then by those in which both are minor (m) descriptors only.

Some information services have gone a little beyond a two point weighting scale. At BIOSIS, for example, Concept Headings were once assigned at any of three "levels of emphasis": primary (the item appears under this heading in printed indexes), secondary (a comparatively strong emphasis), and tertiary—a minor emphasis (Vleduts-Stokolov, 1987).

Note that weighted indexing, in effect, gives the searcher the ability to vary the exhaustivity of the indexing. Returning to Figure 3, it is possible that the first five terms listed would all be considered major descriptors, while the remaining nine terms are considered minor. This being so, a search strategy that specifies major descriptors only would in effect be equivalent to searching on a less exhaustive level of indexing.

It is important to recognize the distinction between *weighted indexing*, of the type described, and *weighted term searching*. The latter need have nothing to do with weighted indexing. Instead, it refers to the construction of a search strategy the logic of which is specified through numerical weights rather than Boolean operators. For example, a search strategy might take the following form:

Term	Weight	
A	10	
B	10	
C	2	Threshold = 20
D	2	
E	1	
F	1	

The lowest acceptable weight is 20, which means that terms *A* and *B* must both be present in a record before it will be retrieved. However, a record may exceed the minimum weight (threshold) so that, conceivably, some records might score 26 (if all six terms were present), some 25, and so on, and these high scoring items would appear first in a printout. In this way, a ranked output can be achieved even though no weighting of index terms is employed. This approach to the searching of databases was quite common in batch processing systems, especially those applied to Selective Dissemination of Information (SDI), but is much less appropriate to searching in the online mode.

The ideal approach to weighting might involve a team approach to indexing (see Chapter 5) with the terms that all indexers agree on given highest weight and those that only one indexer would assign given the lowest weight. Such an ideal can rarely be implemented because of the costs involved. Villarroel et al. (2002) propose such an approach in a digital library environment. The assumption is that a full text record carries a field for user-assigned terms. Users of this record can highlight sections of the digital text that they judge to be of importance and this highlighting can lead to the revision of the weights associated with the index terms (or, indeed, the text words themselves).

Many "automatic" systems include forms of weighting to allow the ranking of output. Systems of this kind are discussed in Chapter 15. In most cases, automatic processing systems weight by frequency criteria: frequency of a term's occurrence in a text and/or frequency of occurrence in a database as a whole; or other methods have been tried, including use of positional criteria (e.g., how far apart two terms are within a text). Keen (1991) compared different approaches and concluded that combined approaches are likely to give superior results.

Linking of Terms

A further examination of Figure 3 will reveal that the document represented could be retrieved in a number of searches for which it is not really an appropriate response. Some of these can be avoided by the use of weighted indexing or by reducing the exhaustivity of the indexing. For example, either approach could avoid the retrieval of this document in a search for information on political leaders in general, for which this item could be considered of only very marginal value.

Other unwanted retrievals could be caused by *false associations*, cases in which the terms that cause an item to be retrieved are really quite unrelated in the document. One example of this is the combination *United States* and *political leaders*. Clearly, this document does not discuss United States political leaders although it is likely to be retrieved in a search on this subject. As previously noted, the probability that false associations of this type will occur increases with the length of the record (i.e., with the number of access points provided or with the exhaustivity of the indexing).

One way of avoiding false associations is by the linking of index terms. That is, the document is, in a sense, partitioned into several subdocuments, each dealing with a separate, although possibly closely related, subject. The document illustrated in Figure 3 might be divided into such links as:

>Middle East, Arab Nations, Political Leaders, Israel, Egypt, Palestine Liberation Organization
>Public Opinion, Telephone Surveys, United States, Attitudes, Middle East
>United States, Foreign Aid, Egypt, Israel
>Peace Conferences, Middle East, Palestine Liberation Organization

and so on.

Note that all terms in each link are directly related and that some terms may appear in several of the links. Each link is identified by some alphanumeric character that is carried in the database itself. In an online retrieval system this would be associated with the document number within the inverted file. Thus, document 12024 may be partitioned into 12024/1, 12024/2, 12024/3, and so on. This gives the searcher the opportunity to specify that two terms should co-occur not only in the document record but in a particular link within that record, thereby avoiding many of the false associations of the *United States/political leaders* type.

A special type of partitioning is that applied to full text documents to reduce spurious relationships and improve retrieval. Williams (1998) refers to this as "passage-level indexing." This is discussed in Chapter 14.

Role Indicators

While links can be effective in avoiding certain unwanted retrievals, they will not solve all problems. Some terms may be directly related in a document, and thus appear in the same link, but not be related in the way the searcher wants them to be related. Figure 3, again, provides an excellent illustration: the item in question could well be retrieved in a search on Middle East attitudes towards the United States, whereas it is exactly the opposite relationship that is dealt with.

To avoid this type of problem (an *incorrect term relationship*), it is necessary to introduce some syntax into the indexing in order to disambiguate. The "traditional" method is to use *role indicators* (or *relational indicators*)—codes that make term relationships explicit. To disambiguate the United States/Attitudes/Middle East situation, only two role indicators would be needed. These would be directional indicators. For example, one might use the letter A to stand for the idea of "recipient, target, or patient" and B to represent "sender, giver, source." In this case, one would associate the *role* A with *Middle East* and B with *United States* since the former is the target of the attitudes while the latter is their source.

Obviously, not all ambiguity problems can be solved through the use of only two roles. If they are kept relatively basic, however, a rather small number of role indicators can solve most problems.

Links and roles were introduced into retrieval systems at the same time, in the early 1960's, when postcoordinate systems were still relatively young and computer-based retrieval was in its infancy. For a while it was very fashionable to index using both links and roles due largely to the influence of the Engineers Joint Council (EJC), which introduced a set of role indicators (see Figure 88) that was quite widely adopted. This type of highly structured indexing did not remain in favor for very long. Not only was it very expensive, because indexers needed much more time to accomplish it, but it proved to be extremely difficult to apply the role indicators consistently. It is difficult enough (see Chapter 5) to achieve consistency in relatively simple approaches to indexing, but the difficulty increases dramatically the more explicit the indexer must be in expressing term relationships. The problems

8   8
The primary topic of consideration is; the principal subject of discussion is; the subject reported is; the major topic under discussion is; there is a description of

1   1
Input; raw material; material of construction; reactant; base metal (for alloys); components to be combined; constituents to be combined; ingredients to be combined; material to be shaped; material to be formed; ore to be refined; sub-assemblies to be assembled; energy input (only in an energy conversion); data and types of data (only when inputs to mathematical processings); a material being corroded

2   2
output; product, by-product, co-product; outcome, resultant; intermediate products; alloy produced; resulting material; resulting mixture or formulation; material manufactured; mixture manufactured; device shaped or formed; metal or substance refined; device, equipment, or appraratus made, assembled, built, fabricated, constructed, created; energy output (only in an energy conversion); data and types of data (only as mathematical processing outputs)

3   3
Undesirable component; waste; scrap; rejects (manufactured devices); contaminant; impurity, pollutant, adulterant, or poison in inputs, environments, and materials passively receiving actions; undesirable material present; unnecessary material present; undesirable product, by-product, co-product

4   4
Indicated, possible, intended present or later uses or applications. The use or application to which the term has been, is now, or will later be put. To be used as, in, on, for, or with; for use as, in, on, for, or with; used as, in, on, for, or with; for later use as, in, on, for, or with

5   5
Environment; medium; atmosphere; solvent; carrier (material); support (in a process or operation); vehicle (material); host; absorbent, adsorbent

6   6
Cause; independent or controlled variable; influencing factor; "X" as a factor affecting or influencing "Y"; the "X" in "Y is a function of X"

7   7
Effect; dependent variable; influenced factor; "Y" as a factor affected or influenced by "X"; the "Y" in "Y is a function of X"

9   9
Passively receiving an operation or process with no change in identity, composition, configuration, molecular structure, physical state, or physical form; possession such as when preceded by the preposition of, in, or on meaning possession; location such as when preceded by the prepositions in, on, at, to, or from meaning location; used with months and years when they locate information (not bibliographic data) on a time continuum

10   10
Means to accomplish primary topic of consideration or other objective

0   0
Bibliographic data, personal names of authors, corporate authors and sources, type of documents, dates of publication, names of journals and other publications, other source-identifying data, and adjectives

FIGURE 88

The EJC system of role indicators.

Reproduced by permission of the American Association of Engineering Societies.

are not so great as long as one thinks only of two or three terms at a time. However, it is frequently very difficult to determine all the relationships that apply to a larger group of terms. Moreover, the addition of a further term to a group may change the relationships somewhat, necessitating a change in the role indicators or, at the very least, increasing the number of roles that apply to each term. In the case of the EJC role indicators, the problems were compounded by the fact that one of them, role 8, was not a relational indicator at all but, rather, a means of weighting the most important term. Searchers found it so difficult to decide what roles an indexer might have applied to a term that they frequently omitted the roles entirely, which is equivalent to requiring that a term appear in any role and completely negates the value of the device. The problems involved in the use of links/role indicators in retrieval systems have been discussed in considerable detail elsewhere (Lancaster, 1964; Sinnett, 1964; Montague, 1965; Van Oot et al., 1966; Mullison et al., 1969).

Even more elaborate than the EJC method of indexing using links and roles was the "semantic code" approach to retrieval introduced by the Center for Documentation and Communication Research at Western Reserve University (Perry and Kent, 1958; Vickery, 1959). The semantic code was applied to a computer-based retrieval system in the field of metals, designed and operated by Western Reserve for the American Society for Metals.

The document surrogate was a "telegraphic abstract." Telegraphic abstracts were prepared in standardized format, according to a set of rules, to eliminate variations and complexities of English sentence structure. Subject analysis forms were specially designed to assist the indexer in recording important aspects of subject matter in the form of telegraphic abstracts. The terms in the telegraphic abstracts were encoded by means of a "semantic code dictionary." The basis of the semantic code was a semantic "stem." The stems (there were about 250 in the system) represent relatively broad concepts. Each stem was given a four-digit code consisting of three characters with a space for interpolation of a fourth character, as in the following examples:

    C-TL Catalyst
    C-TR Container
    C-TT Cutting and drilling
    D-DD Damage
    D-FL Deflection

Individual terms were built up by inserting a one-letter "infix" into the semantic stem and possibly by appending a numerical suffix. For example, DADD represented both "wound" and "decay," where *D-DD* is the semantic stem for "damage" and the infix *A* merely stands for "is a." In other words, a "wound" is a type of damage. A numerical suffix is added merely to distinguish terms having identical stems and infix structure; the suffix in itself has no semantic significance.

The full list of infixes is presented in Figure 89. The use of infixes with a stem allows the expression of various shades of meaning. For example, "bag" and "barrel" were both represented by *CATR*, where the infix *A* indicates that these are *types of* container. "Side wall," on the other hand, was represented by CITR, where the infix *I* indicates *part of* container. An individual complex concept may be built up from several "semantic factors." For example, the topic "telephone" may be expressed by

> DWCM.LQCT.MACH.TURN.001

where

> D-CM represents Information
> L-CT represents Electricity
> M-CH represents Device
> T-RN represents Transmission

and 001 is the unique suffix that distinguishes this term from others (e.g., Telegraph) having the same semantic factors. A maximum of four semantic codes could be combined to form a code for a specific concept.

A	is a
E	is made of
I	is part of
O	is made up of several
Q	makes use of, is produced by means of
U	is used for, produces (frequently used for verbs ending in *ing*
V	acts upon
W	brings about, affected by, is acted upon by (frequently used for verbs ending in *ed*
X	is characterized by the absence of
Y	is connected with, characterized by, characteristically
Z	resembles, but is not
P	is characterized by an increase of
M	is characterized by a decrease of

FIGURE 89

Semantic Infixes in the Western Reserve System.

Source: Aitchison and Cleverdon (1963).

Terms in a telegraphic abstract are syntactically related by means of role indicators. A list of these is given in Figure 90. An example of the application of roles is:

KOV.KEJ	crystal
,KOV.KEJ.KUJ.	metal
,KOV.KEJ.KUJ.	alloy
,KOV.KEJ.KUJ.	beryllium
,KWV	hexagonal close packed
,KWV	elastic

which indicates that metal alloy crystals, specifically beryllium, are being processed in some way, and that they have the properties of being "hexagonal close packed" and "elastic." Note the use of "companion roles" in this system. KOV and KWV are companion or paired roles. When one of these is assigned to a particular term we expect to find the companion assigned to a second term, to tie the terms together and indicate their exact relationship. Thus, "crystal," by the role KOV, is shown to have a property given for it. These given properties are "elastic" and "hexagonal close packed" as indicated by the role KWV.

KEJ	material processed
KUJ	major component
KIJ	minor component
KOV	property given for
KWV	property given
KAM	process
KQJ	means of process
KAH	condition of process
KUP	property affected or determined by process
KAP	property affected by KAL
KAL	factor influencing KAP
KWJ	product

FIGURE 90
Role indicators of the Western Reserve System as used in indexing
the literature of metallurgy.
Source: Aitchison and Cleverdon (1963).

In addition to role indicators, the system used a highly elaborate method of linking terms (and roles) in the telegraphic abstracts. This linking was achieved by various levels of "punctuation":

1. *Subphrase*. A term with one or more role indicators attached.
2. *Phrase*. A set of closely related terms in a particular relationship. A finite number of phrase patterns is recognized. For example:

KAM	(process)
KQJ	(means of process)
KAH	(condition of process)

3. *Sentence*. This is comprised of phrases and is also built up in standard patterns. For example, a sentence may cover a product and its manufacture, or a material tested and the properties determined for it.

4. *Paragraph*. This is a set of sentences, and it may be co-extensive with the abstract itself. It can also be used to distinguish completely different topics within a single telegraphic abstract. A complete telegraphic abstract as it would be recorded on some electronic medium, and showing punctuation, roles, and semantic factors, is illustrated in Figure 91.

```
KOV.KEJ.CARS.009.,KOV.KEJ.CARS.006.,KUJ.KEJ.KOV.MATL.
4.□BQE.,-KAM.CUNG.MWTL.PASS.RQHT.003.,KAM.MAPR.
032.,KAH.DACT.001.*,KAH.LAMN.037.,KAH.DACT.001.*,KAH.
LAMN.024.,KAH.DYFL.6X.PAPR.002.*,KAH.PAPR.PYSH.2X.
001.,-KUP.RANG.009.*,KUP.RAPR.225.,KUP.DASM.006.*,KUP.
PYPR.004.,KUP.DYFL.MATN.002.*,KUP.PYPR.004.,KUP.KAP.
PÅPR.017.,KUP.KAP.PAPR.010.,KAL.PAPR.004.,KAL.RANG.
009.*,KAL.MAPR.041.,KUP.PAPR.45X.PWSH.2X.TYRM.001.
,KUP.KAP.PAPR.001.*,KUP.KAP.PAPR.PYSH.2X.001.,KUP.
KAL.MAPR.114.,KUP.KAL.MAPR.087.*,KUP.KAL.MAPR.041.
,KUP.KAL.RANG.009.*,KUP.KAL.MAPR.041.,KUP.KAP.MAPR.
032.*,KUP.KAP.PAPR.PYSH.2X.001.,KAL.DYFL.6X.PAPR.002.
*,KAL.PAPR.PYSH.2X.001.,KAL.RANG.009.*,KAL.PAPR.058.
*,KAL.BYSS.3X.RAPR.002.
```

FIGURE 91
Telegraphic abstract as stored in electronic form.
Source: Perry and Kent (1958), *Tools for Machine Literature Searching.* Copyright © 1958, John Wiley & Sons, Inc. Reprinted by permission of John Wiley & Sons Inc.

In conducting a search in this system, the request statement was converted to a strategy comprised of semantic factors and role indicators. Various "levels," corresponding to the punctuation of the telegraphic abstracts, were used to restrict criteria to terms occurring within certain units. For example, search level 4 asks merely that a particular term be associated with a particular role indicator. This corresponds to the subphrase in punctuation of the telegraphic abstract.

The Western Reserve system was highly ingenious and was capable of expressing very fine shades of meaning. It had great flexibility. One could search with great precision using punctuation, roles, and specific semantic factors. Alternatively, one could search with relative broadness (for high recall) by ignoring these devices and by using the structure of the semantic codes as a means of generalization (e.g., using the general concept *D-DD* for "damage" wherever it occurs as a component in a complex code).

Unfortunately the system was too ingenious for the intended application. It was complicated to apply, and both indexing and search formulation were time-consuming and expensive operations. Subsequent experience has taught us that, in most retrieval applications, one does not need the level of sophistication built into the Western Reserve system. The system was too complex and expensive to be economically viable, and it was eventually abandoned by the American Society for Metals in favor of a simpler, more cost-effective approach.

Subheadings

The highly structured approach to indexing, exemplified by the use of links and roles or by the semantic code, was prevalent in the early 1960's when computer-based systems were still in a very early state of development. Then it was considered necessary to get very precise retrieval results—to avoid retrieving irrelevant items at any cost. The wild illustration frequently given was the need to distinguish between Venetian blinds and blind Venetians!! The absurdity of this example should be obvious to anyone: what is the likelihood that articles on both subjects would appear in the same database and how much literature exists on blind Venetians anyway? Nowadays one recognizes and accepts the fact that unwanted retrievals due to false or spurious associations will occur. However, their occurrence is usually considered to be within acceptable limits. In the MEDLARS evaluation (Lancaster, 1968a), about 18% of the approximately 3000 precision failures occuring in 302 searches were due to such ambiguous relationships among terms. It is usually considered better to accept some failures of this kind than to try to avoid them through the use of more elaborate and costly indexing methods.

The problems of false or ambiguous associations are now less severe than they were thirty or forty years ago because a higher level of precoordination exists in most systems. These problems are most prevalent in systems based on single word indexing (Uniterms) or in natural language systems (see Chapter 14). As thesauri have incorporated a higher level of precoordination, the probability of false or ambiguous associations declines. To make one simple illustration, the terms *computers* and *design*, applied to a document, are ambiguous: are computers being designed or are they being applied to the design of something else? On the other hand, the more precoordinate combination

> COMPUTERS
> AIRCRAFT DESIGN

is much less ambiguous, and the combination

> AIRCRAFT DESIGN
> COMPUTER-AIDED DESIGN

seems completely unambiguous.

One way of achieving some precoordination, without greatly increasing the size of a controlled vocabulary, is through the use of subheadings. In a postcoordinate system, subheadings can be applied in much the same way that they are in the traditional subject catalogs of libraries. The best candidates for subheadings are those terms that might potentially apply to many of the other terms in the vocabulary. Thus, a vocabulary of 5000 descriptors, plus 20 subheadings, in theory yields 100,000 (5000 x 20) unique terms. In practice, however, each subheading may be applicable to only a particular category of term so the number of possible combinations would not be so great.

To return to the earlier example, the term *design* might be a good candidate to be a subheading in certain databases. Thus, *computers/design* is much less ambiguous than the combination *design* and *computers*. Obviously, the addition of a subheading to a main heading (descriptor) is a rather simple form of linking. In effect, however, subheadings can virtually act as links and simple roles at the same time. For example, consider the combination:

>AIRCRAFT/DESIGN
>COMPUTERS

Not only is the term *design* linked explicitly to *aircraft* but its use as a subheading actually implies the relationship most likely between the term *aircraft* and the term *computers* (i.e., that the computers are used as tools in the design of aircraft).

The National Library of Medicine has been very successful in using subheadings in just this way. In some cases, subheadings complement each other. Thus, the combination

>DISEASE X/CHEMICALLY INDUCED
>DRUG Y/ADVERSE EFFECTS

implies that disease X was caused by drug Y, whereas the combination

>DISEASE X/DRUG THERAPY
>DRUG Y/THERAPEUTIC USE

expresses a completely different relationship between X and Y.

While the main justification for use of subheadings in this way was to facilitate use of the printed *Index Medicus*, they have proven to be effective in reducing ambiguities in the searching of the electronic database also. Although indexing with main heading/subheading combinations will undoubtedly be less consistent than indexing with main headings alone (Lancaster, 1968a), subheadings present fewer problems than role indicators do and, unlike role indicators, are immediately understandable by users.

Index Language Devices

Such devices as weighting, links, and role indicators are considered *precision devices* because they allow the possibility of increased precision in searching a database. Other devices, such as synonym control, on the other hand, are referred to as *recall devices* because they tend to improve recall. The complete array of such devices is sometimes referred to as *index lan-*

guage devices (Raitt, 1980; Lancaster, 1986). This is a little misleading: some of them, such as subheadings and synonym control, are indeed integral components of an index language, while others, such as linking or weighting, are quite independent of the index language. That is, they are operations applied to terms in indexing rather than components of a controlled vocabulary. One could, in fact, separate *index language devices* from *indexing devices* but this might be considered hair splitting.

The indexing devices discussed in this chapter are all precision devices, with the exception of certain components of the semantic code. A precision device essentially increases the size of the vocabulary used to index while a recall device reduces its size. For example, a five point weighting scale virtually increases the size of the vocabulary by a factor of five. Instead of having a single term, *political leaders*, for example, one now has five terms—*political leaders* 5, *political leaders* 4, and so on. Links and role indicators have a similar effect.

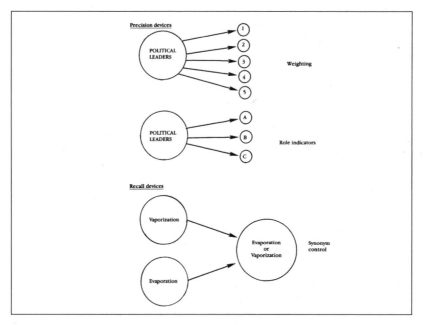

FIGURE 92
Precision devices create smaller classes; recall devices build larger ones.

Another way of looking at this is in terms of class size: precision devices create a greater number of smaller classes while recall devices create a smaller number of larger ones (Figure 92).

It seems likely that the need for a highly structured approach to indexing, especially the use of some form of relational indicators, will vary from one subject field to another. This has never really been studied, although Green (1997) has discussed the applicability of relational structures to indexing in the humanities.

Parallels exist in the computer processing of text for retrieval purposes (see Chapters 14 and 15), where the parsing of text to show syntactic dependencies is equivalent to the use of role or other relational indicators. While such syntactic analysis is probably needed for systems that try to answer questions directly from text, no real evidence exists that it is needed for the less stringent requirements associated with the retrieval of text or text passages. Moreover, syntactic analysis by computer is far from being perfected (McDonald, 1992) and this level of processing would be difficult to justify, on cost-effectiveness grounds, for most retrieval applications.

CHAPTER 12

On the Indexing and Abstracting of Imaginative Works

SUBJECT INDEXING has a very long history, vast experience has been accumulated, and a considerable body of literature on the subject now exists. However, one important application has been rather neglected, at least until very recently: the indexing of imaginative works such as fiction and feature films. The purpose of this chapter is to consider to what extent the indexing and abstracting of an imaginative work presents problems similar to those involved in dealing with "substantive" works such as textbooks, periodical articles, or documentary films.

As we have seen earlier in the book, subject indexing involves two steps—"conceptual analysis" and "translation"—that are quite distinct intellectual processes even though they may seem to be performed as one operation. The conceptual analysis step determines what a document is "about." The subject of "aboutness" as it relates to indexing has been discussed elsewhere, e.g., Maron (1977), Hutchins (1978) and Swift et al. (1978), while Pejtersen (1979) and Beghtol (1994) have specifically dealt with the "aboutness" of fiction. Various aspects of the aboutness of texts in general are discussed by Eco (1979) and by Troitskii (1979, 1981).

These authors raise several theoretical or philosophical issues on the meaning of aboutness, which I will not attempt to repeat here. For present purposes, I will use the word "about" as equivalent to "capable of informing on." That is, if certain people can learn something about farming through reading a book or seeing a film I would say that the book (film) is "about" farming.

Indexing a documentary film that deals with some technique of farming is essentially no different from the indexing of a book, periodical article or technical report on farming. By our definition, all can be considered about farming. But can a feature film that happens to be set on a farm be considered to be about farming, especially if farming is completely incidental to the plot of the film? Can a film that depicts farming in passing be considered about farming? If the hero of a film happens to be a farmer, does this make the film about farming? Does it even make it about farmers?

The indexing of any type of imaginative work—whether a play, a novel or a film—does present problems that are somewhat different from the problems of indexing substantive works. The two types are created for different purposes: the former primarily to entertain or inspire, the latter primarily to convey information. That the former may convey some substantive information is incidental to the major purpose of the medium. That the latter may occasionally entertain is equally incidental to the major purpose of that medium.

If we assign the term *farming* to a documentary film or to a periodical article on this subject, we imply that these items can convey certain information on farming and that users of an index will approach items through this term because they want to learn something about this particular subject.

On the other hand, if someone looks under the term *farming* in an index to imaginative works—say films—it is certainly not to find information about farming. Why, then, would one look under such a term? A number of possibilities exist:

1. to find out which films have a farming setting,
2. to count how many such films have been made in order to study trends in film production over particular periods of time, or
3. to identify the title of a particular film when all one can remember is that it is set on a farm or in a farming community.

The second of these implies some scholarly use. The first suggests some form of "production" use (e.g., film or TV producers seeking to discover how some event, locale, person, activity, or profession has been represented by others). The third type of question represents a more popular use. It is, however, the type of question that one might expect to receive in the reference department of a public library. Insofar as questions of these types do arise, some subject indexing of feature films seems entirely justified, even if the films cannot really be considered "about" the subject matter implied by the index terms. Exactly the same argument can be put forward for some "subject approach" to fiction. "20,000 Leagues Under the Sea" contributes little, if anything, to our knowledge of submarines. It is doubtful if one could reasonably consider the novel "about" submarines. Nevertheless, subject indexing of fiction does have value. A person might legitimately want to know "what novels have been set in submarines?", "how many novels have been set in submarines?", "what was the first novel to be set in a submarine?" or "what was that early classic that predicted the development of submarines?".

This is not to imply that films and novels have no substance, no aboutness. The film "Patton" is clearly about General Patton. It would be about Patton even if it possessed little historical accuracy. Most viewers would agree that the film illustrates Patton's ambition. Whether this makes the film about ambition, or justifies indexing it under the term *ambition*, is entirely another matter. The film also illustrates tank warfare. Does this mean it is about tank warfare? Is it about generals, about generalship, about military strategy? Can it be considered about England or about France just because parts of the film may be set in these two countries?

In practical application, of course, what we are discussing is really a relationship between a work and index terms assigned to represent that work. When we assign an index term to a book or journal article we imply, in almost all cases, that the work conveys some information on the topic represented by that term. In the case of an imaginative work, on the other hand, an index term may be assigned to it for different reasons, most obviously to represent:

1. Its central theme or themes.
2. What it may illustrate, perhaps incidentally.
3. Its environmental setting.

In point of fact, of course, the first two of these are not significantly different. At least, the only difference relates to the extent to which the subject is treated.

The environment of the film may have space, time and "character" dimensions. The space dimension may be quite precise—Pigalle, Paris or France—or imprecise—a jungle, a river, a farming community. The time dimension, likewise, can be precise—e.g., the French Revolution—or ill-defined (e.g., the nineteenth century or "before Christ"). The "character" dimension relates to the environment provided by the types of characters depicted. The fact that a leading character in a film or novel happens to be a nurse does not necessarily make the film about nursing or even about nurses. In the film "Doctor Zhivago," Lara appears at various times as a university student, a nurse and a librarian. Nevertheless, the film is not really about these various roles since it can hardly be considered to convey information on them. On the other hand, in some sense, "The Browning Version" can be regarded as about teachers and teaching since teacher-student relationships are central to the plot of the work. Teaching is not merely a "dressing" or environmental constraint.

From a pragmatic point of view none of this is really important. The central question is not whether a work is about nursing, illustrates nursing, or uses nursing as its setting, but whether the index term *nursing* should be applied to it.

One major difference between the indexing of imaginative works and the indexing of other types is that the former is likely to be more subjective and interpretative than the latter. Studies of indexing consistency have shown that different indexers are unlikely to agree completely on which terms should be assigned to a particular item, even when the subject matter dealt with is reasonably concrete. In the case of imaginative works, the chance that agreement would exist is likely to be much less. This would be particularly true in the case in which the imaginative work deals primarily with some emotion or quality—jealousy, ambition or greed, for example.

Imaginative works have another important characteristic that complicates subject indexing: their scope is essentially open-ended. That is, there are no real limits to what they can depict. In this sense, the indexing of imaginative works has something in common with subject cataloging for a large general library or the indexing of a general newspaper. At least, it has more in common with this situation than it does with a more restricted subject environment such as indexing a collection of items in agriculture or in education. The vocabulary used in indexing must also be open-ended since films and novels are constantly being produced that deal with personalities, events and locations not previously dealt with in these media.

Two major considerations relating to subject indexing include:

1. who is to do the indexing, and
2. what policies the indexers are to follow.

In the indexing of substantive works in a limited subject field, it is clear that some level of subject knowledge may be necessary. How much subject knowledge is needed will depend largely on how esoteric is the subject matter and its terminology. One feels intuitively that indexing in mathematics or applied mechanics may require greater subject expertise than indexing in, say, transportation, where the terminology is more likely to have familiarity to the general public. A good indexer does not necessarily have to be a subject expert; conversely, a subject expert will not necessarily make a good indexer.

Since the content of imaginative works is not restricted by subject matter, subject expertise, in the conventional sense, is irrelevant to the situation. Moreover, what is depicted can be considered to fall in the "general knowledge" category and it has nothing directly to do with the techniques involved in producing imaginative works. One has no reason to suppose, for example, that the indexing of films need be done by scholars of the cinema (although such people could provide valuable input on the types of terms that would be useful, at least to them) or even that it requires any particular knowledge of film making techniques.

Two characteristics of an index that will have a significant impact on its performance are:

1. the exhaustivity of the indexing, and
2. the specificity of the terms used.

As discussed earlier in the book, *exhaustivity* refers to the extent to which the contents of a work are covered by the terms used in indexing. Exhaustivity relates to breadth of coverage. In this context, the opposite of "exhaustive" is "selective." In general, exhaustivity equates to the number of index terms used. If the film "Geronimo" appeared only under the terms *Geronimo* and *Apache Indians* in some index, such indexing would be quite selective. In the subject index to the first edition of the *American Film Institute Catalog*, however, this film was indexed under 17 different terms; the indexing is rather exhaustive.

There are pros and cons associated with high exhaustivity. In theory, exhaustive indexing makes things easier to find: the ability to find an item can be expected to increase as the number of access points (i.e., entries) provided increases. This is true, however, only up to a certain point. Indexing can be overly exhaustive, causing a dilution in the effectiveness of the index—the less significant obscuring the more significant, and making the latter harder to find. To take an extreme example, it would be rather difficult to identify films or novels that deal at a significant level with dogs if the index term *dogs* were assigned to every work in which a dog appears, however briefly. The problem, of course, is that subject indexing usually involves a simple binary decision (a term either is or is not applied) rather than a weighted decision (a term applies with a certain weight). Consequently, for some index uses the chaff may obscure the wheat.

While exhaustivity relates to the breadth of coverage, *specificity* relates to depth of treatment of content. Exhaustivity is established as an indexing policy decision, whereas specificity is a property of the vocabulary used to index. In general, it is good indexing practice to use the most specific term available to describe some feature of a document. This principle, however, needs to be tempered with common sense. In designing an index one should try to arrive at a level of specificity appropriate to the needs of the users of that index. Lassie is presumably a Collie. It would be technically correct to index Lassie movies under *collies*. However, one feels intuitively that users of a film catalog are unlikely to want, or look under, anything more specific than *dogs*. On the other hand, one would want to index much more specifically than *dogs* in an encyclopedia of pets. Clearly, the more specific the terms used, the fewer the entries per term on the average. This makes it easier to find something highly specific but more difficult to perform more general searches.

Fiction in Particular

Although most of the examples used so far have been related to films, the same arguments and principles apply to novels and other imaginative works in printed form. While some authors, notably Pejtersen (see Pejtersen, 1979, 1984; Pejtersen and Austin, 1983, 1984) have experimented with the indexing of fiction over a period of many years, interest in this subject has increased very considerably in the last decade, even leading to the issuance of "guidelines" on the subject by the American Library Association (*Guidelines on Subject Access*, 2000).

Pejtersen (1992), among others, has pointed to the anomaly associated with the fact that librarians have generally done little to improve access to fiction although it can account for half the collection of public libraries and more than half the circulation.

Sapp (1986) and Baker and Shepherd (1987) discuss the classification of fiction on the shelves of libraries and the limitations of existing bibliographic classification schemes or lists of subject headings, which make little provision for topical access to imaginative works. Baker (1988) describes the results of experiments on the classification of fiction in public libraries. Sapp (1986) also discusses approaches used in such printed tools as the *Short Story Index*, the *Cumulated Fiction Index*, and the *Fiction Catalog*. While these publications do index stories under more than one heading, they suffer from the disadvantages of printed indexes in general—not allowing the user to combine headings in a search. Thus, it might be possible to identify detective stories and stories set in China but it will be much more difficult to identify detective stories with a Chinese setting.

Olderr (1991) has pointed out why the indexing of fiction should be important for libraries:

> It is never easy to answer questions as "Do you have any mysteries set in Iowa?"
> or "Are there any contemporary novels about death and dying?" or "Can you suggest a novel about the home front in World War II?" (Page xiii)

Guard (1991) also discusses approaches to fiction needed by typical library users, and Hayes (1992b) gives the results of some experiments on "enhanced catalog access" to fiction in libraries, looking mostly at cataloging times and the types of headings needed. Ranta (1991) presents a different perspective, arguing that subject access to fiction is needed to facilitate various forms of literary scholarship.

A sophisticated approach to the indexing of fiction is described by Pejtersen (e.g., 1979, 1984) and Pejtersen and Austin (1983, 1984). Based on an analysis of how the users of public libraries characterize the contents of books, Pejtersen identified four major "dimensions" of a fictional work: subject matter, frame (time, place, social environment, profession), author's intention or attitude, and accessibility. Building on this, she devised an indexing scheme involving the following dimensions and categories:

1. Subject matter
   a. action and course of events
   b. psychological development and description
   c. social relations
2. Frame
   a. time: past, present, future
   b. place: geographical, social environment, profession
3. Author's intention
   a. emotional experience
   b. cognition and information
4. Accessibility
   a. readability
   b. physical characteristics
   c. literary form

This scheme has been used in Denmark for indexing several online databases, most recently an online, interactive catalog known as the Book House. Searches can be performed using bibliographical data, controlled keywords, classification terms, and words/phrases in a natural language annotation. Figure 93 (from Pejtersen, 1992) illustrates a complete entry from the Book House catalog. Figure 94 is an earlier example, showing a novel completely indexed using keywords.

Author:	Haller, Bent
Title:	Kaskelotternes sang, 1983, 137 pages
Front page:	Blue, sea, whales, icebergs
Names:	Tangeje, Peter
Subject matter:	A sperm whale calf's life in the sea. Its struggle to survive in spite of pollution, hunger, and man's killing of the whales. The sperm whales' sticking together in their struggle against the dangers of the sea.
Setting:	Sea environment.
Time:	1980s
Cognition/ Information:	Criticism of man's pollution of the seas and killing of animals on the point of extinction.
Emotional experience:	Exciting, sad.
Literary form:	Novel, animal story.
Readability:	Age of 11, reading aloud from the age of 7, (happy ending).
Typography:	Large letters.

FIGURE 93
Sample entry from the Book House fiction database.

From Pejtersen (1992) by permission of Emerald.

> **BRANNER, H. C.** *Barnet leger ved stranden*
> *Psychological description:* After a failed marriage, a man isolates himself in a holiday cottage and lives through a deep crisis. He meets two people, who exercise influence on him. *Time:* 1930s. *Place:* Denmark, a holiday cottage near the sea. *Social environment:* Middle classes. *Cognition/ information:* the relationship between the experiences of childhood and the fears and marriage failures of adult life. Psychoanalytical perspective. *Readability:* Difficult. *Typography:* Large. *Form:* Diary. *Bibliog. data:* Copenhagen: Povl Branner, 1937.—379 p.
>
> Access points: 1930-1939
>   Diaries
>   Depression
>   Fear
>   Guilt
>   Psychological descriptions
>   Identity problems
>   Psychological problems
>   Repression

FIGURE 94
Sample of a novel indexed using the Pejtersen approach.
Reprinted from Pejtersen and Austin (1983) by permission of Emerald.

One major advantage of such a highly structured approach to the indexing of fiction is that it will allow searches to be performed in a kind of "pattern matching" mode, catering to the many readers who want books "similar" to one they recently read. The criteria by which imaginative works are sought by library users may be more personal and idiosyncratic than the criteria and characteristics usually associated with subject searches in bibliographic databases covering, say, journal articles. While this presents significant challenges to the designer of retrieval systems, it also suggests innovative approaches to the retrieval problem. One could visualize a public library database that stores information on the fictional works borrowed by each patron. Programs could then be designed to look for groups (perhaps pairs) of patrons who have many books in common. This information could then be used to generate suggested reading lists for library users. For example, if User *A* has borrowed items *a, b, c, d, e* and User *B* has borrowed *a, d, e* and *f*, perhaps *A* might like to know about *f* and *B* about *b* and *c*. Pejtersen's system does allow for searching by "model book"—i.e., finding a novel "similar" to one already found to be entertaining. "Similar" could be in terms of setting, theme, author viewpoint, emotional experience, and so on.

Beghtol (1994) is somewhat critical of the Pejtersen indexing scheme, claiming better results for an alternative and much earlier classification (Walker, 1958), although based on the detailed analysis of a single novel, and putting forward a detailed scheme of her own, using a faceted classification approach.

The American Library Association's publication on the indexing of imaginative works (*Guidelines on Subject Access*, 2000) is less a series of guidelines than a vocabulary, in thesaurus format but based on Library of Congress subject headings, that can be used to index fiction, plays and other forms. The vocabulary covers only types of work (e.g., historical poetry, horror films, Regency novels); users are referred to other sources to standardize names of characters, place names, and other access points.

The guidelines that do appear in the ALA publication are rather imprecise. Besides form terms, the guidelines allow for the assignment of terms for characters, settings and "topics." Setting relates to both place and period, and form subheadings are to be applied (e.g., Paris (France) — Poetry). The guidelines specify that names of fictitious and legendary characters (as opposed to real people) and fictitious places are to be used only "when they appear prominently in three or more different works." While a well educated indexer would presumably know that Sherlock Holmes and Narnia appear in many works, how would one know that a less famous detective or place appears in at least three works, unless one had several of them at hand at once, and what is so special about "three" anyway?

The ALA guidelines on "topical access" are even more vague:

> Assign as many topical headings as the subjects of a work warrant. Dust jackets and book reviews are a good source of information for determining what a given work is about. If these are lacking, "skimming" is often an effective technique for determining topical content.
>
> Themes of fictional works, identified in the critical literature, may be brought out by *LCSH* headings representing qualities or concepts. Since *LCSH* was designed to index nonfiction, however, appropriate headings of this type are comparatively few. (Page 47)

In actual fact, the ALA pamphlet serves no really useful purpose since the guidelines are too vague and a better and more complete thesaurus exists (Olderr, 1991).

In November 1991, OCLC, and the Library of Congress began an experiment in the cooperative subject cataloging of fiction, drama, and other imaginative works. Several public and academic libraries participated in the OCLC/LC Fiction Project by enriching MARC records for selected items. Both genre and subject terms (LC subject headings) were added. More than 15,000 LCMARC records were enriched by OCLC and participating libraries. In addition, some member bibliographic records were also enriched, and many subject heading proposals were submitted to the Library of Congress, which approved over one thousand submissions, mostly headings for fictitious characters (Westberg, 1997). The project was terminated in 1999.

In 1997, the *British National Bibliography* began to include fiction entries with topic subject headings as well as genre and form headings based on the ALA guidelines (MacEwan, 1997).

It is likely that imaginative works present greater difficulties for the indexer than other types of publications. Consistency is likely to be even lower, unless a very small controlled vocabulary of broad terms is used, especially if the indexer is required to express the "viewpoint" of the author. The indexing of fiction (for example) seems inherently more subjective than the indexing of scholarly journals or books about fiction. Another problem is that the skimming of fiction for indexing purposes is not at all easy and the indexer is not aided by the topical headings and subheadings one expects to find in many other types of publication (Jonak, 1978).

Olderr (1991) identifies the problems rather clearly:

> Cataloging fiction requires imagination. A nonfiction work, even if it does not have Cataloging in Publication (CIP) information on the verso of the title page, has a table of contents, an index, topical chapter headings, and other features that will help the cataloger. Even the title is usually an accurate reflection of content. If the book is about envy, it will say so; if it is about jealousy, then it will say that. A fiction work, on the other hand, may be about envy or jealousy and never even use the word in the text. Once the cataloger figures out the theme, there is still the problem of remembering the difference between envy and jealousy. This is not something everyone knows well to begin with. . . (Page xiv)

DeZelar-Tiedman (1996) considered the feasibility of using publisher-supplied copy (e.g., on the dust jacket or book cover) as a source for terms representing character, setting, genre, and topic. In general, she found this satisfactory for most items but the sample she based it on was very small.

Down (1995) discusses some of the problems she encountered in the assignment of subject headings to fiction. Her experience suggests that a superficial examination of a novel, or reliance on publisher-supplied copy, is unlikely to disclose what the main topics illustrated in the work really are.

Beghtol (1994) provides the most complete survey of the problems of indexing fiction, including the matter of "aboutness," as well as presenting her own approach.

Drawing upon the field of literary criticism/literary scholarship, Nielsen (1997) argues that the indexing and abstracting of fiction is a form of literary interpretation. He maintains that approaches to the indexing of fiction, including Pejtersen's, concentrate on *what* a book deals with and pay little attention to *how* the story is told. He mentions such elements as style, narration, discoursive mode, and composition as some of the elements of the *how* aspect of fiction.

Nielsen gives greater detail on what types of things should be considered in indexing the how aspect of a novel:

-Genre, subgenre, literary type. (What kind of literature?)

-Narrative structure, plot. (For example, is it a simple or complex structure? A linear, chronological structure or an alternation between different times? Or is the structure made up of variations of fragment, collage, not chronologically but thematically organized? Is the narrative structured as a puzzle?)

-Narrator(s), way of telling. (For example, how is the narrative delivered? How many narrators? First or third person narrator? Authoritative or involved narrator? "Showing" or "telling"?)

-Points of view. (For example, is the story told from a specific point of view? Or an alternation between different points of view?

-Style, mode of telling, discourse-structure. (For example, specific style: impressionistic, surrealistic etc. Inspired by: Nineteenth-century gothic novel, French nouveau roman, etc. More general: didactic, comic, ironic modes of telling; daily language discourse; or uses of puns, illogical discourse structure, or alternation between most different discourses; intertextuality.)

-Function of the setting. (Is the function documentary? Is it conventional to the specific type of novel? Or is the setting used in a symbolic or allegorical way?)

-Patterns of imagery, leading motifs, symbolism. (Is the symbolism discrete or dominant? What kind of symbols are used? What kind of leading motifs can be found? Which intertextual symbols, motifs, allegories are there? For example, doppelgänger motif, Don Juan motif, the myth of Paradise.) (Pages 174-175)

While indexing of such aspects might well be of value to literary scholars, it is unlikely to be of much concern to the typical readers of fiction. Moreover, indexing of this type would require a detailed textual analysis that only a literary scholar could provide. This would be impractically expensive in any application of significant size.

Work on the indexing and abstracting of fiction is also dealt with in a series of papers by Saarti (1999, 2000a,b, 2002). An indexing consistency study was performed in five Finnish public libraries. The same five novels were indexed by three librarians and three patrons of each library. Terms were drawn from a Finnish thesaurus of fiction and the indexers were required to write abstracts for the novels before indexing. Not surprisingly, consistency was low, and there were great variations from indexer to indexer in the number of terms assigned. The librarian indexers assigned fewer terms than the patrons and were more consistent with each other. Nevertheless, their consistency value was only 19.9 percent compared with 12.4 percent for patrons. The more "complex" novels (e.g., by Dostoyevsky) were indexed with more terms than the less complex (e.g., by Simenon). Abstracts ranged in length from 23 to 186 words (average of 68). About 75% of the 3206 different "elements" in the abstracts dealt with content (such as themes, settings, and characters), 11.9% with the novel's structure, 5.5% with the subjective reading experience, and 5.2% with criticism or evaluation of the novel. Patrons were more evaluative/critical than the librarians (Saarti, 2000a,b).

Saarti (1999) deals with thesauri for fiction indexing and, in particular, with the Finnish thesaurus.

This discussion has so far assumed that fictional works are indexed into some form of database. Bradley (1989) considers a related situation: the need for indexes within individual works of fiction. While a case could be made for including back-of-the-book indexes in certain works, such as established classics, certain historical novels, and other fiction that may be the subject of scholarly research, Bradley's survey showed that little interest was expressed by novelists, reviewers, readers or publishers.

Bell (1991b) identifies the special problems involved in producing indexes to novels. She points out that conveying the "subtlety and complexity" of a novelist's intention is altogether more difficult than conveying what a nonfiction work is about.

Abstracting

Imaginative works require summarization just as much as other types of publication (to make them easier to index if for no other reason) but the characteristics of such *summaries* or *synopses* are quite different from the characteristics of abstracts of scholarly publications as discussed earlier in this book. A good summary should give the essentials of the plot or action, indicating the setting (geographic, chronological) and the emotions depicted where appropriate. The synopsis can be structured as in the example presented in Figure 93 or it can be in simple narrative form as in the example of Figure 95. While the characteristics of the synopsis differ significantly from those of the abstract, the major purpose is similar—to indicate to a reader whether or not be wants to read or view the item described. Moreover, basic

---

A rabbit enters a garden to eat vegetables. The farmer sees him and gives chase. The rabbit escapes.

Peter Rabbit, freed from restraints, enters a garden patch to eat the vegetables. Mr. McGregor, the owner, sees him and attempts to rid his garden of the pest. After a harrowing chase, Peter succeeds in escaping and returning home.

FIGURE 95
Two possible synopses for *The Story of Peter Rabbit* by Beatrix Potter.
Modified from Krieger (1981) by permission of the author.

principles governing the writing of abstracts—accuracy, brevity, clarity— apply just as much to the summarization of imaginative works.

Guidelines on the preparation of synopses for fiction are few and far between. The publishers of *Masterplots* (Magill, 1976) do give some guidance but in very general form:

> Designed primarily for reference, the format of MASTERPLOTS is styled and standardized to afford maximum information in the quickest time. Each of the digests is preceded by carefully checked, concisely stated reference data which furnish at a glance the type of work, authorship, type of plot, time of plot, locale, and first publication date. Following this will be found a list of principal characters and their relationship, often a highly useful feature. Next is the *Critique*, a short, incisive critical analysis of the original book. Then follows the plot summary, given as a well-rounded story and devoid of quotations from the original work. (Page v).

In *Masterplots II* (Magill, 1986) a somewhat different format was adopted:

> . . . along with a summarization of plot, narrative devices are often explored and characterization studied in more depth than before—an aspect useful for younger students. In addition, the major themes of the novel at hand are identified and analyzed, and the overall success of the author's effort is usually discussed in an interpretive summary. (Pages vii-viii).

Figure 96 presents an example from *Masterplots II* (1986).

The revised edition of Masterplots II (Kellman, 2000) adopts a more structured approach to the plot synopsis (conceptually similar to a structured abstract) with four components: Plot, Characters, Themes and Meanings, and Critical Context. Their use is described as follows:

> This analysis begins with a summary of the work's major plot elements and continues with separate sections that explore the work in depth. "The Characters" delves into the motivations and development of the individuals portrayed: "Themes and Meanings" examines the work's larger concerns; and "Critical Context" assesses the work's place in the American literary tradition and summarizes its reception. Each entry concludes with an annotated bibliography that directs readers to recent sources for further study. (Page v)

Pejtersen (1994) recognizes three basic linguistic structures for identifying and expressing the content of fictional works (see Figure 97). Such a framework can be used to guide the writing of annotations, as in the example given, and the annotations are an obvious source of useful index terms. She cautions, however, that "A full description of subject matter may need to combine several structures."

A BLOODSMOOR ROMANCE

Author: Joyce Carol Oates (1938-   )
Type of plot: Historical romance fantasy
Time of plot: 1879-1900
Locale: Bloodsmoor, a valley in Eastern Pennsylvania
First published: 1982

Principal characters:
  JOHN QUINCEY ZINN, a gentleman-inventor and the father of
    a large family
  PRUDENCE KIDDEMASTER ZINN, his wife, mother of the Zinn
    daughters
  CONSTANCE PHILIPPA, their oldest daughter who later
    becomes a son
  MALVINIA, another daughter, later a famous actress
  OCTAVIA, another daughter, later a wife and mother
  SAMANTHA, another daughter who serves as her father's lab-
    oratory assistant
  DEIRDRE, an adopted daughter and spiritualist

The Novel

Joyce Carol Oates's book *A Bloodsmoor Romance* is not a kind of fiction
that is easily named, although it is not hard to recognize. The work combines both realism and fantasy in a display of authorial skill: Oates uses several techniques to achieve this effect. First, she sets her romance in a past
that closely resembles the historical past; in that setting one finds both fictional characters and characters who bear the names of figures from history.
In addition, the characters of the work are interested in many of the things
that interested the real nineteenth century: spiritualism, the theater, the
westward movement, experimental science, abnormal psychology, female
sexuality, and the nature of marriage.

It is Oates's second technique that sets the work apart from historical romances per se: She freely manipulates the order of historical events and
even adds events that could not possibly occur. John Quincey Zinn demonstrates both of these intrusions of fantasy: He invents the ballpoint pen and
solar heating but dismisses them as useless. He invents an operating time
machine, but he destroys it after he uses it to misplace one of his pupils.
Similarly, Zinn's daughter Constance combines fantasy with history. Reared
for marriage, Constance spends her early life accumulating household lin-
ens, but when the wedding night comes, she panics, and placing in her
groom's bed the dress form used to fit her trousseau, she runs away.
Disguising herself as a man, she heads west and tries her hand at being a

FIGURE 96
Example of an entry from *Masterplots II* (1986).

cowboy, an outlaw, a deputy sheriff, and a gambler. During her masquerade, she turns physically into a man as well, and when she returns to the family home at Bloodsmoor, she poses as Philippe Fox, Constance's agent. Eventually, "he" apparently elopes with a childhood girlfriend.

The plot of the book unfolds by following the lives of the daughters as they grow up. In their adventures, the reader meets several characters drawn from history. For example, Deirdre, the Zinns' adopted daughter, is kidnaped by a mysterious stranger in a black balloon who deposits her on the lawn of a character named Madame Elena Blavatsky. This Madame Blavatsky shares the quirks of the historical Madame Blavatsky, cofounder of the American Theosophical Society. Recognizing Deirdre's talents, Oates's Blavatsky teaches Deirdre to become a medium, contacting spirits beyond the grave, and takes her on a world tour. The reader meets other fictional characters with real counterparts as well: Mark Twain, for one.

As may be inferred from the events recounted above, *A Bloodsmoor Romance* is an often hilariously comic work, yet one that at the same time attempts to capture some of the boundless enthusiasm of the late nineteenth century, an enthusiasm that was often as undiscriminating as it was energetic.

FIGURE 96 (continued)
Example of an entry from *Masterplots II*.

Reproduced from *Masterplots II: American Fiction Series*, volume 1, pages 186-187. By permission of the publisher, Salem Press Inc. Copyright © 1986, Salem Press Inc.

Structure 1:

Main character(s) as a noun in genitive—central event as a noun—remaining subject elements as prepositional phrases.

Example: An English lieutenant's carrier [sic] in the military. His dangerous expeditions against smugglers and his job as a captain of a privateer.

Focus: Main character

Structure 2:

Central event(s) as a noun - remaining subject elements as prepositional phrases

Example: Trade with drugs between a CIA agent on a secret mission and the Chinese embassy.

Focus: Central event

Structure 3:

Main characters as a noun—structure 1—remaining subject elements as prepositional phrases.

Example: The Hall Prison. The prisoners' daily life, their drug abuse, their bullying and revolt towards the personnel.

Focus: Relationships among main characters and events

FIGURE 97
Linguistic structures to guide the annotation and indexing of fiction.

From Pejtersen (1994) by permission of ERGON-Verlag Dr. H.-J. Dietrich.

CHAPTER 13

Databases of Images and Sounds

A BOOK EDITED by Feinberg (1983) discusses various special problems in indexing. However, it deals almost exclusively with the indexing of text printed on paper. Every subject area presents somewhat different indexing problems and so do different printed forms such as newspapers and statutes. However, the indexing differences presented by these variants are relatively minor. More significant are the problems caused when one moves from printed text to other forms. This chapter looks at the indexing of images and of recorded sounds. These are difficult areas because they can involve fields, such as speech technology, computer vision, and document understanding, that are well beyond the scope of most indexing applications.

Indexing of Images

The ability to store all kinds of images in databases in digital form, and especially to be able to access millions of these through the Web, has created a tremendous resurgence of interest in images in general, and ways to index them in particular. Jörgensen (2001) refers to this revolution as follows:

> We are, it appears, on the hinge of an important historical swing back towards what may be called the primacy of the image. For the last few centuries, words have been the privileged form of communication, and the preferred means of education. A shift has taken place, however, within the last several decades, and images have been reasserting their primacy as immediate and influential messengers. (Page 906)

All of the indexing discussed so far in this book has been word-based. Of course, word-based descriptions of images are still important. However, digital images can also be indexed (automatically) and retrieved by means of such intrinsic features as color, shape, and texture. The terminology used to distinguish these two approaches is not completely consistent, but word-based descriptions of images, prepared by humans, are generally referred to as *concept-based* indexing, while the indexing of images by their intrinsic features is *content-based* (Rasmussen, 1997). Such features as color, shape, and texture are often referred to as *low-level features. High-level features* are word-based descriptions of the image.[*]

---

[*]Some authors, such as Mostafa (1994), distinguish between verbal indexing (i.e., textual representation of an image) and image-based indexing (the extraction of features, and thus access points, from the image itself) and this seems a clear distinction except, of course, that a single retrieval system can include both types.

Besser (1997) has highlighted the indexing problem associated with images as follows:

> Because most collections of images have very little textual information already accompanying them, our traditional means of retrieval cannot easily be applied to images ...Museums, which collectively house one of the largest bodies of images that do have accompanying text, often assign terms to an image which are not at all helpful to the average layperson. (Page 24)

The retrieval of images differs most closely from the retrieval of text in that database users may wish to search on a wide variety of characteristics, varying from those that are very exact (names of artists, titles of paintings) to those that may be very imprecise (shape, color, texture). Dealing with one particular approach, a database known as MUSEUM, Mehrotra (1997) views these characteristics as varying levels of abstraction. The main levels are illustrated in Figure 98, which Mehrotra explains as follows:

> At the lowest levels are database images or example images. At the next level of description, an image is characterized in terms of its properties such as background/foreground colors, dominant colors, histograms, and texture properties. Description of images in terms of objects—such as image regions, boundary segments, and contours—and relationships among them forms the next level of abstraction. At the next level of abstraction, images are described in terms of generic objects, relationships, and concepts such as man, dog, car, crowd, horizon, sunset, cloudy, colorful, and smile. At the highest level of abstraction, images are described in terms of specific instances of the generic world objects. For example, a man may be described as Joe Smith, a dog may be described as Lassie, an image may be described as the San Francisco skyline. The image descriptions at any of these abstrac-

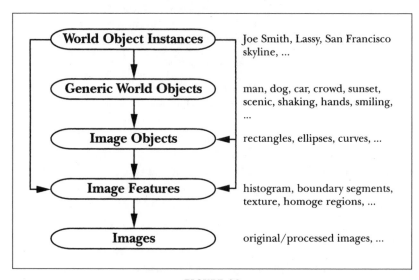

FIGURE 98

Main levels of abstraction in an art museum database.

From Mehrotra (1997) by permission of the Board of Trustees of the University of Illinois.

tion levels can be multilevel and can be derived from—or mapped to—the descriptions at the lower levels of abstraction. (Page 61)

Searching an image database at the middle levels of abstraction involves "content-based image retrieval." Mehrotra goes on to characterize the requirements as follows:

> 1. *Queries involving no image processing/analysis*—in these queries, no processing, or analysis of database images is required, and no query images are given. Examples are: (1) retrieve all images containing at least one automobile in front of a house, (2) retrieve pictures containing a smiling man. The symbolic descriptions (automatically extracted and/or user specified) associated with database images are used to select the desired images. These queries can be processed using traditional approaches.
>
> 2. *Queries involving image processing/analysis*—these queries involve one or more images that are processed to extract the associated desired symbolic information. The extracted description is compared against the description of database images to select images that satisfy the specified constraints. Examples of such queries are: (1) retrieve all images containing one or more objects similar to a given query image in terms of image color and textual features. (Pages 61-62)

It should be obvious that the different levels of abstraction shown in Figure 98 represent, from top to bottom, increasingly complex, and increasingly unconventional indexing problems.

Purely textual representations of a picture have obvious limitations. Heller (1974) gives a rather extreme example of a catalog record for a painting by Picasso (Figure 99). The first group of elements in the record represent "hard" data about the painting but the second group, dealing with what is represented, and how, besides being a matter of interpretation, gives a rather imperfect vision of what the picture looks like; it also fails to cover other important attributes, most obviously the colors.

Schroeder (1999) describes how three different "layers" of indexing are applied to images in the General Motors Media Archives: objects (what is represented—e.g., a 1935 Chevrolet truck), style (e.g., a "candid" versus a "glamour" photograph of a vehicle), and implications (e.g., illustrates the great durability of the vehicle).

It is likely that the indexing of images by verbal description will be even more subjective and, thus, inconsistent than the indexing of text, and there is some evidence that this is true (Markey, 1984). This led Brown et al. (1996) to suggest the possible value of a "democratic" approach to indexing, in which image users suggest their own index terms, and to conduct some experiments with this approach. User contributions to the indexing of video databases are advocated by several writers. Liu and Li (2002), for example, propose a system in which terms appearing in user searches could become index terms associated with the video clips they retrieve (presumably only those judged "relevant").

Group 1
TYPE	oil painting
ACCNO	21.37p
TITLE	The Three Musicians
ARTIST	Picasso, Pablo
VENDOR	Gallerie Rosenberg
MADE	1921
LOC	The Museum of Art, New York
SIZE	79 x 87 3/4"
REF	Our-2
REF	70-164877
MEDIUM	oil
MEDIUM	canvas

Group 2
(5,1)
FIGURE	musician
POSITION	front

(5,1,1)
OBJECT	clarinet
COMMENT	left figure

(5,1,2)
OBJECT	guitar
COMMENT	center figure

(5,1,3)
OBJECT	accordian
OBJECT	music score
COMMENT	right figure

(5,2)
FIGURE	dog
POSITION	side

FIGURE 99
Sample catalog entry for a painting.
From Heller (1974) by permission of the Strong Museum, Rochester, NY.
This illustration was reproduced in Scott (1988).

Agreement on the indexing of pictures is hard to achieve because it is difficult to agree on what a picture really shows. Shatford (1986) makes a distinction between what a picture is *of* and what it is *about*. The former deals, more, or less, in concretes (e.g., the picture depicts a mother with children) while the latter deals more with abstractions (e.g., the picture depicts poverty, suffering, despair). In a later article (Layne, 1994), she identifies various types of "attributes" in the indexing of images, although she suggests that different disciplines may want to use rather different attributes in indexing an image collection. She stresses the importance of using indexing to form useful groups of images rather than thinking only at the single image level. Krause (1988) deals in some detail with the problem of indexing picture collections. He agrees with the *of* and *about* distinction but uses different terms, namely *hard* and *soft* aspects of the picture.

Svenonius (1994) argues that, although some images (e.g., in medical texts) are intended to convey information, this is not really the purpose of paintings, and other artistic forms. While some may depict people or objects that can be represented verbally, others are "linguistically indeterminate."

Markey (1984), Shatford (1986), Svenonius (1994), van der Starre (1995), and Enser (1995), among others, refer to the work of the art historian Panofsky, who suggested that an image could be considered from pre-iconographic, iconographic, and iconological viewpoints. In an experiment conducted with eighteen individuals with varying backgrounds, Enser found that the same picture would be indexed at all three levels. For example, a scene of the Eiffel Tower would receive terms at the pre-iconographic (tower, river, tree), iconographic (Eiffel Tower, River Seine), and iconology (romance, holidays, excitement) levels. The large number of terms assigned to a single picture (eighteen individuals assigned 101 terms to the Paris scene), Enser argues, indicates the need for exhaustive indexing.

Orbach (1990) is one of several writers who have emphasized the need for indexing an image collection from the viewpoint of a particular group of users. She puts it this way:

> The goal of subject analysis is to capture the essence of an image or group of images—its major content and themes—while remaining on the lookout for elements known to be of special interest to the repository's clientele. (Page 184)

For certain types of requirements, such as the retrieval of an image illustrating an emotion, indexing of image databases has something in common with indexing of imaginative works as discussed in the preceding chapter.

Content-Based Approaches

A number of systems have been developed to allow the searching of images by such low-level features as shape, color, and texture. In most cases, the computer (perhaps with human assistance) extracts useful low-level features from images and re-encodes these data in a symbolic form that can be more easily used in later indexing and retrieval operations.

The QBIC (Query by Image Content) system, developed by IBM, is being used experimentally in several applications (Flickner et al., 1995). Holt and Hartwick (1994), who have used it in an art history context, describe the capabilities as follows:

QBIC provides various forms of image queries. The two most general are as an 'object query', or as an 'image query'. Object queries retrieve images containing objects which match query specifications, such as 'Find shapes that are red and circular', whereas image queries match overall image characteristics, for example, 'Find images with mostly red and blue tones'. To do object queries, the objects must be identified in each scene, typically manually by outlining them prior to the queries. The process of outlining objects, and then of computing attributes, or features for each object, and for each image as a whole is referred to as image classification. There are basic drawing tools such as a rectangle, ellipse, polygon, paint brush, and a snake tool, which outline the selected images. A fill tool expedites the masking of high contrast images by automatically outlining pixels of a similar value to one selected. (Pages 82-83)

QBIC permits searches involving colors, textures, and shapes as well as the subject represented in a painting. It also allows query by example ("find other pictures like this one"). Holt and Hartwick report that searches on shapes in paintings can present considerable problems.

A number of other content-based retrieval systems have been developed, although it is not always clear which of these are "operational" and which merely experimental. A typical example is MUSE (Marques and Furht, 2002), a "working prototype" designed to support browsing and query by example. An integral component of the MUSE design is a relevance feedback mechanism.

Techniques for recognizing and matching shapes are still very far from perfect. And, as Picard, and Minka (1995) point out, shape analysis does not solve all query-by-example problems—some sought images (a field, water, crowds of people, fire) have no well-defined shape but must, instead, be matched by "texture." They discuss approaches to identifying "visually similar regions" in a picture, using such characteristics as "directionality, periodicity, randomness, roughness, regularity, coarseness, color distribution, contrast, and complexity." The experimental system they developed seeks to mimic human behavior in the recognition of visually similar scenes. Picard (1996) deals further with vision texture in image retrieval, while Mehrotra and Gary (1995), Mehtre et al. (1997), and Jagadish (1996) all address the shape recognition problem. Examples of systems in which color searching is a major component can be found in Ogle and Stonebraker (1995) and Smith and Chang (1997b).

Mehrotra (1997) discusses some of the problems involved in representing and searching on image shapes, and Huang et al. (1997) discuss shape, color and texture as indexing, and retrieval problems. The image analyzer they describe is able to compute a color histogram for an image as well as a measure of texture based on coarseness, contrast, and directionality. Image segmentation is achieved by means of a clustering technique. The relative position of these clusters allows searches of the database that involve color, texture, and spatial features (e.g., "a red region above and to the right of a large blue region"). Forsyth et al. (1997) give a useful broad overview of the use of color, texture, and geometric characteristics in retrieval from large image databases.

Mehtre et al. (1998) present a method for clustering images based upon a combination of shape and color characteristics. The degree of match between any pair of images can be computed and expressed numerically, thus permitting query by example (i.e., images similar to one already selected can be searched for). They claim high success in retrieval experiments but were working with very small databases (e.g., one of 500 trademark images).

It is important to recognize, however, that the majority of users of image databases are not likely to search on the more abstract features, such as color, shape, and texture, although they may use these to limit a search further. Huang et al. (1997) put it this way:

> In a large number of applications of multimedia retrieval systems, users seldom use low-level image features (i.e., shape, color, texture) directly to query the database. Instead, the user interacts with the system using high-level concepts (e.g., a beach, forest, yellow flowers, a sunset) in specifying a particular image content. (Page 115)

Experiments performed by McDonald et al. (2001) suggest that color may be quite a useful classification and search criterion for a user who does not have a particular image in mind.

Several systems offer the possibility of query by example or "similarity retrieval." Kurita and Kato (1993) describe a number of experimental applications, for example:

1. When a trademark is applied for, it can be scanned by a Patent Office and matched against a database of existing trademarks.*
2. To query museum or art museum databases, a user can sketch an image (e.g., of a landscape or part of a landscape) and the system will look for paintings that best resemble it.**

DiLoreto et al. (1995) discuss work that is somewhat similar to that of Kurita and Kato although in a completely different environment. Their experimental geographic information system, "based only on the pictorial representation

---

*Trademark indexing/retrieval is also dealt with by Wu et al. (1995) and Ravela and Luo (2000), among others.

**Benois-Pineau et al. (1997) describe a similar approach in which images of buildings can be retrieved by matching a "synthesized sketch."

of a query," allows a search that can involve use of geometric attributes, topological relationships, and distances.

Not all content-based systems focus on images in their entirety. Research continues on methods for representing and searching individual regions of an image (see, for example, Moghaddam et al., 2001). A book by Wang (2001) describes in detail a "region-based" approach to content-based image retrieval. The approach is described as follows:

> An image in a database, or a portion of an image, is represented by a set of regions, roughly corresponding to objects, which are characterized by color, texture, shape, and location. The system classifies images into semantic categories, such as textured-nontextured, objectionable-benign, or graph-photograph. The categorization enhances retrieval by permitting semantically-adaptive searching methods and narrowing down the searching range in a database. (Pages xi-xii)

The region-based approach has the advantage that it allows less strict criteria for matching of images: a single region in one image can be matched to several regions in another image. While two images may not match well in their entirety, they may match well enough at the region level.

Jones and Roydhouse (1995) describe an intriguing case-based system for indexing and retrieving of meteorological data. Faced with a current weather situation, a meteorologist can search for past situations of similar conditions. A map of the present conditions (see Figure 100) can be used as a query; the system will then rank earlier situations in order of similarity (see Figure 101). Each graphical object in the query (Figure 100), such as location of the pressure center and its magnitude, is converted into a symbolic representation which is used to search the database where earlier cases are also represented symbolically.

The authors describe their indexing approach as follows:

> Each case represents a slice of time for which meteorological data is available. The data available to us include satellite imagery stored both in digital form and on laser disc, a document archive, and numeric fields ... Some examples of numeric fields include pressure, temperature, relative humidity, wind speed, and relative vorticity, all of which are available at 14 different levels of the atmosphere. [The system] currently possesses 3.5 years of data at 12-hour intervals, making up a case base of about 2,500 cases. We are currently focusing on a region covering about an eighth of the globe, centered on Australasia. We anticipate that a further 10 years of data will soon be available to us, allowing us to expand the case base to about 10,000 cases. Within several years, reanalyses of historical data ... should produce data sets covering a period from World War II to the present, which would permit the construction of a database of over 36,000 past cases.
>
> [The system] retrieves cases by matching queries from a user against explicitly represented *index labels*. Queries identify particular high-level features of the current situation that appear to be meteorologically significant: low- and high-pressure systems, for instance. Index labels are representations of the high-level features of the weather situation in each case. As far as possible, [the system] extracts

these features automatically or semiautomatically from the raw data. We are currently focusing on features such as local minima and maxima that are easy to derive automatically ... (Page 51)

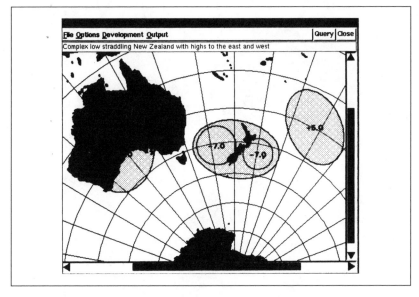

FIGURE 100

A query made to a meteorological database. The query requests a complex low-pressure system over New Zealand with high-pressure systems to east and west.

From Jones and Roydhouse, "Intelligent Retrieval of Archived Meteorological Data," *IEEE Expert*, 10 (6), 1995, 50-57. © 1995, IEEE.

Corridoni et al. (1998) describe an approach to the retrieval of paintings by "color semantics." In essence, paintings are segmented into regions having different chromatic characteristics. The database can then be queried to retrieve paintings having particular color properties and spatial characteristics.

Experiments in the use of texture for indexing and retrieval of aerial photographs are described by Ramsey et al. (1999). Their objective is to produce a "thesaurus" of textures (and perhaps other features of a photograph) that users can browse online. When a user finds a texture that corresponds to an element sought (e.g., an airport runway), he would be able to use the system to browse images to find those having similar textures. Alternatively, it might be possible to make use of query by example; that is, the user could ask the system to look for photographs having textures similar to one already at hand. Texture-based segmentation and retrieval of aerial photographs is discussed by Ma and Manjunath (1998).

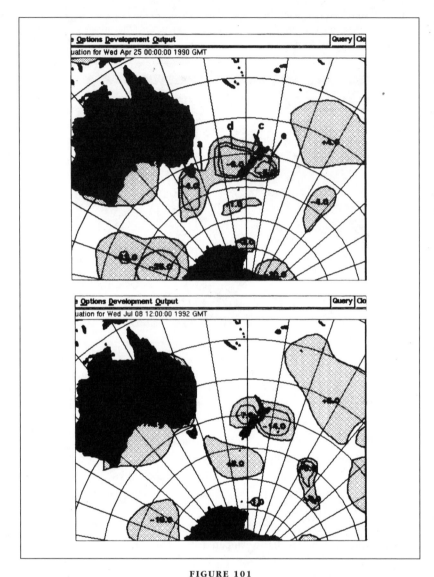

FIGURE 101
Two weather maps retrieved in response to the query in Figure 100.
From Jones and Roydhouse,"Intelligent Retrieval of Archived Meteorological Data,
IEEE Expert,10(6),1995, 50-57. © 1995, IEEE.

Zhu and Chen (2000) point out that an ideal image system should be able to search on low-level features (such as color,shape,and texture) of an image even though the user's query is at a much higher level (e.g., find all images that include orchards). When a user selects some feature (e.g., orchard) on an aerial photograph, their experimental system will look for other images that seem to contain similar features. The system employs only texture in feature matching. They expect that much better results would be obtained if matching were based on shape and color as well as texture.

The word-based indexing of images by humans is expensive, so various suggestions have been made on how concept-based indexing might be achieved automatically, or, at least, with machine aid. Goodrum et al. (2001) suggest how low-level features of images might be used to cluster such images to allow the "inheritance" of terms. Consider a collection of images that has been indexed by terms assigned by humans. A new batch of images is added to this database. The clustering techniques match the incoming images (e.g., by shape) with those already in the database. If new image X is very similar to old image A, A terms might be assigned to X also or, at least, presented as suggestions for the indexing of X. They also propose that this type of matching could be employed in quality control activities. That is, if image X and image Y "look alike" but humans have indexed them very differently, the system could create an alert to cause them to be looked at more carefully. Finally, they propose that users of an image database might be asked to provide a description of the use to which they propose to put an image (or group) and that these descriptions could provide terms that might be useful access points for future retrieval. Patrick et al. (1999) and Frost (2001) have also proposed forms of "inheritance" indexing.

For images appearing in a textual context (e.g., in a newspaper), it may be possible to automatically extract pieces of text to explicate the image. Work of this type has been described by Srihari (1993, 1995a,b, 1997) and Nakamura et al. (1993), among others. The latter discuss the integration of information from text and information from the image (in this case a diagram as it might appear in a textbook or encyclopedia). In their work, as in that of Rajagopalan (1994), the text is used to explicate the diagram. For example (from Rajogopalan) the statement "the disk is rolling down the track" may considerably clarify what is represented in a diagram that is completely static. A number of experimental systems will "annotate" (i.e., index) images based on keywords occurring in text surrounding the image. See, for example, Lieberman et al. (2001).

Srihari addresses more difficult problems and his research is much more sophisticated, drawing on the field of speech recognition as well as those of natural language processing and image understanding. One application uses the text of captions to identify humans represented in newspaper photographs. When the caption can be used to identify an individual, text from the caption can be used to index the image automatically. In one prototype system, Show & Tell (Srihari,1997), a human analyst views a landscape image at a workstation and describes (indexes) it by a combination of mouse input (pointing) and spoken language. A speech recognition system transcribes the input and synchronizes this with the mouse input. This type of "video annotation" has been extended to a system designed for the annotation of video frames with special reference to the indexing and searching of videos in military intelligence applications.

Carrick and Watters (1997) present an approach to a related problem: the automatic recognition of associations among different media, as in the recognition that a particular photograph is related to a particular news story.

It seems likely that some uses of image databases will be so imprecise that only browsing or iterative search approaches will be possible. One obvious example is the search for a face where only general features are known or remembered.* Jain (1997) discusses this problem and the iterative search approach to dealing with it (he calls it "incremental querying"):

> A user looking for certain information, for example, about a person who he vaguely recalls, specifies important things he remembers about the person [see Figure 102]. This specification may be that she has big eyes, wide mouth, long hair, and a small forehead. Based on this information, candidate people's pictures are retrieved. The user can then select the closest person that matches the query and modify the query by either specifying features or by using graphical and image-editing tools on the photo. This refines the query image, which is then sent to the system to provide new candidates to satisfy the query. Thus a query is incrementally formulated starting with the original vague idea. This process will terminate when the user is satisfied. (Page 71)

Price et al. (1992) evaluate an iterative search (relevance feedback) approach to the retrieval of images but based on textual descriptions of the images rather than pattern matching searches of the images themselves. Relevance feedback in the latter situation is dealt with in Gudivada et al. (1996). Ciocca and Schettini (1999) present an approach to automatic search modification based on the low-level features of images selected by a user as useful and of those selected as not useful.

Rowe and colleagues at the U.S. Naval Postgraduate School form one research group that has concentrated on the indexing of photographs and other images. Their approach uses a combination of text (picture captions) and pixel-level image processing. A neural net method is used for region classification applied to photographs and automatic parsing procedures are

---

*Various approaches to the recognition of photographs of faces are discussed in the literature. For example, Rickman and Stonham (1991) propose a neural network approach. The problem is also addressed by Wu et al. (1995), Pentland (1997), Li et al. (1997), Hafed and Levine (2001), and Fleuret and Geman (2001)..

applied to the captions. Their work, which focuses on multimedia data on weapons systems, includes the indexing of photographs forming part of Web pages (Rowe and Guglielmo, 1993; Rowe, 1994, 1996; Rowe and Frew, 1996, 1997; Guglielmo and Rowe, 1996).

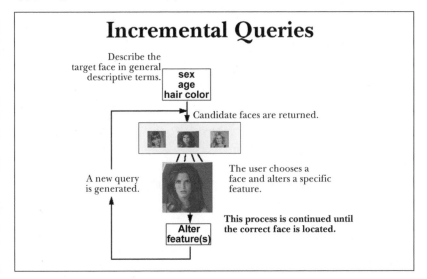

FIGURE 102
Incremental querying of an image database.
From Jain (1997) by permission of the Board of Trustees of the University of Illinois.

Gauch et al. (1999) describe a system, VISION, which will assign video clips to categories based on the terms occurring in their captions. The classification scheme used contains around 2000 categories. Incoming video can be matched against user interest profiles using this set of categories.

Vailaya et al. (2001) have developed procedures that will put images into categories based on their low-level features. The experiments they describe employ a database of almost seven thousand vacation photographs:

> Specifically, we consider the hierarchical classification of vacation images; at the highest level, images are classified as indoor, or outdoor; outdoor images are further classified as city or landscape; finally, a subset of landscape images is classified into sunset, forest, and mountain classes. (Page 117)

Classification is based on color distribution and shape characteristics.

Approaches to the indexing of collections of paintings, and other art objects, are being pursued by various research groups. For example, Ozaki et al. (1996) describe an approach that incorporates information on what is depicted and how it is depicted (e.g., spatial orientation) as well as on aesthetic factors, such as color and style.

More complex problems in image retrieval are also dealt with in the literature. For example, Cromp and Dorfman (1992) discuss an approach to dealing with remote sensing data from orbiting satellites, and Gudivada and Raghavan (1995) identify complex retrieval situations associated with certain types of image database, including the representation and retrieval of three-dimensional images ("retrieval by volume") and "retrieval by motion" (i.e., finding an image that depicts a particular action).

Geisler et al. (2001) describe ongoing work at the University of North Carolina to develop a digital video collection (the Open Video Project) that can be used as a test bed for research on the browsing, retrieval, and use of digital video segments.

A comprehensive (but highly technical) discussion of various aspects of content-based retrieval can be found in a book by Wu et al. (2000).

While some workers in the area of content-based retrieval are rather wild in their claims, others are quite modest. For example, Wang (2001), writing about his work in content-based image retrieval at Stanford University in the 1990s, admits:

> At the time, it seemed reasonable to me that I should discover the solution to the image retrieval problem during the project. Experience has certainly demonstrated how far we are as yet from solving this basic problem. (Page xi)

Images on the World Wide Web

Not surprisingly, a lot of attention is now being devoted to ways of improving the retrieval of images from the World Wide Web. Most of the major search engines do offer the capability for restricting a verbal search to the retrieval of images. However, current research deals with more sophisticated procedures such as the automatic identification of images. A book by Chang et al. (2001) gives a more up-to-date description of multimedia searching approaches within the Web.

Iyenger (2001) has edited a series of articles on image access on the Web. Chen et al. (2001) describe their method for extracting text information from Web images (from URLs, titles, text surrounding an image). These high-level semantic features can then be combined with low-level features. Liu et al. (2001) describe the text extraction in greater detail. Another approach to combining low-level and high-level features is described by Wu et al. (2001).

Rowe and Frew (1998) describe methods developed to automatically identify photographs within the World Wide Web. Photographs can be identified by a combination of characteristics, including shape, size, number of colors, and text references. The second step in this research is to automatically identify captions for these photographs. This is not a trivial task because captions can be separate from the photograph in the Web page, and sometimes embedded in larger text. They locate captions through use of "multimodal clues including the specific words used, the syntax, the surrounding layout of the Web page, and the general appearance of the associated image." They claim "a surprising degree of success" for procedures that avoid full image processing and full natural-language processing.

Several research groups are working on the recognition of photographs of people on the Web. Approaches may be based on face recognition, name occurrence in text, or a combination of these (see, for example, Aslandogan and Yu, 2000).

Agnew et al. (1997) describe an experimental approach to query by example searching of images on the World Wide Web. The system will locate the images, index them (by color, size, and other features), and store the indexes on a server. Smith and Chang (1997a) discuss another approach to indexing Web images using both textual and visual features.

Abstracting of Images

Preparation of an abstract, or other type of surrogate, for an image presents special problems, especially in the case of moving images such as television programs. Basically, two types of abstract are possible: a verbal description of the video (a fairly conventional abstract) or an abstract that is itself an image. Although text abstracts can be prepared to summarize the actions of films or television broadcasts (as demonstrated in the American Film Institute catalog), having a video abstract of scenes from the film itself may be better for some purposes. Geisler et al. (2001) point out that video abstracts can take the form of still images or of moving images. They refer to still-image abstracts as follows:

> Slide shows, storyboards, and filmstrips are examples of this type ... Usually people extract keyframes from each shot to represent it and then arrange all or a subset of the keyframes to form the abstract. The methods of selecting the keyframe and of clustering or assembling the keyframes vary in different projects. (Page 68)

They go on as follows:

> A moving-image abstract is a short video itself and can provide rich and vivid information for the users. The most recognizable example is the movie trailer ... The Movie Content Analysis Project ... selects some clips of a film and then assembles them into the final abstract. Moving-image abstracts incorporate both audio and visual information from a longer source and can be regarded as a short preview for a longer video. (Page 68)

Geisler et al. claim that much more research is needed on how people interact with video abstracts.

Ding et al. (1999) compared three types of video abstract—keyframe, verbal (keyword/phrase), and a combination of the two—on the basis of verbal comprehension (the ability of a person to get the main idea of a videoclip from the abstract) and "visual gisting". In the latter, test subjects were shown images, some from their parent video, and some not, and were asked to select those that belonged to the parent. Related work is reported by Tse et al. (1999), who studied the effects of different keyframe displays on user performance in information seeking tasks. Users judged the static displays (storyboard) easier to use than the dynamic (slide show) display, although no differences in task performance were found.

Goodrum (2001) compared four types of surrogates for videos (title, keywords, still frames, and keyframes) by comparing similarity decisions for each surrogate with similarity decisions for the videos represented, the theory being that the best surrogate is one whose similarity "map" is closest to the map for the videos themselves. Congruence was greater for the image-based surrogates than for the text-based. However, Goodrum concludes that both are needed:

> It seems clear that even though image-based surrogates performed better overall, systems for video retrieval must not exclude textual representations. Each type of surrogate makes a unique contribution to users' perception of information content, and should be included as part of a complete visual information retrieval system. (Page 11)

Lienhart et al. (1997) describe their video abstracting approach in the following terms:

> The abstracting algorithm we developed can be subdivided into three consecutive steps ... In the first step, video segmentation and analysis, the input video is segmented into its shots and scenes. At the same time, frame sequences with special events, such as text appearing in the title sequence, close-up shots of the main actors, explosions, and gunfire, are identified. In the second, clip selection, video clips are selected for inclusion in the abstract. The third, clip assembly, assembles the clips into their final sequences, and produces the presentation layout; this step involves determining the order of the video clips, the type of transitions between them, and other editing decisions. (Page 56)

Systems have ben developed to automatically select keyframes from video and incorporate them into an interface for searching or browsing of video databases (see, for example, Girgensohn et al., 2001). This is more or less equivalent to having abstracts in an interface to facilitate search and browsing of text.

A number of research groups are working to produce effective "dynamic" abstracts of video sequences. One example is the work of Nam and Tewfik (2002), who are critical of video summaries that depend on static arrangements of keyframes presented on a single screen. Such summaries do not "preserve the time-evolving dynamic nature" of the video content. They propose a video summarization approach that produces a dynamic video abstract. This is achieved by a sampling procedure which selects film segments on the basis of the amount of "activity" depicted. The video summary "presents the essential contents of the underlying video data through a fast sequential playback."

Image Attributes

The great increase of interest in image indexing and retrieval has brought with it very many studies of how people view images or react to them. Such studies are intended to reveal what types of approaches people are likely to need in image retrieval and what types of terms will be useful to describe and index images.

Jörgensen (1998) used 48 masters students in "describing tasks" in order to identify attributes of images that would be useful in indexing and retrieval. Students were all shown the same six images and were required to write a "simple description" of each, as well as a query for which the image would be a matching response. Jörgensen reports that, while the attributes occurring most often (terms for objects and people represented, body parts, clothing, color, and location) were predictable, and consistent with earlier studies, terms describing the 'story' in the picture were used much more than expected.

Heidorn (1999) studied the natural language description of objects (in this case, photographs of flowering plants) generated by people "attempting to describe objects in enough detail to allow a listener to recognize the object in a set of similar objects." He discovered that participants made heavy use of analogies in their descriptions (e.g., a plant looking like a butterfly).

Goodrum and Spink (1999) examined more than a million image queries from 211,000 users of a single web search engine, EXCITE. They found that, on the average, there were 3.74 terms per query, and that the great majority of terms used were unique, over half occurring only once.

Frost (2001) studied users searching an image database when both visual and verbal options were available. Subjects were university students, staff, and faculty members. The database comprised images relating to earth and space sciences. A major purpose of the research was to determine if users had a mental image of what they were looking for and if the image retrieved matched their mental image. Based on preliminary results, she concluded that content-based retrieval alone was not good enough for the generalist users, whereas the concept-based retrieval alone was labor-intensive. Costs of an image retrieval system might be reduced if only part of the collection was indexed. Users might then find an acceptable image in this part and use it for a visual search in the larger collection.

Work on the classification of photographs is reported by Burke (2001). She used "Personal Construct Theory" (a technique taken from the field of psychotherapy) in her classification exercises, and found "a high level of consistency among the personal constructs which participants used to distinguish between photographs."

O'Connor et al. (1999) have conducted experiments in which students were asked to view selected images and to record their reactions to them. The underlying assumption was that these reactions might be a useful source of descriptors for organizing a collection of images to facilitate future retrieval (i.e., user-centered indexing). Students were asked to write captions and also to record words or phrases to describe what is in the image and how the image made them feel. One finding of relevance to the indexing of images was the not infrequent occurrence of antonymity: a phrase used to describe an image by one student might be almost diametrically opposite to one used by another (e.g., a duck "just floating" by one, "on a mission" by a second). While the use of "reaction" terms might well be useful in indexing and retrieval of images, at least as a supplement to more conventional, descriptive terms (such as "duck" and "pond"), it is clear that they would have to be provided by a cross-section of viewers in order to capture different interpretations and viewpoints.

Based on an analysis of what types of terms a sample of users choose when looking at selected images, Greisdorf and O'Connor (2002) conclude that "affective/emotion-based query terms appear to be an important descriptive category for image retrieval." It is difficult to follow the logic of this type of statement. The affect/emotion terms (examples given include "beautiful," "ageless," "happy," "strong," "melancholy") must surely be responses that are completely time-dependent. That is, if person A considers that a particular image suggests "strong," is there any likelihood that he will have the same reaction a year or so later? The authors made no attempt to study the stability of this type of reaction or even the consistency of the reaction over a large group of people, so they have absolutely no basis for their conclusion. Moreover, it is very difficult to believe that users of an image database are likely to make much use of such terms in actual searches. "I am looking for a picture of trees that suggests 'strong'" just seems completely implausible.

Choi and Rasmussen (2002) used faculty members and graduate students from departments of history in two universities in their study of criteria by which the relevance of an image to an information need was determined. The queries used were in the field of American history. Not surprisingly, "topicality" (i.e., the image is related to the user's task) was the most important criterion in relevance judgments although other criteria, such as image quality, and clarity, were also important. As with many studies in this area, the conclusions reached by the authors are relatively trivial. For example, they conclude that users are more likely to judge the relevance of images from the images themselves than from textual descriptions of them:

> First, image retrieval systems should allow users to browse through, and compare a set of retrieved images, as viewing images makes relevance judgments easier. (Page 715)

They also conclude that relevance feedback may be more important in image retrieval than it is in text retrieval. While this may be true, no data were collected to support such a conclusion. As documented earlier in this chapter, a number of experimental systems do incorporate relevance feedback.

Chen (2001a,b) studied the queries developed by students to locate images needed to complete term papers in the field of art history. Chen makes a point of telling us that the students "seldom used the concepts of color, shape, and texture in their queries," implying perhaps that such low level features have little relevance to image retrieval in art history. But the topics assigned to the students (e.g., the role of Venice in art history) were not of the type likely to require a content-based approach to retrieval. Moreover, no image retrieval system was actually used in the study, and the image sources available to students (printed tools and Web sites) were not designed to permit content-based searching, so one is left to wonder why this conclusion was given any prominence.

Turner (1995) compared the terms that users selected to apply to images (in this case motion picture shots) with terms already associated with the images in the indexing or in written descriptions of the shot. He found a high level of agreement. Keister (1994) has contributed a useful discussion on types of queries made to an image database, in this case medical prints and photographs of historical interest, and Sutcliffe et al. (1997) have explored information-seeking strategies adopted by users of multimedia databases. Hastings (1995a,b,c) studied the kinds of access points needed by art historians. After viewing a small collection of images of paintings, the historians were interviewed to determine, among other things, what type of access points would be useful to them. Ornager (1997) has studied the needs of journalists using a newspaper image archive.

Jörgensen (1996) found that subjects asked to describe pictures were more likely to select "perceptual" attributes (i.e., rather exact characteristics such as objects depicted and their color) than "interpretive" (e.g., artistic style or "mood" of a picture) or "creative" attributes (i.e., personal reaction to the picture such as judging it ugly or disturbing). However, when prompted by means of a "template" that presented a range of attributes of all types, subjects showed greater diversity in attributes selected. She concludes from this that effective indexing of images requires use of a wide range of attributes, perceptual, interpretive, and reactive.

Concept-based or Content-based?

Layne (2002) is quite critical of the completely automatic approaches to the indexing of images:

> Who or what performs the analysis of the subject in a work of art? For some years there has been strong interest in automated analysis of images, and there have been various attempts to use pattern recognition techniques and iterative methods to identify, and retrieve relevant images. To date, none of these efforts has been particularly successful in retrieving images from heterogeneous groups or in identifying objects, such as horses, that can be depicted in a variety of poses, from many different angles, and under various lighting conditions. Automated systems are most successful in analyzing homogeneous sets of images and in selecting images based purely on color, composition, and texture. Such elements are relatively easy to codify and therefore relatively easy for a computer to identify. With what appears to be significant effort, some systems have had some success in identifying image types such as landscapes that tend to have certain common compositional and color characteristics. But it is safe to say that content-based—that is, automated—image retrieval is still far from being even remotely useful to art historians or art researchers....The ideal at this time would seem to be to let humans do what they do best and to let computers do what they do best. In other words, let humans identify the subjects of an art image, and let computers identify color, shape, and composition. For example, if human indexers were to identify the subjects of art images, a computer could, if desired, then analyze a large retrieved set of images with the same subject (for example, "cathedrals," "dance," "sarcophagi") for similarities in shape, color, or composition. (Pages 14-15)

Most writers seem to agree that effective image retrieval requires both concept-based and content-based approaches, a point put clearly by, Ornager (1994):

> Although the idea of inputting a query-picture has much to recommend it, query-pictures do not always replace the descriptive power of words which may be better for some abstract concepts. For instance it is hard to see how a query-picture could be devised for e.g., "depopulation of small Norwegian villages" or "jealousy". (Page 214)

Cawkell (1993) has addressed the same point:

> Query-pictures will replace word pictures as the techniques are refined although not all concepts can be better queried in this manner. Questions like "What pictures are there showing ladies wearing medals?", or "Are there any 17th century pictures which include animal pets?" might be successful. Abstract concepts may be better handled with word descriptors. (Page 409)

Turner (1990) has pointed out that, even if one can achieve very rapid access to an image (in this case motion picture frames), this does not preclude the need for access to a textual description:

> Furthermore, often the text acts as a guide to the image. In many cases having scanned a synopsis will help the viewer interpret the image; for example it may

be helpful to know that the train one is viewing is the Orient Express, or that the shanty town on screen is just outside Quito. In other words, the text of a visual synopsis can provide useful information not available from the image. Thus, while it is certainly desirable to have instant access to the image, this would not replace the need for a text synopsis. (Page 7)

In a similar vein, Green and Klasén (1993) describe the experiences of Swedish Television with the indexing of television programs, using purely textual descriptions. All scenes that are ten seconds or more in length are described by means of free text annotations, one example being:

Crowded market street. Market stall, oranges, apples, grapes, peaches. Case with potatoes falls. Potatoes rolling on cobble stones. Young girl with face in hands.

Trant (1995) maintains that "Textual description remains the key to retrieval of images." She stresses the need for a standard on how to describe images in image databases and mentions work done toward developing such a standard.

Mostafa and Dillon (1996) tested an interface to an image retrieval system that had both visual and verbal search capabilities. They found that their subjects (eighteen students) were more likely to use the verbal than the visual approach, suggesting that this may be due primarily to lack of familiarity with the latter.

Ogle and Stonebraker (1995), discussing their experience with a large image retrieval system at the University of California, Berkeley, agree that "the best retrieval result is obtained when text-based search criteria are combined with content-based criteria."

Text is still essential to even the most advanced multimedia retrieval applications. For example, Hauptmann and Witbrock (1997) use transcripts of the audio portion of television news broadcasts as a means of retrieving news segments on demand (speech recognition technology is used to create the transcripts and also to allow spoken queries) and Mani et al. (1997), in related research, use closed-caption text in the retrieval of broadcast news video. Closed-caption text is used in a similar way by Takeshita et al. (1997).

Even the experimental art retrieval system discussed by Kurita and Kato (1993) does not rely entirely on visual example for search purposes. An alternative is "query by subjective description," which involves indexing a painting by adjectives representing "impressions" of a viewer (e.g., "warm," "bright,""Japanesque"). Similarly, DiLoreto et al. (1995) incorporate both visual and descriptive query capabilities in their geographic retrieval system.

Cawkell (1994) is one who has highlighted the problem of content-based retrieval on its own:

The more complex the images the more difficult it is for the user to produce a usable visual example and the more difficult it is to effect pattern matching. Three-dimensional patterns may need to be matched; the difficulties are then increased. The order of difficulty is further increased if the user is interested in retrieving pictures containing a particular object within a picture.

For instance, if a user wants to retrieve "all pictures containing a motor car", it should not be too difficult to depict a car aided by currently available software embodying "clip-art" files (containing a large selection of already-drawn objects) and "drawing tool" software. When the "image-query" is submitted to the database for matching, it must be possible to retrieve a car from within any other picture no matter how it is represented, and whatever its attitude—a not impossible, but currently a slow computer-intensive task using expensive equipment. (Page 129)

It is clear that great diversity exists in image retrieval applications and not all of these are likely to benefit much from any form of content-based indexing. A study of journalist needs for photographs, by Markkula, and Sormunen (2000), found very little need for a content-based approach to retrieval, although the investigators did try to dream up some possible uses. The journalists, in fact, exhibited very simple needs (e.g., for photographs of objects or named individuals) but it is not clear how far this may have been influenced by known limitations in the photo archive indexing.

Wang (2001) gives a very useful summary of the types of queries that content-based systems are designed to deal with:

- Histogram query: find pictures with 50% red and 20% yellow . . .
- Layout query: find pictures with a blue object on the top part and a green object on the bottom part . . .
- Shape query: find pictures with three yellow triangular stars arranged in a ring . . .
- Hand-drawn sketch query: find pictures that look like a given drawing . . .
- Query by example: find pictures that look like a given picture . . .

   (Page 19)

However, he goes on to point out that most users of images will be more interested in searching on "high-level semantics":

- *Object*: contains a lesion
- *Object relationship*: contains a lesion near the cerebro-spinal fluid (CSF)
- *Mood*: a happy picture
- *Time/Place*: Yosemite evening

   (Pages 19-20)

Enser (2000) argues that concept-based searching will continue to dominate user requirements in archival image collections but that less traditional visual information needs (e.g., fingerprint and trademark matching, face recognition, texture-based classification of geological images) demand a content-based approach. The ideal is a hybrid system—one in which a verbal search can be used to retrieve relevant images and these can then be used to seek similar images based on content characteristics.

In conclusion, an optimum approach to image retrieval may be one that combines conventional access through text (index terms or descriptive narrative) with image matching. Thus, a search on words (battle, attack, fight) might retrieve an image of a particular type of scene and this, in turn, could be used as input to find others like it. A possible approach is a visual thesaurus—one that stores representative images along with verbal labels (Seloff, 1990) or possibly without the verbal labels. For a discussion of the advantages and characteristics of visual thesauri, for the searching of image databases, see Hogan et al. (1991).

Chu (2001), based on a bibliometric analysis of the literature, concludes that not enough interaction has occurred between those working in the content-based approach, and those in the concept-based, although the situation may be getting better.

Metadata and Indexing Vocabularies

Metadata and controlled vocabularies for describing art images are dealt with in a book edited by Baca (2002). The tools illustrated include Categories for the Description of Works of Art (Harpring, 2002) and ICONCLASS (Hourihane, 2002), the latter a classification scheme, with notation, for describing the people, objects, and activities represented in art works.

Metadata schemes applicable to digital images are reviewed by Greenberg (2001).

Sound Databases

Audio retrieval presents challenges that are even greater than those posed by image retrieval. The field can be divided nicely into speech retrieval and music retrieval (although other types of sounds may also be involved in some cases). Lu (2001) gives a useful concise survey of the field although it is now a little out of date because new developments occur very rapidly.

Because a long soundtrack is likely to have a number of audio components—speech, music, and, possibly, other sounds (e.g., of animal calls or waves lapping on a shore)—the first step is to classify the various components, and Lu describes methods that can be used to achieve this automatically.

Early speech recognition systems could operate only with limited vocabularies and a limited number of speakers but considerable progress has been made since then. Current systems are trained by recording speech sequences from a large number of speakers. The training phase results in several products, most notably a dictionary of words with possible pronunciations. A new sample of recorded speech is matched against this dictionary and the word sequence that is the best match is output as recorded text. This is somewhat oversimplified (for one thing, the speech unit used for matching is below the word level—a phoneme) but gives the general idea. The speech recognition systems are applied to convert the spoken word into text that can be processed in the same way that other text is for retrieval purposes—i.e., words/phrases can be extracted to act as index terms or the entire text can be searched using the types of procedure described in Chapter 14.

The performance of speech recognition systems varies with such factors as the material spoken (ranging from, for example, numbers to general news), whether the speech is read or is spontaneous conversation, and the size of the vocabulary involved. Lu (2001) points out that digit recognition can be better than 99 percent but that word recognition for a general telephone conversation can be as low as 50 percent.

The problems of spoken document retrieval (SDR) have been put very succinctly by Wechsler et al. (2000), as follows:

> The main problem when applying speech recognition for SDR is the accuracy of the recognition output. Automatic speech recognition is a difficult task and accordingly, its output often contains a considerable number of *recognition errors*. The recognition accuracy is mainly dependent on (1) the amount and quality of acoustic *training data*, (2) the number and gender of different speakers, (3) the number of units to recognize, and (4) the recording environment of the speech documents. Moreover, there are no acoustic pauses between words in continuous speech as opposed to blanks in texts.
>
> Recognition errors usually degrade the effectiveness of a SDR system. Strategies against this problem are (1) to improve the speech recognition accuracy, which requires a huge amount of training data, and time, and/or (2) to develop retrieval methods that are more error-tolerant. (Pages 173-174)

One approach is to develop a speech recognizer having a large vocabulary. This is used to convert the speech to text that can then be handled by conventional retrieval methods. This requires a very expensive investment in training the device to recognize words as spoken by different individuals. This implies restriction to a limited domain or application (e.g., patient medical records).

An alternative approach is to go below the word level and recognize and transcribe sounds (phonemes). Phoneme recognition requires less training and, since phonemes are more basic units than words, an unlimited vocabulary is possible. Spoken documents will be indexed and searched under phonemes, which is roughly equivalent to the text retrieval device of breaking words into bigrams, or trigrams for the purpose of searching efficiency. However, phonemes are not really word parts because, in speech, words are frequently run together, so that *phoneme sequences* are the units recognized. That is, the spoken document is transformed into phoneme sequences, and so is the query used to interrogate the database. Typical of current research on phoneme sequence retrieval is the work of Wechsler et al. (2000).

Not surprisingly, speech processing software does better in recognizing words occurring in a training corpus ("in-vocabulary") than it does in recognizing words not encountered before ("out-of-vocabulary"). Srinavasan and Petkovic (2000) explain the problem:

> A well known issue in spoken document retrieval is the concept of in-vocabulary terms and out-of-vocabulary terms. A vocabulary is a set of words that a speech recognition engine uses to translate speech to text. As part of the decoding process, the engine matches the acoustics from the speech input to words in the vocabulary. Therefore, only words in the vocabulary are capable of being recognized. A word not in the vocabulary will often be erroneously recognized as an in-vocabulary word that is phonetically similar to the out-of-vocabulary word. (Page 81)

The breaking of words into subwords, namely phonemes, usually improves the recognition of in-vocabulary words, although not necessarily that of out-of-vocabulary words. The effects of out-of-vocabulary words on the retrieval of spoken documents is investigated by Woodland et al. (2000).

Brown et al. (2001) report word error rates (WER) of 28 percent for conversational telephone speech from a single speaker, and a WER of around 19 percent on prepared speech (i.e., not spontaneous) from a newscaster in a studio. They claim WERs in the range of 35 to 65 percent for "real world speech data" depending on such factors as background noise, degraded acoustics, and whether, or not native speakers are involved. Although redundancy can compensate for some of the errors, retrieval is likely to be significantly degraded in the case of "real-world audio." Brown et al. report recall values of around 26 percent and precision values of around 17 percent for this type of application, although much better results (e.g., precision of 60 to 70 percent) can be achieved in smaller test collections with WERs in the 10 to 30 percent range.

Although considerable progress has been made in speech recognition, transcription errors still occur at a serious level. As Moreno et al. (2002) point out:

> Retrieval systems must compensate for the 20 to 30 percent word error rates that commonly occur when large-vocabulary speech recognizers transcribe unrestricted audio such as broadcast news or informal speech. (Pages 58-59)

Allan (2002), however, claims that even high transcription error rates may be acceptable in retrieval applications:

> Even with a 40 percent recognition error rate, the effectiveness of a typical document retrieval system decreases only 10 percent. (Page 60)

He explains that this is due to a number of factors: (1) words not recognized may not necessarily be words that are important for retrieval purposes;

(2) redundancy (if a word is not recognized in one place, it may be recognized in another), (3) synonyms or near-synonyms of the unrecognized word may occur and be recognized.

Moreno et al. (2002) give a good account of current speech recognition capabilities:

> Word-based speech recognition systems use preset vocabularies including 60,000 to 100,000 words. By definition, the system cannot hypothesize words outside this vocabulary. While a vocabulary of 100,000 words includes most spoken words, every document includes a small percentage of out-of-vocabulary (OOV) words that are likely to be content-bearing terms, and not including them has an adverse effect on retrieval performance.
>
> To circumvent this problem, the system can tailor the vocabulary by examining documents related to the task. For example, a speech recogniser used for court hearings could use legal documents to learn the appropriate dictionary words. While these specialized vocabularies can reduce the number of OOV words, they cannot guarantee their elimination. (Page 59)

They go on to point out that systems based on subword recognition offer advantages:

> Rather than recognizing spoken words, these approaches recognize subword units —typically, phonemes, or syllables—from which all words are constructed. The IR system decomposes search terms into their constituent subword strings, then scans the recognized terms for strings corresponding to the search unit. (Page 59)

Singhal and Pereira (1999) have experimented with "document expansion" to compensate for transcription errors in speech retrieval. Their method involves the expansion of a transcribed text by adding high-frequency words occurring in "related" texts, thus compensating, by redundancy, for words missed in transcription. This seems to be a very labored approach.

Brown et al. (2001), whose paper also provides a useful overview of speech recognition technology, describe work at IBM in "speech mining" applications. One such is an intelligent agent that captures the discussions held during a business or research meeting and "periodically becomes an active participant ... whenever it finds information that it determines is highly pertinent to the current discussion." For example, occurrence of an employee name in the discussion can trigger a search of employee records to retrieve and make available such information as address, phone number, group affiliation, responsibilities, expertise. Meeting support technology has also been investigated by other institutions. Brown et al. also describe work on the mining of telephone sales calls.

Research on spoken document retrieval is now facilitated by the existence of a spoken document database within the TREC (Text Retrieval Conferences) environment (see following chapter). The TREC 7 corpus consisted of about 100 hours of broadcast news programs, representing about 3000 news stories. Participating research groups worked with different quality transcripts of this corpus, including one humanly prepared and assumed to be perfect, one prepared by a speech recognition system with about a 35% word error rate, and one with an error rate of around 50%. The participating research groups tested their retrieval approaches for 23 preselected topics on each of these transcripts (Voorhees and Harman, 1999).

Research on speech interfaces in retrieval applications goes back for several years (see, for example, Smith et al., 1989). More modern approaches are exemplified by the work of Feder and Hobbs (1995). Discussing human speech input to computer operations, Shneiderman (2000) presents reasons why human limitations (e.g., fatigue, impatience, error correction difficulties) may be more significant than technological limitations.

Modern methods for synthesizing and archiving sounds electronically can make large numbers of sounds available (e.g., to the musician), but the retrieval of a particular sound from such an archive presents a significant problem. Feiten and Günzel (1994) describe an approach to indexing and retrieval of sounds through use of neural networks. The retrieval index is created automatically. The ability to recognize and label (i.e., index) sounds automatically has much in common with the processing needed to recognize images automatically. As Picard and Minka (1995) point out, there exists "sound texture" as well as image texture. Thus, it should be possible to develop techniques to identify certain sounds (a bell ringing, water running, applause) automatically using some form of (sound) pattern matching. Retrieval of sounds is discussed in a paper by Blum et al. (1997). They describe a "sound browser" developed to allow fuzzy searches on audio databases. Capabilities include query by example (i.e., "find sounds similar to ...").

Music Retrieval

The objective of modern approaches to the retrieval of music is to "answer music queries framed musically" (Downie and Nelson, 2000)—that is, to allow a search based on a musical input (e.g., sung or hummed).

The history of music information retrieval has been traced back to the 1960s but most of the progress has occurred since the 1990s. It is encapsulated in the proceedings of three annual international symposia on the subject, held in 2000, 2001, and 2002. The 2000 papers are available at this site: <http://ciir.cs.umass.edu/music2000/papers.html> and the 2001 papers at this site: <http://ismir2001.indiana.edu/papers.html>.

An important objective of these symposia is the development of a standard collection of music, queries, and evaluations that can be used to compare different approaches in much the same way that the TREC conferences operate.

Music retrieval is more complex than speech retrieval. Lu (2001) divides the field into (1) structured or synthetic music, and (2) sample based music. In the former, the music notes are recorded in algorithms and control languages, making matching against queries (in the form of a sequence of notes) relatively easy, at least in the case of exact match. Detecting "similar" music passages is more complicated.

Much more complicated is retrieval from music that is not recorded in structured form. Lu (2001) refers to this as "sample-based" because it implies the recognition and extraction of musical samples. He identifies two indexing/retrieval approaches. The first is based on the extraction of "acoustic features" (such as loudness, pitch, brightness, bandwidth, and harmonicity) and these can be calculated for each "frame" of the recorded piece. A piece of music, used as a query (usually a hummed form), is reduced to the same features, allowing a search on a pattern matching basis. In the second approach, indexing and retrieval are based on pitch. The pitch for each note is extracted or estimated. Each pitch can be represented as a change (up, down, or similar) relative to the preceding one so the musical piece (or query piece) is represented by a string of symbols representing these pitch changes. Alternatively, each musical note can be represented by a pitch value selected from a set of "standard" pitch values on a closest match basis. Again, the musical piece will be represented by a string of characters representing the pitch value.

Lippincott (2002) gives a very useful and concise statement of what current approaches to music retrieval are trying to accomplish:

> In the past, users seeking information about music turned to print sources containing metadata hand-recorded, and arranged by title, composer, and other categories. Obviously access methods mirrored print-based retrieval techniques for bibliographic information retrieval of the time and similarly presupposed some prior musical knowledge or access to a librarian. Much current research into automated Music Information Retrieval (MIR) is based upon characterizations of the music itself, rather than information about it. For instance, instead of requiring a search by song title, a user inputs a query in the form of audio, and retrieves results similar to that query. The implications for average users of content-based music retrieval systems are significant because prior bibliographic knowledge of a piece of music is not necessary; rather a bit of music running through one's mind suffices for retrieval purposes. (Page 137)

Her paper is an excellent summary of various methods under investigation. Liu and Tsai (2001) point out that:

> The most straightforward way to query the music databases for a naive user is to hum a piece of music as the query example to retrieve similar music objects. (Page 506)

One of the problems, however, is the great difference in length between this type of query example and a piece of music: a hummed music query is typically a few seconds long whereas a typical pop song is about five minutes in length. They describe an experimental approach in which matching is made more efficient by sequencing a piece of music into "phases" that are roughly the same length as a hummed music query.

In the indexing and retrieval of music, a distinction needs to be made between monophonic music (no new note begins until the current note has finished sounding) and polyphonic music (a note may begin before the previous one ends). Polyphonic music is more usual but more complex for indexing and retrieval operations. The problems of feature selection for indexing and retrieval of polyphonic music are described by Pickens (2001).

Several approaches to the indexing and retrieval of polyphonic music have been described. See, for example, Dovey (2001) and Doraisamy and Rüger (2001).

Downie and Nelson (2000) describe an approach to music retrieval based on pitch, specifically the difference between two pitches, known as the "interval." The melodies from a collection of folksongs were "converted into an interval-only representation of monophonic melodies." These were then fragmented into subsections referred to as "n-grams," which are used to form "musical words." This allows an approach to retrieval that parallels word search in text retrieval and allows a text-based processing system (Salton's SMART), allowing ranked retrieval, to be applied.

Audio input can also be used to search a database of musical scores. McNab et al. (2000) describe an approach to the retrieval of musical scores from a database in response to "a few notes sung or hummed into a microphone." The interface used transcribes the acoustic input into standard music notation which can be used for string matching and ranked retrieval of music. Their "proof of concept" prototype has been tested on a database of folk songs. They conclude that:

> Searching large music databases and retrieving items in which a given theme or sequence of notes occurs is not a trivial undertaking, particularly given the inaccuracies that occur when people sing known melodies, but it is certainly within the scope of current technology. (Page 113)

Byrd and Crawford (2002) review the state of the art of music indexing and retrieval and conclude that rather little progress has been achieved in this area:

> Although a substantial number of research projects have addressed music information retrieval over the past three decades, the field is still very immature. Few of these projects involve complex (polyphonic) music; methods for evaluation are at a very primitive stage of development; none of the projects tackles the problem of realistically large-scale databases. Many problems to be faced are due to the nature of music itself. Among these are issues in human perception and cognition of music, especially as they concern the recognizability of a musical phrase.... the common assumption that searching on pitch (or pitch-contour) alone is likely to

be satisfactory for all purposes ... may indeed be true for most monophonic (single-voice) music, but it is certainly inadequate for polyphonic (multi-voice) music. Even in the monophonic case it can lead to misleading results. The fact, long recognized in projects involving monophonic music, that a recognizable passage is usually not identical with the search pattern means that approximate matching is almost always necessary, yet this too is severely complicated by the demands of polyphonic music. Almost all text-IR methods rely on identifying approximate units of meaning, that is, words. A fundamental problem in music IR is that locating such units is extremely difficult, perhaps impossible. (Page 249)

Multimedia Systems

So far this chapter has dealt with image retrieval and with sound retrieval. However, work is also proceeding on indexing and retrieval problems associated with true multimedia presentations, such as television broadcasts.

A multimedia indexing system described by Kubala et al. (2000) processes spoken language from audio and video sources such as television news broadcasts. The prototype has summarization* and indexing capabilities. The authors describe the former as follows:

> The summarization is a structural representation of the content in spoken language that is very powerful and flexible as an index for content-based information management. This summary, which is automatically produced by the system, includes extracted features such as the names of people, places, and organizations mentioned in the transcript as well as the identities and locations of the speakers in the recording. (Page 49)

The continuous stream of words is automatically broken into "passages that are thematically coherent" and each passage is indexed by the automatic assignment of "topic labels" drawn from a pre-established set of more than 5000 such labels. The labels are ranked by probability of appropriateness and the highest ranked labels for each passage are assigned.

A major multimedia indexing and retrieval initiative is the Informedia Digital Video Library project at Carnegie Mellon University. Wactlar et al. (2000) describe its capabilities as follows:

> [It] uniquely utilizes integrated speech and image and natural language understanding to process broadcast video. ... To enable this access to video, fast, high accuracy automatic transcriptions of broadcast news stories are generated through Carnegie Mellon's Sphinx speech recognition system, and closed captions are incorporated where available. Image processing determines scene boundaries, recognizes faces, and allows for image similarity comparisons. Text visible on the screen is recognized through video OCR and can be searched. Everything is indexed into a searchable digital video library, where users can ask queries, and retrieve relevant news stories as results. ...

---

*The problems involved in automatically creating summaries of spoken dialogue are well presented by Zechner (2001).

The Informedia system allows information retrieval in both spoken language and video or image domains. Queries for relevant news stories may be made with words, images, or maps. Faces are detected in the video and can be searched. Information summaries can be displayed at varying detail, both visually, and textually. Text summaries are displayed for each news story through topics and titles. Visual summaries are given through thumbnail images, filmstrips, and dynamic video skims. (Pages 42-43)

Wactlar et al. claim that an error rate of less than 20 percent in speech recognition is possible and that a transcript of a news broadcast can appear in the database within 2.5 hours of broadcast time.

Brown et al. (2001) present more detail:

The Informedia research project has created a terabyte digital library in which automatically derived descriptors for the video are used for indexing, segmenting, and accessing the library contents. It combines speech recognition, image processing, and natural language understanding techniques for processing video automatically to produce a video "skim," which reduces viewing time without losing content. It offers three ways to view the search results: poster frames, filmstrips, and skims. The poster frame view presents search results in poster frame format with each frame representing a video "paragraph." The filmstrip view reduces the need to view each video paragraph in its entirety by providing storyboard pages for quick viewing. The most relevant subsections of the video paragraph are displayed as key scenes, and key words are clearly marked. Combined word and phonetic retrieval has also been explored in the Informedia project where an inverted index for a phonetic transcript comprising phonetic substrings of three to six phones have been used. During retrieval, the word document index and phonetic transcription index are searched in parallel, and the results are merged. Experiments on a corpus of about 500 ABC News and CNN (Cable News Network) stories using combined word and phone indexes resulted in an average precision of .67 with an overall performance of 84.6 percent of that of a full-text retrieval system. However, for real-world audio with high WER of 70-80 percent, the precision and recall have been reported to drop dramatically to 0.17, and 0.26, respectively. (Pages 989-990)

The image searching capabilities of the Informedia system include color detection (the user specifies colors and regions of interest to be sought among the images). See Wactlar et al. (1999).

Patel and Sethi (1996) describe methods they developed to classify motion picture segments through audio processing. At first, the system could only identify broad categories (such as "musical") but the authors suggest that it could be refined to more specifically identify types of scene (action scene, dancing scene, romantic scene, and so on). Later (Patel and Sethi, 1997), they extended their research to speaker identification (e.g., of actors in video clips from movies).

Adami et al. (2001) propose a system for providing access to multimedia documents by tools analogous to those of a printed book: a hierarchical description of the contents of the item (similar to a conventional contents page) suitable for browsing, and an "analytical index" based on keywords (analogous to a back-of-the-book index).Their research aims to produce such tools automatically and they present an example based on an analysis of a soccer match.

Gauvain et al.(2001) describe a system for automatic partitioning and transcription of television and radio broadcasts.Non-speech segments of the broadcast are identified and removed (automatically) and the remaining segments are clustered and labeled according to bandwith and gender. A "speaker-independent, large vocabulary, continuous speech recognizer" is applied to prepare the transcripts.An average word error of 20 percent is claimed.

Conclusions

Much progress has been made in the indexing and retrieval of images in the last decade, and some progress has occurred in the indexing, and retrieval of sounds. The very many studies done on viewer reaction to images, however, are of variable quality. Some are valuable but others, especially those performed as dissertation research, leave a lot to be desired. Although elaborate statistical analyses of data are presented, too many of these studies arrive at conclusions that are not even addressed by the data collected, giving the impression that the conclusions were arrived at before any study was done.

The fields of image and sound retrieval have attracted many investigators with no previous exposure to text retrieval.This has resulted in the emergence of new terminology for very old ideas, which is really rather unfortunate.A prime example is use of "annotation" to refer to the assignment of a verbal label to an image—i.e., indexing it (see, for example, Picard and Minka.1995).

Clearly,future developments in the retrieval of spoken discourse depend very much on what progress is made in the general field of speech technology.The more popular trade journals tend to be wildly optimistic about future possibilities. For example, the claim of Flynn (1993):

> By the end of the decade, speech recognition systems will let you speak naturally with a virtually limitless vocabulary. (Page 29)

was completely unrealistic as stated.

Haas (1996), citing Rudnicky, makes an important point relevant to future prospects in this area:

> There is a distinction between speech recognition and speech understanding: speech recognition requires that a system identify the words in an utterance, while speech understanding requires that a system also handle the problems of NL understanding, such as anaphora, ellipsis, and other discourse phenomena. Speech recognition is useful for structured tasks such as data entry and issuing simple commands, but a dialogue of any kind requires speech understanding. (Page 98)

The understanding of human speech by computer is not a prospect that is on the immediate horizon.

Even within the community of researchers in this field, there exists a wide divergence of opinion on what speech recognition technology has achieved, and what is likely to come in the near term. Levinson (1995), for example, believes that it will be a long time before systems of real commercial value will emerge:

> The majority opinion holds that technical improvements will soon make large-vocabulary speech recognition commercially viable for specific applications. My prediction ... is that technical improvements will appear painfully slowly but that in 40 to 50 years speech recognition at human performance levels will be ubiquitous. That is, incremental technical advances will, in the near term, result in a fragile technology of relatively small commercial value in very special markets, whereas major technological advances resulting from a true paradigm shift in the underlying science will enable machines to display human levels of competence in spoken language communication. This, in turn, will result in a vast market of incalculable commercial value. (Page 9954)

However, Srinavasan and Brown (2002) point out that, while speech technology was slow to find commercial applications, it now seems poised to take off commercially:

> The Web's connectivity, wireless technology, and handheld devices—combined with effective grammar-based speech recognition ...—may finally bring speech recognition to mass-market prominence. (Page 38)

Exaggerated claims also occur in the image retrieval field. Many investigators in the image retrieval field are completely naive in their beliefs and expectations. To quote but one example, Gupta and Jain (1997), in an otherwise useful overview of image retrieval, encourage us as follows:

> Users can now elicit, store, and retrieve "imagery-based" information content—metadata and visual features—in visual media as easily as they query text documents. (Page 71)

Those of us who have been working in this area for more than forty years know that retrieval from text documents is far from easy in databases of any significant size.

It is important to recognize that research on the retrieval of images or sounds depends much more on techniques for automatic indexing than for indexing by humans. Therefore, the approaches dealt with in the next two chapters are quite closely related to the content of this one.

CHAPTER 14

Text Searching

THE APPLICATION OF COMPUTERS to information retrieval, beginning in the 1950's, made possible the searching of text in electronic form, without the need to apply any form of indexing to this text: the program used for retrieval looks for particular words, or combinations of words, in the text itself, where the words chosen by the searcher are indicative of what the text is discussing. The searching of text by computer may be referred to as "text searching" or as "natural language searching." The text searched can be the complete text of a publication (article, report, or even a book) or some part of it: an abstract, an extract, or only a title. The searching of a complete text is sometimes referred to as "full text search."

The feasibility of text searching has increased considerably over the years as computing power has increased, computing and storage costs have decreased, and more and more text has become available in electronic form, largely as a byproduct of various forms of publishing. The development of the Web, which makes vast quantities of text accessible to huge numbers of users, has made text search the norm rather than the exception. As might be expected from all of this, interest in text searching methods has increased very greatly in the last decade, in the research community as well as in government and commercial sectors.

The field of text searching has been moved forward since 1991 by the TIPSTER program and several other activities related to it. TIPSTER was an initiative of the Defense Advanced Research Projects Agency (DARPA), with the collaboration of the National Institute of Standards and Technology, other government agencies, and several commercial enterprises. The program has had several components, the one most relevant to this chapter being the annual Text Retrieval Conferences (TRECs), of which 11 had been held through 2002. The TREC activities advance the state of the art by allowing different research groups to test and compare their retrieval software under controlled conditions (database, queries, and relevance assessments held constant). Other TIPSTER components are dealt with in the next chapter.

In point of fact, this chapter, and the next one are so closely related that they should really be read as a single unit. Deciding what to include in Chapter 14 and what to defer to Chapter 15 has been a somewhat arbitrary decision at times.

Modern text processing procedures claim to apply techniques drawn from artificial intelligence research, and the term "intelligent text processing" is sometimes used to refer to procedures of this type (see, for example, Jacobs, 1992c).

This chapter will review the relative merits of text (natural language) and controlled vocabulary approaches to information retrieval, survey the development of text searching since the 1950s, and conclude with a discussion on current capabilities in this area.

The term *natural language* can be considered synonymous with "ordinary discourse"—i.e., the language commonly used in writing and conversation, and the opposite of "controlled vocabulary." In the information retrieval context, the term usually refers to the words occurring in printed text and, thus, "free text" can be considered to be a synonym. Free text can consist of:

1. the title,
2. an abstract,
3. an extract, or
4. the full text of a publication.

While "free text" usually refers to some intact portion of a text, it can also be used to refer to words or phrases extracted from the text by a human indexer (or by computer program) and included in a bibliographic record representing the text. In some cases these extracted terms are added to the titles of items indexed and thus form "expanded" or "enriched" titles.

Some History

"Modern" approaches to the use of natural language in information retrieval can be traced back to the Uniterm system described by Taube in 1951. The principles of the Uniterm system had immediate appeal: the subject matter of documents could be adequately represented by single words (uniterms) extracted from the text of documents by indexers of a relatively low level of expertise. By writing or typing, document numbers were "posted" to specially-designed cards, each card representing a single term, and searches were performed by comparing the numbers on two or more cards (in much the same way that a modern online system compares lists of numbers associated with terms).

Taube had considerable influence on the development of information retrieval systems in the 1950s. Unfortunately, however, the Uniterm system proved less attractive than it seemed at first sight. It suffered from all of the problems that controlled vocabularies were set up to solve. Closely related subject matter appeared under several different uniterms, and a comprehensive search on a topic would require that the searcher think of all of the ways that this topic might be represented in text—not always an easy task. These problems led to a return to controlled vocabularies and the development of the information retrieval thesaurus (Holm & Rasmussen, 1961).

Besides the terminological problems, the Uniterm system suffered from mechanical limitations. A human searcher can readily compare numbers on only two cards at a time. Thus, a search on A related to B, where A might be represented by four uniterms and B by ten, would require 4 x 10 separate card comparisons. While possible, this would be a tedious and time-consuming task. Moreover, while the Boolean *and* relationship (involving comparison of numbers) is easy to achieve through the manipulation of Uniterm (or peek-a-boo) cards, it is very difficult in manual systems of this kind to perform a Boolean *or* search (involving the amalgamation of lists) and especially to combine (*and*) sets of terms in an *or* relationship. Such term manipulations, of course, are trivial in computer-based systems. The computer, then, solves the "mechanical" problems involved in manipulating large numbers of uncontrolled terms but does not in itself solve the intellectual problems created by lack of vocabulary control.

Nevertheless, when computers were first applied to information retrieval at a significant level, in the late 1950s and early 1960s, it was recognized that text searching, and even full text searching, had become an attractive possibility. In tracing the history of computer-based systems for information retrieval, two principal lines of development can be recognized. One stems from the large systems, developed by such agencies as the National Library of Medicine (NLM), the Department of Defense (DOD), and the National Aeronautics and Space Administration (NASA), that operated on the basis of index terms drawn from a controlled vocabulary and assigned to documents by human indexers. The other line of development began in the field of law and involved putting complete text (e.g., of statutes) into electronic form and using a computer to search for words or word combinations in this text. Work of this nature actually predated the development of thesauri and the emergence of the large systems based on human indexing. Full text legal retrieval can be traced back to the work of Horty and his colleagues at the Health Law Center of the University of Pittsburgh (Horty, 1960, 1962, Kehl et al., 1961). It was in the legal field that modern techniques for the searching of free text were first developed, and the early work at Pittsburgh laid the foundations for the later legal retrieval systems exemplified by LEXIS and WESTLAW. Myers (1973) prepared a useful review of the state of the art in the searching of legal text by computer. While old, it remains a good account of basic principles. Dabney (1986) acts as an update.

The distinction between those systems based primarily on controlled vocabularies and indexing records created by humans (often misleadingly referred to as "bibliographic" systems) and those based on the searching of text has become increasingly blurred over the years. Gradually, the "bibliographic" systems allowed the searching of words occurring in titles and, later, in abstracts, while some of the full text systems added humanly-assigned index terms to improve access and some databases (e.g., INSPEC) were designed from the beginning to include both controlled terms and uncontrolled "keywords." As more and more text became available in electronic form as a byproduct of publishing or dissemination activities, text searching of abstracts became commonplace and full text searching now extends well beyond law: newspapers, popular magazines, scholarly journals, encyclopedias, and other sources are now accessible in full text form. The Web sites of the Internet consist mostly of text, so it is undoubtedly true that text searches now greatly exceed searches involving controlled vocabulary.

Text searching can be achieved in two ways. In the first approach, nontrivial words are entered into "inverted" files showing, for each word, which document it appears in (and frequently its exact position in that document). Searching is performed in these indexes (which in the original implementation at Pittsburgh were referred to as a "concordance") rather than in the text itself. The other alternative is to search the text sequentially, word by word, with no use of indexes. This was the technique commonly used to provide Selective Dissemination of Information (SDI) services from databases before online systems were widespread. That is, stored profiles of user interests were matched against periodic updates of the database (words in titles or abstracts). This "streaming" approach to the searching of text was more attractive for SDI applications than for retrospective searching because the amount of text to be scanned at any one time is much less in SDI. Later, however, special-purpose computers were developed to search text so rapidly that streaming searches of even very large databases were quite feasible. For example, the Fast Data Finder (Yu et al., 1987) claimed to search text at the rate of 12½ million characters per second, which is equivalent to about 12½ 500-page novels every second.

While the "streaming" approach is no different conceptually from the inverted index approach, it does have improved capabilities. For example, it is much easier to search on word "fragments," especially strings of characters occurring in the middle or end of a word.

The search engines that have been developed within the Internet work by compiling "indexes" of text in the various sites that are nothing more than conventional inverted files.

Searching Aids

Even in the very early days of text searching, various aids were developed to assist the searcher. The most primitive is the alphabetic display (or print-out) of the "significant" words occurring in the database, with an indication of how frequently each one occurs. Some type of word distance indicator (metric operator) was also common. The ability to specify how close two words must be is particularly useful in the searching of full-text databases where words occurring in different paragraphs may not be directly related at all.

Perhaps the most powerful aid to natural language searching is the ability to search on parts of words—that is, to truncate or perform word fragment searching. The value of word fragment searching has been discussed by Williams (1972). The most flexible software allows searching on any fragment: right truncation (e.g., all words beginning with "condens"), left truncation (all words ending with "mycin"), "infix" truncation (the beginning and end of a word are specified but the middle is not), or any possible combination of these (e.g., all words including the character string "magnet," wherever it appears). Although potentially useful in all fields, word fragment searching seems most valuable in science and technology, where the language tends to be more predictable. In a sense, this capability allows one to compensate for lack of a controlled vocabulary by building useful classes of words into a strategy. Thus, searching on the stem "condens" will presumably allow retrieval of a group of documents having something to do with condensers and condensation; searching on the suffix "mycin" will produce documents dealing with antibiotics; and searching on "tri . . . cobaltate" (infix unspecified) will retrieve a related family of chemical compounds.

Word fragment searching achieves some of the capabilities of the conventional thesaurus but does so at the time of output rather than imposing control at the input stage. For example, the ability to search on the suffixes "biotics or illin or mycin or cycline or myxin" goes a long way toward equivalency with a conventional thesaurus entry "antibiotics" that leads to a list of narrower antibiotics terms. The conventional thesaurus is a pre-controlled vocabulary, whereas the building of word or word fragment classes into a search strategy is a kind of "post-controlling" process.

Natural Language Versus Controlled Vocabulary: Some General Considerations

Some major factors influencing the performance of information retrieval systems can be illustrated by further reference to Figure 3. On the left are three free text representations of a document (a title and two abstracts of varying length), while two sets of index terms (selective and exhaustive coverage of the subject matter) appear on the right. The terms are drawn from the *UNBIS Thesaurus* (United Nations, Dag Hammarskjold Library, 1985). One major factor influencing the performance of information retrieval systems is the number of access points provided. Clearly, the expanded abstract provides more than the brief abstract which, in turn, provides more than the title. Likewise, the exhaustive indexing provides almost three times the number of access points provided by the selective indexing.

A text search on the title alone is likely to allow this item to be retrieved only in a search for the central subject matter of the document. As one adds more text, the item becomes retrievable in searches on other aspects. The brief abstract could allow retrieval in searches on: U.S. aid, the PLO, the Palestinian State, Israel, U.S. aid to Israel, and peace conferences, while the expanded abstract adds further access points, such as peace efforts and Middle East leaders. Of course, the same is true of the comparison between the selective indexing and the exhaustive indexing. The selective indexing mirrors only the title of the item and provides no more access points than the title, while the exhaustive indexing is more or less equivalent in breadth to the expanded abstract.

In considering the retrievability of the item depicted, it is the length of the record, rather than type of vocabulary, that is of most importance. The selective indexing is equivalent in this respect to the title, while the exhaustive indexing falls somewhere between the two abstracts in the extent to which it covers the subject matter of the item. Because the brief abstract provides more access points than title or selective indexing, the item it represents will be more retrievable. Likewise, the exhaustive indexing may make this item more retrievable than it would be in a search on the brief abstract but less retrievable than it would be in a search on the expanded abstract.

A database consisting of thousands of items indexed exhaustively, as in the example of Figure 3, is likely to allow a much higher recall than one providing access through titles only. Similarly, a database consisting of "expanded" abstracts is likely to allow higher recall than one based on selective indexing or even, perhaps, exhaustive indexing. This has nothing to do per se with the comparison of natural language versus controlled vocabularies in information retrieval, but relates only to the length of the searchable record.

Unfortunately, several investigators have failed to control for the length of the record in comparing retrieval based on free text with retrieval based on indexing. That exhaustive indexing gives higher recall than titles is hardly surprising and does not prove that human indexing is superior to free text. That a lengthy abstract gives higher recall than selective indexing is hardly surprising and does not prove that free text is superior to human indexing.*

Nevertheless, abstracts will frequently provide more access points than will a set of descriptors assigned by an indexer, and the full text of a document will certainly do so, so one would expect that free text databases will generally allow greater recall than those based on human indexing.

Another important factor affecting the performance of a retrieval system is the specificity with which the subject matter of a document can be described. The *UNBIS Thesaurus* terms are quite specific in describing most aspects of the subject matter of the item depicted in Figure 3 (although the 1995 edition is less so since it drops some terms, such as *telephone surveys*, that were in the 1985 edition). Nevertheless, the free text does provide greater specificity in that it allows retrieval on the names of Middle East leaders, while the indexing allows only a search at the "political leaders" level.

The more access points provided for retrieval, the higher the recall possible but the lower is likely to be the precision. One reason is simply the fact that, the more access points provided, the more likely it is that some of these will relate to rather minor aspects of a document. Thus, a requester receiving the Figure 3 item in a search relating to Arafat might judge it to be of no use because it deals with Arafat too briefly and tangentially.

The more access points provided, also, the greater the possibility that some spurious relationships will exist. As discussed in Chapter 11, these are of two types: (1) false associations and (2) incorrect term relationships. Many possibilities can be seen in Figure 3. For example, the expanded abstract might cause this item to be retrieved in a search on telephone interviews with Middle East leaders (or any of the individual leaders mentioned), and the exhaustive indexing might cause it to be retrieved in a search on political leaders of the United States. These are false associations in that the terms that caused retrieval are essentially unrelated in the document (*telephone interviews* is not directly related to any of the leaders and *United States* is not directly related to *political leaders*).

A more subtle type of spurious relationship is illustrated in the selective indexing or even in the title. Either might cause this item to be retrieved in a search on Middle East attitudes toward the U.S. In this case the terms *Middle East, attitudes*, and *United States* are directly related, but the relationship is ambiguous.

The longer the record, the greater the chance that spurious relationships will occur. Spurious relationships, of course, cause lower precision.

---

*Regrettably, the results of such defective studies are still being put forward as though they had validity (see, for example, Olson, and Boll, 2001).

Some further lessons on the differences between controlled vocabulary and natural language can be learned from Figure 103. In this case the *UNBIS Thesaurus* does a poor job of indexing this item. The abstract is much more specific than the controlled terms: no term exists in the thesaurus for "peer tutoring" or even for "tutoring." This example also illustrates the fact that natural language will tend to be more redundant than controlled indexing terms. For example, the abstract contains the term *programmed learning* as well as the term *programmed instruction* so the item could be retrieved on whichever of these terms a searcher happens to use. The full text of a document is likely to provide considerable redundancy, increasing the chance that it will include an expression used by a searcher and thus improving recall.

Human indexing, of course, is a subjective intellectual process and indexers may not always include a topic that should be included, represent a topic with the best possible term, or make explicit some relationship of potential interest to certain users. The completeness and redundancy of full text avoid this type of problem. Horty (1962), the real pioneer of full text searching, recognized this more than forty years ago:

> When the full text of documents is used as the basis for a retrieval system an inquiry is not bound by the way in which the documents have been indexed. Almost inevitably an indexer is unaware of certain subjects to which the statutory section is applicable or might be applicable in the future. Yet research, by its very nature, dictates that the researcher is looking for novel relationships between a number of subjects; relationships which may not have been anticipated by an indexer. By completely dispensing with an index and going to the original text for each search, such novel relationships can be found. (Page 59)

On the other hand, of course, this very redundancy creates great problems when the text of many documents is combined to form a large database—there are many ways in which a topic can be expressed in full text and, in some cases, the topic is represented implicitly rather than explicitly (O'Connor, 1965), making high recall difficult to achieve. A controlled vocabulary reduces this diversity of terminology. Moreover, by linking semantically related terms, it helps the user to identify all the terms that would be needed to achieve a complete search.

Another factor to be considered is "recency." New terms will enter titles or abstracts long before they appear in a controlled vocabulary. For new topics, then, natural language is likely to win hands down. Precision will be better because the controlled vocabulary will not allow a specific search. Recall is also likely to be better because the searcher will not need to guess what terms to use. Finally, use of the controlled vocabulary will tend to favor the information specialist, who can become fully familiar with the policies

**THE USE OF PEER TUTORING AND
PROGRAMMED RADIO INSTRUCTION;
VIABLE ALTERNATIVES IN EDUCATION**
Hannum, W. H.; Morgan, R. M.
1974, 38p.

Florida State University
College of Education
Center for Educational Technology
Tallahassee, Florida 32306

Educational radio*
Programmed instruction*
Developing countries
Nonformal education
Teachers

Educators in developing countries are likely
to achieve more by applying the principles
rather than the things of educational technology. The principles of program learning have
been shown to be effective in promoting
learning in a wide variety of circumstances.
The most effective instructional materials can
be developed through use of the principles
of programmed instruction and mastery
learning. Radio, when combined with the
use of peer tutors, can be an effective
educational tool in developing countries. The
concepts of programmed learning and
mastery learning can be incorporated in the
design of educational radio programs. Such
programs, accompanied by peer tutors, can
accomplish the total educational effort
within the resources of many developing
countries. This type of educational system is
a viable alternative to traditional formal
education. Such a system should be tried in
several developing countries to explore its
full potential.

FIGURE 103
Comparison of abstract and indexing using a controlled vocabulary.

The abstract is reproduced from *A.I.D. Research & Development Abstracts* by permission of the Center
for Development Information and Evaluation, United States Agency for International Development.
The terms marked * are those the indexer considered most important for this item.

and protocols behind it, while natural language may favor the subject specialist user. Deschâtelets (1986) is one author who has stressed the importance of making a controlled language as close as possible to the natural
language of a field.

So far we have identified several characteristics of free text and also of
human indexing with controlled terms and have related these to their
probable effects on recall and precision. These relationships are summarized

in Figure 104. It is obvious from this that the situation is a complex one in that some factors favor controlled terms and some favor free text. The specificity of text words tends to improve precision but to make it more difficult to achieve high recall, at least in broad "conceptual" searches, while the length of text tends to improve recall but to reduce precision. Whether one is to be preferred to another in a particular situation is very much influenced by the type of search being conducted: a broad conceptual search will favor controlled terms, a highly specific search (particularly one involving named individuals, organizations, and so on) will favor free text, a really comprehensive search on a topic (e.g., every possible reference to some drug) will favor full text, while a highly selective search (only the more important items) is likely to favor controlled term indexing.

In general, other authors have come to similar conclusions. For example, Fugmann (1985) points out that natural language searching may yield good results in the case of "individual concepts" but not for "general concepts"; Dubois (1987) claims that one of the advantages of free text is "no delay in incorporating new terms"; and Perez (1982) states that "a controlled vocabulary may result in a loss of precision" while free text has "no loss of specificity." Knapp (1982) mentions "specific topics," "hot topics" and "new terminology" as examples of cases in which natural language is likely to be more useful.

Of course, cost aspects must also be taken into account in a natural language/controlled vocabulary comparison. The cost of human intellectual processing continues to rise rapidly relative to the cost of machine processing, and indexing with a controlled vocabulary is a labor-intensive, costly proposition. Construction and maintenance of a controlled vocabulary can also be expensive. As more and more text becomes available cheaply in electronic form, as a byproduct of publishing or dissemination activities, it is natural that the managers of information services should look carefully at the situation to decide whether the advantages of controlled vocabulary indexing really justify the additional costs.

From the standpoint of cost-effectiveness one can look at the comparison as a tradeoff between input and output. By abandoning human indexing and controlled vocabularies one is very likely reducing input costs. However, this is achieved at the expense of greater output costs in the sense that an increased intellectual burden is placed upon the user of the database. Among factors that might influence a decision involving this input/output tradeoff are the volumes of documents and searches involved, indexer and searcher costs, and the degree of importance attributable to the results of a search.

Factors favoring recall	*Effect of type of representation*
Length of record (number of access points)	Most free text representations (except for titles only) will be longer than a set of assigned index terms. This will tend to improve recall but reduce precision (cases of "slight mention" and spurious relationships both increase)
Redundancy	Will usually be greater in free text, improving the chance that a particular item will be found. Nevertheless, the great variety of ways in which a topic may be represented in a large text database makes it difficult to achieve high recall.
Presence of broad "concept" terms	Much more likely to appear in a controlled vocabulary representation. May be implicit rather than explicit in text.
Linkage of semantically related terms	Clearly favors the well-constructed controlled vocabulary
Factors favoring precision Specificity	Free text will usually be more specific, favoring precision. The diversity of the way concepts are represented, however, makes it very difficult to achieve a high recall in broad "conceptual" searches. In searches of this kind the relatively broader controlled terms will be much preferable.
Factors affecting both Currency	Free text representations will always be more current. To find a brand new topic in a controlled vocabulary system may require the searcher to experiment with several terms (reducing precision) and he still may not find everything on the topic (reducing recall).
Familiarity	Information specialists, fully familiar with a controlled vocabulary, will use it more effectively than others. The "end user" may do better with the natural language occurring in documents in his or her subject field.

FIGURE 104
The pros and cons of free text versus controlled vocabulary.

Review of Related Studies: Before 1980

Early writings on the experience with full text searching in the legal field were imbued with great enthusiasm for this new capability. However, these writers undertook no experiments to compare full text searching with controlled vocabulary indexing.

Swanson (1960) built a small test collection of 100 articles in nuclear physics and determined which of these were relevant to each of 50 questions. The collection was also indexed using subject headings "designed especially for the field of nuclear physics." The full text searches, which were aided by the use of a "thesaurus-like collection of word and phrase groups," produced, according to Swanson, results superior to those achieved by the searches on subject headings.

The "Cranfield" investigation on the characteristics and performance of index languages seems to have had a profound influence in persuading many information professionals of the advantages of natural language for information retrieval. As reported by Cleverdon et al. (1966), this was a controlled experimental study. A test collection of 1400 research papers, mostly dealing with aerodynamics, was indexed in three different ways: (1) concepts discussed were recorded (e.g., "cascade losses"), (2) concepts were broken into component words in singular form ("cascade," "loss"), and (3) related concepts were grouped together to form "links" or "themes" (e.g., axial flow compressor/cascade loss). The items were indexed exhaustively: 30 to 50 "concepts" per item was not uncommon.

A group of 221 test questions was compiled. These questions were devised by subject experts and were based upon actual research papers that they themselves had authored. The test collection was sifted by postgraduate students at the College of Aeronautics (Cranfield, England) and items of any conceivable "relevance" were sent to the originator of the question to be judged on a 5-point scale (of which one category was "not relevant at all"). As a result, it was known which items in the collection were relevant to each test question (at least in the eyes of the author of that question) and which not.

The entire study was performed as a type of simulation. Different types of vocabularies were "assembled," ranging from the simplest (single words with no controls whatever, singular/plural conflation, word form control [word stem search], simple synonym control) to the complex (grouping of terms into hierarchies as they would appear in a true hierarchical classification). Each question was posed against the test collection 33 times, where each application tested a different vocabulary (33 in all), allowing a comparison of the results achieved by the various vocabularies. When recall and precision measures were combined into a single measure of performance (referred to as "normalised recall"), vocabularies consisting of single-word natural language terms (with word forms controlled, with synonyms controlled, or with no controls whatever) outperformed all others.

The Cranfield study was very controversial and has generated great criticism over the years. However, much of this criticism arises from a lack of understanding of what was actually done in the study. For example, Soergel (1985) has suggested that both the indexing and the index language were of doubtful quality. Since I was one of these indexers, I can attest to the great care that went into the indexing—much more care than is likely in a normal production setting—and that the indexers had very considerable previous experience. Even today the criticisms still surface. Some writers have tried to discredit the Cranfield results on the grounds that, since questions were based on real documents, this would create a bias in favor of natural language. It is hard to understand this criticism in view of the fact that items considered relevant by authors of questions were not the items on which they had based the questions.

In any case, it is not the intention here to defend the Cranfield studies but merely to point out that, flawed or not, they brought many people to the belief that, under certain circumstances at least, natural language systems might do as well as or better than those based on controlled vocabularies. In some of his writings following the Cranfield tests, Cleverdon implied that a natural language system, if properly implemented, would always outperform one based on vocabulary control. Somewhat later, Klingbiel (1970) used the Cranfield results, together with his own experience at the Defense Documentation Center, to claim that "highly structured controlled vocabularies are obsolete for indexing and retrieval" and that "the natural language of scientific prose is fully adequate for indexing and retrieval." A little later, Bhattacharyya (1974) was to state that:

> The findings of various experiments on the testing and evaluation of indexing languages, carried out during the last decade, have demonstrated again and again the strength of the natural language, with minimal or no control, as optimally the best indexing language (that is, taking both retrieval effectiveness and efficiency into account). (Page 235)

Following the Cranfield studies, and influenced by them, a number of other investigators came to similar conclusions on the merits of natural language in information retrieval. For example, Aitchison et al. (1969-1970) undertook some tests to derive data to aid decisions concerning the indexing of the INSPEC database. Results were compared for searches on: (1) title, (2) titles plus abstracts, (3) index terms used in the printed *Science Abstracts*, (4) "free language" human indexing, and (5) controlled terms drawn from a draft thesaurus compiled by the INSPEC staff. The test environment consisted of 542 articles in electronics and 97 questions supplied by researchers. Assessments were made to determine which articles were relevant to which questions. Care was taken to establish some level of "equivalence" among the strategies used in the various search modes. It was found that retrieval based on the draft thesaurus gave better results than any of the other modes of searching. Nevertheless, it was recommended that the assignment of free language terms by human indexers, which ranked second in performance, should be the method adopted. The INSPEC database later incorporated both thesaurus terms and free text terms.

In a major study, Keen and Digger (1972) compared the performance of various types of vocabularies in the field of information science. The major characteristics of the test may be summarized as follows:

1. Five different index languages were used: UL, an uncontrolled postco-ordinate language formed by indexers selecting words from the documents themselves; CT, postcoordinate "compressed term" language of fewer than 300 terms with thesaurus structure imposed; Pre-HS, a precoordinate hierarchically structured language in the form of a faceted classification scheme; HS, a hierarchically structured language (the classification scheme is modified to allow it to be used in a postcoordinate fashion); Pre-RI, a precoordinate language in which terms from the hierarchical classification are combined into indexing phrases ("analets") using the relational operators of Farradane.

2. A test collection of 800 documents on library and information science was indexed, using each of the five vocabularies, by the two investigators.

3. The physical indexes set up were entirely manual, the postcoordinate one on optical coincidence cards.

4. Sixty-three search requests, gathered from librarians and other information specialists, were processed against these indexes.

5. Searches were conducted by nineteen students of library and information science using a Latin square experimental design.

6. Twenty instructors in the subject made relevance judgments for the test requests in relation to each document in the collection.

7. The tests were conducted with different "versions" of the five indexes. These versions reflected changes made to the index language or to indexing policy. The major variables thus examined were the effect of the exhaustivity of indexing (that is, the number of terms assigned per document), the specificity of the vocabulary, differing methods of coordinating terms at the time of search, the degree to which terms are linked (by cross-reference or hierarchical structure) in a vocabulary; linking related terms together at the time of indexing (that is, "partitioning"), the use of the relational operators, and the provision of "context" in the search file (the searcher in an optical coincidence index is led by document number to a "context file" where an alphabetical chain index entry represents the spe-

cific subject matter discussed in the document, this being roughly equivalent to the context provided in a precoordinate index).

The different languages were employed in different comparisons (that is, not all comparisons are relevant to all languages), and for some comparisons a subset of 241 documents and sixty search requests was used. The results of the various comparisons are mostly presented in the form of recall ratios and absolute numbers of nonrelevant items retrieved.

Perhaps not too unexpectedly, this investigation produced results that tend to corroborate findings of earlier studies:

> The Uncontrolled languages tested performed overall just as well as the Controlled languages by providing a consistently good retrieval effectiveness and efficiency performance that was never as bad as the worst controlled language, nor as good as the best, and in no case were these differences statistically significant (Volume 1, pp. 166-67).

The investigators further claim that:

> the prescription for the best index language is clearly one of the highest specificity possible without the use of precision devices more sophisticated than simple coordination (and with little or no pre-coordination of terms). And it does seem that natural language English single words comes close to providing this optimum level of specificity (Volume 1, p. 169).

Keen and Digger went on to suggest that the case against controlled vocabularies was now well proven, going so far as to say that "this should be the last time that traditional controlled index languages are humiliated by being demonstrated to offer no advantage" (Volume 1, p. 170).

Lancaster et al. (1972) performed a study of online searching by biomedical researchers in the Epilepsy Abstracts Retrieval System (EARS). The objective was to determine how well these investigators could search the text of abstracts in the field of epilepsy, and some free text/controlled term comparisons were undertaken. It was found that, over 47 searches, use of the index terms assigned by Excerpta Medica gave about half the recall that searches on abstracts achieved. Note, however, that the abstracts generally provided many more access points so the comparison was more one of record length than a true comparison of free text versus controlled term searching. The investigators concluded that the text search gave better recall because of: (a) number of access points, (b) greater redundancy, (c) better match between user terms and text words, (d) errors and inconsistencies in the human indexing, and (e) overlap among index terms. It was hypothesized that performance might be greatly improved if some type of "search thesaurus" were added to the system.

Using documents and questions assembled in the evaluation of MEDLARS (Lancaster, 1968a), Salton (1972) produced results suggesting that his SMART system could outperform the costly indexing and vocabulary control activities associated with MEDLARS. This comparison is somewhat different from the conventional comparison of searching in natural language and controlled vocabulary databases. SMART operates not on the basis of Boolean algebra but through a type of "pattern matching," the text of abstracts being matched against the text of natural language requests, with the user being given a set of search options of varying levels of sophistication. In Salton's studies, SMART seemed to outperform MEDLARS only when some user feedback was employed. That is, users evaluated preliminary search results and the search was re-run on the basis of relevance feedback from the user. This raises the obvious question of how well MEDLARS would have done with relevance feedback. SMART is mentioned further in the next chapter.

A major study undertaken in this period is one frequently overlooked. Cleverdon (1977) compared natural language and controlled term searching in a subset of the NASA database consisting of 44,000 items. Online searches were performed at four centers, with ten searches conducted at each. Each search was conducted in one mode by one individual and in a different mode by a second individual. The two individuals who searched on the same topic, each in a different mode, first discussed the requirement to get some agreement on what the requester wanted. The modes were: (a) controlled terms only, (b) natural language of titles and abstracts, (c) controlled terms and natural language combined, and (d) natural language search aided by use of a list of "associated concepts." It was found that the natural language searches gave a significantly higher recall and differed little in precision from the controlled term searches. Cleverdon concluded, and rightly so, that it was the length of the abstract that was largely responsible.

Unfortunately, Cleverdon's study is marred by inadequate reporting. For example, those searches in which both controlled terms and natural language were used performed less well on both recall and precision than the searches involving natural language alone. This is quite the opposite of what one would expect and is difficult to explain, especially since these "joint mode" searches retrieved twice as many items as the natural language searches did. Cleverdon fails to explain this anomaly. Another anomaly is that natural language searches aided by the "associated concept file" also performed less well than those conducted using natural language alone. This too is not clearly explained and it is difficult for readers of Cleverdon's report to come to their own conclusions since the "associated concepts file" itself is not fully described. All one can surmise from Cleverdon's description is that it was derived from the co-occurrence of terms in the titles of documents in the collection.

A later paper by Martin (1980) offers some clarification but adds further mystery of its own. He makes clear that the natural language component of the database consisted of single words extracted from titles and abstracts by computer but later edited by humans to remove "stopwords" and to normalize the vocabulary by eliminating variant spellings and word forms. The associated concept file was a file of the keywords extracted from titles only showing, for each, which keywords co-occurred most frequently in titles. Martin summarizes the results as follows:

	Recall (%)	Precision (%)
Controlled terms	56	74
Natural language	78	63
Natural language plus controlled terms	71	45

He then goes on to state that "for every relevant document retrieved by controlled language, natural language alone retrieved 1.4, natural language plus controlled language 1.6 . . .," which is quite incompatible with the recall/precision values given. Martin also makes clear that the "natural language plus controlled term" searches include some that involved controlled terms alone (where the searcher saw no need to augment with natural language) so "they did not represent the full potential of CL plus NL." The inconsistencies in the results and statements about them, as well as concerns regarding the instructions given to the searchers, cast some doubt on the validity of this comparison.

Only one study performed in this period claims to have found superior results for human indexing with a controlled vocabulary. Hersey et al. (1971) used a subset of the Smithsonian Science Information Exchange (SIE) database, consisting of 4,655 project descriptions, in their comparison of free text versus "scientist indexing." The indexing involved the use of subject codes, assigned by subject specialists and drawn from a specially-prepared classification scheme. For 27 searches performed at SIE itself the following results were derived:

	Recall (%)	Precision (%)
Text of project descriptions	66	81
Subject indexing	96	95

Again, poor reporting makes it very difficult for the reader to understand exactly what was done. The questions used were some that had been "previously asked" but it is not clear whether the results for subject indexing were derived when the searches were originally performed for customers or were derived later, at the time the free text searches were performed. The following points are also unclear: on what basis the relevance assessments were made (they were apparently made by SIE staff rather than original requestors), in what form the request was given to the person doing the online free text search, and whether or not any controls were imposed on the searchers to achieve some level of equivalence in search approach between text search and index term search.

Each of these factors could exert a profound influence on the results of the study. For example, if the request used as the basis for the free text search was not in the requester's original words, but had been "compromised" as a result of interaction with SIE personnel, the results of the comparison might well be biased toward the subject codes. The fact that the recall/precision results of this study were very much higher than those achieved in other investigations, and much higher than those achieved in the day-to-day operation of retrieval systems (Lancaster, 1968a), coupled with the rather imprecise reporting, raises serious questions concerning the validity of the comparison. The unusually high precision scores, however, are partly explained by the fact that the test file of project descriptions was really an amalgamation of four separate test files in completely different subject areas.

A supplementary study on this database was performed by the Biological Sciences Communication Project of George Washington University, using twelve SIE questions. Searches on the subject codes retrieved 91 projects of which 74 were judged relevant (precision of 81%), while text searches retrieved 70, of which 43 were judged relevant (precision of 61%). By combining the results for free text and subject code searching one can conclude that recall was about 50% for text and 90% for subject indexing, but some unique items were retrieved by each search mode.

Byrne (1975) used 50 SDI profiles on the COMPENDEX database and compared results when searches were performed on titles, abstracts, and subject headings, and various combinations of these. The results for one search mode were compared with the combined results for all modes. Using this standard, subject headings alone retrieved 21% of the items, abstracts alone 61%, titles plus abstracts 75%, and titles plus subject terms 41%. Not surprisingly, then, the longer representations seemed to give much better recall. However, no real relevance assessments were made in this study: everything retrieved was *ipso facto* considered an appropriate response.

Review of Related Studies: Since 1980

By and large, the comparisons of free text and controlled vocabulary searching performed in the 1960's and 1970's showed that free text could do as well as, if not better than, controlled terms. However, these studies were performed on rather small files, and sometimes trivially small. They were mostly experimental studies rather than involving real information services operating under actual working conditions. Since 1980 some studies have been done with databases of greater size and/or involving real operating services.

Markey et al. (1980) undertook an analysis of controlled vocabulary and free text search statements in online searches of the ERIC database. They also performed "online searching tests" comparing free and controlled vocabulary but only using six topics. They concluded that free text gave higher recall and controlled terms gave higher precision. As in many other studies, reporting of the test is woefully inadequate. No details are given on how the relevance assessments were made and none on how the searches were performed, so the reader does not know if any attempt was made to "control" the search strategies to avoid favoring either search mode. The uncharacteristically high scores (93 percent recall and 71 percent precision for free text, 76 percent recall, and 95 percent precision for the controlled terms) cast doubt on the validity of the study.

A number of studies have been undertaken in the field of law. Coco (1984) used a database of circuit court cases (1960-1969) and 50 actual "research problems" taken from a 1977 Federal Judicial Center study to compare retrieval in the WESTLAW and LEXIS systems. LEXIS includes only the text of the opinions associated with these cases, while WESTLAW adds "editorial components" to the text of the opinions, including various forms of synopses. The stated objective of this study was to compare the results of searches based on the text alone with those achieved with text plus editorial additions. Since the searches on WESTLAW were performed with and without the editorial additions, the comparison with LEXIS was quite unnecessary, and only served to confuse the reader. In any event, the comparison of LEXIS and WESTLAW could not be considered completely valid because the databases were not exactly comparable. As Coco says, "the systems contained *approximately* [italics added] the same number of cases for this period." Moreover, no real systematic attempt was made to determine whether or not the cases retrieved were really relevant to the research problems.

If the one example provided by Coco is representative of all items in the database, the augmented text in WESTLAW is almost twice the length of the opinion text alone. It is hardly surprising, then, that it retrieved more cases (913 versus 728, although we do not know how many were "relevant"). In fact, one might reasonably expect that a doubling of the text would yield more than a 20% increase in the number of cases retrieved. That it did not must in part be attributable to term overlap between the text and the editorial additions. The results of this study were completely predictable from the outset and we hardly needed such an investigation to tell us that doubling the text will increase the number of items retrieved.

Blair and Maron (1985) undertook a rather large study of a legal database on the STAIRS system (about 350,000 pages of text, or 40,000 documents, and

40 information requests). Paralegals performed extensive, iterative searches online and only stopped searching when attorneys for whom they were working were satisfied that at least 75% of the relevant references had been retrieved. By sampling, however, the investigators estimated that no more than 20 percent recall had been achieved. They conclude that their results cast serious doubt on the efficacy of full text searching and, on the basis of some very dubious cost analyses, that full text searching is much more costly than alternative approaches. They completely overlook the fact that large controlled vocabulary systems may not perform any better. For example, a study of 535 MEDLINE searches, performed by 191 different searchers, is said to have produced an average recall of only 23 percent at a precision of 67% (Wanger et al., 1980). Although based largely on Blair and Maron's results, Dabney (1986a) gives an excellent discussion of the problems of full text retrieval in the legal field. Responses to Dabney by McDermott (1986) and by Runde and Lindberg (1986), as well as a follow-up comment by Dabney (1986b), are also worth examination. Salton (1986) contributed a detailed review of the Blair and Maron study. He takes strong issue with their conclusion that humanly indexed databases are likely to outperform text searching.

One of the better studies, comparing full text with abstracts and controlled indexing, was completed by Tenopir (1984). Using the *Harvard Business Review* online, Tenopir achieved the following results, averaged over 31 searches:

	Full text	Abstracts	Controlled terms
Number of documents retrieved (mean)	17.8	2.4	3.1
Relevant documents retrieved (mean)	3.5	1.0	1.2
Recall (relative to union of all methods)	73.9	19.3	28.0
Precision	18.0	35.6	34.0
Cost per search	$20.57	$4.95	$5.32
Cost per relevant item retrieved	$7.86	$3.89	$3.54

Tenopir's cost figures cannot be taken too seriously since she included the costs of obtaining full copies of documents for achieving relevance judgments, whereas in real life this would rarely occur (i.e., users would judge on the basis of titles and/or abstracts viewed online). Perhaps the most significant result of Tenopir's research is her finding that the controlled term searches retrieved some items not retrieved by full text, and vice versa, arguing for the need for both.

Later, Ro (1988) performed a follow-up study on the *Harvard Business Review* database that yielded similar results to those achieved by Tenopir.

Sievert et al. (1992) discovered, not surprisingly, that searches in a database containing the full text of medical journal articles gave better recall than searches in the MEDLINE database, although the full text searches gave much lower precision. In an earlier article, however, they highlighted the problems of searching full text by analyzing the reasons for nonretrieval from the full text database of relevant items retrieved in MEDLINE (Sievert and McKinin, 1989).

The improvements in recall that are possible by using text terms in addition to controlled terms have been demonstrated by several investigators, including McCain et al. (1987), who compared the results of searches in five databases for eleven topics in the medical behavioral sciences.

Various other studies have reported the results of searches on full or partial text, but without comparisons with searches on controlled terms. Some of these studies have involved systems (similar in some ways to SMART) that use probabilistic and/or linguistic methods to rank documents, or paragraphs from them, on the basis of their similarity to request statements or search strategies. For example, Bernstein and Williamson (1984) evaluate such procedures applied to the Hepatitis Knowledge Base and Tong et al. (1985) evaluate artificial intelligence techniques applied to full text retrieval in a database of news items.

Fidel (1992) suggests which factors will favor the controlled vocabulary search and which the text search. From a study of 281 real searches performed by 47 trained searchers, she identified various factors affecting searcher choice of controlled terms versus text words. She found that there is more reliance on text in some subject areas than others (although this may be less related to the characteristics of the subject or its language than to the quality of the controlled vocabularies used in various databases—especially their specificity—and to the quality of the controlled vocabulary indexing).

In order to improve search results, some investigators have studied the effects of partitioning a text into smaller units in an attempt to improve the precision of searches without serious loss of recall. Williams (1998) distinguishes between discourse partitioning (based on sentences, paragraphs, sections) and window partitioning (dividing the text into chunks of arbitrary size). Williams tested retrieval (recall and precision values) for paragraphs, pages, three different windows (250, 500, and 1000 words) and three overlapping windows of 250, 500, and 1000 words. The arbitrary overlapping is designed to avoid the splitting of related text that might otherwise occur with arbitrary partitioning. Williams found that the 500-word overlapping window seemed to offer the best overall result when measured by recall and precision. He concludes that this type of partitioning can substantially improve precision with a moderate decline in recall. Williams refers to this approach as "passage-level indexing." It is not clear how this approach is an improvement on using word proximity search, which was in use in text searching forty years earlier.

The review of the literature included here has focused on studies comparing the performance of free text databases with that of databases indexed by means of controlled vocabularies when searching is performed on Boolean combinations of terms. While some other types of study have been mentioned, no attempt has been made to review all of the literature dealing with the searching of text using non-Boolean approaches. Some approaches of this kind are dealt with in the next chapter.

It is evident from the review that the early extravagant enthusiasm for natural language searching was toned down over the years as the problems involved were more clearly identified. Some of the early studies were based on experimental databases that were trivially small. Because one can tolerate very low precision when only a handful of items are retrieved, it is possible to achieve an acceptable level of recall. This situation changes dramatically when one moves to databases containing hundreds of thousands of items. Low levels of precision are no longer acceptable because of the number of items retrieved ("output overload") and it is correspondingly difficult to achieve high recall at an acceptable level of precision. However, evidence exists (e.g., Wanger et al., 1980) that this is also true of large systems based on controlled vocabularies and not just a peculiarity of free text searching.

It is important to recognize the distinction between the terms *free text* and *full text*. Conclusions reached as a result of studies on full text databases are not automatically transferable to databases containing less than full text (e.g., abstracts). In full text databases the problem of scale is compounded. That is, with a very large database of full text it will be even more difficult to achieve acceptable recall at tolerable precision. Full text should give greater recall, but lower precision, than a database of less than full text. This was demonstrated clearly by Tenopir (1984).

It is an unfortunate fact that most of the studies that purport to compare the retrieval performance of free text with that of a set of index terms selected from a controlled vocabulary do no such thing. Rather, they compare the retrieval performance of records of varying length. A valid comparison of controlled terms versus free text per se would have to hold constant the length of the records (e.g., all of the topics mentioned in an abstract would have to be translated, insofar as possible, into equivalent controlled terms) and also the search strategy (i.e., a "conceptual" strategy would have to be created and then translated exactly into [a] text expressions, and [b] terms selected from the controlled vocabulary). This appears never to have been done since the Cranfield studies. Tenopir controlled her search strategies but, since she was using an existing database, could not control for record length. Consequently, her conclusions relate much more to length of record than they do to the natural language/controlled vocabulary controversy.

Also unfortunate is the fact that the literature includes wild claims, based on anecdotal evidence, from proponents of one or other camp who refuse to accept the fact that natural language and controlled vocabularies each have their own advantages. See Fugmann (1987) for a good example.

A careful examination of the literature included in this review gives me no reason to change my original views on the pros and cons of the two approaches, as summarized in Figure 104. The fact is that each has advantages and disadvantages. Free text records tend to be longer and thus provide more access points, will frequently include some terms more specific or more current than those in any controlled vocabulary, and will usually provide greater redundancy. The controlled vocabulary, on the other hand, imposes consistency in the representation of subject matter among documents, provides the broad "concept" terms that are frequently lacking in text, and, by means of hierarchical and cross-reference structure, gives the user positive aid in identifying appropriate search terms.

Hybrid Systems

Virtually every writer on free text searching, including Henzler (1978), Perez (1982), and Muddamalle (1998), as well as most of the authors already cited, have come to the unsurprising conclusion that the ideal retrieval system will include some controlled terms as well as some free text. The advantages of such hybrid systems are obvious, and they were described and illustrated many years ago by Holst (1966), Uhlmann (1967) and Lancaster (1972). The value of the hybrid approach is supported by the fact that, in most of the studies performed, free text searches retrieved some relevant items not found by controlled vocabulary searches, and vice versa.

The term *hybrid* can be used to refer to any system operating on a combination of controlled terms and natural language, including those in which both sets of terms are assigned by human indexers and those in which a database can be searched on a combination of humanly assigned controlled terms and words occurring in titles, abstracts or full text.

Consider, for example, a system based on three separate vocabulary components:

1. a small vocabulary of broad subject codes, perhaps 300 codes in all;
2. a list of codes representing geographic areas; and
3. keywords or phrases occurring in the titles or texts of documents.

Indexing with such vocabulary elements might represent a significant economy over indexing that uses a large, carefully controlled vocabulary for two reasons:

1. The subject codes would be broad enough to be assigned without much difficulty by an indexer not having a high level of education or subject expertise.
2. The number of codes (subject and geographic) is small enough that the indexer can retain most in memory and avoid having to constantly look them up in a vocabulary listing.

Although any one of the vocabulary elements on its own is relatively crude, the joint use of a keyword (to give specificity) and a subject or geographic code (to give context) is an extremely powerful device. For example, the keyword *plants* may mean something entirely different when combined with a subject code relating to agriculture than when combined with a subject code relating to some industry. Likewise, the keyword *strike* associated with the geographic code for Lebanon may indicate a military operation; when it is coordinated with the geographic code for England, on the other hand, it is more likely to signify a labor dispute. Moreover, the joint use of broad subject codes, geographic codes, and keywords is extremely effective in illustrating relationships, even when these relationships are not explicitly specified. Many of the databases that are now accessible online can be searched on combinations of controlled terms and keywords or phrases occurring in titles or abstracts, the latter permitting greater specificity.

The Post-Controlled Vocabulary

Several authors have pointed out that natural language searching can be considerably improved through the construction and use of various forms of searching aid. Piternick (1984) has described some possible tools of this kind. The most obvious aid would be a "search thesaurus" or "post-controlled vocabulary" as envisioned by Lancaster (1972), Lancaster et al. (1972) and, in more detail, by Lancaster (1986).

The earliest system developed to search large bodies of legal text (at Pittsburgh) used a kind of thesaurus to aid the search process. This was merely a compilation of words with similar meanings, resembling *Roget's Thesaurus* more than the thesaurus structure commonly used in information retrieval. Even without any significant degree of "structure," such a thesaurus could be an extremely valuable searching aid; words with similar meanings are potentially substitutable in a search, and such a tool relieves individual searchers from having to think of all the words that might express a particular idea. Investing in the construction of such a searching aid allows significant economies in a system in which large numbers of searches are performed. This simple type of thesaurus is a kind of controlled vocabulary, with the control applied at output rather than input. It is a post-controlled vocabulary.

The properties of the post-controlled vocabulary can be further illustrated with an example. Consider a public affairs database that is indexed with a thesaurus. The thesaurus includes the term *airlines*, so it is possible to perform a broad search on this subject. It is not possible, however, to limit a search to a particular airline, since specific names do not appear in the thesaurus. Thus, it would be impossible to restrict a search to "financial conditions of Varig"; the best one might do is to retrieve everything on the financial conditions of airlines. The general search tends to be easy in the pre-controlled vocabulary situation, but certain highly specific searches may be virtually impossible.

In contrast, consider an alternative public affairs database that dispenses with indexing but allows searches on titles and abstracts. Retrieving items on Varig or Swissair should be easy. More difficult would be the general search on airlines. To perform a comprehensive search, one would need to go far beyond the use of the word *airlines* and would need such synonyms as *air carriers* and names of individual companies. The search strategy might look like *airlines* or *air carriers* or *Varig* or *Swissair* or *Lufthansa* or . . .," —perhaps a very long list. What the searcher is doing is creating part of a post-controlled thesaurus. Regrettably, in present information services, such thesaurus entries are rarely retained and stored once they have been created and used. Within a large network, much duplication of effort takes place. *Airlines* may appear as a facet of many searches performed during a year, and the work of building the search strategies of varying degrees of completeness will be repeated time and time again. How much more sensible to store it in retrievable form for future use.

A true post-controlled vocabulary consists of tables with names and identifying numbers that can be called up and consulted by users of natural language databases within some online network. Thus, the searcher could retrieve the "airlines" entry, the "financial affairs" entry, and so on. The tables can be viewed online and terms selected from them. Alternatively, the entire table can be incorporated into a search strategy by its identifying numbers. Such tables need not be restricted to words but may incorporate word fragments. Thus, a surgery table might look like "surg . . ., operat . . ., section . . ., . . . section, . . . otomy, . . . ectomy, . . . plasty," and so on. The vocabulary can also be given some minimal structure by cross-referencing of related tables.

A post-controlled vocabulary system can offer all the advantages of natural language with many of the attributes of the pre-controlled vocabulary. Such a system might perform better than one based on a pre-controlled vocabulary. To return to an earlier example, one could search for individual airlines with ease or use the "airlines" table to form the class defined by "airlines" in the conventional thesaurus. One of the advantages of natural language is that it is database-independent. Thus, an "airlines" table would be equally applicable to all databases in the English language. One could visualize a natural-language thesaurus that would be applicable to several hundred databases.

A good example of the post-controlled vocabulary was the TERM database implemented by Bibliographic Retrieval Services (BRS) and described by Knapp (1983). TERM was a database of tables, representing concepts, that include both controlled terms and free-text terms needed to perform searches in a variety of databases in the social and behavioral sciences. A sample table is displayed in Figure 105.

TI	POVERTY AREAS
ER	POVERTY-AREAS+/
ME	POVERTY-AREAS*.
PS	POVERTY-AREAS. CONSIDER ALSO: GHETTOS.
SO	CONSIDER: SLUM. GHETTO, APPALACHIA.
EN	SLUMS.
FT	POVERTY AREAS. SKID ROW. BOWERY. SLUM. INNER CITY. POOR NEIGHBOR-HOODS. MILIEU OF POVERTY. DEPRESSED AREAS. SLUMS. GHETTOS. GHETTO. GHETTOES. APPALACHIA. LOW INCOME AREAS. GHETTOIZATION. STREET CORNER DISTRICT. ETHNIC NEIGHBORHOOD. BLACK NEIGHBORHOOD. BLACK COMMUNITY. SEGREGATED NEIGHBORHOOD. DISADVANTAGED AREA. BLACK SCHOOL DISTRICTS. MINORITY NEIGHBORHOOD. REDLINED AREAS. REDLINING.

FIGURE 105
Example of entry in the TERM database.

The title (TI) of the table is POVERTY AREAS. This term is used to retrieve items on this topic in ERIC (ER), in databases indexed by *Medical Subject Headings* (ME) and in the PsycINFO (PS) database (in which a related term is *ghettos*). In Sociological Abstracts (SO), possible terms are *slum, ghetto*, and *Appalachia*, whereas a narrower ERIC term (EN) is *slums*. Finally, a detailed list of related free text (FT) terms, useful for a search on this subject in any English language database, is given. A strategy could be developed on the TERM database and saved and executed on the bibliographic databases at a later time. Unfortunately, this database is no longer maintained. However, its developer has published a comprehensive printed version for the free text expressions (not the controlled terms). This can be considered as a thesaurus designed for text searching (Knapp, 1993).

A post-controlled vocabulary in a particular subject field can be built by human intellectual effort in much the same way as a conventional thesaurus. The task might be simplified considerably by machine manipulation of the words occurring in relevant databases so that various levels of "statistical association" are derived. Perhaps it would be more sensible, however, to collect and edit the "search fragments" actually entered by users of some online systems (any list of terms entered in an OR relationship would be a candidate), thus producing a kind of "growing thesaurus" as visualized by Reisner (1966), but with some editorial control imposed later. More recently, Besser (1997) has discussed the importance of user-assigned terms in future retrieval applications.

Another possible approach is to construct a thesaurus automatically on the basis of semantic relationships within dictionaries existing in electronic form (Fox et al., 1988; Ahlswede et al., 1988). Anderson and Rowley (1992) describe one approach to building "end-user thesauri" from full text.

Current Approaches

The 1960s saw the initiation of an incredible number of research projects in the use of computers to manipulate text. There were several reasons for the explosion of activity: research institutions (and researchers) found themselves with expensive computing facilities that were looking for applications, research funding was generously available from many government sources, and text processing was widely considered to be a rather simple task for computers viewed as "powerful" (getting significant amounts of text into electronic form was usually regarded as a greater obstacle).

While machine translation was the major goal of much of this research, various approaches to information retrieval were also under investigation. The most ambitious projects in information retrieval sought to develop "question-answering" or "fact retrieval" systems—i.e., systems capable of answering a user question directly rather than retrieving a text that may contain the answer or, more commonly, a reference to such a text.

Of course, the problems turned out to be much greater than anticipated, particularly in the area of machine translation, and interest in text processing rapidly began to wane within the research community as well as the funding agencies, although some of the better projects persisted and, over the years, showed considerable improvement and offered promising results.

The breadth of text processing research today is reminiscent of the activity of the 1960s (see Jacobs (1992a) and Pereira and Grosz (1994) for good overviews of work in the 1990s). This increase in interest and activity stems from the facts that vast quantities of text are now available in electronic form, that computing power is much greater and much cheaper, and that there are now well-recognized needs for viable text processing applications in public and private sectors (e.g., efficient dissemination of information over the Web and the mandated multilingual requirements of the European Community). Current research seeks to develop "text-based intelligent systems."

Paradoxically, the sheer quantity of text available to be processed today presents significant challenges but also offers potential solutions that were not available to the investigators of 30 years ago. For example, lexicons of word roots or word senses can contain many thousands of entries rather than a few hundred (Jacobs and Rau, 1994) and word associations (co-occurrences) in significant bodies of text can be used to recognize significant phrases or disambiguate words preparatory to the more sophisticated linguistic processing of syntactic analysis (Wilks et al., 1992; Haas, 1996). Word frequency can also be used to assign text to various categories (Jacobs, 1992b).

In addition, "statistical filtering," based on the co-occurrence of particular words or roots, can be used to select those sentences that seem most likely to be "relevant" to a particular requirement and, thus, the best candidates for more refined analysis (Wilks et al., 1992).

Charniak (1995) has pointed out that 90% accuracy can be obtained in assigning a part-of-speech "tag" to a word simply on the basis of the most likely (most frequently occurring) case and this accuracy can be increased to 95-96% by some simple context checks (i.e., looking at adjacent words). One example of the corpus-based approach to disambiguation can be found in Leacock et al. (1993). Addison (1991) discusses the use of context to disambiguate in a text retrieval system.

Stanfill and Waltz (1992) compare more modern approaches of today (which claim to incorporate techniques from artificial intelligence—AI) with those of the earlier years, as follows:

> AI as it has been formulated in the past is, if not yet dead, dying; a new AI is taking its place. The old AI was based on rules and logic. The new AI is based on statistics—but not statistics as it has been formulated in the past. The practice of statistics itself is undergoing a substantial transformation. (Page 215)

and Jacobs (1992a) points out that the approaches of today derive "more power from large quantities of stored text than from hand-crafted rules."

Current approaches to text processing can be considered "intelligent" to the extent that computers can be made to "understand" the text.* "Understand"

---

*Although "intelligent" can also be attributed to the process if it performs a task that humans would need intelligence to accomplish.

here means being able to interpret the meaning of a sentence unambiguously. Normally this requires some form of syntactic analysis. Syntactic analysis seeks to determine the role of a word in a sentence (e.g., noun or verb), to recognize the different structural elements (noun phrase, verb phrase, prepositional phrase, and so on), and thus to determine the various dependencies of a sentence (e.g., subject, subject modifier, object, object modifier).

Intelligent text processing is being used, experimentally or operationally, in a number of applications, including text categorization, text extraction, summarization and augmentation, text generation, and enhanced information retrieval, as well as machine translation.*

The purpose of applying more sophisticated natural language processing (NLP) methods to full text searching was explained by Strzalkowski et al. (1999) as follows:

> the main thrust of this project has been to demonstrate that robust if relatively shallow NLP can help to derive better representation of text documents for indexing and search purposes than any simple word and string-based methods commonly used in statistical full-text retrieval. This was based on the premise that linguistic processing can uncover certain *semantic* aspects of document content, something that simple word counting cannot do, thus leading to more accurate representation. (Pages 113-114)

A major approach to dealing with text retrieval, utilized by several of the research groups operating within TREC, is *phrase extraction*—i.e., reducing the entire text to a set of meaningful phrases. One reason for doing this is simply the fact that a phrase may be "significant" even though the component words are not. Thus, "joint venture" may be significant because it occurs relatively infrequently in a database while the component words occur too frequently to be considered significant (Strzalkowski et al., 1999). Many methods of phrase extraction have been used. One such, the "head + modifier" approach, uses syntactic analysis, and subsequent normalization to, for example, recognize that "weapon proliferation" and "proliferation of weapons" are equivalent (Strzalkowski et al., 1999).

Much of the current work in this area seeks to reduce a complete text to a shorter form, by some type of extraction or summarization, for purposes of information retrieval. Such approaches are dealt with in the next chapter, which also attempts to assess the achievements of these approaches.

---

*For some text processing applications it is necessary for the computer to be able to distinguish among logical components of a document (e.g., title, abstract, main text, footnotes, tables, figures) and to determine relationships among them (such as reading order). This has been referred to, somewhat grandiosely, as "document understanding" (see, for example, Semeraro et al., 1994, and *Proceedings of the Third International Conference*, 1995).

The present chapter has been restricted to text search per se, rather than automatic indexing or summarization methods, although the distinction is not always easy to maintain and Chapters 14-15 are closely related.

Text searching is usually based on text in electronic form that has been input at a keyboard or converted from printed form by optical character readers (although it may also be derived from spoken input as discussed in Chapter 13). Some work has also been done on searching and retrieval of handwritten documents (see, for example, Perrone et al., 2002), although it is not clear what the potential applications would be.

What Has Been Achieved?

While the popular trade magazines continue to make rather wild claims, serious authors are much more realistic about what has been achieved in the automatic processing of text. Knight (1999), for example, tells us that:

> Natural-language applications, such as machine translation, speech recognition, information retrieval, and summarization, are reaching a broader range of users today. Anyone who has used these products knows how imperfect they are. Still, people use them because they are desperate for ways to organize, and sift through the vast amount of information available to them—textually—online. (Page 58)

Voorhees (1999), who has been involved in the TREC work for a number of years, is one author who has claimed that the more sophisticated approaches to information retrieval from text have produced disappointing results:

> Currently, the most successful general purpose retrieval methods are statistical methods that treat text as little more than a bag of words . . . attempts to improve retrieval performance through more sophisticated linguistic processing have been largely unsuccessful. Indeed, unless done carefully, such processing can degrade retrieval effectiveness. (Page 32)

However, she does suggest that the more sophisticated levels of text processing may be useful in question answering, and document summarization activities.

Strzalkowski et al. (1999) point out that:

> the use of even the fastest syntactic analysis tools is severely pushing the limits of practicality of an information retrieval system because of the increased demand for computing power and storage. (Pages 117-118)

They claim only modest success for more sophisticated text processing:

> The main observation to make is that thus far natural language processing has not proven as effective as we would have hoped . . . to obtain better indexing and better term representations of queries. Using linguistic terms, such as phrases, head-modifier pairs, names, or even simple concepts does help to improve retrieval precision, but the gains remain quite modest. (Page 143)

Later, Carballo, and Strzalkowski (2000) admit that:

Natural language processing (NLP) techniques may hold a tremendous potential for overcoming the inadequacies of purely quantitative methods of text information retrieval, but the empirical evidence to support such predictions has thus far been inadequate, and appropriate scale evaluations have been slow to emerge. (Page 155)

Blair (2002) maintains that claims for great improvement in TREC results over the years may be greatly exaggerated. In particular, he is critical of the TREC methods of estimating recall (a relative recall approach):

The second effect of unreliable recall estimations concerns the advance of the field of Information Retrieval as a scientific discipline. That is, for research in document retrieval to move forward, we have to know, fairly precisely, where we are now. Any major uncertainty in the comparison of retrieval techniques undermines our sense of what *really* works and what does not, which, in turn, leaves us with no sound reason to choose one technique over another. Currently, most of the automated retrieval techniques used at TREC operate at pretty much the same modest level of recall, and precision. One hoped-for result of more accurate recall estimates might be the uncovering of greater differences in the performance of the systems. Then, we might really start building on the successes of some techniques, and avoid spending more time with unproductive ones. (Page 449)

Saracevic et al. (2003) and Sparck Jones (2003) have refuted some of Blair's criticism, claiming (for example) that evaluation under carefully controlled conditions, based on test collections, is essential for furthering our understanding of retrieval phenomena; that findings from such experiments can carry over to real-life retrieval services; that an absolute recall measure is not necessary for controlled comparisons of the performance of different searching procedures; and that, in the controlled TREC environment, it is possible to document significant improvements in retrieval performance as searching procedures are refined.

Elsewhere, Sparck Jones has consistently claimed that the more sophisticated methods of linguistic processing are hard to justify in retrieval applications. After reviewing the state of the art of linguistic processing of text for information retrieval purposes (she calls this "linguistically-motivated indexing"), she (Sparck Jones, 1999) concludes that this has not proven its superiority over the much simpler approach of combining text words in a search strategy:

It seems that the coordination effect, enhanced by redundancy in simple term indexing, can be quite sufficient for sense disambiguation, at least for single language databases, though whether explicit disambiguation is needed for cross-language searching with multi-lingual databases is an open question. Even where sense discrimination may add something to performance ... this can be achieved by statistical rather than linguistic methods. (Page 21)

Reviewing the TREC work through TREC-6 (1997), she (Sparck Jones, 2000) concludes that "statistically-based methods perform as well as any, and that the nature, and treatment of the user's request is by far the dominant factor in performance." Statistical methods include term weighting, simple phrases as well as single words, query expansion, and relevance feedback.

Smeaton (1999) implies that linguistic processing, while needed for applications that are "exact and precise, such as machine translation," is too fine a tool for information retrieval which he considers "not an exact application and approximation is inherent to its operation because of the many degrees of uncertainty within the processes involved."

Furthermore, sophisticated levels of language processing are still costly. In general, the automatic processing of text requires a rather considerable training of a computer program. That is, the program processes text to do what it is asked to do and its output is examined, and corrected by humans, resulting in program modification. This iterative trial-and-error procedure continues until the program achieves "satisfactory" results. Knight (1999) has indicated how much processing may be needed to train a program to do a task that intelligent humans can do with ease. For example, if definite, and indefinite articles were stripped away from a text, a program could be written to replace them. However, Knight claims that to achieve only a "reasonably good" performance would require the processing of 20 million words of English text.

Knight goes on to claim that:

> Correct parsing of unrestricted text is an exceedingly difficult task, due to ambiguities in part of speech (noun, verb, and so on) and structure ... But despite the existence of promising learning algorithms, no one has yet been able to extract even somewhat accurate syntactic parses from raw text databases. (Pages 59-61)

While more sophisticated language processing may not be needed in text retrieval, it may be in more demanding applications such as question answering.

Question Answering

In very limited domains it should be possible to develop systems that actually answer user questions rather than simply point to potential sources of answers. Systems of this kind would be particularly suitable for knowledge bases that are static or that would change very slowly. For example, an opera database could be developed to answer questions about opera plots, settings, characters, composers, first performances, and so on. While work to develop question-answering systems in very limited fields has gone on for a long time (see, for example, Green etal., 1963), modern technologies make them much more feasible. For instance, Stock (1993) describes a hypermedia system, ALFRESCO, containing images of 14th century Italian frescoes and capable of answering a wide variety of questions concerning them, including the identification of characters or objects depicted in particular paintings. Another example can be found in the work of Kupiec (1999). The approach described can assemble "answer text" from several different documents.

Clarke et al. (2001) describe procedures for automatically answering factual-type questions from the World Wide Web. Their method involves the location and extraction of passages of text likely to contain the answer and the selection of the answer that occurs most frequently in all extracted passages.

A question-answering track was introduced into TREC in 1999 (TREC-8). This work has been reviewed by Voorhees (2001). However, the TREC participants are not required to derive answers from text but, rather, retrieve pieces of text likely to provide the answer.

Knowledge Discovery

An important field of research, that has emerged in recent years, is concerned with methods for extracting unanticipated knowledge from databases. The terminology relating to this area is unusually confusing and inconsistent. A perfectly good and descriptive term is "knowledge discovery." However, the term "mining" is frequently used as a synonym for knowledge discovery or, at least, for the central component of knowledge discovery.* Thus, "data mining" refers to the exploitation (for the purpose of uncovering new knowledge) of numerical/statistical data, "text mining" to the exploitation of text, "speech mining" to the exploitation of recorded speech, and "Web mining" to the exploitation of Web resources. Whatever term is used, the knowledge discovery process essentially involves the identification of meaningful patterns in the sources being exploited.

Data mining in general is reviewed by Benoit (2002) and text mining by Trybula (1999). The use of bibliographic databases in knowledge discovery is covered by Qin and Norton (1999) and Munukata (1999) has also edited a series of articles on knowledge discovery.

Fayyad and Uthurusamy (2002) have edited a journal issue devoted almost exclusively to data mining approaches. Data mining is performed to find interesting patterns in the data. They give the example of finding which products are most frequently purchased together in supermarkets. While mining can be performed to test a hypothesis, it is more useful to develop mining algorithms that essentially suggest the hypotheses.

---

*Freitas (2002) regards mining as a component of knowledge discovery. The latter term includes the preprocessing of data to facilitate the mining and postprocessing of the "discovered knowledge" in order to validate and refine it.

Nasukawa and Nagano (2001) define text mining as "finding valuable patterns and rules in text that indicate trends and significant features about specific topics." They describe a prototype system for mining textual databases within commercial help centers (customer support centers) which, they claim, can:

> automatically detect product failures; determine issues that have led to rapid increases in the number of calls and their underlying reasons; and analyze help center productivity and changes in customers' behavior involving a particular product, without reading any of the text. (Page 967)

Text mining is also dealt with by Knight (1999).

Although Etzioni (1996) maintained that the Web is not useful in mining applications (he considered it too "dynamic and chaotic") , others disagree. At least two books on Web mining (Chang et al., 2001; Chakrabarti, 2003) have been published. The latter is more theoretical than practical and Chakrabarti appears only interested in using the Web for social network analysis. It is not clear that this is "mining" in the way this term is commonly used.

Since knowledge discovery involves the extraction of information, it is closely related to text extraction procedures as discussed in the next chapter.

Conclusions

Systems that dispense with conventional vocabulary control and human indexing can work, and have been proven to do so over a period of more than 40 years. Nevertheless, they do present problems when broad "conceptual" searches must be performed. While there are definite advantages to natural language, it is clear that appropriate enhancements (limited use of indexing and/or development of searching aids) are likely to improve the effectiveness of natural language systems. Moreover, as the Internet has increased by orders of magnitude the amount of full text that is accessible for searching, it has become increasingly necessary to implement systems that will rank retrieved items by "probable relevance" rather than simply dividing into those "retrieved" and those "not retrieved" (Maron, 1988). It is not clear that sophisticated levels of text processing (e.g., involving syntactic analysis) are needed for information retrieval applications although they may be for true question answering and for some of the applications discussed in the next chapter.

CHAPTER 15

Automatic Indexing, Automatic Abstracting, and Related Procedures

A RATHER SIMPLISTIC PICTURE of the information retrieval problem was presented in Figure 1. A more sophisticated version is given in Figure 106. In essence, the problem is that of matching information needs against messages. This can only be done in a rather indirect way. Most messages (what authors want to convey) appear as texts (some are in pictorial, audio, or other nontextual form) while the information needs are presented as requests made to some type of information service. The information service creates representations of the texts, stores these in a database, and provides some device that allows these representations to be searched. The database can be stored in paper, microimage, or electronic form, and the "device" allowing it to be searched can be as simple as the arrangement of entries in a card catalog or printed index or as sophisticated as a computer and a set of computer programs. The information service also creates representations of the requests (search statements of some type) and processes these against the database, retrieving those text representations that match or best match the request representations.

Representations of texts will consist of the full text itself, parts of the text, or some other form of representation humanly or automatically constructed. Representations of requests will consist of terms, terms presented in logical relationships, textual statements, or "items" (e.g., a system may allow a searcher to enter details of an item already known to be relevant and will then look for others that resemble it in some way).

To aid the construction of representations (of texts or requests) various intellectual aids may be made available. The most obvious is the conventional controlled vocabulary, but other aids, such as the postcontrolled vocabulary referred to in Chapter 14, could also be used.

Of course, many variations on the basic theme of Figure 106 are possible. For example, in many situations the information service creating the text representations (i.e., building the database) will not be the same as the services that search it. Moreover, the seeker of information may not delegate the search to an information specialist but may conduct it himself. With the emergence of the Internet, of course, most information retrieval activities involve text searches of Web sites and those who need information perform searches for themselves rather than delegating.

The problems of information retrieval should be obvious from the diagram. Texts may not be perfect representations of messages (while this is a definite communication problem it is not usually considered an information retrieval problem) and, as we have seen from the earlier chapters, the representations of texts may also be imperfect. By the same token, requests are rarely perfect representations of information needs and search statements may not be perfect representations of requests. Moreover, the frame of reference ("schemata") of a requester may not coincide with the frame of reference of an information specialist or, indeed, the frame of reference of authors. The information retrieval problem, then, can be considered essentially one of trying to match approximations of information needs with approximations of messages. Small wonder that the results are not always completely satisfactory.

As Bates (1986) has pointed out, the information retrieval problem is more complex than it appears on the surface; she refers to it as "indeterminate" and "probabilistic." It now seems fashionable to concentrate more on the output side of the activity (information need—request—representation) than on the input side (message—text—representation), the implicit assumption being that the output side is more "complex." In fact, Belkin and Belkin et al. (1980, 1982) refer to matching the "anomalous state of knowledge" of a requester with the more "coherent" state of knowledge of authors. As pointed out as early as Chapter 2, the indexer's role—predicting the types of requests for which a particular document is likely to be a useful response—is not necessarily simpler than that of the search intermediary—understanding what types of documents might satisfy some requester at a given time.

Be that as it may, Figure 106 is presented at this point primarily to illustrate the fact that algorithmic processes can be used in various information retrieval activities as a substitute for human intellectual processing. Computers can be applied in automatic indexing and automatic abstracting, as well as in other operations involving the formation of classes of documents and of terms, in the development of searching strategies, and in establishing networks of associations among terms. As the diagram implies, computers can, to some extent, substitute for humans in virtually all of the activities illustrated. At present they do not independently generate messages or information needs unless specifically programmed to do so by humans, but perhaps some day they may. Since indexing and abstracting are the focal activities of this book, it will be the application of computers to these tasks that will be given most attention in this chapter.

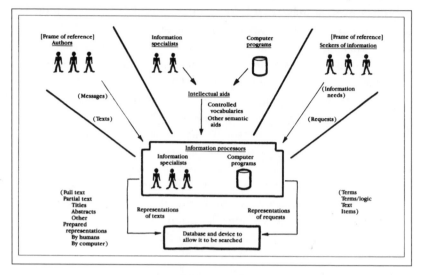

FIGURE 106
The essential problems of information retrieval.

Automatic Extraction Indexing

Early in the book a distinction was made between assignment indexing and indexing by extraction. Most human indexing is assignment indexing, involving the representation of subject matter by means of terms selected from some form of controlled vocabulary. In extraction indexing, words or phrases appearing in a text are extracted and used to represent the content of the text as a whole. Human indexers will try to select textual expressions that appear to be good indicators of what a document is about. Presumably they will be swayed by the frequency with which a term appears in a document and perhaps by where it appears—in title, in summary, in captions to illustrations, and so on—and by its context.

Given that the text exists in electronic form, it is obvious that a computer can be programmed to perform extraction indexing using these same frequency, positional, and contextual criteria. Automatic indexing based on word frequency can be traced back to the 1950's and the work of Luhn (1957) and Baxendale (1958). Simple computer programs count the occurrences of words in a text, once the text has been compared with a "stoplist" to remove non-substantive words (articles, prepositions, conjunctions, and suchlike) from consideration, and then to rank the words by frequency of occurrence. It is the words at the top of the list, of course, that are selected to be the "index terms" for the document. The cutoff point established can observe any of several possible criteria: an absolute number of words, a number related to the length of the text, or words occurring with a frequency above some threshold. A slightly more complicated program can extract phrases occurring significantly often in the text. Thus a document can be represented by a combination of words and phrases, the frequency criterion for the selection of the phrases being less stringent than the one on which significant words are selected.

Rather than selecting words and phrases, the programs can instead be written to select word roots. Thus, the root *heat* might be selected and stored in place of the variants *heat, heating,* and *heated.* Programs for automatic stemming are used to remove only selected word endings (e.g., "ed," "ing"). Of course, words, phrases, or roots can all be given weights reflecting the frequency with which they occur in the document. For example, the root *heat* can be given a numerical weight associated with the fact that it appears in the text, say, twelve times.

Frequency criteria can be supplemented by other criteria. For example, Baxendale (1958) proposed that only the first and last sentences of every paragraph be processed because one of her studies had shown that the first sentence was the "topic sentence" 85 percent of the time and the last sentence was in another seven percent of the cases. The "topic sentence" was the one judged to be that providing the most information concerning the content. In the early days of automatic indexing various other methods for identifying "information rich" segments of text were proposed or tested; computer programs would look for such elements as: prepositional phrases, text following "clue words" like *conclusions* and *summary,* and parts of the text that include the most initial occurrences of nouns.

One obvious disadvantage of using simple word or phrase frequency in the selection of terms is that, even after use of a stoplist, some of the words that occur frequently in a document may not be good discriminators—serving to distinguish this document from others in the database—because they also occur frequently in the database as a whole. To take an obvious example, the words *library* and *information* would not be very good discriminators of individual items within a collection on library and information science. Thus, in a particular document the word *library* may occur twelve times while the word *asbestos* occurs only four times. Nevertheless, the latter is much the better discriminator because it is a term that rarely occurs in the literature of library science. It would be a highly significant term in a collection on this subject even if it occurred only once in a document.

The frequency with which a word occurs in a document is not the only frequency to be concerned with in the computer processing of text. The frequency with which a word occurs in the database as a whole is even more significant. That is, words that are the best discriminators are those that are unexpected and rare in a collection—e.g., *asbestos* in library science, *library* in the database of an asbestos company. In actual fact, it is not necessary to compute the frequency with which a word occurs in a complete database of text but only the frequency with which it occurs in the inverted file used to search the text (i.e., the number of occurrences of a word related to the number of occurrences of all words in the file).

Rather than the absolute frequency with which a word occurs in a document, then, a relative frequency approach to the selection of terms can be used (Oswald et al., 1959). With this approach, words or phrases are selected when they occur in a document more frequently than their rate of occurrence in the database as a whole. This is a bit more complicated than the absolute frequency approach since it requires that a count be maintained of how frequently each word occurs in the database (relative to the total number of word occurrences in the database) and a comparison of this occurrence rate with the rate of occurrence of a word in a particular document.

A list of words or phrases extracted from a document on the basis of relative frequency will be different from a list derived on the basis of absolute frequency but not radically so. Many of the terms will remain the same. The few new terms will be those that occur infrequently in a particular document, perhaps only once, but even more infrequently in the database as a whole—a single occurrence among the 5,000 words of a journal article is highly significant if that word has occurred only five times so far in a database of 10 million words! The terms that disappear, obviously, will be those that, while they may occur frequently in a document, occur frequently in the database as a whole.

Of course, terms selected on the basis of relative frequency should *not* be radically different from those selected on the basis of absolute frequency. For effective information retrieval one wants terms that are good discriminators of documents but also terms that form effective classes of documents. It is useful to be able to zero in on the very rare item—the only document in the database perhaps that discusses the hazards of asbestos in library ceilings—but one also wants to retrieve groups of related documents. Words such as *hazards* or *dangers* may not be quite as rare in a library science database as *asbestos* but they will be useful in retrieving a certain class of document that may interest some users. For effective information retrieval one usually wants classes that consist of more than a single item.

Criteria for the extraction of terms from documents, then, include absolute frequency, relative frequency, or a combination of the two, as well as positional or syntactic criteria.* If a relative approach to the selection of words is used, of course, stoplists are not really necessary: prepositions, conjunctions, and articles will occur frequently in individual items, but they will also occur frequently throughout the database and thus will be rejected, along with the substantive but commonly occurring words (such as *library* in library science).

Terms can also be extracted from text when they match some type of stored dictionary of "acceptable" terms. This was the basis of the important work on machine-aided indexing performed in the 1970s at the Defense Documentation Center (see, for example, Klingbiel, 1971). In essence, word strings occurring in titles and abstracts were matched against a Natural Language Data Base (NLDB). Word strings that matched became candidate index terms. That is, they could cause the assignment of descriptors from the DDC thesaurus. Klingbiel and Rinker (1976) compared the results of the machine-aided indexing with the results of human indexing. As a result of three case studies, they concluded that unedited machine-aided indexing (MAI) can achieve recall levels comparable to those achieved by human indexing and that the precision achieved by the MAI is at least as good as that achieved by the human indexing. Edited machine indexing achieved comparable recall results and better precision than the human indexing. This approach to indexing is now in use at NASA's Center for AeroSpace Information (Silvester et al., 1993, 1994).

Automatic Assignment Indexing

The extraction of words and/or phrases from documents is a task that computers can accomplish rather well. Automatic extraction has one clear advantage over human extraction: it is completely consistent. However, most human indexing is not extraction indexing but assignment indexing and performing this task by computer is altogether more difficult. The obvious way to perform assignment indexing by computer is to develop, for each term to be assigned, a "profile" of words or phrases that tend to occur frequently in documents to which a human indexer would assign that term. This type of profile for the term *acid rain* might include such phrases as acid rain, acid precipitation, air pollution, sulfur dioxides, and so on.

If every term in a controlled vocabulary had such a profile associated with it, computer programs could be used to match the significant phrases in a document (essentially those that would be extracted by the frequency criteria mentioned earlier) with this collection of profiles, assigning a term to

---

*For a complete discussion of various criteria for the selection of terms on the basis of frequency of occurrence see Salton and McGill (1983).

the document when the document profile matches the term profile above some threshold.

This sounds relatively straightforward. In practice, however, it is not that easy. In the first place, the matching criteria would have to be somewhat sophisticated. If *acid rain* occurs ten times in a journal article the index term *acid rain* should almost certainly be assigned. Suppose, on the other hand, that *acid rain* occurs only twice in the document, but *atmosphere*, *sulfur dioxide*, and *sulfuric acid* all occur rather frequently. Should the term *acid rain* be assigned? It is clear that many different combinations of words or phrases could signal the fact that a particular index term should be a candidate for assignment. Moreover, the significance of each combination, as a predictor that a particular term should be assigned, would involve the use of different co-occurrence values. For example, if the words *heat*, *lake*, and *pollution* all occur a few times in a document, this might be enough to cause the term *thermal pollution*, as well as *water pollution*, to be assigned. But *heat* and *lake*, without the appearance of *pollution*, would have to occur together in a document many times before *thermal pollution* would be a good bet for assignment.

The phrase *acid rain* is now very likely to occur frequently in a document dealing with this subject so the correct assignment of the index term *acid rain* may not be as difficult as the above discussion might suggest. The term *thermal pollution* is more of a problem since it is less likely that most of the "thermal pollution" items will include frequent occurrences of this phrase. Some other terms that a human indexer can assign rather easily almost defy assignment by computer. O'Connor (1965) has discussed some of the problems. One good example is the term *toxicity*. A human indexer may legitimately assign such a term on encountering a construction such as "Two days after the substance was ingested several symptoms developed" but it is rather difficult to build all such predictors (that the term *toxicity* should be assigned) into a computer program even if they could all be pre-identified.

Because of such problems, early attempts to assign terms automatically were not very successful, even when very small vocabularies of index terms were involved (for example, Borko and Bernick, 1963). In the past 40 years, however, better procedures have been developed, and it is now possible to perform assignment indexing with greater success.

Automatic indexing and related procedures, then, have a long history. In the remainder of this chapter, some further principles and earlier approaches will first be presented. The more current approaches will be discussed later in the chapter.

Earlier Indexing Studies

A comparison of automatic assignment indexing with manual indexing is reported by Van der Meulen and Janssen (1977). In this case the human indexing used by INSPEC was compared with a scheme for automatic indexing that replaces expressions occurring in abstracts with "concept numbers" drawn from a stored "thesaurus." Although the authors claim that the automatic indexing produced results as good as those achieved by the human indexing, this conclusion was arrived at on the basis of results from only two searches.

One of the more sophisticated programs for automatic assignment indexing, developed at BIOSIS, was discussed by Vleduts-Stokolov (1987). Words appearing in the titles of journal articles were matched against a Semantic Vocabulary, consisting of about 15,000 biological terms, and these in turn were mapped to a vocabulary of 600 Concept Headings (i.e., relatively broad subject headings). Thus, Concept Headings could be assigned by computer on the basis of words/phrases occurring in titles. Vleduts-Stokolov reported that about 61 percent of the Concept Headings assigned by humans could be assigned by computer based on titles alone. If only primary and secondary assignments are considered (BIOSIS used a three level term weighting scheme—primary, secondary, and tertiary), about 75 percent of the assignments could be performed automatically. In fact, however, the programs did not achieve such a high performance level. They achieved about 80-90 percent success in primary and secondary assignments (i.e., assigned 80-90 percent of the 75 percent that could theoretically be assigned based on titles) and almost that level of success in all assignments (i.e., around 80 percent, or a little better, of the 61 percent of assignments that could occur based on titles only). In other words, some *underassignment* occurred; that is, the programs failed to assign some terms that should be assigned and would be assigned by humans. At the same time some *overassignment* also occurred: some terms were assigned that should not be. This is in the same range as the underassignment: between 80 and 90 percent of the term assignments made by computer were correct in the sense that human indexers would also have made them.

A somewhat similar approach, described by Trubkin (1979), was used to automatically index the abstracts in ABI/INFORM (a database in the field of business) for the period 1971-77. A "bridge vocabulary" of almost 19,000 terms was developed to lead from text expressions to the terms of a controlled vocabulary. Since a single occurrence of a term in a title or abstract was enough to cause a controlled term to be assigned, the automatic indexing procedures tended to assign more terms to an item than human indexing would (average of 16 per item as opposed to 8-12).

Again similar to the work at BIOSIS are the procedures for machine-aided indexing implemented by the American Petroleum Institute (Brenner et al., 1984). The goal was to develop methods that will allow the computer to assign the controlled terms of the API thesaurus on the basis of the text of abstracts. Brenner et al. report that an early version of the system assigned only about 40 percent of the terms that human indexers would assign and also assigned many unwanted terms. By learning from this experience, however, they were optimistic that the machine procedures could assign about 80 percent of the terms that should be assigned and that this would be accompanied by a significant reduction in unwanted assignments. In fact, considerable improvements occurred since the first tests. Martinez et al. (1987) discuss the improvements and also describe the problems encountered in mapping from text expressions to thesaurus terms. Later, Hlava (1992) discussed refinements of the API approach in mapping from index terms in one language to index terms in a second (e.g., English to German and vice versa).

A more sophisticated method for mapping text expressions to descriptors was developed at the Technische Hochschule Darmstadt. The most complete description, by Knorz (1983), needs to be supplemented by later references (e.g., Fuhr, 1989; Biebricher et al., 1997). The Darmstadt method is a weighted approach that estimates the probability that a descriptor should be assigned to an item given that a particular text expression occurs in title or abstract. As mentioned earlier in the chapter, one of the most successful applications of machine-aided assignment indexing is now in use at NASA's Center for AeroSpace Information (Silvester et al., 1993, 1994) based on earlier work by Klingbiel.

While automatic assignment indexing has improved considerably in the last 40 years (see final section of this chapter), we have not yet reached a point at which terms from a large vocabulary (say 10,000 descriptors in a thesaurus) could be assigned completely automatically without human intervention. A study by Hersh et al. (1993), dealing with medical text, claims better results from simple text search than from the mapping of text to controlled vocabulary terms (from the Unified Medical Language System).

In point of fact, automatic assignment indexing has little real interest today except in the production of printed indexes. Thirty years ago it was of more general concern. Because it was then very costly to store and process large quantities of text by computer, any method that reduced the text to something shorter was justifiable. Now, of course, if the full text of an item exists in electronic form, or if an adequate abstract exists, it makes little sense to contemplate indexing it unless some form of printed index is to be generated from the database. Nevertheless, as discussed later in the chapter, there do exist special applications in which forms of automatic assignment indexing are still useful. Moreover, the methods of automatic assignment indexing are essentially the same as those used in text categorization (classification) or message routing tasks, as discussed later.

A special form of printed index is the "back of the book" index. Work on producing this type of index by computer also goes back more than 40 years. Artandi (1963) produced book indexes by computer in the field of chemistry. For each index entry ("expression term") she derived a list of associated phrases ("detection terms") the occurrence of any one of which, in a page of text, would cause one of the index entries to be selected for that page. Artandi claimed that an index produced in this way was comparable in quality to a humanly-prepared index but much more expensive. However, a large part of the cost was that of putting the text into electronic form. Since virtually all printing is now done from electronic input the cost factors would no longer favor the human intellectual effort. Nevertheless, the problems of producing indexes to books automatically are more difficult than Artandi's work implies. Even in a restricted subject field a very large vocabulary of expression terms would be needed and, for each, the number of possible detection terms could also be very large. Moreover, both vocabularies would have to be kept up-to-date to reflect new developments and changing terminology in the field.

Of course, Artandi was attempting assignment indexing. Extracting phrases from the text of a book suitable for use as index entries is an easier proposition. Earl (1970) describes a method of producing book indexes by computer that involves the extraction of noun phrases. She claims that "There is every indication that satisfactory back-of-the-book indexes could be produced automatically, with post-editing to delete superfluous terms." Later, Salton (1989) described how syntactic analysis procedures could be used to generate phrases suitable for use in indexes to books. On the other hand, Korycinski and Newell (1990) discuss the reasons why producing book indexes automatically is much more difficult than automatic indexing of journal articles.

Most automatic indexing systems are not really "automatic," in the sense of substituting computers for humans, but are intended to assist the human indexer. A better term for them is "machine-aided." In general, two major approaches to machine-aided indexing can be identified:

1. The computer is used to provide various types of online display and prompts to aid the indexer. Errors made by the indexer (e.g., use of nonstandard terms or invalid main heading/subheading combinations) may be recognized in real time and the indexer immediately notified.

2. Computer programs are used to read text (perhaps only titles and/or abstracts) and to select index terms by extraction or assignment procedures. The terms thus selected may be checked by a human indexer who may add further access points that the programs were unable to assign and/or delete terms erroneously assigned by them.

Current approaches are discussed in the final section of this chapter.

Other Forms of Classification

As discussed in Chapter 2, indexing is a form of classification: the assignment of a term to an item places that item in a class along with others to which that term has been assigned. Other types of classification are possible when various data on bibliographic items exist in electronic form. It is possible to use automatic procedures to generate classes of documents or classes of terms.

In "conventional" retrieval systems, the conduct of a search is aided by the associations among terms made by a human mind, aided perhaps by relationships provided by a thesaurus or some other controlled vocabulary. In a more automatic approach to retrieval—for example, one based on the matching of natural language queries against the full text of items, against abstracts, or against document representations created by computer—it is also desirable to incorporate automatic procedures for developing relationships among terms in order to improve the effectiveness of searches. The obvious relationship to be exploited by computer is co-occurrence. The more frequently two terms occur together (in the text of documents or in lists of terms assigned to documents), the more likely it is that they deal with similar subject matter. To carry this to its logical conclusion, if term A never occurs without B and term B never occurs without A (which would be a very rare situation), the two terms are totally interdependent and would be completely interchangeable in searching. Besides the direct association (X and Y tend to occur together), indirect associations among terms can also be derived on the basis of co-occurrence data. Suppose, for example, that term D almost never occurs in a particular database without W and that term T also tends not to occur without W, yet D and T never co-occur in documents. One concludes that some relationship exists between D and T: they are related by the fact that each one co-occurs strongly with W. In all probability D and T are exactly synonymous in this context: synonyms tend not to occur with each other yet the terms they co-occur with will be very similar. In this hypothetical example D might be "delta," T "triangular," and W "wing."

In fact, the degree of association between two terms should be calculated not on simple frequency of co-occurrence but on the co-occurrence frequency related to the occurrence frequency of each term. For example, if terms A and B co-occur 20 times in a database, while A occurs 10,000 times and B 50,000 times, the "association factor" between A and B will be a weak one. On the other hand, suppose A occurs 50 times, B occurs 25 times, and they co-occur 20 times. The association factor in this case will be great because B is very unlikely to occur without A and almost half the occurrences of A coincide with occurrences of B. Therefore, the relatedness (R) of two terms is usually defined by the simple equation

$$R = \frac{a \ and \ b}{a \ or \ b}$$

When R exceeds some pre-established threshold the two terms are assumed to be related.

Co-occurrence data can be used in two ways: (1) a network of associations among terms can be developed and stored, or (2) discrete classes of terms can be identified and stored, based on associations derived from the network. In the first case the terms input by a searcher, in list form or within a statement in phrase or sentence form, can be elaborated on automatically to produce an expanded list of search terms. In the method Stiles developed (Stiles, 1961; Salisbury & Stiles, 1969), the terms added to a search strategy are those closely related to all of the original search terms on the basis of co-occurrence frequency. For example, A, B, and C occur in the original strategy and X and Y are added because these tend to co-occur with all three of the starting terms. The process could be continued to bring in, say, term P because it is associated with A, B, C, X, and Y. Items in the database can be given a numerical weight, reflecting the number of terms that match between item and search strategy and the strengths of association that exist among these terms (based on co-occurrence), and retrieved items can be ranked by weight. It is thus possible that some items appearing high in the ranking may not contain any terms that the searcher began with.

In the second application, any word occurring in a search statement can be replaced by the class of words to which it belongs. This substitution can be automatic or under the searcher's control. The types of word classes that can be derived from co-occurrence data have been clearly identified by Salton and McGill (1983). In one type, referred to as a *clique*, all words in the group are associated with all other words in the group above some chosen threshold. In a *single-link* group, on the other hand, each word need be linked only to one other word in the group above the established threshold.

The classes formed by statistical procedures will be much less pure than those of a conventional thesaurus. A group of words that strongly co-occur may include genus/species, part/whole, and other relationships, as in the following example:

WING	AERODYNAMICS
AIRFOIL	FLOW
DELTA	
TAIL	
FLUTTER	

The purity of the class is not the main issue. What is important is whether the class is potentially useful in retrieval. For example, is it likely that the hypothetical class of words identified above, if automatically substituted for any one of its members, would improve search results? Depending on the particular query, it seems likely that this type of substitution might improve recall. At the same time, it might cause a severe decline in precision, especially if the class (as in the example) is a very heterogeneous ensemble of terms.

Salton and McGill (1983) give examples of thesaurus entries automatically derived from a document collection in engineering (Figure 107). With such a thesaurus, the query "cryogenic properties of x" could be expanded to "x in relation to concept 415." As a result, items on the superconductivity (i.e., containing the stem "superconduct") of x might be retrieved.

This discussion has so far considered only methods by which classes of terms may be formed on the basis of the documents in which they occur. The data that permit this classification are derived from a matrix showing which terms occur in which documents (term/document matrix). It is clear that the reverse operation can also be performed through use of these data. That is, classes of documents can be formed on the basis of the terms they contain. Salton (1975) and Salton and McGill (1983) have identified various types of such classes:

1 The clique

in which all the items A-E are strongly connected with each other.

2. The star

in which a class $AQRST$ is defined by the fact that Q, R, S, and T are all closely linked with A in some way.

3. The string

$$A<\_\_\_>B<\_\_\_>C<\_\_\_>D<\_\_\_>E$$

in which *B* is closely connected with *A, C* with *B,* and so on up to *E,* which is not closely connected to any other item except *D.*

4. The clump

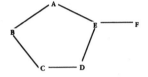

which can be formed on the basis of any of several criteria. In general, however, each member is associated with the other members of the group at a value above some given threshold.

Stars, strings, and clumps are all examples of single-link groups, as defined earlier.

A very similar approach to grouping related items, known as "latent semantic indexing," is based on a classification procedure closely related to factor analysis (see, for example, Dumais, 1995).

Classes of documents can also be formed on the basis of nonterminological characteristics, especially various forms of citation linkage. The possibilities are illustrated in Figure 108. Here *X, Y* and *Z* are recently published documents that cite the earlier items *A, B,* and *C.* A very simple class would consist of a document and the later ones that cite it; e.g., *A, X,* and *Y.* Since *X* and *Y* both cite *A* a good possibility exists that all three have some subject matter in common. This, of course, is the basis of citation indexing. By entering a citation index under *A* the searcher can find *X* and *Y,* the later items that cite *A.* If *A* is an item highly relevant to the searcher's current interests, *X* and *Y* may also be relevant. If so, the searcher has met with some success without the use of conventional subject indexing.

Other classes can be identified in the simple relationships shown in Figure 108. For example, *X* and *Y* can be considered to form a class because they both cite *A* and *B.* This is the principle of *bibliographic coupling* (Kessler, 1962-1965). The more bibliographic references two (or more) items have in common, the more strongly they are coupled. *X* and *Y* are strongly coupled because they both cite *A, B,* and *C. Z* is less strongly coupled to *X* and *Y* because it has only two references in common with the other items. Another way of saying this is that *X* and *Y* form a strong class (strength of 3), while *X* and *Z* and *Y* and *Z* are weaker classes (strength of 2). It is clear that the more alike are the lists of references included in two publications the more likely they are to deal with the same subject. Thus, if *Q* cites *F, G. H* and *I* only, and paper *R* also cites only these four items, *Q* and *R* almost certainly deal with the same subject. If the two papers have these four references in common but each includes, say, ten references that the other does not include, there is less chance that Q and R deal with the same subject although the relationship between Q and R can still be considered fairly close.

408	DISLOCATION	413	CAPACITANCE
	JUNCTION		IMPEDANCE-MATCHING
	MINORITY-CARRIER		IMPEDANCE
	N-P-N		INDUCTANCE
	P-N-P		MUTUAL-IMPEDANCE
	POINT-CONTACT		MUTUAL-INDUCTANCE
	RECOMBINE		MUTUAL
	TRANSITION		NEGATIVE-RESISTANCE
	UNIJUNCTION		POSITIVE-GAP
409	BLAST-COOLED		REACTANCE
	HEAT-FLOW		RESIST
	HEAT-TRANSFER		SELF-IMPEDANCE
			SELF-INDUCTANCE
410	ANNEAL		SELF
	STRAIN		
		414	ANTENNA
411	COERCIVE		KLYSTRON
	DEMAGNETIZE		PULSES-PER-BEAM
	FLUX-LEAKAGE		RECEIVER
	HYSTERESIS		SIGNAL-TO-RECEIVER
	INDUCT		TRANSMITTER
	INSENSITIVE		WAVEGUIDE
	MAGNETORESISTANCE		
	SQUARE-LOOP	415	CRYOGENIC
	THRESHOLD		CRYOTRON
			PERSISTENT-CURRENT
412	LONGITUDINAL		SUPERCONDUCT
	TRANSVERSE		SUPER-CONDUCT
		416	RELAY

FIGURE 107
Example of thesaurus entries derived by automatic methods.
Reprinted from Salton and McGill, *Introduction to Modern Information Retrieval*, 1983, by permission of McGraw-Hill Publishing Company.

A final relationship depicted in Figure 108 is that of *co-citation* (Small, 1973). Items A, B, and C can be considered to form a class because they are cited together (co-cited) by X and Y. As with bibliographic coupling, co-citation can occur with varying strength. In Figure 108 items A, B, and C are weakly related since only two items cite them together. The more items that co-cite them, the more strongly related they are assumed to be.

Classes formed on the basis of citation linkages have some advantages over classes formed through conventional subject indexing. Most obviously, they are independent of language and changing terminology. The name of a disease may change more than once over the course of time but this is no impediment to performing a search on this disease in a citation index, especially if the first paper to identify the disease is known to the searcher and is still frequently cited. The principle of bibliographic coupling, of course, can be used to link papers in completely different languages; for example, identifying papers in, say, Russian and Chinese that are strongly coupled to an English language paper. Likewise, a class of co-cited papers could include items in several languages. More importantly, of course, the classes formed by co-citation change with time as new interrelationships among research results are seen by later investigators. Returning to Figure 108, the authors of X and Y see some relationship among the items A, B, and C, but this relationship may have remained unobserved for very many years. A, B, and C form a class of items for the first time in, say, 1989 because it was in 1989 that X and Y were both published, but A may have been published in the 1930's, C in the 1950's, and B in the 1970's.

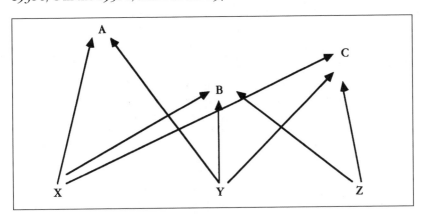

FIGURE 108
Citation/reference linkages.

Studies that have compared the classes formed by conventional subject indexing with those formed on the basis of citation linkages can be traced back for about forty years (Kessler, 1965).Later comparisons include Pao (1988), Pao and Worthen (1989) and Shaw (1990b). A search based on citation linkages (direct citation, bibliographic coupling, or co-citation) may well uncover useful items not found through conventional subject searches in printed indexes or online databases, but the conventional approach is also likely to find useful items that the citation links fail to disclose. The two approaches are complementary rather than competitive.

Kwok (1985a,b) refers to the fact that reference/citation linkages can be used in information retrieval to form an "augmented collection" of retrieved items. That is, when a search strategy is applied to a database in the normal way, using text words or controlled terms, the set of items thus retrieved can be augmented by those items linked to them through bibliographic citations. He suggests that the set of terms associated with the items originally retrieved might be augmented by the addition of terms drawn from the items that they cite. These new terms could be index terms assigned to the cited items or they could be text expressions drawn from abstracts or titles. He suggests that augmentation by drawing terms from the titles of cited items is most practicable. Salton and Zhang (1986) have tested the value of augmenting the set of terms associated with retrieved items by adding title words drawn from "bibliographically related" items. Title words were drawn from (a) items cited by the retrieved items, (b) items citing the retrieved items, and (c) co-cited items. They conclude that, while many "useful" content words can be extracted in this way, many terms of doubtful value will also be extracted, and that the procedure is not sufficiently reliable to warrant inclusion in operating retrieval systems.

It should be obvious that the explicit or implicit links among items in a hypertext or hypermedia network are very similar to the citation linkages discussed here. The indexing implications of hypertext/hypermedia linkages are touched upon in Chapter 16. A book edited by Agosti and Smeaton (1996) is a good source of research on the exploitation of hypertext links in information retrieval.

Automatic Abstracting

If computers can be programmed to select terms from documents according to frequency criteria, they can also be programmed to select sentences from documents. This is the basis of what is usually called "automatic abstracting" although it is more accurately referred to as "automatic extracting." Luhn (1958), the originator of the operation, observed the following procedures:

1. A stoplist eliminates all the nonsubstantive words from further processing.
2. Occurrences of all remaining words are counted and the words ranked by frequency of occurrence (in place of words, roots (stems) can be used).
3. All words occurring more than x times are defined as "high frequency" or "significant" words.
4. Sentences containing concentrations of these high frequency words are located. Two words are considered related within a sentence if there are no more than four intervening words.
5. A "significance factor" for each sentence is calculated, as follows:

a. the number of "clusters" in the sentence is determined (a cluster is the longest group of words bounded by significant words in which the significant words are not separated by more than four intervening words).

b. the number of significant words in the cluster is determined and the square of this number is divided by the total number of words within the cluster,

c. the significance factor for the sentence can be defined either as the value of the highest cluster or the sum of the values of all the clusters in the sentence.

This sounds more complicated than it is in practice and is easily explained through an example. Consider the sentence

$$A\ B\ C\ D^*\ E\ F^*\ G^*\ H\ I\ J^*\ K\ L\ M\ N\ O\ P\ Q\ R$$

where each letter represents a word and the asterisked words are those judged "significant." The cluster formed by the words $D\text{-}J$ contains four significant words so the significance factor for the cluster is $4^2/7$, or 2.3. This is also the significance factor for the sentence since it contains only one cluster.

According to Luhn's procedures, the sentences having the highest significance factors are selected and printed out, in the sequence in which they occur in the text, to form the "abstract." A cutoff point can be established to control the number of sentences selected. This can be based on a fixed number of sentences or on the number of sentences needed to equal a certain percentage of the total document text. Figure 109 is an example of an "auto-abstract" produced by Luhn's procedures.

When dealing with very long documents it may be desirable to have the programs select and print out significant sentences for each section of the publication. Since abstracts should emphasize the particular significance of an item to the organization for which the abstract is prepared, an additional weighting could be given to a certain category or list of words to ensure that sentences containing one or more occurrences of these words will be selected for inclusion in the abstract.

It is clear that an abstract formed in this way will not look much like a humanly prepared abstract. Since some sentences may come from the first paragraph, some from the last, and several others perhaps from the middle of the work, the extract may seem quite disconnected. In point of fact, this is not terribly important as long as the chosen sentences collectively give an accurate picture of what the document deals with. Some investigators, however, disagree with this and insist that automatically-derived extracts should have more continuity (Rush et al., 1971, Mathis et al., 1973).

While Luhn (1958) and Oswald et al. (1959) used word or phrase frequency in the selection of sentences, other investigators have proposed or used alternative criteria. Edmundson (1969) identified four possible methods:

Source: The Scientific American, Vol. 196, No. 2, 86-94, February, 1957

Title: Messengers of the Nervous System

Author: Amodeo S. Marrazzi

Editor's Sub-heading: The internal communication of the body is mediated by chemicals as well as by nerve impulses. Study of their interaction has developed important leads to the understanding and therapy of mental illness.

Auto-Abstract*

It seems reasonable to credit the single-celled organisms also with a system of chemical communication by diffusion of stimulating substances through the cell, and these correspond to the chemical messengers (e.g., hormones) that carry stimuli from cell to cell in the more complex organisms. (7.0)†

Finally, in the vertebrate animals there are special glands (e.g., the adrenals) for producing chemical messengers, and the nervous and chemical communication systems are intertwined: for instance, release of adrenalin by the adrenal gland is subject to control both by nerve impulses and by chemicals brought to the gland by the blood. (6.4)

The experiments clearly demonstrated that acetylcholine (and related substances) and adrenalin (and its relatives) exert opposing actions which maintain a balanced regulation of the transmission of nerve impulses. (6.3)

It is reasonable to suppose that the tranquilizing drugs counteract the inhibitory effect of excessive adrenalin or serotonin or some related inhibitor in the human nervous system. (7.3)

*Sentences selected by means of statistical analysis as having a degree of significance of 6 and over.
†Significance factor is given at the end of each sentence.

FIGURE 109
Example of a Luhn auto-abstract (Luhn 1958).
Copyright © 1958 by International Business Machines Incorporated; reprinted with permission.

1. *Key method.* This was similar to the word frequency criterion used by Luhn. Sentences are given a weight that is the sum of the weights of the component words.

2. *Cue method.* The presence of certain words in a sentence signals the fact that it is likely to be one that is a good indicator of content. A "Cue dictionary" includes a list of words that receive a positive weight and a list of words with a negative weight. The significance value of a sentence is the sum of the weights of the component words.

3. *Title method.* The assumption underlying this method is that words occurring in titles and subheads are good indicators of content. Sentences are given a significance value based on the number of title and subhead words they contain.

4. *Location method.* In this method weights are given to sentences on the basis of where they appear in a document. Sentences appearing in certain sections (first and last sentences of paragraphs, first and last paragraphs, text preceded by headings such as Introduction or Conclusions) are assumed to be more indicative of content than others.

It was discovered that the cue, title, and location methods were more likely to agree on sentences to be selected than any combination of methods involving the key procedure, leading Edmundson to conclude that the key procedure, based on frequency criteria only, was inferior to the other methods.

Rush et al. (1971) make the point that any useful approach to extracting should include criteria for the *rejection* of sentences as well as their *selection*. Their method for evaluating sentences takes into account "contextual influence"—a word or word string, and its surrounding context, offers clues as to whether a sentence should be accepted or rejected. The extracting method they describe is based on the matching of text against a Word Control List (WCL), which includes a list of expressions that, if present in a sentence, would cause it to be rejected and a much smaller list of expressions that would cause it to be selected. Rejection expressions include indicators that the sentence deals with background material rather than the objectives, methods, and results of the present work. Selection expressions are those (such as "this paper," "this study" or "present work") that will almost always signify that the sentence deals with the main thrust of the article. Sentences containing significant words from the title of the item may also be selected. Frequency criteria are not overlooked but they are used only to modify the weights associated with the positive and negative cues in the WCL. The extracting methods developed by Rush et al. offered several advances over earlier procedures, including the ability to modify extracted sentences (e.g., by deleting parenthetical expressions).

Another feature was "intersentence reference": when a sentence was selected for inclusion in an extract it was tested to determine if its meaning was dependent on immediately preceding sentences (e.g., because it includes such expressions as "hence" or "for this reason"). If the meaning was so dependent, the preceding sentences, up to a maximum of three, were included in the abstract even if they did not satisfy other acceptance criteria. This approach to extracting, then, has the potential for creating extracts that have better continuity than those derived by less sophisticated procedures. An example of an extract produced by the Rush et al. procedures (the ADAM automatic abstracting system) is given in Figure 110.

Mathis et al. (1973) introduce improvements on the extracting methods described by Rush et al. The improvements relate primarily to the sentence modification and intersentence reference features of the earlier procedures and are designed to produce representations that are more "readable."

Earl (1970) performed experiments to determine whether or not significant sentences could be identified by syntactic analysis. The assumption was that sentences having certain syntactic structures might be more indicative of content than others. The results were unpromising, due largely to the very great number of sentence types that could be identified. A more promising procedure involved the use of both syntactic and statistical criteria: noun phrases in a text are identified, the substantive words in the phrases are identified, word counts are made, and sentences are selected on the basis of the number of high frequency words they contain.

THE CLAVICHORD AND HOW TO PLAY IT. *MARGERY HALFORD, CLAVIER 9(2), 36-41 (1970).* ESSENTIALLY, THE CLAVICHORD IS A SHALLOW RECTANGULAR BOX WHOSE FRAGILE STRINGS, UNDER LIGHT TENSION, ARE STRUNG HORIZONTALLY FROM A SINGLE BRIDGE OVER A THIN SOUNDBOARD. THE KEYS ARE SIMPLE LEVERS WITH A BRASS BLADE CALLED A TANGENT MOUNTED VERTICALLY ON THE FAR END. THE SOUND PRODUCED IS EXTRAORDINARILY RICH IN OVERTONES. THE TONE OF THE CLAVICHORD DOES NOT EXIST READY-MADE AS IT DOES ON THE PIANO AND HARPSICHORD; IT IS FORMED AND SHAPED BY THE FINGER, AS ON A BOWED STRINGED INSTRUMENT, WITH THE RESULT BEING A GENUINE, DIRECT, LIVING "FEEL OF THE STRINGS". AS LONG AS HIS FINGER REMAINS IN CONTACT WITH THE KEY, THE PLAYER RETAINS CONTROL OF THE SOUND. THE CLAVICHORD IS THE LEAST MECHANIZED AND THE MOST RESPONSIVE OF ALL KEYBOARD INSTRUMENTS IN THAT IT MEETS THE PLAYER HALFWAY IN ITS INSTANT AND FAITHFUL TRANSMISSION OF HIS SLIGHTEST MUSICAL INTENTIONS. EMBELLISHMENTS CAN BE PLAYED CRISPLY AND BRILLIANTLY. SHAKES, SNAPS, APPOGGIATURAS, TRILLS, TURNS, MORDENTS, AND SLIDES—ALL SO CHARACTERISTIC OF THE PERIOD WHEN THE CLAVICHORD ENJOYED ITS GREATEST POPULARITY—ARE IDEALLY SUITED TO THE INSTRUMENT'S EXQUISITE CLARITY AND RICHNESS OF TONE. THE ACTION IS SHALLOW AND VIRTUALLY WEIGHTLESS. IT IS A PHENOMENON OF THE DOUBLE—ENDED LEVER THAT THE TONE PRODUCED BY A STRIKING FORCE WILL SOUND BETTER, SWEETER, AND RICHER AT MAXIMUM LEVER LENGTH. FOR THIS REASON, THE KEYS OF THE CLAVICHORD ARE PLAYED AS NEAR TO THE FRONT EDGES AS POSSIBLE. EXCEPT FOR THE PLAYING OF OCTAVES, THE THUMB IS NEVER USED ON A RAISED KEY; DISPLAY PIECES OF A VIRTUOSO CHARACTER ARE GENERALLY UNSUITED TO THE PERSONAL QUALITIES OF THE CLAVICHORD. CRAMER SAYS THAT THE ESPECIALLY REMARKABLE FEATURES OF CLAVICHORD MUSIC ARE FLUIDITY, SUSTAINED MELODY DIFFUSED WITH EVER-VARYING LIGHT AND SHADOW, THE USE OF CERTAIN MUSICAL SHADING AND ALMOST COMPLETE ABSTINENCE FROM PASSAGES WITH ARPEGGIOS, LEAPS, AND BROKEN CHORDS;

FIGURE 110
Example of an extract produced by the ADAM automatic abstracting system.
Reproduced from Mathis (1972) by permission of the Department of Computer and Information Science, Ohio State University.

Paice (1981) has described automatic extracting procedures based on the identification of sentences likely to be good indicators of what a document is about (e.g., those that contain such expressions as "the principal aim" or "a method is described").

Fum et al. (1982) have described an approach to automatic abstracting in which, they claim, parsing and weighting procedures identify the most important information conveyed in a text, eliminate nonessential elements, and restructure the remainder into a condensed and meaningful summary. They give the example of the sentence

The need to generate enormous additional amounts of electric power while at the same time protecting the environment is one of the major social and technological problems that our society must solve in the next [sic] future being reduced to

> The society must solve in the future the problem of the need to generate power while protecting the environment.

While this is impressive at the sentence level, they fail to demonstrate that the procedures they describe will produce a meaningful and useful summarization of an entire article.

Hahn and Reimer (1984) describe work on the development of an "expert system" approach to text condensation based on the use of a frame knowledge base applied to the parsing of text. They prefer the term *text condensation* to *abstracting* because the methods can, in principle, be used to generate a condensation at various levels of length and detail.

Of course, the more formal and consistent the texts of documents, the more successful extracting procedures are likely to be. For example, Borkowski and Martin (1975) claim better than 90% success in the automatic extraction of case summaries and case dispositions from the text of legal decisions.

Current approaches to automatic extraction, now frequently referred to as "text summarization," are mentioned later in the chapter. While current procedures are capable of doing more sophisticated things, such as successfully combining sentences,* it is possible that the relatively unsophisticated criteria introduced by Luhn and Baxendale may be as good or better than any others in the actual selection of sentences likely to be indicative of document content. For example, Hui and Goh (1996) compared four different criteria in the preparation of abstracts for news articles: location method, indicative process, keyword frequency, and title keyword. Use of indicative phrases (e.g., "in conclusion," "the aim was") to identify significant sentences produced the worst results. The simple keyword frequency criterion was better, but the best results were achieved by methods that gave greater weight to location (e.g., first sentences in a paragraph) or to the selection of sentences containing greater concentrations of words that also occur in titles, subtitles, captions, or bibliographies.

"Automatic" Retrieval Operations

Since indexing and abstracting are the central topics of discussion in this book, automatic indexing and automatic abstracting are the foci of attention in this chapter. Nevertheless, certain other automatic approaches to information retrieval are sufficiently related to warrant some consideration here, if only briefly.

---

*Johnson et al. (1997) present a good example of the state of the art for producing more intelligible abstracts by means of sentence concatenation.

Over the years a major objective of several investigators has been the development of procedures that would allow a request phrased as natural language text to be matched against the text of documents—full text, partial text, or some form of representation. This can be regarded as a kind of pattern matching: the texts in the database can be given some type of score, reflecting the degree to which they match the text of a request, thus allowing them to be presented to the searcher in the form of a ranked output.

Various types and levels of match are possible. Consider this request

Pathology, physiology, radiography, and therapy of radiation pneumonitis or radiation pulmonary fibrosis

and assume that the database consists of the text of abstracts. The simplest method of scoring a match would be one that merely takes into account how many words of the request occur in an abstract. Thus, an abstract might receive a high score if it contained the words "pathology," "physiology," "radiography," "radiation" and "therapy" (i.e., 5 of the 8 significant word occurrences of the request) although, clearly, it is unlikely to be relevant since it contains none of the words of the request that are most discriminating.

Many refinements of this crude level of matching are possible. One is to give each word a score that reflects the number of times it appears in the database as a whole. Thus, "fibrosis" and "pneumonitis" might receive quite high scores since they are likely to be less common in a medical database than the other, more general terms of the request. Consequently, an abstract that contains these two words could receive a high score, even if none of the other request words are present.

The number of occurrences of a word in request and abstract could also be taken into account in the ranking of documents. By this criterion, an abstract that contains the word *radiation* several times is likely to receive a high score because this word is the only one occurring more than once in the request. In the case of a database containing the full text of items, the length of the items needs to be taken into account. Otherwise the very long documents will always have a proportionally greater probability of being retrieved.

Matching can be based on word roots rather than complete words. By this criterion an abstract that includes the words *radiating* and *radiates*, as well as *radiation*, might get a high score in relation to the sample request.

If a machine-generated thesaurus exists in the system it would be possible to substitute for one or more of the request words the thesaurus group (see Figure 107) to which that word belongs. If such a substitution occurred for the request words *radiation* and *pulmonary*, the weights of abstracts containing the words *lung* and *ray* might increase considerably because *lung* and *pulmonary* should belong in the same thesaurus group (along, perhaps, with the root *pneum*), as should *radiography*, *radiation*, and *ray*.

Of course, matching will be more precise if based on phrases rather than single words, so the capability of searching on phrases should definitely exist in any system that matches the text of a request against the text of documents. Abstracts containing the phrase "radiation pneumonitis" should receive a high score in relation to the hypothetical request, as should those containing "radiation pulmonary fibrosis." Abstracts containing the phrase "pulmonary fibrosis" might also receive a high score although they are less likely to be relevant unless the "radiation" aspect is also present. Intermediate between single words and phrases is the use of word proximity—in this case the ability to give higher weight to words that appear close together in text, although not necessarily adjacent.

From this discussion it is obvious that different criteria can be used in assigning a score to a piece of text to reflect the degree to which it matches the text of a request, and that the score assigned can be based on more than one of the criteria discussed (e.g., it could take into account the number of word or phrase matches as well as the rate of occurrence of these words or phrases in the database as a whole). Ideally, then, an "automatic" system should incorporate several possible matching criteria and should allow the user to choose among them.

The most sophisticated system of this general type is the SMART system of Salton, which was developed and refined over a period of more than 30 years. A considerable literature on SMART exists but a good summary can be found in Salton and McGill (1983). While the procedures have been refined since this book was published, it still seems the best account of the basic principles. SMART is designed to assign numerical weights to items, to reflect the extent to which they match request statements, and to present these items to the user in a ranked order, those with highest weights displayed first. SMART incorporates several different matching criteria, including the weighting of terms to reflect their rate of occurrence in a database, phrase matching, and matching on word roots. It also allows for the incorporation of a thesaurus that is arrived at by a combination of computer and human processing. Another essential element in SMART is "relevance feedback." If, in a preliminary output, the user can indicate which items are relevant and which not relevant, the system can recalculate the weight of the items in the database. This is done by reducing the weights associated with the characteristics of the nonrelevant items and increasing the weight of the characteristics associated with the relevant ones. Salton (1989) has also described how the syntactic analysis of the text of book chapters, followed by phrase generation procedures, can be used to generate back-of-the-book indexes.

The methods developed by Salton essentially determine the similarity between two pieces of text and express this closeness as a numerical score, a "similarity measure." In conventional retrieval operations, similarity between the text of a query and texts of documents in a database is measured, the numerical similarity score being used to rank the output. But other uses can be made of this measure of text similarity. For example, the closeness of document texts can be measured, allowing the formation of classes of similar texts. See, for example, the "text relationship map" of Figure 111, based on Salton et al. (1997). While all six of the texts represented can be considered to be semantically related, some are closely related (e.g., 17012 and 17016 are strongly related with a value of 0.57), while the links between other pairs are weak (a value of 0.09 between 19199 and 22387 and a completely nonsignificant link between 22387 and 8907). Salton et al. propose that such procedures for measuring similarity can be used to establish hypertext links within an information network. As discussed later in the chapter, they can also be used to measure the similarity between paragraphs within the same text ("intra-document similarity") and this might then be used as a basis for text summarization.

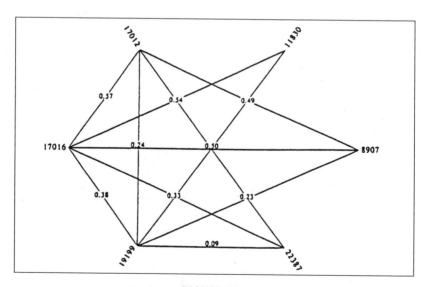

FIGURE 111
Text relationship map based on Salton et al. (1997).
Reprinted by permission of Elsevier Science Inc. The numerical values express the degree of similarity between each pair among the six texts.

Savoy (1995) deals with the establishing of hypertext links through the application of probabilistic methods. He also suggests that the hypertext links can be used to arrive automatically at new search terms. For example, if item *A* is highly relevant to a query and *A* has strong hypertext links to *B*, then *B* may also be relevant. Moreover, the terms strongly associated with *B* may be useful in expanding the search further.

Some other systems have also been developed to allow a user to enter a request in the form of a textual statement. A notable example was the CITE system developed by Doszkocs (1983), which also incorporates relevance feedback. CITE (Computerized Information Transfer in English) has been used as a natural-language interface to the National Library of Medicine's MED-LINE and CATLINE databases. CITE can operate on a database of records consisting of index terms (which is what MEDLINE is) or on one involving free text (e.g., abstracts). The system can stem words automatically (i.e., reduce words to their root forms), assign weights to query terms automatically (the weights reflect the rarity of the term—terms that occur infrequently in the database get the highest weight), and display possible terms for the user's approval or rejection. As in SMART, items in the database are given a numerical score reflecting the degree to which they match the request statement.

In CITE, terms related to those used in a query are identified only when the query has been processed against the database. The raw material worked with is the set of words (terms) associated with the documents retrieved. Thus, in items retrieved on terms *A*, *B*, and *C*, terms *R* and *T* may also occur frequently and may be useful in the expansion of the search. Terms *R* and *T* are not considered significant, however, unless they occur in the retrieved set more frequently than expected. Thus, frequency of occurrence of a term in the database as a whole is also taken into account. For example, a library science database may yield 85 abstracts on the simple query "collection evaluation" (which is interpreted as "collection" *and* "evaluation). The word "library" occurs in 59 of these but is not considered significant because its rate of occurrence in the retrieved set (59/85) does not exceed its occurrence rate in the database as a whole. On the other hand, the word "delivery" might be judged to be significantly associated with "collection" and "evaluation": even though it occurs in only 8 of the 85 abstracts, its rate of occurrence (8/85) greatly exceeds its rate of occurrence in the database as a whole.

A major advantage of the Doszkocs approach is that it does not require the a priori calculation of term associations, a daunting proposition for a very large database. The ability to derive useful term associations a posteriori (after the query has been processed against the database), which requires much less machine processing, makes automatic search optimization procedures viable within very large operating information systems. Systems based on natural language searching and the ranking of retrieved items are now commercially available, as discussed later.

A somewhat different approach is used in the system known as Grateful Med (Snow et al., 1986; Bonham and Nelson, 1988). A formatted online display prompts the user into the formulation of a search strategy. The system will also suggest additional search terms to the user (derived from relevant items already retrieved); a help screen offers suggestions for modifying a search strategy when this has failed to retrieve any items.

Most of the systems described so far are fairly conventional information retrieval systems in the sense that they deal with the searching of bibliographic records (or of bibliographic text), although the methods applied may not be conventional. Other systems were developed to deal with the searching of other types of data. One example of this is an unusual natural language interface, described by Clemencin (1988), which allows a subscriber to query the "yellow pages" in France's online telephone directory using problem statements such as "I would like to repair an old camera," "I want to find a private chauffeur," "My windshield wipers are broken," or "I wrenched my ankle." In response to such a statement the interface will retrieve details on relevant businesses or professionals in the directory.

Current Approaches

As suggested earlier, the Internet has caused a tremendous growth of interest in information retrieval techniques in general and automatic methods in particular. Some systems and procedures that were considered as merely experimental a few years ago are now applied commercially.

As alluded to in the previous chapter, the TIPSTER initiative has been largely instrumental in the progress achieved in the past decade in a variety of automatic text processing activities. This program, and related endeavors, have included several Text Retrieval Conferences (TRECs)—the eleventh was held in 2002—as well as Message Understanding Conferences (MUCs) and, more recently, two Document Understanding Conferences (DUCs), in 2001 and 2002 (see http://www-nlpir.nist.gov/projects/duc/). The DUCs deal with text summarization and are a component of TIDES (DARPA's Translingual Information Detection, Extraction, and Summarization program). Also included was an important conference on the evaluation of summarization methods (Mani, et al., 1998).

Although formal government sponsorship of TIPSTER ended in October 1998 (Gee, 1999), collaborative work in these areas continues, including the continuation of TREC activities. The TIPSTER work, and especially the TREC contributions, have been fully described in the literature (see, for example,

Harman, 1997, Sparck Jones, 1995, and Voorhees and Harman, 1999, 2000). The interactive retrieval track of TREC has been reviewed by Over (2001).

Also contributing significantly to research in this area are the Conferences on Applied Natural Language Processing and the International Conferences on Document Analysis and Recognition.

Automatic text processing procedures related to the subject of this book include machine-aided indexing, completely automatic indexing, message routing (text categorization), text summarization and extraction, and text augmentation and generation.

Research on online machine-aided indexing applied to books, articles and other publications goes back more than thirty years (see, for example, Bennett, 1969 and Bennett et al., 1972). Online aid can take several forms: suggesting terms to indexers (e.g., based on title, abstract, or other text manipulated by the computer or on the basis of terms already entered by the indexer), flagging certain indexer errors (e.g., terms not in the system vocabulary or invalid term combinations), substituting acceptable terms for unacceptable ones, and interfacing with the database to allow an indexer to find how certain terms have been used in the past or how certain items have been indexed in the past.

Online indexing systems in current operational environments offer varying degrees of help and sophistication. For example, the present system in use at the National Library of Medicine, DCMS (Data Creation and Maintenance System) has various prompts for the indexer as mentioned in Chapter 3.

More sophisticated machine-aided indexing systems go beyond these capabilities to, for example, partially index an item or, at least, suggest terms to an indexer. One such, CAIN, was developed for use with AGREP, the European Community's database of ongoing agricultural research projects. Project descriptions include titles, abstracts, and uncontrolled terms indicative of the project scope. CAIN would match this text against two controlled vocabularies (AGROVOC and the CAB Thesaurus) and suggest candidate terms from these sources (Friis, 1992). Some other operating systems have similar capabilities. In the case of systems operating with short texts (e.g., cables) and/or relatively small controlled vocabularies, systems of this kind may be capable of doing much of the indexing correctly before the human indexer reviews to make any necessary corrections or additions.

A fully operational machine-aided indexing system on a large scale exists at the Center for AeroSpace Information (CASI) of NASA, as described by Silvester et al. (1994) and Silvester (1998). A knowledge base of phrases likely to occur in the aerospace literature (128,000 entries as of 1998) is used to map to NASA thesaurus terms. That is, the occurrence of these phrases in input text (usually titles and abstracts) leads the system to produce a list of candidate descriptors for indexer review. Related work at CASI has developed procedures for mapping to terms in the NASA thesaurus from terms assigned to records by other agencies and using other vocabularies (Silvester et al., 1993).

There remains considerable interest in automatic indexing for small specialized applications, especially in the biomedical field. In one example (Borst et al., 1992), the text of patient discharge summaries is analyzed in order to assign relevant clinical descriptors automatically. Somewhat similar is a system, described by Oliver and Altman (1994), that will analyze medical records and assign SNOMED (Systematized Nomenclature of Human and Veterinary Medicine) terms to them.

While reasonable performance is claimed for assignment indexing of this type in specialized subject areas, such automatic procedures generally fail to reach the level of performance achieved by human indexers (see, for example, Chute and Yang, 1993). Nevertheless, automatic indexing of this type should be able to reduce the burden on the human indexers by doing a preliminary assignment. Rindflesch and Aronson (1994) discuss some of the ambiguity problems involved in mapping from text to medical vocabularies (in this case, the Unified Medical Language System) and present several disambiguation rules.

Completely automatic assignment indexing (i.e., with no human intervention) for article-length texts dealing with complex subject matter (e.g., in medicine, chemistry, or physics) is far from realization, especially when the controlled vocabulary used is a very large one, so work has been performed to produce more sophisticated expert systems to aid the indexer. A notable example was MedIndEx, which was under development at the National Library of Medicine for a number of years (Humphrey, 1992). This is a conventional frame-based expert system approach. The user, who need not be an experienced indexer but should have at least some understanding of the medical literature and its terminology, is led to various relevant frames (e.g., type of disease, type of treatment) and prompted to complete them effectively. The system can prompt an indexer to assign a particular term and can also correct the indexer when a term is used inappropriately. For example, an indexer who assigns a neoplasm (cancer) term reflecting the site of the disease (e.g., *bone neoplasms*) can be reminded to assign a companion term representing the histologic type of the neoplasm (e.g., *adenocarcinoma*). Or, the indexer who assigns an inappropriate combination, such as *femur* and *bone neoplasms*, can be informed of the correct term, in this case *femoral neoplasms*. MedIndEx has been abandoned in favor of work on more fully automatic approaches.

Other expert systems have been developed to assist in the training of index-ers rather than to aid the indexing process on a day-to-day basis; one sys-tem of this type, CAIT (Computer-Assisted Indexing Tutor), was developed at the National Agricultural Library (Irving, 1997).

Any computer-based system that helps in the task of subject indexing can be thought of as an expert system, at least in the loosest sense of that term, especially if it helps a less experienced person to approximate the work of an expert indexer. And systems that suggest terms to indexers, or correct certain indexer errors, can be considered to offer at least a modicum of "intel-ligence."

Some systems or programs described in the literature are referred to as "artificially intelligent." Examples can be found in Driscoll et al. (1991) and Jones and Bell (1992). The system described by the latter two authors is designed to extract words or phrases from text in order to form index entries. It works largely on the basis of stored lists: of words to be ignored, of words/phrases/names of known interest, and lists to aid in the disam-biguation of homographs, to conflate singular/plural forms, and to allow sim-ple parsing (a list of word endings). The lists are combined to form a dictionary, which also includes information to allow other facilities such as limited generic posting.

The system described by Driscoll et al. is also designed to find useful index terms in text. Text is processed against a list of rather more than 3,000 phrases. Occurrence of one of these in a text triggers the use of insertion and dele-tion rules. The deletion rules merely avoid further processing of words or phrases that are ambiguous, whereas the insertion rules can generate a lim-ited set of sought terms (to complete a "template") by implication. For exam-ple, the words "time," "over," and "target" will generate AIR WARFARE if they appear within x words of each other. Malone et al. (1991) present a statis-tical model for predicting the performance of this system.

Systems of the type described by Driscoll et al. and by Jones and Bell are ingenious. They may be capable of performing extraction indexing, or extraction with limited assignment, at a level comparable to that achieved by human indexers and at less cost. At the very least, they are useful for pro-ducing candidate terms for human review. Nevertheless, one cannot really agree that they exhibit true intelligence. The same may be said for programs that develop "thesauri" and other searching aids on the basis of term co-occurrence (e.g., Chen et al., 1995).

Research to identify improved statistical association criteria for assign-ing controlled vocabulary terms, based on word occurrences in text, con-tinues to be reported in the literature. Plaunt and Norgard (1998), for example, describe experiments in the assignment of INSPEC thesaurus terms based on a "lexical collocation" technique.

The National Library of Medicine (NLM) is now putting considerable resources into the development of procedures for automatically assigning Medical Subject Headings (*MeSH*) to journal articles. This is becoming a critical need because of the volume of processing involved: about 400,000 articles per year from about 4300 biomedical journals, with more than 19,000 terms in the *MeSH* vocabularies. The problem is addressed by the NLM Indexing Initiative. Aronson et al. (2000) justify this as follows:

> As more and more documents become available in electronic form, and as more and more organizations develop "digital libraries" for their collections, automated techniques for accessing the information are required. It is not possible to index each document by hand, and new methods must be developed. These considerations led to the instigation of the Indexing Initiative at the library. Automated methods developed and implemented within the project will have an important impact on NLM's ability to continue to provide high-quality services to its constituents. (Page 17)

Three principal methods of automatic indexing are under investigation at NLM. Each method can generate a list of candidate subject headings in ranked order; alternatively, the ranking can be achieved by combining two of the methods or, indeed, all three. Two of the methods involve the mapping of phrases, in article titles and abstracts, to *MeSH* terms. The Unified Medical Language System is used as a tool in this mapping (see also Wright et al., 1999, and Aronson, 2001). The third method arrives at candidate terms by matching the words, in title and abstract, of a "new" article with the words occurring in title and abstract of articles already indexed. The terms assigned to the matching articles become candidates for assignment to the new one.

Humphrey (1999) studied the relationship between text words in titles and abstracts of medical articles and the subject category of the journal in which they appear. For example, if a certain group of keywords is strongly associated with the category "cardiology," because they occur frequently in cardiology journals, the term CARDIOLOGY could be automatically assigned to any text in which this keyword group occurs. While such general categorization may not be adequate for many purposes, it may have useful applications. For example, it could be used to automatically categorize biomedical sites on the Web (Humphrey, 2000; Humphrey et al., 2003).

Other groups of researchers, not affiliated with the National Library of Medicine, have developed approaches to automatic assignment indexing in biomedicine. Roberts and Souter (2000) describe techniques for assigning descriptors based on word strings in article titles and word occurrences in abstracts (a keyword must occur at least three times to be judged significant). After processing one hundred records, the automatic descriptor assignment was compared with humanly assigned descriptors. The automatic methods omitted many descriptors that humans assigned correctly and added many that should not have been assigned, although they also added an average of slightly more than one descriptor per record that humans should have assigned but did not. Of the 5.5 descriptors per record assigned automatically, only 3.5 were judged correct. The conditions under which they operated were very simple compared with those of MEDLINE (e.g., a much smaller vocabulary and many fewer terms assigned per item) which serves to illustrate the great problems involved in trying to fully automate assignment indexing within a real database environment.

Bradshaw and Hammond (1999) describe a system in which citations from one publication to another can lead to the extraction of text that might be a useful description for retrieval purposes. That is, if publication *A* cites publication *B*, *A* may include text that indicates what *B* is about or, at least, what *A* thinks *B* is about. For example, a paper by Harpring (2002) cites a book by Panofsky and states:

> Panofsky identified three main levels of meaning in art: pre-iconographic *description*, iconographic *identification*, and iconographic *interpretation* or "iconology."

Clearly, this text does provide some useful "index terms" for Panofsky: meaning, art, iconography, iconology, and so on. The method is intriguing but it is difficult to see any real practical application except, perhaps, for a database of text in a highly specialized subject area. The examples of search successes used by Bradshaw and Hammond (for queries "Java" and "common lisp") are quite trivial, the more so because keyword-in-title searches would have done just as well.

Woodruff and Plaunt (1994) describe a novel system for automated geographic indexing. It is designed:

> . . . to extract place names as well as more general geographic indicators from documents, and use the intersection of these referents to generate estimations of the area to which a document refers. (Page 648)

Place names identified in text can be matched with a database that will supply latitude/longitude coordinates and also associated "features" such as "forest," "reserve," harbour," and "swamp."

It seems likely that, in most applications at least, there will always be some items that cannot be indexed automatically. For example, Ribeiro-Neto et al. (2001) describe their procedures for the automatic assignment of International Code of Diseases (ICD) categories to patient medical records. The text of the records is matched against terms associated with each of the ICD categories and subcategories (from the ICD index, together with synonym and acronym dictionaries). Based on the indexing of more than 20,000 records, the authors claim "excellent" results. While very few of the codes assigned were judged to be "wrong," more than 3000 of the records did not receive the "ideal" code. Of these, 918 received no code at all (i.e., the algorithm could not index them). The vast majority of these, they state, "represent cases that can only be fully categorized with the assistance of a human subject (because, for instance, they require specific knowledge of a given pathology)."

Work continues in the area of "latent semantic indexing." Anderson and Pérez-Carballo (2001) describe the method as follows:

> Latent semantic indexing (LSI) is one of the most sophisticated modern attempts at high quality automatic indexing. It is based on clustering of terms based on co-occurrence and the identification of documents associated with these clusters. By relying on co-occurrence data, LSI is also able to deal with the problem of the variety of terms that can be used to express similar ideas. . . .
>
> As an example of LSI's capability of dealing with divergent terminology, let's imagine documents on the repair and maintenance of automobiles. Different documents may use a number of different terms like "automobile," "car," "motor vehicle," "sedan," plus the names of particular brands and models—"Buick," "Plymouth," "Cherokee." The LSI program is likely to associate these terms together because of their high level of co-occurrence with terms like "oil," "gasoline," "fuel," "carburetor," "tires," "air-conditioning," etc. The LSI program creates clusters of highly related (through co-occurrence) terms, so that when a sufficient number of these terms occurs in a document, the document can be linked to that cluster. In this way, a search for the care and maintenance of carburetors in gasoline-powered automobiles can be made without regard to the particular words used for automobile. All words that mean more or less the same thing as automobile will be linked to the same cluster, as long as a sufficient number of other co-occurring terms match with terms in the cluster. (Page 266)

Actually, latent semantic indexing is not really an indexing method but a way of elaborating automatically on a search strategy in order to bring in semantically related terms. For example, term A may be somehow related to term Y if both occur frequently with term Q. By using this approach, one may retrieve possibly relevant documents whose index terms differ from the query terms but are statistically associated with them. Gordon and Dumais (1998) put it this way:

> Practically, this means that two documents that use strongly overlapping vocabulary may both be retrieved even if a particular query only uses the terms that index one of them. Similarly, terms will be considered "close" to each other if they occur in overlapping sets of documents. (Page 677)

They discuss use of this approach as a means of identifying "disconnected" literatures (see, for example, Swanson, 1990): literature A may be related to literature Y if A's index terms are similar to Q's and Y's are also similar to Q's, although the connecting terms in each case are different. Note the similarities between latent semantic indexing and the associative retrieval described much earlier by Stiles (1961).

An important element in the automatic processing of text is the recognition and extraction of phrases likely to be good indicators of content. Extracted phrases can be used as index terms, can be listed to form a type of abstract, or can be used to map to the terms of a controlled vocabulary. Many approaches have been investigated.

Kim and Wilbur (2001) have studied three different statistical approaches to the selection of content-bearing phrases in text, compared them, and evaluated their combined use in phrase extraction.

Godby (2001) compared phrase extraction by linguistic procedures (parsing to identify noun phrases) with extraction based on frequency statistics, concluding that the simpler frequency approach gives results that are just as good as the parsing method. The statistical approach can identify word pairs that occur frequently in a particular corpus, their frequency in a particular document, and their occurrence in the document within larger phrases (Godby and Reighart, 2001).

Automatic indexing procedures are very closely related to text categorization (or, better, text classification) procedures.* In essence, various characteristics of a text, especially the occurrence of various words or phrases, are used by computer to assign the text to one or more pre-established categories. The conceptual origin of this were the programs developed for the Selective Dissemination of Information (SDI). In SDI, the characteristics of newly published items are matched against the "interest profiles" of individuals or groups. When a match of a certain strength occurs, the selected item is brought to the attention of the individual or group. This type of current awareness service can actually be traced back to 1959.

This matching of incoming documents against stored profiles of interest is referred to as "filtering and routing" within the TREC environment. Robertson (2002) reviews this component of the TREC research.

One important routing application is the categorization of incoming news items. The CONSTRUE system, developed for Reuters Ltd., classifies a stream of news stories using a scheme of up to 674 categories (Hayes and Weinstein, 1991; Hayes, 1992a). Chen et al, (1994) describe procedures for identifying concepts occurring in the text of electronic meetings; in this case the concepts are determined by the procedures rather than being pre-established. Yang (1999) has compared the performance of several text categorization methods, using different evaluation criteria, on various collections of Reuters newswires.

Automatic text categorization is now incorporated within a number of operational publishing systems. A good example can be found in the work

*See Guthrie et al. (1999) for a discussion of frequency criteria for text categorization.

of Al-Kofahi et al. (2001). The application involves the assignment of case law summaries to a classification scheme based on more than 13 thousand legal concepts. About 12 thousand such summaries are produced each week. Categorization is based primarily on the nouns and noun-noun, noun-verb, and noun-adjective pairs occurring in the summary text, which are matched against nouns/noun pairs associated with each of the categories. The assignment is not completely automatic—the procedures produce categorization suggestions for review by an editorial team. The automatic procedures are said to compare favorably with the manual procedures they replace in terms of the number of summaries that can be processed each week. From a weekly feed of 12 thousand summaries, the automatic categorization makes about 1600 suggestions, of which 900 are accepted, 170 rejected, and 530 not used for editorial reasons (precision is quoted at 89%—1430/1600).

Software is now available to perform some level of automatic classification of Web resources (Trippe, 2001; Reamy, 2002). Reamy, who refers to the process as "auto-categorization," summarizes some of the approaches:

> The first and best thing auto-categorization software can do is to very quickly scan every word in a document and analyze the frequencies of patterns of words and, based on a comparison with an existing taxonomy, assign the document to a particular category in the taxonomy.
>
> Some other things that are being done with this software are "clustering" or "taxonomy building" in which the software is simply pointed at a collection of documents, say 10,000 to 100,000, and it searches through all the combinations of words to find clumps or clusters of documents that appear to belong together. (Page 18)

Trippe mentions several products of this type, including one from Eprise described as follows:

> According to Hank Barnes, vice president of strategy for Eprise, "A key aspect of making content more effective is metatags for classification. These tags enable content users to more easily find relevant information and to get more in-depth information on specific subjects." Barnes notes that Eprise uses these types of tags to dynamically locate information in response to user actions, such as following a certain path through a Web site. Adds Barnes, "Often, this approach of content delivery based on classification is much more effective than full-text or general-purpose searching." (Page 46).

Kwon and Lee (2003) also deal with the classification of Web sites, while Lawrence et al. (1999) describe procedures for the automatic citation indexing of science literature on the Web.

The text categorization procedures so far described represent forms of automatic classification—i.e., the assignment of items to pre-established classes or categories. Some work has been done over the years on automating the type of classification more familiar to librarians, namely the assignment of class numbers to books, but no fully operational systems have emerged. Iyer and Giguere (1995) have done work toward development of an expert system to map from one classification scheme to another, in this case from the mathematics scheme of the American Mathematical Society to the mathematics section of the Dewey Decimal Classification. They claim that "An interface that enables mathematicians to access library collections organized with the Dewey Decimal Classification using the AMS scheme as an interface will certainly be useful." Nevertheless, this type of application seems of very limited value.

Of more general interest would be an interactive system to aid in the actual assignment of class numbers. Some work of this type has been done but not on a very great scale. For example, Gowtham and Kamat (1995) developed a prototype system for classifying in the field of metallurgy using the Universal Decimal Classification. While much less ambitious and sophisticated than the MedIndEx system described earlier, the prototype they describe operates in a similar way in that it prompts the user to construct a class number having all the necessary facets (type of metal, property, type of process applied, and so on). Cosgrove and Weimann (1992) also discuss an expert system approach to classification by the UDC but from a theoretical perspective—there is no evidence that any system, even an experimental one, was implemented.

Significant work on automatic classification has been performed at OCLC. The Scorpion project at OCLC has experimented with the automatic classification of Web pages using the Dewey Decimal Classification (Thompson et al., 1997). Assignment is based on the matching of Web text against the text headings associated with the DDC class numbers using algorithms developed for use in Salton's SMART system.

Earlier, Larson (1992) had experimented on a small scale with the automatic assignment of class numbers from the Library of Congress Classification. His objective was different: the automatic assignment of a single number to a book based on titles and subject headings appearing in MARC records. As in the OCLC work, his algorithm ranks class numbers in order of probability of "correctness." Larson concluded that fully automatic classification may not be possible, although semi-automatic classification may be. That is, his program could produce a list of candidate (highly ranked) numbers from which a classifier could select the most appropriate one.

Research on automatic classification also takes place in completely different fields. For example, Bailin et al. (1993) have discussed work on the classification of software components (for a repository of reusable software); machine learning capabilities are claimed. Savić (1995) deals with the possibilities for automatic classification of office correspondence.

Work on automatic thesaurus construction proceeds in a number of research centers outside the library/information science field. The tools thus constructed, while they do reveal possibly useful relationships among terms, are much less highly structured than thesauri created by humans. Examples can be found in Gao et al. (1995), Chen et al, (1995), and Lu et al. (1995).

While computer-aided indexing has a long history, computer-aided abstracting (as opposed to fully automatic methods) has received rather little attention. Craven (2000, 2001), however, has described a system that will automatically generate keywords or phrases from full text and display these in windows to aid someone preparing an abstract for this text. Phrases are selected on the basis of a numerical score that reflects the number of "frequent" keywords in the phrase, the length of the phrase, and the number of times the phrase occurs. The subjects in his experiments judged extracted phrases as no more useful than keywords in the writing of abstracts.

The term "automatic abstracting" has given way to the term "text summarization." In point of fact, no research group has been able to produce automatically the type of abstract that can be written by a human. Automatic summarization is still a matter of sentence selection and the aims of research in this area are to optimize this selection (in the sense of choosing the sentences that best represent the content of the present text) and to organize the selected sentences (possibly modifying them by some form of conflation) to optimize the clarity and utility of the extract.

Summarization can involve various transformations of the text to condense it further. For example, statements can be aggregated by syntactic and semantic analysis. Mani (2001 gives the very simple example of "John and Mary had dinner" and "Then John proposed" being aggregated to "John proposed to Mary after dinner."

The limitations of current summarization methods were well put by Hahn and Mani (2000):

> . . . their application is limited to *extraction*—selecting original pieces from the source document and concatenating them to yield a shorter text. *Abstraction*, in contrast, paraphrases in more general terms what the text is about.
>
> The concatenation approach to extraction does little to ensure that the summary is coherent, which can make the text hard to read. Moreover, the source may not always have text—for example, a sports event on videotape or tables displaying economic data—and current tools cannot summarize nontextual media. Finally, these tools do. not currently handle multiple sources. For example, there may be many stories on the Web about a particular news event, and it would be useful if the summarizer could capture common and new information. (Page 29)

The last two limitations mentioned are no longer really valid because various approaches to video abstracting (see Chapter 13) and multi-document abstracting (discussed later) now exist.

Hahn and Mani (2000) point out that current methods of extraction make use of a linear weighting model that has a number of components such as location in the text, number of occurrences in the database as a whole, and appearance of cue phrases. So, a text unit (usually a sentence) would be selected based on a model of the following type:

Weight of sentence = location weight + cue phrase weight + text occurrence weight + database occurrence weight

Of course, the last component is a negative weight: words or phrases get higher scores the less frequently they occur elsewhere in the database. Hahn and Mani also suggest use of an additional weight for words/phrases based on occurrence elsewhere in the text (e.g., higher weight if it also occurs in the title) or even occurrence in a list of terms representing current interests.

One approach to producing summaries of complex texts automatically has been described by Salton et al. (1997). The methods used to measure the similarity between pairs of documents (see Figure 111) can also be used to measure the similarity between pairs of paragraphs within the same document. Thus, text clusters can be formed, where a cluster consists of paragraphs, possibly drawn from completely different parts of the text, that appear to deal with the same theme. It is claimed that this allows the formation of meaningful summaries of texts by means of paragraph extraction. Note that their work is somewhat different from the majority of work on automatic abstracting, which is based on the sentence as a unit, rather than the paragraph. The Salton et al. procedures produce longer text summaries than the more conventional approaches.

Summaries of text produced by this paragraph extraction were compared with summaries produced by the extraction of "significant" paragraphs by humans. The investigators judge the automatic procedures as acceptable because the resulting summary is as likely to agree with a humanly extracted summary as two humanly extracted summaries are to agree with each other, while the automatic procedures should be much cheaper.

McKeown et al. (1995) and Maybury (1995) describe highly specialized summarization activities. The former generate narrative summaries from stored data (rather than narrative text) relating to basketball games and to telephone network planning activity, while Maybury's system generates textual summaries from highly condensed and structured military messages (battle event data).

Nomoto and Matsumoto (2001) describe a method of creating summaries in which "diversity" is taken into account in forming the extract. That is, the various topics covered in the text are identified, and the most representative sentence for each topic is selected.

Saggion and Lapalme (2000) describe a summarization approach based on "selective analysis." The approach is a two-step process. In the first step, an indicative abstract is presented to the user (really just a list of extracted key terms); if the user wants more, salient text passages are retrieved and presented.

The method used by Lehmam (1999) is based on the selection of sentences that contain the highest concentration of "content-indicating" words or phrases such as "in this research," "the method," and "is discussed."

There is still strong interest in the automatic preparation of extracts. For example, Moens and Dumortier (2000) describe procedures for producing extracts from magazine articles. The purpose of these "highlight abstracts" is to arouse sufficient interest that readers, browsing online in the abstracts, would want to order the entire article. They describe the desirable characteristics as follows:

> The highlight abstract is indicative of the content of the original text. It must suggest the main topics of the article without going into too much detail, which might make the reading of the complete text superfluous. The highlight abstract has an added dimension. It must not only be factual and suggest what the article is about, but it must also encourage the purchase of the complete article. The abstract consists of clippings of text, i.e., sentences and statements extracted from the text. It preferably contains short, easily readable sentences, which do not rely upon the context of the surrounding article text for a correct interpretation. It is important to include conversational language (e.g., quoted speech, questions) in the abstract, because this makes it interesting. (Page 521)

Their summarization process makes use of the discourse patterns that are typical of news stories to develop a "text grammar" that is used in the parsing of text. "Signalling linguistic cues" identify sentences relevant for inclusion in the abstract.

Moens et al. (1999) argue that knowledge of the discourse structure of various types of texts is helpful in the design of systems for text generation or text extraction. They deal particularly with legal texts.

Software for automatic extracting of key sentences from text is now commonplace. A number of products are available for preparing such extracts for text accessible on the Web. Several such products that are free or inexpensive have been reviewed by Jacsó (2002).

Allan et al. (2001) describe methods for producing "temporal summaries" of news stories. The situation is that of a stream of news stories on a particular topic where the news is changing rapidly and it would be difficult to keep up with the changes by reading every item. The procedures are intended to produce a revised summary at regular intervals (e.g., every hour or at the start of each day). Each summary is intended to show only what has changed since the preceding summary. With temporal summarization, "novelty" becomes a useful criterion in sentence selection. That is, a new sentence that is quite unlike the sentences occurring in the past is a promising candidate for selection. Selection of sentences to appear in the summaries is based on a combination of novelty and "usefulness" (probability of relevance to the topic). This type of automatic tracking of the development of a news story over time has been referred to as "event tracking." See, for example, Yang et al. (2000). Gong and Liu (2001) refer to summaries that are related to a particular topic as "query relevant."

Mani (2001) provides a review of work on various forms of summarization applied to multimedia presentations, including both audio and video summarization. Automatic summarization can also be used in conjunction with other automatic procedures, such as use of the summaries produced as input to text categorization (see, for example, Kolcz et al., 2001).

As text summarization methods have become increasingly refined, more specialized applications have emerged. These include multidocument summarization and text miniaturization.

Text summarization need not be restricted to a single text. In automatic multidocument summarization (Mani, 2001), sentences from many separate sources can be merged to form a summary. For example, all references to a particular person or event can be located in a database of text, and these references can be compared to remove redundancy and conflate the residue into a few salient sentences.

Schiffman et al. (2001) describe a system to create a biographical dossier for a person featured in the news by drawing references from a range of texts. It will "select and merge descriptions of people from a document collection, removing redundant descriptions." A high level of conflation and summarization is achieved. Here is one example (the text underlined is taken directly from the sources; the connectives, not underlined, are supplied by the system):

> **Henry Hyde** is a _Republican chairman of House Judiciary Committee_ and a _prosecutor in Senate impeachment trial. He will lead the Judiciary Committee's impeachment review. Hyde urged his colleagues to heed their consciences, "the voice that whispers in our ear, 'duty, duty, duty.'"_

This summary was created from a collection of 1300 wire service news items (707,000 words) containing 503 sentences mentioning Hyde.

Another multidocument summarization application, described by Elhadad and McKeown (2001), relates to medical records. The procedures they describe are designed to examine the results sections of journal. articles retrieved in a search, locate article text that appears directly related to the findings in a patient record, and produce a patient-related summary.

The problem of multidocument summarization, as well as various possible approaches, is discussed by Goldstein et al. (2000) and by Mani (2001).

A lot of attention is now being devoted to the summarization of text (e.g., of e-mail) to appear on very small screens such as those of cellular telephones or personal digital assistants. Corston-Oliver (2001) describes one such approach to what he calls the *compaction* of text. The compaction techniques include sentence selection, character and punctuation deletion, and the substitution of abbreviations for full words or phrases. Thus, this sentence

> *The problem of automatic summarization poses a variety of tough challenges in both NL understanding and generation.*

is compacted into

> *PrblmOfAutmtcSmmrzinPssVrtyOfTghChllngsInBthNL Undrstndng&Gnrin.*

Buyukkokten et al. (2001) describe methods for summarizing Web pages for browsing on handheld devices. Their procedures involve the partitioning of Web pages into "semantic textual units." These can be displayed completely or partially (e.g., first line only, or first three only). Alternatively, the software developed can identify and display (a) the most important keywords extracted from the unit, (b) its most significant sentence, or (c) both keywords and significant sentence. Keyword selection is based on number of occurrences in the text unit and estimates of its occurrence in the Web as a whole (based on the sampling of 20 million Web pages). Sentence selection uses a modified version of Luhn's method for recognizing significant sentences, as described earlier in the chapter. The relative performance of the various summaries was evaluated using human subjects in several information search tasks. The combination of keyword and key sentence was most effective in task completion. Miniaturized summarization of news for handheld devices is also dealt with by Boguraev et al. (2001).

The recent upsurge of activity in text summarization has also brought about a renewal of interest in methods of evaluation (see also Chapter 9). Mani (2001) divides the evaluation of automatically-prepared summaries into intrinsic and extrinsic methods. Intrinsic methods include:

a. use of a panel of judges to decide which sentences are worth selection and which not (*agreement*)
b. judging the readability of the summary in terms of such criteria as word and sentence length and grammatical quality; human judges or grammar and style checkers can be used in this (*quality*)
c. comparing an automatically-prepared summary against an "ideal" summary prepared by humans (*informativeness*)

d. judging a summary in terms of whether it is capable of answering a particular set of questions; the summary can be compared with the full text for this evaluation (*content-based approach*)

e. judging how much of the information in the full text is preserved in the summary (*fidelity to source*).

The extrinsic methods recognized by Mani include (1) judging the summary in terms of its ability to correctly predict the relevance of the full text, (2) judging its ability to allow a human analyst to classify the full text correctly, and (3) reading comprehension evaluation. Mani also recognizes "mature system evaluation," which involves the evaluation of summaries within the context of a fully operating system (e.g., in terms of user satisfaction).

Text summarization usually involves the extraction of sentences but other types of extraction are possible, such as the extraction of particular terms or types of terms, and perhaps the placement of extracted terms into some type of template. To take a completely hypothetical example, a system might monitor movement of business executives through analysis of news items, and the sentence

"John F. Ritter, Vice President of Sales at ABC for the past 5 years, has been appointed Executive Vice President at XYZ" might be reduced to the following structure:

Executive: John F. Ritter
Former position: Vice President of Sales
Former employer: ABC
New position: Executive Vice President
New employer: XYZ
Date: November 5, 1996 (date of news item)

Cowie and Lehnert (1996) provide a useful overview of text extraction and Grishman (1994) discusses problems involved in evaluating the results of extraction tasks. Shuldberg et al. (1993) give a detailed description of one approach. Template design considerations have been discussed by Onyshkevych (1994) and Hobbs and Israel (1994), among others. Lawson et al. (1996) consider this type of data extraction/template filling as a form of "data mining." However, this term is more often applied to procedures and programs that seek to discover significant patterns and correlations in data (e.g., sales records or medical records) without directions on what to look for (see preceding chapter).

There are many potential applications for this type of text extraction and template (frame) filling, perhaps the most obvious being the production of summaries of current news. Haug and Beesley (1992) discuss another application in which data from patient records can be recognized automatically, extracted, and placed under a limited number of headings (e.g., "patient complains of," "patient denies") to aid a radiologist in the interpretation of x-rays. Paice and Jones (1993) discuss the use of a frame-filling approach in the construction of automatic abstracts. Another specialized application of the template approach is the extraction of bibliographic citations from the text of patents (Lawson et al., 1996). Humphreys et al. (2000) describe how template-filling procedures can be applied to the extraction of particular data from science journals.

Modern extraction procedures can identify candidate texts (i.e., those whose keywords indicate a high probability that the text will contain the type of data to be extracted) and portions of the text that are good candidates for the extraction procedures, based on a combination of syntactic and semantic analysis. Jacobs and Rau (1990) describe one such system applied to the extraction of information on corporate mergers. Information extraction in general is dealt with in a book edited by Pazienza (1999).

In some retrieval situations, a limited set of text features may be paramount. For example, dates and names (of places, people, organizations) are especially useful in searches for news items. Watters and Wang (2000) describe a system that can extract "name phrases" from news items and categorize these (as event location, event date, personal name, organizational name). Capitalization in text is the cue for identifying name phrases. The system is designed for real time, interactive retrieval based on a matching algorithm: an online user who finds a news item of interest can ask the system to find others that are similar. The experimental system is intended for Web application "using regular web browsers.as the interface."

Several procedures have been developed at the National Library of Medicine (NLM) for identification/extraction involving medical text. Bodenreider and Zweigenbaum (2000) deal with identification of proper names, Wilbur et al. (1999) with chemical names, Rindflesch et al. (1999) with molecular binding terminology, Rindflesch et al. (2000a) with drug and gene terminology, and Sneiderman et al. (1998) with anatomical terms. In many cases, the identified or extracted terms are further processed (e.g., mapping to the Unified Medical Language System (UMLS). Other research projects at NLM are intended to develop linguistic tools to aid these types of processing. For example, Weeber et al. (2001) deal with the word sense disambiguation problem, and McCray et al. (2001) with the use of the UMLS in the identification of text expressions deserving of further natural language processing.

Of course, extractive summarization does not work well with certain types of text, including Web pages, which Berger and Mittal (2000) describe as "a chaotic jumble of phrases, links, graphics and formatting commands." They describe their work to develop "gists" of Web pages that are not text extracts (i.e., sentences or paragraphs) but, rather, concatenations, of words, such as (a real example) "the music business and industry artists raise awareness rock and jazz."

Jones and Paynter (2002) describe procedures for the automatic extraction of keywords or phrases from document text, the objective being to produce surrogates that can be used to browse through large retrievals of text on the Web. "Keyphrase" extraction is achieved through machine learning procedures. The extraction algorithm learns from a training set of texts to which keyphrases have already been assigned (e.g., by their authors). Based on human evaluation, Jones and Paynter conclude that the phrases extracted by their procedures were "no worse, statistically, than those provided by authors" Earlier, Hui and Goh (1996) experimented with the automatic generation of abstracts of newspaper articles as part of a Web retrieval and filtering interface.

Software for extraction of various forms of data from Web sites is now commercially available. For example, Ojala (2002) refers to a product that will search for changes in corporate affiliations, companies bought and sold, the results of corporate restructuring, and other evidence of corporate change (among other applications).

Related text processing applications include text linkage, text augmentation, and text generation.

Text linkage uses statistical and/or syntactic analyses to determine similarities between different passages of text, usually from completely different documents, and thereby link them (Salton and Buckley, 1992; Maarek, 1992; Salton et al., 1997). In essence, the approach can be applied to produce hypertext links automatically.*

Text augmentation can be considered an extension of text linkage. Systems designed for this purpose attempt to integrate pieces of text from several sources into a coherent narrative—e.g., by following news on some event, such as a corporate merger or natural disaster, in newspapers (and thus applicable to template filling or multidocument summarization tasks). A variation of this is research to develop tools that integrate text and pictorial input—e.g., relate a descriptive passage in a textbook to elements in a diagram and extract text to elucidate the diagram itself (Rajagopalan, 1994). Chen (1993) describes a computer "model" for the integration of related text from different sources.

Text generation here refers both to tools that generate limited types of text automatically and expert systems that aid humans in the writing of var-

---

*A practical linkage application, involving correspondence and other office documents, is discussed by Pozzi and Celentano (1993).

ious types of reports. Systems of the latter type exist, for example, to aid in the generation of product documentation in industry by providing online access to text and graphics that may be repetitively applicable in the creation of various types of reports (see Smith, 1991, as one example). More sophisticated systems are exemplified by the "editor's workbench," described by Bateman and Teich (1995), which will extract text and structure it in response to editorial requirements. Modern "intelligent writing assistants" will do much more than check spelling; they will give advice on word choice and correct grammar and usage (Oakman, 1994).

Stock (1993) and Stock et al. (1997) describe an interesting hypermedia system (ALFRESCO) for retrieving images on fourteenth century Italian frescoes and information concerning them. Among other features, the system incorporates a natural language search interface and the ability to generate coherent answers from "canned texts" associated with different images of frescoes stored within a hypermedia network. Stock gives an example of the question "Can you show and describe to me a fresco by Ambrogio Lorenzetti in Siena?" which could generate the following response:

> **The Effects of Good Government is a fresco by Ambrogio Lorenzetti in the Public Palace. The Effects of Good Government was painted in 1338. A fresco from the same period is S. Silvestro and the Holy Kings by Maso di Banco, painted in 1330-1340. Another work by Ambrogio Lorenzetti in a monument of Siena is the Announcement, of 1344, in the Pinacoteca.**

The various components of this answer are drawn from canned texts appearing in different parts of the hypermedia network.

A specialized text-generation application has been described by Demasco and McCoy (1992). They work to develop an interface to help people with severe motor impairments to compose text. A "virtual keyboard" allows users to select from displays of letters, words, or phrases and a semantic parser is then used to generate a "well-formed sentence." They use the term "sentence compansion" to refer to this process which could, for example, take the selected words "John," "study," "weather," "big," and "university" and form a sentence "John studies weather at a big university."

Kerpedjiev (1992) deals with another specialized text generation situation. In this case, meteorological data can be used to generate "multimodal" weather reports; the reports can be in the form of narrative text, maps, tables, or a combination of these, according to the requirements of the user.

Information retrieval technologies are spreading to a wide range of applications where they were formerly little used, especially in the business world. In fact, some of the more sophisticated of information retrieval approaches have been better accepted by commercial enterprises than they have by the information service industry. One important application is in the help desk area.

A help desk is a telephone service designed to deal with customer questions and problems. Initially, the term referred to a service within the computer industry, established to handle problems encountered within computer networks. While help desks are still strongly associated with the computer industry, services of this kind now exist in a wide range of companies producing consumer products.

The heart of a typical help desk is a "problem-resolution component" in which information is stored on problems previously encountered and possible resolutions to them. The help desk can be considered a true expert system: the support staff who receive the calls are not experts, at least not on all aspects of the situation, but the system gives them problem-solving knowledge. Help desks economize on the number of staff needed to deal with customer questions and reduce the level of the staff assigned to the service. They are made particularly valuable by the fact that many of the problems occur time and time again.

One good example of a help desk, in place at Compaq Computer Corporation, as described by Acorn and Walden (1992), employs a version of the SMART retrieval system developed by Salton. Use of the system is illustrated in Figures 112 through 115. The cases dealt with in the past (i.e., problems and resolutions) are stored as text descriptions, although described in a brief and formalized way. The staff member receiving a call from a customer enters a text statement of the current problem (Figure 112). The system then looks for similar cases by text search and produces (1) a list of best-matching cases and (2) questions to put to the customer in order to focus the search and thus retrieve the correct case and resolution. Answers to the questions narrow the scope of the search although the searcher can browse information on the stored cases (see Figure 113) to supplement the questions. As a result of this interactive process, the cases in the database are given numerical scores which allow them to be ranked according to probable relevance. A score of 70 or above indicates a case that is highly likely to be relevant.

Figure 114 shows an example of a query, with system-generated questions answered by the customer, and the results presented as ranked cases, and Figure 115 shows the final record of the process: the problem, the questions, the case retrieved, and the action recommended to the customer. Unresolved cases are analyzed later by specialists and lead to new additions to the database.

Help desks are usually based upon interaction involving the customer, the customer representative, and the database. Questions generated by the system are necessary to focus the search more precisely. In some cases, the answer to a broad question (Is this a frost-free refrigerator?) may restrict further activity to a particular segment of the database (Danilewitz and Freiheit, 1992; Hart and Graham, 1997).

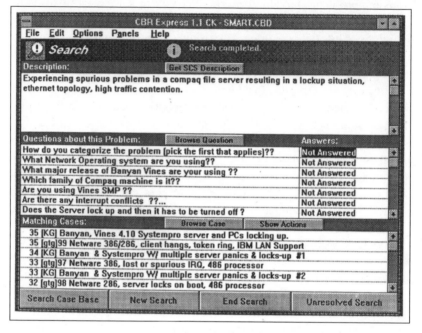

FIGURE 112
Initial search of help desk database.

From T. L. Acorn and S. H. Walden. In Scott and Klahr, eds. *Innovative Applications of Artificial Intelligence* 4, pp. 3-18. Cambridge, MA, MIT Press, 1992.

Help desks of the type referred to above operate through *case-based reasoning*. While there is nothing particularly new in a ranking capability, these systems are unique in that they focus on the most likely solution by generating questions to the user drawn from the cases themselves (e.g., Is this a newly-installed printer? Have you tried changing the X? Have you tried cleaning the Y?). The cases in this type of database may be constructed by "case-base authors" and software tools are commercially available to aid in this task.

Some help desks incorporate sophisticated approaches to natural language processing. For example, Anick (1993) describes such a system, which also includes a form of thesaurus to help users identify alternative search terms, and Uthurusamy et al. (1993) describe a diagnostic system that includes highly-developed procedures for making ambiguous or poorly-formed descriptions (motor vehicle repair records) more intelligible—by correcting spelling errors, disambiguating abbreviations, and refining grammar.

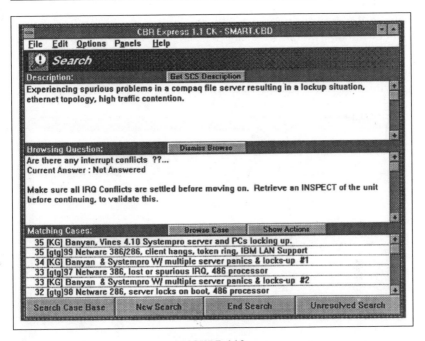

FIGURE 113
Browsing help desk database for further information.
From T. L. Acorn and S. H. Walden. In Scott and Klahr, eds. *Innovative Applications of Artificial Intelligence* 4, pp. 3-18. Cambridge, MA, MIT Press, 1992.

Commercially available software for help desks may incorporate hyper-media capabilities, with text, graphics, audio, and video files accessible to aid in the diagnostic process. The integration of hypermedia and expert system technologies is reviewed by Ragusa and Turban (1994). Thé (1996) gives a useful survey of commercially-available help desk software as of early 1996.

Increasingly, companies heavily involved in customer support activities are seeking to develop help desks that customers can use for themselves, especially help desks that can be implemented through the World Wide Web. Software is now commercially available to aid implementation of Web-based help desks (Varney, 1996; Rapoza, 1996), including software that allows consumers to report problems to a help desk from browsers on their workstations (Walsh, 1996).

A rather complete description of the procedures discussed in this chapter (and, to a lesser extent, the preceding one) can be found in a book by Moens (2000).

Conclusions

Information retrieval is implied in all of the text processing activities already mentioned. In terms of sophistication, retrieving sentences or paragraphs falls midway between retrieving bibliographical references (typical of most online searching performed in libraries) and the retrieval of actual answers to questions. Croft and Turtle (1992) maintain that significant improvements in retrieval will require techniques that "understand" the contents of documents and queries and can thus infer whether an item will be useful.*

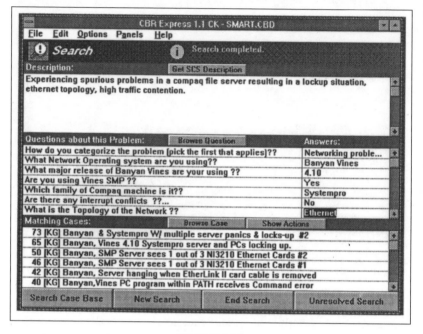

FIGURE 114
Most highly ranked cases selected on the basis of critical query and customer answers to questions.

From T. L. Acorn and S. H. Walden. In Scott and Klahr, eds. *Innovative Applications of Artificial Intelligence* 4, pp. 3-18. Cambridge, MA, MIT Press, 1992.

The methods used in much of text processing today are not particularly new. Most of them were used, perhaps in a more rudimentary form, thirty or more years ago by Luhn, Baxendale, Edmundson, Borko, Maron, Simmons, Salton, and many other investigators (see Chapter 9 of Lancaster (1968b) for an overview of this area in the 1960s). As suggested earlier, better results can be achieved today because much greater bodies of electronic

---

*For some text processing applications it is necessary for the computer to be able to distinguish among logical components of a document (e.g., title, abstract, main text, footnotes, tables, figures) and to determine relationships among them (such as reading order). This has been referred to, somewhat grandiosely, as "document understanding" (see, for example, Semeraro et al., 1994, and *Proceedings of the Third International Conference*, 1995).

text are now available and the power of present-day computers allows the processing of such text with reasonable efficiency.

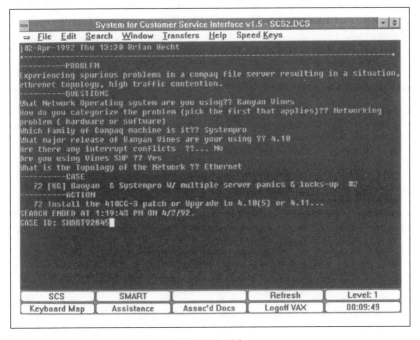

FIGURE 115

Case summary with action recommended to customer.

From T. L. Acorn and S. H. Walden. In Scott and Klahr, eds. *Innovative Applications of Artificial Intelligence* 4, pp. 3-18. Cambridge, MA, MIT Press, 1992.

Nevertheless, even the most sophisticated of current methods are far from ideal in terms of results achieved, processing time, and processing costs. Moreover, there are still relatively few systems that are truly "operational" in the sense that they provide a real service on an everyday basis.

Jacobs (1992a) sees the situation as follows:

> While there has been some visible progress toward text-based intelligent systems, we aren't very close to a desirable state of technology. (Page 5)

Hobbs et al. (1992) claim that the ultimate objective is to develop a system that will:

> . . . recover all information that is implicitly or explicitly present in the text, and it should do so without making mistakes. This standard is far beyond the state of the art. It is an impossibly high standard for human beings, let alone machines. (Pages 13-14)

McDonald (1992) points out that, in general, the best of modern parsers can only deal with relatively short and simple sentences. For longer and more complex sentences, the best they can do is identify component fragments (e.g., noun phrases); they are far from being able to produce a complete, unambiguous analysis. For a typical newspaper-length sentence of 20-25 words, current parsers could potentially come up with hundreds of possible analyses. In McDonald's words, "no parser even comes close to understanding everything in a real text, such as a news article."

Even with relatively small corpora (around 1500 messages) of short texts (typically around 14 sentences), the best of current methods are far from producing perfect results—e.g., in a text extraction exercise, not all relevant sentences are selected and not all selected sentences are relevant. Under controlled evaluation conditions, many modern systems operate only around the 50/50 mark (Jacobs and Rau, 1994; Sundheim, 1995)—e.g., they produce about half the templates (structured representations based on text extracted from the messages) they should produce and about half those produced are wanted (i.e., match the pre-established standard).* While some text processing systems report much better results, they do so for much simpler tasks. For example, Hayes (1992a) reports 94% recall and 84% precision for CONSTRUE but the task performed—putting news items into up to 200 categories—is simpler than the text extraction/template filling tasks.

Yang (1999) claims that CONSTRUE is able to achieve such good results through the use of "manually-developed domain-specific or application-specific rules" and that this approach is too expensive for most applications.

Under controlled conditions, much better scores can be obtained in simpler extraction tasks (e.g., finding named entities in text) or simpler template filling tasks—involving extraction of text related to named entities (Sundheim, 1995).

The 50/50 level of performance in sentence extraction/template completion needs also to be put into context. These results are achieved in very limited domains (e.g., terrorist activity in Latin America). To achieve the sentence selection, a domain-specific dictionary must be created. Even in a very limited domain, this can be labor-intensive (1500 person hours quoted for one), although tools have been developed to construct such dictionaries automatically or semi-automatically (see Riloff and Lehnert, 1993, for an example).**

The routing task in TREC-6 (1997) achieved, at best, only 42% precision (Voorhees and Harman, 2000) with only 47 topics.

---

*It is worth noting that modern researchers in text processing use the same measures — recall and precision—first described in the information retrieval literature in the 1950s.

**A tool of this type "learns" from a training corpus of text. For example, given a representative set of text extracts known to deal with topic x, it will build a dictionary capable of selecting topic x sentences from a new corpus of text.

In general, even the most sophisticated of current automatic indexing procedures compare unfavorably with skilled human indexing. For example, Chute and Yang (1993), dealing with surgical case reports, found that humanly assigned procedure codes produced better results than a variety of automatic procedures, including latent semantic indexing. Earlier, Hersh and Hickam (1991) reported that searching on text words (titles and abstracts only) gave better results than the searching of humanly-indexed (MEDLINE) or automatically processed records in a medical setting. Later (Hersh and Hickam, 1995a) they reported "no significant differences" in searching a medical textbook by two automatic processing methods (word-based and "concept-based") and a Boolean text search approach. Hersh and Hickam (1995b) summarize the evaluation studies they performed over a period of four years.

Moens and Dumortier (2000) describe a method of assigning categories to articles from popular magazines. The success rate reported is very modest. With only 14 broad categories to assign, the best of their procedures can achieve no more than 74% recall and 64% precision. That is, it assigned 74% of the categories that should be assigned while 64% of the assignments actually made were judged to be correct

Fidel (1994) claims that automatic indexing is document-oriented rather than user-centered. While this is true in general, certain approaches can be made more user-centered—for example, the use of lists of terms to be specifically looked for in a text. As Fidel herself points out too, a fully automated system may be more user-centered on the output side, through allowing natural language queries, relevance feedback, and ranked output.

Also, many of the automatic systems use a form of weighting to produce a ranked output. While some studies (e.g., Salton, 1972) have claimed successful ranking, others have not. In an information retrieval study, Marchionini et al. (1994) got rather poor ranking results. This has also been true in completely different applications. For example, automatic diagnostic systems in medicine rarely put the "correct" diagnosis at the top of the ranking and it frequently appears rather low down (Berner, et al., 1994; Kassirer, 1994).

More modern approaches to producing "intelligent" summaries (automatic abstracts) of documents may be less than impressive. The system developed by Brandow et al. (1995), and evaluated by them, produced summaries that were judged significantly less acceptable than "leading text." What this means is that human analysts, on the average, judge the first 250 words (say) of a text to be a better indicator of its content than a 250-word abstract composed of sentences selected from the text automatically.

Moens (2000), who has worked for some time in the area of automatic summarization, agrees that an abstract that is generated automatically is only "an approximation of an ideal one."

Gaizauskas and Wilks (1998), after an excellent review of the field of text extraction (they refer to it as information extraction (IE)), conclude that the levels of performance typical of information retrieval systems is unlikely to be adequate for most purposes:

> Combined precision and recall scores for IR systems have rested in the mid-50% range for many years, and it is in this range that current IE systems also find themselves. While users of IR systems have adapted themselves to these performance levels, it is not clear that for IE applications such levels are acceptable. Clearly what is tolerable will vary from application to application. But where IE applications involve building databases over extended periods of time which subsequently form the input to further analysis, noise in the data will seriously compromise its utility. (Page 97)

The greatly renewed interest in automatic procedures applied to various aspects of information retrieval brings many research groups to this field for the first time. Lacking any historical perspective, they are likely to duplicate work done in the past or, at least, fail to build upon earlier research. To mention just one example, Fowler et al. (1996) and Zizi (1996) describe work on online concept displays very similar to the work of Doyle (1961) performed 40 years earlier.

In the preceding chapter it was pointed out that many research studies that compare text retrieval with retrieval from indexed databases are seriously flawed. Unfortunately, the same can be said for comparisons of automatic versus human indexing procedures. One example can be found in Hmeidi et al. (1997). Based on retrieval results from a small database of Arabic abstracts in the field of computer science, the authors conclude that "automatic indexing is at least as effective as manual indexing and more effective in some cases." In point of fact, there was no manual indexing involved: the comparison was between an automatic indexing procedure based on the work of Salton and text searching applied to the abstracts. Since the Saltonesque procedures are intended to improve both recall and precision (e.g., by eliminating words of greatest frequency and those of lowest frequency), it is hardly surprising that they achieved better results than doing nothing with the text other than perhaps reducing it to stem/root form.

Despite the fact that the cost of computing continues to drop, modern text processing is not necessarily an inexpensive proposition. Hayes (1992a) puts things in perspective, using CONSTRUE as an example. In 1992, this system processed text at about 1800 words per minute (an average Reuters message of 151 words in just under 5 seconds). At this rate, he points out, "a gigabyte of text would take almost two months of cpu time to categorize." This refers simply to putting news items into around 200 categories. More sophisticated text extraction and manipulation, clearly, would take more processing. Dramatically, Hayes points out that CONSTRUE would use 20 years or more of cpu time to process a 100 gigabyte database of the size of NEXIS. While this point is a valid one, it is a little misleading. A system such as CONSTRUE is designed to operate on relatively small corpora at a time—e.g., all messages arriving in a single day—and not for the analysis of huge retrospective databases. This is similar to the distinction between retrospective searching of large bibliographic databases in the 1960s, based on batch processing, and the use of updates of these same databases for current awareness (SDI) purposes. SDI was economically attractive; retrospective searching was certainly not.

Development of the limited systems in existence is also very expensive. CONSTRUE, for example, required 9.5 person years of effort (Hayes and Weinstein, 1991).

It is interesting to note that the 50/50 type of results reported for some modern text processing systems are very close to the performance level reported for large bibliographic retrieval systems (e.g., MEDLARS) in the 1960s (Lancaster, 1968a). While, on the surface, the comparison seems unfair, since the text extraction/template filling tasks are clearly more complex than the reference retrieval task, it must also be recognized that the corpora used in the more sophisticated tasks are quite small compared with the size of the bibliographic databases of even 30 years ago.[*]

The fact is that the relatively crude Boolean search methods most commonly used to search large bibliographic databases today, despite their many critics, produce remarkably good results considering the size of the corpora dealt with, a point made very cogently by Stanfill and Waltz (1992):

> The surprising thing (from the point of view of AI) is that the statistical approach, using no domain-specific knowledge at all, works. And it works for quantities of information (gigabytes) that are unimaginably large by the standards of AI. (Page 217)

Note that they were referring to simple Boolean search approaches as used in indexed (e.g., MEDLINE) or full text (e.g., NEXIS) databases and not the more sophisticated ranked output approaches.

Jacobs (1992a) has identified several challenges facing researchers in the area of text processing today: making systems more robust (greater accuracy, faster, cheaper in linguistic analysis), refining capabilities (e.g., going from document retrieval to passage retrieval to answer retrieval), and making outputs more cost-effective or attractive to the user (by highlighting, text extraction, or summarization).

While some progress has certainly been made in applying computers to various tasks related to information retrieval, little evidence exists that auto-

---

[*]In more conventional retrieval exercises, modern text searching methods do not even reach the 50/50 level of performance when much larger databases (hundreds of thousands of items) are involved (Harman, 1997; Sparck Jones, 1995).

matic procedures can yet outperform humans in such intellectual tasks as index-ing, abstracting, thesaurus construction, and the creation of search strategies.

Kuhlen (1984) suggests that we do not know enough about the intellectual processes involved in abstracting (and, by analogy, indexing and related pro-cedures) to develop programs whereby these activities could be simulated by computer:

> Abstracting . . . is an intellectual art and as such not directly transferable to auto-matic procedures. Cognitive psychology and artificial intelligence have, so far, not provided us with sufficient knowledge about the processes really going on in abstracters' minds when they understand texts and condense them. Thus the direct imitation of an intellectual procedure such as abstracting seems to be out of reach. (Page 98)*

Despite the research and development of the last decade or so, Kuhlen's words seem just as relevant today.

---

*Some authors make the mistake of claiming that the types of automatic processing of text discussed in this chapter (e.g., extraction activities) constitute "automatic under-standing" of text (see, for example, Moens et al. (1999). Nothing could be further from the truth.

CHAPTER 16

Indexing and the Internet

THE WORLD WIDE WEB has become so large, unwieldy, and complex in the last few years that it is well beyond the scope of this book to attempt to explain the myriad components— browsers, search engines, metasearch engines, search agents, crawlers, and so on—that make up its apparatus. The overview by Schwartz (1998) is still conceptually useful although outdated in many details. An excellent technical description of how Web crawlers and search engines actually operate can be found in Arasu et al. (2001). A more readable (i.e., simpler) approach can be found in Liddy (2002). Changes now occur so rapidly that any published account will be at least partially obsolete as soon as it appears. To keep up with changes, it is necessary to use a service such as

<http://extremesearcher.com/news.htm>

and

<http://searchenginewatch.com>

available on the Web itself. This chapter will restrict itself to Web issues most relevant to the subjects of indexing and abstracting.

From a retrieval perspective, the information resources accessible through the Web are very much different from the bibliographic records of a "conventional" system as illustrated in Figure 1 at the beginning of this book. Nevertheless, there are some similarities. Web sites may contain several different searchable elements: URL, site name, any metadata included in the site, content pages (where the terms occurring may be considered somewhat analogous to the index terms of conventional bibliographic records), and all the text occurring within the site.

These searchable elements do bear some similarities to the different searchable elements in records within a bibliographic database: title, classification numbers (perhaps), index terms, text of abstract (although the amount of text in the Web site may be considerably more). Web sites differ most from bibliographic records in that they may also contain pointers (hypertext links) to other sites, with the link terms also being searchable. In this sense, a site is not a discrete unit (as is a typical bibliographic record) but a node in a network.

Lynch (2001) has pointed out one significant difference between a database of bibliographic records, such as MEDLINE, and the collection of sites that comprise the World Wide Web. The organizations producing bibliographic databases are "neutral" towards the records they process. The surrogates they develop—abstracts and index terms—are intended to be accurate and unbiased representations of documents. On the other hand, many Web sites are the creations of commercial enterprises that want their site to be retrieved instead of a site produced by a competitor. "Index spamming" and "page jacking" (discussed later) are two ways of doing this.

Web Search Services

Hock (2001) gives a clear overview of the Web as an information retrieval system:

> For our purposes, a Web search engine is a service provided through the World Wide Web that allows a user to enter a query, and search a database that covers a very substantial portion of the Web's content. Being a bit more specific, a search engine allows the user to enter one or more terms, with optional qualifiers, in order to locate Web pages of interest. The term is almost interchangeable with "Web search services," which … will usually refer more to the overall site, and which in turn may provide the search engine as one of multiple options. The search engine may even be just one offering in a collection of offerings that together aim to provide the user with a general starting place or "portal" to the Web. (Page xxii)
>
> The search engine itself can be considered to have five main functional parts: (1) the engine's "crawlers," which go out and find Web sites and pages; (2) the database of information gathered about those pages and about other pages that have been gathered from other sources; (3) the indexing program, which indexes the content of the database; (4) the "retrieval engine," the algorithm and associated programming, devices, etc. that, upon request, retrieve material from the index/database; and (5) the graphical (HTML) interface, which gathers query data from the user to feed to the retrieval engine. (Page 6)
>
> *Crawlers,* or *spiders,* are the programs that go out to the Web to (1) identify new sites that are to be added to the search engine and (2) to identify sites already covered that have changed. Crawlers gather information about the content of pages from sites and feed that information to the search engine's database. (Page 6)
>
> The total collection of information that's stored about all the individual Web pages constitutes the search engine's database. The collection includes pages that have been identified by crawlers but increasingly also includes pages identified by other sources or techniques. A very large number of sites added to search engines come from direct submissions by Web page publishers. (Page 7)
>
> In terms of which pages will actually be retrieved by a query, indexing can be even more critical than the crawling process. The indexing program examines the information stored in the database and creates the appropriate entries in the index. When you submit a query, it is this index that's used in order to identify matching records.
>
> Most search engines claim to index "all" of the words from every page. The catch is what the engines choose to regard as a "word." Some have a list of "stop words" … that they don't index. (Page 8)
>
> All major engines index the "high value" fields such as the title and the URL. Metatags are usually indexed, but not always. (Metatags are words, phrases, or sen-

tences that are placed in a special section of the HTML (Hypertext Markup Language) code as a way of describing the content of the page. Metatags are not displayed when you view a page, though you can view them if you wish by telling your browser to show the "page source." ... However, some engines purposely do *not* index some metatags because metatags are the part of the page that's most susceptible to abuse by spammers. This caution is taken at the considerable expense of ignoring extremely valuable indexing information. (Pages 8-9)

Schwarz (1998) has mentioned the variability of indexing among the various services:

> Some services index every word on a page ... Positional and markup tag information may be stored with indexed text to improve retrieval and ranking effectiveness. Others index only frequently occurring words, or only words occurring within certain markup tags, or only the first so many words or lines ... Stopwords may be or not be applied, and if applied, may include words of very high frequency ... (Page 975)

Hert et al. (2000) is one of the few studies to look at a Web site from an indexing perspective. The investigators developed three alternative approaches to the indexing actually used on an existing site and compared the different approaches by means of searching tasks performed by twenty university students. Comparisons were made on the basis of both retrieval effectiveness and user preferences.

Although several search engines now claim databases of over 200 million records, no single engine covers every site in the Web. Lawrence and Giles (1999) estimated coverage to be no more than 16 percent for the most comprehensive engine, with many covering only 10 percent or less. Moreover, they reported that coverage seemed to be declining over the years. That is, the Web was growing faster than the engines could cope with.

Retrieval Capabilities

Although the unsophisticated Internet user is likely to search by entering a simple string of terms (which different search engines will treat differently— some putting terms in an OR relationship, others in an AND relationship), search engines may actually offer several more advanced options—such as use of:

1. Boolean logic, including nesting capabilities
2. Truncation
3. Phrase searching
4. Word proximity
5. Field searching (i.e., being able to limit the search to a specified field in a record, such as title or URL)
6. Hypertext links (i.e., searching for pages that link to a particular URL)
7. Image search (ability to look only for pages that contain images)
8. Query by example (ability to find records similar to one already known to be of interest).

Of course, not all search engines have all these capabilities.

The records retrieved in a Web search are ranked, based on a numerical score, and presented to the user in ranked order. Several factors may be taken into account in the scoring, including:

1. Frequency of occurrence of search terms in the record. Relative frequency may be used (the number of occurrences is related to the length of the record so that, for example, a search term occurring five times in a 100-word record will carry more weight than one occurring five times in a record of 1000 words). There is likely to be a limit to the number of occurrences taken into account in the score because of index spamming.
2. Number of term matches. Records that match all three terms in a query (say) should score more highly than those that match only two.
3. Term location. Terms occurring in title may get more weight than those occurring elsewhere.
4. Rarity. Very unusual terms—those that occur very few times in the database—are likely to get a higher score.
5. Proximity. If search terms occur close together in text, this may count more than if they are far apart.
6. Term order. A term entered first by a searcher may get more weight than the subsequent entries.
7. Date. More recent records get higher weight.
8. Popularity of the source based either on the number of times it has been accessed or the number of other sources linked to it.

Some search engines also allow alternative output formats—essentially short versus long display options.

Eastman (2002) discovered that items appearing at the top of the ranking in relatively unsophisticated searches (a string of search terms) had higher relevance (precision) than those at the top of the ranking when more sophisticated Boolean searches were used for the same topics. She concludes that the search engine ranking procedures must work rather well.

Nevertheless, Hock (2001) maintains that Web searching is still fairly crude compared with the use of a carefully indexed database, such as MEDLINE, by a skilled searcher. However, he recognizes that Web searching capabilities are improving all the time:

> The gap between traditional retrieval expectations and Web search expectations is further narrowed when a couple of other factors are considered. Recognition of both of these factors is important for the searcher who wants to get the most out of either kind of search service.
>
> First, Web search engines are dealing with very unstructured data, or at least data with very little consistency of structure. Indeed, there is a definite structure to the HTML behind the Web pages, but for the actual intellectual content, about the only

"intellectual" structure is found in the titles and metatags. The body of the pages has little consistent structure that the Web search service can use for structured searching. . . .

Second, the sheer volume of data currently on the Web—in combination with the volume added every day—should add a degree of respect for what the Web search engines have accomplished in a very short period of time. The fact that there's at least an elementary level of access to the hundreds of millions of pages of material is a feat that should inspire much more awe than disappointment. (Pages 20-21)

Other writers are more critical of Web searching capabilities. Wheatley and Armstrong (1997) for example, present the situation as follows:

Within the body of a Web page, there is no provision for fielded data, and so it is not possible . . . to limit searches to . . . parts of the page. Thus a search will discover the search term(s) with equal ease in the very final paragraph, in an explanations footnote or in material found near the top of the page. With the advent of metadata, a slightly different approach is . . . [possible] . . . However, as metadata is not displayed, and there is often no publisher/authority to impose constraints, the keywords and description pairs can easily be abused, and seeded with terms designed to gain them high apparent relevance or frequent location . . . There is, as yet, no standard for labeling networked resources, and while work continues on metadata, actual use of metadata in the head area of Web pages is still uncommon, and inconsistent. (Page 206)

However, things have improved to some extent, in both fielding and metadata, since this was written.

Of course, different search engines will produce different results for the same query because of differences in coverage, in search algorithms, and in ranking criteria. Many performance comparisons have appeared in the literature over the past several years, going back at least to 1995, but these are of limited value because of the constantly changing situation in the Web itself.

Evaluative comparisons may compare search results only on the basis of overlap/uniqueness or they may attempt to establish relevance of the items retrieved. Leighton and Srivastava (2000) and Su and Chen (1999) are examples of the latter. A review of earlier studies is provided by Jansen and Pooch (2001). Other evaluations have been made for special purposes. Thelwall (2001) compares search engines for their potential use in data mining applications, which he seems to define as "the aggregation of information from large numbers of Web pages in order to create new knowledge."

Oppenheim et al. (2000) provide an excellent review of previous evaluations of search engines. They recommend the development of a standardized set of procedures for such evaluations so that "comparisons can be made between search engines more effectively, and that variations in performance of any given search engine over time can be tracked."

To some extent, it is possible to compensate for capabilities among the search engines through the use of metasearch engines, services that search several individual engines, and then combine the results. According to Hock

(2001), there are now more than 100 metasearch engines in use. Hock is clear about their limitations:

> In particular, if there are more than a handful of relevant sites to be found in the search engines, the meta-search engines often miss most of them. This is caused by a number of factors, including limits imposed by the service on the number of records retrieved from individual engines, time-outs where the meta-search service simply cuts off the search within an engine if it takes too long, failure to adequately translate the query into the specific syntax required by the target engine, and other factors. Fortunately, some meta-search engines do return all of the records that are really there (but have other drawbacks).
>
> The three major weaknesses of meta-search engines are that (1) they often strictly limit the number of records they'll retrieve from any single engine (sometimes to as few as 10); (2) they often will not transfer even slightly sophisticated queries to the engines; and (3) in most cases, they don't search more than two or three of the five largest search engines....
>
> For the most part, the meta-search engines differ from one another in the following ways:
>
> - The specific search engines they cover
> - The number of search engines that can be searched at a time
> - Their ability to transfer more-sophisticated queries—such as those including phrases, Boolean statements, etc.—to the "target" search engines
> - Their limits on how many records they retrieve from each engine (which can be as low as 10)
> - The length of time they're willing to spend searching each engine (before they time-out)
> - How output is presented, including whether or not they eliminate duplicate hits from the various engines. (Pages 186-187)

Hock points out that the metasearch engines are most useful when looking for something obscure—i.e., topics to which very few sites are likely to contribute.

At the beginning of the chapter, a distinction was made between Web resources, and traditional bibliographic databases. Of course, many such databases are accessible via the Web. While a database such as MEDLINE can be located and searched, its contents are not included in the results returned by any one of the search engines, a point made explicitly by Zich (1998):

> Searching for information on the Web suffers from two debilitating deficiencies—Web searching is shallow and narrow. It is shallow in that existing Web-wide search engines go only to what I will call first level documents—i.e., to documents that reside on servers in HTML. There is a world of additional information just beyond. I am referring to information in library catalogs and other data files to which the Web offers entry. The Library of Congress catalog, for instance, is never searched by any of the Web-wide search engines. The millions of meticulously organized and rigorously authenticated bits of information that lie within it and are available go unexplored by these engines. The descriptions of the materials in digital form in the Library's American Memory program and those digital materials themselves—the pictures, sounds, and image-based text documents in their hundreds of thousands—do not appear in Web engine search results, nor do comparable materials, and files from myriads of other institutions. Present search engines skim the surface of Web content. (Page 107)

This point has also been made by Han and Chang (2002):

> In July 2000, analysts estimated that searchable databases on the Web numbered at least 100,000. These databases provide high-quality, well-maintained information, but are not effectively accessible. Because current Web crawlers cannot query these databases, the data they contain remains invisible to traditional search engines. (Page 64)

Metadata

There are several possible definitions of the term "metadata." Cleveland and Cleveland (2001) deal with it this way:

> Metadata is repeatedly defined as *data about data*. While this is a necessary definition, it is not quite sufficient. Metadata is data about data that is structured to describe an information object or resource. It characterizes source data and describes their relationships. Authors of resources, publishers, librarians, and other information professionals can create metadata. It can be embedded in the resource or held in separate metadata repositories. (Page 223)

Hock (2001) prefers the term "metatags" which he defines as:

> The portion (field) of the HTML coding for a Web page that allows the person creating the page to enter text describing the content of the page. The content of metatags is not shown on the page itself when the page is viewed in a browser window. (Page 220)

The so-called Dublin Core is a set of metadata items (metatags) to describe networked resources. It has become a de facto standard for describing resources within the Web. Cleveland and Cleveland (2001) point out that the Dublin Core:

> ... provides for indexing information for document-like sources including indicators for title, creator, subject, description, publisher, co-contributors, data, type, format, resource identifier, language, relationship to related resources, and rights management....
>
> The concept of *core* refers to a consensus by information handlers and subject specialists of what elements are basic or fundamental to support information representation, especially for electronic forms....
>
> One purpose in the development of the Dublin Core was to create a scheme that would be an alternative to complex cataloging techniques and would be usable by catalogers, noncatalogers, and searchers of information. Creators of electronic databases could, in a sense, have *do-it-yourself* cataloging by filling in the blanks. Searchers could use it to traverse within and across disciplines, in an international environment on the Web. (Page 224)

Hearst (1999) makes a distinction between "external metadata" and "contentful metadata." The former is defined as data "associated with the production and use of the document," such as author, place of publication, and date of publication. "Contentful metadata," of course, are data that refer to the content (subject matter) of the document. Clearly, this book is more concerned with contentful metadata.

A different distinction is made by O'Neill et al. (2001). The metadata types they recognize are: "that which is explicitly provided by the Web document author, and that which is supplied automatically by the HTML editor with which the document is created." Based on a sampling of Web records performed in June 1998, they conclude:

> The results ... suggest that metadata usage is quite common in Web documents. However, a number of caveats must be attached to this conclusion. First, it is evident that much of current metadata usage can be attributed to the automatic generation of META tags by HTML editors. It is not clear that metadata of this kind is particularly useful for facilitating resource discovery and description. Second, metadata is often used to describe only the site itself, or at the most a small subset of the site's documents. Current metadata usage patterns are a long way from comprehensive document description at the page level. Finally, most metadata usage is still *ad hoc*; with a few exceptions, most sites do not adhere to a well-defined set of metadata elements. (Page 374)

About 17% of the sites sampled were found to contain "keywords." However, these were not necessarily very useful terms for retrieval purposes:

> The most notable feature was that the keywords, while usually pertinent in some way to the site's content, nonetheless, were often extremely broad. For example, a university Web site might have "education" as a keyword, or an Internet service provider might use "Web" as a keyword. The use of keywords in this manner suggests that the purpose of the metadata is to cast as wide a net as possible in terms of the site's perceived relevancy to search engine queries, rather than to assist in the discovery of the site by itself or as a member of a relatively small search query result set. Of course, the generality of some of these keywords can be mitigated by combining two or more of them in a search query. Furthermore, it is not necessarily the case that nonspecific keywords were chosen to enhance the probability of retrieval for the site. It is likely that in some cases, the use of extremely general terms is simply the result of poor indexing practice. (Page 366)

Dempsey and Heery (1998) have stressed the increasing importance of metadata as follows:

> Metadata will be pervasive of viable digital information environments, to the extent that ... it may be difficult to sustain a general conversation about it. Sensible discussion will involve metadata for particular purposes or within particular communities. (Page 168)

The importance of metadata for digital video archives has been discussed by Wactlar and Christel (2002).

Drott (2002) has studied the extent to which the Web sites of large corporations include "indexing aids" (i.e., aids in the text that guide robots in what to look at for indexing purposes). He looked both at positive aids (embedded metatags that identify "keywords" or "description" in the text) and negative (use of a robots.txt file that may prevent a robot from indexing some part of a Web site). Between 2000 and 2002 he detected an increase in the use of metatags.

Some writers have pointed to the fact that metadata may have some disadvantages as well as advantages. DeRuiter (2002) is one of these:

To guide search engines without confusing humans, certain information was placed in metatags that are not immediately visible in the Web presentation of a screen. This has proven to be a mixed blessing. On the one hand, a search engine can find the information efficiently, but on the other hand it often is unclear for users why a page has come up in the search. (Page 205)

Craven (2001a) has examined the stability of metadata on the Web. He summarized his findings as follows:

Four sets of Web pages previously visited in the summer of 2000 were revisited one year later. Of 707 pages containing metatag descriptions in 2000, 586 retained descriptions in 2001, and, of 1,230 pages lacking descriptions in 2000, 101 had descriptions in 2001. Home pages appeared to both lose and change descriptions more than other pages, with about 19% of descriptions changed in the two sets where home pages predominated versus about 12% in the other two sets. (Page 1)

In a related study (Craven, 2001b), he looked at the appearance of "descriptions" (essentially a type of abstract) in Web metadata. He describes his findings in these terms:

Random samples of 1,872 web pages registered with Yahoo! and 1,638 pages reachable from Yahoo!-registered pages were analyzed for use of meta tags and specifically those containing descriptions. Seven hundred twenty-seven (38.8 percent) of the Yahoo!-registered pages and 442 (27.0 percent) of the other pages included descriptions in meta tags. Some of the descriptions greatly exceeded typical length guidelines of 150 or two hundred characters. A relatively small number (ten percent of the registered and seven percent of the other pages) duplicated exactly phrasing found in the visible text; most repeated some words and phrases. Contrary to documented advice to web-page writers, pages with less visible text were less likely to have descriptions. Keywords were more likely to appear nearer the beginning of a description than nearer the end. Noun phrases were more common than complete sentences, especially in non-registered pages. (Page 1)

A major initiative for applying metadata to Web resources was established as CORC (Cooperative Online Resource Catalog), a joint program of OCLC and a large cadre of participating libraries. In 2002, it was renamed "Connexion." It comprises a database of Web resource descriptions and a database of "pathfinders" which provide browsable access to the resources by means of the Dewey Decimal Classification (DDC) (Vizine-Goetz, 2001; Hickey and Vizine-Goetz, 2001). Resources selected by member libraries for inclusion in the database may be assigned DDC numbers automatically by means of the Scorpion software (Shafer, 2001). Scorpion operates by looking for the best matches between key phrases in text and the text associated with DDC numbers. The Scorpion assignments can be considered as suggestions for human review. While they will frequently be "correct" (i.e., agree with human classification), they will not always be. Godby and Reighart (2001a) describe their research on applying automatic indexing (the WordSmith system) to CORC records. WordSmith can select candidate phrases from Web documents to act as possible index terms, presenting these as suggestions to the cataloger creating a CORC record. As of October 2002, around 700,000 records had been contributed by about 500 institutions.

Another initiative for quality filtering of the Web is the Open Directory Project (<http://dmoz.org>), which intends to be a directory of Web resources selected as of good quality in a wide range of subject areas. It is maintained through the efforts of volunteers who undertake to select sites in their area of expertise. As of 1/18/2003 the project claimed to include more than 3.8 million sites selected by more than 54,000 contributors, and organized into more than 460,000 categories.

Of course, the library profession has been dealing with metadata for a very long time—in the form of descriptive entries in catalogs in card, printed, and online form. Nevertheless, metadata needed for Web resources differ in some ways from the metadata used traditionally to describe books and other printed materials, including the fact that they may have to describe whole collections of records rather than individual items (Hill et al.,1999) and that they may refer to objects (e.g., museum items) rather than text (see, for example, Zeng,1999). Moreover, different levels of metadata may be needed for the same materials in order to meet the needs of different audiences including, perhaps, children (see, for example, Sutton,1999).

A discussion of recent metadata developments, including MODS (Metadata Object and Description Schema) and METS (Metadata Encoding and Transmission Standard) can be found in Guenther and McCallum (2003).

Abstracting on the Web

The metadata included in a Web site may include text that is somewhat akin to an abstract—at least an annotation or scope note. If nothing of this kind exists, some search engines will use the first few lines of the text itself as a kind of abstract.

Some of the search services first construct "abstracts" for the resources they find, and then make the words of the abstract searchable, or extract words from the abstract rather than the full text. However, the companies involved tend not to be very informative on how their automatic abstracting procedures actually work.

Wheatley and Armstrong (1997) have pointed out that resources accessible through the Web may require a somewhat different approach to abstracting, especially since they are likely to refer to *collections* of text (or, in fact, images) rather than individual items:

> An ideal "Internet abstract" might include, for example, user guidance, assessment of authority, discussion of physical attributes (the design of the site or the ease of navigation), judgements on quality, or pointers to alternative sources. (Page 212)

They compare Internet-derived abstracts or extracts with abstracts from conventional bibliographic databases and abstracts or descriptions from Internet gateways. Comparisons were made on readability, content, and style.

Some Web items include keywords or phrases assigned by authors, which can act as surrogates for browsing purposes. However, the great majority do not, and this has prompted work to extract such phrases from Web text automatically, as described in the previous chapter (see, for example, Jones, and Paynter, 2002).

For a discussion of the characteristics of Web page "descriptions" (a type of abstract), see Craven (2001b). He found, for example, that many tend to use noun phrases instead of complete sentences.

Index Spamming and Related Deceptions

A potentially serious problem within the Web is caused by the fact that the developers of Web sites want their sites to be found, which is particularly true of profit-making concerns. Some years before the Internet even emerged, Price (1983) warned that network access to electronic resources could tempt authors, personal and corporate, to make their work more attractive to readers, or more retrievable. This is now occurring on the Internet in a phenomenon that has been variously referred to as "spoofing" or "index spamming."

Lynch (2001) has dealt in some detail with the subject of trust and provenance in the Internet. He points out that:

> Digital documents in a distributed environment may not behave consistently; because they are presented both to people who want to view them and software systems that want to index them by computer programs, they can be changed, perhaps radically, for each presentation. Each presentation can be tailored for a specific recipient. Further, the information that a human takes away from a presentation of a document through mediating software such as a Web browser may be very different from what an indexing program extracts even from the identical source document, unless the indexing program is designed to consider the perceptual impact of the document on human beings....
>
> Sites interested in manipulating the results of the indexing process rapidly began to exploit the difference between the document as viewed by the user and the document as analyzed by the indexing crawler through a set of techniques broadly called "index spamming." For example, a document might be stuffed with thousands of words that the user would not see because they blended into the page background in a tiny font, but which would be found by the indexing crawler. The result has been an ongoing arms race between indexers and Web site developers, with the indexing services adding greater sophistication in word extraction, statistical analysis, natural language processing, and other technology. The indexing services also supplement direct indexing of content with contextual information, such as how many other sites link to a page, as a way of trying to identify important pages.
>
> It is important to understand that when a crawler requests a page for indexing it is not simply reading a file in some sort of network file system; it is making a request for a page to a Web server through the http protocol. The request includes

identification of the request source (at several levels—the software that is asking, and the machine that is sent the request), and the Web server can be programmed to respond differently to identical requests from different sources. The reasons for this may be fairly benign; for example, some servers provide pages that are tuned to index effectively with the indexing algorithms used by different crawlers. Other reasons for source-sensitive responses are more actively malicious, such as the practice of pagejacking. This is most easily illustrated by an example. Suppose you have a product X that competes with another product Y made by another company. When people issue queries to Web search engines asking for Y you would like to get the search engine to return your page advertising X instead. You take a copy of the page for Y, and give this to the Web indexing service, but when a user (as opposed to the indexing service) clicks on the URL, you return the page for your product X instead of the copied page for Y. Competition is not the only motive; for example, perhaps you would like to ensure that the pages of an organization you do not like are returned in response to requests for explicit sexual material. Pagejacking might be defined generally as providing arbitrary documents with independent arbitrary index entries. Clearly, building information retrieval systems to cope with this environment is a huge problem, and Web crawlers are beginning to integrate a wide range of validity checks (such as looking at link networks between pages and sites) to attempt to identify and filter likely pagejacking attempts. (Pages 13-14)

Drott (2002) has also addressed the spamming problem:

One major insurance company employed the ruse of repeating the same word over and over. That is, their "keywords" entry repeated each word six times (e.g., annuities annuities annuities annuities annuities annuities). This kind of attempt to secure better indexing position is frequently found in the text of pornographic websites where the words are hidden by making text and background the same color. To their credit, the insurance company has not used this questionable device. Most search services discount repetitions so that keyword repetition is useless. More to the point, it is hard to imagine a legitimate business reason why a reputable company would want to engage in such a practice. (Pages 214-215)

Introna and Nissenbaum (2000) maintain that, in terms of access, the Web favors the wealthy, the unscrupulous, and the technologically proficient. The last two are able to promote access to Web sites by spamming and other deceptions. The wealthy are able to pay the search engines for achieving "prominence" in output ranking.

Mowshowitz and Kawaguchi (2002) have alerted us to the existence of bias in the Web. That is, the various search engines may create bias by their selection of the sites they provide access to. They illustrate bias through searches on product information (a search on refrigerators shows bias towards certain manufacturers in some search engines) and on euthanasia. While they do not attempt to explain why bias occurs, they refer to it as a "socially significant issue."

Floridi (1996) may have been first to point to the dangers of the Internet as a source of disinformation. The subject has since been dealt with in some detail in a book edited by Mintz (2002), who refers to it as misinformation, which is defined as information that is "intentionally wrong or misleading." Examples include unauthenticated medical and business information, charity scams, e-mail fraud, and dangerous legal advice.

While the problems addressed in this section are not indexing problems per se, they clearly illustrate the need for quality filtering and the fact that a substantial chunk of the Web is just not worth any indexing attention.

Hypertext/Hypermedia Linkage

It is obvious that a form of indexing is implicit in the structure of the Web. The fact that two sources, *A* and *B*, are linked within the Web implies that both belong, in some sense, to the same class, and that the terms associated with *A* may also be useful in the retrieval of *B*, and vice versa (Savoy, 1995).

Not surprisingly, indexing problems associated with hypertext, and hypermedia sources have received considerable attention. Some papers (e.g., Salton and Buckley, 1992; Savoy, 1995; Salton et al., 1997) discuss procedures for establishing hypertext links automatically. This is also dealt with in a book edited by Agosti and Smeaton (1996). Agosti et al. (1995) describe methods for establishing hypermedia links automatically, using statistical association criteria, in real time, browsing interaction with the Web. They refer to this as "automatic authoring" of hypermedia. Although they do not explicitly advocate it, the hypertext links established by one searcher, if recorded, might be useful to later searchers. The idea is conceptually similar to the idea of a "growing thesaurus."

Arents and Bogaerts (1996) review the literature on hypermedia retrieval. Although they make frequent mention of "indexing," the majority of the (mostly experimental) approaches they review involve browsing or "navigation" in hypernetworks, following pre-established links or links formed during the search process itself. The graphical "browsers" or "maps," designed to give the user a visual overview of linkages in the network (see Zizi, 1996, for example), are reminiscent of the "semantic road maps" proposed by Doyle (1961) more than forty years ago.

As pointed out early in the book, hypertext, and hypermedia networks create information sources that have no clearly defined boundaries. Chiaramella and Kheirbek (1996) address this issue. They point out that "documents are no longer atomic units" and this changes our ideas about what constitutes not only "document" but "corpus" and "index" as well.

Tessier (1992), Ellis et al. (1994, 1996) and Chu (1997) are some of the authors who have addressed indexing/hypertext relations. Tessier discussed the similarities between hypertext linking and conventional indexing. She claims that hypertext authors link text in ways that are very similar to the ways they would be linked in conventional indexing. Ellis et al. found that humans, asked to insert hypertext links in a collection of texts, like conventional indexers, do not exhibit much consistency in this task. In a later article (Ellis et al.,1996), they test the effect of this consistency of linking on retrieval effectiveness. Chu (1997) has attempted to apply the principles of exhaustivity and specificity to hypertext links. While the measure of the former can be precise (number of links to number of words in a document), the measure of specificity is much more difficult to apply successfully.

Srinavasan et al. (1996) address the problems associated with indexing and retrieval of items within the Web. Their work suggests that techniques that may work well in more stable environments (e.g., inverse term frequency for the ranking of retrieved items) may be less effective in such a "heterogeneous and dynamic context." Some of the problems associated with use of a hypertext database in information retrieval activities are discussed by Dimitroff and Wolfram (1993). Later, Wolfram (1996) explored hypertext inter-record linkages using three different models.

Blair and Kimbaugh (2002) extol the virtues of "exemplary documents" in the design of retrieval systems. Exemplary documents are those (such as review articles, standard textbooks, and legal depositions) that best "describe or exhibit the intellectual structure of a particular field." They suggest a number of possible uses (one is as a source of representative terminology for the field), including their possible value to the Web searcher. If a searcher first retrieves an exemplary document, hypertext links embedded in it can be used to extend a search in various directions.

Melucci (1999) has evaluated the retrieval effectiveness of automatically-constructed hypertext links, and Blustein, and Staveley (2001) provide a review of studies on the generation and evaluation of hypertext.

Somewhat related to hypertext is the capability for users of Web resources to annotate them in much the same way that they would annotate a textbook. This capability is dealt with in some detail by Marshall (2000).

Classification in the Internet

Several of the search engines include some form of categorization of the resources they provide access to. These "directories" employ some form of hierarchical classification. In some cases, several search engines share use of a directory produced elsewhere. Yahoo regards itself as primarily a Web directory although it is essentially a directory/search engine combination.

In addition, some agencies are working towards the organization of Internet resources by means of a form of classification. OCLC, for example, has several related initiatives. One of these, Scorpion, is an experimental system for assigning Dewey Decimal class numbers to Web resources automatically (Vizine-Goetz,1998, 2001; Hickey and Vizine-Goetz, 2001). The OCLC NetFirst database (no longer maintained) also used the hierarchical structure of the Dewey classification to provide access to selected Web resources.

Zins (2002) examined the types of classification used in major portals and Web classified directories. He identified eight principles of classification used in these resources, judging five of them to be "content-related": subjects, objects (e.g., people and organizations), applications (e.g., shopping), users (for whom a resource is intended), and locations (place). The other three principles he categorized as format-related: media (e.g., pictures), "reference" (e.g., dictionaries, maps), and languages. Zins suggests the need to integrate these different principles into a faceted classification for Internet application. While such integration may be theoretically attractive, Zins seems to overlook the fact that the classification of Web resources is essentially pragmatic and practical, and that the unidimensional schemes now used may be all that is required for successful exploitation by users.

A few libraries are beginning to assign classification numbers to the Web resources they provide access to. Elrod (2000) has summarized an online discussion of this issue. One contributor to this discussion gives a good, concise justification of the practice:

> By assigning classification numbers to materials accessible via your online catalog but not physically housed in your stacks (Internet resources), and if your OPAC allows browsing by call number, then the patron can 'browse' not only the materials you have in your collection but also those Internet resources on the same or closely-related subject. Since this same patron can access the Internet resource through the link provided in the bib record, having this record show up in a call number search is a method by which we can provide greater access to information. (Elrod, page 23)

While the Web search engines provide access at the page level, directories, and portals generally provide access at the level of the Web site. Casey (1999) has discussed the need for an analytical index to the Web—i.e., one that uses some form of classification or other controlled vocabulary to index resources below the site level. She recognizes "the impossibility of a comprehensive analytical index to the Internet" but believes that the "creation of small, focused indexes may be the best solution for accessing specific types of digital information." This is precisely what the portals discussed in the next section aim to do.

The need for more classification of Web resources has been stressed by many writers. Trippe (2001) puts it this way:

> According to some, the path to improved information retrieval on the Web lies in intelligently applied taxonomies. In this view, content needs to be more accurately identified by category in such a way that search engines, and other navigational aids

can be better tuned to help the user. As content moves increasingly to the Web, these data sources need to benefit from technologies, and techniques that allow people to view, navigate, and search data by broadly understood categories. (Page 44)

He goes on to describe several commercial products designed to perform various categorization activities on Web sources automatically.

Portals

Although bibliographic databases, such as those of the National Library of Medicine, may be accessible through the Internet, the great majority of Web resources are not "indexed" as the term is used in this book—i.e., by human or computer assignment of terms, perhaps from a controlled vocabulary. Nevertheless, special libraries and information centers can provide an important service by identifying those Web resources of greatest relevance and value to their users, indexing these resources in some way, and developing a gateway that provides access to these resources through the metadata elements. A number of such gateways or "portals" are described and illustrated in Wells et al. (1999), who refer to them as "virtual libraries."

A typical gateway or portal of this type is EEVL, which is a joint venture of several universities in the United Kingdom. According to Breaks and Guyon (1999), this:

> ... is a gateway to quality engineering Internet sites ... [that] aims to enable U.K. engineering academics, researchers, and students to make better use of available Internet resources by improving access to these resources. We achieve this by a process of identifying, filtering, describing, classifying, and indexing quality sites before they are added to a database that is freely available over the World Wide Web. (Page 76)

The database contains searchable descriptions of, and links to, Internet sites of interest. A specially-developed classification scheme is used to categorize the resources. EEVL (<http://www.eevl.ac.uk/>) originally stood for the Edinburgh Engineering Virtual Library. It was later renamed the Enhanced and Evaluated Virtual Library when its scope was extended to include mathematics and computing. As of 9/21/2002, EEVL provided access to over 9000 sites.

A somewhat similar portal is the Agriculture Network Information Center (AgNIC), which is maintained by the National Agricultural Library and several other institutions. AgNIC (<http://www.agnic.org/>) provides access to Web resources in fifteen broad categories, all related to agriculture in the broadest sense.

INFOMINE (<http://infomine.ucr.edu/>) describes itself as:

> ... a virtual library of Internet resources relevant to faculty, students, and research staff at the university level. It contains useful Internet resources such as databases, electronic journals, electronic books, bulletin boards, mailing lists, online library ... catalogs, articles, directories of researchers, and many other types of information.

INFOMINE is librarian built. Librarians from The University of California, Wake Forest University, California State University, The University of Detroit - Mercy, and other universities, and colleges have contributed to building INFOMINE.

As of 9/21/02, it claimed to provide access to more than 23,000 resources. The sites included are annotated and subject headings (Library of Congress) are assigned to improve access (Mitchell and Mooney, 1999).

Other portals are designed to facilitate access to Web resources likely to be of interest to public library users. The Librarians' Index to the Internet (<http://lii.org/>) is described by Hinman and Leita, 1999, as:

> a searchable and annotated subject directory of ... Internet resources that have been selected and evaluated for their usefulness to the public library user's information needs. Resources are selected and indexed by a cadre of trained volunteer librarians from California libraries. (Page 144)

More than 10,000 Internet resources are covered. These are organized into categories and subcategories. Modified Library of Congress subject headings are used.

The Getty Information Institute is another organization active in this type of endeavor. Busch (1998) has described how Getty's controlled vocabularies can be used to provide improved access to art resources.

Portals of this kind are important as filters to network resources. The "value-added" or "quality filtering" component—of selection, annotation, indexing—is paramount. This point is emphasized in EEVL:

> Searching EEVL will retrieve high quality resources, but because EEVL's resources are hand-picked, you will not find as many resources as with some services, but they will be the best!

The portals referred to in this chapter are designed for access by a wide range of potential users. However, more restricted, and specialized portals are possible. Individual libraries can create their own portals to Web resources. Hurt and Potter (2001) give an example:

> On Georgia State University's campus, the liaison librarians (who are also reference and collection development librarians) are actively identifying and creating Web sites, particularly in their subject areas, and are developing individual Web sites on various topics that incorporate reputable Web sites. Another important group of librarians deeply involved in the Web are library faculty in special collections and archives, many of who are creating digital archives to add to the content of the Web's virtual library. (Page 23)

Medeiros et al. (2001) describe an academic medical library's approach to a portal, using the Cooperative Online Resource Catalog (CORC) as a base. They refer to the advantages as follows:

> The library can use CORC to select sites that offer quality content. The library patron is served by being able to go effortlessly to the exact resource needed and can avoid sifting through search engine results that often consist of pages of irrelevant

links. Standard CORC features, such as authority control for name access, assist with resource location. (Page 112)

An industrial information center can develop a portal to point to Web resources of greatest interest and value to the company and can integrate this with its own company intranet using the same mode of subject access (e.g., classification scheme). See, for example, Crandall (2000). Bannan (2002) deals with the subject of company portals but she sees these as providing access to internal information, and possibly for allowing outsiders access to selected company resources, rather than as gateways to useful (to the company) information elsewhere on the Web.

Campbell (2000) has described his vision of a more general "scholars' portal" designed to:

promote the development of and provide access to the highest quality content on the Web. [It would] facilitate the addition of high quality material by fostering standards, searching across databases, and offering a variety of supporting tools. As a result, libraries, corporations, and many other organizations would be empowered to contribute to an accessible distributed digital library. (Page 3)

While Campbell does not address indexing issues directly, they are implicit in his recognition that the portal "might also offer sophisticated electronic thesauri to guide researchers toward areas of interest with precision." The Association of Research Libraries is now active in this development through its Scholar's Portal Project (<http://www.arl.org/access/scholarsportal/>). See Jackson (2002) for developments in this area as of the middle of 2002.

A brief review of recent portal developments in the UK can be found in Awre and Wise (2002).

Place (1999) gives a prediction of the future of subject gateways as follows:

Users can already take advantage of subject gateways, which together describe tens of thousands of high-quality Internet resources. In the future, users can expect to see the existing subject gateways grow considerably in size as more librarians and information professionals contribute to them and as automated, and human solutions to resource discovery are integrated. They can also expect new gateways to appear and to be able to cross-search different gateways simultaneously and seamlessly.

Also on the horizon, user profiles may be used to enable subject gateways to deliver a personalized information service. Users will be asked to enter their information preferences into a database, enabling the gateways to notify them of new resources when and as they appear in the catalog. (Pages 243-244)

The future of indexing and abstracting is discussed in more detail in the next and final chapter.

CHAPTER 17

The Future of Indexing and Abstracting

Writing almost 50 years ago, Fairthorne (1958) claimed that "Indexing is the basic problem as well as the costliest bottleneck of information retrieval." Indexing is still the central problem of information access and Fairthorne's mind would surely have boggled at the immensity of the information access problems posed by the World Wide Web.

Missingham (1996) has given a very clear explanation of the problems:

> The Internet cannot be considered to be just another step in the history of index-ing. It offers huge challenges and needs a very different approach to indexing to enable effective information retrieval.... Indexing the Internet offers many chal-lenges: it contains millions of documents or files; the location of Internet docu-ments/files changes frequently; there is no quality control for Internet information, no consistency in use of terminology, or even in the use of titles; keeping up with new sources is very difficult; indexes are complicated by the fact that many rely on self-reporting by publishers (somewhat similar to the current cataloguing in pub-lication process).... There are no standards which require that authors or titles should be used, nor a requirement that heading information should include title or subtitle information. Internet indexing is therefore quite different from journal article indexing, where this identifying information is usually clear. (Page 35)

She goes on to point out that the biggest problem of all may be:

> ... the volatile nature of the web where indexing a resource can really be like pin-ning jelly to the wall, as it may be there today and gone or completely changed tomorrow. Not only can the resource's name, contents and location change regu-larly, but its accessibility and format change easily as well. (Page 36)

The major defect of the Internet as an information source, apart from its sheer size, is the fact that it lacks any form of quality control. That informa-tion services work reasonably effectively in the world of print on paper is due to the fact that various institutions are in place to perform a quality fil-tering function. Publishers of scholarly books and journals apply review-ing/refereeing procedures that are, at least to some extent, effective in eliminating the most worthless of what is written. The published indexing and abstracting services provide the next level of quality filtering, mostly by choosing the journals, report series, or other publications that they cover on a regular basis. Finally, libraries, particularly those serving the research and scholarly communities, put into place the filters closest to the actual users by purchasing those materials judged of most value to these users and by arranging collections by levels of accessibility, the most accessible materials (physically and perhaps also intellectually) being those that users will be most likely to want frequently.

It is clear that the vast expanse of poorly organized resources that are accessible, at least in a theoretical sense, through the Internet makes the construction of effective filters a daunting proposition, whether at individual or institutional levels. Moreover, we are assured that the situation will get much worse (Weld et al., 1995).

While many Web documents may be of low value, others may simply disappear, as Missingham pointed out. Spinellis (2003) found that around 28% of the URLs referenced in two major computer science journals between 1995 and 1999 were no longer accessible in 2000, and this figure increased to 41% in 2002. The rate of disappearance of Web documents may roughly parallel the rate of obsolescence of the computer science literature (i.e., decline in use with age). Nevertheless, the fact that items disappear, or perhaps reappear in another form without reference from the original, does not encourage an investment in costly indexing.

At the present time, it does not seem likely that the current chaotic situation caused by the "every man his own publisher" phenomenon is likely to be reversible. In other words, it is hard to visualize the possibility that anyone could or would impose overall quality standards on network publication or distribution. Consequently, the viability of a vast network as an information resource must depend upon the imposition of quality filters similar to those of the print-on-paper world.

There is no doubt that the filtering function is just as important in the electronic environment as it was in a publishing environment dominated by print on paper. Because indexing and abstracting, in one form or another, are essential elements in information filtering, it follows that they must have a future. The only remaining questions, then, are:

1. What form will these activities take, and
2. Who will or should perform them?

It is interesting to note that Odlyzko, who for some years has predicted that both libraries and scholarly journals will become obsolete, at least in their traditional forms (see, for example, Odlyzko, 1995), is quite positive on the future of indexing and abstracting services. He claims (Odlyzko, 1999) that such services will survive because they make a substantial intellectual contribution and are comparatively inexpensive relative to that contribution.

Jacsó (2002) disagrees somewhat about the services, but he remains a firm believer in the need for abstracts within the Web:

The increasing availability of full-text databases has decreased the importance of A&I databases in the past 10 to 15 years, but not the need for abstracts. Full-text databases require abstracts for efficient use. The obvious reason for this is that scanning the search-results lists with short abstracts helps tremendously to select the most promising source documents, even when the abstracts leave much to be desired.

He goes on to say:

> The less obvious reason for having abstracts with these databases is that limiting a search in a full-text database to the abstract field is guaranteed to make it more precise than searching hundreds of thousands of full-text documents. (Page 22)

Of course, Jacsó is not necessarily referring to humanly prepared abstracts but to abstracts or extracts that are automatically prepared. In fact, his article reviews commercially available software designed for "document summarization."

Mani (2001) is another writer who has emphasized the importance of summarization:

> The explosion of the World Wide Web has brought with it a vast hoard of information, most of it relatively unstructured. This has created a demand for new ways of managing this rather unwieldy body of dynamically changing information. Some form of automatic summarization seems indispensable in this environment. Increased pressure for technology advances in summarization is coming from users of the web, on-line information sources, and new mobile devices, as well as from the need for corporate knowledge management. Commercial companies are increasingly starting to offer text summarization capabilities, often bundled with information retrieval tools. (Page 529)

Proposals concerning indexing of Web resources cover an extremely wide range, including claims that it is not possible at all. For example, Wellisch (1994) maintained that "Electronic journals are unlikely to be indexed because of the instability of their texts." Since most sources on the Internet are much less stable than the journals, he presumably feels that the whole enterprise—i.e., indexing text that is subject to frequent change—is a lost cause.

It is obvious that human professional indexing of the entire Web is completely impractical. Even if it were, much of what appears on the Web is too impermanent or of too low quality to merit such indexing attention. Selective professional indexing, of course, is possible. Owen (1994) and Weinberg (1996) are two writers who have advocated professional indexing on a selective basis. Weinberg specifically recommended back-of-the-book type of indexing and this kind of indexing could certainly be applied to individual Web sites. Indeed, it has already been applied in this way, and Browne (2001) has discussed and illustrated the processes. Casey (1999) recognizes that her dream of a full "analytical index" to the Web (i.e., one that indexes below the level of the Web site) is utopian and that "small, focused indexes may be the best solution."

Ellis et al. (1998) suggest that a major problem in any approach to Web indexing is the fact that the indexer will always be very remote from the user:

> ... [in] the World Wide Web ... there is no closeness at all between designer or creator (which could be anyone) and potential user (which could be anyone or everyone). This is compounded by the lack of any clear understanding on the part of most searchers as to what it is the various search engines are actually doing when they search. So that the real source of problems in searching distributed online or Internet sources arises not from technical indexing problems but from the easy access provided by online services and the World Wide Web to information selected, structured and indexed for one group of users (with one set of characteristics and information requirements) by quite different sorts of users with quite different characteristics and requirements.
>
> This may be expected to exacerbate existing problems of indexer-user concept matching as users encounter many different files or sites, with differing characteristics, indexing practices and vocabularies, none of which can be expected to meet all, or even some, of the needs of any potential user or user group. This is a key issue, for the more distant users are, in characteristics and information needs, from the types of user conceived of and catered for by those creating or indexing a database, the more likely there are to be problems in accessing relevant information by users from that database. The problem is that of indexing for the unknown user. (Page 44)

Web documents can be considered to be "dynamic," rather than static, in the sense that they can be changed by the creator, or even by others. Bishop (1999) has discussed how researchers can manipulate electronic journal articles (for example) to create new documents. She refers to this as disaggregation (pulling apart the article) and reaggregation (putting all or parts of the article into a different organization). Moreover, some Web documents are "virtual" —documents "for which no persistent state exists" (they are created on the way to the user. (Watters, 1999). Giordano (2000) points out that:

> ... document structure itself is problematic because, in a Web-based environment, a document that appears on a user's workstation as a single object may in fact be an assembly of linked, yet discrete, documents residing in distributed databases. (Page 243)

This type of fluid situation is confusing for people used to the rather solid, permanent publishing environment of print on paper but it will not always present indexing/abstracting problems. Author changes to an "authoritative" text could, of course, necessitate some changes in any abstract or index terms associated with this text (e.g., in portals pointing to it). The "virtual" document (as described by Watters) would only qualify for indexing or abstracting if it were captured and stored in a database as a new item. Likewise, the reaggregated document (as described by Bishop) would presumably be an informal one not deserving of indexing or abstracting attention. The impermanence of electronic documents is more likely to be a problem in company intranets, where documents may disappear completely, be radically altered, or aggregated/disaggregated without any control.

Professional Approaches

Two major approaches to providing intellectual access to the more important Web resources are already in place, and were discussed in the preceding chapter: the CORC (Cooperative Online Resource Catalog) initiative (renamed "Connexion" in 2002) and the various specialized portals that have emerged. Although the majority of portals have been developed in "academic" areas, the importance of this type of activity for the public library was highlighted by Holt (1995) as follows:

> ...public library staff can save time for their constituents by organizing the mass of electronic information available on local, national, and international servers ... [and] can develop electronic guides to help searchers through the metadata and megafiles with which they must deal online. (Pages 555-556)

He specifically mentions the importance of providing annotations for users, and sees the public library as an information clearinghouse staffed with "information agents."

All of these activities relate to the filtering of Web resources and they all imply some form of subject access provision through indexing or classification, and perhaps some form of abstracting. Trippe (2001) stresses the need for more classification of Web resources and Elrod (2000) summarizes an online discussion on the desirability of libraries assigning class numbers to the Web resources they provide access to (some already do).

Several authors (see, for example, MacDougall, 2000, and Studwell, 2000) urge the use of controlled vocabularies in indexing Web resources but are either vague about the application or seem to greatly underestimate the application problems.

Anderson and Perez-Carballo (2001) argue that the tremendous increase in the amount of indexable text, especially in the Web, makes a selective approach to human indexing essential:

> What we cannot afford to continue to do is to treat all documents that enter our collections and our IR databases as if they were all equally important and equally deserving of our expert analysis and indexing. They simply are not, and to continue to do so is to waste precious resources. (Page 274)

They make suggestions as to how these elite items may be identified.

Alternative Approaches

Drott (2002) proposes a completely different solution. He has highlighted the Web indexing problem, as follows:

> Finding information on specific topics on the web is hard and getting harder. New advances in automated web searching and algorithmic indexing have been largely offset by the enormous growth in the amount of material available. The estimates of search engine coverage of the web by Lawrence and Giles (1999) suggest the impossibility of using robots to index all of the web, and clearly, the more analyt-

ical time that a robot must devote to extracting index terms for a single page, the smaller the amount of the available material that can be indexed. Further, while strides are being made in improving the accuracy of automatic indexing, the fact remains that assigning index terms to a database as diverse as the web remains a problem with few promising solutions. (Pages 209-210)

He goes on to suggest, however, that, while the use of professional indexers may not be an economically attractive proposition, those responsible for creating Web pages should be able to do an acceptable job of indexing themselves:

> Would encouraging web site creators to assign their own index terms be a good thing? The current model of indexing, such as that found in the major journal indexing services, is based on the use of skilled indexers with extensive training. There is, however, encouraging research by Coombs (1998) on indexing State Government web pages in Washington State. Coombs used the people who created and worked with the documents as indexers. The results of this study showed that, when the lay indexers share a common understanding of the content and uses of their documents, the keywords which they produce are reasonable subject location aids. (Page 218)

And, finally:

> Our model of web indexing may well become one of "global chaos, local order" in which the author indexing of specific subject fields is adequate within narrow subject fields but only poorly integrated into any overall scheme of knowledge. This view suggests a two-tiered indexing system in which distributed processing of Meta tags by large number of computers running rather simple software is supported on the next level by more complex indexing robots. These robots should be designed not to extract specific content description from individual pages, but focus on placing groups of pages or entire sites into specific subject categories and leaving the details of content to the creators of the tags. (Page 218)

Another possibility is to promote the indexing of Web resources by their users. Besser (1997) discussed the need for this. Although he was dealing specifically with images on the Web, the approach is applicable to any resources:

> If we can develop systems for user-assigned terminology, collection managers can rely upon users to assign terms or keywords to individual images. Under such a system, when a user finds an image, the system would ask them what words they might have used to search for this image. Those words are then entered into the retrieval system, and subsequent users searching on these words will find the image. As the number of people using such a system grows, so do the number of access points for many of the images.
>
> It is essential that such systems allow searches against officially-assigned terms both independently of user-contributed terms and in conjunction with them. We can expect two types of searches: one that only looks at terms assigned by catalogers, and the other that looks at both cataloger-assigned terms and at user-assigned terms. Systems like this will also be able to serve as aids to catalogers. One can envision a system where periodically user-contributed terms will be "upgraded" to officially assigned terms by a cataloger (and will then be retrievable by both methods).

As systems like this grow, future users may want to limit their searches to terms assigned by people who they trust (perhaps because they come from the same field, or because they assign terms more reliably). So these systems will likely develop both a searchable "ownership" feature for each term assigned and a "confidence level" that a user can set which applies to a group of owners. Design of systems like this will also have to be sensitive to the privacy of term contributors. Users setting confidence levels for term-assigners may locate these people through basic profiles of their subject expertise and position (but not name), or they may locate them by finding correlations between other term-assigners and how the user him/herself assigns terms to other images ... (Pages 24-25)

User indexing of Web documents has also been advocated by Villarroel et al. (2002).

Automatic Approaches

Software is available to perform some indexing or abstracting of Web resources automatically. Jacsó (2002) evaluates some commercially-available summarization programs, and Reamy (2002) refers to "auto-categorization" software (i.e., programs that put electronic resources into categories automatically) and predicts major developments in this area in the future. The state of the development of automatic methods was discussed in Chapter 15.

Conclusion

From all of this, one might conclude that indexing and abstracting activities are increasing in importance rather than decreasing, and that professionals in these areas can make a substantial contribution at the level of the individual Web site or at broader levels such as portal design and implementation.

They could also have important roles to play in the operation of company intranets. In fact, Reamy (2002), a specialist in the area of knowledge management, while predicting the growth of "auto-categorization," presents a very compelling case for the need for professionals in intellectual access activities:

Companies don't want to pay librarians to categorize their content because they think it's too expensive. They are wrong, at least when you factor in the time employees waste trying in vain to find that document that they must have in order to answer that customer's question, without which the customer will scram and go with a competitor who had the answer instead. Despite that, many companies still won't pay for humans to categorize their content, but they are more likely to pay anywhere from 250K to 750K for software that frequently does a less effective job. (Page 18)

He goes on as follows:

First and foremost, auto-categorization cannot completely replace a librarian or information architect although it can make them more productive, save them time, and produce a better end-product. The software itself, without some human rules-based categorization, cannot currently achieve more than about 90% accuracy—which sounds pretty good until you realize that one out of every ten documents listed in the results of a search or browse interface will be wrong. And more importantly, it will be wrong in inexplicable ways—ways that will cause users to lose confidence in the system.

While it is much faster than a human categorizer and doesn't require vacation days and medical benefits, auto-categorization is still simply not as good as a human categorizer. It can't understand the subtleties of meaning like a human can, and it can't summarize like a human, because it doesn't understand things like implicit meaning in a document and because it doesn't bring the meaningful contexts that humans bring to the task of categorization. One thing that early AI efforts taught us is that while speed is significant, speed alone cannot make up for a lack of understanding of meaning. (Page 21)

And finally:

Rather than a danger to information professionals, auto-categorization can, in fact, not only enhance their ability to solve user's information problems, it may even elevate their status to something closer to the level it should be. Not only will librarians and information architects produce more and more economically, but they will have expensive software associated with the task and, as we all know, in today's corporations, unless there is expensive software involved, no one will think you're valuable.

Well, OK, maybe that's a bit overstated, but auto-categorization software has the potential to highlight what should already be clear—that the information professional is engaged in a fundamental infrastructure activity. Information professionals are or should be involved in the creation and maintenance of the intellectual infrastructure of their organization. While technology and organizational infrastructures have received more attention and resources, some of the imbalance could be righted through the intelligent utilization and integration of new software, new methods of working with both content providers and content consumers, and new ways of presenting information.

So, in conclusion, I think it's likely that auto-categorization will ultimately enhance both the power and the prestige of the information professional. (Page 22)

It seems clear that the continued growth of network-accessible information resources will make subject analysis activities of greater importance than ever before. Moreover, it is likely that more and more individuals will be involved in these functions. To be sure, methods for indexing and abstracting automatically will continue to improve. However, as Lancaster and Warner (2001) point out in their review of this area, it will probably be a very long time before machines are intelligent enough to completely replace humans in these important activities, if indeed they ever are.

Part II

Practice

CHAPTER 18

Indexing Exercises

PRACTICE MAKES PERFECT in indexing and abstracting as in other activities. The last two chapters of this book contain some exercises in indexing and abstracting. Clearly, the few exercises that can be included in a book of this kind are far from enough to produce accomplished indexers and abstractors. Nevertheless, they are presented in the hope that they will at least provide some concrete illustrations of major points made in the earlier chapters.

On the next few pages appear several abstracts of reports or journal articles. Some are actual abstracts of real publications. Others are abstracts of "hypothetical" articles, although they are based on actual publications.

You are to index each of these items using terms from the *UNBIS Thesaurus* (New York, United Nations, Dag Hammarskjöld Library, 1995). If you wish, you may first write down words or phrases representing your conceptual analysis of each item and then attempt to translate each of these statements into a term or terms from the thesaurus. In any case, divide up your descriptors into *major* and *minor* descriptors, the former being terms that you consider most important in representing the subject matter.

Following the abstracts you will find my suggested indexing for each item so that you can check your indexing against mine. Remember, however, that indexing is a somewhat subjective process. While I believe in my indexing, I cannot claim that it is "correct" in any absolute sense. Explanations of why indexing was done in a particular way are included.

Items 6-13 first appeared in the January 1977 issue of *A.I.D. Research and Development Abstracts* and are reproduced with the permission of the Center for Development Information and Evaluation, United States Agency for International Development.

Items to Be Indexed

1. *Alcohol fuel today.* (Based on an article appearing in *Smithsonian*, March 1981, pp. 44-53)

Describes the various sources from which ethanol can be distilled, including crops of various types, agricultural waste products, municipal wastes, and industrial sludge. Compares production costs of ethanol with those of gasoline and discusses problems involved in converting from pilot plant production of ethanol to full-scale commercial production. Discusses the advantages and disadvantages of gasohol, a blend of gasoline and alcohol fuel, and explores the problems that must be solved before alcohol-powered cars become practical.

2. *Erosion and the farmer.*

Describes how wind, rain and melting snow can erode valuable farmland and assesses the extent of agricultural losses from these causes in Northern Europe. Discusses possible solutions, namely the alternation of grain crops with soil-conserving grasses and the use of trees and terraces as windbreakers.

3. *Aerial photography and what it can do.* (Based on an article appearing in Smithsonian, March 1984, pp. 150-155)

Reviews several possible uses of aerial photography, including satellite photography, military surveillance, disarmament verification, the study of archaeological sites, census applications (e.g., the counting of homes), weather and flood forecasting, and mapmaking (photogrammetry).

4. *The end of the sugar maple?* (Based on articles appearing in Blair & Ketchum's Country Journal, March 1986, pp. 46-49 and American Forests, November-December 1987, pp. 26-34)

Large numbers of sugar maple trees in Canada and the Northern United States are dead or dying, causing a serious reduction in sugar production. Acid rain, causing defoliation, is suspected to be the principal cause.

5. *Can a plane fly forever?* (Based on an article appearing in Newsweek, September 28, 1987, pp. 42, 47)

A prototype of an electric-powered aircraft, requiring no conventional fuel, is to be tested in Canada. Electricity is tranmitted from the ground as microwave energy and reconverted to electricity by "rectennas" on the plane. Theoretically, the plane could remain aloft for months without pilots. Applications might include scientific research, surveillance (military, police, or civilian), weather forecasting, and passenger transport. Microwaves might also power spacecraft. Possible health hazards from the microwaves could deter widespread application.

6. *Nutrition education in child feeding programs in the developing countries* (Agency for International Development 1974, 44p.)

This simply-worded booklet, supplemented by many cartoon drawings, is intended for village workers and others involved in child feeding in the developing countries in assisting them to teach mothers and children about the foods children need for growth and health and how to use local foods to improve their diets. Chapters cover: The Double Purpose of Child-Feeding programs; What you Should Know about Food; Setting Goals to Fit Your Community; Some General Rules for Teaching; Working with Mothers of Preschool Children; and Teaching Children in School Feeding Programs. It is felt that the nutrition education which grass roots workers provide may have a more lasting effect and may do as much for the prevention of malnutrition as the actual foods contributed, important as these are to the health of the mothers and children receiving them.

7. *Improvement of the nutritive quality and productivity of barley for semi-arid regions; annual report, 1975/1976.* (Montana State University, College of Agriculture 1976, 70p.)

This is the second annual report for a three-year project designed to increase the nutritive value of barleys consumed in less developed countries, increase barley yields, and decrease losses caused by barley diseases. During the first year of work, several LDC's were visited to establish contacts and collect isolates of the major disease organisms. The work with diseases has progressed to the point where a significant outreach program can be initiated. In work on nutritive value, the microbiological assay technique for determining lysine has been perfected to the point where it is a reliable screening tool. No significant differences were found in the feed value of waxy and normal Compana isogenic pairs due to starch type or amino acid composition of the protein. Preliminary results indicate that peoples who consume primarily rice would much prefer and probably consume more of a waxy endosperm barley than the normal endosperm barley. The High Amylose Glacier variety was slightly lower in energy value than normal Glacier but the former has a higher quality protein due to an increase in the protein of several amino acids. Animal performance data (Growth, PER, and BV) support the chemical analyses for protein and amino acid composition of Hiproly and Hiproly Normal barleys. Lysine content of the protein has been found to be environmentally influenced differentially, dependent on the gene present, and is reflected in animal performance. Animal performance is highly correlated to the essential amino acid content of the barleys. Lysine usually accounts for over 50% of the animal variation in growth and PER and 60% of the variation in biological value. A double translocation has been located that should be effective in transferring the Hiproly gene to a population as well as disease resistance genes (scale, net-blotch, barley yellow dwarf) on chromosome 3. Fertile, plump, high-lysine lines from Hiproly crosses have been developed to serve as parents in further variety development work with this gene.

8. *African women in agricultural development, a case study in Sierra Leone.* (Spencer, D. S. C., 1976, 41p. Department of Agricultural Economics, Michigan State University)

A study of the labor effects on farm families of an I.A.D.P. loan for developing inland swampland for rice production. The study was a small part of a national study of rural employment problems in Sierra Leone. One village, Benduma, in one of the three operational areas of the I.A.D. project was selected for intensive study of the daily work performed by males, females, and children in 23 selected households. From May, 1974 to June, 1975, interviews were conducted twice a week at selected households, and an input-output questionnaire was used to provide daily records of hours worked per family member and non-farm output, farm and non-farm sales, loans given and received, and gifts given and received. From this data were calculated household income by source and its distribution, labor utilization, returns to labor, and seasonal profiles of farm and non-farm enterprises. The author concludes that women worked slightly harder in the development project than women not participating in it, but that the increase in their work load was much less than the increase in the work load of adult males and children. Women play a substantial role in the cultivation of a "development" crop (swamp rice) using improved technology. However, the results of the study negate the hypothesis that such agricultural development projects place an uneven burden on women vis-a-vis men.

9. *Science and technology policy; research management and planning in the Arab Republic of Egypt 1976,* 103p. (National Academy of Sciences, National Research Council, Washington, D.C. 20418)

Report of a Symposium on Science Policy Planning and a Workshop on the Management and Planning of Research. The conference focused on scientific and technology policy, planning, and research management. A "workshop" format was chosen as the best method to bring together a representative group of Egyptian and American physical, natural, and social scientists, economists, engineers, and development planners. It was found that although Egypt lacks a formally enunciated national science policy, the various science-oriented agencies it has established and the funds it provides for research and science education constitute a significant, implicit national policy. Management of this large and complex set of organizations is a formidable task, and every effort should be made for their effectiveness and efficiency. Managing university research is a very different problem from managing applied research institutes and should be solved as quickly as possible. Even though Egypt's applied research program is a sizable effort, its execution probably requires considerable restructuring and redirection if it is to be fully effective. Transfer of technology to Egyptian industry from other nations and from multinational corporations has been and will continue to be a major element in Egypt's industrial development. To ensure effective transfer of technology and to minimize its costs there should be appropriate revisions of national legislation and practices.

10. Utilization of underutilized marine species for human consumption (Constantinides, S. M.; Figueroa, Jose; Kaplan, Harvey, 1974, 11p. International Center for Marine Resource Development, University of Rhode Island)

At a time when the prices of fish are rising and protein malnutrition is prevailing in many developing countries, fishermen around the world are throwing back millions of tons of protein-rich fish to die. These fish are thrown back because they are considered "trash" or "discards" or are unfamiliar species of no economical value. In the United States fishermen throw back up to 70% of the fish trapped in the nets while fishing for other market species such as flounder and shrimp. Man cannot afford any more to ignore the protein-rich marine species. Markets for under-utilized species have to be created and expanded as alternative resources to the declining supply of commercially established species, thereby augmenting the industry, encouraging resource conservation, and revitalizing the familiar and long-exploited species. Conventional and nonconventional ways can be employed to utilize these species which are considered discards. The utilization of these species can be developed along these main lines: minced fish flesh (mixed species or single species), fish pastes, and dried fish products. The production of minces from many small and medium-size fish is made possible by the use of separators, which produce meat free of bones. The meat is washed and then frozen in blocks. A combination of fatty and non-fatty fish may yield a desirable end product acceptable to the consumer. Fish pastes, shrimp pastes, and crab pastes can be prepared by various methods. To the washed, minced flesh, salt, starch, and polyphosphates are added to produce a paste from which sausages and other products can be prepared. Other products can be made such as fish mixed with potatoes, fish in spreads, dips, and soups, or several kinds of minced fish mixed together or with other ingredients to produce exciting new flavors. Species that have not been exploited yet by man must be utilized in the future and all so-called trash species must be regarded as edible species fit for direct human consumption.

11. The use of peer tutoring and programmed radio instruction: viable alternatives in education (Hannum, W. H.; Morgan, R. M. 1974, 38p. Florida State University, College of Education)

Educators in developing countries are likely to achieve more by applying the principles rather than the things of educational technology. The principles of programmed learning have been shown to be effective in promoting learning in a wide variety of circumstances. The most effective instructional materials can be developed through use of the principles of programmed instruction and mastery learning. Radio, when combined with the use of peer tutors, can be an effective educational tool in developing countries. The concepts of programmed learning and mastery learning can be incorporated in the design of educational radio programs. Such programs, accompanied by peer tutors, can accomplish the total educational effort within the resources of many developing countries. This type of educational system is a viable alternative to traditional formal education. Such a system should be tried in several developing countries to explore its full potential.

12. Cultural and social factors affecting small farmer participation in formal credit programs (Gillette, Cynthia; Uphoff, Norman 1973, 40p. Rural Development Committee, Center for International Studies, Cornell University)

This paper presents three basic assumptions which, with one exception, are its focus. The exception is the issue of "economic rationality," which is familiar to all concerned with development in the Third World, but which is seen as warranting a brief discussion in the introduction. Part II deals with the cultural context of small farmers as borrowers, i.e., various factors affecting the demand for credit. Following this, Part III treats the cultural context of credit programs as lenders, i.e., factors conditioning the supply of credit available in functional terms to small farmers. Part IV shows various implications of the preceding Parts II and III—what happens when these two cultural systems interact and what are the likely points of difficulty. Part V concludes by comparing general differences between formal and informal sources of credit.

13. Development of low-cost roofing from indigenous materials in developing nations; annual report, 1974/1975 (Monsanto Research Corporation, Dayton, Ohio, 1975, 335p.)

This report discusses the second phase (May 1974 through September 1975) of a three-phase, 3.5 year research effort to produce improved roofing for developing countries by matching indigenous fibers and fillers with low-cost binders. The ultimate goal of the program is to make available, in at least three countries, one each in Latin America, Asia, and Africa, an economically and technically acceptable roofing system that requires less foreign exchange than existing alternatives. The program objective is to be demonstrated within each of the participating countries through construction of at least four prototype roofs and transfer of the necessary technology to qualified organizations. Current collaborating countries are Jamaica, the Philippines, and Ghana. The project emphasis during Phase III was on development of roofing materials and establishing the mechanism for the technology transfer. Primary objectives of the materials development included establishing a generalized set of criteria for roofing; defining composite material ingredients; determining the most promising sets of materials, processes, and products; and analyzing the cost and practicality of the candidate systems. Four candidate composite roofing material systems were defined that use from 70 to 100% indigenous material. Outstanding as a filler is the sugar cane residue, bagasse. The primary candidate binders include natural rubber, phenolic, and commercial thermoplastic resins. Accelerated and outdoor aging are demonstrating the viability of the candidate systems. The objectives of the technology transfer aspects included defining potential collaborative institutions and individuals in Jamaica, the Philippines, and Ghana; forming Advisory and Technical Working Committees in each of these countries that would participate in the roofing development program; and locating qualified organizations interested in future commercial production of the roofing. Those institutions, committees, and working groups were defined in the three countries and are functioning to various degrees, with Jamaica taking the lead. Private industry organizations that may become future manufacturers of the roofing have been located in each of the three countries. During Phase III, October 1975 through December 1976, the program will be brought to completion through material optimization, design, fabrication, testing, and evaluation of prototype roofing; and field manufacture, installation, and evaluation of full-scale roofing.

Author's Indexing and Explanations
(Major descriptors are identified with an asterisk*)

1. Alcohol fuel today.
   Alcohol fuels*
   Gasohol*
   Production costs
   Gasoline
   Crops

Agricultural wastes
Refuse derived fuels
Domestic wastes
Industrial wastes
Pilot projects
Waste utilization

Ethanol is not a term in UNBIS but is referred to *alcohol fuels*, which seems the single most pertinent term for this item. If the term *ethanol* existed in the thesaurus, this term and not *alcohol fuels* should be used, despite the title, because the abstract indicates that the article deals exclusively with ethanol. Do not rely too heavily on titles; they are sometimes misleading.

The abstract suggests that the article deals quite heavily with gasohol so this term is also used in the selective indexing. The thesaurus does not allow one to express the idea of "alcohol-powered cars." Nevertheless, this is implied quite clearly in *gasohol* so use of the term *automobiles*, while not wrong, seems unnecessary. Using the term *motor fuels* would be quite wrong because the article deals exclusively with gasohol, a type of motor fuel, and *motor fuels* is a broader term (BT) above *gasohol* in UNBIS.

In more exhaustive indexing it would be necessary to cover the other ideas summarized in the abstract. The sources of ethanol can be well covered by use of the term *crops* plus several specific "waste" terms. Because specific types of waste are mentioned, it is better to use the specific terms rather than the more generic *wastes*. To illustrate, suppose someone was looking for information on possible applications of agricultural wastes. This item seems highly relevant but might not be found if indexed under the more general term.

The term *municipal wastes* does not exist in UNBIS, but municipal wastes are usually domestic wastes (see scope note under *domestic wastes* in UNBIS) so *domestic wastes* should be used. If the article deals heavily with the "waste" aspect, *waste utilization* seems a good term; *refuse derived fuels* is certainly appropriate.

Since costs of ethanol and gasoline are compared, the term *gasoline* should probably be included in the exhaustive indexing. *Production costs* certainly should.

In UNBIS terms, it is not possible to precisely express the idea of "scaling up" from pilot plant to commercial production. The most relevant term would seem to be *pilot projects*.

It is also impossible to express the idea of "advantages/disadvantages" or "problems" (associated with gasohol or alcohol-powered cars). Most controlled vocabularies fail to cover more nebulous ideas of this kind.

2. Erosion and the farmer.
   Soil erosion*
   Rain
   Soil conservation*
   Snow
   Wind
   Crop rotation
   Windbreaks
   Crop yields
   Europe

The essential term here is *soil erosion*. *Soil conservation* is the single term that best covers "possible solutions." Defects in the UNBIS thesaurus make the exhaustive indexing more difficult. *Rain, snow*, and *wind* are all appropriate terms, and necessary if one wants to be able to search specifically for articles on erosion of soil by rain, snow, or wind. For the specific solutions discussed, *crop rotation* and *windbreaks* are appropriate.

In UNBIS one cannot express the idea of "agricultural losses" but *crop yields* is sufficiently close to be worth assigning (i.e., the effect of erosion on yields). The term *Northern Europe* does not exist in UNBIS (although *Southern Europe* does!) so the term *Europe* must be assigned. This illustrates an important point: if the precise term needed is not available, use the most specific term that the thesaurus allows.

3. Aerial photography and what it can do.
   Aerial photography*
   Aerial photogrammetry
   Image analysis
   Aerial surveys*
   Hydrographic surveys
   Flood control
   Military surveillance
   Satellite monitoring
   Geodetic satellites*
   Archaeology
   Censuses
   Weather forecasting
   Weather maps

This article seems to deal with the use of aircraft and satellites in the performance of various types of photographic surveys. *Aerial photography* and *aerial surveys* are important terms. The term *satellite photography* does not exist in UNBIS. The idea could be expressed, however, by combining *aerial photography* with a "satellite" term. The most appropriate seems to be *geodetic satellites*, especially since UNBIS links (by RT) the term *aerial photogrammetry* with *geodetic satellites*.

As to the applications, UNBIS covers some well and some not so well. *Verification* is a thesaurus term that looks good for this article until one discovers that *satellite monitoring* is a narrower term to *verification*. *Satellite monitoring* should be used because the type of verification discussed (disarmament verification) could only be achieved through satellite photography. Remember, always use the *most specific* term available in the thesaurus even though another term may "sound" more appropriate. This illustrates another important point: the "context" of a term in a thesaurus may reveal the meaning of a term even if no scope note is given. The context of *satellite monitoring* in UNBIS makes clear that it is the use of satellites in verification, not the monitoring of satellites, that is intended.

The study of archaeological sites is probably better covered by *archaeology* than by *archaeological excavations*. Since "counting of homes" is used merely as an example of a census application, the general *censuses* is a safer term than *housing censuses*. Moreover, the latter term is somewhat ambiguous and may refer to the occupancy of buildings rather than the number of homes.

Weather forecasting translates exactly in UNBIS. Since this implies the development of *weather maps*, this term might also be applied, although it is marginal. Flood forecasting cannot be covered as such. The purpose is prevention of floods so *flood control* should be used. Since the movement of water or ice is implied, *hydrographic surveys* might also be considered a good term.

Mapmaking is well covered by *photogrammetry*. Finally, since these various applications all strongly imply the interpretation of photographs, *image analysis* seems entirely appropriate.

4. *The end of the sugar maple?*
   Sugar crops*
   Sugar industry
   Trees*
   Defoliation
   Acid rain*
   Canada
   United States
   Plant diseases

The UNBIS thesaurus recognizes only sugar cane and sugar beets as sources of sugar so it is necessary to use *sugar crops* here. Since few terms for specific types of trees exist in the thesaurus, it is necessary to use the general *trees*. Pollution is likely to be the cause of the defoliation but it is unnecessary to use *air pollution* because *acid rain* is more precise.

5. *Can a plane fly forever?*
    Aircraft*
    Electric vehicles*
    Microwaves*
    Scientific research
    Prototypes
    Spacecraft
    Radiation sickness
    Military surveillance
    Canada

The idea of an electric-powered aircraft using microwaves is well covered by the three starred terms. More attention is given in the article to possible scientific and military applications so an attempt has been made to cover those aspects. Unfortunately, the idea of surveillance in general is missing from UNBIS but *military surveillance* does exist. The other possible applications mentioned—e.g., weather forecasting—are touched upon so briefly in this article that they seem unworthy of coverage in indexing. Since the health hazard discussed is microwave radiation, the term *radiation sickness* looks appropriate.

6. *Nutrition education in child feeding programs.*
    Child feeding*
    Nutrition education*
    Child nutrition*
    Developing countries
    Infant nutrition
    School meals

The subject of this report can be covered perfectly adequately by terms available in the thesaurus.

7. *Improvement of the nutritive quality and productivity of barley.*
    Barley*
    Arid zones*
    Nutrition*
    Crop yields

Developing countries
Plant breeding
Plant genetics
Plant diseases
Plant protection
Proteins
Arid zones is as close as one can get in UNBIS to "semi-arid regions."

8. *African women in agricultural development.*
Rice
Sierra Leone
Women in agriculture*
Women workers*
Women in development
Women's rights
Hours of work*
Working time arrangement
Labour productivity
Division of labour

Do not be misled by the title. This is about women in Sierra Leone, not African women in general. The main focus of the study is employment conditions of women, not the cultivation of rice. While *rice* is a relevant term, it is the women worker and hours of work terms that are most important. *Rice* is not a major term because someone looking for items on the cultivation of rice might not be very interested in this type of social study. The term *division of labour* is probably relevant, since the male/female relationship in labor is discussed, but the scope note in the thesaurus gives a very inadequate indication of how and when this term is to be used.

9 *Science and technology policy.*
Egypt*
Science and technology policy*
Science and technology planning*
Research and development*
Technology transfer
Scientific research
Public administration
Management
Science and technology financing

Quite a few terms are needed to adequately cover this report. Note that *research and development* and *management* are both needed to cover the idea of "research management." *Egypt* is regarded as a major term because the entire report is about the Egyptian situation. This is quite different from the article on "African women" where the setting (Sierra Leone) is almost incidental to the purpose of the study.

10. Utilization of underutilized marine species for human consumption.
> Food consumption*
> Fish*
> Fish processing
> Fishery products
> Fishery conservation*

This is an example of an article that cannot be adequately indexed because the thesaurus cannot express the idea of "underutilized fish species." The terms used here do not give a good picture of what the item is about, but they are the best available.

11. The use of peer tutoring and programmed radio instruction.
> Educational radio*
> Programmed instruction*
> Developing countries
> Nonformal education
> Teachers

Again, not well covered because the thesaurus lacks terms to express the idea of "peer tutoring" or even of "tutoring."

12. Cultural and social factors affecting small farmer participation in formal credit programs.
> Credit policy*
> Farmers*
> Small farms*
> Developing countries
> Agricultural credit*
> Cultural values
> Social values

This is an excellent example of a relatively long report that can be well covered by a small number of terms. To express the idea of "small farmers" it is necessary to use both *farmers* and *small farms. Developing countries* is assigned because it is obvious that this is the context in which agricultural credit is being discussed.

13. Development of low-cost roofing.
> Roofs*

Traditional technology
Bagasse
Fibres
Building materials*
Technology transfer
Rubber
Plastic products
Jamaica
Ghana
Philippines
Developing countries

The indexing of this is not completely satisfactory because the the-saurus does not allow us to express "indigenous materials." Nevertheless, indigenous materials can be considered closely related to indigenous tech-nology, so the term *traditional technology* is justified, if not exactly ideal.

CHAPTER 19

Abstracting Exercises

PART 1

TO UNDERTAKE THIS EXERCISE it is first necessary to assemble the periodical articles listed. Most of these are readily available through libraries in the United States. For each article prepare an abstract or abstracts (see note below) and compare what you write with my suggested abstracts and with my notes. How do my abstracts differ from yours? Which are better? Why?

Articles to be abstracted:

1. Can a plane fly forever? (*Newsweek*, September 28, 1987, pp. 42, 47).
2. Pluto: limits on its atmosphere, ice on its moon (*Science News*, September 26, 1987, p. 207)
3. Plastic shocks and visible sparks (*Science News*, September 5, 1987, p. 152).
4. Moscow's chemical candor (*Newsweek*, October 19, 1987, p. 56).
5. Stereotypes: the Arab's image (*World Press Review*, June 1986, p. 39).
6. Ads require sensitivity to Arab culture, religion. (*Marketing News*, April 25, 1986, p. 3).
7. France, racism and the Left (*The Nation*, September 28, 1985, pp. 279-281).
8. Compassion for animals. (*National Forum*, Winter 1986, pp. 2-3).

Note: For item 1, prepare indicative abstracts. For 2, 5 and 7 prepare informative abstracts. For 3 and 4 prepare both. For 6 and 8 use the form that seems most appropriate.

Author's Abstracts

1. Can a plane fly forever? (Newsweek, September 28, 1987, pp. 42, 47)

Abstract (Indicative)

A prototype of an electric-powered aircraft, requiring no conventional fuel, is to be tested in Canada. Electricity is transmitted from the ground as microwave energy and reconverted to electricity by "rectennas" on the plane.

Theoretically, the plane could remain aloft for months without pilots. Applications might include scientific research, surveillance (military, police, or civilian), weather forecasting and passenger transport. Microwaves might also power spacecraft. Possible health hazards from the microwaves could deter widespread application.

Notes

Clarity takes precedence over brevity. The phrase "requiring no conventional fuel" is needed to make clear that the craft is *entirely* powered by electricity. The abstract should not go beyond what is claimed in the article. Thus, "is to be tested" is appropriate even if the abstractor knows that the tests have already taken place. Try to avoid use of extraneous words. For example, "Microwaves might also power spacecraft" is shorter than "Microwaves might also be used to power spacecraft" yet is no less clear. Because no real results are presented it would be difficult to write a true informative abstract for this item.

2. Pluto: limits on its atmosphere, ice on its moon (*Science News*, September 26, 1987, p. 207)

Abstract (Informative)

Recent estimates indicate that Pluto may be no more than 2290 km across, with its moon, Charon, no more than 1284 km across. Pluto's infrared spectrum seems to be radically different from Charon's. Pluto has a methane-rich surface but Charon, with relatively little methane, appears to be dominated by water-ice. Charon's average reflectivity is only about one half that of Pluto, suggesting that Pluto has a lower surface temperature: perhaps 50 kelvins for Pluto and 58 for Charon. Vapor pressure on Pluto could be only 3.5 microbars compared with 59 on Charon. Pluto appears to have nonstatic polar caps of methane ice whose coverage of the planet varies with time.

Notes

This is a true informative abstract that tries to summarize all of the major data reported in the article. Try to avoid redundancy. For example, it is accurate but not necessary to say "Infrared spectral measurements suggest that Pluto's infrared spectrum seems to be radically different from Charon's" because the reference to "infrared spectrum" itself indicates that infrared spectral measurements have been made.

3. Plastic shocks and visible sparks (*Science News*, September 5, 1987, Vol. 132, No. 10, p. 152)

Abstract (Indicative)

Describes conditions under which static electricity may cause fires or explosions in the handling of powders or liquids and mentions two recently-developed instruments that can be used to monitor materials handling operations.

Abstract (Informative)

In filling or emptying containers, static electricity may generate sparks that can cause fires or explosions. Plastic bottles containing flammable liquids may receive a charge from a surrounding plastic bag or coat pocket, causing a spark when the liquid is poured. Charges can also occur when chemical powders are conveyed, when plastic-lined metal drums are filled with conductive liquids or receive rags soaked with conductive solvents, or when solvent-based semiconductive coatings are applied to one surface of a nonconductive film. The human body itself can generate sparks that can ignite flammable vapors. New instruments now allow the monitoring of filling and emptying operations involving powders or liquids. Using electronic image-intensification or the measurement of charge polarity and magnitude, they record sparking and identify conditions most likely to cause ignition. Powders with fine particles are more hazardous than coarse ones. The most dangerous liquids have low conductivity, are negatively charged, are highly flammable, and evaporate easily to form a vapor-air mixture that supports ignition.

Notes

This is a good illustration of the difference between indicative and informative abstracts. The former merely mentions what the article is about while the latter tries to be a true summary—which type of operations, what type of hazard, which type of instrument, and so on. Brevity can often be achieved, without sacrificing clarity, by omitting articles or conjunctions. For example, "In filling or emptying containers . . ." is shorter and just as clear as "In the filling or emptying of containers . . ."

4. Moscow's chemical candor (*Newsweek*, October 19, 1987, p. 56)

Abstract (Informative)

The Soviet Union openly admits to a stockpile of chemical weapons but claims to no longer produce them. Western observers have been permitted at the formerly secret Shikhany base but Western experts feel that the weapons displayed are old ones—the Soviets have more modern weapons that they do not admit to. The U.S. claims to have ceased production of chemical weapons in 1969 but Western intelligence believes that the Soviets are still producing them and have stockpiled as much as 300,000 tons. The U.S. has provided a detailed report on size and location of U.S. stockpiles but the Soviets refuse to reciprocate until a treaty is signed. The U.S. proposal of a ban on chemical weapons was not pursued by the Soviets in 1984 but they now claim to want a treaty and on-site verification. The Soviets say that the U.S. decision to produce "binary" weapons will obstruct the signing of a treaty but the U.S. feels that this new generation of weapons will actually force the Soviets to negotiate.

Abstract (Indicative)

Describes steps the Soviet Union has taken recently to promote a treaty banning use of chemical weapons. Mentions the new generation of "binary" weapons now being produced by the U.S. and the possible effect of this development on the signing of a treaty.

Notes

Again, a good illustration of the difference between indicative and informative abstracts. The latter tries to summarize the substance of the article while the former merely indicates what it is about.

5. Stereotypes: the Arabs' image (*World Press Review*, June 1986, p. 39)

Abstract (Informative)

The American media, especially television, promotes a negative image of Arabs and Arab countries. Hostility towards Arabs, exacerbated by the Arab-Israeli conflict and the oil crisis of the 1970's, extends to the more than one million Arabs living in the United States. The interests of truth, peace and brotherhood require that steps be taken to change this image.

Notes

The abstractor must decide what is significant and what is not. The substance of this brief article seems well covered by these three sentences. It is unnecessary to summarize the details on the stereotypes, which occupies about half of the article. Inclusion of the names of organizations mentioned in the article would make the abstract too detailed.

6. Ads require sensitivity to Arab culture, religion (*Marketing News*, April 25, 1986, p. 3)

Abstract

Because of the decline in oil prices, spending by Arab countries must be stimulated by effective advertising. Advertisers must understand the religious, social and cultural mores governing Arab life. Some examples of things to avoid are presented.

Notes

Despite being very brief, this is less an indicative abstract than one attempting to summarize what the author says, rather than describing what the article is about. Only the last sentence is truly indicative. This illustrates that abstracts can be made to combine informative and indicative elements.

7. France: racism and the Left (*The Nation*, September 28, 1985, pp. 279-281)

Abstract (Informative)

The ultrarightist party, National Front, actively promotes racial hatred in France, especially against North Africans, but the Communists and Socialists have done little to fight racial prejudice. Campaigns against racism are organized by unofficial groups, mostly youth groups.

Notes

As in the previous example, this abstract is more informative than indicative. A comparison of abstracts 5-7 with abstracts 1-4 will show that it is more difficult to write true informative abstracts in the social sciences than it is in the sciences. Articles in the social sciences tend to be more abstract and to contain less hard data.

8. Compassion for animals (*National Forum*, Winter 1986, pp. 2-3)

Abstract

The close bond between humans and animals, which tended to exist in earlier times, has been eroded by urban development and industrialization, leading to a disregard for animal life in many quarters. But a strong people-animal bond is essential for the health of the individual, the community and society. Suggests ways in which society could improve its sensitivity and compassion toward animals.

Notes

Again, a combined indicative/informative abstract seems most appropriate. The first two sentences, by trying to encapsulate the message of the authors, are really informative, while the last sentence is clearly indicative. The abstract could be made fully informative by summarizing all of the methods for raising compassion, as mentioned on page 3 of the article, but these are so diverse that a rather lengthy abstract would be needed and this seems unjustified by the brevity of the article itself.

PART 2

Reproduced below are eight abstracts that appeared in *Irricab*, April 1980, volume 5, number 2), an abstracting publication in the field of irrigation once published by the International Irrigation Information Center. Can you find anything wrong with these abstracts? How can you improve them? See the author's notes on each below.

Abstracts

[The abstracts are reproduced by kind permission of the International Irrigation Information Center, Bet Dagan, Israel, and Pergamon Press Inc. The selection of these abstracts was made from this source as a matter of convenience and in no way implies that the abstracts in *Irricab* are of low quality. In fact, they are usually very good and it is difficult to find any that could be greatly improved.]

1. Anon. Clarification of highly turbid waters by means of acoustic filters (Rus) Gidrotekh Melior, 1977, (9): 98-99

   Development of a method for water clarification with acoustic filters is briefly reported. Hydraulic characteristics of various screens were studied with and without vibration and the resistance coefficient of various screens was determined. The method is proposed for water clarification without the use of chemical reagents.

2. Vaneyan, S.S.; Makoveev, V.P. (Volzhanka side roll sprinkler for irrigation of vegetable crops) (Rus) Gidrotekh Melior, Mar 1979, (3): 67-68, 1 photo, 2 tab (All-Union Research Institute for Vegetable Growing, USSR)

   Experience obtained with the irrigation of various vegetable crops using the Volzhanka sprinkler are reported. The paper contains an equation for calculation of the duration of irrigation and the number of sprinkler units necessary for irrigating a given area. Data are given on crop damage by the sprinkler wheels.

3. Rhoades, J.D. Determining soil salinity and detecting saline seeps using an inductive electromagnetic soil conductivity sensor (Eng) In: *Agronomy Abstracts: 1978 Annual Meeting of the Soil Science Society of America*: 183 (USDA, SEA, Riverside, CA, USA)

   A new instrument has been developed for determining soil salinity and detecting saline seeps from the measurements of soil electrical conductivity without probes or ground contact using an inductive magnetic technique. The conductivity can be directly read on the instrument and measurements can be made by walking over the ground. Equipment and results are discussed. Advantages and limitations of the new and previous methods are discussed.

4. Gisser, M.; Pohoryles, S. Water shortage in Israel: long-run policy for the farm sector (Eng) *Water Resources*, Dec 1977, 13(6): 865-872, 1 fig. 10 tab, 4 ref (University of New Mexico, Dept of Economics, Albuquerque, NM 87131, USA)

Israel faces a situation of a limited amount of water supply and increasing demands. Since agriculture uses a large fraction of the water available, one potential policy is to reduce allocations of water to agriculture in order to permit the growth of use in other sectors. Estimates of the total loss in income to agriculture from reduction in current allocations are made by using a linear programming model.

5. Debrivna, I. Ye. (Sulfate reducing bacteria of rice irrigation systems in the southern Ukrainian SSR) (Ukr, summary Eng) *Mikrobiologii Zhurnal*, 1977, 39(5): 627-629, 2 tab, 9 ref (Academy of Sciences of the Ukrainian SSR, Institute of Microbiology and Virology, Kiev, USSR)

The studies reported have shown a very intensive development of sulfate-reducing bacteria in the subsoil of the rice irrigation systems characterized by a high water table. It is suggested this may account for the reduced rice yields under these conditions.

6. Koo, J.W.; Ryu, H.Y. (A study on the determination method of pumping rates in tubewells for irrigation) (Kor, summary Eng) *Journal of Korean Society of Agricultural Engineers*, Dec 1976, 18(4): 1-9, 8 fig, 4 tab, 20 ref (Seoul National University, Suweon, Republic of Korea)

In order to find a method to calculate the pumping rates in tubewells for irrigation, pumping tests were conducted in 12 tubewells. A 3" centrifugal pump, a 5 hp motor and a 90 degree V-notch were used in the test and the depths, static water levels, pumping levels and yields of tubewells were measured. A negative correlation between pumping rate and drawdown, and a positive correlation between pumping rate and the coefficient of transmissibility were found. A formula derived from Thiem's theory was found to be satisfactory for calculation of the pumping rates from tubewells.

7. Shanmugarajah, K.; Atukorale, S.C. Water management at Rajangana scheme—lessons from cultivation—Yala 1976 (Eng) *Jalavrudhi* (Sri Lanka), Dec 1976, 1(2): 60-65, 5 tab (Water Management Division, Irrigation Dept. Sri Lanka)

This is a description of how it was proven that rice farmers of a certain area had always been wasting water. Water managers were called in during a drought because of the fear of crop failure, and by improved water use efficiency, consumption was drastically reduced without reducing crop yield.

8. Arbarb, M.; Manbeck, D.M. Influence of lateral depth and spacing on corn yield and water use in subsurface irrigation system (Eng) *Annual Meeting, ASAE, North Carolina State University, Raleigh, NC, USA, Jun 26-29, 1977, Paper No. 77-2021*, 21 p., 8 fig, 1 tab, 9 ref. Available from ASAE, POB 410, St. Joseph, MI 49085, USA (University of Nebraska, Agricultural Engineering Dept, NB, USA)

The aims of this experiment were to study the influence of different lateral depths and spacings on corn yield and water use, and to study the practical use of a sub-surface irrigation system and the water distribution pattern.

Author's Notes

1. The first sentence adds nothing to the title. The abstract could be further condensed, with no loss of meaning, as follows:

   Proposes a method that requires no chemical reagents. Hydraulic characteristics of various screens were studied, with and without vibration, and their resistance coefficients were determined.

2. Again some duplication of the title. Could be made more compact, as follows:

   Experiences with various vegetable crops are reported. Presents an equation for calculating, for a given area, the required number of sprinkler units and duration of irrigation. Gives data on crop damage by the sprinkler wheels.

   (NB. Would be much better to identify the crops; e.g., "Experiences with cabbages, beets and carrots are reported").

3. Unnecessary duplication can be avoided and the abstract made more "tight":

   The new instrument described operates by measuring electrical conductivity of soil without probes or ground contact. Conductivity can be read directly and measurements made by walking over the ground. The instrument and its results are compared with previous methods.

4. Unnecessarily verbose. Could be reduced to:

   Reducing the allocations to agriculture (a major consumer), to allow increased use in other sectors, would be one way of alleviating water shortage. A linear programming model is used to estimate agricultural income that would be lost were present allocations reduced.

   (NB. Since the title provides the context—water shortage in Israel—it is not necessary to repeat it in the abstract. Title and abstract complement each other; the latter should not exist separately from the title. This abstract is quite longwinded: "a limited amount of water supply and increasing demands" is a roundabout way of saying "water shortage," which is already explicit in the title).

5. This one can be reduced almost 50%:

   A very intensive development of the bacteria in the subsoil of high-water-table irrigation systems may be responsible for reduced rice yields.

6. Can be further abbreviated:

   A 3″ centrifugal pump, a 5 hp motor and a 90 degree V-notch were used to measure the depths, static water levels, pumping levels and yields of 12 tubewells. Pumping rate correlates positively with the coefficient of transmissibility and negatively with drawdown. A formula derived from Thiem's theory can be used in calculating the pumping rates.

7. A very longwinded abstract. The substance can be stated as follows:

   Water managers, called in during a drought, showed that efficiency in water use could be greatly improved, leading to drastically reduced consumption without reducing rice yield.

   NB. Various parts of the original abstract are superflous. The first sentence is implicit in the later "by improved water use efficiency." The "because of the fear of crop failure" is self-evident and adds nothing to the abstract. On the other hand, because the title is nonspecific, the particular crop (rice), rather than "crop" in general, should be specified. Of course, one could not replace "crop" with "rice" without seeing the original article.

8. A rare example of a very poor abstract in *Irricab*. It adds essentially nothing to the information in the title. It would not be possible to improve on this without seeing the original.

Summary of Abstracting Principles[*]

General Principles

1. No restriction should be placed on absolute length of the abstract. The abstract should be of the length necessary to make it the most direct, concise, unified statement possible, which includes all the plus information from the article and none of the zero information. By zero information is meant (1) that material which is judged to have no reasonable likelihood of directly or indirectly supporting any job decision, (2) that material which is redundant to other material already included, and (3) that material which is common knowledge to those competent in the field.

2. Short, well-written, complete sentences are required for easy access to the information.

3. The abstract may either paraphrase the original article or selectively and carefully lift from it. The better organized, the more well-written the original article, the more dependence may be placed on the latter method, a form of "extracting."

4. Technical words and phrases should be those currently used in the science under consideration.

5. New terms or names should be reported with definitions.

6. To avoid confusion and provide readability, only the most common abbreviations and standard symbols should be used.

Content Principles

1. If not apparent from the title, the introductory statement should give an accurate indication of the subject dealt with and the methods used. However, this statement is wasteful redundancy if the title has well represented the subject matter and method of investigation.

2. If not apparent from the title and/or the introductory statement, the following statement should indicate the article's scope and author's purpose and objectives. If the abstract-user is seeking some specific infor-

---

*Summary of abstracting principles as presented by Payne et al (1962). Reprinted by permission of the American Institutes for Research

mation, these two statements should indicate to him the likelihood of finding his information.

In effect, these opening statements should constitute a concise descriptive abstract used in most cases to help the reader determine whether he should go back to the original article, but in this instance to determine for him if the information contained is what he is seeking or appropriate to his task.

3. Whether the article is experimental or theoretical in nature, the author's hypothesis should be explicitly stated if not apparent from the opening statements.

4. The investigative methods used should be identified. If standard techniques or procedures are used, these need not be described. If the procedures are new or contain novel characteristics applied to well-known procedures, these features should be clearly described. The basic principles of new methods or technologies, their uses and qualities, operational ranges, and degrees of accuracy should be stated.

5. Data gathering methods, methods of measurement, rotation of variables, method of isolating the data, identification of indices, data summarizing techniques, etc., must be explicitly described. The abstracter must depend upon the data collection method, along with the method of investigation in evaluating the quality of the author's work and the reliability and validity of the results and conclusions.

6. Data, whether a collection of experimental results or theoretical arguments, must be presented to the extent, and only to the extent, that they fully represent all significant aspects of the article, and must be sufficient to lead logically to the author's conclusions. Data of an absolute nature should be presented in sufficient detail to satisfy the anticipated use to be made of it in projected scientific endeavor.

   Data may be presented in any form, the criterion for format being: use the most economical yet most lucid presentation possible. Precisely labeled tables, charts, graphs, etc., may be included, but data presented in this fashion should be self-sufficient, i.e., understandable without reference to the text of the abstract.

7. Qualitative and/or quantitative data manipulation methods, when used, should be indicated. Standard, well-known techniques need not be described. Variations or special applications of known techniques should be presented to the extent necessary to completely represent the significant aspects of the study and to fully substantiate the conclusions drawn.

8. The logical conclusions must be presented. Hypotheses and theories must be re-examined as proven or disproven, accepted or rejected. At this point, the abstracter has the responsibility for discriminating between substantiated and unsubstantiated conclusions and real conclusions vs. inferences. Above all, he must not present conclusions that cannot be verified from the previous sections of the abstract. Erroneous statements contained in the article must not be included unless accompanied by a statement sharply calling attention to the error, and the error correction, if possible.

9. Valid and significant interpretations the author makes of the results and/or conclusions presented can be included if they further knowledge in such ways as showing new relationships or reaffirming old relationships.

10. Throughout the abstract, the abstracter must exercise his right to clarify and simplify material contained in the article.

APPENDIX 2

Modular Content Analysis
with Subject Modules

Citation

STOLL, A. M., CHIANTA, M. A., and MUNROE, L. R. Flame-contact studies. *Transactions of the ASME, Series C, Journal of Heat Transfer*, vol. 86, No. 3, August 1964, pp. 449-456.

Abstract

Flame impingement heating apparatus and methods, applied successfully to determine destruction temperatures and thermal characteristics of fiber-type and plastics materials, are described. Test results confirming the analysis are presented. Results for a polyamide fiber, and for the insulation effect of air spaces between fabric layers, are given.

Composite slab models were injected into the flame of a Meker burner and the backside wall temperatures determined optically or by thermocouples. The heat flux to the surface was determined optically. On the flame side of the composite wall a polyamide fabric (du Pont HT-1) of varying weights per unit surface area (3 oz – 5 oz/sq yd.) was evaluated. The backside, or reference material, in the wall consisted of a resinous compound (simulated skin) with known thermal and optical properties. Destruction temperatures of the HT-1 fabric were 427±3°C as determined optically and 423±27°C as determined by thermocouple measurements. Flame temperature was 1200°C. Burn-through occurred in 3-6 seconds depending on the weight. In investigating the use of air spaces as insulating layers between layers of the fabric, 4 mm. gaps appeared to be optimum for the 3 oz/sq yd material. It was concluded that for short-time, high-temperature applications, insulating materials of this form would tend to be optimum for personnel protection. Very thin (.050-.100 cm) RTV-20 silicone rubber samples were used in validation tests of the mathematical analysis. Excellent agreement was obtained between calculated and measured wall temperatures (% difference of < 0.5%); the analysis used was that of Griffith and Horton.

The use of these analytical and experimental techniques is discussed in relation to determining thermal diffusivity and thermal conductivity from flame-contact type tests. It is concluded that the techniques provided a sensitive and accurate means of determining thermal properties.

Specialized Subject Modules
(paragraphs supplementary to basic abstract)

Physiology and Medicine
Apparatus is described, and mathematical expressions developed, which may allow an analysis of tissue damage, due to exposure to flame, from knowledge of the properties and temperature-time history of an overlying fabric layer. This constitutes a relatively simple means of studying thermal properties (including diffusivity and conductivity) of intact living tissue without alteration of the tissue itself.

Plastics Industry
HT-1, an experimental heat-resistant polyamide textile fiber of du Pont, was exposed to flame impingement in a Meker burner with a flame temperature of 1200°C. Destruction temperature of fabrics of 3, 4, 5 and 6 oz/sq yd weight was 427±3°C, as measured radiometrically. Burn-through occurred in 3-6 seconds, depending on the weight.

Rubber Industry
Transient heat flow through a two-layer assembly of RTV-20, a silicone rubber manufactured by General Electric, backed by simulated skin, was measured by means of a flame-impingement calorimeter. Three-second temperature rise for rubber layers of 0.95, 0.55 and 0.52 mm. was measured within the backing layer and agreed excellently with theoretical values.

Protective Clothing and Aircraft Industries
The experiments described, on the destruction temperatures and thermal characteristics of fabrics under flame impingement heating, are of great significance to the design of clothing for burn protection. In particular they help to explain why, in experiments on flight coveralls, greatly increased burn protection is offered by double-layer clothing as compared to single-layer suits.

Index Entries
Physical and Mathematical Systems
SLABS, COMPOSITE
SLABS, SINGLE-LAYER

Heat Transfer
CONDUCTION, TRANSIENT, ANALYTICAL
CONDUCTION, TRANSIENT (GRIFFITH-HORTON)
CONDUCTION, ONE-DIMENSIONAL

Means and Methods
EXPERIMENTAL APPARATUS
CALORIMETERS, FLAME-IMPINGEMENT

Other Subject Tags
PROTECTIVE CLOTHING
FLIGHT CLOTHING
BURNS

Environment
TEMPERATURE: 0-1000°F
MEKER BURNER
FLAME IMPINGEMENT

Materials and Properties
FABRICS
HT-1
POLYAMIDES
RTV-20
SILICONE RUBBER
SKIN
INSULATING PROPERTIES
THERMAL CONDUCTIVITY
THERMAL DIFFUSIVITY
BURN PROTECTION

Authors
STOLL, A.M.
CHIANTA, M.A.
MUNROE, L.R.

Affiliations
Aviation Medical Acceleration Laboratory, U.S. Naval Air Development Center, Johnsville, Pennsylvania

REFERENCES

Acorn, T. L. and Walden, S. H. SMART: support management automated reasoning technology for Compaq customer service. In: *Innovative Applications of Artificial Intelligence 4*; ed. by A. C. Scott and P. Klahr, pp. 3-18. Cambridge, MA, MIT Press, 1992.

Acton, P. Indexing is *not* classifying—and vice versa. *Records Management Quarterly*, 20(3), 1986, 10-15.

Adami, N. et al. The ToCAI description scheme for indexing and retrieval of multimedia documents. *Multimedia Tools and Applications*, 14, 2001, 153-173.

Addison, E. R. Large scale full text retrieval by concept indexing. In: *Proceedings of the Twelfth National Online Meeting*, pp. 5-15. Medford, NJ, Learned Information, 1991.

Agnew, B. et al. Multi-media indexing over the Web. In: *Storage and Retrieval for Image and Video Databases V*; ed. by I. K. Sethi and R. C. Jain, pp. 72-83. Bellingham, WA, International Society for Optical Engineering, 1997.

Agosti, M. and Smeaton, A. F., eds. *Information Retrieval and Hypertext*. Boston, Kluwer, 1996.

Agosti, M. et al. Automatic authoring and construction of hypermedia for information retrieval. *Multimedia Systems*, 3, 1995, 15-24.

Ahlswede, T., et al. Automatic construction of a phrasal thesaurus for an information retrieval system from a machine readable dictionary. *RIAO 88 Conference Proceedings*. Volume 1, pp. 597-608. Paris, C.I.D., 1988.

Aitchison, J. and Cleverdon, C. W. *A Report on a Test of the Index of Metallurgical Literature of Western Reserve University*. Cranfield, UK, College of Aeronautics, 1963.

Aitchison, T. M. et al. *Comparative Evaluation of Index Languages*. London, Institution of Electrical Engineers, 1969-1970. 2 vols.

Ajiferuke, I. and Chu, C. M. Quality of indexing in online databases: an alternative measure for a term discriminating index. *Information Processing & Management*, 24, 1988, 599-601.

Al-Kofahi, K. et al. Combining multiple classifiers for text categorization. In: *Proceedings of the Tenth International Conference on Information and Knowledge Management*, pp. 97-103. New York, Association for Computing Machinery, 2001.

Albright, J. B. *Some Limits to Subject Retrieval from a Large Published Index*. Doctoral thesis. Urbana-Champaign, University of Illinois, Graduate School of Library Science, 1979.

Allan, J. Knowledge management and speech recognition. *Computer*, 35(4), 2002, 60-61.

Allan, J. et al. Temporal summaries of news topics. *Proceedings of the 24th Annual International ACM SIGIR Conference on Research and Development in Information Retrieval*, pp. 10-18. New York, Association for Computing Machinery, 2001.

Anderson, J. D. and Pérez-Carballo, J. The nature of indexing: how humans and machines analyze messages and texts for retrieval. *Information Processing & Management*, 37, 2001, 231-277.

Anderson, J. D. Indexing systems: extensions of the mind's organizing power. In: *Information and Behavior*. Volume 1; ed. by B. D. Ruben, pp. 287-323. New Brunswick, NJ, Transaction Books, 1985.

Anderson, J. D. and Rowley, F. A. Building end-user thesauri from full-text. *Advances in Classification Research*, 2, 1992, 1-13.

Anderson, M. D. *Book Indexing*. Cambridge, UK, Cambridge University Press, 1971. (Reprinted with corrections in 1979.)

Anick, P. G. Integrating natural language processing and information retrieval in a troubleshooting help desk. *IEEE Expert*, 8(6), 1993, 9-17.

Arasu, A. et al. Searching the Web. *ACM Transactions on Internet Technology*, 1, 2001, 2-43.

Arents, H. C. and Bogaerts, W. F. L. Concept-based indexing and retrieval of hypermedia information. In: *Encyclopedia of Library and Information Science*. Volume 58, Supplement 21, pp. 1-29. New York, Marcel Dekker, 1996.

Armitage, J. E. and Lynch, M. F. Some structural characteristics of articulated subject indexes. *Information Storage and Retrieval*, 4, 1968, 101-111.

Armstrong, C. J. and Keen, E. M. *Workbook for NEPHIS and KWAC*. Boston Spa, British Library, 1982. British Library Research and Development Reports Number 5710. (Microcomputer Printed Subject Indexes Teaching Package, volume 1)

Aronson, A. R. Effective mapping of biomedical text to the UMLS Metathesaurus: the MetaMap program. *Proceedings of the 2001 Annual Symposium of the American Medical Informatics Association*, pp. 17-21. Philadelphia, Hanley and Belfus, 2001.

Aronson, A. R. et al. The NLM Indexing Initiative. *Proceedings of the 2000 Annual Symposium of the American Medical Informatics Association*, pp. 17-21. Philadelphia, Hanley and Belfus, 2000.

Artandi, S. *Book Indexing by Computer*. Doctoral thesis. New Brunswick, NJ, Rutgers, the State University, 1963.

Aslandogan, Y. A. and Yu, C. T. Multiple evidence combination in image retrieval: Diogenes searches for people on the Web. *Proceedings of the 23rd Annual International ACM SIGIR Conference on Research and Development in Information Retrieval*, pp. 88-95. New York, Association for Computing Machinery, 2000.

Austin, D. *PRECIS: a Manual of Concept Analysis and Subject Indexing*. Second edition. London, British Library, 1984.

Austin, D. and Digger, J. A. PRECIS: the Preserved Context Index System. *Library Resources & Technical Services*, 21, 1977, 13-30.

Awre, C. and Wise, A. Portal progress *Update*, 1(6), 2002, 46-47.

Azgaldov, E. G. A framework for description and classification of printed subject indexes. *Libri*, 19, 1969, 275-291.

Baca, M., ed. *Introduction to Art Image Access*. Los Angeles, Getty Research Institute, 2002.

Bailin, S. et al. Application of machine learning to the organization of institutional software repositories. *Telematics and Informatics*, 10, 1993, 283-299.

Baker, S. L. Will fiction classification schemes increase use? *RQ*, 27, 1988, 366-376.

Baker, S. L. and Shepherd, G. W. Fiction classification schemes: the principles behind them and their success. *RQ*, 27, 1987, 245-251.

Bakewell, K. G. B. Reference books for indexers. *The Indexer*, 15, 1987, 131-140.

Bannan, K. J. Personalization and portals. *EContent*, 25(10), 2002, 16-21.

Bateman, J. and Teich, E. Selective information presentation in an integrated publication system: an application of genre-driven text generation. *Information Processing & Management*, 31, 1995, 753-767.

Bates, M. J. Indexing and access for digital libraries and the Internet. *Journal of the American Society for Information Science*, 49, 1998, 1185-1205.

Bates, M. J. Subject access in online catalogs: a design model. *Journal of the American Society for Information Science*, 37, 1986, 357-376.

Bates, M. J. System meets user: problems in matching subject search terms. *Information Processing & Management*, 13, 1977, 367-375.

Baxendale, P. B. Machine-made index for technical literature—an experiment. *IBM Journal of Research and Development*, 2, 1958, 354-361.

Bearman, T. C. and Kunberger, W. A. *A Study of Coverage Overlap Among Fourteen Major Science and Technology Abstracting and Indexing Services*. Philadelphia, National Federation of Abstracting and Indexing Services, 1977.

Beghtol, C. Bibliographic classification theory and text linguistics: aboutness analysis, intertextuality and the cognitive act of classifying documents. *Journal of Documentation*, 42, 1986, 84-113.

Beghtol, C. *The Classification of Fiction*. Metuchen, NJ, Scarecrow Press, 1994.

Belkin, N. J. Anomalous states of knowledge as a basis for information retrieval. *Canadian Journal of Information Science*, 5, 1980, 133-143.

Belkin, N. J. et al. ASK for information retrieval. *Journal of Documentation*, 38, 1982, 61-71, 145-164.

Bell, H. K. Bias in indexing and loaded language. *The Indexer*, 17, 1991a, 173-177.

Bell, H. K. Indexing fiction: a story of complexity. *The Indexer*, 17, 1991b, 251-256.

Bennett, J. L. On-line access to information: NSF as an aid to the indexer/cataloger. *American Documentation*, 20, 1969, 213-220.

Bennett, J. L. et al. *Observing and Evaluating an Interactive Process: a Pilot Experiment in Indexing*. San Jose, CA, IBM Research Laboratory, 1972.

Benois-Pineau, J. et al. Query by synthesized sketch in an architectural database. In: *Storage and Retrieval for Image and Video Databases V*; ed. by I. K. Sethi and R. C. Jain, pp. 361-367. Bellingham, WA, International Society for Optical Engineering, 1997.

Benoit, G. Data mining. *Annual Review of Information Science and Technology*, 36, 2002, 265-310.

Berger, A. L. and Mittal, V. O. OCELOT: a system for summarizing web pages. *Proceedings of the 23rd Annual International ACM SIGIR Conference on Research and Development in Information Retrieval*, pp. 144-151. New York, Association for Computing Machinery, 2000.

Berner, E. S. et al. Performance of four computer-based diagnostic systems. *New England Journal of Medicine*, 330, 1994, 1792-1796.

Bernier, C. L. and Yerkey, A. N. *Cogent Communication: Overcoming Reading Overload*. Westport, CT, Greenwood Press, 1979.

Bernstein, L. M. and Williamson, R. E. Testing of a natural language retrieval system for a full text knowledge base. *Journal of the American Society for Information Science*, 35, 1984, 235-247.

Bertrand, A. and Cellier, J.-M. Psychological approach to indexing: effects of the operator's expertise upon indexing behaviour. *Journal of Information Science*, 21, 1995, 459-472.

Bertrand-Gastaldy, S. et al. Convergent theories: using a multidisciplinary approach to explain indexing results. *Proceedings of the American Society for Information Science*, 32, 1995, 56-60.

Besser, H. Image databases: the first decade, the present, and the future. In: *Digital Image Access & Retrieval*; ed. by P. B. Heidorn and B. Sandore, pp. 11-28. Urbana-Champaign, University of Illinois, Graduate School of Library and Information Science, 1997.

Bhattacharyya, G. The effectiveness of natural language in science indexing and retrieval. *Journal of Documentation*, 30, 1974, 235-254.

Bhattacharyya, G. Elements of POPSI. In: *Indexing Systems: Concepts, Models and Techniques*; ed. by T. N. Rajan, pp. 73-102. Calcutta, Indian Association of Special Libraries and Information Centres, 1981.

Biebricher, P. et al. The automatic indexing system AIR/PHYS—from research to application. In: *Readings in Information Retrieval*; ed. by K. Sparck Jones and P. Willett, pp. 513-517. San Francisco, Morgan Kaufmann, 1997.

Bishop, A. P. Document structure and digital libraries: how researchers mobilize information in journal articles. *Information Processing & Management*, 35, 1999, 255-279.

Bishop, A. P. et al. Index quality study, part I: quantitative description of back-of-the-book indexes. In: *Indexing Tradition and Innovation*, pp. 15-51. American Society of Indexers, 1990.

Blair, D. C. Some thoughts on the reported results of TREC. *Information Processing & Management*, 38, 2002, 445-451.

Blair, D. C. and Kimbrough, S. O. Exemplary documents: a foundation for information retrieval design. *Information Processing & Management*, 38, 2002, 363-379.

Blair, D. C. and Maron, M. E. An evaluation of retrieval effectiveness for a full-text document-retrieval system. *Communications of the ACM*, 28, 1985, 289-299.

Blum, T. et al. Audio databases with content-based retrieval. In: *Intelligent Multimedia Information Retrieval*; ed. by M. T. Maybury, pp. 113-135. Menlo Park, CA, AAAI Press, 1997b.

Blustein, J. and Staveley, M. S. Methods of generating and evaluating hypertext. *Annual Review of Information Science and Technology*, 35, 2001, 299-335.

Bodenreider, O. and Zweigenbaum, P. Identifying proper names in parallel medical terminologies. *Studies in Health Technology and Informatics*, 77, 2000, 443-447.

Boguraev, B. et al. Summarisation miniaturisation: delivery of news to hand-helds. *Proceedings of the NAACL 2001 Workshop on Automatic Summarization*. New Brunswick, NJ, Association for Computational Linguistics, 2001.

Bonham, M. D. and Nelson, L. L. An evaluation of four end-user systems for searching MEDLINE. *Bulletin of the Medical Library Association*, 76, 1988, 22-31.

Booth, A. and O'Rourke, A. J. The value of structured abstracts in information retrieval from MEDLINE. *Health Libraries Review*, 14, 1997, 157-166.

Borko, H. Toward a theory of indexing. *Information Processing & Management*, 13, 1977, 355-365.

Borko, H. and Bernick, M. Automatic document classification. *Journal of the Association for Computing Machinery*, 10, 1963, 151-162.

Borko, H. and Bernier, C. L. *Abstracting Concepts and Methods*. New York, Academic Press, 1975.

Borko, H. and Chatman, S. Criteria for acceptable abstracts: a survey of abstractors' instructions. *American Documentation*, 14, 1963, 149-160.

Borkowski, C. and Martin, J. S. Structure, effectiveness and benefits of LEXtractor, an operational computer program for automatic extraction of case summaries and dispositions from court decisions. *Journal of the American Society for Information Science*, 26, 1975, 94-102.

Borst, F. et al. TEXTINFO: a tool for automatic determination of patient clinical profiles using text analysis. In: *Fifteenth Annual Symposium on Computer Applications in Medical Care*, pp. 63-67. New York, McGraw Hill, 1992.

Bourne, C. P. *Characteristics of Coverage by the Bibliography of Agriculture of the Literature Relating to Agricultural Research and Development*. Palo Alto, CA, Information General Corporation, 1969a. PB 185 425.

Bourne, C. P. *Overlapping Coverage of the Bibliography of Agriculture by Fifteen Other Secondary Sources*. Palo Alto, CA, Information General Corporation, 1969b. PB 185 069.

Boyce, B. R. and McLain, J. P. Entry point depth and online search using a controlled vocabulary. *Journal of the American Society for Information Science*, 40, 1989, 273-276.

Bradley, P. Indexes to works of fiction: the views of producers and users on the need for them. *The Indexer*, 16, 1989, 239-248.

Bradshaw, S. and Hammond, K. Constructing indices from citations in collections of research papers. *Proceedings of the American Society for Information Science*, 36, 1999, 741-750.

Brandow, R. et al. Automatic condensation of electronic publications by sentence selection. *Information Processing & Management*, 31, 1995, 675-685.

Breaks, M. and Guyon, A. Edinburgh Engineering Virtual Library (EEVL). In: *The Amazing Internet Challenge*; ed. by A. T. Wells et al., pp. 76-96. Chicago, American Library Association, 1999.

Brenner, C. W. and Mooers, C. N. A case history of a Zatocoding information retrieval system. In: *Punched Cards: Their Applications to Science and Industry*. Second edition; ed. by R. S. Casey et al., pp. 340-356. New York, Reinhold, 1958.

Brenner, E. H. et al. American Petroleum Institute's machine-aided indexing and searching project. *Science and Technology Libraries*, 5(1), 1984, 49-62.

Breton, E. J. Indexing for invention. *Journal of the American Society for Information Science*, 42, 1991, 173-177.

Breton, E. J. Why engineers don't use databases. *Bulletin of the American Society for Information Science*, 7(6), 1981, 20-23.

Brettle, A. J. et al. Comparison of bibliographic databases for information on the rehabilitation of people with severe mental illness. *Bulletin of the Medical Library Association*, 89, 2001, 353-362.

Brew, C. and Thompson, H. S. Automatic evaluation of computer generated text: a progress report on the TextEval project. In: *Proceedings of the Human Language Technology Workshop, March 8-11, 1994*, pp. 108-113. San Francisco, Morgan Kaufmann, 1994.

Brittain, J. M. and Roberts, S. A. Rationalization of secondary services: measurement of coverage of primary journals and overlap between services. *Journal of the American Society for Information Science*, 31, 1980, 131-142.

Broer, J. W. Abstracts in block diagram form. *IEEE Transactions on Engineering Writing and Speech*, 14, 1971, 64-67.

Brown, E. W. et al. Toward speech as a knowledge resource. *IBM Systems Journal*, 40, 2001, 985-1001.

Brown, M. S. et al. A new comparison of the *Current Index to Journals in Education* and the *Education Index*: a deep analysis of indexing. *Journal of Academic Librarianship*, 25, 1999, 216-222.

Brown, P. et al. The democratic indexing of images. *New Review of Hypermedia and Multimedia*, 2, 1996, 107-120.

Browne, G. M. Indexing Web sites: a practical guide. *Internet Reference Services Quarterly*, 5(3), 2001, 27-41.

Bruza, P. D. et al. Aboutness from a commonsense perspective. *Journal of the American Society for Information Science*, 51, 2000, 1090-1105.

Burgin, R. The effect of indexing exhaustivity on retrieval performance. *Information Processing & Managemment*, 27, 1991, 623-628.

Burgin, R. The retrieval effectiveness of five clustering algorithms as a function of indexing exhaustivity. *Journal of the American Society for Information Science*, 46, 1995, 562-572.

Bürk, K. et al. *INIS: Manual for Subject Analysis*. Vienna, International Atomic Energy Agency, 1996. IAEA-INIS-12 (Rev. 3)

Burke, F. G. The application of automated techniques in the management and control of source materials. *American Archivist*, 30, 1967, 255-278.

Burke, M. The use of repertory grids to develop a user-driven classification of a collection of digitized photographs. *Proceedings of the American Society for Information Science and Technology*, 38, 2001, 76-92.

Burnett, K. et al. A comparison of the two traditions of metadata development. *Journal of the American Society for Information Science*, 50, 1999, 1209-1217.

Busch, J. A. Building and accessing vocabulary resources for networked discovery and navigation. In: *Visualizing Subject Access for 21st Century Information Resources*; ed. by P. A. Cochrane and E. H. Johnson, pp. 93-105. Urbana-Champaign, University of Illinois, Graduate School of Library and Information Science, 1998.

Buyukkokten, O. et al. Seeing the whole in parts: text summarization for web browsing on handheld devices. *Proceedings of the Tenth International Conference on the World Wide Web*, 2001. (http://www-db.stanford.edu/~orkut/papers/www10b/index.html)

Byrd, D. and Crawford, T. Problems of music information retrieval in the real world. *Information Processing & Management*, 38, 2002, 249-272.

Byrne, J. R. Relative effectiveness of titles, abstracts, and subject headings for machine retrieval from the COMPENDEX services. *Journal of the American Society for Information Science*, 26, 1975, 223-229.

Campbell, J. D. The case for creating a scholars portal to the Web. *ARL*, 211, August 2000, 1-4.

Carrick, C. and Watters, C. Automatic association of news items. *Information Processing & Management*, 33, 1997, 615-632.

Carroll, K. H. An analytical survey of virology literature reported in two announcement journals. *American Documentation*, 20, 1969, 234-237.

Casey, C. An analytical index to the Internet: dreams of Utopia. *College & Research Libraries*, 60, 1999, 586-595.

Cawkell, A. E. *A Guide to Image Processing and Picture Management*. Brookfield, VT, Gower, 1994.

Cawkell, A. E. Picture-queries and picture databases. *Journal of Information Science*, 19, 1993, 409-423.

Chakrabarti, S. *Mining the Web: Discovering Knowledge from Hypertext Data*. San Francisco, Morgan Kaufmann, 2003.

Chang, G. et al. *Mining the World Wide Web*. Boston, Kluwer, 2001.

Charniak, E. Natural language learning. *ACM Computing Surveys*, 27, 1995, 317-319.

Chen, H. et al. Automatic concept classification of text from electronic meetings. *Communications of the ACM*, 37 (10), 1994, 56-73.

Chen, H. et al. Automatic thesaurus generation for an electronic community system. *Journal of the American Society for Information Science*, 46, 1995, 175-193.

Chen, H.-I. An analysis of image queries in the field of art history. *Journal of the American Society for Information Science and Technology*, 52, 2001a, 260-273.

Chen, H.-l. An analysis of image retrieval tasks in the field of art history. *Information Processing & Management*, 37, 2001b, 701-720.

Chen, Z. Let documents talk to each other: a computer model for connection of short documents. *Journal of Documentation*, 49, 1993, 44-54.

Chen, Z. et al. Web mining for Web image retrieval. *Journal of the American Society for Information Science and Technology*, 52, 2001, 831-839.

Chiaramella, Y. and Kheirbek, A. An integrated model for hypermedia and information retrieval. In: *Information Retrieval and Hypertext*; ed. by M. Agosti and A. F. Smeaton, pp. 139-178. Boston, Kluwer, 1996.

Chien, L.-F. et al. A spoken-access approach for Chinese text and speech information retrieval. *Journal of the American Society for Information Science*, 51, 2000, 313-323.

Choi, Y. and Rasmussen, E. M. Users' relevance criteria in image retrieval in American history. *Information Processing & Management*, 38, 2002, 695-726.

Chu, C. M. and Ajiferuke, I. Quality of indexing in library and information science databases. *Online Review*, 13, 1989, 11-35.

Chu, C. M. and O'Brien, A. Subject analysis: the critical first stage in indexing. *Journal of Information Science*, 19, 1993, 439-454.

Chu, H. Hyperlinks: how well do they represent the intellectual content of digital collections? *Proceedings of the American Society for Information Science*, 34, 1997, 361-368.

Chute, C. G. and Yang, Y. An evaluation of concept based latent semantic indexing for clinical information retrieval. *Sixteenth Annual Symposium on Computer Applications in Medical Care*, pp. 639-643. New York, McGraw Hill, 1993.

Ciocca, G. and Schettini, R. A relevance feedback mechanism for content-based image retrieval. *Information Processing & Management*, 35, 1999, 605-632.

Clarke, C. L. A. Exploiting redundancy in question answering. *Proceedings of the 24th Annual International ACM SIGIR Conference on Research and Development in Information Retrieval*, pp. 358-365. New York, Association for Computing Machinery, 2001.

Clemencin, G. Querying the French Yellow Pages: natural language access to the directory. *Information Processing & Management*, 24, 1988, 633-649.

Cleveland, D. B. and Cleveland, A. D. *Introduction to Indexing and Abstracting*. Third edition. Englewood, CO, Libraries Unlimited, 2001.

Cleverdon, C. W. *A Comparative Evaluation of Searching by Controlled Language and Natural Language in an Experimental NASA Data Base*. Frascati, European Space Agency, Space Documentation Service, 1977.

Cleverdon, C. W. et al. *Factors Determining the Performance of Index Languages*. Cranfield, UK, College of Aeronautics, 1966. 3 vols.

Cluley, H. J. *Analytical Abstracts*: user reaction study. *Proceedings of the Society for Analytical Chemistry*, 5, 1968, 217-221.

Coates, E. J. *Subject Catalogues: Headings and Structure*. London, Library Association, 1960.

Coco, A. Full-text versus full-text plus editorial additions. *Legal Reference Services Quarterly*, 4 (2), 1984, 27-37.

Collison, R. L. *Abstracts and Abstracting Services*. Santa Barbara, CA, ABC-Clio, 1971.

Collison, R. L. *Indexes and Indexing*. Fourth edition. New York, deGraaf, 1972.

Conaway, C. W. *An Experimental Investigation of the Influence of Several Index Variables on Index Usability and a Preliminary Study Toward a Coefficient of Index Usability*. Doctoral thesis. New Brunswick, NJ, Rutgers University, Graduate School of Library Service, 1974.

Connolly, D. and Landeen, C. Toward a standard measure of index density. *KEYWORDS*, 9(2), 2001, 52-56.

Cook, M. *Archives and the Computer*. London, Butterworths, 1980.

Cooper, W. S. Expected search length: a single measure of retrieval effectiveness based on the weak ordering action of retrieval systems. *American Documentation*, 19, 1968, 30-41.

Cooper, W. S. Indexing documents by gedanken experimentation. *Journal of the American Society for Information Science*, 29, 1978, 107-119.

Cooper, W. S. Is inter-indexer consistency a hobgoblin? *American Documentation*, 20, 1969, 268-278.

Corridoni, J. M. et al. Image retrieval by color semantics with incomplete knowledge. *Journal of the American Society for Information Science*, 49, 1998, 267-282.

Corston-Oliver, S. Text compaction for display on very small screens. *Proceedings of the NAACL 2001 Workshop on Automatic Summarization*, 2001. (http://research.microsoft.com/nlp/publications/NAACL2001)

Cosgrove, S. J. and Weimann, J. M. Expert system technology applied to item classification. *Library Hi Tech*, 10(1/2), 1992, 33-40.

Cowie, J. and Lehnert, W. Information extraction. *Communications of the ACM*, 39(1), 1996, 80-91.

Crandall, M. Microsoft. In: *Linkage Inc's Best Practices in Knowledge Management and Organizational Learning Handbook*, pp. 89-123. Lexington, MA, Linkage Inc., 2000.

Craven, T. C. Abstracts produced using computer assistance. *Journal of the American Society for Information Science*, 51, 2000, 745-756.

Craven, T. C. Changes in metatag descriptions over time. *First Monday*, 6(10), 2001a (http://firstmonday.org/issues/issue6_10/craven/index.html)

Craven, T. C. A coding scheme as a basis for the production of customized abstracts. *Journal of Information Science*, 13, 1987, 51-58.

Craven, T. C. DESCRIPTION meta tags in public home and linked pages. *LIBRES: Library and Information Science Research Electronic Journal*, 11(2), 2001b (http://libres.curtin.edu.au/LIBRE11N2/craven.htm)

Craven, T. C. An experiment in the use of tools for computer-assisted abstracting. *Proceedings of the American Society for Information Science*, 33, 1996, 203-208.

Craven, T. C. NEPHIS: a nested-phrase indexing system. *Journal of the American Society for Information Science*, 28, 1977, 107-114.

Craven, T. C. Presentation of repeated phrases in a computer-assisted abstracting tool kit. *Information Processing & Management*, 37, 2001c, 221-230.

Craven, T. C. *String Indexing*. Orlando, FL, Academic Press, 1986.

Craven, T. C. A thesaurus for use in a computer-aided abstracting tool kit. *Proceedings of the American Society for Information Science*, 30, 1993, 178-184.

Craven, T. C. Use of words and phrases from full text in abstracts. *Journal of Information Science*, 16, 1990, 351-358.

Cremmins, E. T. *The Art of Abstracting*. Second edition. Arlington, VA, Information Resources Press, 1996.

Croft, W. B. and Turtle, H. R. Text retrieval and inference. In: *Text-Based Intelligent Systems*; ed. by P. S. Jacobs, pp. 127-155. Hillsdale, NJ, Lawrence Erlbaum, 1992.

Cromp, R. F. and Dorfman, E. A spatial data handling system for retrieval of images by unrestricted regions of user interest. *Telematics and Informatics*, 9, 1992, 221-241.

Crowe, J. D. *Study of the Feasibility of Indexing a Work's Subjective Viewpoint.* Doctoral thesis. Berkeley, University of California, 1986.

Cutter, C. A. *Rules for a Dictionary Catalog.* Washington, D.C., Government Printing Office, 1876.

Dabney, D. P. The curse of Thamus: an analysis of full-text legal document retrieval. *Law Library Journal*, 78, 1986a, 5-40.

Dabney, D. P. A reply to West Publishing Company and Mead Data Central on *The Curse of Thamus. Law Library Journal*, 78, 1986b, 349-350.

Dahlberg, I. On the theory of the concept. In: *Ordering Systems for Global Information Networks*; ed. by A. Neelameghan, pp. 54-63. Bangalore, International Federation for Documentation, 1979.

Danilewitz, D. B. and Freiheit, F. E., IV. A knowledge-based system within a cooperative processing environment. In: *Innovative Applications of Artificial Intelligence 4*; ed. by A. C. Scott and P. Klahr, pp. 19-36. Cambridge, MA, MIT Press, 1992.

David, C. et al. Indexing as problem solving: a cognitive approach to consistency. *Proceedings of the American Society for Information Science*, 32, 1995, 49-55.

Davison, P. S. and Matthews, D. A. R. Assessment of information services. *Aslib Proceedings*, 21, 1969, 280-284.

Defense Documentation Center. *Abstracting of Technical Reports.* 1968. AD 667 000.

Demasco, P. W. and McCoy, K. F. Generating text from compressed input: an intelligent interface for people with severe motor impairments. *Communications of the ACM*, 35 (5), 1992, 68-78.

Dempsey, L. and Heery, R. Metadata: a current view of practice and issues. *Journal of Documentation*, 54, 1998, 145-172.

De Ruiter, J. Aspects of dealing with digital information: "mature" novices on the Internet. *Library Trends*, 51, 2002, 199-209.

Deschâtelets, G. The three languages theory in information retrieval. *International Classification*, 13, 1986, 126-132.

DeZelar-Tiedman, C. Subject access to fiction: an application of the *Guidelines. Library Resources & Technical Services*, 40, 1996, 203-210.

Di Loreto, F. et al. A visual object-oriented query language for geographic information systems. In: *Database and Expert Systems Applications*; ed. by N. Revell and A. M. Tjoa, pp. 103-113. Berlin, Springer-Verlag, 1995. (Lecture Notes in Computer Science, Number 978).

Dimitroff, A. and Wolfram, D. Design issues in a hypertext-based information system for bibliographic retrieval. *Proceedings of the American Society for Information Science*, 30, 1993, 191-198.

Ding, W. et al. Performance of visual, verbal, and combined video surrogates. *Proceedings of the American Society for Information Science*, 36, 1999, 651-664.

Diodato, V. P. *Author Indexing in Mathematics.* Doctoral thesis. Urbana-Champaign, University of Illinois, Graduate School of Library and Information Science, 1981.

Diodato, V. P. User preferences for features in back of book indexes. *Journal of the American Society for Information Science*, 45, 1994, 529-536.

Diodato, V. P. and Gandt, G. Back of book indexes and the characteristics of author and nonauthor indexing: report of an exploratory study. *Journal of the American Society for Information Science*, 42, 1991, 341-350.

Doraisamy, S. and Rüger, S. M. An approach towards a polyphonic music retrieval system. Paper presented at the Second Annual International Symposium on Music Information Retrieval, 2001. (http://ismir2001.indiana.edu/papers.html)

Doszkocs, T. E. CITE NLM: natural-language searching in an online catalog. *Information Technology and Libraries*, 2, 1983, 364-380.

Dovey, M. J. A technique for "regular expression" style searching in polyphonic music. Paper presented at the Second Annual International Symposium on Music Information Retrieval, 2001. (http://ismir2001.indiana.edu/papers.html)

Down, N. Subject access to individual works of fiction: participating in the OCLC/LC fiction project. *Cataloging & Classification Quarterly*, 20(2), 1995, 61-69.

Downie, S. and Nelson, M. Evaluation of a simple and effective music information retrieval method. *Proceedings of the 23rd Annual International ACM SIGIR Conference on Research and Development in Information Retrieval*, pp. 73-80. New York, Association for Computing Machinery, 2000.

Doyle, L. B. Semantic road maps for literature searchers. *Journal of the Association for Computing Machinery*, 8, 1961, 553-578.

Drage, J. F. User preferences in technical indexes. *The Indexer*, 6, 1969, 151-155.

Driscoll, J. R. et al. The operation and performance of an artificially intelligent keywording system. *Information Processing & Management*, 27, 1991, 43-54.

Dronberger, G. B. and Kowitz, G. T. Abstract readability as a factor in information systems. *Journal of the American Society for Information Science*, 26, 1975, 108-111.

Drott, M. C. Indexing aids at corporate websites: the use of robots.txt and META tags. *Information Processing & Management*, 38, 2002, 209-219.

Dubois, C. P. R. Free text vs. controlled vocabulary; a reassessment. *Online Review*, 11, 1987, 243-253.

Dumais, S. T. Latent semantic indexing (LSI): TREC-3 report. In: *Overview of the Third Text Retrieval Conference* (TREC-3); ed. by D. K. Harman, pp. 219-230. Gaithersburg, MD, National Institute of Standards and Technology, 1995. NIST Special Publication 500-225.

Dutta, S. and Sinha, P. K. Pragmatic approach to subject indexing: a new concept. *Journal of the American Society for Information Science*, 35, 1984, 325-331.

Dym, E. D. Relevance predictability: I. Investigation, background and procedures. In: *Electronic Handling of Information: Testing and Evaluation*; ed. by A. Kent et al., pp. 175-185. Washington, D.C., Thompson Book Co., 1967.

Earl, L. L. Experiments in automatic extracting and indexing. *Information Storage and Retrieval*, 6, 1970, 313-334.

Eastman, C. M. 30,000 hits may be better than 300: precision anomalies in Internet searches. *Journal of the American Society of Information Science and Technology*, 53, 2002, 879-882.

Ebinuma, Y. et al. Promotion of keyword assignment to scientific literature by contributors. *International Forum on Information and Documentation*, 8(3), 1983, 16-20.

Eco, U. *The Role of the Reader: Explorations in the Semiotics of Texts*. Bloomington, Indiana University Press, 1979.

Edmundson, H. P. New methods in automatic extracting. *Journal of the Association for Computing Machinery*, 16, 1969, 264-289.

Edmundson, H. P. et al. *Final Report on the Study for Automatic Abstracting*. Canoga Park, CA, Thompson Ramo Wooldridge, 1961. PB 166 532.

Edwards, T. A comparative analysis of the major abstracting and indexing services for library and information science. *Unesco Bulletin for Libraries*, 30, 1976, 18-25.

Elchesen, D. R. Cost effectiveness comparison of manual and on-line retrospective bibliographic searching. *Journal of the American Society for Information Science*, 29, 1978, 56-66.

Elhadad, N. and McKeown, K. Towards generating patient specific summaries of medical articles. Presentation at the NAACL 2001 Workshop on Automatic Summarization.

Ellis, D. et al. In search of the unknown user: indexing, hypertext and the World Wide Web. *Journal of Documentation*, 54, 1998, 28-47.

Ellis, D. et al. On the creation of hypertext links in full-text documents: measurement of interlinker consistency. *Journal of Documentation*, 50, 1994, 67-98.

Ellis, D. et al. On the creation of hypertext links in full-text documents: measurement of retrieval effectiveness. *Journal of the American Society for Information Science*, 47, 1996, 287-300.

Elrod, J. M. Classification of Internet resources: an AUTOCAT discussion. *Cataloging & Classification Quarterly*, 29(4), 2000, 19-38.

Endres-Niggemeyer, B. A naturalistic model of abstracting. In: *Advances in Knowledge Organization*, 4, 1994, 181-187.

Endres-Niggemeyer, B. *Summarizing Information*. Berlin, Springer-Verlag, 1998.

Enser, P. G. B. Pictorial information retrieval. *Journal of Documentation*, 51, 1995, 126-170.

Enser, P. G. B. Visual information retrieval: seeking the alliance of concept-based and content-based paradigms. *Journal of Information Science*, 26, 2000, 199-210.

ERIC Processing Manual. Section 7: Indexing. Washington, DC, U.S. Department of Education, Educational Resources Information Center, 1980.

Etzioni, O. The World-Wide Web: quagmire or gold mine? *Communications of the ACM*, 39(11), 1996, 65-68.

Fairthorne, R. A. Automatic retrieval of recorded information. *Computer Journal*, 1(1), 1958, 36-41.

Falk, J. D. and Baser, K. H. ABC-Spindex: a subject profile, rotated string indexing system. *Proceedings of the American Society for Information Science*, 17, 1980, 152-154.

Farradane, J. A comparison of some computer-produced permuted alphabetical subject indexes. *International Classification*, 4, 1977, 94-101.

Farradane, J. Concept organization for information retrieval. *Information Storage and Retrieval*, 3, 1967, 297-314.

Farradane, J. Relational indexing. *Journal of Information Science*, 1, 1979, 267-276; 1, 1980, 313-324.

Farradane, J. and Yates-Mercer, P. A. Retrieval characteristics of the index to *Metals Abstracts*. *Journal of Documentation*, 29, 1973, 295-314.

Fayyad, U. and Uthurusamy, R. Evolving data mining into solutions for insights. *Communications of the ACM*, 45(8), 2002, 28-31.

Feder, J. D. and Hobbs, E. T. Speech recognition and full-text retrieval: interface and integration. *Proceedings of the Sixteenth National Online Meeting*, pp. 97-104. Medford, NJ, Learned Information, 1995.

Fedosyuk, M. Yu. Linguistic criteria for differentiating informative and indicative abstracts. *Automatic Documentation and Mathematical Linguistics*, 12(3), 1978, 98-110. [English translation of *Nauchno-Tekhnicheskaya Informatsiya*, Seriya 2, volume 12, number 9, 1978, pp. 11-17.]

Feinberg, H., ed. *Indexing Specialized Formats and Subjects*. Metuchen, NJ, Scarecrow Press, 1983.

Feiten, B. and Günzel, S. Automatic indexing of a sound database using self-organizing neural nets. *Computer Music Journal*, 18(3), 1994, 53-65.

Fidel, R. Individual variability in online search behavior. *Proceedings of the American Society for Information Science*, 22, 1985, 69-72.

Fidel, R. User-centered indexing. *Journal of the American Society for Information Science*, 45, 1994, 572-576.

Fidel, R. Who needs controlled vocabulary? *Special Libraries*, 83, 1992, 1-9.

Fidel, R. Writing abstracts for free-text searching. *Journal of Documentation*, 42, 1986, 11-21.

Fleuret, F. and Geman, D. Coarse-to-fine face detection. *International Journal of Computer Vision*, 41, 2001, 85-107.

Flickner, M. et al. Query by image and video content: the QBIC system. *Computer*, 28(9), 1995, 23-32.

Floridi, L. Brave.Net.World: the Internet as a disinformation superhighway? *Electronic Library*, 14, 1996, 509-514.

Flynn, M. K. Take a letter, computer: speech recognition is coming of age. *PC Magazine*, 12(13), 1993, 29.

Forrester, M. A. Hypermedia and indexing: identifying appropriate models from user studies. In: *Online Information 93*, pp. 313-324. Medford, NJ, Learned Information, 1993.

Forsyth, D. A. et al. Finding pictures of objects in large collections of images. In: *Digital Image Access & Retrieval*; ed. by P. B. Heidorn and B. Sandore, pp. 118-139. Urbana-Champaign, University of Illinois, Graduate School of Library and Information Science, 1997.

Fowler, R. H. et al. Visualizing and browsing WWW semantic content. In: *Proceedings of the First Annual Conference on Emerging Technologies and Applications in Communications*, pp. 110-113. Los Alamitos, CA, IEEE Computer Society Press, 1996.

Fox, E. A. et al. Building a large thesaurus for information retrieval. *Proceedings of the Second Conference on Applied Natural Language Processing*, pp. 101-108. Morristown, NJ, Association for Computational Linguistics, 1988.

Freitas, A. A. *Data Mining and Knowledge Discovery with Evolutionary Algorithms*. Berlin, Springer, 2002.

Fridman, E. P. and Popova, V. N. Otrazhenie mirovoi literatury po eksperimental'noi primatologii v *Referativnykh Zhurnalakh SSSR*. *Nauchno-Tekhnicheskaia Informatsiia*, Seriya 1, No. 2, 1972, 34-36.

Fried, C. and Prevel, J. J. *Effects of Indexing Aids on Indexing Performance*. Bethesda, MD, General Electric Co., 1966. RADC-TR-66-525.

Friis, T. Assisted INdexing (CAIN). *IAALD Quarterly Bulletin*, 37, 1992, 35-37.

Froom, P. and Froom, J. Deficiencies in structured medical abstracts. *Journal of Clinical Epidemiology*, 46, 1993a, 591-594.

Froom, P. and Froom, J. Response to commentary by R. B. Haynes on "Deficiencies in structured medical abstracts." *Journal of Clinical Epidemiology*, 46, 1993b, 599.

Frost, C. The role of mental models in a multimodal image search. *Proceedings of the American Society for Information Science and Technology*, 38, 2001, 52-57.

Fugmann, R. The five-axiom theory of indexing and information supply. *Journal of the American Society for Information Science*, 36, 1985, 116-129.

Fugmann, R. Review of second edition of *Vocabulary Control for Information Retrieval* by F. W. Lancaster. *International Classification*, 14, 1987, 164-166.

Fugmann, R. Toward a theory of information supply and indexing. *International Classification*, 6, 1979, 3-15.

Fuhr, N. Models for retrieval with probabilistic indexing. *Information Processing & Management*, 25, 1989, 55-72.

Fum, D. et al. Forward and backward reasoning in automatic abstracting. In: *COLING 82, Proceedings of the Ninth International Conference on Computational Linguistics*; ed.by J. Horecky, pp. 83-88. Amsterdam, North Holland Publishing, 1982.

Funk, M. E. et al. Indexing consistency in MEDLINE. *Bulletin of the Medical Library Association*, 71, 1983, 176-183.

Gaizauskas, R. and Wilks, Y. Information extraction: beyond document retrieval. *Journal of Documentation*, 54, 1998, 70-105.

Gao, Y. J. et al. Fuzzy multilinkage thesaurus builder in multimedia information systems. In: *Proceedings of Third International Conference on Document Analysis and Recognition*. Volume 1, pp. 142-145. Los Alamitos, CA, IEEE Computer Society Press, 1995.

Gardiner, D. et al. TREC-3: experience with conceptual relations in information retrieval. In: *Overview of the Third Text Retrieval Conference* (TREC-3); ed. by D. K. Harman, pp. 333-352. Gaithersburg, MD, National Institute of Standards and Technology, 1995. NIST Special Publication 500-225.

Gauch, J. M. et al. Real time video scene detection and classification. *Information Processing & Management*, 35, 1999, 381-400.

Gauvain, J.-L. et al. Audio partitioning and transcription for broadcast data indexation. *Multimedia Tools and Applications*, 14, 2001, 187-200.

Gee, F. R. TIPSTER Phase III accomplishments. In: *Proceedings of the TIPSTER Text Program, Phase III*, pp. 7-13. San Francisco, Morgan Kaufmann, 1999.

Geisler, G. Interface concepts for the Open Video Project. *Proceedings of the American Society for Information Science and Technology*, 38, 2001, 58-75.

Gilchrist, A. Documentation of documentation: a survey of leading abstracts services in documentation and an identification of key journals. *Aslib Proceedings*, 18, 1966, 62-80.

Girgensohn, A. et al. Keyframe-based user interfaces for digital video. *Computer*, 34(9), 2001, 61-67.

Godby, C. J. Two techniques for the identification of phrases in full text. *Journal of Library Administration*, 34, 2001, 57-65.

Godby, C. J. and Reighart, R. Terminology identification in a collection of Web resources. In: *CORC: New Tools and Possibilities for Cooperative Electronic Resource Description*; ed. by K. Calhoun and J. J. Riemer, pp. 49-65. Binghampton, NY, Haworth Press, 2001a.

Godby, C. J. and Reighart, R. The WordSmith indexing system. *Journal of Library Administration*, 34, 2001b, 375-384.

Goldstein, J. et al. Multi-document summarization by sentence extraction. *Proceedings of the ANLP 2000 Workshop on Automatic Summarization*, pp. 40-48. New Brunswick, NJ, Association for Computational Linguistics, 2000.

Gong, Y. and Liu, X. Generic text summarization using relevance measure and latent semantic analysis. *Proceedings of the 24th Annual International ACM SIGIR Conference on Research and Development in Information Retrieval*, pp. 19-25. New York, Association for Computing Machinery, 2001.

Goode, D. J. et al. Comparative analysis of *Epilepsy Abstracts* and a MEDLARS bibliography. *Bulletin of the Medical Library Association*, 58, 1970, 44-50.

Goodrum, A. A. Multidimensional scaling of video surrogates. *Journal of the American Society for Information Science and Technology*, 52, 2001, 174-182.

Goodrum, A. A. and Spink, A. Visual information seeking: a study of image queries on the World Wide Web. *Proceedings of the American Society for Information Science*, 36, 1999, 665-674.

Goodrum, A. A. et al. An open source agenda for research linking text and image content features. *Journal of the American Society for Information Science and Technology*, 52, 2001, 948-953.

Gordon, M. D. and Dumais, S. Using latent semantic indexing for literature based discovery. *Journal of the American Society for Information Science*, 49, 1998, 674-685.

Gowtham, M. S. and Kamat, S. K. An expert system as a tool to classification. *Library Science with a Slant to Documentation and Information Studies*, 32(2), 1995, 57-63.

Green, A. Keeping up with the times: evaluating currency of indexing, language coverage and subject area coverage in three music periodical index databases. *Music Reference Services Quarterly*, 8(1), 2001, 53-68.

Green, B. F. et al. BASEBALL: an automatic question-answerer. In: *Computers and Thought;* ed. by E. Feigenbaum and J. Feldman, pp. 207-216. New York, McGraw Hill, 1963.

Green, E.-L. and Klasén, L. Indexing and information retrieval of moving images—experiences from a large television information database. In: *Online Information 93*, pp. 129-136. Medford, NJ, Learned Information, 1993.

Green, R. The role of relational structures in indexing for the humanities. *Knowledge Organization*, 24, 1997, 72-83.

Greenberg, J. Metadata generation. *Bulletin of the American Society for Information Science and Technology*, 29(2), 2003, 16-19.

Greenberg, J. A quantitative categorical analysis of metadata elements in image-applicable metadata schemas. *Journal of the American Society for Information Science and Technology*, 52, 2001, 917-924.

Greisdorf, H. and O'Connor, B. C. Modelling what users see when they look at images: a cognitive viewpoint. *Journal of Documentation*, 58, 2002, 6-29.

Grimson, W. E. L. and Mundy, J. L. Computer vision applications. *Communications of the ACM*, 37(3), 1994, 45-51.

Grishman, R. Whither written language evaluation? In: *Proceedings of the Human Language Technology Workshop, March 8-11, 1994*, pp. 120-125. San Francisco, Morgan Kaufmann, 1994.

Guard, A. An antidote for browsing: subject headings for fiction. *Technicalities*, 11(12), 1991, 10-14.

Gudivada, V. N. and Raghavan, V. V. Content-based image retrieval systems. *Computer*, 28(9), 1995, 18-22.

Gudivada, V. N. and Raghavan, V. V. Modeling and retrieving images by content. *Information Processing & Management*, 33, 1997, 427-452

Gudivada, V. N. et al. A unified approach to data modeling and retrieval for a class of image database applications. In: *Multimedia Database Systems;* ed. by V. S. Subrahmanian and S. Jajodia, pp. 37-78. Berlin, Springer-Verlag, 1996.

Guenther, R. and McCallum, S. New metadata standards for digital resources: MODS and METS. *Bulletin of the American Society for Information Science and Technology*, 29(2), 2003, 16-19.

Guglielmo, E. J. and Rowe, N. C. Natural-language retrieval of images based on descriptive captions. *ACM Transactions on Information Systems*, 14, 1996, 237-267.

Guidelines for Abstracts. Bethesda, MD, National Information Standards Organization, 1997. ANSI/NISO Z39.14-1997. Reissued 2002.

Guidelines for Indexes and Related Information Retrieval Devices (by James D. Anderson). Bethesda, MD, National Information Standards Organization, 1997. NISO-TR02-1997.

Guidelines on Subject Access to Individual Works of Fiction, Drama, Etc. Second edition. Chicago, American Library Association, 2000.

Gupta, A. and Jain, R. Visual information retrieval. *Communications of the ACM*, 40(5), 1997, 71-79.

Guthrie, L. et al. Document classification and routing: a probabilistic approach. In: *Natural Language Information Retrieval*; ed. by T. Strzalkowski, pp. 289-310. Boston, Kluwer, 1999.

Haas, S. W. Natural language processing: toward large-scale, robust systems. *Annual Review of Information Science and Technology*, 31, 1996, 83-119.

Hafed, Z. M. and Levine, M. D. Face recognition using the discrete cosine transform. *International Journal of Computer Vision*, 43, 2001, 167-188.

Hagerty, K. *Abstracts as a Basis for Relevance Judgment*. University of Chicago, Graduate Library School, 1967. Working paper no. 380-5.

Hahn, U. and Mani, I. The challenges of automatic summarization. *Computer*, 33(11), 2000, 29-36.

Hahn, U. and Reimer, U. Heuristic text parsing in 'TOPIC': methodological issues in a knowledge-based text condensation system. In: *Representation and Exchange of Knowledge as a Basis of Information Processes*; ed. by H. J. Dietschmann, pp. 143-163. Amsterdam, North-Holland, 1984.

Hall, A. M. *Case Studies of the Use of Subject Indexes*. London, Institution of Electrical Engineers, 1972a.

Hall, A. M. *User Preferences in Printed Indexes*. London, Institution of Electrical Engineers, 1972b.

Han, J. and Chang, K. C.-C. Data mining for Web intelligence. *Computer*, 35(11), 2002, 64-70.

Hanson, C. W. and Janes, M. Coverage by abstracting journals of conference papers. *Journal of Documentation*, 17, 1961, 143-149.

Harman, D. The TREC conferences. In: *Readings in Information Retrieval*; ed. by K. Sparck Jones and P. Willett, pp. 247-256. San Francisco, Morgan Kaufmann, 1997.

Harpring, P. The language of images: enhancing access to images by applying metadata schemas and structured vocabularies. In: *Introduction to Art Image Access*; ed. by M. Baca, pp. 20-39. Los Angeles, Getty Research Institute, 2002.

Harris, D. et al. *The Testing of Inter-Indexer Consistency at Various Indexing Depths*. University of Chicago, Graduate Library School, 1966. Working paper no. 380-2.

Hart, P. E. and Graham, J. Query-free information retrieval. *IEEE Expert*, 12(5), 1997, 32-37.

Harter, S. P. Psychological relevance and information science. *Journal of the American Society for Information Science*, 43, 1992, 602-615.

Hartley, J. Are structured abstracts more or less accurate than traditional ones? *Journal of Information Science*, 26, 2000a, 273-277.

Hartley, J. Clarifying the abstracts of systematic literature reviews. *Bulletin of the Medical Library Association*, 88, 2000b, 332-337.

Hartley, J. Do structured abstracts take more space? And does it matter? *Journal of Information Science*, 28, 2002, 417-422.

Hartley, J. Is it appropriate to use structured abstracts in non-medical science journals? *Journal of Information Science*, 24, 1998, 359-364.

Hartley, J. Three ways to improve the clarity of journal abstracts. *British Journal of Educational Psychology*, 64, 1994, 331-343.

Hartley, J. Typographic settings for structured abstracts. *Journal of Technical Writing and Communication*, 30, 2000c, 355-365.

Hartley, J. and Benjamin, M. An evaluation of structured abstracts in journals published by the British Psychological Society. *British Journal of Educational Psychology*, 68, 1998, 443-456.

Hartley, J. and Sydes, M. Which layout do you prefer? An analysis of readers' preferences for different typographic layouts of structured abstracts. *Journal of Information Science*, 22, 1996, 27-37.

Hartley, J. et al. Obtaining information accurately and quickly: are structured abstracts more efficient? *Journal of Information Science*, 22, 1996, 349-356.

Hastings, S. K. An exploratory study of intellectual access to digitized art images. *Proceedings of the Sixteenth National Online Meeting*, pp. 177-185. Medford, NJ, Learned Information, 1995a.

Hastings, S. K. Index access points in a study of intellectual access to digitized art images. In: *Multimedia Computing and Museums*; ed. by D. Bearman, pp. 299-309. Pittsburgh, Archives and Museum Informatics, 1995b.

Hastings, S. K. Query categories in a study of intellectual access to digitized art images. *Proceedings of the American Society for Information Science*, 32, 1995c, 3-8.

Haug, P. and Beesley, D. Automated selection of clinical data to support radiographic interpretation. In: *Fifteenth Annual Symposium on Computer Applications in Medical Care*, pp. 593-597. New York, McGraw Hill, 1992.

Hayes, P. J. Intelligent high-volume text processing using shallow, domain-specific techniques. In: *Text-Based Intelligent Systems*; ed. by P. S. Jacobs, pp. 227-241. Hillsdale, NJ, Lawrence Erlbaum, 1992a.

Hayes, P. J. and Weinstein, S. P. Construe-TIS: a system for content-based indexing of a database of news stories. In: *Innovative Applications of Artificial Intelligence 2*; ed. by A. Rappaport and R. Smith, pp. 51-64. Cambridge, MA, MIT Press, 1991.

Hayes, S. Enhanced catalog access to fiction: a preliminary study. *Library Resources & Technical Services*, 36, 1992b, 441-459.

Haynes, R. B. More informative abstracts: current status and evaluation. *Journal of Clinical Epidemiology*, 46, 1993, 595-597.

Haynes, R. B. et al. More informative abstracts revisited. *Annals of Internal Medicine*, 113, 1990, 69-76.

Haynes, R. B. et al. Online access to MEDLINE in clinical settings: a study of use and usefulness. *Annals of Internal Medicine*, 112, 1990, 78-84.

Hearst, M. A. The use of categories and clusters for organizing retrieval results. In: *Natural Language Information Retrieval*; ed. by T. Strzalkowski, pp. 333-374. Boston, Kluwer, 1999.

Heidorn, P. B. The identification of index terms in natural language object descriptions. *Proceedings of the American Society for Information Science*, 36, 1999, 472-481.

Heller, J. On logical data organization, card catalogs, and the GRIPHOS management information system. Rochester, NY, Margaret Woodbury Strong Museum, 1974. Museum Data Bank Research Report Number 3.

Henzler, R. G. Free or controlled vocabularies: some statistical user-oriented evaluations of biomedical information systems. *International Classification*, 5, 1978, 21-26.

Herner, S. Subject slanting in scientific abstracting publications. In: *International Conference on Scientific Information, Washington, D.C., Proceedings*. Volume 1, pp. 407-427. Washington, DC, National Academy of Sciences, 1959.

Hersey, D. F. et al. Free text word retrieval and scientist indexing: performance profiles and costs. *Journal of Documentation*, 27, 1971, 167-183.

Hersh, W. R. and Hickam, D. H. A comparative analysis of retrieval effectiveness for three methods of indexing AIDS-related abstracts. *Proceedings of the American Society for Information Science*, 28, 1991, 211-225.

Hersh, W. R. and Hickam, D. H. An evaluation of interactive Boolean and natural language searching with an online medical textbook. *Journal of the American Society for Information Science*, 46, 1995a, 478-489.

Hersh, W. R. and Hickam, D. H. Information retrieval in medicine: the SAPHIRE experience. *Journal of the American Society for Information Science*, 46, 1995b, 743-747.

Hersh, W. R. et al. Words, concepts, or both: optimal indexing units for automated information retrieval. *Sixteenth Annual Symposium on Computer Applications in Medical Care*, pp. 644-648. New York, McGraw Hill, 1993.

Hert, C. A. et al. A usability assessment of online indexing structures in the networked environment. *Journal of the American Society for Information Science*, 51, 2000, 971-988.

Hickey, T. B. and Vizine-Goetz, D. The role of classification in CORC. *Journal of Library Administration*, 34, 2001, 421-430.

Hidderley, R. and Rafferty, P. Democratic indexing: an approach to the retrieval of fiction. *Information Services & Use*, 17, 1997, 101-109.

Hill, L. L. Collection metadata solutions for digital library applications. *Journal of the American Society for Information Science*, 50, 1999, 1169-1181.

Hinman, H. and Leita, C. Librarians Index to the Internet (LII). In: *The Amazing Internet Challenge*; ed. by A. T. Wells et al., pp. 144-160. Chicago, American Library Association, 1999.

Hjørland, B. Relevance research. *Journal of the American Society for Information Science and Technology*, 51, 2000, 209-211.

Hjørland, B. Towards a theory of aboutness, subject, topicality, theme, domain, field, content . . . and relevance. *Journal of the American Society for Information Science and Technology*, 52, 2001, 774-778.

Hjørland, B. and Nielsen, L. K. Subject access points in electronic retrieval. *Annual Review of Information Science and Technology*, 35, 2001, 249-298.

Hlava, M. M. K. Machine-aided indexing (MAI) in a multilingual environment. In: *Online Information 92*, pp. 297-300. Medford, NJ, Learned Information, 1992.

Hmeidi, I. et al. Design and implementation of automatic indexing for information retrieval with Arabic documents. *Journal of the American Society for Information Science*, 48, 1997, 867-881,

Hobbs, J. R. and Israel, D. Principles of template design. In: *Proceedings of the Human Language Technology Workshop, March 8-11, 1994*, pp. 177-181. San Francisco, Morgan Kaufmann, 1994.

Hobbs, J. R. et al. Robust processing of real-world natural-language texts. In: *Text-Based Intelligent Systems*; ed. by P. S. Jacobs, pp. 13-33. Hillsdale, NJ, Lawrence Erlbaum, 1992.

Hock, R. E. *The Extreme Searcher's Guide to Web Search Engines*. Second edition. Medford, NJ, Information Today, 2001.

Hock, R. E. Sizing up HotBot: evaluating one Web search engine's capabilities. *Online*, 21 (6), 1997, 24-33.

Hodges, P. R. Keyword in title indexes: effectiveness of retrieval in computer searches. *Special Libraries*, 74, 1983, 56-60.

Hogan, M. et al. The visual thesaurus in a hypermedia environment. In: *Hypermedia & Interactivity in Museums*; ed. by D. Bearman, pp. 202-221. Pittsburgh, Archives and Museum Informatics, 1991.

Holm, B. E. and Rasmussen, L. E. Development of a technical thesaurus. *American Documentation*, 12, 1961, 184-190.

Holmes, N. The KWIC and the dead: a lesson in computing history. *Computer,* 34(1), 2001, 142-144.

Holst, W. Problemer ved strukturering og bruk av den polytekniske tesaurus. *Tidskrift for Dokumentation*, 22, 1966, 69-74.

Holt, B. and Hartwick, L. 'Quick, who painted fish?': searching a picture database with the QBIC project at UC Davis. *Information Services & Use*, 14, 1994, 79-90.

Holt, B. et al. The QBIC project in the Department of Art and Art History at UC Davis. *Proceedings of the American Society for Information Science*, 34, 1997, 189-195.

Holt, G. E. On becoming essential: an agenda for quality in twenty-first century public libraries. *Library Trends*, 44, 1995, 545-571.

Hooper, R. S. Evaluation and analysis of indexing systems. In: *The Second Institute on Technical Literature Indexing*, Session 1. Washington, DC, American University, Center for Technology and Administration, 1966.

Hooper, R. S. *Indexer Consistency Tests—Origin, Measurements, Results and Utilization*. Bethesda, MD, IBM, 1965.

Horký, J. Shoda mezi zpracovateli pri vyberu klicovych slov z odbornych textu, [Agreement in the selection of keywords from specialised texts]. *Ceskoslovenska Informatika*, 25, 1983, 275-278.

Horty, J. F. Experience with the application of electronic data processing systems in general law. *Modern Uses of Logic in Law*, 60D, 1960, 158-168.

Horty, J. F. Legal research using electronic techniques. In: *Literature of the Law—Techniques of Access*, pp. 56-68. South Hackensack, NJ, F. B. Rothman & Co., 1962.

Hourihane, C. It begins with the cataloguer: subject access to images and the cataloguer's perspective. In: *Introduction to Art Image Access*; ed. by M. Baca, pp. 40-66. Los Angeles, Getty Research Institute, 2002.

Hovy, E. Using an ontology to simplify data access. *Communications of the ACM,* 46(1), 2003, 47-49.

Huang, T. et al. Multimedia Analysis and Retrieval System (MARS) project. In: *Digital Image Access & Retrieval*; ed. by P. B. Heidorn and B. Sandore, pp. 100-117. Urbana-Champaign, University of Illinois, Graduate School of Library and Information Science, 1997.

Hui, S. C. and Goh, A. Incorporating abstract generation into an online retrieval interface for a library newspaper cutting system. *Aslib Proceedings*, 48, 1996, 259-265.

Humphrey, S. M. Automated indexing. *Bulletin of the American Society of Indexers*, 8, 2000, 157-159.

Humphrey, S. M. Automatic indexing of documents from journal descriptors: a preliminary investigation. *Journal of the American Society for Information Science*, 50, 1999, 661-674.

Humphrey, S. M. Interactive knowledge-based systems for improved subject analysis and retrieval. In: *Artificial Intelligence and Expert Systems: Will They Change the Library?*; ed. by F. W. Lancaster and L. C. Smith, pp. 81-117. Urbana-Champaign, University of Illinois, Graduate School of Library and Information Science, 1992.

Humphrey, S. M. Personal e-mail communication, November 20, 1995.

Humphrey, S. M. et al. Automatic indexing by discipline and high-level categories. To be published in *Advances in Classification Research*, 11, 2003 (in press).

Humphreys, K. et al. Bioinformatics applications of information extraction from scientific journal articles. *Journal of Information Science*, 26, 2000, 75-85.

Hurt, C. and Potter, W. G. CORC and the future of libraries. In: *CORC: New Tools and Possibilities for Cooperative Electronic Resource Description*; ed. by K. Calhoun and J. J. Riemer, pp. 17-27. Binghampton, NY, Haworth Press, 2001.

Hutchins, W. J. The concept of "aboutness" in subject indexing. *Aslib Proceedings*, 30, 1978, 172-181.

Intner, S. S. Censorship in indexing. *The Indexer*, 14, 1984, 105-108.

Introna, L. and Nissenbaum, H. Defining the Web: the politics of search engines. *Computer*, 33(1), 2000, 54-62.

Irving, H. B. Computer-assisted indexing training and electronic text conversion at NAL. *Knowledge Organization*, 24, 1997, 4-7.

Iyengar, S. S. Visual based retrieval systems and Web mining. *Journal of the American Society for Information Science and Technology*, 52, 2001, 828-875.

Iyer, H. and Giguere, M. Towards designing an expert system to map mathematics classificatory structures. *Knowledge Organization*, 22, 1995, 141-147.

Jackson, M. E. The advent of portals. *Library Journal*, 127(15), 2002, 36-39.

Jacobs, P. S. Introduction: text power and intelligent systems. In: *Text-Based Intelligent Systems*; ed. by P. S. Jacobs, pp. 1-8. Hillsdale, NJ, Lawrence Erlbaum, 1992a.

Jacobs, P. S. Joining statistics with NLP for text categorization. In: *Proceedings of the Third Conference on Applied Natural Language Processing*, pp. 178-185. San Francisco, Morgan Kaufmann, 1992b.

Jacobs, P. S., ed. *Text-Based Intelligent Systems: Current Research and Practice in Information Extraction and Retrieval*. Hillsdale, NJ, Lawrence Erlbaum, 1992c.

Jacobs, P. S. and Rau, L. F. Innovations in text interpretation. In: *Natural Language Processing*; ed. by F. C. N. Pereira and B. J. Grosz, pp. 143-191. Cambridge, MA, MIT Press, 1994.

Jacobs, P. S. and Rau, L. F. SCISOR: extracting information from online news. *Communications of the ACM*, 33(11), 1990, 88-97.

Jacoby, J. and Slamecka, V. *Indexer Consistency Under Minimal Conditions*. Bethesda, MD, Documentation Inc., 1962. RADC-TDR-62-426.

Jacsó, P. Document-summarization software. *Information Today*, 19(2), 2002, 22-23.

Jagadish, H. V. Indexing for retrieval by similarity. In: *Multimedia Database Systems*; ed. by V. S. Subrahmanian and S. Jajodia, pp. 165-184. Berlin, Springer-Verlag, 1996.

Jahoda, G. and Stursa, M. L. A comparison of a keyword from title index with a single access point per document alphabetic subject index. *American Documentation*, 20, 1969, 377-380.

Jain, R. Visual information retrieval in digital libraries. In: *Digital Image Access & Retrieval*; ed. by P. B. Heidorn and B. Sandore, pp. 68-85. Urbana-Champaign, University of Illinois, Graduate School of Library and Information Science, 1997.

Janes, J. W. Relevance judgments and the incremental presentation of document representations. *Information Processing & Management*, 27, 1991, 629-646.

Jansen, B. J. and Pooch, U. A review of Web searching studies and a framework for future research. *Journal of the American Society for Information Science and Technology*, 52, 2001, 235-246.

Johnson, F. C. et al. The application of linguistic processing to automatic abstract generation. In: *Readings in Information Retrieval*; ed. by K. Sparck Jones and P. Willett, pp. 538-551. San Francisco, Morgan Kaufmann, 1997.

Jonak, Z. Problemy informacni analyzy pri Popisu Beletristickeho Dila. (Problems of information analysis in describing a work of fiction). *Kniznice a Vedecke Informacie*, 10(1), 1978, 16-21.

Jones, E. K. and Roydhouse, A. Intelligent retrieval of archived meteorological data. *IEEE Expert*, 10(6), 1995, 50-57.

Jones, K. P. Towards a theory of indexing. *Journal of Documentation*, 32, 1976, 118-125.

Jones, K. P. and Bell, C. L. M. Artificial intelligence program for indexing automatically (AIPIA). In: *Online Information 92*, pp. 187-196. Medford, NJ, Learned Information, 1992.

Jones, S. and Paynter, G. W. Automatic extraction of document keyphrases for use in digital libraries. *Journal of the American Society for Information Science and Technology*, 53, 2002, 653-677.

Jonker, F. *Indexing Theory, Indexing Methods and Search Devices*. New York, Scarecrow Press, 1964.

Jörgensen, C. Indexing images: testing an image description template. *Proceedings of the American Society for Information Science*, 33, 1996, 209-213.

Jörgensen, C. Introduction and overview. *Journal of the American Society for Information Science and Technology*, 52, 2001, 906-910.

Kaiser, J. O. *Systematic Indexing*. London, Pitman, 1911.

Karasev, S. A. Abstracting scientific and technical literature: elements of a theory. *Automatic Documentation and Mathematical Linguistics*, 12(4), 1978, 1-7. [English translation of *Nauchno-Tekhnicheskaya Informatsiya*, Seriya 2, volume 12, number 10, 1978, pp. 1-4.]

Kassirer, J. P. A report card on computer-assisted diagnosis—the grade: C. *New England Journal of Medicine*, 330, 1994, 1824-1825.

Katzer, J. et al. A study of the overlap among document representations. *Information Technology: Research and Development*, 1, 1982, 261-274.

Keen, E. M. On the generation and searching of entries in printed subject indexes. *Journal of Documentation*, 33, 1977a, 15-45.

Keen, E. M. On the processing of printed subject index entries during searching. *Journal of Documentation*, 33, 1977b, 266-276.

Keen, E. M. Query term weighting schemes for effective ranked output retrieval. *Online Information 91*, pp. 135-142. Medford, NJ, Learned Information, 1991.

Keen, E. M. A retrieval comparison of six published indexes in the field of library and information science. *Unesco Bulletin for Libraries*, 30, 1976, 26-36.

Keen, E. M. and Digger, J. A. *Report of an Information Science Index Languages Test*. Aberystwyth, College of LibrarianshipWales, 1972. 2 volumes.

Kehl, W. B. et al. An information retrieval language for legal studies. *Communications of the ACM*, 4, 1961, 380-389.

Keister, L. H. User types and queries: impact on image access systems. In: *Challenges in Indexing Electronic Text and Images*; ed. by R. Fidel et al., pp. 7-22. Medford, NJ, Learned Information, 1994.

Kellman, S. G., ed. *Masterplots II: American Fiction Series*. 6 volumes. Pasadena, CA, Salem Press, 2000.

Kent, A. et al. Relevance predictability in information retrieval systems. *Methods of Information in Medicine*, 6, 1967, 45-51.

Kerpedjiev, S. M. Automatic generation of multimodal weather reports from datasets. In: *Proceedings of the Third Conference on Applied Natural Language Processing*, pp. 48-55. San Francisco, Morgan Kaufmann, 1992.

Kessler, M. M. Bibliographic coupling between scientific papers. *American Documentation*, 14, 1963, 10-25.

Kessler, M. M. *Bibliographic Coupling Extended in Time*. Cambridge, MA, Massachusetts Institute of Technology, 1962.

Kessler, M. M. Comparison of the results of bibliographic coupling and analytic subject indexing. *American Documentation*, 16, 1965, 223-233.

Kim, W. and Wilbur, W. J. Corpus-based statistical screening for content-bearing terms. *Journal of the American Society for Information Science and Technology*, 52, 2001, 247-259.

King, R. A comparison of the readability of abstracts with their source documents. *Journal of the American Society for Information Science*, 27, 1976, 118-121.

Klement, S. Open-system versus closed-system indexing. *The Indexer*, 23, 2002, 23-31.

Klingbiel, P. H. *The Future of Indexing and Retrieval Vocabularies*. Alexandria, VA., Defense Documentation Center, 1970. AD 716 200.

Klingbiel, P. H. *Machine-aided Indexing*. Technical progress report for period July 1969-June 1970. Alexandria, VA., Defense Documentation Center, 1971. AD 721 875.

Klingbiel, P. H. and Rinker, C. C. Evaluation of machine-aided indexing. *Information Processing & Management*, 12, 1976, 351-366.

Knapp, S. D. BRS/TERM: database for searchers. *Online '83 Conference Proceedings*, pp. 162-166. Weston, CT, Online Inc., 1983.

Knapp, S. D. *The Contemporary Thesaurus of Social Science Terms and Synonyms: a Guide for Natural Language Computer Searching*. Phoenix, AZ, Oryx Press, 1993.

Knapp, S. D. Free-text searching of online databases. *Reference Librarian*, 5/6, 1982, 143-153.

Knight, K. Mining online text. *Communications of the ACM*, 42(11), 1999, 58-61.

Knorz, G. *Automatisches Indexieren als Erkennen abstrakter Objekte*. Tubingen, Max Niemeyer Verlag, 1983.

Kolcz, A. Summarization as feature selection for text categorization. In: *Proceedings of the Tenth International Conference on Information and Knowledge Management*, pp. 365-370. New York, Association for Computing Machinery, 2001.

Korotkin, A. L. and Oliver, L. H. *The Effect of Subject Matter Familiarity and the Use of an Indexing Aid upon Inter-Indexer Consistency*. Bethesda, MD., General Electric Company, Information Systems Operation, 1964.

Korycinski, C. and Newell, A. F. Natural-language processing and automatic indexing. *The Indexer*, 17, 1990, 21-29.

Krause, M. G. Intellectual problems of indexing picture collections. *Audiovisual Librarian*, 14, 1988, 73-81.

Krieger, T. *Instructor Influences Versus Text Influences in the Selection of Subject Descriptors by Undergraduate Students*. Doctoral thesis. Urbana-Champaign, University of Illinois, Graduate School of Library Science, 1981.

Kubala, F. et al. Integrated technologies for indexing spoken language. *Communications of the ACM*, 43(2), 2000, 48-56.

Kuhlen, R. Some similarities and differences between intellectual and machine text understanding for the purpose of abstracting. In: *Representation and Exchange of Knowledge as a Basis of Information Processes*; ed. by H. J. Dietschmann, pp. 87-109. Amsterdam, North-Holland, 1984.

Kupiec, J. M. Murax: finding and organizing answers from text search. In: *Natural Language Information Retrieval*; ed. by T. S. Strzalkowski, pp. 311-332. Boston, Kluwer, 1999.

Kurita, T. and Kato, T. Learning of personal visual impression for image database systems. In: *Proceedings of the Second International Conference on Document Analysis and Recognition*, pp. 547-552. Los Alamitos, CA, IEEE Computer Society Press, 1993.

Kwok, K. L. A probabilistic theory of indexing and similarity measure based on cited and citing documents. *Journal of the American Society for Information Science*, 36, 1985a, 342-351.

Kwok, K. L. A probabilistic theory of indexing using author-provided relevance information. *Proceedings of the American Society for Information Science*, 22, 1985b, 59-63.

Kwon, O-W. and Lee, J.-H. Text categorization based on k-nearest neighbor approach for Web site classification. *Information Processing & Management*, 39, 2003, 25-44.

LaBorie, T. et al. Library and information science abstracting and indexing services: coverage, overlap, and context. *Library and Information Science Research*, 7, 1985, 183-195.

Lam-Adesina, A. M. and Jones, G. J. F. Applying summarization techniques for term selection in relevance feedback. *Proceedings of the 24th Annual International ACM SIGIR Conference on Research and Development in Information Retrieval*, pp. 1-9. New York, Association for Computing Machinery, 2001.

Lancaster, F. W. *Evaluation of the MEDLARS Demand Search Service*. Bethesda, MD, National Library of Medicine, 1968a.

Lancaster, F. W. *Information Retrieval Systems: Characteristics, Testing and Evaluation*. New York, Wiley, 1968b.

Lancaster, F. W. Some observations on the performance of EJC role indicators in a mechanized retrieval system. *Special Libraries*, 55, 1964, 696-701.

Lancaster, F. W. *Vocabulary Control for Information Retrieval*. Second edition. Arlington, VA, Information Resources Press, 1986.

Lancaster, F. W. *Vocabulary Control for Information Retrieval*. Washington, DC, Information Resources Press, 1972.

Lancaster, F. W. and Sandore, B. *Technology and Management in Library and Information Services*. Urbana-Champaign, University of Illinois, Graduate School of Library and Information Science, 1997.

Lancaster, F. W. and Warner, A. J. *Information Retrieval Today*. Arlington, VA, Information Resources Press, 1983.

Lancaster, F. W. and Warner, A. J. *Intelligent Technologies in Library and Information Service Applications*. Medford, NJ, Information Today, 2001.

Lancaster, F. W. et al. Evaluating the effectiveness of an on-line, natural language retrieval system. *Information Storage and Retrieval*, 8, 1972, 223-245.

Lancaster, F. W. et al. Evaluation of interactive knowledge-based systems: overview and design for empirical testing. *Journal of the American Society for Information Science*, 47, 1996, 57-69.

Lancaster, F. W. et al. Identifying barriers to effective subject access in library catalogs. *Library Resources & Technical Services*, 35, 1991, 377-391.

Lancaster, F. W. et al. *Modular Content Analyses*. Final report to the National Science Foundation. Washington, DC, Herner and Company, 1965.

Larson, R. R. Experiments in automatic Library of Congress classification. *Journal of the American Society for Information Science*, 43, 1992, 130-148.

Lawrence, S. and Giles, C. L. Accessibility of information on the Web. *Nature*, 400, 1999, 107-109.

Lawrence, S. et al. Digital libraries and autonomous citation indexing. *Computer*, 32(6), 1999, 67-71.

Lawson, M. et al. Automatic extraction of citations from the text of English-language patents—an example of template mining. *Journal of Information Science*, 22, 1996, 423-436.

Layne, S. S. Some issues in the indexing of images. *Journal of the American Society for Information Science*, 45, 1994, 583-588.

Layne, S. S. Subject access to art images. In: *Introduction to Art Image Access*; ed. by M. Baca, pp. 1-19. Los Angeles, Getty Research Institute, 2002.

Leacock, C. et al. Corpus-based statistical sense resolution. In: *Human Language Technology: Proceedings of a Workshop held at Plainsboro, New Jersey, March 21-24, 1993*, pp. 260-263. San Francisco, Morgan Kaufmann, 1993.

Lehmam, A. Text structuration leading to an automatic summary system: RAFI. *Information Processing & Management*, 35, 1999, 181-191.

Leighton, H. V. and Srivastava, J. First 20 precision among World Wide Web Search Services (Search Engines). *Journal of the American Society for Information Science*, 50, 1999, 870-881.

Leininger, K. Interindexer consistency in PsycINFO. *Journal of Librarianship and Information Science*, 32(1), 2000, 4-8.

Leonard, L. E. *Inter-Indexer Consistency and Retrieval Effectiveness: Measurement of Relationships*. Doctoral thesis. Urbana-Champaign, University of Illinois, Graduate School of Library Science, 1975.

Levinson, S. E. Speech recognition technology: a critique. *Proceedings of the National Academy of Sciences*, 92, 1995, 9953-9955.

Li, Y. et al. Semantic image retrieval through human subject segmentation and characterization. In: *Storage and Retrieval for Image and Video Databases V*; ed. by I. K. Sethi and R. C. Jain, pp. 340-351. Bellingham, WA, International Society for Optical Engineering, 1997.

Liddy, E. D. How a search engine works. In: *Web of Deception: Misinformation on the Internet*; ed. by A. P. Mintz, pp. 197-208. Medford, NJ, Information Today, 2002.

Liddy, E. D. and Jörgensen, C. Modeling information seeking behaviors in index use. *Proceedings of the American Society for Information Science*, 30, 1993a, 185-190.

Liddy, E. D. and Jörgensen, C. Reality check! Book index characteristics that facilitate information access. In: *Indexing, Providing Access to Information*; ed. by N. C. Mulvany, pp. 125-138. Port Aransas, TX, American Society of Indexers, 1993b.

Liddy, E. D. et al. Index quality study, part II: publishers' survey and qualitative assessment. In: *Indexing Tradition and Innovation*, pp. 53-79. American Society of Indexers, 1990.

Lieberman, H. et al. Aria: an agent for annotating and retrieving images. *Computer*, 34(7), 2001, 57-62.

Lienhart, R. et al. Video abstracting. *Communications of the ACM*, 40(12), 1997, 55-62.

Lippincott, A. Issues in content-based music information retrieval. *Journal of Information Science*, 28, 2002, 137-142.

Liu, C.-C. and Tsai, P.-J. Content-based retrieval of MP3 music objects. In: *Proceedings of the Tenth International Conference on Information and Knowledge Management*, pp. 506-511. New York, Association for Computing Machinery, 2001.

Liu, W. et al. A media agent for automatically building a personalized semantic index of Web media objects. *Journal of the American Society for Information Science and Technology*, 52, 2001, 853-855.

Liu, Y. & Li, F. Semantic extraction and semantics-based annotation and retrieval for video databases. *Multimedia Tools and Applications*, 17, 2002, 5-20.

Loukopoulos, L. Indexing problems and some of their solutions. *American Documentation*, 17, 1966, 17-25.

Lu, C. et al. TheSys—a comprehensive thesaurus system for intelligent document analysis and text retrieval. In: *Proceedings of Third International Conference on Document Analysis and Recognition*. Volume 2, pp. 1169-1173. Los Alamitos, CA, IEEE Computer Society Press, 1995.

Lu, G. Indexing and retrieval of audio: a survey. *Multimedia Tools and Applications*, 15, 2001, 269-290.

Luhn, H. P. The automatic creation of literature abstracts. *IBM Journal of Research and Development*, 2, 1958, 159-165.

Luhn, H. P. *Keyword-in-Context Index for Technical Literature (KWIC Index)*. Yorktown Heights, NY, IBM Advanced Systems Development Division, 1959.

Luhn, H. P. A statistical approach to mechanized encoding and searching of literary information. *IBM Journal of Research and Development*, 1, 1957, 309-317.

Lunin, L. The development of a machine-searchable index-abstract and its application to biomedical literature. In: *Three Drexel Information Science Research Studies*; ed. by B. Flood, pp. 47-134. Philadelphia, Drexel Press, 1967.

Lynch, C. A. When documents deceive: trust and provenance as new factors for information retrieval in a tangled web. *Journal of the American Society for Information Science and Technology*, 52, 2001, 12-17.

Lynch, M. F. and Petrie, J. H. A program suite for the production of articulated subject indexes. *Computer Journal*, 16, 1973, 46-51.

Ma, W.-Y. and Manjunath, B. S. A texture thesaurus for browsing large aerial photographs. *Journal of the American Society for Information Science*, 49, 1998, 633-648.

Maarek, Y. S. Automatically constructing simple help systems from natural language documentation. In: *Text-Based Intelligent Systems*; ed. by P. S. Jacobs, pp. 243-256. Hillsdale, NJ, Lawrence Erlbaum, 1992.

MacDougall, S. Signposts on the information superhighway: indexes and access. *Journal of Internet Cataloging*, 2(3/4), 2000, 61-79.

MacEwan, A. Where do you keep the dystopias? *Library Association Record*, 99, 1997, 40-41.

Magill, F. N., ed. *Masterplots: 2,010 Plot Stories & Essay Reviews from the World's Fine Literature*. Revised edition. Englewood Cliffs, NJ, Salem Press, 1976.

Magill, F. N. ed. *Masterplots II: American Fiction Series*. Volume 1. Englewood Cliffs, NJ, Salem Press, 1986.

Mai, J.-E. Deconstructing the indexing process. *Advances in Librarianship*, 23, 2000, 269-298.

Mai, J.-E. Semiotics and indexing: an analysis of the subject indexing process. *Journal of Documentation*, 57, 2001, 591-622.

Malone, L. C. et al. Modeling the performance of an automated keywording system. *Information Processing & Management*, 27, 1991, 145-151.

Mani, I. *Automatic Summarization*. Philadelphia, John Benjamins Publishing, 2001a.

Mani, I. Recent developments in text summarization. In: *Proceedings of the Tenth International Conference on Information and Knowledge Management*, pp. 529-531. New York, Association for Computing Machinery, 2001b.

Mani, I. et al. *TIPSTER SUMMAC Text Summarization Evaluation. Final Report.* MTR 98W0000138. McLean, VA, MITRE Corporation, 1998.

Mani, I. et al. Towards content-based browsing of broadcast news video. In: *Intelligent Multimedia Information Retrieval*; ed. by M. T. Maybury, pp. 241-258. Menlo Park, CA, AAAI Press, 1997.

Marchionini, G. et al. Extending retrieval strategies to networked environments: old ways, new ways, and a critical look at WAIS. *Journal of the American Society for Information Science*, 45, 1994, 561-564.

Marcus, R. S. et al. The user interface for the Intrex retrieval system. In: *Interactive Bibliographic Search: the User/Computer Interface*; ed. by D. E. Walker, pp. 159-201. Montvale, NJ, AFIPS Press, 1971.

Markey, K. et al. An analysis of controlled vocabulary and free-text search statements in online searches. *Online Review*, 4, 1980, 225-236.

Markey, K. Interindexer consistency tests: a literature review and report of a test of consistency in indexing visual materials. *Library and Information Science Research*, 6, 1984, 155-177.

Markkula, M. and Sormunen, E. End-user searching challenges indexing practices in the digital newspaper photo archive. *Information Retrieval*, 1, 2000, 259-285.

Maron, M. E. Depth of indexing. *Journal of the American Society for Information Science*, 30, 1979, 224-228.

Maron, M. E. On indexing, retrieval and the meaning of about. *Journal of the American Society for Information Science*, 28, 1977, 38-43

Maron, M. E. Probabilistic design principles for conventional and full-text retrieval systems. *Information Processing & Management*, 24, 1988, 249-250.

Maron, M. E. and Kuhns, J. C. On relevance, probabilistic indexing and information retrieval. *Journal of the Association for Computing Machinery*, 7, 1960, 216-244.

Maron, M. E. et al. *Probabilistic Indexing—a Statistical Technique for Document Identification and Retrieval*. Los Angeles, Thompson Ramo Wooldridge, 1959.

Marques, O. and Furht, B. MUSE: a content-based image search and retrieval system using relevance feedback. *Multimedia Tools and Applications*, 17, 2002, 21-50.

Marshall, C. C. The future of annotation in a digital (paper) world. In: *Successes & Failures of Digital Libraries*; ed. by S. Harum and M. Twidale, pp. 97-117. Urbana-Champaign, University of Illinois, Graduate School of Library and Information Science, 2000.

Martin, W. A. Toward an integral multi-file on-line bibliographic database. *Journal of Information Science*, 2, 1980, 241-253.

Martinez, C. et al. An expert system for machine-aided indexing. *Journal of Chemical Information and Computer Science*, 27, 1987, 158-162.

Martyn, J. Tests on abstracts journals: coverage, overlap, and indexing. *Journal of Documentation*, 23, 1967, 45-70.

Martyn, J. and Slater, M. Tests on abstracts journals. *Journal of Documentation*, 20, 1964, 212-235.

Massey-Burzio, V. The MultiPlatter experience at Brandeis University. *CD-ROM Professional*, 3(3), 1990, 22-26.

Mathis, B. A. *Techniques for the Evaluation and Improvement of Computer-Produced Abstracts*. Columbus, Ohio State University, Computer and Information Science Research Center, 1972. OSU-CISRC-TR-72-15. PB 214 675.

Mathis, B. A. et al. Improvement of automatic abstracts by the use of structural analysis. *Journal of the American Society for Information Science*, 24, 1973, 101-109.

Maybury, M. T. Generating summaries from event data. *Information Processing & Management*, 31, 1995, 735-751.

McCain, K. W. et al. Comparing retrieval performance in online data bases. *Information Processing & Management*, 23, 1987, 539-553.

McCray, A. T. et al. Evaluating UMLS strings for natural language processing. *Proceedings of the 2001 Annual Symposium of the American Medical Informatics Association*, pp. 448-452. Philadelphia, Hanley & Belfus, 2001.

McDermott, J. Another analysis of full-text legal document retrieval. *Law Library Journal*, 78, 1986, 339-343.

McDonald, D. D. Robust partial-parsing through incremental, multi-algorithm processing. In: *Text-Based Intelligent Systems*; ed. by P. S. Jacobs, pp. 83-99. Hillsdale, NJ, Lawrence Erlbaum, 1992.

McDonald, S. et al. Evaluating a content based image retrieval system. *Proceedings of the 24th Annual International ACM SIGIR Conference on Research and Development in Information Retrieval*, pp. 232-240. New York, Association for Computing Machinery, 2001.

McKeown, K. et al. Generating concise natural language summaries. *Information Processing & Management*, 31, 1995, 703-733.

McNab, R. J. et al. Tune retrieval in the multimedia library. *Multimedia Tools and Applications*, 10, 2000, 113-132.

Medeiros, N. et al. Utilizing CORC to develop and maintain access to biomedical Web sites. In: *CORC: New Tools and Possibilities for Cooperative Electronic Resource Description*; ed. by K. Calhoun and J. J. Riemer, pp. 111-121. Binghampton, NY, Haworth Press, 2001.

Mehrotra, R. Content-based image modeling and retrieval. In: *Digital Image Access & Retrieval*; ed. by P. B. Heidorn and B. Sandore, pp. 57-67. Urbana-Champaign, University of Illinois, Graduate School of Library and Information Science, 1997.

Mehrotra, R. and Gary, J. E. Similar-shape retrieval in shape data management. *Computer*, 28(9), 1995, 57-62.

Mehtre, B. M. et al. Content-based image retrieval using a composite color-shape approach. *Information Processing & Management*, 34, 1998, 109-120.

Mehtre, B. M. et al. Shape measures for content based image retrieval: a comparison. *Information Processing & Management*, 33, 1997, 319-337.

Melucci, M. An evaluation of automatically constructed hypertexts for information retrieval. *Information Retrieval*, 1, 1999, 91-114.

Meng, W. et al. Concept hierarchy-based text database categorization. *Knowledge and Information Systems*, 4, 2002, 132-150.

Methods for Examining Documents, Determining Their Subjects, and Selecting Indexing Terms. Geneva, International Organization for Standardization, 1985. ISO 5963-1985 (E).

Milstead, J. L. *Subject Access Systems: Alternatives in Design*. Orlando, Academic Press, 1984.

Milstead, J. L. and Feldman, S. Metadata: cataloging by any other name ..., *Online, 26(1)*, 1999, 66-74.

Mintz, A. P., ed. *Web of Deception: Misinformation on the Internet*. Medford,NJ, Information Today, 2002.

Missingham, R. Indexing the Internet: pinning jelly to the wall? *LASIE*, 27(3), 1996, 32-42.

Mitchell, S. and Mooney, M. INFOMINE. In: *The Amazing Internet Challenge*; ed. by A. T. Wells et al., pp. 97-120. Chicago, American Library Association, 1999.

Mizzaro, S. Relevance: the whole history. In: *Historical Studies in Information Science*; ed. by T. B. Hahn and M. Buckland, pp. 221-244. Medford, NJ, Information Today, 1998.

Moens, M.-F. *Automatic Indexing and Abstracting of Document Texts*. Boston, Kluwer, 2000.

Moens, M.-F. and Dumortier, J. Text categorization: the assignment of subject descriptors to magazine articles. *Information Processing & Management*, 36, 2000a, 841-861.

Moens, M.-F. and Dumortier, J. Use of a text grammar for generating highlight abstracts of magazine articles. *Journal of Documentation*, 56, 2000b, 520-539.

Moens, M.-F. et al. Information extraction from legal texts: the potential of discourse analysis. *International Journal of Human-Computer Studies*, 51, 1999, 1155-1171.

Moghaddam, B. et al. Regions-of-interest and spatial layout for content-based image retrieval. *Multimedia Tools and Applications*, 14, 2001, 201-210.

Montague, B. A. Testing, comparison and evaluation of recall, relevance and cost of coordinate indexing with links and roles. *American Documentation*, 16, 1965, 201-208.

Montgomery, R. R. An indexing coverage study of toxicological literature. *Journal of Chemical Documentation*, 13, 1973, 41-44.

Moreno, P. J. et al. From multimedia retrieval to knowledge management. *Computer*, 35(4), 2002, 58-59, 62-66.

Mostafa, J. Digital image representation and access. *Annual Review of Information Science and Technology*, 29, 1994, 91-135.

Mostafa, J. and Dillon, A. Design and evaluation of a user interface supporting multiple image query models. *Proceedings of the American Society for Information Science*, 33, 1996, 52-57.

Mowshowitz, A. and Kawaguchi, A. Bias on the Web. *Communications of the ACM*, 45(9), 2002, 56-60.

Muddamalle, M. R. Natural language versus controlled vocabulary in information retrieval: a case study in soil mechanics. *Journal of the American Society for Information Science*, 49, 1998, 881-887.

Mullison, W. R. et al. Comparing indexing efficiency, effectiveness, and consistency with or without the use of roles. *Proceedings of the American Society for Information Science*, 6, 1969, 301-311.

Mulvany, N. C. *Indexing Books*. Chicago, University of Chicago Press, 1994.

Munakata, T., ed. Knowledge discovery. *Communications of the ACM*, 42(11), 1999, 26-67.

Myers, J. M. Computers and the searching of law texts in England and North America: a review of the state of the art. *Journal of Documentation*, 29, 1973, 212-228.

Nakamura, Y. et al. Diagram understanding utilizing natural language text. In: *Proceedings of the Second International Conference on Document Analysis and Recognition*, pp. 614-618. Los Alamitos, CA, IEEE Computer Society Press, 1993.

Nam, J. and Tewfik, A. H. Event-driven video extraction and visualization. *Multimedia Tools and Applications*, 16, 2002, 55-77.

Nasukawa, T. and Nagano, T. Text analysis and knowledge mining system. *IBM Systems Journal*, 40, 2001, 967-984.

Nielsen, H. J. The nature of fiction and its significance for classification and indexing. *Information Services & Use*, 17, 1997, 171-181.

Nomoto, T. and Matsumoto, Y. A new approach to unsupervised text summarization. *Proceedings of the 24th Annual International ACM SIGIR Conference on Research and Development in Information Retrieval*, pp. 26-34. New York, Association for Computing Machinery, 2001.

Oakman, R. L. The evolution of intelligent writing assistants: trends and future prospects. In: *Proceedings* (of the) *Sixth International Conference on Tools With Artificial Intelligence*, pp. 233-234. Los Alamitos, CA, IEEE Computer Society Press, 1994.

O'Connor, B. C. *Explorations in Indexing and Abstracting: Pointing, Virtue, and Power.* Englewood, CO, Libraries Unlimited, 1996.

O'Connor, B. C. et al. User reactions as access mechanism: an exploration based on captions for images. *Journal of the American Society for Information Science*, 50, 1999, 681-697.

O'Connor, J. Automatic subject recognition in scientific papers: an empirical study. *Journal of the Association for Computing Machinery*, 12, 1965, 490-515.

O'Connor, J. G. and Meadows, A. J. *Physics Abstracts* as a source of abstracts in astronomy. *Journal of Documentation*, 2, 1968, 107-112.

Odlyzko, A. M. Abstracting and reviewing in the digital era. *NFAIS Newsletter*, 41(6), 1999, 85, 90-92.

Odlyzko, A. M. Tragic loss or good riddance? The impending demise of traditional scholarly journals. *International Journal of Human-Computer Studies*, 42, 1995, 71-122.

Ogle, V. E. and Stonebraker, M. Chabot: retrieval from a relational database of images. *Computer*, 28(9), 1995, 40-48.

Oh, S. G. Document representation and retrieval using empirical facts. *Journal of the American Society for Information Science*, 49, 1998, 920-931.

Ojala, M. Web content extraction. *EContent*, 25(4), 2002, 39-41.

Olafsen, T. and Vokac, L. Authors' reply to R. Moss. *Journal of the American Society for Information Science*, 34, 1983, 294.

Olason, S. C. Let's get usable: usability studies for indexes. *The Indexer*, 22, 2000, 91-95.

Olderr, S. *Olderr's Fiction Subject Headings: a Supplement and Guide to the LC Thesaurus.* Chicago, American Library Association, 1991.

Oliver, D. E. and Altman, R. B. Extraction of SNOMED concepts from medical record texts. In: *Eighteenth Annual Symposium on Computer Applications in Medical Care*, pp. 179-183. Philadelphia, Hanley & Belfus, 1994.

Oliver, L. H. et al. *An Investigation of the Basic Processes Involved in the Manual Indexing of Scientific Documents.* Bethesda, MD, General Electric Co., Information Systems Operation, 1966. PB 169 415.

Olson, H. A. and Boll, J. J. *Subject Analysis in Online Catalogs.* Second edition. Englewood, CO, Libraries Unlimited, 2001.

O'Neill, E. T. and Aluri, R. Library of Congress subject heading patterns in OCLC monographic records. *Library Resources & Technical Services*, 25, 1981, 63-80.

O'Neill, E. T. et al. Web characterization project: an analysis of metadata usage on the Web. *Journal of Library Administration*, 34, 2001, 359-374. This article originally appeared in the *Annual Review of OCLC Research 1988*, the full text of which is available online from <http://www.oclc.org/research/publications/arr/>

Onyshkevych, B. Issues and methodology for template design for information extraction. In: *Proceedings of the Human Language Technology Workshop, March 8-11, 1994*, pp. 171-176. San Francisco, Morgan Kaufmann, 1994.

Oppenheim, C. The patents coverage of *Chemical Abstracts. Information Scientist*, 8, 1974, 133-138.

Oppenheim, C. et al. The evaluation of WWW search engines. *Journal of Documentation*, 56, 2000, 190-211.

Orbach, B. So that others may see: tools for cataloging still images. *Cataloging & Classification Quarterly*, 11(3/4), 1990, 163-191.

Ornager, S. The image database: a need for innovative indexing and retrieval. *Advances in Knowledge Organization*, 4, 1994, 208-216.

Ornager, S. Image retrieval: theoretical analysis and empirical user studies on accessing information in images. *Proceedings of the American Society for Information Science*, 34, 1997, 202-211.

Oswald, V. A., Jr. et al. *Automatic Indexing and Abstracting of the Contents of Documents*. Los Angeles, Planning Research Corporation, 1959. RADC-TR-59-208.

Over, P. The TREC interactive track: an annotated bibliography. *Information Processing & Management*, 37, 2001, 369-381.

Owen, P. Structured for success: the continuing role of quality indexing in intelligent information retrieval systems. In: *Online Information 94*, pp. 227-231. Medford, NJ, Learned Information, 1994.

Ozaki, K. et al. Semantic retrieval on art museum database system. In: (Proceedings of the) *1996 IEEE International Conference on Systems, Man and Cybernetics*, pp. 2108-2112. Piscataway, NJ, Institute of Electrical and Electronics Engineers, 1996.

Paice, C. D. The automatic generation of literature abstracts: an approach based on the identification of self-indicating phrases. In: *Information Retrieval Research*; ed. by R. N. Oddy et al., pp. 172-191. London, Butterworths, 1981.

Paice, C. D. and Jones, P. A. The identification of important concepts in highly structured technical papers. In: *SIGIR-93: Proceedings of the Sixteenth Annual International ACM SIGIR Conference on Research and Development in Information Retrieval*, pp. 69-78. New York, Association for Computing Machinery, 1993.

Pao, M. L. Term and citation searching: a preliminary report. *Proceedings of the American Society for Information Science*, 25, 1988, 177-180.

Pao, M. L. and Worthen, D. B. Retrieval effectiveness by semantic and citation searching. *Journal of the American Society for Information Science*, 40, 1989, 226-235.

Patel, N. V. and Sethi, I. K. Audio characterization for video indexing. In: *Storage and Retrieval for Still Image and Video Databases IV*; ed. by I. K. Sethi and R. C. Jain, pp. 373-384. Bellingham, WA, International Society for Optical Engineering, 1996.

Patel, N. V. and Sethi, I. K. Video classification using speaker identification. In: *Storage and Retrieval for Image and Video Databases V*; ed. by I. K. Sethi and R. C. Jain, pp. 218-225. Bellingham, WA, International Society for Optical Engineering, 1997.

Patrick, T. B. et al. Text indexing of images based on graphical image content. *Proceedings of the American Society for Information Science*, 36, 1999, 675-680.

Payne, D. et al. *A Textual Abstracting Technique: a Preliminary Development and Evaluation Support*. Pittsburgh, Americans Institutes for Research, 1962. 2 volumes. AD 285081-285082.

Pazienza, M. T., ed. *Information Extraction*. New York, Springer-Verlag, 1999.

Pejtersen, A. M. Design of a computer-aided user-system dialogue based on an analysis of users' search behaviour. *Social Science Information Studies*, 4, 1984, 167-183.

Pejtersen, A. M. A framework for indexing and representation of information based on work domain analysis: a fiction classification example. *Advances in Knowledge Organization*, 4, 1994, 251-263.

Pejtersen, A. M. The meaning of "about" in fiction indexing and retrieval. *Aslib Proceedings*, 31, 1979, 251-257.

Pejtersen, A. M. New model for multimedia interfaces to online public access catalogues. *Electronic Library*, 10, 1992, 359-366.

Pejtersen, A. M. and Austin, J. Fiction retrieval: experimental design and evaluation of a search system based on users' value criteria. *Journal of Documentation*, 39, 1983, 230-246; 40, 1984, 25-35.

Pentland, A. Machine understanding of human behavior in video. In: *Intelligent Multimedia Information Retrieval*; ed. by M. T. Maybury, pp. 175-188. Menlo Park, CA, AAAI Press, 1997.

Pereira, F. C. N. and Grosz, B. J. *Natural Language Processing*. Cambridge, MA, MIT Press, 1994.

Perez, E. Text enhancement: controlled vocabulary vs. free text. *Special Libraries*, 73, 1982, 183-192.

Perrone, M. P. Machine learning in a multimedia document retrieval framework. *IBM Systems Journal*, 41, 2002, 494-503.

Perry, J. W. and Kent, A. *Tools for Machine Literature Searching*. New York, Interscience Publishers Inc., 1958.

Petrarca, A. E. and Lay, W. M. The double-KWIC coordinate index: a new approach for preparation of high-quality printed indexes by automatic indexing techniques. *Journal of Chemical Documentation*, 9, 1969, 256-261.

Picard, R. W. A society of models for video and image libraries. *IBM Systems Journal*, 35, 1996, 292-312.

Picard, R. W. and Minka, T. P. Vision texture for annotation. *Multimedia Systems*, 3, 1995, 3-14.

Pickens, J. Feature selection for polyphonic music retrieval. *Proceedings of the 24th Annual International ACM SIGIR Conference on Research and Development in Information Retrieval*, pp. 428-429. New York, Association for Computing Machinery, 2001.

Pinto, M. Documentary abstracting: toward a methodological model. *Journal of the American Society for Information Science*, 46, 1995, 225-234.

Pinto, M. Interdisciplinary approaches to the concept and practice of written text documentary content analysis (WTDCA). *Journal of Documentation*, 50, 1994, 111-133.

Pinto, M. *El resumen documental*. Second edition. Madrid, Fundación Germán Sánchez Ruipérez, 2001.

Pinto, M. and Gálvez, C. Paradigms for abstracting systems. *Journal of Information Science*, 25, 1999, 365-380.

Pinto, M. and Lancaster, F. W. Abstracts and abstracting in knowledge discovery. *Library Trends*, 48, 1999, 234-248.

Piternick, A. Searching vocabularies: a developing category of online search tools. *Online Review*, 8, 1984, 441-449.

Pitkin, R. M. and Branagan, M. A. Can the accuracy of abstracts be improved by providing specific instructions? *Journal of the American Medical Association (JAMA)*, 280, 1998, 267-269.

Pitkin, R. M. et al. Accuracy of data in abstracts of published research articles. *Journal of the American Medical Association (JAMA)*, 281, 1999, 1110-1111.

Pitkin, R. M. et al. Effectiveness of journal intervention to improve abstract quality. *Journal of the American Medical Association (JAMA)*, 283, 2000, 481.

Place, E. Social Science Information Gateway (SOSIG). In: *The Amazing Internet Challenge*; ed. by A. T. Wells et al., pp. 223-244. Chicago, American Library Association, 1999.

Plaunt, C. and Norgard, B. A. An association-based method for automatic indexing with a controlled vocabulary. *Journal of the American Society for Information Science*, 49, 1998, 888-902.

Pozzi, S. and Celentano, A. Knowledge-based document filing. *IEEE Expert*, 8(5), 1993, 34-45.

Prabha, C. The large retrieval phenomenon. *Advances in Library Automation and Networking*, 4, 1991, 55-92.

Preschel, B. M. *Funk & Wagnalls New Encyclopedia* Indexing Manual. New York, Funk & Wagnall, 1981. (Unpublished)

Preschel, B. M. *Indexer Consistency in Perception of Concepts and in Choice of Terminology*. New York, Columbia University, School of Library Service, 1972.

Price, D. S. Possible impact of electronic publishing on abstracting and indexing. *Journal of the American Society for Information Science*, 34, 1983, 288.

Price, R. et al. Applying relevance feedback to a photo archival system. *Journal of Information Science*, 18, 1992, 203-215.

Proceedings of the Third International Conference on Document Analysis and Recognition. Los Alamitos, CA, IEEE Computer Society Press, 1995. 2 volumes.

Qin, J. Semantic similarities between a keyword database and a controlled vocabulary database. *Journal of the American Society for Information Science*, 51, 2000, 166-180.

Qin, J. and Norton, M., eds. Knowledge discovery in bibliographic databases. *Library Trends*, 48(1), 1999 (entire issue).

Ragusa, J. M. and Turban, E. Integrating expert systems and multimedia: a review of the literature. *International Journal of Applied Expert Systems*, 2(1), 1994, 54-71.

Raitt, D. Recall and precision devices in interactive bibliographic search and retrieval systems. *Aslib Proceedings*, 32, 1980, 281-301.

Rajagopalan, R. The Figure Understander: a tool for the integration of text and graphical input to a knowledge base. In: *Proceedings* (of the) *Sixth International Conference on Tools With Artificial Intelligence*, pp. 80-87. Los Alamitos, CA, IEEE Computer Society Press, 1994.

Ramsey, M. C. et al. A collection of visual thesauri for browsing large collections of geographic images. *Journal of the American Society for Information Science*, 50, 1999, 826-834.

Ranta, J. A. The new literary scholarship and a basis for increased subject catalog access to imaginative literature. *Cataloging & Classification Quarterly*, 14(1), 1991, 3-26.

Rapoza, J. A smart way to put help on the Web. *PC Week*, 13(39), 1996, 93.

Rasheed, M. A. Comparative index terms. *International Library Review*, 21, 1989, 289-300.

Rasmussen, E. M. Indexing images. *Annual Review of Information Science and Technology*, 32, 1997, 169-196.

Rath, G. J. et al. Comparison of four types of lexical indicators of content. *American Documentation*, 12, 1961a, 126-130.

Rath, G. J. et al. The formation of abstracts by the selection of sentences. *American Documentation*, 12, 1961b, 139-143.

Ravela, S. and Luo, C. Appearance-based global similarity retrieval of images. In: *Advances in Information Retrieval*; ed. by W. B. Croft, pp. 267-303. Boston, Kluwer, 2000.

Reamy, T. Auto-categorization—coming to a library or intranet near you! *EContent*, 25(11), 2002, 16-22.

Reich, P. and Biever, E. J. Indexing consistency: the input/output function of thesauri. *College & Research Libraries*, 52, 1991, 336-342.

Reisner, P. *Evaluation of a "Growing" Thesaurus*. Yorktown Heights, NY, IBM, Thomas Watson Research Center, 1966. Research Paper RD-1662.

Resnick, A. Relative effectiveness of document titles and abstracts for determining relevance of documents. *Science*, 134, 1961, 1004-1006.

Resnikoff, H. L. and Dolby, J. L. *Access: a Study of Information Storage and Retrieval with Emphasis on Library Information Systems*. 1972. ERIC Document ED 060 921.

Ribeiro-Neto, B. et al. An experimental study in automatically categorizing medical documents. *Journal of the American Society for Information Science and Technology*, 52, 2001, 391-401.

Rickman, R. M. and Stonham, T. J. Image retrieval from large databases using a neural network coding scheme. In: *The Structuring of Information: Informatics II*; ed. by K. P. Jones, pp. 147-159. London, Aslib, 1991.

Riloff, E. and Lehnert, W. Automated dictionary construction for information extraction from text. In: (Proceedings of the) *Ninth Conference on Artificial Intelligence for Applications*, pp. 93-99. Los Alamitos, CA, IEEE Computer Society Press, 1993.

Rindflesch, T. C. and Aronson, A. R. Ambiguity resolution while mapping free text to the UMLS metathesaurus. In: *Eighteenth Annual Symposium on Computer Applications in Medical Care*, pp. 240-244. Philadelphia, Hanley & Belfus, 1994.

Rindflesch, T. C. et al. EDGAR: extraction of drugs, genes and relations from the biomedical literature. *Pacific Symposium on Biocomputing*, 5, 2000a, 514-525.

Rindflesch, T. C. et al. Extracting molecular binding relationships from biomedical text. *Proceedings of the Sixth Conference on Applied Natural Language Processing*, pp. 188-195. San Francisco, Morgan Kaufmann, 2000b.

Rindflesch, T. C. et al. Mining molecular binding terminology from biomedical text. *Proceedings of the 1999 Annual Symposium of the American Medical Informatics Association*, pp. 127-131. Philadelphia, Hanley & Belfus, 1999.

Ro, J. S. An evaluation of the applicability of ranking algorithms to improve the effectiveness of full-text retrieval. 1. On the effectiveness of full-text retrieval. *Journal of the American Society for Information Science*, 39, 1988, 73-78.

Roberts, D. and Souter, C. The automation of controlled vocabulary subject indexing of medical journal articles. *Aslib Proceedings*, 52, 2000, 384-400.

Robertson, S. E. Introduction to the special issue: overview of the TREC routing and filtering tasks. *Information Retrieval*, 5, 2002, 127-137.

Robertson, S. E. The parametric description of retrieval tests. *Journal of Documentation*, 25, 1969, 1-27, 93-107.

Robinson, J. and Hu, M. DOE's Energy Database (EDB) versus other energy related databases: a comparative analysis. *Database*, 4(4), 1981, 10-27.

Rodgers, D. J. *A Study of Inter-Indexer Consistency.* Washington, DC, General Electric Co., 1961.

Rolling, L. Indexing consistency, quality and efficiency. *Information Processing & Management*, 17, 1981, 69-76.

Rowe, N. C. Inferring depictions in natural-language captions for efficient access to picture data. *Information Processing & Management*, 30, 1994, 379-388.

Rowe, N. C. *Precise and Efficient Access to Captioned Picture Libraries: the MARIE Project.* Monterey, CA, Naval Postgraduate School, Computer Science Department, 1996.

Rowe, N. C. and Frew, B. Automatic caption localization for photographs on World Wide Web pages. *Information Processing & Management*, 34, 1998, 95-107.

Rowe, N. C. and Frew, B. Automatic classification of objects in captioned depictive photographs for retrieval. In: *Intelligent Multimedia Information Retrieval*; ed. by M. Maybury, pp. 65-79. Palo Alto, CA, AAAI Press, 1997.

Rowe, N. C. and Guglielmo, E. J. Exploiting captions in retrieval of multimedia data. *Information Processing & Management*, 29, 1993, 453-461.

Runde, C. E. and Lindberg, W. H. The curse of Thamus: a response. *Law Library Journal*, 78, 1986, 345-347.

Rush, J. E. et al. Automatic abstracting and indexing. II. Production of indicative abstracts by application of contextual inference and syntactic coherence criteria. *Journal of the American Society for Information Science*, 22, 1971, 260-274.

Saarti, J. Consistency of subject indexing of novels by public library professionals and patrons. *Journal of Documentation*, 58, 2002, 49-65.

Saarti, J. Fiction indexing and the development of fiction thesauri. *Journal of Librarianship and Information Science*, 31, 1999, 85-92.

Saarti, J. Fiction indexing by library professionals and users. *Scandinavian Public Library Quarterly*, 33(4), 2000a, 6-9.

Saarti, J. Taxonomy of novel abstracts based on empirical findings. *Knowledge Organization*, 27, 2000b, 213-220.

Saggion, H. and Lapalme, G. Selective analysis for the automatic generation of summaries. In: *Dynamism and Stability in Knowledge Organization*; ed. by C. Beghtol et al., pp. 176-181. Würzburg, ERGON Verlag, 2000.

Salager-Meyer, F. Medical English abstracts: how well are they structured? *Journal of the American Society for Information Science*, 42, 1991, 528-531.

Salisbury, B. A., Jr. and Stiles, H. E. The use of the B-coefficient in information retrieval. *Proceedings of the American Society for Information Science*, 6, 1969, 265-268.

Salton, G. Another look at automatic text-retrieval systems. *Communications of the ACM*, 29, 1986, 648-656.

Salton, G. *Dynamic Information and Library Processing.* Englewood Cliffs, NJ, Prentice-Hall, 1975.

Salton, G. A new comparison between conventional indexing (MEDLARS) and automatic text processing (SMART). *Journal of the American Society for Information Science*, 23, 1972, 75-84.

Salton, G. *A Syntactic Approach to Automatic Book Indexing.* Ithaca, NY, Cornell University, Department of Computer Science, 1989. Technical Report TR 89-979.

Salton, G. and Buckley, C. Automatic text structuring experiments. In: *Text-Based Intelligent Systems*; ed. by P. S. Jacobs, pp. 199-210. Hillsdale, NJ, Lawrence Erlbaum, 1992.

Salton, G. and McGill, M. J. *Introduction to Modern Information Retrieval.* New York, McGraw Hill, 1983.

Salton, G. and Zhang, Y. Enhancement of text representations using related document titles. *Information Processing & Management*, 22, 1986, 385-394.

Salton, G. et al. Automatic text structuring and summarization. *Information Processing & Management*, 33, 1997, 193-207.

Santini, S. Using language more responsibly. *Computer, 35(12)*, 2002, 126-128.

Sapp, G. The levels of access: subject approaches to fiction. *RQ*, 25, 1986, 488-497.

Saracevic, T. Comparative effects of titles, abstracts and full texts on relevance judgements. *Proceedings of the American Society for Information Science*, 6, 1969, 293-299.

Saracevic, T. et al. Letter to the editor. *Information Processing & Management*, 39, 2003, 153-156.

Saracevic, T. et al. A study of information seeking and retrieving. *Journal of the American Society for Information Science*, 39, 1988, 161-216.

Šauperl, A. *Subject Determination during the Cataloging Process.* Lanham, MD, Scarecrow Press, 2002.

Savić, D. Automatic classification of office documents: review of available methods and techniques. *Records Management Quarterly*, 29(4), 1995, 3-6, 8-18.

Savoy, J. A new probabilistic scheme for information retrieval in hypertext. *New Review of Hypermedia and Multimedia*, 1, 1995, 107-134.

Schiffman, B. et al. Producing biographical summaries. *Proceedings of the 39th Annual Meeting of the Association for Computational Linguistics,* pp. 450-457. New Brunswick, NJ, Association for Computational Linguistics, 2001.

Schreiber, A. Th. et al. Ontology-based photo annotation. *IEEE Intelligent Systems,* 16(3), 2001, 66-74.

Schroeder, K. A. Layered indexing of images. *The Indexer*, 21, 1998, 11-14.

Schwartz, C. Web search engines. *Journal of the American Society for Information Science*, 49, 1998, 973-982.

Scott, D. W. Museum Data Bank research report. *Library Trends*, 37, 1988, 130-141.

Sekerak, R. J. A comparison of journal coverage in *Psychological Abstracts* and the primary health sciences indexes: implications for cooperative serials acquisition and retention. *Bulletin of the Medical Library Association*, 74, 1986, 231-233.

Seloff, G. A. Automated access to the NASA-JSC image archives. *Library Trends*, 38, 1990, 682-696.

Selye, H. *Symbolic Shorthand System.* New Brunswick, N.J., Rutgers State University, Graduate School of Library Service, 1966.

Selye, H. and Ember, G. *Symbolic Shorthand System for Physiology and Medicine.* Fourth edition. Montreal, Université de Montreal, 1964.

Semeraro, G. et al. Learning contextual rules for document understanding. In: *Proceedings* (of the) *Tenth Conference on Artificial Intelligence for Applications*, pp. 108-115. Los Alamitos, CA, IEEE Computer Society Press, 1994.

Shafer, K. E. Evaluating Scorpion results. *Journal of Library Administration*, 34, 2001, 237-244.

Shafer, K. E. Scorpion helps catalog the Web. *Bulletin of the American Society for Information Science*, 24(1), 1997, 28-29.

Sharp, J. R. The SLIC index. *American Documentation*, 17, 1966, 41-44.

Shatford, S. Analyzing the subject of a picture: a theoretical approach. *Cataloging & Classification Quarterly*, 6(3), 1986, 39-62.

Shaw, W. M., Jr. An investigation of document partitions. *Information Processing & Management*, 22, 1986, 19-28.

Shaw, W. M., Jr. An investigation of document structures. *Information Processing & Management*, 26, 1990a, 339-348.

Shaw, W. M., Jr. Subject indexing and citation indexing. *Information Processing & Management*, 26, 1990b, 693-718.

Shirey, D. L. and Kurfeerst, M. Relevance predictability: II. Data reduction. In: *Electronic Handling of Information: Testing and Evaluation*; ed. by A. Kent et al., pp. 187-198. Washington, DC, Thompson Book Co., 1967.

Shneiderman, B. The limits of speech recognition. *Communications of the ACM*, 43(9), 2000, 63-65.

Shuldberg, H. K. et al. Distilling information from text: the EDS TemplateFiller system. *Journal of the American Society for Information Science*, 44, 1993, 493-507.

Sievert, M. and McKinin, E. J. Why full-text misses some relevant documents: an analysis of documents not retrieved by CCML or MEDIS. *Proceedings of the American Society for Information Science*, 26, 1989, 34-39.

Sievert, M. et al. Retrieval from full-text medical literature: the dream & the reality. In: *Fifteenth Annual Symposium on Computer Applications in Medical Care*, pp, 348-352. New York, McGraw Hill, 1992.

Silvester, J. P. Computer supported indexing. In: *Encyclopedia of Library and Information Science*. Volume 61, Supplement 24, pp. 76-90. New York, Marcel Dekker, 1998.

Silvester, J. P. et al. Machine-aided indexing at NASA. *Information Processing & Management*, 30, 1994, 631-645.

Silvester, J. P. et al. *Machine Aided Indexing from Natural Language Text. Status Report*. Linthicum Heights, MD, RMS Associates, 1993. NASA-CR-4512.

Singhal, A. and Pereira, F. Document expansion for speech retrieval. *Proceedings of the 22nd International Conference on Research and Development in Information Retrieval*, pp. 34-41. New York, Association for Computing Machinery, 1999.

Sinnett, J. D. *An Evaluation of Links and Roles Used in Information Retrieval*. Dayton, Air Force Materials Laboratory, Wright Patterson Air Force Base, 1964. AD 432 198.

Slamecka, V. and Jacoby, J. *Effect of Indexing Aids on the Reliability of Indexers. Final Technical Note*. Bethesda, MD, Documentation Inc., 1963. RADC-TDR-63- 116.

Small, H. Co-citation in the scientific literature: a new measure of the relationship between two documents. *Journal of the American Society for Information Science*, 24, 1973, 265-269.

Smalley, T. N. Comparing *Psychological Abstracts* and *Index Medicus* for coverage of the journal literature in a subject area in psychology. *Journal of the American Society for Information Science*, 31, 1980, 143-146.

Smeaton, A. F. Using NLP or NLP resources for information retrieval tasks. In: *Natural Language Information Retrieval*; ed. by T. Strzalkowski, pp. 99-111. Boston, Kluwer, 1999.

Smith, F. J. et al. Voice access to BLAISE. In: *Online Information 89*, pp. 1-12. Medford, NJ, Learned Information, 1989.

Smith, G. L. Generation of electronic product documentation. In: *Innovative Applications of Artificial Intelligence 2*; ed. by A. Rappaport and R. Smith, pp. 189-200. Cambridge, MA, MIT Press, 1991.

Smith, J. R. and Chang, S.-F. An image and video search engine for the World-Wide Web. In: *Storage and Retrieval for Image and Video Databases V*; ed. by I. K. Sethi and R. C. Jain, pp. 84-95. Bellingham, WA, International Society for Optical Engineering, 1997a.

Smith, J. R. and Chang, S.-F. Querying by color regions using the VisualSEEK content-based visual query system. In: *Intelligent Multimedia Information Retrieval*; ed. by M. T. Maybury, pp. 23-41. Menlo Park, CA, AAAI Press, 1997b.

Sneiderman, C. A. et al. Identification of anatomical terminology in medical text. *Proceedings of the 1998 Annual Symposium of the American Medical Informatics Association*, pp. 428-432. Philadelphia, Hanley & Belfus, 1998.

Snow, B. et al. Grateful MED: NLM's front end software. *Database*, 9(6), 1986, 94-99.

Soergel, D. *Indexing Languages and Thesauri: Construction and Maintenance*. Los Angeles, Melville, 1974.

Soergel, D. *Organizing Information: Principles of Data Base and Retrieval Systems*. Orlando, Academic Press, 1985.

Soergel, D. The rise of ontologies or the reinvention of classification. *Journal of the American Society for Information Science*, 50, 1999, 1119-1120.

Solov'ev, V. I. The aspective method of abstracting. *Automatic Documentation and Mathematical Linguistics*, 5(1), 1971, 30-35. (English translation of *Nauchno-Tekhnicheskaya Informatsiya*, Seriya 2, Number 2, 1971, pp. 14-17.)

Solov'ev, V. I. Functional characteristics of the author's abstract of a dissertation and the specifics of writing it. *Scientific and Technical Information Processing*, 3, 1981, 80-88. (English translation of *Nauchno-Tekhnicheskaya Informatsiya*, Seriya 1, Number 6, 1981, pp. 20-24.)

Sparck Jones, K. Does indexing exhaustivity matter? *Journal of the American Society for Information Science*, 24, 1973, 313-316.

Sparck Jones, K. Letter to the editor. *Information Processing & Management*, 39, 2003, 156-159.

Sparck Jones, K. Reflections on TREC. *Information Processing & Management*, 31(3), 1995, 291-314.

Sparck Jones, K. What is the role of NLP in text retrieval? In: *Natural Language Information Retrieval*; ed. by T. Strzalkowski, pp. 1-24. Boston, Kluwer, 1999.

Spinellis, D. The decay and failures of Web references. *Computer*, 46(1), 2003, 71-77.

Srihari, R. K. Automatic indexing and content-based retrieval of captioned images. *Computer*, 28(9), 1995a, 49-56.

Srihari, R. K. Automatic indexing and content-based retrieval of captioned photographs. In: *Proceedings of Third International Conference on Document Analysis and Recognition*. Volume 2, pp. 1165-1167. Los Alamitos, CA, IEEE Computer Society Press, 1995b.

Srihari, R. K. Intelligent document understanding: understanding photographs with captions. In: *Proceedings of the Second International Conference on Document Analysis and Recognition*, pp. 664-667. Los Alamitos, CA, IEEE Computer Society Press, 1993.

Srihari, R. K. Using speech input for image interpretation, annotation, and retrieval. In: *Digital Image Access & Retrieval*; ed. by P. B. Heidorn and B. Sandore, pp. 140-156. Urbana-Champaign, University of Illinois, Graduate School of Library and Information Science, 1997.

Srinavasan, P. et al. An investigation of indexing on the WWW. *Proceedings of the American Society for Information Science*, 33, 1996, 79-83.

Srinavasan, S. and Brown, E. W. Is speech recognition becoming mainstream? *Computer*, 35(4), 2002, 38-41.

Srinavasan, S. and Petkovic, D. Phonetic confusion matrix-based spoken document retrieval. *Proceedings of the 23rd Annual International ACM SIGIR Conference on Research and Development in Information Retrieval*, pp. 81-87. New York, Association for Computing Machinery, 2001.

Stanfill, C. and Waltz, D. L. Statistical methods, artificial intelligence, and information retrieval. In: *Text-Based Intelligent Systems*; ed. by P. S. Jacobs, pp. 215-225. Hillsdale, NJ, Lawrence Erlbaum, 1992.

Stiles, H. E. Machine retrieval using the association factor. In: *Machine Indexing: Progress and Problems*, pp. 192-206. Washington, DC, American University, 1961.

Stock, O. ALFRESCO: enjoying the combination of natural language processing and hypermedia for information exploration. In: *Intelligent Multimedia Interfaces*; ed. by M. T. Maybury, pp. 197-224. Cambridge, MA, MIT Press, 1993.

Stock, O. et al. Explorations in an environment for natural-language multimodal information access. In: *Intelligent Multimedia Information Retrieval*; ed. by M. T. Maybury, pp. 381-398. Menlo Park, CA, AAAI Press, 1997.

Strzalkowski, T. et al. Evaluating natural language processing techniques in information retrieval. In: *Natural Language Information Retrieval*; ed. by T. Strzalkowski, pp. 113-145. Boston, Kluwer, 1999.

Stubbs, E. A. et al. Internal quality audit of indexing: a new application of interindexer consistency. *Cataloging and Classification Quarterly*, 28(4), 1999, 53-69.

Studwell, W. E. USE, the Universal Subject Environment: a new subject access approach in the time of the Internet. *Journal of Internet Cataloging*, 2(3/4), 1998, 197-209.

Su, L. T. and Chen, H-l. Evaluation of Web search engines by undergraduate students. *Proceedings of the American Society for Information Science*, 36, 1999, 98-114.

Sundheim, B. M. Overview of results of the MUC-6 evaluation. In: *Proceedings of the Sixth Message Understanding Conference (MUC-6)*, pp. 13-31. San Francisco, Morgan Kaufmann, 1995.

Sutcliffe, A. et al. Empirical studies in multimedia information retrieval. In: *Intelligent Multimedia Information Retrieval*; ed. by M. T. Maybury, pp. 449-471. Menlo Park, CA, AAAI Press, 1997.

Sutton, S. A. Conceptual design and deployment of a metadata framework for educational resources on the Internet. *Journal of the American Society for Information Science*, 50, 1999, 1182-1192.

Svenonius, E. Access to nonbook materials: the limits of subject indexing for visual and aural languages. *Journal of the American Society for Information Science*, 45, 1994, 600-606.

Swanson, D. R. Medical literature as a potential source of new knowledge. *Bulletin of the Medical Library Association*, 78, 1990, 29-37.

Swanson, D. R. Searching natural language text by computer. *Science*, 132, 3434, 1960, 1099-1104.

Swanson, D. R. Subjective versus objective relevance in bibliographic retrieval systems. *Library Quarterly*, 56, 1986, 389-398.

Swift, D. F. et al. 'Aboutness' as a strategy for retrieval in the social sciences. *Aslib Proceedings*, 30, 1978, 182-187.

Taddio, A. et al. Quality of nonstructured and structured abstracts of original research articles in the *British Medical Journal*, the *Canadian Medical Association Journal*

431

and the *Journal of the American Medical Association*. *Canadian Medical Association Journal*, 150, 1994, 1611-1615.

Takeshita, A. et al. Topic-based multimedia structuring. In: *Intelligent Multimedia Information Retrieval*; ed. by M. T. Maybury, pp. 259-277. Menlo Park, CA, AAAI Press, 1997.

Tancredi, S. A. and Nichols, O. D. Air pollution technical information processing—the microthesaurus approach. *American Documentation*, 19, 1968, 66-70.

Tell, B. V. Document representation and indexer consistency. *Proceedings of the American Society for Information Science*, 6, 1969, 285-292.

Tenopir, C. *Retrieval Performance in a Full Text Journal Article Database*. Doctoral thesis. Urbana-Champaign, University of Illinois, Graduate School of Library and Information Science, 1984. (Condensed versions appear as: Tenopir, C. Full text database retrieval performance. *Online Review*, 9, 1985, 149-164 and Tenopir, C. Searching *Harvard Business Review*. *Online*, 9(2), 1985, 1-8.)

Tessier, J. A. Hypertext linking as a model of expert indexing. *Advances in Classification Research*, 2, 1992, 171-178.

Thé, L. Morph your help desk into customer support. *Datamation*, 42, January 15, 1996, 52-54.

Thelwall, M. A survey of search engine capabilities useful in data mining. *Proceedings of the American Society for Information Science and Technology*, 38, 2001, 24-29.

Thompson, C. W. N. The functions of abstracts in the initial screening of technical documents by the user. *Journal of the American Society for Information Science*, 24, 1973, 270-276.

Thompson, R. et al. Evaluating Dewey concepts as a knowledge base for automatic subject assignment. http://orc.rsch.oclc.org:6109/eval_c.html February 12, 1997.

Thorpe, P. An evaluation of *Index Medicus* in rheumatology: coverage, currency, and efficiency. *Methods of Information in Medicine*, 13, 1974, 44-47.

Tibbo, H. R. Abstracting across the disciplines: a content analysis of abstracts from the natural sciences, the social sciences, and the humanities with implications for abstracting standards and online information retrieval. *Library and Information Science Research*, 14, 1992, 31-56.

Tibbo, H. R. Indexing for the humanities. *Journal of the American Society for Information Science*, 45, 1994, 607-619.

Tinker, J. F. Imprecision in indexing. *American Documentation*, 17, 1966, 93-102; 19, 1968, 322-330.

Todeschini, C. Personal communication, November 11, 1997.

Todeschini, C. and Farrel, M. P. An expert system for quality control in bibliographic databases. *Journal of the American Society for Information Science*, 40, 1989, 1-11.

Todeschini, C. and Tolstenkov, A. Expert system for quality control in the INIS database. Paper presented at the International Symposium on the Future of Scientific, Technological and Industrial Information Services, Leningrad, May 1990. IAEA-SM-317/58.

Tong, R. M. et al. *RUBRIC: an Environment for Full Text Information Retrieval*. Mountain View, CA, Advanced Information and Decision Systems, 1985.

Torr, D. V. et al. *Program of Studies on the Use of Published Indexes*. Bethesda, MD, General Electric Co., Information Systems Operation, 1966.

Trant, J. Framing the picture: standards for imaging systems. In: *Multimedia Computing and Museums*; ed. by D. Bearman, pp. 347-367. Pittsburgh, Archives & Museum Informatics, 1995.

Trawinski, B. A methodology for writing problem structured abstracts. *Information Processing & Management*, 25, 1989, 693-702.

Trippe, B. Taxonomies and topic maps: categorization steps forward. *EContent*, 24(6), 2001, 44-49.

Troitskii, V. P. An extrapolation approach to the concept of information. *Automatic Documentation and Mathematical Linguistics*, 13(6), 1979, 49-60. (English translation of *Nauchno-Tekhnicheskaya Informatsiya*, Seriya 2, 13(12), 1979, 1-7.)

Troitskii, V. P. Text, information and epistemology. *Automatic Documentation and Mathematical Linguistics*, 15(1), 1981, 20-27. (English translation of *Nauchno-Tekhnicheskaya Informatsiya*, Seriya 2, 15(2), 1981, 1-5.)

Trubkin, L. Auto-indexing of the 1971-77 ABI/INFORM database. *Database*, 2(2), 1979, 56-61.

Trybula, W. J. Text mining. *Annual Review of Information Science and Technology*, 34, 1999, 385-419.

Tse, T. et al. An exploratory study of video browsing user interface designs and research methodologies. *Proceedings of the American Society for Information Science*, 36, 1999, 681-692.

Turner, J. M. Comparing user-assigned terms with indexer-assigned terms for storage and retrieval of moving images: research results. *Proceedings of the American Society for Information Science*, 32, 1995, 9-12.

Turner, J. M. Representing and assessing information in the stockshot database at the National Film Board of Canada. *Canadian Journal of Information Science*, 15(4), 1990, 1-19.

Uhlmann, W. A thesaurus *Nuclear Science and Technology*: principles of design. *Teknisk-Vetenskaplig Forskning* (TVF), 38, 1967, 46-52.

UNHCR Refugee Documentation Centre. *A Guide for Abstractors*. Geneva, United Nations High Commissioner for Refugees, 1985.

Uthurusamy, R. et al. Extracting knowledge from diagnostic databases. *IEEE Expert*, 8(6), 1993, 27-38.

Vailaya, A. et al. Image classification for content-based indexing. *IEEE Transactions on Image Processing*, 10, 2001, 117-130.

van der Meij, H. Styling the index: is it time for a change? *Journal of Information Science*, 28, 2002, 243-251.

Van der Meulen, W. A. and Janssen, P. J. F. C. Automatic versus manual indexing. *Information Processing & Management*, 13, 1977, 13-21.

van der Starre, J. H. E. Ceci n'est pas une pipe: indexing of images. In: *Multimedia Computing and Museums*; ed. by D. Bearman, pp. 267-277. Pittsburgh, Archives & Museum Informatics, 1995.

Van Oot, J. G. et al. Links and roles in coordinate indexing and searching: an economic study of their use, and an evaluation of their effect on relevance and recall. *Journal of Chemical Documentation*, 6, 1966, 95-101.

Varney, S. Link your help desk to the Web. *Datamation*, 42(10), 1996, 64-67.

Vickery, B. C. The structure of semantic coding: a review. *American Documentation*, 10, 1959, 234-241.

Villarroel, M. et al. Obtaining feedback for indexing from highlighted text. *The Electronic Library*, 20, 2002, 306-313.

Vinsonhaler, J. F. Some behavioral indices of the validity of document abstracts. *Information Storage and Retrieval*, 3, 1966, 1-11.

Virgo, J. A. An evaluation of *Index Medicus* and MEDLARS in the field of ophthalmology. *Journal of the American Society for Information Science*, 21, 1970, 254-263.

Vizine-Goetz, D. Dewey in CORC: classification in metadata and pathfinders. In: *CORC: New Tools and Possibilities for Cooperative Electronic Resource Description*; ed. by K. Calhoun and J. J. Riemer, pp. 67-80. Binghampton, NY, Haworth Press, 2001.

Vizine-Goetz, D. OCLC investigates using classification tools to organize Internet data. In: *Visualizing Subject Access for 21st Century Information Resources*; ed. by P. A. Cochrane and E. H. Johnson, pp. 93-105. Urbana-Champaign, University of Illinois, Graduate School of Library and Information Science, 1998.

Vleduts-Stokolov, N. Concept recognition in an automatic text-processing system for the life sciences. *Journal of the American Society for Information Science*, 38, 1987, 269-287.

Voorbij, H. J. Title keywords and subject descriptors: a comparison of subject search entries of books in the humanities and social sciences. *Journal of Documentation*, 54, 1998, 466-476.

Voorhees, E.M. Natural language processing and information retrieval. In: *Information Extraction*; ed. by M. T. Pazienza, pp. 32-48. New York, Springer-Verlag, 1999.

Voorhees, E. M. Question answering in TREC. In: *Proceedings of the Tenth International Conference on Information and Knowledge Management*, pp. 535-537. New York, Association for Computing Machinery, 2001.

Voorhees, E.M. and Harman, D. The Text Retrieval Conferences (TRECS). In: *Proceedings of the TIPSTER Text Program, Phase III*, pp. 241-267. San Francisco, Morgan Kaufmann, 1999.

Wactlar, H. D. and Christel, M. G. Digital video archives: managing through metadata. In: *Building a National Strategy for Digital Preservation: Issues in Digital Media Archiving*, pp. 80-95. Washington, DC, Council on Library and Information Resources, 2002.

Wactlar, H. D. et al. Complementary video and audio analysis for broadcast news archives. *Communications of the ACM*, 43(2), 2000, 42-47.

Wactlar, H. D. et al. Lessons learned from building a terabyte digital video library. *Computer*, 32(2), 1999, 66-73.

Walker, R. S. Problem child: some observations on fiction, with a sketch of a new system of classification. *Librarian and Book World*, 47(2), 1958, 21-28.

Walsh, J. Intel LANDesk lets users cry for help from Web browsers. *InfoWorld*, 18(39), 1996, 12.

Wang, J. Z. *Integrated Region-Based Image Retrieval*. Boston, MA, Kluwer, 2001.

Wanger, J. et al. *Evaluation of the On-Line Process*, Santa Monica, CA, Cuadra Associates, 1980. PB81-132565.

Watters, C. Information retrieval and the virtual document. *Journal of the American Society for Information Science*, 50, 1999, 1028-1029.

Watters, C. and Wang, H. Rating news documents for similarity. *Journal of the American Society for Information Science*, 51, 2000, 793-804.

Wechsler, M. et al. New approaches to spoken document retrieval. *Information Retrieval*, 3, 2000, 173-188.

Weeber, M. et al. Developing a test collection for biomedical word sense disambiguation. *Proceedings of the 2001 Annual Symposium of the American Medical Informatics Association*, pp. 746-750. Philadelphia, Hanley & Belfus, 2001.

Weil, B. H. et al. Technical-abstracting fundamentals. *Journal of Chemical Documentation*, 3, 1963, 86-89, 125-136.

Weinberg, B. H. Complexity in indexing systems—abandonment and failure: implications for organizing the Internet. *Proceedings of the American Society for Information Science*, 33, 1996, 84-90.

Weinberg, B. H. A theory of relativity for catalogers. In: *Cataloging Heresy: Challenging the Standard Bibliographic Product*; ed. by B. H. Weinberg, pp. 7-11. Medford, NJ, Learned Information, 1992.

Weinberg, B. H. Why indexing fails the researcher. *The Indexer*, 16, 1988, 3-6.

Weinberg, B. H. Why postcoordination fails the searcher. *The Indexer*, 19, 1995, 155-159.

Weld, D.S., et al., eds. The role of intelligent systems in the National Information Infrastructure. *AI Magazine*, 16(3), 1995, 45-64.

Wellisch, H. H. Book and periodical indexing. *Journal of the American Society for Information Science*, 45, 1994, 620-627.

Wells, A. T. et al. *The Amazing Internet Challenge*. Chicago, American Library Association, 1999.

Westberg, S. Faxed communication of October 9, 1997.

Wheatley, A. and Armstrong, C. J. Metadata, recall, and abstracts: can abstracts ever be reliable indicators of document value? *Aslib Proceedings*, 49(8), 1997, 206-213.

White, H. D. and Griffith, B. C. Quality of indexing in online data bases. *Information Processing & Management*, 23, 1987, 211-224.

Wilbur, W. J. et al. Analysis of biomedical text for chemical names. *Proceedings of the 1999 Annual Symposium of the American Medical Informatics Association*, pp. 176-180. Philadelphia, Hanley & Belfus, 1999.

Wilkinson, D. and Hollander, S. A comparison of drug literature coverage by *Index Medicus* and *Drug Literature Index*. *Bulletin of the Medical Library Association*, 61, 1973, 431-432.

Wilks, Y. et al. Combining weak methods in large-scale text processing. In: *Text-Based Intelligent Systems*; ed. by P. S. Jacobs, pp. 35-58. Hillsdale, NJ, Lawrence Erlbaum, 1992.

Williams, M. An evaluation of passage-level indexing strategies for a technical report archive. *LIBRES: Library and Information Science Electronic Journal*, volume 8, issue 1, March 31, 1998 (www.infomotions.com/serials/libres/libres-v8n01-williams-evaluation.txt)

Williams, M. E. Experiences of IIT Research Institute in operating a computerized retrieval system for searching a variety of data bases. *Information Storage and Retrieval*, 8, 1972, 57-75.

Wilson, P. Situational relevance. *Information Storage and Retrieval*, 9, 1973, 457-471.

Wilson, P. *Two Kinds of Power: an Essay on Bibliographical Control*. Berkeley, University of California Press, 1968.

Winkler, M. A. The need for concrete improvement in abstract quality. *Journal of the American Medical Association (JAMA)*, 281, 1999, 1129-1130.

Witbrock, M. J. and Hauptmann, A. G. Speech recognition for a digital video library. *Journal of the American Society for Information Science*, 49, 1998, 619-632.

Wolfram, D. Inter-record linkage structure in a hypertext bibliographic retrieval system. *Journal of the American Society for Information Science*, 47, 1996, 765-774.

Wolfram, D. and Zhang, J. An investigation of the influence of indexing exhaustivity and term distributions on a document space. *Journal of the American Society for Information Science and Technology*, 53, 2002, 943-952.

Wong, K.-F. et al. Application of aboutness to functional benchmarking in information retrieval. *ACM Transactions on Information Systems*, 19, 2001, 337-370.

Wood, J. L. et al. Overlap among the journal articles selected for coverage by BIOSIS, CAS, and Ei. *Journal of the American Society for Information Science*, 24, 1973, 25-28.

Wood, J. L. et al. Overlap in the lists of journals monitored by BIOSIS, CAS, and Ei. *Journal of the American Society for Information Science*, 23, 1972, 36-38.

Woodland, P. C. et al. Effects of out of vocabulary words in spoken document retrieval. *Proceedings of the 23rd Annual International ACM SIGIR Conference on Research and Development in Information Retrieval*, pp. 372-374. New York, Association for Computing Machinery, 2000.

Woodruff, A. G. and Plaunt, C. GIPSY: automated geographic indexing of text documents. *Journal of the American Society for Information Science*, 45, 1994, 645-655.

Wooster, H. Optimal utilization of indexing personnel. *Research Review* (U.S. Air Force, Office of Aerospace Research), 3(4), 1964, 22-23.

Wright, L. W. et al. Hierarchical concept indexing of full-text documents in the Unified Medical Language System Information Sources Map. *Journal of the American Society for Information Science*, 50, 1999, 514-523.

Wu, J. K. et al. CORE: a content-based retrieval engine for multimedia information systems. *Multimedia Systems*, 3, 1995, 25-41.

Wu, J. K. et al. *Perspectives on Content-Based Multimedia Systems*. Boston, Kluwer, 2000.

Wu, Q. Web image retrieval using self-organizing feature map. *Journal of the American Society for Information Science and Technology*, 52, 2001, 868-875.

Xu, H. and Lancaster, F. W. Redundancy and uniqueness of subject access points in online catalogs. *Library Resources & Technical Services*, 42, 1998, 61-66.

Yang, Y. An evaluation of statistical approaches to text categorization. *Information Retrieval*, 1, 1999, 69-90.

Yang, Y. Improving text categorization methods for event tracking. *Proceedings of the 23rd Annual International ACM SIGIR Conference on Research and Development in Information Retrieval*, pp. 65-72. New York, Association for Computing Machinery, 2000.

Yerkey, A. N. Models of index searching and retrieval effectiveness of keyword-in-context indexes. *Journal of the American Society for Information Science*, 24, 1973, 282-286.

Yu, K.-I. et al. Pipelined for speed: the Fast Data Finder system. *Quest*, Winter 1986-1987, 5-19.

Zechner, K. Automatic generation of concise summaries of spoken dialogues in unrestricted domains. *Proceedings of the 24th Annual International ACM SIGIR Conference on Research and Development in Information Retrieval*, pp. 199-207. New York, Association for Computing Machinery, 2001.

Zeng, M. L. Metadata elements for object description and representation: a case report from a digitized historical fashion collection project. *Journal of the American Society for Information Science*, 50, 1999, 1193-1208.

Zholkova, A. I. Applying facet analysis methods in abstracting. *Scientific and Technical Information Processing*, 2, 1975, 70-74. (English translation of *Nauchno-Tekhnicheskaya Informatsiya*, Seriya 1, Number 6, pp. 26-28.)

Zhu, B. and Chen, H. Validating a geographical image retrieval system. *Journal of the American Society for Information Science*, 51, 2000, 625-634.

Zich, B. Visualizing digital libraries. In: *Visualizing Subject Access for 21st Century Information Resources*; ed. by P. A. Cochrane and E. H. Johnson, pp. 106-109. Urbana-Champaign, University of Illinois, Graduate School of Library and Information Science, 1998.

Zins, C. Models for classifying Internet resources. *Knowledge Organization*, 29, 2002, 20-28.

Zizi, M. Interactive dynamic maps for visualisation and retrieval from hypertext systems. In: *Information Retrieval and Hypertext*; ed. by M. Agosti and A. F. Smeaton, pp. 203-224. Boston, Kluwer, 1996.

Zunde, P. and Dexter, M. E. Factors affecting indexing performance. *Proceedings of the American Society for Information Science*, 6, 1969a, 313-322.

Zunde, P. and Dexter, M. E. Indexing consistency and quality. *American Documentation*, 20, 1969b, 259-267.

INDEX

Because the entire volume is about indexing and abstracting, the use of these terms as entry points has been minimized in this index.